LACAN
THE SILENT PARTNE

WO ES WAR

A series from Verso edited by Slavoj Žižek

Wo es war, soll ich werden – Where it was, I shall come into being – is Freud's version of the Enlightenment goal of knowledge that is in itself an act of liberation. Is it still possible to pursue this goal today, in the conditions of late capitalism? If 'it' today is the twin rule of pragmatic-relativist New Sophists and New Age obscurantists, what 'shall come into being' in its place? The premise of the series is that the explosive combination of Lacanian psychoanalysis and Marxist tradition detonates a dynamic freedom that enables us to question the very presuppositions of the circuit of Capital.

In the same series:

Alain Badiou, *Ethics: An Essay on the Understanding of Evil.* Translated and introduced by Peter Hallward
Alain Badiou, *Metapolitics.* Translated and introduced by Jason Barker
Jeremy Bentham, *The Panopticon Writings.* Edited and introduced by Miran Booviè
Alain Grosrichard, *The Sultan's Court: European Fantasies of the East.* Translated by Liz Heron and introduced by Mladen Dolar
Renata Salecl, *(Per)Versions of Love and Hate*
Slavoj Žižek, *Did Somebody Say Totalitarianism?*
Slavoj Žižek, *The Fragile Absolute*
Slavoj Žižek, *Iraq: The Borrowed Kettle*
Slavoj Žižek, *The Metastases of Enjoyment: Six Essays on Women and Causality*
Slavoj Žižek, *The Indivisible Remainder: An Essay on Schilling and Related Matters*
Slavoj Žižek, *The Plague of Fantasies*
Slavoj Žižek, *The Ticklish Subject: The Absent Centre of Political Ontology*
Alenka Zupančič, *Ethics of the Real: Kant, Lacan*

LACAN

The Silent Partners

Edited by

Slavoj Žižek

VERSO
London • New York

First published by Verso 2006

1 3 5 7 9 10 8 6 4 2

Verso
UK: 6 Meard Street, London W1F 0EG
USA: 180 Varick Street, New York, NY 10014-4606
www.versobooks.com

Verso is the imprint of New Left Books

ISBN 1–84467–065–3 (hbk)
ISBN 1–84467–549–1 (pbk)

British Library Cataloguing in Publication Data
A catalogue record for this book is available from the British Library

Library of Congress Cataloging-in-Publication Data
A catalog record for this book is available from the Library of Congress

Typeset in Minion by RefineCatch Limited, Bungay, Suffolk
Printed and bound in the US by Quebecor World Fairfield

Contents

Introduction: Lacan with (x)

Jacques Lacan wrote that a theoretical breakthrough always misrecognizes itself, its true dimension – and this holds for Lacan himself, for his renewal of psychoanalytic theory. Perhaps the best way to discern this misrecognized dimension is to focus on Lacan's 'silent partners'. Lacan developed his thought in a constant dialogue with the great names, both past and present, of European thought and art: Plato, Aristotle, Saint Thomas Aquinas, Descartes, Kant, Hegel, Kierkegaard, Marx, Heidegger; or Sophocles, Shakespeare, Racine, Goethe, Claudel, Joyce, Duras. . . . What, however, if there is another series of names which are rarely mentioned or not mentioned at all by Lacan, but are connected to his thought by a secret link, and are crucial for a proper understanding of his work? What if these other names provide the key to what Jacques-Alain Miller called the 'other Lacan', the dimension of Lacan's thought, which explodes the received image of 'Lacanian theory', and whose (philosophical *and* political) consequences are much more radical than is usually surmised? Far from aiming at a complete list of these 'silent partners', this volume takes the first steps in this direction, with the underlying goal of recuperating Lacan for Marxist theory. It is divided into two parts: silent partners in the history of *thought*; and silent partners among *artists*.

Although the earliest philosophical figure interpreted by Lacan is the couple Socrates/Plato, a new text by Alain Badiou brings to light Lacan's neglected pre-Socratic references. Miran Božovič discovers the lost Lacanian pearls hidden in the theories of sexuality of eighteenth-century French materialism, especially in the writings of Denis Diderot. Eclipsed by Hegel, the philosophy of Schelling uncannily adumbrates some key Lacanian themes, as Adrian Johnston shows in his close analysis. It may seem strange to count Hegel among Lacan's 'silent partners' – in the index of names in *Écrits*, Hegel appears more often than Freud himself! If, however, there is a philosopher who deserves this title, it is Hegel: Lacan's almost exclusive

Hegelian reference is the *Phenomenology of Spirit* in its reading by Alexandre Kojève (and, to a lesser degree, Jean Hyppolite), so that, in a digitalized version of *Écrits*, one can, almost with impunity, enact the operation 'Replace Hegel with Kojève'. This massive reference overshadows the hidden – but much more crucial – links between Lacan's 'logic of the signifier' and Hegel's *Logic*, as Timothy Huson amply demonstrates. In contrast to Hegel, Nietzsche is rarely mentioned by Lacan, and as a rule rather disparagingly; here, Silvia Ons restores the balance by bringing to light Freud's and Lacan's debt to Nietzsche. Another author ignored by Lacan, but one whose themes are often reminiscent of Lacan's, is Levinas; here Joan Copjec sets the record straight by articulating the link between shame and anxiety. Among contemporary philosophers, Lacan's only true 'silent partner' is Alain Badiou: although he is critical of (what he perceives as) Lacan's 'anti-philosophy', his entire work is marked by a deep fidelity to and incessant dialogue with Lacan – the topic of Bruno Bosteels's contribution, which concludes Part I.

Part II begins with another text on Hegel: although Lacan's famous reading of Antigone's tragedy is thoroughly anti-Hegelian, Alenka Zupančič shows how, in a kind of *futur antérieur*, Hegel's neglected theory of comedy not only reverberates with Lacanian themes, but also provides a basis for a critical rejection of the fashionable contemporary 'philosophy of finitude'. The comic is also the topic of Robert Pfaller's insightful Lacanian investigation of thought experiments and other scientific fictions. After these two general approaches to aesthetic topics, the volume then turns to individual artists. It is difficult to imagine a more 'anti-Lacanian' artist than Richard Wagner; however, François Regnault's Lacanian reading of Wagner and his participation in Patrice Chéreau's legendary centenary Bayreuth staging of the *Ring* in 1976–80 hint at the possibility of a new approach, developed in detail by Slavoj Žižek. The great nineteenth-century Russian realist tradition seems to be even further from Lacan than Wagner – or is it? Sigi Jöttkandt's close reading of Turgenev's 'First Love' has some surprises in store. While the absence of Turgenev's name from Lacan's work is to be expected, Lacan's almost total silence on Kafka is the big enigma – why Joyce (to whom Lacan dedicated a whole seminar), not Kafka, *the* writer of obscene *jouissance*? Mladen Dolar fills in this gap in his extraordinary politico-ideological reading of Kafka's three animal short stories. Lacan also neglects to mention his contemporary Antonin Artaud, although, as Lorenzo Chiesa demonstrates, Artaud's texts throw a new light on Lacan's late topic of *jouis-sens*. The volume concludes with a more synthetic approach: Fredric Jameson's substantial contribution, which provides a long and detailed reading of Lacan as a social and art theorist.

The ultimate aim of the volume is therefore not, as one usually puts it, to enable readers to approach Lacan in a new way but, rather, to *instigate a new wave of Lacanian paranoia*: to push readers to engage in work of their own, and start to discern Lacanian themes everywhere – from politics to trash culture, from obscure ancient philosophers to Franz Kafka.

I Thought

1
Lacan and the Pre-Socratics

Alain Badiou

It is always perilous to approach Lacan from a philosophical point of view. For he is an anti-philosopher, and no one is entitled to take this designation lightly.

Considering him in relation to the Pre-Socratics is a still more risky undertaking. References to these thinkers in Lacan's work are rare, scattered, and above all mediated by something other than themselves. There is, moreover, the risk of losing one's thought in a latent confrontation between Lacan and Heidegger, which has all the attractions of a rhetorical impasse.

Having arrived at this perspective on the scope of Lacan's texts, one should not lose sight of the fact that it is a localization, the disinterested examination of a symptom.

The revelatory power of Lacan's references to the Pre-Socratics is secret – I would almost say encoded. Three thinkers are invoked: Empedocles, Heraclitus and Parmenides. The invocation is itself caught up in four principal problems. The first can be formulated as follows: to what originary impulse of thought is psychoanalysis the heir? The question reaches far beyond the point where, with Descartes, we enter the modern epoch of the subject, or what Lacan calls the subject of science. Of course, psychoanalysis could appear only within the element of this modernity. But as a general figure of the will to thought [*vouloir-penser*], it enigmatically bears a confrontation with what is most originary in our site. Here it is a question of knowing what is at stake when we determine the place of psychoanalysis in the strictly Western history of thought, in which psychoanalysis marks a rupture, and which is not at all constituted by but, rather, punctuated by philosophy.

The second problem concerns the relation – which is decisive for Lacan – between psychoanalysis and Plato. Driven by rivalry and contestation, this relation is unstable. Lacan's references to the Pre-Socratics clarify the principle behind this instability.

The third problem is, of course, that of providing an exact delimitation of

Lacan's relation to Heidegger. It is to Heidegger that we owe the reactivation of the Pre-Socratics as the forgotten source from which our destiny took flight. If it is not a matter here of 'comparing' Lacan to Heidegger – which would be meaningless – the theme of origins alone compels us to search for some measure of what led one to cite and translate the other.

Finally, the fourth problem concerns the polemical dimension of psychoanalysis. With respect to what primordial division of thought does psychoanalysis make its stand? Can one inscribe psychoanalysis within an insistent conflict that long preceded it? There is no doubt that Lacan here makes use of the canonical opposition between Parmenides and Heraclitus. Lacan opts, quite explicitly, for the latter.

Freud's work was a new foundation, a rupture. But it was also the product of an orientation within thought that rests on divisions and territories that pre-existed it.

Lacan's references to the Pre-Socratics thus attest – and herein lies their difficulty – not so much to what is truly revolutionary in psychoanalysis as to what inscribes it within dialectical continuities of what we might call continental reach.

1.

Those of Lacan's psychoanalytic discoveries that can be made to enter into resonance with the Pre-Socratics can be grouped around two themes: the primacy of discourse and the function of love in the truth-process.

On several occasions Lacan praises the innocent audacity of the Pre-Socratics, who identified the powers of discourse with the grasping of being [*la prise sur l'être*]. Thus, in the seminar on transference, he writes: 'Beyond Plato, in the background, we have this attempt, grandiose in its innocence – this hope residing in the first philosophers, called physicists – of finding an ultimate grasp on the real under the guarantee of discourse, which is in the end their instrument for gauging experience.'[1]

How are we to characterize this peculiar balancing of the 'grandiose' and the 'innocent'? The grandiose aspect lies in the conviction that the question of the Real is commensurable with that of language; the innocence is in not having carried this conviction as far as its true principle, which is mathematization. You will recall that Lacan holds mathematization to be the key to any thinkable relation to the Real. He never varied on this point. In the seminar *Encore*, he says, without the slightest note of caution: 'Mathematization alone reaches a real.'[2] Without mathematization, without the grasp of the letter [*la prise de la lettre*], the Real remains captive to a mundane reality driven by a phantasm.

Is this to say that the Pre-Socratic physicists remain within the bounds of the mythic narrative which delivers us the phantasm of the world? No, for they outline a genuine rupture with traditional knowledge, albeit one innocent with regard to the matheme.

The latter point is essential. Lacan does not conceive of the Pre-Socratics as the founders of a tradition, or as a lost tradition in themselves. A tradition is what 'tra-dicts' [*fait tra-diction*] the reality of the phantasm of the world. In placing their trust in the pure supremacy of discourse, the Pre-Socratics had the grandiose audacity to break with all traditional forms of knowledge.

This is why their writings prefigure mathematization, although the latter is not present in its literal form. The premonition appears in its paradoxical inversion, the use of poetic form. Far from opposing, as Heidegger did, the Pre-Socratic poem to Plato's matheme, Lacan has the powerful idea that poetry was the closest thing to mathematization available to the Pre-Socratics. Poetic form is the innocence of the grandiose. For Lacan, it even goes beyond the explicit content of statements, because it anticipates the regularity of the matheme. In *Encore*, he writes:

> Fortunately, Parmenides actually wrote poems. Doesn't he use linguistic devices – the linguist's testimony takes precedence here – that closely resemble mathematical articulation, alternation after succession, framing after alternation? It is precisely because he was a poet that Parmenides says what he has to say to us in the least stupid of manners. Otherwise, the idea that being is and that nonbeing is not, I don't know what that means to you, but personally I find that stupid.[3]

This text indeed registers an innocence in its trace of stupidity. There is something unreal in Parmenides' proposition on being, in the sense of a still unthought attachment to phantasmatic reality. But the poetic form contains a grandiose anticipation of the matheme. Alternation, succession, framing: the figures of poetic rhetoric are branded, as if by an unconscious lightning flash, with the features of a mathematization to come; through poetry, Parmenides attests to the fact that the grasp of thought upon the Real can be established only by the regulated power of the letter. It is for this reason that the Pre-Socratics should be praised: they wished to free thought from any figure that involves the simple transmission of knowledge. They entrusted thought to the aleatory care of the letter, a letter that remains poetic for temporary lack of mathematics.

The Pre-Socratics' second foundational innovation was to pose the power of love as a relation of being wherein lies the function of truth. The seminar on transference is, of course, our guiding reference here. Take the following passage: 'Phaedraos tells us that Love, the first of the gods imagined by the Goddess of Parmenides, and which Jean Beaufret in his book on Parmenides identifies more accurately, I believe, with truth than with any other function, truth in its radical structure . . .'.[4] In fact, Lacan credits the Pre-Socratics with binding love to the question of the truth in two ways.

First of all, they were able to see that love, as Lacan himself says, is what brings being face to face with itself; this is expressed in Empedocles' description of love as the 'power of cohesion or harmony'. Secondly, and above all, the Pre-Socratics pointed out that it is in love that the Two is unleashed, the enigma of the difference between the sexes. Love is the appearance of a non-relation, the sexual non-relation, taken to the extent that any supreme relation is punctured or undone. This puncturing, this undoing of the One, is what aligns love with the question of the truth. The fact that we are dealing here with what brings into being a non-relation in place of a relation permits us also to say that knowledge is that part of the truth which is experienced in the figure of hate. Hate is, along with love and ignorance, the very passion of the truth, to the extent that it proceeds as non-relation imagined as relation.

Lacan emblematically ascribes to Empedocles this power of truth as the torsion that relates love to hate. Empedocles saw that the question of our being, and of what can be stated of its truth, presupposes the recognition of a non-relation, an original discord. If one ceases to misconstrue it according to some scheme of dialectical antagonisms, the love/hate tension is one of the possible names of this discord.

Freud, as Lacan emphasizes, had recognized in Empedocles something close to the antinomy of drives. In the 'Rome Report', Lacan mentions 'the express reference of [Freud's] new conception to the conflict of the two principles to which the alternation of universal life was subjected by Empedocles of Agrigentum in the fifth century BC'.[5] If we allow that what is at stake here is access to being in the shape of a truth, we can say that what Empedocles identifies in the pairing of love and hate, *philia* and *neikos*, is something akin to the excess of the passion of access.

Lacan, one suspects, recalibrates this reference in such a way as to put increasing emphasis on discord, on non-relation as the key to truth. To this end, he fleetingly pairs Empedocles and Heraclitus. Empedocles isolates the two terms through which the necessity of a non-relation is inscribed; Empedocles names the two passions of access, as deployed by a truth. Heraclitus sustains the primacy of discord; he is the thinker of non-relation's chronological priority over relation. Take, for example, the following lines on the death drive in 'Aggressivity in Psychoanalysis': 'a vital dehiscence that is constitutive of man, and which makes unthinkable the idea of an environment that is preformed for him, a "negative" libido that enables the Heraclitean notion of Discord, which the Ephesian believed to be prior to harmony, to shine once more'.[6] In Lacan's work, the negative libido is constantly connected to Heraclitus. In short, the connections between love, hate, truth and knowledge were established by Empedocles and then radicalized by Heraclitus, the originary thinker of discord, of non-relation.

A further proof of the Pre-Socratics' anticipation of the death drive lies in the consequences that can be drawn from their writings regarding God. Since the God of Empedocles knows nothing of hate, and therefore nothing of the nodal point of excess for the passion of access, one would therefore expect such a God's access to truth to be correspondingly restricted. This is precisely what Lacan, adducing Aristotle's commentary in support, attributes to Empedocles in *Encore*:

> There was someone named Empedocles – as if by chance, Freud uses him from time to time like a corkscrew – of whose work we know but three lines, but Aristotle draws the consequences of them very well when he enunciates that, in the end, God was the most ignorant of all beings according to Empedocles, because he knew nothing of hatred. . . . If God does not know hatred, according to Empedocles, it is clear that he knows less about it than mortals.[7]

For the startling consequences that can be drawn from these considerations of God's ignorance, I refer the reader to François Regnault's marvellous book *Dieu est inconscient*.[8]

What matters here, however, is that we observe that, after noting the poetic anticipation of the free functioning of the matheme, Lacan credits the Pre-Socratics with an intuition that has far-reaching implications for the resources of truth inherent in sexual discord.

2.

Let us turn to the problem of stabilizing the relationship between psychoanalysis and Platonism.

In Heidegger's strategy, the Pre-Socratics were deployed largely in order to deconstruct Plato and, as a side-effect, to plot the emergence of the system of metaphysics. Does Lacan conduct a similar operation? The answer is complex.

Lacan never pursues purely philosophical objectives. His intention, then, is not to dissect Plato. Rather, Lacan maintains an ambiguous rivalry with Plato.

For Plato and psychoanalysis have at least two conceptual undertakings in common: thinking love as transference, and exploring the sinuous trajectory of the One. On these two points, it matters a great deal to Lacan to establish that what he called the 'Freudian way' is different from the Platonic.

In the end, however, it remains the case that Lacan summons the Pre-Socratics to his aid while struggling to mark the boundary between psychoanalysis and Platonism. And it is also clear that the central wager in this attempt at demarcation once more concerns the theme of non-relation, of discord, of alterity without concept; and, consequently, concerns the delinking of knowledge and truth.

Lacan attributes to Plato a desire for being to be completed by knowledge, and therefore an identification (itself entirely a product of mastery) of knowledge with truth. The Idea, in Plato's sense, would be an equivocal point which is simultaneously a norm of knowledge and a *raison d'être*. For Lacan, such a point can only be imaginary. It is like a cork plugging the hiatus between knowledge and truth. It brings a fallacious peace to the original discord. Lacan holds that Plato's standing declines in the light of Empedocles' and Heraclitus' propositions on the primacy of discord over harmony.

It is therefore certain that, for Lacan as for Heidegger, something has been forgotten or lost between the Pre-Socratics and Plato. It is not, however, the meaning of being. It is, rather, the meaning of non-relation, of the first separation or gap. Indeed, what has been lost is thought's recognition of the difference between the sexes as such.

One could also say that between the Pre-Socratics and Plato, a change takes place in the way difference is thought. This is fundamental for Lacan, since the signifier is constituted by difference. Empedocles and Heraclitus posit that, in the thing itself, identity is saturated by difference. As soon as a thing is exposed to thought, it can be identified only by difference. Plato could be said to have lost sight of this line of argument, since he removed the possibility of identifying difference within the identity of the Idea. We could say that the Pre-Socratics differentiate identity, while Plato identifies difference. This is perhaps the source of Lacan's preference for Heraclitus.

Recalling, in his very first seminar, that the relation between the concept and the thing is founded on the pairing of identity and difference, Lacan adds: 'Heraclitus tells us – if we introduce absolute mobility in the existence of things such that the flow of the world never comes to pass twice by the same situation, it is precisely because identity in difference is already saturated in the thing'.[9] Here we see how Lacan contrasts the eternal identification of differences according to the fixed point of the Idea – as in Plato – with the absolute differential process constitutive of the thing itself. The Lacanian conception of the relation between identity and difference – and therefore, in the thing, between the one and the multiple – finds support, *contra* Plato, in the universal mobilism of Heraclitus. This is what Lacan observes with regard to the God of President Schreber in the text 'On a Question Preliminary to Any Possible Treatment of Psychosis'. For Schreber, the Creator is 'Unique in his Multiplicity, Multiple in his Unity (such are the attributes, reminiscent of Heraclitus, with which Schreber defines him).'[10]

In fact, what Heraclitus allows us to think – and what Plato, on the contrary, prohibits – is the death drive. The Platonic effort to identify difference through the Idea leaves no room for it; Heraclitean discord, on the other hand, anticipates its every effect. In Seminar VII, when he discusses Antigone's suicide in her tomb, and our ignorance of what is happening inside it, Lacan declares: 'No better reference than the aphorisms of Heraclitus.' Among these aphorisms, the most useful is the one which states the correlation of the Phallus and death, in the following, striking form: 'Hades and Dionysus are one and the same'. The authority of difference allows Heraclitus to perceive, in the identity of the god of the dead with the god of vital ecstasy, the double investment of the Phallus. Or, as Lacan notes of Bacchic processions: 'And [Heraclitus] leads us up to the point where he says that if it weren't a reference to Hades or a ceremony of ecstasy, it would be nothing more than an odious phallic ceremony.'[11] According to Lacan, the Platonic subordination of difference to identity is incapable of arriving at such a point.

The Pre-Socratics, then, provide ample material from which to reconstruct, from its origins, a far-reaching disorientation of Plato. In this sense, they form part of the polemical genealogy of psychoanalysis.

3.

Turning to Heidegger, we should of course recall that Lacan translated his *Logos*, which deals in particular with Heraclitus. I believe that three principal connections can be drawn between Lacan and Heidegger. They involve repression, the One, and being-for-death [*l'être-pour-la-mort*]. All three are mediated by the Pre-Socratics.

First, Lacan believes he can go so far as to say that there is at least a similarity between the Freudian theme of repression and the Heideggerian articulation of truth and forgetting. It is significant for Lacan that, as Heidegger remarks, the name of the river of forgetting, Lethe, can be heard in the word for truth, *aletheia*. The link is made explicit in the first seminar where, in his analysis of repression in the Freudian sense, we come across the following observation: 'In every entry of being into its habitation in words, there's a margin of forgetting, a *lethe* complementary to every *aletheia*.'[12] Such a repression, then, can with good reason be called 'originary'. Its originary character accords with the correlation in origins Heidegger establishes between truth and veiling, a correlation constantly reinforced through etymological exegesis of the Pre-Socratics.

Secondly, Lacan takes from Heidegger's commentary on Heraclitus the notion of an intimate connection between the theme of the One and that of Logos. This, for Lacan, is an essential thesis. It will later be formulated in structural fashion: the aphorism 'there is something of (the) One' [*il y a d'l'Un*] is constitutive of the symbolic order. But starting in Seminar III, in a discussion of the Schreber case, Lacan confirms Heidegger's reading of Heraclitus. Commenting on the fact that Schreber only ever has one interlocutor, he adds:

> This *Einheit* [oneness] is very amusing to consider, if we think of this text on 'Logos' by Heidegger I have translated, which is going to be published in the first issue of our new journal, *La Psychanalyse*, and which identifies the logos with Heraclitus's *En* [One]. And in fact we shall see that Schreber's delusion is in its own way a mode of relationship between the subject and language as a whole.[13]

It is in the most intimate part of clinical practice – that which deals with psychoses – that the clarificatory power of Heraclitus' aphorisms, supported by Heidegger, now reappears.

Finally, Lacan believes he can also connect the Freudian concept of the death drive to Heidegger's existential analysis, which defines *Dasein* as being-for-death. The emblematic figure of Empedocles serves, in the 'Rome Report', as the vector for this connection: 'Empedocles, by throwing himself into Mount Etna, leaves forever present in the memory of men this symbolic act of his being-for-death'.[14]

You will note that in all three occurrences of Heidegger – truth and forgetting, One and Logos, being-for-death – the Pre-Socratics are a required reference. Indeed, they are necessary to the extent that one cannot decide if the Pre-Socratics are a point of suture, or projection, between Lacan and Heidegger; or if, on the contrary, it is Heidegger who allows Lacan access to a more fundamental concern with the Pre-Socratic genealogy of psychoanalysis. I, for one, tend towards the second hypothesis.

4.

For Lacan intends to inscribe psychoanalysis within a destiny of thought that is determined by oppositions and divisions originally informed by the Pre-Socratics. On this view there are two crucial oppositions: one, as we have seen, contrasting the Pre-Socratic sense of discord to the dominance of identity in the Platonic schema. But there is also an opposition, perhaps still more profound, within the ranks of the Pre-Socratics, that sets Heraclitus against Parmenides. The clearest text is in Seminar XX:

> The fact that thought moves in the direction of science only by being attributed to thinking – in other words, the fact that being is presumed to think – is what founds the philosophical tradition starting from Parmenides. Parmenides was wrong and Heraclitus was right. That is clinched by the fact that, in fragment 93, Heraclitus enunciates *oute legei oute kruptei alla semainei*, 'he neither avows nor hides, he signifies' – putting back in its place the discourse of the winning side itself – *o anax ou to manteion este to en Delphoi*, 'the prince' – in other words, the winner – 'who prophesies in Delphi'.[15]

It is interesting to note that Lacan attributes the foundation of the philosophical tradition not to Plato, but to Parmenides.

I said at the outset that the grandiose innocence of the Pre-Socratics was to have broken with the traditional forms of knowledge. But Parmenides himself is also the founder of a tradition. We need, then, to locate two ruptures. On the one hand, the Pre-Socratics break with the mythic enunciation, with the tradition of myth that 'tra-dicts' the imaginary reality of the world. But on the other, at least one of the Pre-Socratics founds a tradition with which Lacan in turn breaks: the philosophical tradition. For Lacan is an anti-philosopher. This anti-philosophy, however, is already manifested, in a certain sense, by Heraclitus. The philosophical idea is that being thinks, for want of a Real [*l'être pense, au manque le réel*]. Against this idea, Heraclitus immediately puts forward the diagonal dimension of signification, which is neither revelation nor dissimulation, but an act. In the same way, the heart of the psychoanalytic procedure lies in the act itself. Heraclitus thus puts in its place the pretension of the master, of the oracle at Delphi, but also the pretension of the philosopher to be the one who listens to the voice of the being who is supposed to think.

Finally, Lacan has a dual, even duplicitous relation to the Pre-Socratics, as he does to the entire history of philosophy. It is embodied by the relationship between two proper names: Heraclitus and Parmenides. Parmenides covers the traditional institution of philosophy, while Heraclitus refers to components of the genealogy of psychoanalysis. Lacan will adopt the same procedure to stabilize his relationship to Plato, distributing it between two proper names: Socrates, the discourse of the analyst, and Plato, the discourse of the master.

But this duplicitous split is an operation carried out within the signifier. 'Parmenides is wrong, Heraclitus is right,' says Lacan. Should we not take this to mean that, as thought from the point of view of psychoanalysis, philosophy appears as a form of reason that stagnates within the element of this wrong? Or as a wrong which, within the maze of its illusion, none the less makes sufficient contact with the Real to then fail to recognize the reason behind it?

The Pre-Socratics, then, who remain for us little more than an assortment of proper names to whom scattered phrases are ascribed, serve for Lacan as a formal reservoir. These names – Empedocles, Heraclitus, Parmenides – have just enough literal weight, just enough aura of significance, to allow him to separate out, to draw together and, finally, to formalize the internal dialectics of anti-philosophy.

Notes

1. Jacques Lacan, *Le Séminaire de Jacques Lacan, Livre VIII Le transfert, 1960–1961* (ed. Jacques-Alain Miller) (Paris: Seuil, 2001), pp. 98–9.
2. Lacan, *The Seminar of Jacques Lacan Book XX: On Feminine Sexuality, the Limits of Love and Knowledge, 1972–1973*, trans. Bruce Fink (New York, 1999), p. 131.
3. Lacan, *The Seminar of Jacques Lacan Book XX*, p. 22.
4. Lacan, *Le Séminaire, Livre VIII*, pp. 66–7.
5. Jacques Lacan, 'The Function and Field of Speech and Language in Psychoanalysis', in *Écrits: A Selection* (London, 2001), p. 112.
6. Lacan, 'Aggressivity in Psychoanalysis', in *Écrits*, p. 24.
7. Lacan, *Seminar XX*, p. 89.
8. François Regnault, *Dieu est inconscient* (Paris: Navarin, 1986).
9. Jacques Lacan, *The Seminar of Jacques Lacan, Book I: Freud's Papers on Technique 1953–1954*, ed. Jacques-Alain Miller (Cambridge, 1988), p. 243.
10. Lacan, 'On a Question Preliminary to Any Possible Treatment of Psychosis', in *Écrits*, p. 225.
11. Jacques Lacan, *The Seminar of Jacques Lacan Book VII: The Ethics of Psychoanalysis, 1959–1960*, (New York, 1992), p. 299.
12. Lacan, *Seminar I*, p. 192.
13. Jacques Lacan, *The Seminar of Jacques Lacan Book III: The Psychoses, 1955–1956* (New York, 1993), p. 124; translation modified.
14. Lacan, 'Function and Field', p. 114.
15. Lacan, *Seminar XX*, p. 114.

2

The Omniscient Body

Miran Božovič

While the majority of Denis Diderot's most important works – for example *Le Rêve de d'Alembert*, and the two philosophical novels, *Le Neveu de Rameau* and *Jacques le fataliste*, that is, the works that he is mainly famous for today – were only published posthumously, one of the works that acquired a certain international fame and even notoriety in his lifetime, but is rarely read today, is his first novel, *Les Bijoux indiscrets* (1748).

In this novel, the philosophy is expounded by the body itself. In this philosophical fantasy, the body itself has come to speak. The body has a speech organ of its own: it speaks through the organ traditionally considered to be the least submissive to the soul or mind – that is, through the organ that also serves as the reproductive organ, called euphemistically by Diderot *le bijou*, the jewel. These are perhaps the only words in the history of philosophy not spoken by the soul or the mind, but by the body (for this reason alone, this exceptional document would deserve a place in the history of philosophy). The philosophy expounded by the body reflecting upon itself and its soul is one of materialism, that is to say, Diderot's own philosophy. This work marks the author's transition from the deism of the early *Pensées philosophiques* (1746) to the fully fledged materialism of *Lettre sur les aveugles* (1749) and his later works. It was, then, in considering how to make out the case for the philosophy of materialism that Diderot came up with the idea of the speaking body. Firmly believing that the body knows more about itself and its soul than the soul knows about itself and its body, Diderot presents the philosophy of materialism as the body's discourse on itself. In contrast to spiritualism, where the soul is distinct from the body it animates, in materialism, where the soul is nothing other than 'the organization and life' of the body itself, we encounter a body that is its own soul. Once the body is given the power of speech, the philosophy it will develop is sure to be one of materialism, just as the philosophy embraced by fictitious – in other words, literary or film – characters reflecting upon their own ontological status within the universe of a novel or film is most often a version of Berkeley's immaterialism.[1]

The plot of the novel is extraordinary, but fairly simple. In the African empire of the Congo, a most unusual phenomenon occurs: all of a sudden, women begin recounting their most intimate activities through the most intimate parts of their bodies in the most public of places: at the Opera, at the theatre, at the ball, and so forth. In women, the speech organs have been duplicated – that is, the power of speech has been transferred to their sex organs. The explanation of this bizarre phenomenon is simple: the sultan Mangogul, racking his brains over the question of feminine fidelity, has come into possession of a magic ring by means of which he is able to make talk the 'principal instruments'[2] of the activities in which he is interested – that is to say, the 'jewels'. In order to find out whether the virtue of the women of his empire is, perhaps, only an illusion, he conducts a series of 'interviews' in which every woman asserts fidelity to her partner. However, on the basis of the testimony obtained during 'cross-examination' – that is to say by alternately questioning the women's jewels by means of the magic ring – it turns out that none of them has been speaking the truth – they all prove to be sexually promiscuous. The virtue of the women of the Congo, in short, is nothing but an illusion. And this is more or less all the story there is.

It is, perhaps, because of its premise of 'talking jewels' or sex organs that the novel has been characterized as pornographic; however, nothing could be further from the truth. As Aram Vartanian has observed, all the jewels do is talk;[3] furthermore, we do not even *see* them talk – we only hear them. The civilized 'chatter of the jewels'[4] cannot even be compared to what the jewels do, for example, in *Thérèse philosophe*, a no less philosophically inspired erotic novel of the same year. In his later philosophical and theoretical works, Diderot is incomparably more 'indiscreet' – in *Le Rêve de d'Alembert*, for example, we actually witness the eponymous character experiencing sexual climax in his sleep.

In the gallery of literary characters found in Diderot's works, 'the talking jewels' do not stick out as much as it might seem: the central characters of some of his key philosophical and theoretical works are blind or deaf and mute, Siamese twins, two-headed monsters, various medical curiosities, and so forth.[5] Likewise, the fact that it is the female genitals that expound Diderot's own philosophy in the novel, and that it is therefore Diderot himself who, as a radical materialist, is speaking through them, should come as no surprise either. Consider again the example of *Le Rêve de d'Alembert*, where Diderot's own philosophical system is expounded not by someone who would be cautiously choosing his words, weighing the arguments with care and thoughtfully refuting objections as befits a formal philosophical treatise, but by the delirious d'Alembert, who is babbling thoughtlessly in his sleep (experiencing an orgasm in the process), and in this way comes to develop the central themes of Diderot's materialism (a minimal commentary is provided by his mistress, who has been noting down the words of the sleeping d'Alembert, and the medical doctor she summons to his bedside because she fears he has lost his mind).

In an important chapter, the novel presents a curious theory of the soul and its migration, developed by the sultan's mistress, Mirzoza. It is not a theory of the immortal soul migrating from one body to another – a version of this theory can be found, for example, in Crébillon's 1742 novel *Le Sopha*, in which the main character's soul, in one of his previous lives, was condemned to migrate from one sofa to another (the entire novel consists of the character recounting the amorous adventures he had surreptitiously observed from his abode) – but a theory of the soul that migrates within one and the same body, and is extinguished together with it. Thus developments in philosophy – the quarrel between the spiritualists and the materialists concerning the human soul – are reflected in the erotic fiction of that period; while the universe of Crébillon's novel is still governed by the spiritualist system of the human soul – the soul that survives the destruction of its body and migrates from one body to another is clearly a spiritual substance, distinct from the body it animates – the universe of *Les Bijoux indiscrets* is already unmistakably governed by the materialist system: in Mirzoza's 'experimental metaphysics',[6] the soul is nothing but a function of the organ or of the bodily part that it presently inhabits.

Contrary to the court philosophers who claim that 'the soul is in the head', Mirzoza believes that 'most men die without it ever having dwelt there, for its first place of residence is in the feet'.[7] The soul has not come to its 'first abode' from without: 'it is in the feet that it begins to exist'.[8] Leaving the feet, it then advances through the body; it 'leaves one spot, comes back to it only to leave it again'.[9] Every change of the soul's seat in the body brings about a change in the economy of the bodily mechanism, so that, in Mirzoza's words, 'the other limbs are always subordinated to the one in which the soul resides'.[10] Accordingly, everyone is characterized by the main function of the bodily part or organ in which their soul resides: a woman whose soul resides in the tongue is 'a tiresome prattler'; a woman whose soul resides in the eyes is 'a flirt'; a woman whose soul is 'now in her head, now in her heart, but never elsewhere' is a 'virtuous woman'; a woman whose soul resides in her heart, or, according to another of Mirzoza's definitions, 'usually in her heart, but sometimes also in her jewel', is an 'affectionate woman', that is, a 'faithful and constant lover'; and a woman whose soul resides 'in her jewel, and never strays from there', is a 'voluptuous woman'.[11] It is against the background of Mirzoza's theory of 'vagabond souls'[12] that the novel, which readers have most probably started to read as an intriguing, piquant account of sexual mores in an exotic African empire, turns out to be a serious philosophical treatise concerning the true seat of the soul. It presents a series of female characters whose souls have, on their journey through the body, become stuck in their jewels: although they all claim to be either virtuous – that is, sexually inactive – or faithful to their partners, they are, in fact, all 'voluptuous', that is, sexually promiscuous. Therefore, what the women asserting their fidelity or virtue really assert is that their souls are 'usually in [the] heart, but sometimes also in [the] jewel', or 'now in [the] head, now in [the] heart, but never elsewhere' – whereas in truth, the soul of each and every one of them 'resides in her jewel, and never strays from there'.

The women assert their fidelity or virtue through the voice that comes from their head – and it is *the body itself* that contradicts these false accounts of its encounters with the bodies of the other sex, literally raises *its* voice and, in front of everyone present, spitefully enumerates all its encounters with other bodies. That is to say: the voice coming from the head, traditionally held to be the seat of the soul, is, in cross-examination, contradicted by a voice which comes from that part of the body which is traditionally considered to be the least submissive to the head or mind. What the novel depicts is therefore the confrontation between the spiritualist and the materialist systems of the human soul. The main plot device, the doubling of speech organs, enables Diderot to confront two different conceptions of the soul, the spiritual and material, in one and the same body: a soul that resides in the head and/or the heart (traditionally considered to be the seats of the immaterial soul), but 'never' (or, according to Mirzoza's first definition of the 'affectionate woman', only 'sometimes') in the jewel, is clearly a spiritual substance distinct from the body to which it is united; on the other hand, the soul that resides in the jewel, that is, in that part of the body which is the least submissive to the mind, 'and never strays from there', is a soul that is identical with the body – it is none other than a function of the organ in which it manifests itself: an effect of corporeal organization. Therefore, when the body rebels against the women who believe themselves to be spiritual substances in command of the body to which they are united, it is in fact the soul which is identical with the body or with its organization that really rebels against them, and *objects to the false portrayal of its seat – and function – in the body.* Strictly speaking, by unmasking the women's fidelity as a lie, the jewels expose the very spiritualist position itself as a lie. Unlike the spiritualism propounded by the head, the spontaneous philosophy of the 'indiscreet jewels' is one of forthright materialism.

1 Hysterical materialism

The phenomenon of the doubling of the organs of speech is widely discussed and written about in the Congo: the Academy of Sciences convenes an extraordinary session to examine the phenomenon; the exact transcriptions of some of the jewels' discourses are published and then meticulously studied word by word;[13] in short, the talk of the jewels generates 'a great number of excellent works' in the empire, some of them even deemed to be 'the most advanced efforts of the human mind'.[14] Since the real cause of the phenomenon is unknown to everyone except the sultan and his mistress, certain African authors ascribe the talk of the jewels to 'the blind workings of nature',[15] and begin to seek for its explanation 'in the properties of matter',[16] while others recognize in it 'the hand of Brahma'[17] at work, and even a new proof of God's existence.[18]

Since the 'new tellers of tales'[19] or 'interlocutors'[20] – that is, the organs themselves that have come to speak – are never seen speaking, the exact source of this 'strange voice'[21] – the voice that is 'not exactly the same'[22] as the voice of the woman whose body is emitting it – can only be guessed at. But as the things that are spoken of are presented by this 'indiscreet voice' – which comes 'from the lower region',[23] from beneath the women's clothes – unmistakably from the point of view of the jewel itself, 'it was not very difficult to guess whence this extraordinary sound issued'.[24]

This never-seen voice that the women produce 'without opening [the] mouth',[25] which causes such a great stir in the empire, is a perfect example of what Michel Chion calls 'the acousmatic voice'.[26] In the mind of someone who hears it, such a voice – and the *acousmêtre*, that is, its invisible bearer – is automatically assigned exceptional powers: it seems to have 'the ability to be everywhere, to see all, to know all, and to have the complete power'.[27] This unseen, bodiless voice – a typical cinematic example is the voice of a stranger threatening his victim over the telephone – functions as a formless, unlocatable threat lurking everywhere in the background; since we do not see its bearer we cannot hide from it; for all we know, the bearer of this unseen voice himself sees everything: the one whom we ourselves do not see is believed to see us and everything that we do not see; while we know nothing about its bearer, the voice seems to know everything about us. This, in short, is a voice possessed of divine attributes. And the voice retains these powers as long as it remains unseen; the moment the voice finds its body – that is, the moment the source of its production is seen – it loses these powers. Although the voice of Diderot's jewels is attached to a body, it is nevertheless, strictly speaking, still unseen – we never *see* the jewels speak. Accordingly, its bearer could perhaps be characterized more adequately as a semi-*acousmêtre*, the designation used by Chion to describe that stage in the process of de-acousmatization in which we see other parts of the speaker's body, but we have not yet seen his mouth.[28] And de-acousmatization is incomplete as long as we do not verify 'the co-incidence of the voice with the mouth',[29] that is to say, as long as the speaker is not completely revealed. And as long as the de-acousmatization is incomplete, the voice – and its bearer – retains its exceptional powers. The last stage of de-acousmatization, that is, the stage immediately preceding the complete revealing of the speaker, is compared by Chion to the last stage in the undressing of the female body: 'in much the same way that the female genitals are the end point revealed by undressing (the point after which the denial of the absence of the penis is no longer possible), there is an end point of de-acousmatization – the *mouth* from which the voice issues'.[30] In Diderot, the process of de-acousmatization itself would *be* literally the undressing, the revealing of 'the mouth from which the voice issues' would reveal the genitals themselves.

That the concept of the acousmatic voice and its 'magical powers' were not unknown to Diderot is evident from at least two of his *Encyclopédie* articles devoted to Pythagoras and his disciples. In the article on 'Pythagorisme', he says that Pythagoras 'taught a double doctrine', and had 'two kinds of disciples': some 'only heard him' – to them he spoke from behind a curtain – while the others 'saw and heard him'.[31] For the first group his philosophy was 'enigmatic and symbolic', while for the others it was 'clear, explicit, stripped of obscurities and enigmas'.[32] In the article on 'Acousmatiques' – that is, the article about those of his disciples who 'have not yet deserved ... to see Pythagoras speak' – Diderot is even more precise: to those who 'only heard him' Pythagoras presented things merely 'emblematically', that is, symbolically or allegorically, while to those who 'saw and heard him' he revealed things as they were, without obfuscation; moreover, to the latter he even gave reasons for the things he spoke about. While he disregarded the objections of the first group – the only answer given to the acousmatics was simply 'Pythagoras has said so' – the objections of the others were resolved by 'Pythagoras himself'.[33]

As Diderot's enumeration of characteristics of the two groups of Pythagoras' disciples makes abundantly clear, the moment they do not only hear him speak from behind the curtain – that is, the moment they are 'admitted into the sanctuary' where they see him 'face to face' – Pythagoras himself loses his divine status, and his voice loses its magical power. As long as the disciples 'only heard him', they were clearly willing to believe his cryptic utterances: it was as though every word heard from behind the curtain, 'from the sanctuary', was a word coming directly from God and had, for the acousmatics, the status of a divine revelation; a sufficient guarantee of the truth of the revealed propositions, unintelligible in themselves, was provided by the mere fact that 'Pythagoras has said so'. When the disciples 'saw and heard him', however, the picture changes completely: although Pythagoras now speaks without obfuscation and presents things such as they truly are, the disciples are apparently no longer willing to believe his words – he now has to give them reasons for the things that are spoken of (his words have, therefore, lost the status of divine revelation). From now on, appealing to the all-knowing voice – that is, claiming that 'Pythagoras has said so' – is clearly no longer sufficient, as Pythagoras is forced to address their objections himself (he has, therefore, lost his divine attributes). Here, the fact that the second doctrine is clear and explicit, and no longer merely emblematic, is made to depend on the master's visibility: the moment his disciples also 'see him speak', Pythagoras has to abandon his enigmatic and symbolic language – since, for his disciples, he has lost the aura of the all-knowing philosopher that he had while he spoke from behind the curtain, they would probably no longer be willing to believe him. Furthermore, abandoning the cryptic formulas is clearly not enough, as he now struggles with additional elucidations, clarifying things and giving reasons for them; he himself answers the objections that he had arrogantly disregarded before, and so forth.

That the words uttered by the unseen voice of the jewels have a special weight for the people of Congo – no less weight than the master's words had for the Pythagorean acousmatics – which words uttered by a seen voice do not have can best be seen in cases where the unseen voice and the seen voice contradict each other. In such cases it is, as a rule, the unseen voice of the jewels that definitely convinces them. They believe the unseen voice not only when its testimony contradicts the testimony of the seen voice of another individual, but also when its testimony is contrary to the testimony of the seen voice of the *same* person.

The infidelity of a certain woman (who asserts the contrary, that is, asserts her fidelity or virtue) could also be revealed by her lover who, no doubt, would be able to tell exactly the same things as her jewel: 'For what difference does it make, after all, whether it be a woman's jewel or her lover that proves indiscreet? Is one any the less exposed?'[34] While this may well be true, the unseen voice of the jewel nevertheless possesses a 'power' that the seen voice of the mouth does not have even when it speaks about exactly the same things as the unseen voice. Where the testimony of the man and that of the jewel are contrary to each other, for the people of Congo the truth is always on the side of the unseen voice of the jewel. Thus, for example, the testimony of men boasting about having affairs with certain women is considered a lie solely on the grounds that 'the jewels of these women' assert the contrary – that is, they deny having anything to do with these men (yet, at the same time, they are truthful enough to admit to affairs with several *other* men).[35] It is, then, clearly the testimony of the jewels that proves decisive; it is the jewels that have the last word. As far as the people of Congo are concerned, it is none other than Brahma himself who has spoken through the acousmatic voice of the jewels: in the above case they expect Brahma 'to do justice to truth through their mouths',[36] that is, through the 'mouths' of the jewels. They treat the jewels as if they were *fons veritatis*, a supreme source of truth, whereas they completely disregard the testimony of the women themselves whose jewels have spoken (because they expect the women to deny such relationships even if they are not fictitious). When the testimonies of both voices are consistent – and therefore the man also speaks the truth – the thing which, in their view, in fact 'convicts' the unfaithful woman is 'not so much the relevance of the testimony as its source': a lover, through his talk, 'dishonors the altar upon which he has sacrificed', but if the jewel speaks, it is as if 'the altar itself raises its voice'.[37] While the words of the unseen voice of the jewels are regarded as divine revelation, the words of men can only be a lie or, if true, a sacrilege.

Since they believe that it is Brahma who causes the jewels to speak – and God, surely, 'would not suffer them to lie'[38] – the people of Congo believe the jewels even when the testimony of their unseen voice is in contradiction with the testimony of the seen voice of one and the same body, that is, when the organs of speech contradicting each other belong to the same person. It would be impious to think the jewels could lie. In a word, they believe the jewels 'as if they were oracles'.[39] For them, the unseen voice of the jewels – considered to be 'the most honest part'[40] of women – obviously has such weight that anyone disputing its testimony could, no doubt, be silenced in the same way as the Pythagorean acousmatics were said to be silenced – that is, simply by the words 'the jewel has said so'.

Let us now take a closer look at a woman whose jewel has spoken. Although she is at first the least willing to accept its testimony, she ends up being the one most transfixed by the unseen voice of the jewel: of all those who hear it, the woman whose jewel has spoken is the only one who directly experiences the exceptional, 'oracular' powers of its unseen voice. The 'unknown voice'[41] disclosing her amorous adventures – this voice is 'unknown' even to the woman whose jewel has spoken; she herself is not sure where exactly it comes from; she looks around nervously, suspecting that it might be coming from the mouth or a jewel of another woman – is obviously aware of her innermost, secret thoughts, that is, the thoughts she firmly believes no one else but she is aware of. Yet, at the same time, this voice is neither an inner voice nor a voice of conscience, as it is also heard by all those present. Ultimately, her resistance is crushed by the fact that this voice's knowledge far surpasses her own: this voice seems to be aware also of her body's encounters with the bodies of the opposite sex that she herself has already forgotten – and was therefore telling the truth when she claimed to have no knowledge of those encounters[42] – but when the invisible voice reminds her of those encounters, she can only realize with horror that this voice knows more about her than she knows about herself. Not only does this voice read her thoughts; not only does it know things about her that she herself does not know; moreover, this voice is also more powerful than she is: it speaks independently of, and even against, her will – although the voice speaks through a part of her own body, she has no power over it, and cannot silence it. In short, once her jewel has spoken, the woman can only listen helplessly as it exposes her misdeeds. The fact that this voice is more powerful than she is, and that it is therefore not she who is in command of the voice but the voice that is in command of her, soon becomes evident to everyone who hears her speak 'without opening her mouth'. These people now reason as follows: 'judging from the circumstances under which most of the jewels spoke, and from the things that they said' – the woman's jewel confesses in the presence of everyone to things that she herself would never be willing to confess to – 'there is every reason to believe that it is involuntary and that these parts would have remained mute had it been within the power of their owners to silence them'.[43]

This voice presents the women with a 'bitter' alternative: either they renounce their unrestrained lovemaking and truly become what they claim to be (i.e. virtuous or faithful), or they must be regarded as what they truly are (i.e. sexually promiscuous) – 'there is no middle course' any more; pretence is no longer possible.[44] In short, once the jewels have spoken, nothing in the empire of the Congo is as it had been before: women live in constant fear that 'at any moment a jewel might join in the conversation'[45] and, in front of everybody, expose their lies, while men are walking around pricking up their ears in the hopes of overhearing more of the involuntary confessions.

'The chatter of jewels' that the people of Congo have come to associate with 'altars', 'oracles', and so on is interpreted by the Brahmins as 'a divine punishment', and even as the 'latest proof' of Brahma's existence. The law of Brahma prohibits and condemns, among other things, 'perjury, lying and adultery', which are precisely the sins of which the women are guilty. Brahmins have been warning against these sins all along, but in vain; as a result, 'heaven's wrath has wrought new punishments'. As a just and wise judge, Brahma punishes adultery and lying about it by a voice which, against the will of the sinners, reveals the truth about their misdeeds. The punishment for the sin is therefore nothing other than the truth about it, the truth voiced by the 'principal instruments' of the sin itself. Hitherto, the people of Congo have been saying 'in their hearts' that 'Brahma does not exist'; now, however, Brahmins believe, they will come to see and 'cease to deny the existence of Brahma, or determine the limits to his power. Brahma is! He is almighty, and he shows himself to us no less clearly in these terrible scourges than in his ineffable favors.'[46]

2 Les femmes-machines

And therein lies the subversive materialist message of Diderot's novel: the unseen voice of the jewels, in which most people in the empire – with the exception of those few who begin to seek an explanation for the speech of the jewels in the properties of matter – recognize the God Brahma, is in fact nothing other than the voice through which, by the help of the sultan's magic ring, the body has come to speak.

The powers actually reflected in the unseen voice of the jewels are thus not the powers of God but the powers of the body itself. Accordingly, these powers are not pure divine attributes, but proportionally weaker in accordance with the status of the body as a semi-*acousmêtre.* Although the voice of the jewels is attached to a body, it is, strictly speaking, still unseen, since the co-incidence of the voice with the 'mouth' from which it issues is never verified. Although this voice cannot be said to see and to know everything, it nevertheless still sees and knows more than the woman whose jewel has come to speak; although its power is not absolute, it is nevertheless more powerful than the woman herself. Although the voice cannot be said to be ubiquitous, it is nevertheless impossible to escape or hide from it: the voice will find the women wherever they may go, since they literally carry the source of its production within themselves. In other words, with regard to the body from which it issues and its affections, this voice is as all-seeing, all-knowing and omnipotent as God is all-seeing, all-knowing and omnipotent with regard to the universe. That which sees and knows more than we do, that which is more powerful than we are, is therefore not the all-seeing, all-knowing, omnipotent and omnipresent God, but our own body. In short, that in which the Brahmins have recognized the power of Brahma is, to the materialist, nothing other than the despotism of the body.

None of the exceptional powers manifest in the unseen voice of the jewel results from the workings of the sultan's magic ring – all these powers are the body's own powers. The sole magic effect is the power of speech itself, that is, the body's ability to verbalize these powers. Thus, by means of the fiction of the magic ring, Diderot merely bestows the power of speech on the body or, more precisely, on that bodily part traditionally thought of as the least submissive to the soul or mind. At this point, the magical power of the sultan's ring ends, and the 'magical power' of the acousmatic voice (and that of the body as its never completely revealed bearer) takes over. Unlike Chion's *acousmêtre* – which, as a rule, loses its powers at de-acousmatization – the body actually possesses the powers manifested by its unseen voice, and would retain them even if it were completely revealed – these powers are not themselves an effect of the unseen voice.

Wherein lies the 'magical power' of the body? What does that power boil down to? A single example should suffice: how does the body 'read' the mind of the woman it embodies? Or, more precisely, how does the jewel 'know' that the woman – in this particular case a nun and therefore, by definition, a virtuous woman – is thinking impure thoughts? The answer is provided by her jewel itself: 'her little finger told me so'.[47] It is in this manner – that is, on the basis of their own affections – that the jewels know everything they know. And everything they say is known to them in like manner: their 'indiscreetness' is limited to the 'matters with which they are most familiar',[48] that is, to the interpretation of their own affections. Or, in the words of one of the courtiers: the jewels 'speak only of what they know'.[49] There is nothing in what the jewels say that any other organ could not say about itself if it could be made to speak. The jewels, in other words, speak as the mouth would speak if it limited itself to speaking only of what it really 'knows', that is, if it described only its own affections, for example, the sensations accompanying the ingestion of food. In a word, the jewels speak in the same way as the mouth would speak if it were *not* an organ of speech.

The fact that the jewels never digress from the narrowly delineated topic is analysed by the anatomist Orcotomus, one of 'the great minds', who began to seek in the properties of matter an explanation for the chatter of jewels, as follows: if the jewels all speak about the same things, it is because 'this is the only topic on which they have an opinion'; if they never utter a single word about anything else, it is because 'they lack ideas or terms'; if they keep silent, it is because 'they have nothing to say'.[50] That is, whatever the source of their power of speech may be – the power of the sultan's magic ring, the hand of God, or the blind workings of nature – the jewels merely verbalize their own 'empirical knowledge'. This is also why the jewels 'easily repeat themselves'[51] – sooner or later, they are bound to exhaust their 'knowledge' and experiences, which are not unlimited; they have already told everything about what they know, and they can neither invent nor express anything that they have not experienced themselves, since they lack ideas or terms.

In the view of the radical materialist, then, the jewels owe their credibility to the fact that they – unlike the women themselves, who never lack either ideas or terms, and are therefore able to confabulate indefinitely – inevitably run short of either ideas or terms, that is, they owe it to the fact that they speak dispassionately, involuntarily, mechanically, that they blindly stick to a single topic, that more often than not they repeat themselves – in short, to the fact that they speak like machines.

It is not because their mechanical manner of speaking does not indicate the presence of a spiritual soul, however, that the jewels should be regarded as 'merely machines', as an African Cartesian mistakenly concludes in the novel, applying Descartes's 'metaphysical argument against the souls of animals' to the jewels' speech ('[the] jewels speak the way birds sing').[52] Rather, they should be regarded as machines because a soul that is itself nothing other than an effect of bodily organization speaks through them. While a soul as a substance distinct from the body is likely to have an 'opinion' on several other things besides the body it animates, the talk of a soul identical with the body is limited to verbalization and minimal interpretation of the affections of that body. All modalities of the soul, which is 'nothing without the body',[53] are mere manifestations of that body itself. It is, then, the body itself that has come to speak through the soul. To say *je veux*, I wish, is, in Diderot's opinion, tantamount to saying *je suis tel*,[54] this is how I am. Thus, my wishing cannot be distinguished from my physical makeup; in a word, as a modality of the soul, my wishing is but a state of my corporeal organization. Unlike Descartes's *bête-machine*, Diderot's *homme automate* and La Mettrie's *homme-machine* are not soulless – their soul is their bodily organization itself: just as for Diderot the soul is nothing but 'the organization and life'[55] of the body itself, so for La Mettrie 'all the soul's faculties depend so much on the specific organization of the brain and of the whole body that they are clearly nothing but that very organization'.[56]

As far as Diderot is concerned, women are trustworthy only in so far as they are machines – that is, in so far as it is the soul which is identical to their body or its organization that speaks through them. So also, for La Mettrie, people in general are worthy of his respect and affection only in so far as they are machines. 'Do you know why I still have some respect for men?', he asks in his last work, *Système d'Épicure*. 'Because I seriously believe them to be machines. If I believed the opposite hypothesis, I know few of them with whom I would wish to associate.'[57]

This idea could be seen as La Mettrie's commentary on Diderot's *Les Bijoux indiscrets*, with which he was familiar and which he hailed enthusiastically as 'more learned than indiscreet'.[58] Here, La Mettrie is developing his notorious man–machine ethics according to which 'lack of faithfulness in a wife or a mistress' is 'only a slight defect', just as theft is 'a bad habit rather than a crime'.[59] Why is this so? Simply because people are machines, that is, because their soul is nothing other than an effect of their bodily organization. According to La Mettrie, we are driven in our actions by our bodily organization, while we ourselves are literally powerless: 'when I do good or evil . . . it is the fault of my blood . . . which makes me will and determines me in everything'.[60] Thus, a criminal is 'the slave of the blood galloping in his veins, as the hand of a watch is the slave of the works which make it move'.[61] It is because the criminal 'was not free not to be guilty'[62] – it was no more in his power to stop the 'galloping' of his bodily fluids, and his thoughts with them, 'than it is in the power of a thermometer or a barometer to check the liquid that heat or air pressure must push up';[63] therefore he 'only deserves compassion'[64] – that La Mettrie is trying to free him of the remorse accompanying his crimes (which is, perhaps, his most scandalous thesis – the only one to embrace it wholeheartedly was the Marquis de Sade[65]). La Mettrie is therefore able to tolerate the people around him only because he firmly believes that they are driven in all their actions – in fornication, in theft, and so on – by their bodily organization. (It was, perhaps, in order for others to be able to tolerate *him* and *his* excesses[66] that he occasionally referred to himself as 'Mr Machine'.[67]) If people were not machines – that is, if they had a spiritual soul which did not depend so closely on their bodily organization – he would find them repellent. Or, more precisely, he would find people repellent if they indulged in fornication, theft, and so forth despite the fact that they were able to wish what they wish more or less independently of their bodily organization – that is, despite the fact that for them, 'I wish' was not synonymous with 'this is how I am'.

That they, too, are driven in their fornication by their bodily organization ('everyone is driven by their organization',[68] says Diderot in another of his works) and that therefore, strictly speaking, it is not they themselves who want to fornicate but, rather, their jewels – or, in short, that they themselves are nothing other than *femmes-machines* – is something the heroines of Diderot's novel come to realize for themselves when they say: 'our conduct is dictated by our jewels'.[69] The materialist lesson of the novel is therefore as follows: it is not the soul that is in command of the organs; rather, it is the organs that 'often despotically command the soul'.[70] The despotism of the organs or of the body itself, is nowhere so obvious as it is in the jewels or in those bodily parts which, as we read in Diderot's *Salon de 1767, veulent quand le fils d'Adam ne veut pas*, wish when the son of Adam does not, *et qui ne veulent pas quand le fils d'Adam voudrait bien*,[71] and do not wish when the son of Adam would like to. Or, as Diderot puts it in his *Éléments de physiologie*:

> It is never you who wishes to eat or to vomit, it is the stomach; for urinating, it is the bladder; and likewise for the other functions. However much you may wish it, nothing will happen unless the bodily organ wishes it also to be. You may wish to enjoy the woman you love, but when will you have that enjoyment? When the organ wishes it to be.[72]

La Mettrie concludes his reflections on man–machine ethics with the maxim: 'Materialism is the antidote to misanthropy.'[73] The moral that could be extracted from Diderot's *Les Bijoux indiscrets* is pretty much the same: materialism is the antidote to – *misogyny*.

The novel should not be dismissed as a youthful literary experiment; rather, it should be considered an integral part of the author's philosophical canon. Apart from the criticism of spiritualism, it also offers a provisional way out of an impasse the materialist sage has reached while thinking about his mind. According to Diderot, the insurmountable difficulty of thinking about one's mind is that the mind – like the eye – cannot see itself:

> Many times, with the intention of examining what was going on in my head, and of *surprising my mind in the act*, I cast myself into the deepest meditation, withdrawing into myself with all the application that I am capable of. But these efforts led to nothing. It seemed to me that one would need to be simultaneously both inside and outside oneself, while at the same time performing not only the role of observer but also that of the machine observed. But as with the eye, so too it is with the mind: it cannot see itself. . . . A monster with two heads attached to the same neck might perhaps teach us something novel. One must therefore wait until nature, which combines all and which, over the centuries, bears along the most extraordinary phenomena, shall give us a dicephalus who contemplates himself, and one of whose heads observes the other.[74]

While waiting for the genuine dicephalus to emerge,[75] Diderot has, in *Les Bijoux indiscrets*, by doubling the speech organs, himself created *un monstre à deux têtes*, a two-headed monster, 'one of whose heads observes the other':

'the discourse of [the] jewel'[76] is simply testimony given by one of the two heads – the one that is 'dispassionate, and adds nothing to the truth'[77] – on the other, or, in short, a first-hand account of *a mind that has surprised itself in the act.*

Notes

1. Thus, for example, the two central characters in Jostein Gaarder's novel *Sophie's World*, or the main character in Woody Allen's film *The Purple Rose of Cairo*, that is, the actor in the film-within-a-film who walks off the screen into the 'real world', are aware that they exist only as a fiction in the writer's imagination. When they realize that they are living their lives in a fictional reality of a book or film, it is the writer who created them and wrote their lines that these characters typically recognize as God (the character who steps out of the cinema screen is able to grasp the role of God in the real world only on the basis of the creative, demiurgic role of the writer with respect to the fictional universe of the film).
2. Denis Diderot, *The Indiscreet Jewels*, trans. Sophie Hawkes (New York: Marsilio, 1993), 49.
3. Aram Vartanian, 'Introduction', *Les Bijoux indiscrets*, in Denis Diderot, *Œuvres complètes*, ed. Herbert Dieckmann, Jacques Proust and Jean Varloot (Paris: Hermann, 1975–), 3: 12.
4. Diderot, *The Indiscreet Jewels*, 33.
5. For a detailed catalogue of these characters, see Emita B. Hill, 'The Role of "le monstre" in Diderot's thought,' *Studies on Voltaire and the Eighteenth Century* 97 (1972), 149–261.
6. Diderot, *The Indiscreet Jewels*, 122.
7. Diderot, *The Indiscreet Jewels*, 121.
8. Diderot, *The Indiscreet Jewels*, 122.
9. Diderot, *The Indiscreet Jewels*, 125.
10. Diderot, *The Indiscreet Jewels*, 125.
11. Diderot, *The Indiscreet Jewels*, 126.
12. Diderot, *The Indiscreet Jewels*, 126.
13. Diderot, *The Indiscreet Jewels*, 19.
14. Diderot, *The Indiscreet Jewels*, 28.
15. Diderot, *The Indiscreet Jewels*, 49.
16. Diderot, *The Indiscreet Jewels*, 28.
17. Diderot, *The Indiscreet Jewels*, 47.
18. Diderot, *The Indiscreet Jewels*, 49.
19. Diderot, *The Indiscreet Jewels*, 21.
20. Diderot, *The Indiscreet Jewels*, 36.
21. Diderot, *The Indiscreet Jewels*, 22.
22. Diderot, *The Indiscreet Jewels*, 110.
23. Diderot, *The Indiscreet Jewels*, 19.
24. Diderot, *The Indiscreet Jewels*, 22.
25. Diderot, *The Indiscreet Jewels*, 22.

26. Michel Chion, *The Voice in Cinema*, trans. Claudia Gorbman (New York: Columbia University Press, 1999), 23–8.
27. Chion, *The Voice in Cinema*, 24.
28. Chion, *The Voice in Cinema*, 28.
29. Chion, *The Voice in Cinema*.
30. Chion, *The Voice in Cinema*, (original emphasis).
31. Diderot, *Encyclopédie*, in *Œuvres complètes*, 8: 163.
32. Diderot, *Encyclopédie*.
33. Diderot, *Encyclopédie*, in *Œuvres complètes*, 5: 272. In tracing the history of the term 'acousmatic', Chion himself refers to this article; see *The Voice in Cinema*, 19, note 5.
34. Diderot, *The Indiscreet Jewels*, 22.
35. Diderot, *The Indiscreet Jewels*, 154.
36. Diderot, *The Indiscreet Jewels*. 154.
37. Diderot, *The Indiscreet Jewels*, 23.
38. Diderot, *The Indiscreet Jewels*, 34.
39. Diderot, *The Indiscreet Jewels*, 24.
40. Diderot, *The Indiscreet Jewels*, 13.
41. Diderot, *The Indiscreet Jewels*, 35.
42. Diderot, *The Indiscreet Jewels*, 35–6.
43. Diderot, *The Indiscreet Jewels*, 31–2.
44. Diderot, *The Indiscreet Jewels*, 22.
45. Diderot, *The Indiscreet Jewels*, 21.
46. Diderot, *The Indiscreet Jewels*, 49–50.
47. Diderot, *The Indiscreet Jewels*, 27.
48. Diderot, *The Indiscreet Jewels*, 24.
49. Diderot, *The Indiscreet Jewels*, 24.
50. Diderot, *The Indiscreet Jewels*, 32.
51. Diderot, *The Indiscreet Jewels*, 105.
52. Diderot, *The Indiscreet Jewels*, 198.
53. Denis Diderot, *Éléments de physiologie*, in *Œuvres*, ed. Laurent Versini, 5 vols (Paris: Robert Laffont, 1994–97), 1: 1282.
54. Diderot, *Observations sur Hemsterhuis*, in Diderot, *Œuvres*, 1: 718.
55. Diderot, *Éléments de physiologie*, 1: 1316.
56. La Mettrie, *Machine Man*, in *Machine Man and Other Writings*, trans. Ann Thomson (Cambridge: Cambridge University Press, 1996), 26.
57. La Mettrie, *The System of Epicurus*, in *Machine Man and Other Writings*, 103.
58. La Mettrie, *Ouvrage de Pénélope*, ed. Francine Markovits (Paris: Fayard, 2002), 591; see also Aram Vartanian, 'La Mettrie and Diderot Revisited: An Intertextual Encounter', *Diderot Studies* XXI (1983), 170.
59. La Mettrie, *The System of Epicurus*, 103.
60. La Mettrie, *Anti-Seneca or the Sovereign Good*, in *Machine Man and Other Writings*, 141.
61. La Mettrie, *Anti-Seneca or the Sovereign Good*, 143.
62. La Mettrie, *Anti-Seneca or the Sovereign Good*, 143.
63. La Mettrie, *Anti-Seneca or the Sovereign Good*, 140.
64. La Mettrie, *Anti-Seneca or the Sovereign Good*, 143.
65. See Jacques Domenech, *L'Éthique des Lumières: Les fondements de la morale dans la philosophie française du XVIIIe siècle* (Paris: J. Vrin, 1989), 173.

66. For a description of some of La Mettrie's excesses at the court of Frederick the Great, see Giles MacDonogh, *Frederick the Great: A Life in Deed and Letters* (New York: St. Martin's Press, 2000), 214.

67. See, for example, La Mettrie *Épître à Mlle A. C. P. ou la machine terrassée*, in *Œuvres philosophiques*, ed. Francine Markovits, 2 vols (Paris: Fayard, 1987), 2:215 and *passim*.

68. Diderot, *Réfutation d'Helvétius*, in *Œuvres*, 1: 805.

69. Diderot, *The Indiscreet Jewels*, 34.

70. Diderot, *Observations sur Hemsterhuis*, 1: 712.

71. Diderot, *Les Salons*, in *Œuvres*, 4: 726.

72. Diderot, *Éléments de physiologie*, 1: 1308.

73. La Mettrie, *The System of Epicurus*, 103.

74. Diderot, *Additions à la Lettre sur les sourds et muets*, in *Œuvres*, 4:55 (original emphasis). This was also the opinion of Buffon, who wrote in a letter of 6 January 1739 to Dutour: 'in the same way as the tip of the finger cannot touch itself and as the eye cannot see itself, so the thought cannot comprehend itself'; quoted in Jacques Roger, *Buffon: un philosophe au Jardin du Roi* (Paris: Fayard, 1989), 72.

75. The deformations Diderot was still expecting nature to produce were known to have occurred centuries before Diderot; see Jan Bondeson, 'The Tocci Brothers, and Other Dicephali', in *The Two-headed Boy, and Other Medical Marvels* (Ithaca, NY and London: Cornell University Press, 2000), 160–88.

76. Diderot, *The Indiscreet Jewels*, 19.

77. Diderot, *The Indiscreet Jewels*, 23.

3

Ghosts of Substance Past: Schelling, Lacan, and the Denaturalization of Nature

Adrian Johnston

Introduction

In his 1958 *écrit* 'The Direction of the Treatment and the Principles of Its Power', Jacques Lacan declares that the object of psychoanalysis ('our particular subject matter') is '*antiphusis*' (anti-nature).[1] Years later, in a session of the twenty-fourth seminar, Lacan again makes reference to a 'counter-nature' [*contre-nature*], maintaining there that this is a notion easier to comprehend than what is imprecisely signified by the term 'nature'.[2] Analysis deals with something other than nature, with something opposed to or set against that which is commonly identified as natural. At this stage in his teaching (the quasi-structuralist phase during the 1950s), it is not difficult to guess what Lacan means by this: Given that human nature, as the specific nature with which psychoanalysis occupies itself, is shot through with non-natural influences, analysts are restricted to handling manifestations of a denaturalized nature.[3] And, of course, the reason why human nature is (from an analytic perspective) invariably denaturalized is that individuals are submerged in a world of images and signifiers from their earliest beginnings onwards. What is more, Lacan repeatedly emphasizes that the big Other, as a non-natural symbolic order, precedes the birth of the individual, preparing in advance a place for him or her in a system obeying rules other than the laws of nature. Thanks to these representational mediators and their central role in the processes of subjectification, the Lacanian subject exists as a (non-)being alienated from its corporeal-material substratum.

But what allows for these Imaginary-Symbolic structures to take root in the first place? What permits them to colonize bodies, to overwrite the being of individuals and thereby denaturalize their natures? Why are these structures, often involving modifications apparently moving in directions contrary to the presumed default trajectories of the libidinal economy, not rejected by this economy in a manner analogous to failed organ transplants? An incredibly important theoretical issue of direct concern to Freudian–Lacanian psychoanalytic metapsychology is at stake here: the very conditions of possibility for the genesis of the subject, for the ontogenetic emergence of a being situated on the plane of *antiphusis*. One might be tempted to respond to these questions by insisting that, as far as Freud and Lacan are concerned, an external imposition, coming from an Other (whether this Other be the Freudian Oedipal family unit or the Lacanian symbolic order), is solely responsible for fashioning unnatural subjectivity out of natural animality, for transubstantiating an organic being with instincts and needs into a speaking being with drives and desires. The (symbolic) 'castration' dictated by the socio-structural *Umwelt* is, according to this response, a transformative traumatic blow descending upon the individual from elsewhere. However, human nature must be, in its intrinsic essence, configured in such a way as to be receptive to this blow and its repercussions. In other words, it must be in the nature of this particular nature to be open to and capable of undergoing the dynamics of denaturalization involved in the processes of subjectification. A psychoanalytically influenced theory of the subject that fails to furnish a basic delineation of human nature as the precondition for the genesis of subjectivity is groundless, incapable of explaining a foundational dimension of its object of enquiry.

In the later seminars of the 1970s, a series of somewhat cryptic remarks testifies to Lacan's awareness of the need to redefine nature itself in order to account for why human nature is predisposed to being thoroughly altered by the denaturalizing mediation of socio-symbolic structures. In both the twenty-first and twenty-fourth seminars, Lacan contends that nature is far from being entirely natural.[4] However, this is not just a slightly reworded reiteration of his earlier remarks from the 1950s about humanity's denaturalized nature. Rather than grounding his assertions here by invoking the externally imposed intrusion of images and signifiers as the ultimate cause of the denaturalization involved in subjectification, Lacan takes the additional step of pointing to something within nature itself that inclines it in the direction of its own effacement. In the twenty-third seminar, Lacan posits that '*la nature se spécifie de n'être pas une.*'[5] That is to say, nature (at least human nature) should not be envisioned as an integrated organic wholeness, a co-ordinated sphere of components interrelating according to the laws of an eternally balanced harmony.

In fact, Lacan's contemporaneous meditations on the nonexistence of the '*rapport sexuel*' (sexual relationship)[6] are directly tied to these broader reflections on the nature of nature. One of the rudimentary lessons of psychoanalysis is that the sexual is never simply sexual. Hence the notion of the *rapport sexuel* is bound up with a whole series of themes and implications concerning matters seemingly far removed from carnal interactions between males and females. The (nonexistent) sexual relationship, as Lacan repeatedly insists, is the paradigm for the pervasive themes of harmony and wholeness that colour, at a global level, fundamental conceptualizations regarding the essence of reality and material being.[7] *'Il n'y a pas de rapport sexuel'* implies, among other things, that balanced co-ordination is missing, that nature, within the realm of human existence, is anything but a harmonious and whole 'One–All'. As Lacan expresses it in the seventeenth seminar, nature does not 'copulate' in order to generate the fictitious, perfected unity of a spherical totality.[8] Perhaps this fractured field of material being ought to be designated as a 'barred Real' (corresponding to Lacan's 'barred Other' as the inconsistent, conflict-ridden symbolic order).

What are the consequences of these reflections regarding the disharmonious 'not-wholeness' of (human) nature? More specifically, how is this barred Real relevant to a theory of subjectivity informed by psychoanalysis? Lacan's late work provides only a few hints. At one point, he identifies 'liberty' [*liberté*] with 'the nonexistence of the sexual relationship',[9] which, in the light of the above, can be understood as indicating that the freedom enjoyed by the autonomous subject is made possible by the lack of an integrated organic foundation as the grounding basis of this subject's being. Similarly, several years later, Lacan speaks of nature as not all that natural because it is internally plagued by 'rottenness' [*pourriture*], by a decay or defect out of which culture (as *antiphusis*) bubbles forth [*bouillonner*].[10] Viewed thus, human nature is naturally destined for denaturalization. To put it differently, immaterial subjectivity immanently arises out of the dysfunctionality of a libidinal-material ground.[11] Moving forward with the development of these sketchily outlined Lacanian propositions requires going back to a thinker Lacan never mentions even once anywhere in either the nine-hundred-page *Écrits* or the twenty-seven-year course of *le Séminaire*: the German idealist philosopher F.W.J. von Schelling.

A synthesis of Schelling and Lacan enables the argument to be advanced that certain properties of an asubjective, heteronomous libidinal-material foundation (as the barred Real of human nature) function as fundamental conditions of possibility for the ontogenesis of subjective autonomy (as a transcendence of this same 'natural' foundation). These properties are the meta-transcendental conditions for the event of the advent of the Schellingian–Lacanian transcendent(al) subject *qua* $. A psychoanalytic theory of subjectivity informed by German idealism is able to contend that, strange as it may sound, autonomy immanently emerges out of heteronomy as an excess or a surplus that cannot be reinscribed back within the ontological register out of which it grew. As Lacan indicates in his later seminars, the freedom of autonomous subjectivity is possible only if being is inherently incomplete and internally inconsistent, asymmetrical and out of joint with itself. If, by contrast, being is entirely at one with itself, if material nature is a perfectly functioning machine in which each and every cog and component is organically co-ordinated into the single, massive whole of an uninterrupted One–All, then no space remains, no clearing is held open, for the emergence of something capable of (at least from time to time) transcending or breaking with this stifling ontological closure. Being must be originally and primordially unbalanced in order for the subject as a trans-ontological excess to become operative.[12] As Schelling himself succinctly states: 'Were the first nature in harmony with itself, it would remain so. It would be constantly One and would never become Two.'[13] Those points and moments where being becomes dysfunctional (that is, when, to put it loosely, 'the run of things' breaks down) signal the possibility for the genesis of subjectivity as that which cannot be reduced to a mere circuit in the machinery of a base material substratum in which everything is exhaustively integrated with everything else.

Schelling, in his *Clara* dialogue, speaks of the 'horror of nature',[14] claiming that 'within nature there was something nameless and frightful'.[15] He then points to the 'hideous' necessity of nature's transient nature.[16] In *The Ages of the World*, he maintains that intuiting the 'inner life' lying beneath the 'peaceful' façade of reality's appearances is liable to provoke 'terror'.[17] This Schellingian theme, which comes to the fore in his later post-idealist texts starting in 1809, is vitally important for a metapsychologically based transcendental materialist theory of subjectivity in so far as it tacitly advances two axiomatic theses crucial for such a theory. One: the underlying onto-genetic base of the subject consists of the materiality of a certain Real – more specifically, of an internally conflicted libidinal economy at odds with itself from the very beginning (in other words, the Schellingian 'vortex of drive' [*Trieb*] as the volatility of, so to speak, substance against itself); two: the subject is genetically produced as a consequence of the fact that the disturbing discontent of this initial state prompts efforts at taming and domesticating this 'corpo-Real',[18] efforts that come to constitute and define the fundamental contours of subjectivity itself (as a subject-position characterized by a [pseudo-]transcendence of embodied materiality).[19]

Part One: From spiritual corporeality . . .

In his 1809 essay on human freedom, Schelling describes how an occluded-yet-insistent underbelly, an anarchic base, forever lies just beneath the calm, smooth surfaces of rationally governed, conceptually well-structured reality (surfaces that arose out of this same obscured foundation – even though, once they have arisen, a sustained tension is generated between surface and depth, between, in Schelling's terms, the Ideal and the Real).[20] At least as far as human existence is concerned, Schelling posits a law of reverse entropy: Chaos comes first, and any established order is necessarily preceded by this same chaos from which it emerges and subsequently excludes.[21] He consistently maintains that the Real is necessarily prior to the Ideal,[22] namely, that the palpitations of an archaic, shadowy (proto-)materiality come before and condition the subsequent blossoming forth of the luminous flower of a more evanescent, spiritualized dimension of existence rooted, none the less, in this dense, heavy soil.[23] The crucial caveat Schelling attaches to the delineation of this basic dynamic, however, is that 'Dependence does not determine the nature of the dependent, and merely declares that the dependent entity, whatever else it may be, can only be as a consequence of that upon which it is dependent; it does not declare what this dependent entity is or is not.'[24] In other words, acknowledging that the Ideal is (ontogenetically) conditioned by the Real is not tantamount to a reductionistic assertion to the effect that the Ideal is merely epiphenomenal in relation to the Real. Here, in conformity with a general tenet of dialectical thought, (Ideal) effects can outgrow their (Real) causes. This allows for the possibility that the ground of the material Real can internally/immanently give rise to a process of 'de-materialization' eventually resulting in the emergence of an immaterial form of subjectivity, a subject that enjoys a relative degree of autonomy in relation to the ground (that is, the Schellingian *Grund*) from which it splits itself off in the process of being created.

Furthermore, Schelling's invocation of the notion of a 'primal longing' in the passages from the 1809 *Freiheitschrift* cited above refers to an aspect of his later works that is of major importance for the present discussion: the proposition that such forces as drives, desires and passions play an absolutely foundational role in the constitution of reality (a proposition that is central to any psychoanalytic explanation of the human condition). In the 1810 'Stuttgart Seminars', Schelling proclaims that 'desire' [*Begierde*] is the primordial manifestation of spiritual ideality[25] (he characterizes desire as 'an unremitting striving' and 'an eternally insatiable obsession'[26]). This desirous, passionate spirit [*Geist*] both 'fuels itself' and 'is addicted to matter'.[27] That is to say: Ideal spirituality, initially incarnated in desire, is simultaneously independent of and dependent upon Real materiality (or, as he phrases it in *The Ages of the World*, 'coveting' is halfway between nothingness and being as a non-being that, none the less, is not a mere nothing[28]). Is this not an untenable contradiction?

This puzzling paradox becomes comprehensible once one understands that, according to Schelling, a paradoxical antagonism/tension always-already perturbs being from the heart of its inner core. There is something 'in being more than being itself'. As he tirelessly asserts again and again, the Real of natural being contains within itself the Ideal of spiritual negativity as that which comes to break away from and transcend this ground. Schelling's treatment of desire here is an outgrowth of his general tendency to chart the immanent genesis of the transcendent in its various forms and modes. He proclaims that 'nature . . . liberates itself from the inside out'.[29] Apropos desire as the original embodiment of the spiritual dimension, this means that a passionate longing proper to the Real of natural being (rather than this being's collision with the otherness of a pre-existent external agency or force) internally generates the momentum needed for that which is eternally in being more than being itself to break out of the ontological closure of what Schelling portrays as the sterile cycles of expansion and contraction. The momentum behind the 'escape velocity' from the prison-house of the vortex of *Trieb* comes from within the confines of this same prison. The *Weltalter* manuscripts are quite explicit on this matter. Primal life is haunted by 'the wish to escape from the involuntary movement and from the distress of pining', by an 'obsession' or a 'yearning' to attain freedom from the rotary motion of the drives[30] (with Schelling identifying this rotary motion, this circulating movement, as the 'first nature'[31]). Moreover, this primordial state involves, as part of its very essence, the imbalance of contradiction. The 'fire of contradiction' as the 'discontent' of a 'self-lacerating rage' immanent to the materiality of being prompts/triggers the emergence of and striving towards a 'higher' plane of existence standing above the roiling, seething cauldron of driven matter.[32] If by 'desire' Schelling is referring to this basic impulse within the material Real, then it should now be clear why desire, as the basis of Ideal spirituality, is simultaneously independent of and dependent upon the Real materiality of being: Being gives birth to the non-being of a desire which, although it owes its existence to being, seeks to achieve a relative autonomy with respect to it.

Having set the stage in this manner, it is possible to examine Schelling's *Weltalter* productively from a Lacanian angle. The narrative sketched in

The Ages of the World can be interpreted as a metapsychological story of the ontogenesis of psychic subjectivity told in theosophical terms. Schelling himself offers an explanation for why he feels forced to resort to allegories and metaphors that might seem less clear and unambiguous than the discourse of late modern philosophy employed in his earlier writings. The three drafts of the *Weltalter* manuscript represent an unfinished project aiming to treat the three temporal epochs of past, present and future. The three extant abortive versions of this project deal exclusively with the past. And, by 'past', Schelling means the 'eternal past', that is, a time before (linear) time that forever precedes the present temporal period.[33] The philosopher has no choice but to struggle to conceptualize this eternal past, a past differing radically from the present, from within the confines and constraints of the era of the present.[34]

During Schelling's 'Stuttgart Seminars', there are moments when preliminary outlines of the *Weltalter* endeavour are quite visible. He explicitly asserts there that a definite parallel exists between, on the one hand, the genetic dynamics involved in the formation of individual subjectivity and, on the other, the process of God's creation of the existent natural world through the elevation of Himself above the murky fray of His own drive-ridden being.[35] With both the singular subject and the divine creator, a 'coming-to-consciousness' proceeds out of a prior 'preconscious state [*Bewusstlosigkeit*]' devoid of 'any consciousness of division and distinction [*Scheidung und Unterscheidung*]'.[36] What is more, in this same text Schelling maintains that consciousness itself requires separation, discord, conflict, antagonism, and so on – in short, 'division and distinction'.[37]

In *The Ages of the World*, Schelling's theosophical narrative refers to a primordial condition (as the 'preconscious state' mentioned in the 'Stuttgart Seminars') characterized by a sterile pulsation, a recurrent oscillation, between the opposed forces of expansion and contraction[38] (as the rotary circulation of archaic drives). He even indicates that this condition, marked by an opposition of forces, involves being trapped in the closure of a vicious circle.[39] What finally breaks this deadlock? If this pulsating oscillation between expansion and contraction were in perfect balance, involving a strict complementarity, then this initial state would persist indefinitely. Schelling surmises, however, that some sort of disturbing imbalance, an unsettling tension disrupting the cyclical movement of drives, intervenes to prompt this originary condition to sunder itself, to give rise to something other: 'contradiction . . . is alone what drives, nay, what coerces, action. Therefore, without the contradiction, there would be no movement, no life, and no progress. There would only be eternal stoppage, a deathly slumber of all of the forces.'[40]

Schelling proposes here that there never was a primordial state of balanced equilibrium between diametrically opposed tendencies to begin with, not even in the eternal past. If, in the beginning, such a satisfying equilibrium had been in place, then there would never have been a genuine beginning as the start of a trajectory of movement departing from and leaving behind this point of origin. Schelling unambiguously maintains that, in the beginning, there is 'contradiction' (that is, antagonism, imbalance, strife and tension).

Consequently, the *Grund* of the drives is not a cohesive, solid, unified ontological foundation of harmoniously integrated natural energies and impulses, a homogeneous, monolithic mass of dense corporeality at one with itself, but, rather, a fragmented and perturbed hotchpotch of conflicting elements lacking overall symmetrical measure, proportion or ratio. In order to account for the (hypothesized) transition from the Real of ground (past) to the reality of existence (present), this past must be presumed to be (in Lacanian parlance) a barred Real (that is, a Real always-already out of joint with itself). One must assume that, as it were, the ground fails to ground – that *Grund* is *Ungrund*, an abyssal groundlessness.

Part Two: . . . to corporeal spirituality

In the *Weltalter* narrative, the unbalanced *Grund*-as-*Ungrund*, due to its dissatisfying instability and desire-provoking contradictions, catalyses the sudden event of a gesture of negation (with ground's internal inconsistency being a vital precondition allowing for the very occurrence of this gesture – the cracks within the foundation of *Grund* are the open spaces, the clearing, within and out of which can burst forth something other than this ground's own drives). According to Schelling, this exit from (via immanent negation of) the inconsistent ground of the barred Real is the true moment of beginning (rather than the eternal past of the vortex of *Trieb* qualifying as a proper beginning). He asserts that the beginning of any movement whatsoever is predicated upon a negation of a point that becomes a starting point through this negation.[41] In combined theosophical and psychoanalytic terms, God must 'abject' His unconscious, quasi-material side in order to become Himself as an actualized subject; in fact, it is through this expulsive act of abjection, this violent taking of distance from the drives, that God comes to (be) Himself.[42]

For a metapsychological interpretation, the event of rupture with the bog of the drives is of special interest. The Schellingian act (as a decision [*Entscheidung*] to divorce, part or separate [*scheiden*] – hence the term

'*Ent-Scheidung*', signifying a separating decision or decision to separate), like the Lacanian Real, is an occurrence that has never taken place within the field of fully constituted reality (as the domain of 'existence' opposed to that of ground, as per Schelling's ground-versus-existence distinction). None the less, this act must be presupposed as having happened in order to account for the status quo of the present.

In the 'Stuttgart Seminars', Schelling bluntly asserts that the event of the *Ent-Scheidung* is not to be thought of as an act that occurs at some point within the linear flow of chronological time. He maintains that this intervention is itself atemporal.[43] One key effect of the *Ent-Scheidung* is to give rise to chronological temporality, to initiate the linear movement of time. This decision–separation is not in time; it creates time. Although it is treated as archaic and primordial (albeit not archaic and primordial in the sense of a now-past-but-once-present moment), the rotary motion of the drives is not to be mistaken for the 'true Beginning' as such. That is to say: only with the cancellation/negation of this vortex of *Trieb* via the gesture of the *Ent-Scheidung* is a genuine beginning possible, an initiation of a (temporal) movement of change and flux (instead of cyclical repetition) flowing away from its thereafter-surpassed past point of origin. Schelling's act of breaking away from the Real of ground cannot itself be included within the parameters of the reality of existence that it generates as an outcome (here, one encounters the logic according to which the cause is necessarily obfuscated by its effects – the domain of the cause's effects is structurally unable to accommodate or integrate its own 'lost cause'[44]).

Along these lines, Schellingian philosophy makes a crucial contribution to psychoanalytic theory by struggling to shed light on the relationship between, on the one hand, the unconscious dimension of psychic subjectivity and, on the other, the initiation and execution of decisions and deeds. Here and there, Freud occasionally mentions what he puzzlingly designates as the 'choice of neurosis'.[45] What does it mean to say that an individual 'chooses' his or her psychopathological character structure, especially for a model of mind based upon the axiom that an unconscious beyond conscious control (and, hence, presumably outside the parameters of any decision-making agency capable of choice) overdetermines mental life? Do not psychopathologies, at least according to psychoanalysis, befall individuals, instead of being opted for through some sort of strange deliberative procedure? In certain ways, the Lacanian 'subject of the unconscious' exhibits a similar perplexing oddness: Is not the unconscious fundamentally asubjective, that which eludes or escapes the domain of subjectivity?

For Schellingian philosophy as well as Freudian–Lacanian metapsychology, prior to the advent of repression (itself conditioned by a prior establishment of the rudiments of representational-structural mediation), there is no distinction to be made between that which is conscious and that which is unconscious; neither psychic system exists yet *per se*. Through a certain 'cut', two new strata are simultaneously created: the unconscious and the subject. The advent of representational-structural mediation permits subjectivity (that is, the *parlêtre qua* $) to arise as what detaches itself from and transcends the turbulent immediacy of the drives, with this immediacy having correlatively become what forever after must be permanently repressed (that is, unconscious). The unconscious and the subject are co-emergent, owing their existence to the same ontogenetic factors. Thus, Lacan's phrase 'subject of the unconscious' might be interpreted as, in one sense, pointing to the claim that the processes of subjectification and the movements/mechanisms generating the unconscious are co-dependent. In other words, no subject(ification) is possible without the creation of an unconscious.

In *The Ages of the World*, Schelling describes a deed that can never be brought before conscious awareness. More specifically, he identifies the mythical moment when an individual 'decides' upon the nature of his or her essential character (strikingly akin to Freud's idea that someone 'chooses' his or her neurosis) as precisely such a deed.[46] At this juncture, two important questions demand answers. First, are the drives and their rotary motion the distinctive content of the temporal epoch of the eternal past, or, alternatively, does this eternal past (also) contain the act–decision that breaks with these same drives? Second, although this 'choice' might be a priori or transcendental in relation to fully constituted experiential reality (in other words, this separating decision is a constitutive possibility condition for the emergence of the reality of existence out of the Real of ground), what are the meta-transcendental conditions of possibility for the occurrence of this decisive moment itself – that is to say, what clears the space, within the Real of ground, for the irruption of the *Ent-Scheidung*? As will become increasingly evident, these two questions are bound up with each other.

So why is it that the Schellingian deed, as viewed through the lens of Freud's 'choice of neurosis' and/or Lacan's 'act', must be unconscious? Why cannot the *Ent-Scheidung* be brought back before the subject's consciousness? The complementary inverse of the Hegelian effect that exceeds its cause is operative here: namely, the Kantian cause that exceeds (or recedes behind) its effect. The transcendental act/deed founding consciousness cannot be (re)introduced into the circumscribed reality of the experiential field to which it gives rise.

Consequently, the Schellingian–Lacanian unconscious is not to be identified exclusively as the vortex of *Trieb* (in orthodox Freudian terms, the unconscious is not simply the id). Instead, what remains unconscious in the constituted subject is, above all else, the cutting, disruptive gesture of the act/deed *qua Ent-Scheidung* founding subjectivity itself in its (attempted) jettisoning of the drives. Subjectivity's ownmost origin is the most foreign and inaccessible thing for it. The Schellingian temporal category of the eternal past contains the vortex of *Trieb* as well as the act of the *Ent-Scheidung*. The unconscious is not just the thriving mass of the id-body and its multitude of libidinal impulses, although they too are part of it. Prior to the 'cision' of the act–decision generating the subject through a splitting off from the Real of its own *Grund*, there is no distinction whatsoever between the unconscious and consciousness. Hence the unconscious, along with consciousness, is created by the *Ent-Scheidung*, and this act–decision itself is almost instantaneously absorbed into one of the products of its very own intervention (that is, this act–decision creates the unconscious, and is then swallowed up by this same unconscious which it produced, devoured by its own progeny).[47]

This recasting of the unconscious leads to the pivotal contention that the unconscious, concealed behind the veils of repression, is not to be understood merely as an aggregate of overdetermining factors and forces compromising or impeding the individual's autonomous capacities as a free agent (this being a crude yet common depiction of the psychoanalytic unconscious). Rather, repression frequently conceals the opposite: namely, the Schellingian 'abyss of freedom', a radical indeterminacy and groundlessness covered over by various psychic layers seeking to avoid this void. Confronting the unconscious, instead of involving a realization that one is a puppet dancing on the end of personal-historical strings held firmly in the grasp of a libidinal puppet-master, might very well amount, in certain instances, to coming face to face with an abyssal autonomy, an anonymous nothingness/negativity situated as the extimate kernel of one's subjective existence. Paraphrasing Freud ('the normal man is not only far more immoral than be believes but also far more moral than he knows'[48]), one could say that the normal man is not only far more determined than he believes, but also far freer than he knows.[49]

One might think that human freedom, an apparent autonomy seen nowhere else in the natural world, is something individuals prize as singularly emblematic of their humanity, as a quasi-divine gift forming the core of a sense of dignity and worth. One of Schelling's post-Kantian innovations is his reversal of this impression as regards freedom. Already in Kant's practical philosophy, the status of human autonomy, itself an innate property of beings endowed with reason, is somewhat ambiguous. Although it deserves esteem, this autonomy is, at least phenomenologically speaking, experienced by those to whom it is bequeathed as, more often than not, a painful burden, a guilt-inducing voice commanding obedience and demanding the sacrifice of the comfortable pursuit of pleasure-orientated inclinations.[50] Schelling goes much further: The true extent of human freedom is such that encountering it is apt to provoke horror or terror. In the *Clara* dialogue, the dialogue's namesake observes that 'the sight of freedom – not the freedom that is usually so-called, but the true and real one – would have to be unbearable to man, even though people talk about it continually and praise it at every instant'.[51] The *Weltalter* manuscripts echo Clara's remark: 'most people are frightened precisely by this abyssal freedom . . . where they see a flash of freedom, they turn away from it as if from an utterly injurious flash of lightning and they feel prostrated by freedom as an appearance that comes from the ineffable, from eternal freedom, from where there is no ground whatsoever'.[52]

Psychoanalytically speaking, this would suggest that abyssal freedom is not 'unconscious' simply in the sense of being structurally incompatible with consciousness. Rather, the spectre of this freedom is barred from consciousness more for defensive than for structural reasons. In other words, such autonomy is unconscious not just because the groundless founding act generating consciousness cannot itself become conscious; this autonomy is kept unconscious through repressive strategies also because it is disturbing – even, in some cases, terrifying.

Schelling asserts that human autonomy is a freedom for evil as well as for good, that individuals contain an a priori propensity for the diabolical as well as the angelic.[53] Evil too is spiritual, and not just pathological *qua* material-phenomenal. Given that Schellingian freedom is, in essence, groundless, there is no transcendent law, no higher, normative principle of ethico-moral reason, governing its employment (as Lacan would put it: 'there is no Other of the Other' or 'the big Other does not exist'). The 'good' side of this freedom is frequently a source of pain in so far as it obliges individuals to do what does not feel pleasurable in the name of a moral rule. But the 'evil' side is also painful, albeit for different reasons. Schelling's treatment of this topic suggests that individuals, if they truly stopped to ponder what they are capable of thanks to the void of abyssal freedom situated at the groundless core of their very being, would realize that they possess the capacity to engage in the most monstrous of atrocities: 'it would be desirable if the rottenness in man could only go so far as animality; but unfortunately man can only stand above or beneath animals'.[54] One aspect of autonomy that renders it disturbing is the fact that there is no guarantee whatsoever that those endowed with it will act 'properly', in ways that are amenable to others (or even to themselves – one must keep in mind the various links conjoining the autonomous subject with the Freudian–Lacanian *Todestrieb*, especially in so far as the death drive involves masochistic self-destructiveness, the human capacity to deviate from the paths laid down by natural and/or rational self-interest).

Much of the preceding analysis has been quietly and steadily building to the following assertion: The opposition between *Grund* and *Urgrund*, between the vortex of *Trieb* and the abyss of freedom – in his later writings, Schelling, on a certain reading, proposes that the nothingness of the *Urgrund* precedes the plentitude of the *Grund* – is a false dichotomy. The domain of the drives is itself the domain underpinning human autonomy. *Trieb* is freedom – or, at a minimum, it is the contingent material condition of possibility for the emergence of full-fledged autonomy.[55] In Schellingian parlance, *Grund* is *Ungrund*; the ground is incapable of functioning in a grounding capacity in so far as it is unstably divided against itself. The ground is not a ground as something grounded or grounding (Heidegger declares that, from Schelling's standpoint, 'the nature of man is grounded in freedom',[56] which would now, in this present context, require being interpreted as saying that the ground of humanity's distinctly human essence is the very lack of a grounding nature).

An authentic materialist paradigm must be based upon the axiomatic contention that material being itself (whether as body, nature, world, and so forth) is internally inconsistent, shot through with antagonisms, fissures, gaps and tensions. For a Schellingian–Lacanian materialist, the foundations of the ontological edifice must contain cracks. In other words, the materiality of the Real is not homogeneous and harmoniously at one with itself; the Real is barred. Why is this thesis so crucial? Why is it essential for advancing a materialist theory of the subject that is not vulnerable to relapses into idealist models? If one maintains that the Real of material being is not barred (that is, that body, nature and world are organically integrated substances in which the functions of their various constituent elements are co-ordinated and operate in tandem), then one must either deny the existence of subjectivity (at a minimum, dismissing it as an epiphenomenal residue of physical reality) or regress back into crude versions of the Real-versus-Ideal dichotomy. Given its stifling ontological closure, the materiality of vulgar materialism cannot give rise to a non-epiphenomenal subjectivity. Thus, if one wishes to assert the materialist thesis concerning the primacy of the material Real while simultaneously positing the effective existence of a non-epiphenomenal subjectivity, either one immediately betrays materialism by endorsing the idealist contention that an entirely separate domain 'above' material being 'exists' on its own, or, alternatively, one struggles to find a means of delineating the material genesis of the immaterial subject.[57] The ultimate meta-transcendental condition for the transcendental subject is the material Real of being as 'not All'. The substance of being must contain splits within itself, splits within whose crack-like clearings is held open the possibility for the self-sundering of this same substance. This sundering is a vital part of what produces the subject.

For Schelling, the ideality of subjectivity arises from the Real of a fractured, conflicted being as a means of overcoming, surmounting or transcending this tortured, writhing mass of drive-ridden matter. And for Lacan, the Real exhibits various quasi-Hegelian properties. In it, one can discern certain convergences of opposites. For instance, the Real is simultaneously the positive plentitude of material, bodily being as well as the negative void of absence evading incarnation and defying representation; it both overflows and withdraws from the register of the Symbolic, being a surplus and a deficit all at once. Treating the Schellingian Real in a similar manner means asserting that the primordial ground, the (pre-)ontological foundation of reality, is simultaneously the 'plenitude' or 'surplus' of the vortex of *Trieb* and the 'void' or 'deficit' of the abyss of freedom, with these two dimensions being combined together in the notion of *Grund*-as-*Un/Ur-grund*. What if, instead of a chronological sequence running from nothing [*Un/Ur-grund*] to being [*Grund*] – sequencing itself should be highly problematic here, since linear temporality allegedly does not exist in the mythical Schellingian epoch of the eternal past – this void (as the abyss of freedom) is embedded in the materiality of being as the fissures and inconsistencies subsisting within the latter?

One way to interpret Heidegger's remarks, in his 1936 seminar on Schelling's *Freiheitschrift*, apropos the Schellingian 'spiritualization of nature'[58] is along these very lines: 'Nature' *qua* the ontological ground of material being is not to be opposed to 'Spirit' *qua* the pre- and/or trans-ontological groundlessness of immaterial autonomy; the 'spiritualization of nature' signifies that the *Ungrund* of autonomy inheres within the *Grund* of material being. Translated into psychoanalytic terms, the libidinal economy (as the ontogenetic ground out of which full-fledged subjectivity emerges) is linked to the embodied existence of the individual. And yet, at the same time, this ground is riddled with antagonisms and tensions right from the beginning – as conflicts within each and every drive, between different drives, and between drives and their *Umwelt*. The psychoanalytic appropriation of Schelling enables one to argue that the inner inconsistency of the libidinal ground of the individual's being is a condition of possibility for the subsequent genesis of a subject linked to, but distinguishing itself from, this same ground. Moreover, this emergent subjectivity possesses a degree of freedom in so far as its drive-ridden 'nature' bequeaths to it the absence of a natural programme:

namely, the absence of a deterministic agenda automatically orientated around the co-ordinated pursuit of a set configuration of closely related means and ends – this could be described as a gift of lack. This missing mandate of nature, its original lack in relation to the conflicted libidinal being of human beings, is a (pre-)condition for the coming-to-be of the 'unnatural' subject of freedom.[59] In terms of its clinical dimension, psychoanalysis tends to associate conflict with psychopathological difficulties that rob the individual of autonomy (such as, for instance, intrapsychic conflicts prompting repressions that result in neurotic rigidity). In terms of the broader implications of Freudian–Lacanian metapsychology for philosophical theories of human freedom, however, conflict is a double-edged sword, since it also serves as a fundamental possibility condition for this freedom.

In his thorough examination of Badiou's œuvre, Peter Hallward contrasts Kant and Badiou via their treatment of autonomy. Whereas the Kantian notion of transcendental freedom entails that autonomous subjectivity is an abiding, underlying constant (even in instances where it does not intervene and thereby manifest its presence), Badiouian autonomous subjectivity, as 'evental' (that is, as conditioned by and contingent upon events), is 'exceptional' and 'rare'.[60] In other words, the freedom of the subject is not part of an invariant noumenal bedrock but, rather, an evanescent occurrence that flashes fleetingly into existence only occasionally. What is being proposed here is, in a sense, a transient transcendence, a momentary break, from time to time, with the run of things (whether natural or social). In Lacanian terms, one could say that the freedom of autonomous subjectivity is provided the chance briefly to emerge at those junctures where the Real and/or the Symbolic become (temporarily) barred – more specifically, when the libidinal economy and/or the big Other become internally inconsistent, unable to solidly dictate a course to be followed (when neither *Trieb* nor *Umwelt* moves with clear, directed authority due to the interference of conflictual disharmonies between or within themselves – it should also be noted that, on the basis of the explanations formulated in this discussion, one ought to reject Hallward's Badiousian step of straightforwardly opposing, along the lines of Badiou's overarching dichotomy between being and event, the drive-as-asubjective and the domain of evental truth promising the possibility of subjectification[61]).

To use an example that is familiar to Lacanians, Sophocles' *Antigone* nicely illustrates this position. Antigone is forced to be free in so far as she confronts a deadlock in her surrounding symbolic order. Caught between two competing obligations (the familial-religious duty to bury the dead and the civic-political duty to obey the laws of the state), Antigone, unable immediately to invoke an overarching third principle that would unproblematically adjudicate between these two competing duties (duties forced into competition by unusual circumstances), subjectifies herself by responding to the event of this rupture (her brother's death followed by Creon's edict) with a resolute decision whose consequences she is compelled to assume – consequences that carry her far beyond the 'pleasure principle' (whether as Kantian pathological inclination or Freudian libidinal satisfaction). This deadlock in the big Other (that is, the fact that contradictions can and do arise between its various injunctions, that it does not always speak with one voice) interpellates Antigone so as to transform her, transubstantiating a mere human individual into an almost inhuman subject. To be more precise, one could think of this as the exact inverse of Althusserian interpellation. Whereas, for Althusser, 'interpellation' designates a process wherein the positive, functional dimensions of 'Ideological State Apparatuses' (or facets of Lacan's big Other as the symbolic order) imprint/impress themselves upon the individual and thereby subjugate him or her – subjectivity here amounts to subjection, to anything but autonomy[62] – this analysis now underway points to a similar yet different process, the process of 'inverse interpellation', wherein the negative, dysfunctional dimensions of the big Other as the symbolic order (that is, the necessary structural incompleteness and inconsistency of this Other/order, denoted by its 'barring') sometimes, due to various factors, 'hail' the individual and thereby force him or her to (temporarily) become an autonomous subject, to be jarred out of the comfortable nonconscious habits of the automaton of quotidian individuality and plunged into an abyss of freedom devoid of the solid ground of unproblematic, taken-for-granted socio-normative directives and guarantees. When it is not plagued by snags in the threads of its fabric, the symbolic order forms an implicit backdrop, a sort of second nature, quietly yet effectively governing the flow of the individual's life in socially and linguistically mediated reality; it tacitly steers both cognition and comportment. However, in becoming temporarily dysfunctional owing to loopholes in its programmes (that is, the inconsistencies subsisting within the structures of the symbolic order), the barred big Other's inherent incompleteness, activated by crises or unforeseen occurrences, offers the sudden opening/opportunity for a transient transcendence *qua* momentary, transitory break with this Other's deterministic nexus.

The example of Antigone highlights the link between the barring of the Symbolic and autonomous subjectivity.[63] However, these cracks and gaps in the big Other, as the barring of the Symbolic, can be exploited as openings/opportunities for the exercise of a transcendent freedom only by an entity preconfigured with a constitution that is itself barred: namely, an entity lacking a homogeneous, unified nature whose programme would be activated automatically in instances where the big Other's determining function breaks down (in other words, a natural fallback position, a certain default steering direction for individual action reverted to when clear socio-normative mandates are inoperative). What is required is again a barred Real: 'human nature' as an inconsistent and conflict-ridden corpo-Real, a libidinal economy intrinsically lacking in balanced cohesiveness and co-ordination. The transient transcendence of freedom is sparked into being when the cracks and gaps of the Real overlap with those subsisting within the Symbolic. This explosive combination of antagonisms ignites the bursting forth of exceptional subjectivity out of mundane individuality.

Another crucial difference with Kant deserves mention. Whereas Kant's practical philosophy maintains that autonomy is an attribute or property possessed by rational beings at the level of their inalienable noumenal essence,[64] the analysis offered here treats autonomy as an insubstantial phenomenon bound up with the faltering or failure of this essence. In other words, freedom does not arise from a special faculty with an innate capacity for autonomy hard-wired into the individual's constitution; instead, the capacity for autonomy is a consequence of the deficient and incomplete harmonization of the various faculties forming the individual's constitution. This represents a 'negative' account of human freedom – an account based on the absence, rather than the presence, of certain attributes and properties (by contrast, Kant could be said to pursue a 'positive' account in which a noumenal faculty for subjective autonomy is added to the otherwise overdetermined phenomenal individual). The surplus of autonomy is made possible by the deficit of heteronomy. Freedom emerges from the dysfunctioning of determinism.

Conclusion

Perhaps Schelling's key post-Kantian theoretical contribution is the asking and answering of the question regarding what, exactly, underlies the structural scaffolding of fully formed transcendental subjectivity as portrayed in Kant's critical apparatus. Whereas the Kantian transcendental system implicitly treats the subject, ensconced in experiential reality and its world of constituted objects, as always-already existent and operative, Schelling seeks to account for the very emergence of such subjectivity, for the origins of this agent-function. That is to say: Schelling, especially in his texts from 1809 and after, attempts to sketch the (transcendental) subject's (ontogenetic) pre/proto-history (a task largely neglected by Kant – however, an examination of the connections between the pre-critical *Anthropology from a Pragmatic Point of View* and the *Critique of Pure Reason* reveals an awareness on his part of this problematic matter[65]). As Andrew Bowie observes, Schelling identifies a 'fundamental problem that goes to the heart of the Kantian project: how does one explain the genesis of transcendental subjectivity itself?'[66]

Generally speaking, Schelling seeks to specify the process wherein immaterial subjectivity (as a spiritual transcendence or transcendental ideality) immanently emerges out of a substantial material base (as the Real ground of 'productive' nature). Yet, although Schelling maintains that subject arises from substance, he none the less insists that, following this movement of genetic emergence, the subject thus produced remains thereafter irreducible to the materiality of its (now-occluded) source(s).[67] This search for the first-order genetic conditions of possibility for transcendental subjectivity (a subjectivity which itself, once formed, operates as a set of second-order possibility conditions for experiential reality) is tantamount to the quest for a meta-transcendental account of the subject, for the genetic possibility conditions underlying those static possibility conditions outlined in the Kantian critical system. The Freudian–Lacanian concept of drive deserves to be elevated to the philosophical dignity of just such a meta-transcendental, genetic possibility condition for subjectivity.

Through a startling reversal running contrary to the vulgar perspective that views psychoanalysis as a fatalistic discourse of determinism, the notion of *Trieb* must be reconceived as precisely that which promises to yield a positive theoretical conceptualization of human freedom.[68] Rather than being the final psychoanalytic barrier to positing the potential of liberation from the deterministic nexus of (physical or psychic) nature, the Freudian drive is, in and of itself, the very possibility condition for what comes to present itself as a transcendent form of freedom. The psychoanalytic drive is the dysfunctional instinct of human nature, destining this nature for denaturalization. As Joan Copjec accurately articulates it: 'the notion of drive . . . implies not an overriding so much as a redefinition of nature . . . The question one must ask is: how does drive determine human embodiment as both a freedom from nature and a part of it?'[69]

In his seminar on Schelling, Heidegger discusses the fundamental implications of the Schellingian dissolution of the traditional dichotomy between 'system' (more specifically, nature as the exhaustive theoretical model of the necessary relations between phenomenal entities/appearances) and freedom (as an unconditioned agency incapable of reduction to the deterministic, causal chains of natural necessity). In Schelling's view, overcoming the standard conceptual antagonism between these two spheres is the most pressing and important task facing philosophy.[70] His rhetoric concerning the mutually reinforcing efforts to 'naturalize' freedom and, correlatively, to 'liberate' nature implies that the very foundations of philosophy in general (above and beyond practical philosophy alone) are at stake here. Following this line, Heidegger notes that Schelling's reassessment of freedom has consequences that go far beyond treating it either as a mere sub-component of ethical philosophy or as a simple empirical feature of human beings. Fundamental ontological issues hinge upon the German idealist vision of an always-already 'spiritualized' natural ground out of which springs everything that is, including autonomous subjectivity. No doubt Heidegger sees in Schelling a precursor of his own notion of *Dasein*, a notion declaring the essence of man to reside in an open 'clearing' of temporally structured possibilities.[71] One could say, regarding the Heideggerian conception of human being, that temporality and possibility are not qualities or attributes of the subject, but, inversely, that subjectivity is a residual, particular determination occurring within the overarching domains of being and time. Similarly, Heidegger alleges that Schelling's naturalization of human freedom entails that the subject is itself an outgrowth of an unconditioned *Urgrund*, an abyssal openness within which empirical human nature gradually constructs and constrains itself.

Freudian–Lacanian psychoanalysis, despite the usual conclusions drawn from it, must be properly situated within this Schellingian lineage. Freud concretizes Schelling's speculations about 'natural freedom' through his basic, foundational concept of *Trieb*. In the 1905 *Three Essays on the Theory of Sexuality*, which is Freud's first sustained treatment of the drives, the crucial thesis of the book (a thesis absolutely central to the theoretical edifice of psychoanalysis) is that human beings do not have constitutionally predetermined instincts invariantly correlated with fixed types of natural objects. By insisting on the need 'to loosen the bond that exists in our thoughts between instinct and object',[72] Freud problematizes, in a decisive fashion, standard conceptualizations of human nature. For psychoanalysis, humans are naturally unnatural.

Individuals are capable of achieving the ideality of a freedom that transcends material determination precisely because their drives are constitutionally divorced from a strict anchoring to the innerworldly domain of natural objects (and this 'loosening' of the ties to objects is only the most basic feature of *Trieb* involved in engendering autonomous subjectivity – as indicated, the multiple axes of conflict dwelling within the psychic ground of the libidinal economy are vital factors here too). Instead of hindering the development of a theory of human freedom, this conceptualization of the initial, primordial *Urgrund* of the drives (as formulated specifically by psychoanalytic metapsychology) is what makes possible an account of the autonomous subject that is none the less capable of acknowledging the emergent, genetic essence of subjectivity in relation to an underlying heteronomous, material origin.[73] Psychoanalysis brings to full theoretical fruition Schelling's obscure theosophical ruminations, moving from abstract, poetic speculations about God and *Grund* to a richly elaborated vision of the tension-ridden rapport between the Real and the Ideal as manifest in the lives of flesh-and-blood human beings.

Notes

1. Jacques Lacan, 'The Direction of the Treatment and the Principles of Its Power', in *Écrits: A Selection*, trans. Bruce Fink (New York: W.W. Norton and Company, 2002), p. 241.
2. Jacques Lacan, *Le Séminaire de Jacques Lacan, Livre XXIV: L'insu que sait de l'une-bévue, s'aile à mourre, 1976–1977* (unpublished typescript), session of 19 April, 1977.
3. Jacques Lacan, *Le Séminaire de Jacques Lacan, Livre IV: La relation d'objet, 1956–1957*, ed. Jacques-Alain Miller, (Paris: Éditions du Seuil, 1994), p. 254.
4. Jacques Lacan, *Le Séminaire de Jacques Lacan, Livre XXI: Les non-dupes errent, 1973–1974* (unpublished typescript), session of 21 May, 1974. Lacan, *Le Séminaire de Jacques Lacan, Livre XXIV*, session of 17 May, 1977.
5. Jacques Lacan, *Le Séminaire de Jacques Lacan, Livre XXIII: Le sinthome, 1975–1976*, ed. Jacques-Alain Miller, (Paris: Éditions du Seuil, 2005) p. 12.
6. Jacques Lacan, *The Seminar of Jacques Lacan, Book XX: Encore, 1972–1973*, ed. Jacques-Alain Miller, trans. Bruce Fink, (New York: W.W. Norton and Company, 1998), pp. 6–7, 9–12.
7. Jacques Lacan, *Le Séminaire de Jacques Lacan, Livre VIII: Le transfert, 1960–1961*, ed. Jacques-Alain Miller (Paris: Éditions du Seuil, 2001 [seconde édition corrigée]), p. 117. Jacques Lacan, *Le Séminaire de Jacques Lacan, Livre XVIII: D'un discours qui ne serait pas du semblant, 1971* (unpublished typescript), session of 17 February, 1971. Jacques Lacan, *Le Séminaire de Jacques Lacan, Livre XIX: Le savoir du psychanalyste, 1971–1972* (unpublished typescript), session of 3 March, 1972.
8. Jacques Lacan, *Le Séminaire de Jacques Lacan, Livre XVII: L'envers de la psychanalyse, 1969–1970*, ed. Jacques-Alain Miller (Paris: Éditions du Seuil, 1991), p. 36.
9. Lacan, *Le Séminaire de Jacques Lacan, Livre XVIII*, session of 17 February, 1971.
10. Lacan, *Le Séminaire de Jacques Lacan, Livre XXIV*, session of 17 May, 1977.
11. Adrian Johnston, 'Against Embodiment: The Material Ground of the Immaterial Subject', *Journal for Lacanian Studies*, vol. 2, no. 2, December 2004, pp. 230, 243, 250–1.
12. F.W.J. Schelling, *The Ages of the World: Third Version (c. 1815)*, trans. Jason M. Wirth (Albany, NY: State University of New York Press, 2000), pp. 60–61.
13. Schelling, *The Ages of the World*, p. 12.

14. F.W.J. Schelling, *Clara – or, On Nature's Connection to the Spirit World*, trans. Fiona Steinkamp (Albany, NY: State University of New York Press, 2002), p. 19.
15. Schelling, *Clara*, p. 21.
16. Schelling, *Clara*, p. 22.
17. Schelling, *The Ages of the World*, pp. 20, 49.
18. Adrian Johnston, *Time Driven: Metapsychology and the Splitting of the Drive* (Evanston IL: Northwestern University Press, 2005).
19. Adrian Johnston, 'Revulsion is not without its subject: Kant, Lacan, Žižek and the Symptom of Subjectivity', *Pli: The Warwick Journal of Philosophy*, no. 15, Spring 2004, pp. 201, 205, 228.
20. F.W.J. Schelling, *Philosophical Inquiries into the Nature of Human Freedom and Matters Connected Therewith*, trans. James Gutmann, (Chicago: The Open Court Publishing Company, 1936), p. 34.
21. Schelling, *Philosophical Inquiries into the Nature of Human Freedom*, p. 35.
22. F.W.J. Schelling, 'Stuttgart Seminars', *Idealism and the Endgame of Theory: Three Essays by F.W.J. Schelling*, trans. Thomas Pfau (Albany, NY: State University of New York Press, 1994), p. 202.
23. Schelling, *Clara*, p. 54.
24. Schelling, *Philosophical Inquiries into the Nature of Human Freedom*, p. 18.
25. Schelling, 'Stuttgart Seminars', p. 230.
26. Schelling, *The Ages of the World*, p. 21.
27. Schelling, 'Stuttgart Seminars', p. 230.
28. Schelling, *The Ages of the World*, p. 48.
29. Schelling, *The Ages of the World*, p. 58.
30. Schelling, *The Ages of the World*, pp. 27–8.
31. Schelling, *The Ages of the World*, pp. 20, 92.
32. Schelling, *The Ages of the World*, pp. 90–91.
33. Schelling, *The Ages of the World*, pp. 38–9.
34. Schelling, *The Ages of the World*, p. 100.
35. Schelling, 'Stuttgart Seminars', pp. 206–7.
36. Schelling, 'Stuttgart Seminars', p. 206.
37. Schelling, 'Stuttgart Seminars', p. 200.
38. Schelling, *The Ages of the World*, pp. 5–6.
39. Schelling, *The Ages of the World*, p. 11.
40. Schelling, *The Ages of the World*, p. 12.
41. Schelling, *The Ages of the World*, p. 16.
42. Schelling, 'Stuttgart Seminars', pp. 207–8; Schelling, *The Ages of the World*, p. 31.
43. Schelling, 'Stuttgart Seminars', p. 205.
44. Jacques Lacan, *The Seminar of Jacques Lacan, Book XI: The Four Fundamental Concepts of Psycho-Analysis, 1964*, ed. Jacques-Alain Miller, trans. Alan Sheridan (New York: W.W. Norton and Company, 1979), p. 128.
45. James Strachey, ed., *The Standard Edition of the Complete Psychological Works of Sigmund Freud* (London: Hogarth Press, 1953–73) (hereafter *SE*), *SE* 1: 231, 270–71, 279; *SE* 3: 220, 255.
46. Schelling, *The Ages of the World*, p. 85.
47. Schelling, *Clara*, p. 28.
48. *SE* 19: 52.

49. Alenka Zupančič, *Ethics of the Real: Kant, Lacan* (London and New York: Verso, 2000), pp. 28, 39. Alenka Zupančič, *Das Reale einer Illusion: Kant und Lacan*, trans. Reiner Ansén, (Baden-Baden: Suhrkamp, 2001), pp. 35, 46.

50. Immanuel Kant, *Critique of Practical Reason*, trans. Lewis White Beck, (New Jersey: Prentice-Hall, Inc., 1993), pp. 76–7. Immanuel Kant, *Fundamental Principles of the Metaphysics of Morals*, trans. Thomas K. Abbott, (Indianapolis: The Bobbs–Merrill Company, Inc., 1949), pp. 13–14.

51. Schelling, *Clara*, p. 28.

52. Schelling, *The Ages of the World*, p. 78.

53. Schelling, *Philosophical Inquiries into the Nature of Human Freedom*, pp. 44–5, 47–8.

54. Schelling, *Philosophical Inquiries into the Nature of Human Freedom*, p. 49.

55. Johnston, *Time Driven.*

56. Martin Heidegger, *Schelling's Treatise on the Essence of Human Freedom*, trans. Joan Stambaugh, (Athens: University of Ohio Press, 1985), p. 9.

57. Johnston, 'Against Embodiment'.

58. Heidegger, *Schelling's Treatise on the Essence of Human Freedom*, p. 60.

59. Johnston, *Time Driven.*

60. Peter Hallward, *Badiou: A Subject to Truth* (Minneapolis: University of Minnesota Press, 2003), pp. xxxii, 167.

61. Hallward, *Badiou*, p. 144.

62. Louis Althusser, 'Ideology and Ideological State Apparatuses (Notes towards an Investigation)', in *Mapping Ideology*, ed. Slavoj Žižek, (London and New York: Verso, 1994), pp. 130–31, 135–6.

63. Zupančič, *Ethics of the Real*, pp. 29–30.

64. Kant, *Critique of Practical Reason*, pp. 3, 6.

65. Adrian Johnston, 'The Genesis of the Transcendent: Kant, Schelling, and the Ground of Experience', *Idealistic Studies*, vol. 33, no. 1, Spring 2003, pp. 59, 60–61.

66. Andrew Bowie, *Schelling and Modern European Philosophy: An Introduction* (New York: Routledge, 1993), p. 34.

67. Adrian Johnston, 'The Soul of *Dasein*: Schelling's Doctrine of the Soul and Heidegger's Analytic of *Dasein*', *Philosophy Today*, vol. 47, no. 3, Fall 2003, pp. 228, 230.

68. Adrian Johnston, *Freedom from Nature: Drive between Heteronomy and Autonomy* (unpublished manuscript).

69. Joan Copjec, *Imagine There's No Woman: Ethics and Sublimation* (Cambridge, MA: MIT Press, 2004), p. 180.

70. Schelling, *Philosophical Inquiries into the Nature of Human Freedom*, pp. 3, 24.

71. Johnston, 'The Soul of *Dasein*', pp. 229, 241–2.

72. *SE* 7: 148.

73. Johnston, *Freedom from Nature.*

4

Truth and Contradiction: Reading Hegel with Lacan

Timothy Huson

Dedicated to my teacher, Ed Lawrence[1]

Jacques Lacan correctly recognized in Freud, beyond the scientist in the narrow sense, the speculative philosopher, the thinker driven to grasp the ultimate principles of human reality and, indeed, of reality itself. Part of what he found in Freud's writings touches the heart of Hegel's thought: located beneath the level of everyday consciousness and governed by radically different principles, there is a realm bearing a symbolic relation to our everyday world and containing, as the essential other of that world, our repressed desire – the truth excluded by the social order but manifested in everyday life in the form of the dream, the joke, the slip or mistake, and the symptom (the non-linguistic symbol, as Lacan has termed it). In these forms, the unconscious truth encroaches upon and interrupts our logically consistent everyday experience, revealing its contradiction and betraying the deception of this seeming coherence. It may be a neurotic twitch, an uncontrollable gesture – one might not even be aware of it – the symptom breaking forth, expressing the truth of the unconscious, a truth in this way manifesting its absence in the 'rational' order of everyday logical consistency, disrupting it and forming in it a hole, an inexplicable stain. And this stain, this logical impossibility in the social discourse, is also essential to it, sustains it, for behind it is the choice of the individual's self-negation – negation of her desire – that gives rise to that social order. This immanent negation of the finite social order relates to it in a contradictory way: it stands to it in a relation of reciprocal determination, being both a product of the order and its creator, as well as in a relation of mutual indifference and independence – it can negate it. This relation between the unconscious and everyday reality is conceptually parallel to Hegel's understanding of the contradictory relation between finite reality and the absolute. The apparent logical consistency of the finite, more carefully examined, turns into a fundamental incoherence. If we look beyond the finite to the absolute, the problem of the self-contradiction of the finite is resolved by understanding the essentially contradictory relation of the finite to the absolute, a contradictory relation that forms its truth – truth as contradiction. Standing to the finite in the conflicting relations of reciprocal determination, and, at the same time, mutual indifference and independence, the absolute shows the structure of Hegel's *Voraussetzung*, 'posited as not posited'.[2]

Throughout the history of philosophy, truth has often been seen as some kind of correspondence – of proposition to fact, of concept to reality, of reality to concept. For Hegel, however, truth's correspondence is also a contradictory one: reality corresponds to the concept only in so far as it also at the same time does not correspond. Truth, composed of two contradicting relations, is a contradiction. As the basic structure of reality, this contradiction illuminates the role of human individuals in that reality, for human thought is the metaphysical basis for being and change towards what is not. When one's thought is true in the sense of serving as the principle of change, one stands in a contradictory relationship to society – being both a product of that society and its negation. Social critique is the negation, the truth, and the very product of that which it negates – Hegel's determinate negation. In this respect, Socrates' conflict with old Athens involves – more fundamental than the social contract issue – the fundamental paradox of human existence itself: one can exist as an individual in society only by giving up one's essential core, yet it is only by virtue of society that one exists at all. At this metaphysical level, the truth of human existence is a contradiction, a synthesis of two contradictory relationships: I exist independently of society only because I am also at the same time determined by society; in other words, society creates me as independent, as the negation of all determination. Socrates deals with this contradiction through his genuinely human act of carrying out this negation in the Real, realizing through his own death his truth, the truth of subjectivity, and making explicit the negation, the immanent contradiction, already existing in potentiality in Athens. Read in this way, Hegel's discussion of Socrates touches on the act of psychoanalysis, the act that changes the very symbolic basis of reality, as opposed to 'action' that simply moves within the given parameters of a particular social order.[3]

In this discussion so far, the term 'truth' has been used to refer not only to the two contradicting relations between reality and its immanent negation – thought, repressed desire – but also to that negation as the key moment sustaining those relations. While these clearly different aspects of truth can be distinguished, as a speculative identity the confusion is inevitable and, indeed, essential. The negation does not exist independently of the contradictory relations to that which it negates. The negation is, as Hegel puts it, a moment of a whole of which it is a constitutive part. Here the term 'truth' can refer to either of these essential aspects, the moment or the whole. (Regarding *Moment* and *Ganze*, see Hegel's *Logik* II, *Werke* 6,166.f.)

These different senses of contradiction are ultimately at play in Lacan's understanding of what it means to be a master or a slave. Lacan offers conceptions of slavery, self-deception, authenticity, mastery and truth that can make sense of our contradictory social reality, serve as a metaphysical critique of today's culture – today's 'civilization of hate', as Lacan has termed it[4] – and bring out again the critical spirit of Hegel's thought. For Lacan, the slave lives in self-deception, fearing to confront her true desire, fearing to live the truth of human existence as being-towards-death in opposition to a life and desire determined in the social order. Manifesting today's social neurosis, she waits, accepting the social order and hiding from herself her own true being, this death – the 'absolute master' (Hegel's metaphor from the *Phänomenologie des Geistes, Werke* 3, 153). In waiting, however, this slave has none the less chosen this order and, consequently, also chosen her being as determined by this order, though in self-deception she hides this choice from herself. But her choice in accepting is not, as Lacan has insinuated, on the same ontological level as that of rejecting. Accepting the throne is not on the same ontological level as renouncing it, for to refuse is to truly act, as shown so clearly in Shakespeare's *King Lear* with Cordelia's simple speech act, the simple word of refusal, the negation that changes the very parameters of the social world. In response to Lear's request as to what (flattering) words she can offer to prove herself worthy of her most opulent share of his kingdom, she performs the most authentic deed in the tragedy, the symbolic act that turns the world upside down and fundamentally restructures the reality in which action takes place, when she utters the simple words: 'Nothing, my lord.' In following one's desire, in refusing the loss demanded by the social order, one lives consistent with one's true being, leading a life no longer based on a contradiction one denies but, rather, on a contradiction embraced at the heart of human existence itself. This sincere act embodies the structure Hegel attributes to speculative thinking, which 'holds fast the contradiction and in it itself' (*Werke* 6, 76).

I HEGEL: 'THE NON-BEING OF THE FINITE IS THE BEING OF THE ABSOLUTE'

It is important not to forget that Hegel's discussion of contradiction in the *Logic* ends with the absolute itself, and that it is identified – in Hegel's speculative sense – with the finite's non-being. When it comes to Hegel's absolute, there is a tendency to hypostatize, to reify, to make it into a positive entity somehow existing prior to the world and independent of it, like the Christian God's existence before the creation of the world. While there is a measure of truth in this interpretation, textual evidence also supports another reading of Hegel's absolute, a reading more closely aligned with psychoanalysis, a reading that allows Hegel's thought to be utilized in analysing and criticizing the contradictions of today's social reality.

For Hegel, a single meaning of any term can be discussed only at the risk of losing the full meaning the term has as but one of a variety of interrelated moments. Bearing in mind this limitation, I will none the less attempt, drawing on the section on contradiction in Hegel's *Logic*, to delineate the idea of a contradiction of relationships, and then use it to discuss the absolute as negativity, the absolute as the other of the social order.

A contradiction of relations

Contradiction is usually thought to involve a concept, substance or attribute and its negation, and indeed Hegel does discuss such forms of contradiction, considering them at distinct conceptual levels, at different levels of reflection. But his discussions ultimately involve the level of reflection at which emerges what we call a contradiction of relationships or a contradiction of relations. This contradiction takes forms such as unity and difference (negative unity), or reciprocal determination and indifference. We find this even with finite reality, where the self-contained self-contradiction means that a finite object like a house, as to its very being, is involved in two contradictory relations between two parts of itself, for example, between its infinite manifold and its essence. A formulation of the contradiction of relationships appears in the opening paragraph of Hegel's discussion of contradiction in the *Logic*:

> Distinction [*Unterschied*] in general contains its two sides as moments [*Momente*]; in difference [*Verschiedenheit*] they are indifferently separate from each other; in opposition [*Gegensatz*] as such they are the sides of the distinction, one determined by the other, and thus only moments; but they are just as much determined in themselves, indifferent to each other, and reciprocally excluding each other: self-standing reflective determinations [*die selbständigen Reflexionsbestimmungen*]. (*Werke* 6, 64)

The concept of distinction is composed of two contradictory relationships between its moments: reciprocal determination and indifference. The analysis of distinction moves at the level of reflection that involves relations rather than concrete entities. Formally expressed as 'A & ~ A' (with 'indifference' meaning 'non-determination'), the 'A' stands for a relation. It is these relations which, as the essential conflicting components of the contradiction, on the one hand are embodied in and on the other themselves constitute one and the same whole, one and the same 'substance' (paralleling the role of substance that, for Aristotle, underlies the different senses in the sophistic contradiction). That is to say: this self-contradictory entity, this substance, is on the one hand that of which is predicated two conflicting relations and on the other that which is itself constituted by these contradictory relations – a formulation generally consistent with Hegel's discussion of substance in the *Logic*, where what underlies is seen as both independent of and determined by its predicates (see *Werke* 6, 219).

In Hegel's examples of contradiction, it is also at the level of relations that the explanatory analysis is ultimately found. In the third remark in the section on contradiction, Hegel introduces what he calls 'the most trivial examples' – 'up and down, right and left, father and son' – to demonstrate an 'opposition in one': 'Above is what is not below; above is determined only as not being below, and it has being [*ist*] only in so far as a below has being [*ist*], and vice versa; within the one determination is its opposite' (*Werke* 6, 77). It might seem that the point is simply that some things necessarily contain and refer to their opposites. With Hegel's discussion of the opposition of father and son, however, it becomes clear that a different level of analysis is at issue. This discussion begins much the same as the one about up and down: 'Father is the other of son and son the other of father, and each has being [*ist*] only as this other of the other. . . .' But then, Hegel continues: 'and, at the same time, the one determination has being [*ist*] only in reference to the other; their being [*Sein*] is one existence [*Bestehen*]'. The 'one existence' mentioned here indicates what in this structure plays the role parallel to the one substance plays in Aristotle's theory of contradiction. For Aristotle, the predicates of a substance shall not, at the same time, contradict. For Hegel, however, this substance (if we so call it) involves a contradiction.

One might think that the contradiction found in the unity or substance discussed here results from the two individuals contradicting one another. The next sentence, however, makes it clear that the formulation of a substance or unity containing father and son as moments essentially related to each other – father essentially relates to son and son to father, with the father relating to the son as to one relating to the father – is not the basis of the contradiction, rather, the contradiction consists in the father relating to the son in a contradictory way – that is, his existence is constituted by a unity of two contradictory relations: 'The father is also something for himself outside of the relation to the son; but thus he is not father, but a man in general [*ein Mann überhaupt*]; just as above and below, right and left, are also something when reflected in themselves outside of the relationship, but [what they are is] only place in general.' The moment of father, then, is constituted by a contradiction, being independent of (thus indeterminate) and at the same time determined by the relation to the other. This provides a conceptual account of the fact that our most unique self-identity is empty of determination and synonymous with 'human in general', while our concrete identity is constituted by what we are in relation to some subset of humanity – class, race, gender, profession, nationality, and so forth. Hegel concludes this paragraph by noting that opposing things like father and son, up and down, contain a contradiction – need I point out that father does not contradict son, nor does up contradict down? – due to their contradictory relations: 'The opposed entities contain contradiction in so far as they are in one and the same respect things relating to one another negatively or things sublating each other reciprocally and things indifferent to each other' (*Werke* 6, 77). That two things are both indifferent and not indifferent to each other constitutes a contradiction of relations.

Hegel's use of the expression 'in one and the same respect' seems to mark the form of the contradiction that Aristotle would insist on rejecting rather than reformulating in a non-contradictory way – for example, by using the separate terms 'A' and 'B' – as he would the sophistic contradiction, which was not qualified with 'at the same time', 'in the same respect', and so on. But does Hegel's contradiction have to be either a sophistic contradiction or a meaningless statement? Is there a third possibility? The indifference and reciprocal determination in Hegel's contradiction distinguish it from the sophistic variety in that these terms are integrally related and mutually conditioning aspects of a unity. For example, Hegel's well-known statement: 'Nature is the other-being of spirit [*Geist*]' (see, for example, *Werke* 5, 127; *Werke* 9, 24) captures in a unity two contradictory and yet integral relations, for nature is external to spirit (and external in itself) precisely by being posited as such by spirit. In this unity constituted by a contradiction of relationships, nature's indifference to spirit is essentially determined by spirit, for it is posited as such by spirit.

Another way to look at this unity appears in Hegel's discussion of the excluded middle. Apart from '+A' and '~A' there is the (supposedly excluded) middle, 'A' (*Werke* 6, 74). Besides the asserted A and the denied A, there is also the A embodying the determinations of assertion and denial in one unity, one substance (in the sense indicated above). The A common to +A and ~A can be seen either as an abstraction from determination or as the concrete whole containing the contradictory relations. The latter constitutes the self-contradictory reality. The 'A' that encompasses both '+A' and '~A' is not a specific thing, nor does it exist independent of the contradictory relations that constitute its content. 'A' is a contradiction in the form: '~A is at the same time reciprocally determined by and indifferent to +A'. The excluded middle, A, is 'the unity of reflection to which the opposition returns as to its reason or basis [*Grund*]' (*Werke* 6, 74).

The example of father and son further bears this out. Father is determined in opposition to son, yet is also something outside of that relation – human in general. The contradiction involving father and son consists in the fact that father is a determination of the substance 'humanity' (like +A of A). This unity, the excluded middle, does not exist in abstraction. It exists only as the essential non-being of the conflicting moments, and consists in their simultaneous indifference and reciprocal determination. This unity is a 'substance' that is no thing, nor an abstract definition or essence, but a contradiction of relationships. So human substance would be the unity of the concrete contradicting relationships of indifference and reciprocal determination between the various moments of human reality.

Contradiction in finite being

Finite things are marked in their very existence with their negation, their limit – the Latin 'finis'. As Hegel puts it: 'non-being constitutes the nature, the being [of finite things]' (*Werke* 5, 139). Finite things are destined to pass away. 'They are, but the truth of this being is their end' (*Werke* 5, 139). 'The hour of their birth is the hour of their death' (*Werke* 5, 140). Their very existence is marked by a being that is essentially non-being. They no longer have an affirmative being independent of their passing away. 'Finitude is', writes Hegel, 'the most stubborn category of understanding,' because it is marked in its very essence with a direct opposition to being (*Werke* 5, 140).

When the finite is grasped speculatively, its limit [*Grenze*] comes to be seen as a barrier [*Schranke*] – that is, something which points beyond itself: 'The very limit of something, thus something posited by it as something negative that is at the same time essential, is not only a limit [*Grenze*] as such, but rather a barrier [*Schranke*]' (*Werke* 5, 142.f). This barrier is in itself a concrete contradiction, being both something's limit and its other, pointing beyond the limit. Wherever there is a barrier, there is a beyond. And the beyond is the basis of an ought. As Hegel emphasizes in the *Logic* section entitled 'Barrier and Ought' [*die Schranke und das Sollen*]: 'What should be is and at the same time is not. If it were to be, it shouldn't merely be. Thus ought essentially possesses a barrier' (*Werke* 5, 143).

Hegel construes this ought as a contradiction of the formal variety: 'The in-itself-being [*Ansichsein*] of something in its determination thus reduces itself to ought because that which constitutes its in-itself-being is in one and the same respect non-being' (*Werke* 5, 144). The barrier is not just a barrier; it is the duty to remove it: 'Something has a barrier to the extent that it has negation in its determination, and this determination is also the state of the barrier's being sublated [*Aufgehobensein*]' (*Werke* 5, 144). The finite here is a contradiction of relations. Its barrier is its limit, its determination, and also, in pointing beyond, its indifference, its infinity, its freedom. The barrier is determined by the finite, and also indifferent to it in its pointing beyond. So it is without limit. With the concept of *Sollen*, the limit is both a limit and not a limit; something relates to its limit as limiting and as what indicates the freedom from the limit (see *Werke* 5, 144). Here finite being forms a relational pair with the infinite constituting a contradiction of relations.

Let us consider Hegel's statement: 'The non-being of the finite is the being of the absolute' (*Werke* 6, 80). The finite, seen in its truth, is the absolute, the contradiction of relations, the subject that, as nothing, underlies the finite. Within the realm of understanding [*Verstand*], the finite's passing away is taken simply as non-being. In this respect, finite being is characterized by the expression '*zugrundegehen*' in one of the aspects Hegel attributes to the expression: 'Language unifies . . . the meaning of disappearance [*Untergang*] and basis [or "reason for", *Grund*] . . .' (*Werke* 6, 128). For understanding, reality is seen in its finitude and 'passes away in contradiction' [*geht in dem Widerspruch zugrunde*] (*Werke* 6, 76) according to the contradiction expressed in 'the finite is'. Seen in itself, finite reality's contradiction is simply its limitation. It is determined from outside, given its concept by another, and so is limited. Seen in this way, it does not correspond to its concept. Accepting the role of the social order, spirit itself is finite. But when the finite is seen as positing its own concept, the concept is its other; then its lack of correspondence is an ought, a beyond, and its contradiction is its truth and its freedom. So with reason [*Vernunft*], the negation of the finite becomes the substance, the contradiction of relations underlying finite reality.

In some sense finite beings must correspond to their concept, or they would not even exist at all. They correspond in so far as they contain in themselves the beyond of the barrier in the form of a lack (corresponding to Aristotle's *sterêsis*). For example, a child possesses rationality as lack, existing as yet only in the form of potentiality. This is the impetus for development and change. And, so long as this correspondence exists, a bad reality is potentially good. As Hegel says, even the worst political state, so long as it exists, still bears some relation to the idea, and is still its manifestation. Even in the worst political state, 'individuals still hearken to a powerful concept' (*Werke* 6, 466). The individual is moulded by and related to the political state in two ways. On the one hand, she is determined by its laws, if even unawares, and reflects its structure – dialectically, this means that she and the state are being prepared for a change – and, on the other, she is the negation of the present order; she is this negation by virtue of having the potential to act, to effect a leap in the grid in which reality takes on meaning, and thus to enable the emergence of a new social concept, and hence a new social order. And the point is that in any case it is the free choice of an individual to accept the given order or to perform the symbolic act and utter the simple 'No!' When she does this, the finite, the potentially infinite, becomes actually infinite. As I would develop Kant's discussion on the origin of evil in *Religion within the Limits of Reason Alone* (B39.ff), the first free choice is always the choice of whether or not to act according to the causality of freedom, whether or not to act freely. Similarly, Hegel would tell us, *mutatis mutandis*, that the slave, in choosing her slavery, is also free. But again, as Lacan has implicitly told us, renouncing the kingship and accepting it, though both have symbolic implications, are not of the same ontological status – to put it simply, in the one there is a change, while in the other things stay the same. We exist within the limits of a social order, for a social order contradicts part of our being and forces us to give up our desire. But, in rejecting one's truth, one has freely chosen and is still the radical source, the unconscious other, upon which the social order rests. No matter how bad the social order is, no matter how little it recognizes the individual as its source, the individual is still its source in the choice to accept it. In this choice, radical freedom fails to realize its true potential and effect a symbolic change; it manifests itself only as a fantasy-distortion of the authentic choice of freedom, as the diversion of that potential, the frenzy of random destruction by the USA in Afghanistan and Iraq or, more subtly, as the forgotten word, the forgotten name, the forgotten scene around the curve of the road.

Contradiction and freedom in the absolute

Hegel distinguishes between a form of being that is able to comprehend its underlying contradiction, its principle of life and motion, and thus is alive and in motion, and one that cannot grasp this contradiction as its principle but, rather, passes away in the contradiction [*geht in dem Widerspruch zugrunde*] (*Werke* 6, 76). Hegel calls 'speculative thinking' that which holds fast to itself in holding to this contradiction and is not mastered by it (as is the thought that uncritically accepts the given of the senses). Here as well, Hegel uses the expression 'in one and the same respect', indicating the formal contradiction rejected by Aristotle. Extended beyond the mere biological sense, human substance and life include two conflicting senses: what I am as a member of society according to the empirical laws of the social order and what I am independent of this social order. My being includes both my finite existence as well as an infinite, that which is not determined. These two facets of human existence constitute the contradiction of relations. I am independent of the finite social order, and also stand to it in a relation of reciprocal determination. I have being as independent, as the other of the social order, only by virtue of my being in that order, for the independent self came to be through its exclusion from that order. Similarly, the self as independent, through its acceptance, sustains the order that creates the socially determined self. Here human substance is not what is opposed to society, but the contradiction of relations itself. Spiritual substance constitutes – as Kierkegaard put it in *Sickness Unto Death* – the paradox of a relation that relates to itself. Spirit is not simply the infinite or the finite, nor the infinite bound to the finite; rather, it is the fact that the infinite is both determined by the finite and indifferent to it, the paradoxical relationship of the infinite to itself. The infinite is not present as a positive thing; rather, it appears as a blemish, a structural stain on finite reality: 'The non-being of the finite is the being of the absolute.' Without positive existence, it is yet manifested in finite reality.

A reality that is truly contradictory contains freedom. But reality, as the absolute that is free, cannot be completely comprehended. Something must be left over at the heart of the absolute that has the potential fundamentally and freely to reconfigure the very structure of reality. So the true and conceptually developed absolute, the absolute containing distinct conceptual moments, appears in time and is in time (synchronically) marked with its negation, its other, the other that sustains it as absolute. This posited absolute – today's social reality – encompasses and creates its own other, and is also both sustained and threatened by it. As for this double role of the other within the absolute, the absolute's synchronic contradiction of relations has as its counterpart a contradiction involving the origin of a new symbolic order. In other words, the absolute is synchronically sustained by its other – renounced desire – and diachronically changes into a new order through the act of negation, renunciation. What is at play here is similar to the distinction between accepting or rejecting kingship. In accepting kingship one sustains the social order as it is, while in rejecting it, one transforms it. These are two different choices: one is synchronic – it never really occurs, but is implicit according to a sort of application of Kant's view in *Religion within the Limits of Reason Alone* (B42f) that evil resulting from acting according to the phenomenal laws is also a result of a free choice; the other is diachronic in that the old order is transformed into the new one. Since this change occurs in a symbolic leap in which the laws of reality themselves change, it cannot be comprehended by empirically derived laws of social science. This second choice corresponds to the Kantian choice to act according to laws of freedom, laws not grounded in or comprehensible as the phenomenal laws one follows when one accepts acting according to natural motives.

Following Kant, Hegel's analysis of freedom unites freedom and necessity. We are both determined and free. Some would say that this expression indicates the well-known Stoic resolution of freedom and determination, and Plekhanov – as I read him – has formulated an instructive dialectical conception of freedom and determinism along these lines. But I would resist this approach and insist that Hegel's concept of freedom includes – sublates by sustaining, not merely by annihilating and leaving behind – the concept of freedom rejected by Hume in the *Treatise* as the 'freedom of indifference'. For the Hegelian approach developed here, the freedom of indifference, the freedom of real choice between *a* and *b* where one could have chosen otherwise, is not the choice between a Big Mac and a Quarter-Pounder but, rather, the choice as the act that alters the symbolic order giving shape to reality itself. In this way, freedom also unites the freedom and necessity of individuals and the freedom and necessity of the whole. On the universal concept, Hegel writes: 'Even the determined concept thus remains in itself an infinitely free concept' (*Werke* 6, 278). The contradiction of the absolute – determined and free – is grounded in the fact that the absolute's other, both product and sustainer/creator of the absolute, is not determined by the absolute to act. And that other of the absolute is composed of individuals – determined and free. This other can just as well continue to sustain the given order and leave its mark only as the forgotten word, the neurotic twitch, the all-too-clearly remembered event that did not happen, and so on. In this case, we are still free. The absolute of Hegel's idealism must be understood in terms of the contradiction of relations – the determined as indifferent, free.

II LACAN: TRUTH, *LA PAROLE* AND THE SYMBOLIC ORDER

If we look at the closing chapters of Lacan's first published seminar (1953–54), we can see that the contradiction of relations can be used to clarify his discussion of the relation of truth to language, deception, falsehood, error, and repressed desire and its manifestation in everyday discourse, providing a structure for understanding the authentic subject.

Truth's relation to language, deception and error

In Lacan's discussion, truth is found beyond consciousness, beyond the realm of the sign, beyond language, yet it is manifested in language. The problem is how to move from the system of signs, from the relation of sign to sign, to that to which they refer, to truth, 'the authentic master' (399). It is with *la parole* that this connection between language and truth emerges. As soon as someone attempts to understand the truth beyond language, she has already assumed truth as the basis of the investigation. Of course, one might be deceived as to what it is. But deception itself presupposes truth and, in the course of time, can reveal the truth it is attempting to hide. Error, on the other hand, is different in that there is nobody attempting to deceive another. Error and truth – like, I would add, Hegel's pairs up/down, master/slave – are determined in reference to each other. But, as Lacan notes, the connection entails much more than 'saying that, if there had been no truth, there would have been no error' (401). Since deception and falsehood are external distortions of truth, the truth might indeed be thought to exist without them. For Lacan, however, this is not the case with error, for it is only in error that truth can be manifested in discourse. Truth must pass through error. Lacan expresses this in many ways: 'There is no error which does not present and reveal itself as truth.' '[E]rror is the usual incarnation of truth.' 'If we want to be quite rigorous, we will say that, to the extent that truth will not be entirely revealed, that is to say, by all probability, until the end of the ages, it will be its nature to propagate under the form of error.' '[P]aths of truth are essentially paths of error' (401). Truth must ultimately be explicated in terms of what, in reference to Hegel, has here been called a contradiction of relations, according to which the realm of error itself gives rise to, generates and presupposes the truth – that is, in the Hegelian sense of *Voraussetzung*, posited as not posited, as independent. Truth is both independent of and not independent of error. But how can we determine what is true in discourse?

Freud's discovery and *la parole*

For Lacan, Freud's project is directed towards finding truth and detecting error. As a test for truth, Lacan considers the criterion of experience and that of the 'illumination of inner truth' (401). The former is governed by the principle of contradiction – in rejecting what is contradictory, we would reject error. But the various symbolic systems – 'religious, legal, scientific, political' (402) – stand in irresolvable conflict with each other, making impossible a concept of truth in the sense of a system of logically consistent statements in discourse corresponding to the objects of experience. And more importantly, as Lacan puts it, 'the symbolic system is not like a garment that sticks to things, it is not without its effect on them and on human life' (403). A language system does not simply reflect things, but also in some sense makes them what they are. For Lacan, language stands to things in much the same way as, in German idealism, conceptual categories stand to objects. Instead of seeing language as labels standing for reality, one must see that a symbolic system develops as an independent order moving according to principles independent of the things it would represent and then, when it none the less is used in reference to reality, reality is changed.

For Lacan, the answer Freud gives us does not involve looking to the outside world for the criterion, but turning within and seeing in language, the realm of error, an immanent manifestation of the inner truth. As Lacan reads Freud, in psychoanalysis 'the discourse of the subject normally develops . . . in the order of error, of misunderstanding, of denial – it is not simply falsehood. It is between error and falsehood' (403.f). In error, nobody is consciously deceiving. One has unintentionally made a mistake. But in the mistake there may indeed be an unconscious self-deception. And where there is deception, there is also the truth. To discover this truth, we must understand the nature of the falsehood that appears in the form of a mistake. A mistake, for Freud, is a distorted truth, such as the so-called Freudian slips. If you can learn what causes the mistake, you can get at the truth behind it. The truth that emerges in the realm of error is identified with what Lacan calls *la parole*, while the realm of error is identified with the socially determined subject, the conscious subject. *La parole* appears in discourse, for example, through the function of condensation (*Verdichtung*), as illustrated in Freud's work on dream interpretation. The underlying signified content is manifested in many elements in the dream content, while each element in the dream content can refer to several different things in the latent, unconscious content. *La parole* appears in everyday discourse in the same way, in a disguised way; its purpose is hidden from the awareness of the subject. Freud's method – his discovery of the unconscious – involves the attempt to find the distorted truth in discourse: 'We are thus led by the Freudian discovery to hear in discourse this *parole* which is manifested through, or even in spite of, the subject' (405). While the subject functioning in the symbolic order is a self-deception and a departure from truth, she also causes the truth to appear. This appearance of truth in what she says is *la parole*. In expressing *la parole – parole de vérité*, as Lacan puts it – the subject is not aware of expressing the deeper meaning. In speaking *la parole*, the subject 'always says more than she means, more than she knows she is saying' (405).

The 'structure and function' of *la parole* is captured by the contradiction of relations. Truth is not something that exists completely independently of error, since its basic manifestation occurs in 'the discourse of error'. For Lacan, *la parole* is not first in time, but comes in arrears – just as, I would add, Hegel's absolute is misunderstood when it is taken as temporally prior. Its independence is posited (in the sense of Hegel's '*vorausgesetzt*') in and by discourse. Lacan says of the gap in the real caused by its founding truth: 'This being and this nothing are essentially tied to the phenomenon of *la parole*' (412). Paralleling Hegel's expression, one might call *la parole* the 'non-being of discourse', that which can account for the 'discourse of error', explaining why I forgot that name, that number, took that false turn, and so on. In unwittingly uttering this deeper and (to everyday consciousness) hidden meaning of *la parole*, the subject expresses truth in the only form it can take in the discourse of error. It is this structure – speaking a 'truth' as *la parole* appearing in our manifest discourse – which characterizes human existence, human experience. As Lacan puts it: 'If it is not in this way that our experience is structured, then it has no strict sense at all' (405).

La parole appears in discourse, yet it is not discourse. It is not, as Jung made the unconscious, '*le lieu réel d'un autre discours*' (406). In this context, Lacan asks: 'Are these archetypes, these hypostatized symbols residing in permanent fashion in the basement of the human soul, truer than that which is presumably at the surface? Is that which is in the cellars truer than that which is in the granary?' (406). Lacan, in the manner of Hegel, avoids the error of hypostatizing, reifying, naturalizing a foundation. For Lacan, *la parole* is not another discourse separate from the errant one, not an ineffable reality that should exist prior to and be privileged over the surface reality; rather, *la parole* – like Hegel's concept of substance or the absolute as non-being of the finite – is what must exist for the surface discourse to work as it does. *La parole* points to the truth of that surface discourse – for example, in a failure of the usual flow of social discourse.

Contradiction and the truth of the unconscious

The unconscious Freud discovered behind *la parole* does not recognize the law of contradiction. By displacement, a character in a dream, for example, in terms of the latent dream content, can be both another person and the dreamer herself. In *Verneinung*, the word 'no' can mean 'yes'. Does this mean that the unconscious is unthinkable? The word 'thinkable' has different meanings. If 'thinkable' means 'according to the law of contradiction', then empirical reality as treated by positive science – for Hegel, the realm of *Verstand* – is the 'thinkable'. But the unconscious – like the realm of Hegel's *Vernunft*, whose unconscious aspect is captured with the expression 'the cunning of reason' [*die List der Vernunft*] – is not subject to the same laws of contradiction. As Lacan puts it: 'The authentic *parole* has other modes, other means, than usual discourse' (406). So how does it function? Truth is not the consistency of everyday discourse, but precisely its inconsistency, the emergence in discourse of something that disrupts it, negates it. The unconscious truth not only contradicts everyday discourse, but in itself constitutes a contradiction of relations in reference to that discourse. Truth ultimately involves repressed desire created by its very exclusion from discourse by the restrictions of the social order. Discourse itself creates the truth as something beyond that discourse, independent, the other of the speaking subject. This repressed (re)appears in discourse as its negation, as a *parole* 'that surpasses the subject of discourse' (407). Determined by discourse as its beyond, as independent, *la parole* involves a contradiction of relations. Like Hegel's *Schranke und Sollen*, appearing in the finite as what points beyond it to the infinite, *la parole* is a product of finite discourse that points beyond to – even gives rise to – a truth independent of discourse. It is only in and by means of discourse that truth exists independent of it. Truth is both determined by discourse and independent of it, not determined – a contradiction of relations.

Desire and being

For Freud, the pivot on which the world turns and takes shape is desire – paralleling the metaphysical role of the first mover for Aristotle, or the ego cogito for Descartes. On the one hand desire is repressed, on the other it is a product of the repression. And it is produced both as desire 'named by the Other' (the desire one has in playing a role in the social order) and as desire negated by the Other (desire excluded from the social order). This often takes the form of *Verdrängung*, repression, manifested in an interruption, a break or a failure in social discourse – as in failures to remember, or saying what one does not consciously intend to say – and can be characterized as a place where the repressed desire breaks through into the social discourse in disguised form, creating a slip of the tongue, and so forth – recall, for example, Freud's legislator opening a meeting of parliament with the words: 'I hereby declare this meeting adjourned' – or pulls some part of that discourse with it into the unconscious, thus interrupting the discourse. In the opening example from *The Psychopathology of Everyday Life*, Freud discusses at length the variety of associations by which the repressed content of sex and death interrupted his conversation and distorted his train of thought in talking about the painter of the frescoes in the cathedral at Orvieto. The repressed content of death pulled the name of the painter, Signorelli (containing the word '*signor*,' master) down into the unconscious, interrupting discourse, while the remembered – but incorrect – substitute names, Botticelli and Boltraffio, were forced into consciousness as compromise formations of the repressed content. Forgetting induced by repression occurs when a repressed desire, in a variety of ways (perhaps only phonetically, as in a rebus, or through a sort of folk etymology, a completely valid connection in the unconscious), is associated with a word, and the word is pulled down into the unconscious as well, whereas words we end up using may contain displaced but normally unrecognizable repressed content. Thus, words in social discourse are 'never simply words', as Lacan tells us (411). They are charged through a multitude of associations with repressed content from the unconscious, which at points can break through into the social discourse and disrupt it, causing it to stop or malfunction. The law of contradiction then fails on the surface level, at the level of discourse, because *la parole* breaks in. *La parole* functions in discourse when shifts in the cross-references of words in discourse, in their association with the repressed content of a desire, change the symbolic structure of that content. When the nature of the distortion that hides the desire is understood and worked through, a symbolic shift can occur, resulting in a change in being itself, since this is shaped by the symbolic order. For Lacan, desire is both the key to being and the goal of his seminar: 'the repressed desire manifested in the dream is identified at the register to which I am in the process of trying to show you entry – it is being which awaits to be revealed' (411).

III THE ABSOLUTE MASTER AND SOCIAL CRITIQUE

The resolve to 'be oneself' – 'I am, I will be, I have been, I want to be' – always involves 'a leap, a gap' (424), the symbolic leap that separates being from the real. What I am is always more than what is immediately real (say, in the mechanical or chemical configuration of the world). To be a human being at all involves this symbolic leap. Playing a particular human role takes it further. This symbolic leap is at play in being an analyst, just as it is in being a king. The analyst's ability, like that of the king, depends on the symbolic role she plays. Accepting a symbolic role involves such a leap in the real. But the refusal of a symbolic role constitutes an act, something different from mere acceptance of a role. In accepting the kingship, one takes on a role offered by the symbolic order, one exists as an individual by means of the given symbolic order. But in the act of refusing to accept the role of king, 'by the very fact that one refuses, one is not king' (424). And, as Lacan could have added, the kingdom lacks a king, and so it is not a kingdom; reality itself has changed by means of the act. In rejecting one's symbolic role, one can change the symbolic order, and thereby reality.

In the last session of the 1953–54 seminar, Lacan uses as an example the archaic system of qualifying exams employed in the symbolic leaps in academia. In terms of their content, these exams are meaningless. But, as Lacan puts it, 'a competition, to the extent that it invests the subject with a qualification which is symbolic, cannot have an entirely rational structure, and it cannot be inscribed quite frankly in the register of the adding up of qualities' (425). Anyone who knows about the exam system in China can appreciate what this is about. A third or so of the questions in a national English exam will have more than one correct answer, so even a native English speaker could only guess at the correct answer. Since the exams serve only to give some arbitrary ranking to students – owing to the limited number of positions, they cannot all be promoted to the next educational level – why should they reflect any real knowledge? What they do measure is willingness to cram for pointless exams – that is, the ability to accept a meaningless exam system, to accept the world as it is: for some in today's world, of course, a desirable trait. But, in a way, those who simply criticize the exams for their meaninglessness miss the point. Lacan compares those who criticize such exams with 'people who tap at the walls of the prison they have themselves constructed' (425). He is thinking of the tapping by the prisoners inside. We are the builders of our own prison, of our own symbolic order. We criticize particular institutions, not realizing that our whole social order is constructed out of the same irrational fiction and that it is we who, through our act of acceptance, have built it. And what would it take to give it up? Would we?

How does a person become aware that she has built her own prison? The analyst is needed here to play the role of that Other. The subject always sees herself within the symbolic order, that is, from the standpoint of the Other. But the Other is also oneself, as Freud has shown in his analysis of the ego-ideal. The analyst serves as a reflection of the analysand in the Other through the mechanism of transference. Transference, involving the neurotic's shift of focus from the original object of neurosis to the analyst (in the form of either love or hate), is often seen as a breakdown of the treatment, coming as it does at the moment when the patient is beginning to break through to insight regarding her illness. For Lacan, however, this turn to the analyst is essential to the cure. In the analytic identification with the analyst as Other, the analyst is the reflection of the analysand within the social order, echoing her own discourse back to her and allowing her, by means of transference, to see what she has repressed – her truth.

This role in self-reflection played by the analyst seems to parallel the role of the master in the symbolic order. But there is a difference. The master in the symbolic order sustains that order, while the analyst is a master who enables the slave to free herself from that order. The master as analyst occupies a symbolic position of authority from which he 'bestows' upon the analysand, the slave, the symbolic shift of perspective that enables her to see her own truth. As with the dialectic of Plato's Socrates, as with Hegelian dialectic, transference entails a sort of 'self-cure', because the analyst is not an external norm but, rather, the disclosure of the subject's own unconscious, of her own *parole*, whose truth she has formerly misperceived in errant discourse.

The transference, then, is a sort of contradiction in the cure itself, for it is a delay by the patient to avoid cure and continue the symptoms in reference to the analyst; at the same time, it is the means to cure through the neurotic's self-reflection in the analyst. The process should not happen too quickly, for it takes time to overcome the inhibitions and bring the unconscious to the surface. As Lacan notes, if the analyst gets too close, the reflection of the unconscious becomes too intense, and resistance results in the form of silence. In that case, the transference becomes an obstacle.

Another well-known neurotic symptom brought up in Lacan's seminar is the endless waiting that serves to avoid a confrontation with the repressed. With reference to waiting, Lacan's discussion of the obsessive neurotic can be seen at many levels. First, there are individual neurotics. But, paralleling Freud's extension of neurosis to society itself in *The Future of an Illusion* and in *Civilization and its Discontents*, there is a sense in which we are all obsessive neurotics and a sense in which our society itself, the Other, is neurotic. All these levels of interpretation are no doubt also correctly paralleled with nuances of Hegel's master–slave discussion. Lacan associates the obsessive neurotic's waiting through life and during treatment with the slave's situation after submission in Hegel's master–slave dialectic: 'What does the obsessed wait for? For the death of the master. What purpose does the waiting serve? The waiting is interposed between the obsessed and death. When the master dies, everything will begin' (435). This slave lives in a false hope, a false consciousness, a bad faith – a bad contradiction, in fact, for she can wait in hope only so long as she remains waiting. She lives with the contentment of a slave as long as she can delude herself and conceal the self-contradiction of the hope, the hope caused by hiding from herself the fact that, upon the death of the finite master, she herself must face death: 'It is precisely the obsessed who does not assume his being-towards-death; he is in reprieve' (436). The neurotic's cure is crucial. The act of the 'neurotic', the 'slave' in all her forms, is the only hope. The compromise ending the battle to death in Hegel's dialectic – a sort of one-sided peace agreement – is the resulting slave society. In order to live, one member in the battle to death made the choice to accept being a slave. Only her reversal of her decision can end that situation. It therefore devolves upon the 'slave' to sustain the order by continuing to accept it or, in revolt, to withdraw her support and destroy it.

When Marx – viewing the practical situation of wage-slaves confronting a symbolic order, capitalism, and those filling the master-slots in it, the capitalists – appealed to the workers in concluding *The Communist Manifesto*, he thought the choice should be obvious: 'The proletarians have nothing to lose but their chains. They have a world to win.' For Lacan, however, there are good psychological reasons for not refusing the social order, for acquiescing – psychological reasons inherent to the slave-consciousness, this false consciousness. It is only the slave who is in a position to commit the true act, the act of refusal, the symbolic act that would undermine the social order and, in Marx's words, 'win the world'. At any given moment, the slave can act and withdraw her original acceptance of the social order. But what does she do? – She waits.

Analysis should allow the neurotic to arrive at the point where she can put an end to the waiting, give up the illusion, and pull her support from under the master. The slave, prisoner of this order, must come to realize that this temporal master's authority does not really exist, that what keeps her true desire, her own *parole*, in check is not external, that the temporal master is sustained in the errant discourse as the product of an unconscious logic, a social order that is ultimately found in the slave herself. She controls the master, both the individual playing the role of the master and the symbolic order itself, for it exists only because of the choice the slave has always already eternally made to acquiesce and accept it as the rule for what she says and does. To become free, the slave, the neurotic, must work out 'some imaginary exits from the master's prison' in order to realize 'what they signify', that is, to realize that the temporal master is not the true master, that the temporal master depends upon her: 'The subject, thinking the thought of the other, sees in the other the image and the sketch of his own movements. Now, each time that the other is exactly the same as the subject, there is no master except the absolute master, death' (436). But this is precisely what is so difficult for the slave to realize: 'For', as Lacan says, 'he is indeed quite content being a slave, like everyone' (436).

Lacan's concept of slavery involves a special sense of recognition found in Hegel. In Hegel's concept of recognition, the activity of one person should be simultaneously and reciprocally the activity of the other: 'The doing not only contains a double meaning in so far as it is just as much a doing to oneself as to the other, but also in so far as it is inseparably just as much the doing of one as that of the other' (*Werke* 3, 147). Each does something both to himself and to the other, and the doing of each is performed by himself as well as by the other. But this reciprocity is missing at the end of the battle for recognition, a battle that results in the submission of one, becoming the slave, to the other, becoming the master. The master contains the purpose, the enjoyment, the essence, the principle of negation of the object as immediately given, and so he contains the principle or purpose of the deed; while the slave is simply the deed without the purpose, without the essence, without the principle of negation. Indeed, two of the moments of recognition are present, since the slave does to herself what the master does to her and does the master's deed in doing her own. But this recognition is 'one-sided and unequal', as Hegel notes, because it is not reciprocal (*Werke* 3, 152). The slave does to herself what the master does to her, and herself does the master's deed in doing her own; but, unlike in genuine recognition, the master does not do to himself what he does to the slave, nor does the slave do to the master what she does to herself.

The psychoanalytic self-concept, the ego-ideal, is found in a relation of identity and opposition between self and other that maps a logically similar landscape to Hegel's master–slave dialectic, particularly as regards this failure of reciprocity in recognition. The slave does what the master desires – not only according to the formula 'human desire is the desire of the other', which Lacan, as is well known, distinguished into the two senses of *de*, the desire for the Other and the Other's desire, but, as he also notes: 'It is in the other, by the other, that desire is named' (277). Desire named as desire in this Other is what we think we have chosen, while in fact, by a logic we are not aware of, it was the only choice allowed. But the unconscious contains not only this desire of unwitting 'forced choices', but also the repressed desire, the desire that is not named. These two desires parallel two senses of the absolute found in Hegel's individual: the absolute of the given social order, along with the individual's self-negating choice to sustain it, and the absolute of her refusal. The slave's master parallels the symbolic order, the Other who names desire. But here, carrying the master–slave dialectic further, there really is no master: 'each time that the other is exactly the same as the subject, there is no master except. . . .' The temporal master, the symbolic order, does not exist. The 'recognition' is not reciprocal. The enigma of the battle for recognition lies in the fact that the recognition is purely symbolic in a more extreme sense than usually thought. The Other cannot recognize anyone, because the Other does not exist. In a genuine recognition, one only recognizes oneself, the Other as one's own Other.

When, in the Hans Christian Andersen story, the king continues to parade down the street and his subjects continue to praise his 'clothes', it is for the Other, of course, not for the king, that this scene is produced. And the parade does not stop when the king also realizes that he is not wearing clothes. The Other for whom the show is performed is found only among the performers. This show addresses the desire of the Other in the sense that each individual takes as her own desire the desire named by the Other – in fact by herself, for she deceives herself that there is an Other. She deceives herself because she has become accustomed to this desire. It is convenient and secure. So she has good psychological reasons not to want to give up that order. It need not even be unconscious – hence today's cynicism. To motivate the slave to act, it is not enough simply to point out to her that the social order is in her, that there is no master, and that a better order can be established. She may well know this already. The problem is deeper. Even knowing there is no master, that the slave pulls the strings, still, since the desire she has come to know is named within that social order, the slave has good psychological motives – conscious or unconscious – to deceive herself, or simply to pretend. She is accustomed to the Other's desire. Yet there is another desire that is also essential to that order: its negation. But that desire, from the perspective of the social order, is death.

The situation of this slave – the subject in the process – is precisely that of a self-relation in the Hegelian sense (the relation of slave to master) and in the Freudian sense (the relation of ego to ego-ideal). The social theatre is being performed for an Other who exists only as the 'presupposed' (posited as not-posited) ruler of the actors' actions. The recognition by the Other should be a liberating recognition, ultimately a self-recognition – the slave's recognition that the Other is herself. Yet this self-recognition will not suffice. Since the Other names desire, one must leap without support – the ultimate leap, the other desire: death.

This is the final enigma in Lacan's seminar. Adding the ending, the last quoted sentence above continues: '. . . there is no master except the absolute master, death'. Lacan is certainly correct to bring together Freud's reference to the repressed Signor – ultimately the death drive, the drive for truth, the drive to breach the limits of the errant social order – and Hegel's reference to death as absolute master (*Werke* 3, 153). It is dialectically cogent to develop Hegel's master–slave situation further. The ground or truth of the master–slave relationship is its dissolution as developed through the concept of the master. Both Lacan's and Hegel's dialectic of the master move through three stages: the master as another individual; the social order as master sustained by the slave's own acquiescence; and the authentic master, the absolute master, identified with the truth and pure negativity as an immanent recognition within the slave herself. In her confrontation with the other's arbitrariness and meaninglessness, the slave's consciousness has already experienced the absolute master, death, for this is why she submits. Death has become object to the slave, and it leaves memory traces in the slave's consciousness. While the master is the 'essence' governing development of being-in-itself, the slave, in fear of death, is the one who knows the truth, if only unconsciously. At the heart of her being, as the very cause of her becoming a slave, she has seen through the illusion of the social order – she knows the finite master's dependency on her, she knows that beyond the finite master the absolute master awaits; deep down, she knows this because she has confronted death. But she represses this uncomfortable knowledge and lives a consciousness of self-deception, waiting for a liberation which in fact she does not want, for it would reveal the truth that, beyond the threat of her slavery to the finite master, the absolute master – death – still waits for her.

It is common, of course, to naturalize Hegel's absolute master. But when we speak of the highest dialectical stage, where truth and the absolute are invoked in the same gesture, why should this mean anything but what, in psychoanalytic terms, is called 'symbolic death'? The real basis for the fear of death is the fear of the loss of the father's love and, by extension, the absolute negativity experienced at the loss of the Other's love that would result from the destruction of the symbolic order. When we wait and acquiesce in the errant discourse, the order of the temporal master, we experience the passive form of death through the loss of our true being; while when we embrace our own truth and transform ourselves from slaves into masters – not temporal masters, but absolute masters – we take the active form of death as our being.

This continuation of Hegel's master–slave dialectic corresponds to Lacan's seemingly cryptic conclusion to his seminar. In the end we must all meet our truth, a truth that destroys the self-deception of waiting, that inauthentic gesture, hiding from ourselves the fate that is most our own, death, remaining slaves with the empty hope that beyond the master's death everything will be possible, that our finite being has no limit, no *finis*. Our limit is our end, our truth, our essence. Here we act because there is no meaning. Precisely here, where there is no meaning, our *creatio ex nihilo* is possible. It is the object of our unnamed desire that we can fulfill only by a leap. Our authentic truth contains its own contradiction. As finite subjects playing out our subject roles within a slave order, we can select from among its roles, though survival requires that we not reject the system of roles. But we are also produced and determined by that order as its necessary other, an other incomprehensible to the principles of that order. In this sense, I am a subject as the substance underlying this social order, its sustaining principle or – and here is my real choice – its principle of negation. Determined as indifferent, as free, I can act, I can destroy it. The true subject exists only in this act of refusal. This subject that constitutes Hegel's absolute has no positive existence, no existence as a positive entity within the social order; it exists only in the act of negation. Quite different from the subject role one plays by fulfilling the desire named in the symbolic order, keeping one's perceived comfortable life, high salary, social prestige, retirement fund, and so on, the true subject is the subject who – like Socrates in Athens of old – has found her own *parole*, her voice, her *daimonion*, as other than the discourse of error.

Notes

1. This chapter originated as a paper written for a meeting in December 2002 in honour of Edwin Lawrence at Southern Illinois University at Edwardsville. I owe thanks to Sang Ki Kim for advice, and to Craig Gallup for assistance and a careful critique.

2. See *Georg Wilhelm Friedrich Hegel: Werke* (Frankfurt am Main: Suhrkamp, 1986), vol. 5, p. 188; hereafter cited in the text as *Werke* volume, page. Translations of Hegel and Lacan are mine throughout.

3. For the concept of 'act' used in this chapter, my contemporary source is Slavoj Žižek's treatment in *The Ticklish Subject: The Absent Centre of Political Ontology* (London and New York: Verso, 1999).

4. Jacques Lacan, *Les écrits techniques de Freud. Le séminaire livre I 1953–1954*, ed. Jacques Alain Miller (Paris: Éditions du Seuil, 1975) p. 422; throughout this essay all page numbers for Lacan's writings refer to the book and edition given in this footnote, unless otherwise indicated.

5

Nietzsche, Freud, Lacan

Silvia Ons

There are few references to Nietzsche in Freud's or Lacan's works.

'I have denied myself the very great pleasure of reading the works of Nietzsche,' says Freud, 'with the deliberate object of not being hampered in working out the impressions received in psychoanalysis by any sort of anticipatory ideas. I had therefore to be prepared – and I am so, gladly – to forgo all claims to priority in the many instances in which laborious psychoanalytic investigation can merely confirm the truths which the philosopher recognized by intuition.'[1] This argument clearly reveals the force he accorded to these ideas, which might become an obstacle because they cannot be ignored, since they are powerful and attract attention. Freud admitted to Arnold Zweig that Nietzsche had been unattainable for some time: 'When I was young, Nietzsche was a noble and distinguished person inaccessible for me.'[2] When Freud says that he has refused himself the great pleasure of Nietzsche's work, he implies that he has experimented with such pleasure. Some passages show that Freud did not altogether disregard reading Nietzsche, and that what he read deeply marked his work. When, for example, in *The Ego and the Id*,[3] Freud elaborates on the second topic and refers to the id, he does so by including a notion that came to him from Nietzsche via Groddeck. He records the origin of the concept in a footnote: 'Groddeck himself doubtlessly follows Nietzsche's example of the habitual use of this grammatical expression for whatever is impersonal and responds, as it were, to a natural need, a need of our being.' At other times Freud refers to Nietzsche without quoting him. In *Beyond the Pleasure Principle*, his greatest theoretical paper, he alludes to repetition as the 'eternal return', using quotation marks without reference to the author.

Lacan,[4] like Freud, mentions the luminary intensity of Nietzschean thought, describing it as a nova that is as bright as it is quick to return to darkness. Freud and Lacan agree when they define Nietzsche's thinking in terms that have much affinity with the Thing-in-itself: a sudden flash, a disturbing brightness, a blaze, a meteor. Perhaps Freud turned to Nietzsche hoping that the latter would have the appropriate words to express what he was unable to articulate. In one of his letters to Fliess, he says: 'Now I have found Nietzsche's book in which I hope to find the words for much of what remains silent in me, but I have not yet opened it.'[5]

But, as I said above, there are few references to Nietzsche's work in Freud's and Lacan's writings. The silence of psychoanalysis with regard to Nietzsche is both surprising and symptomatic. Surprising, because Nietzsche is the philosopher who is closest to psychoanalysis, the one who no longer believes in metaphysical philosophy, and holds out more hopes for the medical doctor of the future than for the philosopher. Nietzsche did not know of psychoanalysis, yet we could say that his work had psychoanalysis as its target: 'I continue to hope that a philosopher-doctor . . . will some day dare to fully develop the idea that I can only suspect or risk.'[6]

It is worth recalling Arnold Zweig's words to Freud:

> In the last few years I have again come closer to him [Nietzsche] for the mere fact of having recognized in you, dear father Freud, the man who has been able to achieve that which in Nietzsche was only a painting: the man who has brought light back to Antiquity, who has re-evalued all values, the one who has put an end to Christianity, the true immoralist and atheist, the man who has given a new name to human drives, the critic of all cultural evolution up to the present and the one who has done all the other things attributable only to you, who has always managed to avoid all distortions and madness because you have invented psychoanalysis and not Zarathustra.[7]

We are interested in demonstrating to what extent the deconstruction of morality carried out by psychoanalysis has this philosopher as its great precursor. We could even go so far as to say that if Marx invented the symptom, Nietzsche also did so by having discovered the symptom in morality.

Nietzsche is close to Freud as regards the deconstruction of morality, his criticism of Christianity, the invention of the symptom, the notion of the id and the idea of drives and repetition. And Nietzsche is close to Lacan in his conception of truth as having the structure of fiction and the status of appearance that derives from this structure, the rupture of language as grammar to produce new values, in the pragmatism resulting from the dismantling of metaphysics and in the conception of *jouissance* as a different concept from pleasure. This last aspect is extremely important as an indication of how this philosopher anticipated psychoanalysis. We should say that although there are some studies on the link between Freud and Nietzsche, there are no studies so far on Nietzsche and Lacan. We believe that the intensity of the interconnections, and their implications, deserve such attention.

Kant with Sade

Few texts infuriate philosophers so much as Lacan's 'Kant with Sade'.[8] This undertaking, which consisted in connecting a monumental work about morality with that of a libertine theorist, is in itself irritating. When this text is discussed, Kantians believe that psychoanalysts read it from the point of view of psychoanalysis, which is untenable in the philosophical field. The main arguments of the text, however, have their antecedents not only in Freud but also in Nietzsche. The deconstruction of morality carried out by psychoanalysis has its great precursor in this philosopher, perhaps because he was more an analyst than a philosopher. I will take this viewpoint to establish one of the many connections between his work and psychoanalysis. I will then commit myself to proving that, as with Freud, Nietzsche discovers the symptom in morality, and that this discovery was of capital importance in the dismantling of metaphysics.

I will start from 'Kant with Sade', and then trace its precedents in Nietzsche's work. Antecedents of this text have been found in the Excursion II ('Juliette or Enlightenment and Morality') of Adorno's and Horkheimer's *Dialectic of Enlightenment*, but there has never been any discussion of the way in which Nietzsche anticipates the arguments of Lacan's text.

Kant builds an ethics which, in contrast with ancient ethics, is divorced from pleasure.[9] Pure practical reason imposes itself as universal, and does not depend on the particularities of our happiness: 'So act in that the maxim of your will could always hold at the same time as the principle giving universal law.' Pure reason is in itself practical and is the origin of a universal law, a moral law. Moral law constitutes an imperative whose determining character highlights the modality of command with which it imposes itself on the will. The categorical and unconditional nature of the imperative is autonomous inasmuch as it does not serve the aim, the object or subject of love. Kantian ethics takes shape, in Freudian terms, beyond the pleasure principle.

Kant defines pleasure as the conformity between the subject and the representation of the object. As a consequence, every 'material' practical principle – that is to say, that which proposes an object or a content to the will, as the object or content which would determine it – is a necessarily empirical principle incapable of founding a morality. Kantian formalism maintains that universal practical laws are the bases of determination of the will – not according to matter or contents, but according to form. This means: not according to the principle of love of oneself or one's own happiness. Hence, the object will never determine an action.

It is important to emphasize the coercive nature of the command, the unconditional constriction of the command, the compulsive nature (Kant emphasizes the word compulsion) of duty. The coercion of the imperative injures feeling, causes damage, humiliates, wounds one's pride, and pierces the *sensorium.* The law arises beyond pleasure, and the spectre of pain appears in what is supposedly pure. The motor of the moral imperative should be free of any perceptible condition, yet its correlate in the sensory realm is pain. The moral law 'completely excludes the influence of self-love from the highest practical principle and forever checks self-conceit, which decrees the subjective conditions of self-love as laws. If anything checks our self-esteem in our own judgment, it humiliates.'[10]

Lacan says that where Kant believes that he has seen the object eliminated from the phenomenal field, this object none the less becomes apparent, and it is Sade who proves it. In the imperative the object is revealed as a voice, one which takes shape in its deadly depths. The law imposes itself as autonomous order, independent of the material nature of the desired object. In this operation, however, another object appears as an intimidating agent. We know that whatever imposes itself, compels and coerces, frequently takes the form of a voice in the conscience, which arises as if from outside the subject.

Sade unmasks this object when he enunciates the right to enjoyment as a universal rule – this is how Lacan reconstructs the implicit basic premises of Sade's ethics: ' "I have the right to enjoy your body," anybody can tell me, "and I will exercise that right, without any limits preventing me from the whimsical exactions I feel like satisfying." ' Lacan explicates the logic of this phrase by making it clear that the insertion 'anybody can tell me' does not refer to any or all of the speaker's intersubjective partners;[11] rather, it stands for the voice in the mouth of the Other, as an object which is different from the objects that appear in the field of phenomena.

But it is not a question of approving the law and the imperative of Sadeian enjoyment/*jouissance.* Kant and Sade are often identified with each other in psychoanalysis, an idea that is the result of hasty reading and a position lacking the proper sense of perspective. Lacan does not present them as equivalent, but indicates the way in which the imperative shows the aspect of enjoyment which exists, but is suppressed in the unconditional practice of reason. Freud suspected early on – and wrote of this to Fliess – that there must be something in sexual life that strongly nourished morality.[12]

Sadeian frames

There is a little-explored remark in Lacan's *Encore*[13] that has many repercussions and is rich in consequences: Lacan takes a word to pinpoint the peculiarity of perversion: *almoralité* (amorality-of-the-soul/*alma*/). Love [*amor*] is different from almorality. Such a designation can be properly understood only if we notice that this word contains a link between *objet petit a* as the object of *jouissance* and love. On the other hand, there is a link between *objet petit a* and morality. We can thus speak of the possibility of *amor* in neuroses, since the conditions of *jouissance* can be connected with love; and we can speak of *almoralité* in perversion, since the conditions of *jouissance* are connected with morality.

It is not possible to think of love in perversion, neither is it possible in Kantian ethics. This is not a coincidence. We should note that the universal and the necessary are at odds with its modality, which is always contingent. Sade says that love is a madness of the soul, because it satisfies two individuals, and therefore does not have universal scope.[14] On eliminating it from his topos – the way Kant does, considering the subject's private happiness incapable of founding an ethics – the call of the libertine is to morality. An ever-present guest, never missing an appointment, a witness to all excesses, morality will be questioned for its inconsistency. Sade denounces a morality that is forgotten, and if we read his work carefully, we perceive that he does not accept the futility of principles – in sum, amnesia on the ethical plane. Strengthening morality implies appealing to a voice that does not tire the ear, reaching a definitive agreement between behaviour and the law; a copula, then, between *jouissance* and morality. Such an amalgam will make *jouissance* take on the character of an unavoidable universal law, valid in all cases.

Thus the Sadeian ghost denies chance, rejects the unforeseen, and is boringly static. Notice, for instance, that in no scene does failure of the sexual act appear, nor does *detumescence*, or anything that indicates the presence of the unexpected in a woman. They are a priori schemes; lust should not confuse us as to their nature, which is, in an unprecedented way, formal. A passage from *Juliette* clearly illustrates this dimension: two young people want to satisfy their appetites, but when they are on the point of making love, the depraved nun stops them, telling them that they should wait, that order is necessary, that *jouissance* is achieved only by specifying one's pleasures beforehand. On the one hand we see, in this as in other Sadeian scenes, that the agent is not fundamentally the one who has the power or the pleasure, but the one who is in control of the scene and the phrase or, further still, the direction of meaning. On the other hand, we can thus detect that there is repression in so-called libertinage, repression of the non-prescribed, of the unframed, of *tyché*. The pervert wants to eliminate the unexpected event that shakes a previous assumption; his desire to break the law conceals the pervert's deepest wish: to substitute himself for it. Sadeian society is a codified one, with guidelines and rules but devoid of eroticism, if by eroticism we mean allusive, ambiguous, suggestive language that is home to the unexpected.

There is religiosity in this deterministic kind of logic if we, like Nietzsche, think that the religious person (basically the Christian) rejects the world of the unexpected because the hiatus between cause and effect has to be suppressed in order to perpetuate the bond between guilt and punishment. We find a similar omission in the Sadeian view. After all, does Lacan not say that the pervert is a crusader? Lacan also states that, in religion, the cause rests in the hands of God.[15] Do we not find in Sade an omnipresent, governing will?

Naturally, this will to *jouissance* always needs tension to resist it. It is a matter of causing outrage, and this kind of transgression needs a victim, which for Lacan would be represented by the brutal subject of pleasure, the one considered pathological by Kant, since it is attracted to an object that concerns its happiness. Sade's Manichaeism is truly incredible, the regiments of sadists and victims are absolutely delimited, and there is no crossing from one side to the other. This scene needs polarity, the scheme must be imposed; it is always a question of education, of turning the poor brutal subject into a subject divided by the imperative. This is an impossible passage; we need only recall that crime will not suffice, since the shift must be perpetuated in the great beyond. Sade likes to identify himself with nature, and supposes that nature wants to elevate destruction as its supreme law. But total annihilation can never be proven, given that death is only a change in form. For such annihilation to be possible, it would be necessary to prove the existence of one instant of inaction of matter, but this can never be discovered. Life itself opposes this, and the more Sade approaches crime, the more he encounters its impossibility.

Nietzsche and the discovery of morality as a symptom

Nietzsche says that morality turns against life. In *On the Genealogy of Morals*,[16] he wonders how to imprint something on the living capacity of forgetfulness, in such a way that it always remains present. It is impossible not to connect such an undertaking with Sade's aspiration.

Nietzsche, then, points out that for something to remain in the memory, it must be branded on it; only that which does not cease to hurt will remain. This is always done through bloodshed. All that is ascetic belongs to this field: several ideas must become indelible, so that the whole system is left hypnotized. In this conception, ascetic ways of life are the means to prevent all those ideas from competing with the others, to make them unforgettable. For Sade, moral principles should be in accord with the voice of nature. This is achieved by locating certain ideas outside the self, as is done in the morality described by Nietzsche.

We are not unaware of the transition between seemingly dissimilar terms such as perversion and asceticism. Nietzsche anticipated psychoanalysis when he pointed out the connection between the two. He speaks of ascetic voluptuousness, of the ascetic self-derision of reason, of ascetic self-contempt, of the lascivious nature of asceticism, to mention only some of the many ways in which he points out the morbidity of this ideal. This line of thought would not have been possible if sexuality had not been situated in the centre of the debate on reason and morality; as if the operation performed by Freud in the clinic were parallel and related to that performed by Nietzsche in philosophy. Silvio Maresca groups them together as positivists who collaborate actively in the process of the dissolution of transcendental subjectivity, extracting from this dissolution a previously unknown dimension of drives.[17] Nietzsche investigates the libidinal reasons that are at issue in asceticism. The anchorite worships part of his self as God, and in order to do so he has to render the remaining part of himself diabolical. The spectre of the pathological appears in morality, as Lacan observed with regard to Kantian law. Notably, Nietzsche concludes that if these men repudiate what is natural in them, it is because they have derived some kind of enjoyment from it. Together with Lacan, Nietzsche refers to enjoyment to designate a pleasure beyond the pleasure principle:

> pleasure is felt and sought in ill-constitutedness, decay, pain, mischance, ugliness, voluntary deprivation, self-mortification, self-flagellation, self-sacrifice. All this is in the highest degree paradoxical: we stand before a discord that *wants* to be discordant, that *enjoys* itself in this suffering and even grows more self-confident and triumphant the more its own presupposition, its physiological capacity for life, *decreases*. 'Triumph in the ultimate agony.'[18]

It is not, then, pure reason that fights drives, it is always one drive that fights another. Much of what is considered rational is morality in disguise. Neither is it a rational 'I' that undertakes the struggle. What animates it are questions of *jouissance*. And are these the same reasons that Nietzsche refers to regarding Kant's violence in connection with the tyranny of the philosopher in pursuit of a unifying formula capable of condensing the problem of the world? Philosophy 'always creates the world in its own image, it cannot do otherwise; philosophy is this tyrannical drive itself, the most spiritual will to power, to "creation of the world", to *causa prima*'. It is impossible not to notice the echo with Lacan's description of the relation between the discourse of the master and philosophy.

Violence is disclosed in the search for ultimate notions that attack the chance aspect of the future, in building universals that ferociously annul particularities. The metaphor of the spider-philosopher is, in this sense, very meaningful: like a spider, the philosopher creates a conceptual web in cavernous darkness, captures reality in his nets, paralyses it, renders it static to inject its poison into it and deprives it of its last remnants of life. Or the philosophy that fears meanings itself becomes a vampire that leaves only the bones and the rattling they produce: categories, formulas, words. The connection between violence and metaphysics has been established, and the *jouissance* aspect of foundations has been unmasked.

Heidegger's interpretation of Nietzsche's philosophy consists of including this philosophy in the history of metaphysics, as its fulfilment and completion. In contrast to Heidegger, who stresses man's relationship with Being as the connecting thread, Maresca highlights the dimension of drives that results from the dissolution of the transcendental subject; he considers that the dismantling of metaphysics was not possible without the dismantling of morality, a deconstruction that implies deepening the matrix of drives into that morality. Morality is metaphysical, and it is organized by creating pyramids with a supreme principle at the top. When the nomadic character of 'transformation' is rejected, values are created generating unshakeable certainties, Archimedean points that require incompatible antitheses. The metaphysician wants things of supreme value to have an origin that is distinct, their own, and immutable. That is why Nietzsche disrupts the moral antitheses upon which metaphysics is based.

'It could even be possible', he says in *Beyond Good and Evil*,

> that the value of those good and honoured things consists precisely in the fact that in an insidious way *they are related* to those bad, seemingly opposite things, linked, knit together, even identical perhaps. Perhaps! But who is willing to worry about such dangerous Perhapses? We must wait for a new category of philosophers to arrive, those whose taste and inclination are the reverse of their predecessors' – they will be in every sense philosophers of the dangerous Perhaps.[19]

Is it not Freud who occupies this position, as if it had been the one required by Nietzsche, as if the creation of psychoanalysis had been urged by his work, as if there had been a previous claim, a call *through which Freud was interpellated*? Dismantling metaphysics (as Maresca clearly explains) is not possible without dismantling morality; in principle, it will be a question of disengaging the antitheses on which it is founded. Nietzsche says: 'The metaphysicians' fundamental belief is *the belief in the opposition of values.*'[20] Questioning this belief makes him approach the truth of the Freudian unconscious. In his short essay 'The Antithetical Meaning of Primal Words',[21] Freud shares Nietzsche's interest in philology. He finds in Karl Abel's work on languages with more ancient roots than Egyptian a discovery that coincides with the discovery of the dream-work: these words, which can designate opposed values, behave like the dream itself. 'The dream's conduct towards the category of opposition and contradiction is striking. This category is omitted altogether; the "no" (negation) does not seem to exist in the dream. It clearly prefers to compose opposites in a unit or to represent them as an identical element.'

Metaphysics, as opposed to the unconscious, divides, separates, renders absolute, and generates antitheses suitable for unidirectional thinking. In this sense, neither Freud nor Nietzsche could avoid being admirers of Goethe, enemy of the disunity of reason, sensibility and will envisioned by Kant.

Metaphysics presupposes irreconcilable polarities. Its dismantling is not possible without the inclusion of what we would call energetics in philosophical analysis. Nietzsche's thinking delves into the thermodynamics of illusion, it tracks the idea and its appetite. Corporeality has arisen in thought, so physicalist concepts permeate Freud's and Nietzsche's work. The inclusion of sexuality in morality causes true commotion. Once repressed, displaced, elided and ignored, sexuality brings about the collapse of convictions based on a supposedly pure *episteme*: 'Thus I do not believe that an "instinct for knowledge" is the father of philosophy, but rather that here as elsewhere a different instinct has merely made use of knowledge (and kNOwledge!) as its tool.'[22]

Nietzsche revealed the symptom; taking our cue from him, we can say that metaphysics was its defence. No dismantling is possible without this discovery of symptom in morality. 'In short, we believe that the intention is but a sign or a symptom, first of all requiring interpretation, and furthermore that it is a sign with so many meanings that as a consequence it has almost none in and of itself; we believe that morality in its earliest sense, intention-morality, was a prejudice, something precipitous . . .'.[23]

Neither the discovery of the repression of sexuality nor that of the unconscious would by themselves be able to make the metaphysical postulates collapse. It is only the symptom that demolishes the antithesis. What is to be condemned appears disguised in the condemnation itself. It is no longer possible to speak of two poles separated by a dividing line: a new topology is required. For Freud, the virtuous man bears within his character the trace of the drives he tries to impugn. The symptom as substitute satisfaction shows the failure of the metaphysical defence that divides the areas it wants to keep uncontaminated.

Nietzsche considers morality a will towards nothingness, life against life, exposing its anorexic nature. '– all this means – let us dare to grasp it – a *will to nothingness*, an aversion to life, a rebellion against the most fundamental presuppositions of life; but it is and remains a *will!*'[24] And by anticipating the great symptom of our times, he will say that man prefers willing nothingness itself to not willing.

The deconstruction of metaphysical morality is in unison with the recovery of a sensibility that has been anaesthetized, undermined, and confined to its lethal destiny. If morality has made an attempt on life, its commotion should free the tormented body. But such a consequence should not make us believe that we are dealing with a form of thought focused on the body; neither is it a way of using the physical against the spiritual but, rather, a corporeal spirituality that arises from the post-metaphysical universe. Metaphors of fragrance, sounds, outbursts, births, earthquakes, undercurrents, dawns, storms and lights indicate along the path of thought, and within its very fabric, the resonance of the sensory realm.

The contrast with Sade is evident: Sade wants to found a morality which, coupled with sexuality, would remain unforgettable. The voluptuous toughness that is aimed at here is not the result of the sensible order because it is, rather, superimposed on the latter, as a second nature. The initiate should acquire the habit of doing evil by apathetic repetition of an act perpetrated in cold blood.

Nietzsche, on the other hand, dismantles morality. This dismantling has deep connections with psychoanalysis; the deconstruction disturbs the metaphysical defence. In Nietzsche, such an operation is the condition for the creation of new values which, far from rejecting life, draw sustenance from it. Such a condition needs work, a path, which we could connect with psychoanalysis. Lacan, together with Nietzsche, is Aristotelian when he states that what comes after this condition is an enjoyment he likes to call the enjoyment of life.

Notes

1. Sigmund Freud, 'On the History Of the Psychoanalytic Movement', *The Penguin Freud Library*, vol. 15. (Harmondsworth: Penguin, 1993), p. 73.
2. Letter to Arnold Zweig of 12 May 1934, in *The Letters of Sigmund Freud and Arnold Zweig* (London: Tavistock, 1970).
3. See Sigmund Freud, *The Ego and the Id*, in James Strachey, ed., *The Standard Edition of the Complete Psychological Works of Sigmund Freud* (London: Hogarth Press, 1953–73) (hereafter *SE*), vol. 19.
4. Jacques Lacan, *Écrits* (New York: Norton, 2002), p. 112.
5. Letter to Wilhem Fliess of 1 February 1902 in Sigmund Freud, *Letters 1873–1939* (London: Tavistock, 1960).
6. Friedrich Nietzsche, *Daybreak: Thoughts on the Prejudices of Morality* (Cambridge: Cambridge University Press, 1997), p. 19.
7. Letter to Freud of 28 April 1934, in *The Letters of Sigmund Freud and Arnold Zweig.*
8. See Jacques Lacan, 'Kant avec Sade', in *Écrits* (Paris: Éditions du Seuil, 1966).
9. Immanuel Kant, *Critique of Practical Reason*, Book I, Chapter 1, Theorems I, II, and III (New York: Macmillan, 1993).
10. Kant, op. cit., p. 77.
11. Lacan, 'Kant avec Sade', pp. 769 ff.
12. See Sigmund Freud, *The Origins of Psycho-Analysis*, K manuscript (London: Tavistock, 1954).
13. Jacques Lacan, *Le Séminaire de Jacques Lacan. Livre XX: Encore* (Paris: editions du Seuil, 1975), p. 80.
14. See D.A.F. de Sade, 'Yet Another Effort, Frenchmen, If You Want to Become Republicans', in *Justine, Philosophy In the Bedroom, and Other Writings* (New York: Grove Press, 1966).
15. See Lacan, *Écrits*, p. 870.
16. Friedrich Nietzsche, *On the Genealogy of Morals* (New York: Vintage, 1989), p. 58.
17. See Silvio Maresca, *Nietzsche y Illuminismo* (Buenos Aires: Alianza Publishers, 2004).
18. Nietzsche, *On the Genealogy of Morals*, p. 118.
19. Friedrich Nietzsche, *Beyond Good and Evil* (Oxford: Oxford University Press, 1998), p. 6.
20. Nietzsche, *Beyond Good and Evil*, p. 6.
21. See Sigmund Freud, 'The Antithetical Meaning of Primal Words', *SE* 11.
22. Nietzsche, *Beyond Good and Evil*, p. 9.
23. Nietzsche, *Beyond Good and Evil*, p. 33.
24. Nietzsche, *On the Genealogy of Morals*, p. 163.

6

May ’68, The Emotional Month

Joan Copjec

Emotions ran high in Paris in May ’68, particularly among students in the universities. Sensing the peril of ignoring the groundswell of emotion, faculty responded immediately, but variously. Some conservative old fossils attempted to quash the rebellion, while more liberal-minded, avuncular types ‘took to the barricades’, casting their lot with the student radicals. Both camps permitted themselves a little more passion than usual, precisely because ‘usual’ seemed to have evaporated in the hurly-burly of dissent. In the upheaval, everything seemed to have been turned upside down and inside out, including reason, which – suddenly agitated – became clouded with roily sediment. Less cool-headed and clear, reason became crimson-faced.

The response of Jacques Lacan did not fit, however, into either camp. Aligning himself neither against nor on the side of the student radicals, he simply accused them of not being radical enough, of behaving like unwitting flunkies of the university against which they imagined themselves to be in revolt. Detecting in their cries a plea for a new Master, he warned that they were on the verge of getting one. The monitory finger he held in their faces assumed the form of a year-long seminar, *Séminaire XVII: L’envers de la psychanalyse [The Underside (or Reverse) of Psychoanalysis]*.[1] In this seminar Lacan maintained that although the students wanted to believe they were abandoning the university for the streets, the university was not so easily abandoned; it had already begun to take them over – as well as the streets. Which is why even certain elements of their revolt reflected academic business as usual.

For the most part, the reversals or upendings referred to in the seminar’s title produce something *other than* psychoanalysis, another kind of discourse, namely, that of the Master, the Hysteric, or the University. That is, the specific operation of ‘reversal’ referred to in the title is that of the ‘quarter-turns’ or rotations which produce the four discourses, of which psychoanalysis is only one.[2] Yet there is also a sense in which the reversal does take place *within* psychoanalysis itself, as Lacan turns classical Freudian theory upside down and inside out to produce a more revolutionary version of it, and thus to redefine the 'analytic discourse' as a new social bond. At the end of the seminar, this social tie is rendered in a distilled formula that exposes the ultimate ambition of the analyst – who, in her impossible role as analyst, operates on the analysand – as rather unseemly. The final aim of psychoanalysis, it turns out, is the production of shame. That which Lacan himself describes as unmentionable, even improper to speech as such, is mentioned (and mentioned only) on the threshold of the seminar's close. The seamy underside of psychoanalysis, the backside towards which all the twists and turns have led, is finally shame: that affect whose very mention brings a blush to the face.[3] Why is shame given such a place of honour, if we may put it that way, in the seminar? And what should the position of the analyst be with respect to it? Should she try to reduce it, get rid of it, lower her eyes before it? No; Lacan proposes that the analyst make herself the agent of it. Provoke it. Looking out into the audience gathered in large numbers around him, he accounts for their presence in his final, closing remarks thus: if you have come here to listen to what I have to say, it is because I have positioned myself with respect to you as analyst, that is: as object-cause of your desire. And in this way I have helped you to feel ashamed. End of seminar.

I want to allow what Lacan is saying to sink in. In response to May '68, a very emotional month, he ends his seminar, his long warning against the rampant and misguided emotionalism of the university students, with an impassioned plea for a display of shame. Curb your impudence, your shamelessness, he exhorts, cautioning: you should be ashamed! What effrontery! What a provocation is this seminar! But then: what are we to make of it? Because the reference to shame appears so abruptly only in the final session and without elaboration, this is not an easy question to answer. One hears echoes of the transferential words of Alcibiades, who has this to say in *The Symposium* about Socrates: 'And with this man alone I have an experience which no one would believe was possible for me – the sense of shame.'[4] But to detect the vibrations of this precedent is a far cry from understanding what to make of it.

To sort matters out, one looks for hints that might be seen in retrospect to have been dropped along the way, and might now steer us in the proper direction. Shame did emerge as a topic of interest in earlier seminars. In *Seminar VII: The Ethics of Psychoanalysis*, for example, Lacan compared shame to beauty, noting that the two functioned similarly to mark a limit; and in *Seminar XI: The Four Fundamental Concepts of Psycho-Analysis*, in his discussion of Sartre's scenario of the voyeur at the keyhole, he dwells for a time on the phenomenon of shame as if trying to justify Sartre's contention that it marks the 'birth of the social'. In *L'envers*, Lacan adjusts that claim slightly, arguing that shame marks not the social link as such, but that particular link which analysis is intent on forging. One of the most fruitful paths to follow, however, is the one laid down by Lacan's remarks on affect, precisely because an affect is what shame is.

That the return to Freud via Saussurean linguistics was guilty of a disastrous neglect of affect was, by May '68, not a new charge. Lacan had dealt with it before, particularly in *Seminar X*, the seminar on anxiety. But it is not difficult to understand why the charge was resurrected by the students who confronted him, during the course of this very seminar, on the steps of the Pantheon. The perceived hyperrationality of the formulas drawn on blackboards by their structuralist professors seemed arid and far removed from the turmoil that surrounded them, from the newness of extraordinary events, the violence of police beatings, and from their own inchoate feelings of solidarity with the workers. A grumbling sense that something had been left out, that something inevitably escaped these desiccated and timeless structures, was expressed in the renewed demand that Lacan begin redressing the university's failures by recognizing the importance of affect. They had had it up to their eyeballs with signifiers and all the talk of signifiers, which only left a whole area of their experience unacknowledged: precisely the fact of their being agitated, moved by what was happening here and now.

Lacan responded by drawing more formulas on the backboard. But let us at least credit him with this: he bent over backwards to point out that he was not simply talking the talk, he was . . . well, he was fitting his structures with feet. Indeed, he mentions this over and over: my structures have legs. They *do* march; they *do* move, my four-legged creatures. If he keeps repeating this joking reference to his four-footed structures, it is not because he is delighted with his little metaphor, but because it is not a metaphor. The movement in these signifying structures is real, which is how we know they do not ignore affect, as many had charged.

Affect is included in the formulas of the four discourses. But where? A negative answer first: one misses the point if one tries to locate affect – or *jouissance*, in Lacan's preferred vocabulary – in any of the individual symbols that compose the structure; affect (again, affect) is not to be treated as a local element that can simply be added to the chain of signifiers like that. This is in fact what Lacan himself did in his earlier work, when he theorized *jouissance* as an outside discourse. Defining the relation between the signifier and *jouissance* as antinomic, he localized the latter in a beyond. A positive answer begins by noting that what is new in *Seminar XVII* is the emphasis Lacan gives to Freud's critical assertion that only ideas are ever repressed; affect never is. Affect remains on the surface. This does not mean that repression has no effect on affect [*jouissance*]; it means, rather, that this effect is something other than the removal of affect from consciousness. The specific effect of repression on affect is displacement. Affect is *always* displaced, or: always out of place. The question is: in relation to what? The first temptation is to answer: in relation to the signifier or representation. This would mean that representation and affect are out of phase with one another. The problem with this answer is that it tends to reinstate the old antinomy between *jouissance* and the signifier, and to insist finally on the deficit or failure of representation.

One way of gaining perspective on this manoeuvre, I suggest, is to take a brief detour through an essay published by Gilles Deleuze in 1967 – that is, between the years of Lacan's XIth and XVIIth seminars. Consider this passage from that essay:

> The first effect of Others is that around each object that I perceive or each idea that I think there is the organization of a marginal world, a mantle or background, where other objects and other ideas may come forth. . . . I regard an object, then I divert my attention, letting it fall into the background. At the same time, there comes forth from the background a new object of my attention. If this new object does not injure me, if it does not collide with me with the violence of a projectile (as when one bumps against something unseen), it is because the first object had already at its disposal a complete margin where I had already felt the preexistence of objects yet to come, and of an entire field of virtualities and potentialities which I already knew were capable of being actualized.[5]

In this description perceptions, or representations, are conceived less as limited than as wrapped in a mantle of indetermination; they are fringed by something like peripheral vision. A surplus of perception, an indeterminate 'more', creates a kind of buffer zone which ensures that perceptions do not simply follow antecedent perceptions, but emerge smoothly from their penumbra. The source of this mantle or surplus is what Deleuze calls here 'the Other'; it is an Other who 'assures the margins and transitions of the world' and 'fills the world with a benevolent murmuring'. In his later work, Deleuze rebaptizes this benevolent Other with another term, 'affect', and he will define affect (specifically in the books on cinema) as the participation of the actual in the virtual and the virtual in the actual, as seen from the side of the actual thing. In this later work, he will argue that an actual, individual perception participates simultaneously in a pre-individual or impersonal field, just as in the 1967 Tournier essay he claims that it participates in the field of the Other.

But something changes in the later work, when the Other comes to be called affect; to put it succinctly, Deleuze's account becomes less Merleau-Pontyesque. In other words, affect is not quite as 'benevolent' as the Other was in so far as the claim is no longer that affect serves to confirm the existence of a stable world – to guarantee, for example, that the back of a house meets up with its front in some consistent way – or to protect the subject from 'assaults from behind', as Deleuze puts it in his earlier essay. In that essay, Merleau-Ponty's account of the relation between the gaze and the visible is invoked as critique of the analysis given by Sartre in *Being and Nothingness*; it is as if Deleuze had wanted to overturn Lacan's argument in *Seminar XI*, in which Sartre is used against Merleau-Ponty. The later Deleuze is more 'Sartrean' in the sense that he conceives affect as more disruptive, more murderous than murmuring; it is less a mantle surrounding perception than perception's inner division, its dislocation from itself. While I began by wondering if Freud's insistence that affect is always displaced implied an out-of-phase relation between affect and representation, the present line of argument suggests that this formulation suffers from an overly sharp separation of the two terms, a division that antagonizes them. Is not affect, rather, in this account, representation's own essential 'out-of-phaseness' with itself? A marginal difference opens up, separating the individual perception from itself – and it is this difference which is called affect. Not something added to representation or the signifier, but a surplus produced by its very function, a surplus of the signifier over itself.

According to the most common misunderstanding, the displacement of affect means that perception is liable to distortion whenever a quantum of affect wanders inappropriately into an otherwise objective field, and burdens or blocks it with a subjective excess of feeling. This misunderstanding is skilfully put to rest in Brian Massumi's Deleuzian-inspired analysis of an experiment in which subjects were instructed to match a colour swatch with some cherished object about which they were invited to reminisce. Massumi notes that the subjects in the experiment frequently mismatched the fondly remembered object with a 'too-blue' swatch. In the common misunderstanding, the excess of colour would be viewed as a sure sign of the affected character of the choice in the sense that it would be read as an excess *quantity* of feeling, a surplus or addition of personal feeling that would not have been elicited had the subject maintained a purely objective relation to the object. If affect is understood, however, not as a quantitative but as a *qualitative* surplus – that is, if the excessiveness of affect is seen as its opening on to another dimension (in Deleuze, the virtual) or another register (in Lacan, the Real) – the overly saturated colour becomes readable as an indication of something other than its limitation, that is, its being only a particular or subjective *aspect* rather than a clear and full view of the object, as in: '*To me* his eyes seem very blue.'

Affect does not familiarize, domesticate or subjectivize – on the contrary, it estranges. The cherished memories of the subjects in the experiment lose what Lacan once called 'that belong-to-me-aspect so reminiscent of property'. The overly saturated colour is the sign that perception has begun to overspill the narrow grooves of the associations or recollections that once bound the object to these subjects. The memory becomes moving, affective, only to the extent that it becomes independent of the subjects, becomes less recognizable through its participation in an extra-individual dimension.

Freud and Lacan both associate affect with movement. And Massumi, following Deleuze, states that 'affect inhabits passage', adding this metaphor: in the same way, 'an excess of activity over each successive step' constitutes the 'momentum of walking'.[6] Just as walking would grind to a halt if there were no excess of movement over and above the simple addition of one step to another, so, too, would signification and thinking stop dead in their tracks if thought did not exceed the simple succession of signifiers or logical steps. Each step, signifier or thought must not merely follow its antecedent, but emerge from within it. That Freud tried to theorize this movement of thought by insisting on affect's displacement is a truth nearly lost on his readers, mainly because he reserved the much-maligned word 'discharge' to describe the process. Attempting to forestall this casualty, Lacan rescues the word from the biochemical context that obscures Freud's insights, emphatically stating in *Television* that 'What affect discharges is not adrenalin but thought.'[7]

Affect is the discharge, the movement, of thought. If readers of Freud, blinded by the word 'discharge', failed to see that it was the term by which he attempted to theorize affect as the movement of thought, readers of Lacan, blinded by the word 'signifier', were misled into believing that he had neglected affect altogether. Counting only signifiers among the elements of his system, they saw no room for affect, never noticing that one of these signifiers, the one Freud called *Vorstellungrepräsentanz*, was not like all the rest. If it has a 'signifying' name, nevertheless, this is because it designates not something other than the signifier, but the signifier's otherness to itself. In brief, it names the inner displacement of the signifier, its misalignment with itself. We become estranged from our memories and thoughts because the signifier, hence thought, can be estranged from itself or can move in a new direction.

Anxiety: Sister of Shame

It sometimes happens, however, that thinking does grind to a halt, stops moving, becomes inhibited. At these times movement is reduced to agitation, a kind of inexpedient-tentative running in place. When this happens, affect is known by a more specific name; it is called anxiety. Before we can understand affect in general as the movement of thought, it is necessary to understand this specific affect, which is its obstacle, the arrest of thought. According to one of Freud's formulations, anxiety occurs when what was repressed and should have remained hidden becomes visible. We are now able to revise this. What erupts into awareness in moments of anxiety is not something that was formerly repressed (since affect never is), but the disjunction that defines displacement, which suddenly impresses itself as a gap or break in perception. As Lacan will put it: anxiety is the experience of an encounter with *objet petit a*. Let us agree to suspend what we think about this object until we examine it *in situ*, in the setting Lacan gives it in *Seminar XVII*.

Never more inventive than when speaking of *objet petit a*, the concept he touts as his major innovation, Lacan went so far in *Seminar XI* as to invent a modern myth, the myth of the lamella, to showcase it. In *Seminar XVII* this mythical lamella, a kind of anarchic, runaway organ, let loose from any imaginary body that might contain it, undergoes some biotechnological tinkering; the little organ is made over into a small gadget or gizmo. The neologism employed to designate this little genetically engineered device, this little nothing, is 'lathouse'. In Lacan's new ultra-modern myth, there is no heavenly sphere, naturally; it has been demolished. All that remains of the world beyond the subject is the 'alethosphere', which is a kind of high-tech heaven, a laicized or 'disenchanted' space filled none the less with every techno-scientific marvel imaginable: space probes and orbiters, telecommunications and telebanking systems, and so on. The subject is now a 'terminal' subject, plugged into various circuitries, suited with wearable computers and fitted with artificial, remotely monitored and controlled organs, implants.[8]

The myth is probably inspired by the section of *Civilization and its Discontents* where Freud speaks of modern man's capacity to remake himself as 'a kind of prosthetic God', to replace every lost appendage or damaged organ with another, superior one endowed with fantastic powers.[9] In this alethosphere (*alethosphere* because this space and everything in it is built on the demonstrable *truths*, rigorous and mathematical, of modern science) the prosthetically enhanced, plugged-in subject does not need to flee reality in order to indulge his pleasure principle, for he is now able to remould reality in accordance with it. In other words, in the ultra-modern, advanced capitalist world, the pleasure principle and the reality principle are no longer in competition, but have merged to form a kind of corporation. The image Freud paints is of a friendly takeover of reality by the pleasure principle, which presents the former with a set of blueprints for the global cyber-city of its dreams. But Lacan stresses the underside of this merger. As the twentieth century wore on, and the utopian view of science gave way to dystopian visions, while capitalism grew more muscular, it became more difficult to hold on to the idea that pleasure had the power to programme reality. The reality (of the market) principle was clearly calling the shots, telling the pleasure principle in what to invest and what pleasures ought to be sacrificed to get the best returns on those investments.

One of the best depictions of the takeover of pleasure by reality is still to be found in Walter Benjamin's notion of aura. Benjamin writes as though aura was *destroyed* when we began, by means of capitalist production, to bring things closer to us, yet he taught us enough to know that it could not have existed *before* capitalism, that aura appeared for the first time only *with* capitalism, specifically as that which had been lost. This loss, however, had a rather odd effect, since the eradication of the intervening existence between us and things *created* 'the unique phenomenon of a distance' and a now more rigid, indestructible aura. How are we to understand this logic if not in the terms Freud gave us: an original loss, the difference between satisfaction anticipated and satisfaction obtained, is recuperated by being embodied or imagined in objects with a certain sheen which we no longer simply want, but want more of. Prosthetic gods, we do not simply bring our fantasies closer to reality, more within reach, we experience their remodelling by the market into *mise en scènes* of the postponement of desire. The gleaming, globalized city erected in the alethosphere turns out to be ruled, as in Fritz Lang's *Metropolis*, by an occult, maimed wizard, Rot[z]wang, the S_1 placed in the bottom-left corner of the University Discourse, the master, castrated, fallen to the level of superegoic urgings to 'Keep on yearning'.

In the alethosphere, the merger of the principles of reality and pleasure is coextensive with a merger of subject and Other. Patched into a surface network of social circuitry, the subject 'interfaces' with the Other. This interface is not to be confused, however, with what is in Lacanian terms referred to as 'extimacy'. The notion of interface (which pretends to antiquate the psychoanalytic conception of the subject) is only the most recent retooling of that phenomenological assumption against which Lacan repeatedly railed: namely, that the whole of the subject's corporeal presence is engaged or chiasmically intertwined with the Other, 'directed in what is called [its] total intentionality'.[10] At a certain historical moment, that moment when the social configuration Lacan calls the 'University Discourse' was first set in place, reality – including man – began to be conceived as fully manipulable. Man came to be viewed as a being without foundation, without roots, or as so intertwined with the Other as to be infinitely mouldable. This is the heart of the conception of the cosmopolitical subject, nomadic, homeless man of the world. Capitalism drives and profits from this conception of the malleability of man, but we have not yet said enough to know how it does so, how it gets us to surrender ourselves to it, or what it is we surrender. The first point that needs to be made is this: if the subject becomes conceivable as completely intertwined with the Other, this is because modern science comes to be conceived as universal, as having triumphed over and supplanted every other realm and every other form of truth. Man is totally taken up, then, *without exception*, into the Other of the scientific world.[11]

Without exception? This is, of course, the interesting issue, and one Lacan will persistently mine. According to a long tradition that includes Freud himself, anxiety is distinguished from fear on the grounds that, unlike fear, it has no object. Anxiety is intransitive, while fear is transitive. Lacan goes against this tradition, however, to assert instead that anxiety is 'not without object'. Why? What does he gain by this? The standard criterion, 'with or without object', offers a simple choice between two contradictory or mutually exclusive terms which exhaust the field of possibilities. Between the two there is a strict boundary. The choice of one or the other (object or not) decides on which side of the boundary the phenomenon is situated. Freud seems to have intuited that this boundary did not only divide fear and anxiety, but had the potential to divide the scientific and reason from the unscientific and irrational. And Freud did not want this. He never wanted his science, psychoanalysis, to be construed as a study of irrational phenomena; the workings of the psyche, no matter how troubled, did not fall outside the pale of science. This is surely why Freud kept trying to model anxiety on some form of actual threat, even proposing at one point a 'realistic anxiety' after which signal anxiety might be patterned. The sentiment of anxiety is one of hard certainty, and he felt no impulse to question it, to characterize that feeling as a delusion: that is, to dismiss this certainty as unfounded, as having no basis in reason.

Lacan's formula, 'not without object', is fashioned out of the same concern as Freud's. The first thing to observe is that the formula has a definable rhetorical structure: namely, that of a litotes or understatement. Through the rhetorical figure of litotes one expresses an affirmation by negating its contrary. If someone were to say to you, for example, 'I am not unhappy with the way things turned out,' you would be able to discern an affirmation of the following sort: 'It would be an understatement to say I am happy; I am, in fact, ecstatic.' Likewise, when Lacan asserts that anxiety is 'not without object', he tells us, in effect, that it would be an understatement to say it has an object. For anxiety is precipitated by an encounter with an object of a level of certainty superior to that of any object of fact, to any actual object. And this is so despite the fact that the object affirmed by this figure of speech is nowhere present in the statement but is, rather, a surfeit of signification beyond what is explicitly said. Not stated, by – once again – being understated, in and by a negation.[12]

Far from being an abstract idea, the insistent affirmation of a negative contrary is a central fact with which modern philosophy and politics tries to come to grips. I noted earlier that the historical proposition that everything, including man, is malleable implies that he is without foundation, without roots. Deterritorialization therefore reigns, or should be expected to reign, in the scientific/capitalist world. Yet no political fact has asserted itself with such ferocity than that man is '*not* without foundation', '*not* without roots'.[13] Something insists on disrupting the progress of deterritorialization, time and time again.

Now, to say that one is 'not without roots' is different from saying that one has roots in some racial, ethnic or national tradition, as those who engineered the turn to 'identity politics' are wont to say. But by way of exploring this critical difference, I want to return to Lacan's myth of the lathouses, the non-objectified objects that appear from time to time in the alethosphere. Man, the prosthetic God of this alethosphere, is uprooted from every foundation, ungrounded, thus malleable or at one with the Other, but from time to time, and without warning, he encounters one of these lathouses, which provokes his anxiety. The chiasmic intertwining of man and Other, the absorption of the former in the latter, suddenly falters; man is pulled away, disengaged *from* his foundationless existence in the Other; he grows deaf or indifferent to the Other's appeal. This disruption is not followed, however, by a retreat from the publicity of 'pleasure-reality incorporated' into privacy, simply. For what we encounter in this moment is not the privacy of a self, but the other within the alethospheric. *This* is the moment of extimacy in which we discover an 'overpopulated' privacy, where some alien excess adheres to us.

It may now be apparent why *objet petit a*, as lathouse, has more mechanical connotations than the lamella does. Within the seemingly well-oiled, smooth-functioning alethosphere, the impossible, mythic *objet petit a* assumes the character of a malfunctioning, mechanical nuisance, a toy-like, mechanical thing that does not quite work. An example of such an object is found in

Charlie Chaplin's *City Lights*. In this film, the little tramp – who merely wants to blend seamlessly into modern city life, to give himself over to it – is thwarted by the importunate sound of a whistle he previously swallowed, which keeps calling him back to himself. In an early text, *On Escape*, Emmanuel Levinas draws our attention precisely to this scene, proposing that this ingested whistle 'triggers the scandal of the brutal presence of [Charlie's] being; it works like a recording device, which betrays the discrete manifestations of a presence that Charlie's legendary tramp costume barely dissimulates'.[14] This whistle is the equivalent of Lacan's *objet petit a* in the technological field of modernity. If Charlie cannot be totally absorbed into the world of his surroundings, this is because he is, in Levinas's phrase 'riveted to his being', and thereby uprooted from the uprootedness of modern life.

As Levinas puts it, in the capitalist world, where man feels himself 'liable to be mobilized – in every sense of the term', there insists nevertheless a palpable counterweight, a disturbance that lends our 'temporal existence . . . the inexpressible flavor of the absolute . . . [and gives rise to] an acute feeling of being held fast', or being able to desert or escape being.[15] In other words, Levinas associates the feeling of being riveted, of the inescapablity of being, to life under capitalism, as though the counterweight preventing us from becoming totally absorbed within the universal world of capitalism also acted, in some paradoxical way, as the driving force of our full participation in the latter. I will examine this proposition in a moment, after saying a bit more about the central concept of this text.

The phrase 'riveted to being' is revealing. Rather than simply and immediately being our being, coinciding with it, we are ineluctably fastened, stuck to it – or it to us. (Levinas describes this being 'adhering to' us, just as Lacan, in his own myth of the lamella, describes the object as 'sticking to us'.) The sentiment of being riveted to being is one of being in the forced company of our own being, whose 'brutality' consists in the fact that it is impossible either to assume it *or* to disown it. It is what we are in our most intimate core, that which singularizes us, that which cannot be vulgarized and yet also that which we cannot recognize. We do not comprehend or choose it, but neither can we get rid of it; since it is not of the order of objects – but, rather, of the 'not-without-object' – it cannot be objectified, placed before us and confronted.

The sentiment of being doubled by an inhuman, impersonal partner, who is at the same time me and disquietingly alien, is, of course, the psychoanalytic equivalent of Levinas's sentiment of being riveted. In each case we feel ourselves 'enclosed in a tight circle that smothers'[16] (in each case everything transpires as if we bore engraved on our backs or scalps a defining mark we could not read or even see).

Riveted to *Jouissance*: Levinas with Sartre and Lacan

In his commentary on Sartre's voyeur, Lacan makes the strong point that the gaze that 'assaults [the voyeur] from behind' (to recall Deleuze's dismissal of this idea, as mentioned above), or looks at him from a place he cannot see, is the voyeur's own, not another's. This brings Lacan's reading close to that of Levinas: the gaze that looks at me is that of my own being, to which I am riveted. But Lacan goes further in his revision of Sartre, and this revision has no precedent in Levinas. Sartre is adamant that the gaze must always be 'manifested in connection with . . . a sensible form'.[17] If he insists that the accidental sound of rustling, or some other sensible disturbance, is necessary to evoke the gaze, it is because he – like Freud before him – does not want anxiety to be confused with an imaginary phenomenon. Lacan would concur that a sensible experience is required for the feeling of anxiety to arise, but is reluctant to attribute this experience to accident in the same way. Is it an accident, he asks, that the gaze manifests itself at the very moment the voyeur peers through the keyhole?

Lacan's suspicion has a traceable provenance. An almost identical suspicion is voiced by Freud in one of his case studies. When a young woman patient of his makes the delusional accusation that her lover has planted hidden witnesses to photograph their lovemaking in order to disgrace her and force her to resign her position, he questions her closely and discovers that the onset of the delusion coincided with a specific accident. Lying half-dressed beside her lover, the woman suddenly 'heard a noise like a click or a beat'. It was this click which the woman later interpreted as that of the camera photographing her and her lover. From the beginning, Freud does not doubt that there was a click or beat, but he does protest that he cannot believe that had the 'unlucky noise' (which the woman's lover identifies as coming from a clock on the far side of the room) *not* occurred, the delusion would not have formed. After further speculation, however, he summons up the courage to go 'further in the analysis of this ostensibly real "accident." ' He now risks the following hypothesis: 'I do not believe that the clock ever ticked or that there was a noise to be heard at all. The woman's situation [that is, her lying half-naked on the sofa] justified a sensation of a knock or beat in her clitoris. And it was this that she subsequently projected as a perception of an external object.'[18]

Lacan follows Freud in rejecting an explanation that would link the onset of the delusion of being photographed, in the one case, or the feeling of being gazed at, in the other, to an accidental external sound. Yet, like Sartre, Freud and Lacan both insist on locating a *sensible* cause for the uncanny sense of being observed by another. The sensible disturbance for Freud and Lacan, however, is the subject's own surplus-*jouissance*, the libidinal knock or beat of the signifier on some part of the body. We summarize the difference Lacan introduces this way: while Sartre likens our sudden awareness of the presence of the gaze to the opening of a kind of drain hole in our world,[19] James Joyce, in 'The Portrait of an Artist', identifies this drain hole with the obscene sound it makes: 'Suck!' Joyce thus approaches more closely Lacan's view. And in relation to Levinas's argument, we can now make the point that the being to which we are riveted or stuck is, specifically, *jouissance*. It is our own *jouissance* which cannot be escaped, got rid of, even though we never manage to claim it as our own. It is *jouissance* that not only singularizes us, but also doubles and suffocates us. If in the crawl space of our solitude we bump up against an otherness that refuses to leave us alone with ourselves, it is because of *jouissance* that we can say – as Sartre says of the Other's gaze – that it 'delivers me to myself as unrevealed.'[20] *Jouissance* makes me me, while preventing me from knowing who I am.

This is what we have thus far: Freud's half-clothed patient reclined in an erotic attitude beside her lover; Chaplin's little tramp in his legendary costume; a voyeur peering through a keyhole. All three, concentrated in some activity, are caught off-guard by a disturbance (audible in all three cases) that thwarts their willed concentration, seems to come from outside, from some other place, but actually comes from the very core of their being. In each case the disturbance functions as a counterweight, an unexpected resistance that causes a swerve in the main flow of activity. Freud speaks in his essay 'On Narcissism' of an easy exchange between object libido and narcissistic libido, as though the one could be converted into the other without loss. But at a certain point he insists that there is a residue of non-convertible narcissistic libido that does not enter into the exchange, the back-and-forth flow. At the point of disturbance, the moment of anxiety, it is this non-convertible narcissistic libido – this *jouissance* which cannot be vulgarized or distributed – which we encounter.

Outside the experience of anxiety, this inalienable remainder of narcissistic libido is never directly experienced but remains hidden behind its object-libido 'emanations', or behind our absorption in the activities and objects in which we are concentrated. One might have imagined that the direct experience of this surplus, this abrupt uprooting from our rooted absorption in everyday life, might have brought with it a sense of mastery rather than this sense of inescapable anxiety. But instead of breathing freely, we begin to asphyxiate in the air of an overly proximate otherness. This sense of being overburdened and doubled by *jouissance*, of an embarrassed enchainment to an excessive body, or (once again) of being 'enclosed in a tight circle that smothers', is the automatic result of the encounter with our own *jouissance*, with *jouissance* in its status – we can now state – as the object-*cause* of our desire.

Anxiety Is Not Simple

Hitherto I have simplified matters somewhat, pretended it was simply anxiety that was in question all this while. In fact, anxiety has almost imperceptibly shaded over into moral anxiety and shame anxiety, or guilt and shame, in the various discussions we have been following. Let us take the last first. In truth, Sartre did not define the encounter with the gaze as an experience only of 'pure monition' or anxiety, but also as one of shame. And Levinas did not define the experience of being riveted to being only as nausea or anxiety – 'this fact of being riveted constitutes all the anxiety or nausea',[21] – but also as shame: 'What appears in shame is thus precisely the fact of being riveted to oneself.'[22] The conflation of anxiety and shame is almost total, as when Levinas says, for example, 'the phenomenon of shame of a self confronted with itself . . . is the same as nausea'.[23]

The only gap Levinas opens between nausea and shame is a brief moment of hope in which we imagine we might be able, through pleasure, to escape. Shame simply underscores the disappointment of this hope; shame is, in his view, the affective recognition that escape is impossible, that we remain tethered, without any hope of escape, to something we cannot assume as our own. It is precisely at this point that Lacan parts ways with Levinas. For Lacan, it is not a matter of going beyond ontology or escaping being but, rather, of transforming our relation to it. As is well known, in his later work Levinas seeks to open an escape route by going 'behind' being, as it were, proposing an ethical relation with the Other prior to the ontological relation. In the final session of *Seminar XVII*, Lacan offers an alternative strategy by advocating what he calls his *hontology*. One must take this pun seriously, for what Lacan proposes in making it, I argue, is that shame offers not an escape from the ontology *per se*, but an escape from ontology's 'pre-comprehension' of the subject. For Lacan, shame is the subject's ethical relation towards being, his own and the other's.

An analysis of shame will have to await an examination of the pressure to take flight that accompanies anxiety, and of the flight path carved out by guilt. Anxiety is not only the feeling of suffocation that accompanies the encounter with being, but the felt need to escape it. Lacan described anxiety as an 'edge' phenomenon in the seminar he devoted to the concept; Levinas called it a 'limit situation'.[24] Edge, limit, of what? Some surplus, I have been arguing, asserts itself in the field of the Other, and thus provides the subject with an opportunity to break from the grip of the Other, from the intersubjective relations the Other defines and in which it catches us up. And yet, in so far as this surplus evades assimilation by us, it binds us in turn in an even stronger, more terrifying grip. Anxiety restrains the hand of the writer, preventing her from composing her thoughts; it stays the sword of Hamlet, preventing him from avenging his father. It stuns and immobilizes the protagonists of that postwar cinema which Deleuze designates the 'cinema of the voyeur', converting the would-be action heroes into passive witnesses of an incomprehensible and unassimilable event. But it was the paralyses of the hysterics that led to the most famous diagnosis of the ailment of anxiety. For the conclusion Freud reaches regarding the hysterics holds true for all cases of anxious paralysis: what its sufferers suffer from are reminiscences.

Why invoke these reminiscences at this point, after all the effort expended thus far on convincing you that it is the subject's own defining or narcissistic *jouissance* which provokes her anxiety? Or: what is the relation between *jouissance* as the intimate core of being, the object-cause of desire, and reminiscences? In that anxious moment when we encounter the very core of our being, we encounter ourselves, in Heidegger's language, as *gewesend* – that is to say, as being the one who thus has been. If the moment of anxiety is experienced as one in which we are uncannily doubled by an alien and yet intimate other, this is because the confrontation with *jouissance* as the 'origin of [our] own person' confronts a doubled or forked time where who I am in the present converges with who I was in the past. The unassimilability of the experience is due to the fact that this past is not a modality of the present, of actual or realized events that once happened, but, rather, of 'that portion of the powers of the past that has been thrust aside at each crossroads where [actual events] made [their] choices'.[25]

In other words, the edge on which anxiety touches is that of the unrealized, the 'thrust-aside' powers of the past that might have caused my personal history or history *tout court* – and thus me – to be otherwise. I am tempted to say that this past is a burden that can never be laid to rest, but the everyday meaning of 'burden' would be strained here – less because the 'lightness' of unrealized events and actions belies the 'heaviness' of burdens than because the subject who must support the weight is at risk of annihilation, of being devoured by the very insubstantiality of the unrealized. This makes anxiety 'the supreme instant from which we can only depart'.[26]

This discussion of the emergence of an 'immemorial past' within moments of anxiety permits me to observe an intuition that barely surfaces in Levinas's text, where the sentiment of 'being riveted' seems sometimes to relate to issues of race, ethnicity and national identity. The immemorial past that shadows me and compels my anxiety also reawakens me to the fact that I was born into an identity that I did not choose, but which chose me. That this intuition does indeed subtly haunt the argument is verified when, in the first annotation to *On Escape*, Jacques Rolland reveals a striking similarity between the language of this text and an essay Levinas wrote in the same year, 1935. In 'The Religious Inspiration of the Alliance', Levinas wrote these sentences: 'Hitlerism is the greatest trial . . . through which Judaism has had to pass. . . . The pathetic destiny of being Jewish becomes a fatality. One can no longer flee it. The Jew is ineluctably riveted to his Judaism.' And also these: a youth 'definitely attached to the sufferings and joys of the nations to which it belongs . . . discovers in the reality of Hitlerism all the gravity of being Jewish'; 'In the barbarous and primitive symbol of race . . . Hitler recalled that one does not desert Judaism.'[27]

The phrasing of these sentences is indeed eerily similar to *On Escape*'s description of the manner by which, as Rolland translates it, 'the existent is compelled to its existence', the manner in which one is riveted to one's being. It is none the less a mistake to confuse the racist, anti-Semitic view of race invoked in Levinas's essay with the experience of being riveted to the enjoyment that composes the core of one's being. For, in the experience of anxiety, one has a sense not only of being chained to an enjoyment that outstrips and precedes one, but also of the opacity of this enjoyment, its incomprehensibility and unassumability, which is dependent, I have argued, on its being grounded in nothing actual, in a 'thrust-aside' past that never took place. In the envious eye of the anti-Semite, the situation is different: the Jew is, to be sure, riveted to his *jouissance*, but if this *jouissance* is opaque, it is so only to others, to the anti-Semites, *not* (the latter is convinced) to the Jews. The anti-Semite thus reduces the Jew to just one pole of the oscillation between the certainty and inhibiting indecisiveness that constitutes anxiety, the painful, irresolvable tension occasioned by the certainty that one is called and the impossibility of knowing what one is called to. But according to the anti-Semite, being a Jew is an uncomplicated compulsion; a Jew knows what it is to be a Jew, and cannot be otherwise. He lives his life serving the irremissible fate which has chosen him. In brief, a

Jew *is* a Jew, not only irremediably but immediately – this according to the anti-Semite.

Moral Anxiety

In *Seminar XVII*, Lacan claims that anxiety is the 'central affect' around which every social arrangement is organized; every social link is approachable as a response to or transformation of anxiety, the affect which, as we have noted, functions as a counterweight to existing social relations. The intolerable inhibition, the debilitating helplessness induced by the encounter with one's own *jouissance*, must admit of some escape if society is to be possible. Opposing the Analytic to the University Discourse, Lacan opposes the response or exit strategy of the latter in terms that bear ominously on the questions of race, ethnicity and national identity at which Levinas's text hinted. The question now is: in what kind of response does the University Discourse, the discourse Lacan linked to the rise of capitalism, consist? A scene from psychoanalytic literature gives us some insight. The curious behaviour manifested in this well-known scene by Freud's patient, the Rat Man, occurs at a time when he

> was working for an examination and toying with his favourite phantasy that his father was still alive and might at any moment reappear. [The Rat Man] used to arrange that his working hours should be as late as possible in the night. Between twelve and one o'clock at night he would interrupt his work, and open the front door of the flat as though his father were standing outside it; then, coming into the hall, he would take out his penis and look at it in the looking-glass.[28]

What was the Rat Man trying to glimpse in the mirror? That bit of surplus or narcissistic *jouissance*-being to which he felt himself, in his bouts of anxiety, riveted. If he could assure himself that this *jouissance*-being were here now in front of him, reflected in this mirror, then it would no longer be behind, an unreadable hieroglyph occupying his blind spot. He could grasp it, possess it, which would mean it no longer possessed him; that is: he no longer had to identify himself with it in its status as unassumable, foreign thing. What interposed itself between the Rat Man and his anxiety, Freud explained, was a principle of renunciation that took shape around the patient's father, and was experienced as the internal voice of conscience. This voice uttered prohibitions in the form of demands for implementable cost–benefit assessments: 'What sacrifice am I prepared to make in order to . . .?'[29] The impossibility of escaping *jouissance*-being was transformed into a prohibition that sounded more like an investment strategy, while what Freud frequently referred to as 'moral anxiety' substituted itself for originary anxiety. The danger from which the Rat Man felt compelled to flee was no longer his unassumable narcissistic enjoyment, as in originary anxiety, but a hostile and obscene superego. One flees – or attempts to flee – the superego by obeying its commands to enjoy in a productive way, or by banking one's '*jouissance* credits' in anticipation of some 'cash out' to come in a new, improved high-tech future. You see what happened: the rat of a foreign, surplus-*jouissance* has been exchanged for the florins of a countable, accumulative surplus-value; a question of being converted into a problem of having – or, more precisely, of having more.

In the Rat Man's mirror, *jouissance* becomes a spectacle, something to be seen not only by the Rat Many but by others as well, a kind of merit badge that announces his value. One cannot help being reminded of 'The Impromptu at Vincennes', which took place during the period *Seminar XVII* was being delivered, where Lacan warned a group of students that they were playing the role of helots, serfs of the state, by parading their zealous enjoyment for all – especially the state – to see and enjoy.[30] There is compulsion in this display of enjoyment-as-identity, but not the same compulsion experienced in the state of originary anxiety. I noted above that in *On Escape*, Levinas suggested that an intimate connection exists between the sentiment of being riveted and capitalism. We can now see more clearly why this connection is made and how, finally, it misses the mark. The problem is that Levinas fails to distinguish originary and moral anxiety, anxiety and guilt. For capitalism is founded on a *transformation* of anxiety – the originary feeling of being riveted – into guilt. This transformation is undertaken in an attempt to escape the unbearable condition of anxiety, but in doing so it indentures the subject to a cruel, insatiable superego and to a past that is no longer immemorial but, on the contrary, compulsively memorialized.

We were pursuing hints in Levinas's text that the sentiment of being riveted was connected to the question of race, and all those forms of identity which are ours by virtue of birth rather than choice. This connection is suggested in relation to a specific characterization of anxiety or being riveted as the feeling of being burdened by a 'non-remittable *obligation*'. From this sentiment to that of being weighed down by an inexpiable *debt* is a short step, but to take it without being aware of the distance traversed leads to the inappropriate conflation of originary and moral anxiety. That Levinas makes the error of too quickly conflating the experience of being riveted with experiences of culpability and debt proves nothing so much as the effectiveness of the superego, of guilt, in the modern world. Why *should* our admittedly infrangible attachment to that which precedes us and drenches our enjoyment in its indelible colours be characterized as a guilty one? There is no good reason for it; but if the equation of the past with guilt and debt is endemic to modern thought, it is because the superegoic evasion or recoil from anxiety retains so much influence over thought, up to and including Freud's. Critiquing the familiar Freudian myth of the murder of the primordial father by sons who try to atone for their crime by reinstating him in an idealized form (as all-loving and loved by all), Lacan disentangles guilt from originary anxiety, and prepares the way for an alternative escape from the latter.

What is the point of Lacan's critique? This myth of the father underwrites the reign of the superego. The first thing one needs to recognize is that the superego is nothing other than that very narcissistic *jouissance* – *jouissance* as the core of being – which we encounter in anxiety, *in an altered form*. The transformation that produces it could be described as the conversion of a *force* (that of *jouissance* as core of being and object-cause of desire) into a *power* (that of the superego). What is the difference? Steven Connor puts it this way: 'For something we want to call a power, there is a notion of an agent that precedes and deploys the power, a who looming through the what. A force, by contrast, exerts itself, and exerts itself on itself.' The difference between force and power lies, in other words, primarily in this distinction between exertion, which does not imply any wielding or willed coercion of one thing by another, and exercise, which does. 'A power is exercised as one exercises a right, or one's right arm, a prerogative or property, something apart from ourselves.' Power 'possesses its own potentiality', while force, crucially, does not.[31] The old term 'phallomorphic *power*' is precise; for to say that power possesses its potentiality is to say that it is wielded in order to imprint itself, its form, on external objects. Power seizes possession of that on which it is exercised, it realizes itself in its objects by appropriating them, stamping them with its identifying mark. Creation, on the other hand, is a force, not – properly speaking – a power.

The painful split – or tension – experienced in anxiety gives way in moral anxiety, or guilt, to a different sort of split, one more easily imaginarized by *dramatis personae* engaged in a power struggle. In fact, the second topology of Freud, in which he thinks the psyche as a struggle among agents – ego, id, superego – is to a large extent the result of his increasing fascination with the superego. The feeling of guilt is the sentiment that a power – the superego – internal to the subject and acting on him or her is exercised by an external agent. Freud thought of this external agent as parental interdictions that had been internalized by the subject; in *Seminar XVII*, Lacan instead attributes the role of agent to accumulated knowledge. This improves on Freud by locating the authority of parental interdictions in a wider social source.

The Lacanian reidentification of the agent of power also permits us to see more clearly what happens in the transformation of anxiety into guilt. Freud described the power of the superego as that of prohibition, specifically the prohibition of *jouissance*. But Lacan sees this power less as a prohibition of *jouissance* as such than as prohibition or, better, dissolution or blockage of the disturbing enigma, the enigma of being, which *jouissance* poses. The unmistakable and baffling certainty that forms the ground of anxiety vanishes in guilt in favour of a pursuit of knowledge. Let me reiterate this point: certainty is transformed not only into knowledge but also into the relentless pursuit of ever more knowledge. The 'inexpressible flavour of the absolute' which Levinas discerned as a feature of temporal existence under capitalism finds its explanation here. For the 'acute feeling of being held fast' no longer comes – as Levinas indicates in his confusion – from being stuck or doubled by a *jouissance* we cannot assume because it remains opaque to us but, rather, from being riveted to the pursuit of ideals and goals we cannot obtain because they withdraw from us.

To continue translating into the terms of the present discussion: guilt takes flight from the enigma of our *jouissance*-being, not from *jouissance* as such. The guilt-laden, anxiety-relieved subject still experiences *jouissance*, but this *jouissance* is characterized by Lacan in *Seminar XVII* as a 'sham', as 'counterfeit'.[32] The fraudulent nature of this *jouissance* has everything to do with the fact that it gives one a false sense that the core of one's being is something knowable, possessable as an identity, a property, a surplus-value attaching to one's person. Sham *jouissance* intoxicates one with the sense that all our inherited, unchosen identities – racial, national, ethnic – root us in an actual past that may be lost, but is not for all that inaccessible in so far as we can have knowledge about it, and about how to restore it in an ideal future. What anxiety exposes as ungraspable or unclaimable *jouissance* is that which the guilty shamelessly grasp for in the obsequious respect they pay to a past sacralized as their future. The feverish pursuit of this future – conceived both as their due and as repayment of their (unpayable) debt to the past – is the poor substitute, the Sweet'n' Low, the guilty acceptance in the place of the real sweetness of *jouissance*.

Let us permit ourselves a little surprise, however, at finding that the universalizing tendency of the University Discourse does not end up forsaking these inherited identities or differences, but welcoming them with open arms, those of the idealized father. At the moment the university students stepped forward on the political stage as presumptive actors, Lacan responded by agreeing with them that the university had ill-prepared them for the role. On the contrary, it had inducted them into the inglorious role of serfs of the superego, compelled to add mortar to the thickening barricade against anxiety, against the enigma it poses. With reference to their feeling of fraternity with the workers, he warned that we are always alone together, and that the students ought to mind the gathering storm clouds of segregation already visible in the alethosphere. The mounting threat of segregation was a major concern for Lacan during this period. He had written in 1967, for example: 'Our future as common markets will find its equilibrium in a harsher extension of the processes of segregation.' And in 1968: 'We think that universalism ... homogenizes the relations among men. On the contrary, I believe that what characterizes our time ... is a ramified and reinforced segregation that produces intersections at all levels and that only multiplies barriers.'[33] He reiterated his concern about the rise of racism in his television interview a few years later. Lacan's point was not that segregation would re-emerge in the form of a return of the repressed, but that it was being positively fomented by the universalism of the university and the occult power of the superego. Since 1970 segregationism has indeed returned in the form Lacan predicted, curiously partnered rather than at odds with universalism, and with the universities which became home to 'identity politics'. One of the most remarkable instantiations of this association in recent years has been, as Jacques Rancière was the first to point out, the extension of humanitarian aid to the very ethnic enemies with whom we are simultaneously at war.[34]

Here the logic of the psychic transformation we have tried to describe plays itself out on the big screen of world events. We shore up our increasingly fractious identities, exercise our rights in the name of identities we believe we possess, while locating our underlying 'humanity' in our basic impotence in need of aid, our powerlessness before – what? Our own internal power. Our feeling of powerlessness, in other words, stems from conceiving ourselves as possessors of power.

Shame Anxiety

It is only against this background that Lacan's call to shame makes any sense. His is a recommendation not for a renewed prudishness but, on the contrary, for relinquishing our satisfaction with a sham *jouissance* in favour of the real thing. The real thing – *jouissance* – can never be 'dutified', controlled, regimented; rather, it catches us by surprise, like a sudden, uncontrollable blush on the cheek. It is not possible here, in this brief conclusion, to do justice to the concept of shame, as I am doing elsewhere. I do not want, however, to end quite so abruptly as Lacan ends his seminar, so I will say a few more words – only.

Alain Badiou has identified a dominant trait of the last century as its 'passion for the Real', its frenzied desire to remove every barrier that frustrates our contact with the Real. If this has a familiar ring, it is because a similar diagnosis was proffered by Nietzsche, who complained that our age was one in which we sought to 'see *through* everything'. Nietzsche further characterized this passion as a lack of reverence or discretion, a tactless desire 'to touch, lick, and finger everything'.[35] The passion for the Real treats every surface as an exterior to be penetrated, a barrier to be transgressed, or a veil to be removed. The violence of this passion insists in each penetration, transgression, and in removal, which is only exacerbated by the fact that each arrives on the other side, only to find that the Real has fled behind another barrier.

It is hard not to recognize in this the logic subtending the University Discourse as Lacan presents it in *Seminar XVII*. Nor is it difficult to see, in this context, that the antidote of shame which Lacan proposes also follows Nietzsche's leads, in addition to Freud's. Shame is, as Freud put it, a 'mental dam' against the 'aggressive instinct' or the destructive passion for the Real.[36] Unlike guilt, shame does not seek to penetrate surfaces or tear away veils; rather, it seeks comfort in them, hides itself in them as in a safe haven. Our relationships to the surface change in shame, as compared to guilt; we become fascinated with its maze-like intricacies, its richness and profundity.

This is where Lacan's *hontology*, his suturing of ontology and shame, comes in, as if in answer to Levinas. Shame is not a failed flight from being, but *a flight into being*, where being – the being of surfaces, of social existence – is viewed as that which protects us from the ravages of anxiety, which risk drowning us in its borderless enigma. Unlike the flight or transformation of guilt, however, shame does not sacrifice *jouissance*'s opacity, which is finally what 'keeps it real'. True *jouissance* never reveals itself to us, it remains ever veiled. But instead of inhibiting us, this opacity now gives us that distance from ourselves and our world that allows us creatively to alter both; it gives us, in other words, a privacy, an interiority unbreachable even by ourselves.

Notes

1. Jacques Lacan, *Séminaire XVII: L'envers de la psychanalyse*, text established by Jacques-Alain Miller (Paris: Éditions du Seuil, 1991).

2. Lacan borrows the concept of the 'quarter-turn' from the mathematical theory of groups. It is interesting to note that there are *eight* such turns possible in group theory, since the four terms can be 'flipped' or 'reversed', like a sheet of paper; Lacan develops only *half* of the possibilities. Perhaps one of his followers will one day. . . .

3. Shame, and the blush to the face that is its most persistent sign, must be distinguished from the other passions that reddened the faces and rhetoric of those who participated in the events of May '68. Long before Lacan, Charles Darwin had designated shame (and its accompanying blush) as *the* affect (and passionate sign) of the human subject as such. 'Monkeys redden from passion,' he noted, 'but it would require an overwhelming amount of evidence to make us believe that any animal could blush.' Darwin, *The Expression of the Emotions in Man and Animals* (Chicago: University of Chicago Press, 1965), p. 309.

4. Cited in Helen Merrell Lynd, *On Shame and the Search for Identity* (New York: Harcourt, Brace and World, 1958), p. 51.

5. Gilles Deleuze, 'Michael Tournier and the World without Others', published as an appendix in *The Logic of Sense* (New York: Columbia University Press), 1990, p. 305.

6. Brian Massumi, *Parables for the Virtual: Movement, Affect, Sensation*, (Durham, NC and London: Duke University Press, 2002), p. 217.

7. Jacques Lacan, *Television: A Challenge to the Psychoanalytic Establishment*, ed. Joan Copjec, trans. Denis Hollier, Rosalind Krauss and Annette Michelson (New York: W. W. Norton, 1990), p. 20. In this television interview, Lacan makes precisely the same points about the relation between affect and displacement he makes in *Seminar XVII*. On Freud's notion of discharge as an attempt to theorize the movement of thought, see also Monique David-Menard, *Hysteria from Freud to Lacan: Body and Language in Psychoanalysis*, trans. Catherine Porter (Ithaca, NY: Cornell University Press, 1989), especially the remarkable final chapter, 'Jouissance and Knowledge'.

8. Lacan's description of the alethosphere, written as it was at the very end of the 1960s, now sounds a bit quainter than the description I give; think 'Sputnik' rather than space probes. The myth of the alethosphere and the lathouses is presented in the 20 May, 1970 seminar, which is titled '*Les sillons de l'aléthosphère*' in the book published from the seminar.

9. Sigmund Freud, *Civilization and its Discontents, in The Complete Psychological Works of Sigmund Freud*, trans. James Strachey and Alix Strachey (London: The Hogarth Press and the Institute of Psycho-Analysis, 1953-1974) (hereafter *SE*) 21: 92.

10. Jacques Lacan, *Séminaire X: L'Angoisse* (unpublished), 26 June, 1963.

11. Jacques Lacan, *Seminar XI: The Four Fundamental Concepts of Psycho-Analysis*, trans. Alan Sheridan, ed. Jacques-Alain Miller, (London: The Hogarth Press and the Institute of Psycho-Analysis, 1977), p. 71.

12. Feminists have always noticed that there is something suspicious, a little too empirical, in the way Freud relates the story of the boy's sudden anxiety at the sight of the mother's missing genitals. Everything depends on a simple, naked perception without symbolic mediation of her missing penis. In *L'Angoisse*, Lacan already employs the phrase, 'not without object', to rethink this notorious scenario. He adds the necessary element of mediation by contending that the whole scene plays out against the backdrop of a universal proposition, 'No human being is without a penis.' If woman, then, becomes a source of anxiety, it is not because she gives direct evidence of a particular exception to a universal rule, but because she is for the boy 'not without a penis'. What is affirmed is nothing visible. The important point is that the negation of the contrary does not attack the universal from without, providing contradictory evidence of what falls out or escapes from

it; it attacks it from within, serving as evidence of the universal's inconsistency, its lack of self-identity.

The form of negation to be found in the rhetorical figure of litotes is clearly the same as that which Kant calls 'indefinite judgement'.

13. In his superb book *Truth and Singularity: Taking Foucault into Phenomenology* (Dordrect/Boston/London: Kluwer Academic Publishers, 1999), Rudi Visker several times uses the phrase 'not without roots' to describe this same notion of an ungrounded grounding, but without excavating the Lacanian background, which we obviously share. My own thesis is very similar to Visker's; I want to thank Jill Robbins for recognizing this similarity and recommending this book to me while I was writing this chapter.

14. Emmanuel Levinas, *On Escape*, trans. Bettina Bergo (Stanford, CA: Stanford University Press, 2003), p.65.

15. Levinas, *On Escape*, p. 52.

16. Levinas, *On Escape*, p. 66.

17. See Jean-Paul Sartre, *Being and Nothingness*, trans. Hazel Barnes (New York: Washington Square Press, 1992).

18. Sigmund Freud, 'A Case of Paranoia Running Counter to the Psycho-Analytic Theory of the Disease', *SE* 14: 269–70.

19. Jacques Lacan, 'The Function and Field of Speech and Language in Psychoanalysis', in *Écrits*, trans. Alain Sheridan, ed. Jacques-Alain Miller, (New York: W. W. Norton, 1977), p. 47. This essay, commonly known as 'The Rome Discourse', was delivered at Rome Congress in 1953; Lacan's phrase 'the powers of the past' later becomes Deleuze's 'powers of the false'.

20. Sartre, *Being and Nothingness*, p. 359.

21. Levinas, *On Escape*, p. 66.

22. Levinas, *On Escape*, p. 64.

23. Levinas, *On Escape*, pp. 67–8.

24. Levinas, *On Escape*, p. 67.

25. Lacan, 'The Function and Field of Speech and Language in Psychoanalysis', p. 47.

26. Levinas, *On Escape*, p. 67.

27. Levinas, *On Escape*, p. 75.

28. Sigmund Freud, 'Notes Upon a Case of Obsessional Neurosis', *SE* 10:204.

29. Sigmund Freud, *SE*, 10: 271.

30. 'The Impromptu at Vincennes' was translated into English by Jeffrey Mehlman and published in Lacan, *Television*; it appears also as Annex A, 'Analyticon', in Lacan, *L'envers*.

31. Steven Connor, 'The Shame of Being a Man', *http://www.bbk.ac.uk/eh/skc/shame/*. This is an expanded version of the essay published in *Texual Practice* 15 (2001). It is interesting to note that in *L'angoisse*, Lacan similarly explicates the concept of the object-cause of desire by critiquing those conceptions of cause that resort to images of a will exercising itself on some part of the body, such as an arm, conceived as external to will. This reduces the arm, Lacan argues, to something as forgettable as an umbrella. In other words, one exercises one's arm only at a gym, where – it can be argued – one treats one's own body as an object external to oneself; one raises one's arm, however, through the exertion or force of one's will, which is inconceivable as an external power.

32. Juliet Flower MacCannell highlights the counterfeit nature of capitalist or superegoic *jouissance* in her excellent reading of the seminar; see 'More Thought on War and Death: Lacan's Critique of Capitalism in *Seminar XVII*', forthcoming in *Reading Seminar XVII*, ed. Russell Grigg, SIC Series, vol. 6 (Durham, NC: Duke University Press, 2006).

33. The 1967 reference is to Jacques Lacan, 'Proposition of 9 October 1967 on the Psychoanalyst of the School', trans. Russell Grigg, *Analysis*, no. 6 (1995), p. 257; the 1968 quotation is translated from Jacques Lacan, 'Nota sul padre e l'universalisimo', *La Psicoanalisi*, no. 33 (2003).

34. See Jaques Rancière, *Dis-agreements: Politics and Philosophy*, trans. Julie Rose (Minneapolis and London: University of Minnesota Press, 1999).

35. Friedrich Nietzsche, *Beyond Good and Evil*, trans. Walter Kaufman (New York: Random House, 1966) section 263, p. 213.

36. Sigmund Freud, *Three Essays on the Theory of Sexuality, SE* 7: 178.

7

Alain Badiou's Theory of the Subject: The Recommencement of Dialectical Materialism*

Bruno Bosteels

An Old Name for Some New Ways of Thinking

> I hold that the concepts of event, structure, intervention, and fidelity are the very concepts of the dialectic, insofar as the latter is not reduced to the flat image, which was already inadequate for Hegel himself, of totalization and the labor of the negative.[1]

Despite the complacent if not downright reactionary trend of our times, which would rather condemn the orthodox vocabulary to oblivion instead of tarrying with its untimely potential, it is not exaggerated to say that all of Alain Badiou's work constitutes a prolonged effort to contribute to the renewal of the philosophical tradition of dialectical materialism, or of the materialist dialectic. Not only do we find that one of Badiou's first publications – his own contingent beginning as a philosopher – is a review of Louis Althusser's two canonical works *For Marx* and *Reading Capital*, programmatically titled 'Le (re)commencement du matérialisme dialectique', but what is more, in the preface to his new major book, *Logics of Worlds*, which is the much-awaited follow-up to *Being and Event*, Badiou also reaffirms his overall position in the name of a certain materialist dialectic: 'After much hesitation I have decided to name my enterprise – or, rather, the ideological atmosphere in which it gives vent to its most extreme tension – a *materialist dialectic*'.[2] Badiou's lifelong and ongoing contribution to the reconstitution of a materialist dialectic, in turn, is indissociable from that peculiar French version of Freudo-Marxism that is the school of Lacano-Althusserianism.

* A longer version of this article appeared in two parts in *PLI: The Warwick Journal of Philosophy* 12 (2001): 200–29; and 13 (2002): 173–208. Reprinted with permission of the editors.

Structural Causality: Science and Ideology Revisited

> Every truly contemporary philosophy must start from the singular theses with which Althusser identifies philosophy.[3]

Althusser's theses serve Badiou in his early review to redefine the nature and object of dialectical materialism in relation to historical materialism. We know that for Althusser, Marx's greatest discovery entails a double theoretical foundation in a single epistemological break, or two ruptures in a unique inaugural act: 'It is by founding the theory of history (historical materialism) that Marx, in one and the same movement, has broken with his earlier ideological philosophical consciousness and founded a new philosophy (dialectical materialism).'[4] In fact, it is not too much to say that the difference between these two disciplines continues to be a real enigma today, albeit under different guises. The struggle to pull Marx from under Hegel's prolonged shadow is only the dramatic form of appearance of this wider debate within Marxism. Everything seems to revolve then around the complex difference between historical and dialectical materialism: how are we to articulate the intricate unity of this difference?

A first articulation implies the response to a question raised by Althusser: 'By what necessity of principle should the foundation of the scientific theory of history imply and include *ipso facto* a theoretical revolution in philosophy?'[5] The principle in question holds that after every major scientific breakthrough, which produces new forms of rationality, there occurs a revolutionary transformation in philosophy. The classical example, of course, refers to the discovery of mathematical science as the very condition of the beginning of philosophy in Ancient Greece, but similar encounters take place in the cases of Descartes, Leibniz or Kant. In his later work Badiou himself will always subscribe to this principle, with two caveats: not every scientific break is always registered in philosophy; sometimes its impact goes unnoticed, or for a long time is driven underground, as in the case of set theory; and, more importantly, the formation of a philosophy is always conditioned not just by scientific discoveries but also by emancipatory politics, by artistic experiments, and by the encounter of a truth in love, as in psychoanalysis. These clarifications allow us to postulate that Marxism, defined as a doctrine that intervenes politically in a history of singular sequences, can still be a condition for modern philosophy, even if historical materialism does not achieve the status of a science, as is indeed no longer the case for Badiou in his later work.

Althusser's dilemma, by contrast, as he seems to admit in his many self-criticisms, is to have mistaken a political condition for a scientific one. To be more precise: there is an unarticulated tension between politics as the fundamental practice conditioning philosophy from the outside, and science as the only safeguard, within philosophy, against the ideological reinscription of this political invention, the importance of which is then obscured. The result is a mixture of 'scientism' and 'theoreticism' which we somewhat lazily identify – following, among others, the melancholy views of the author himself – with Althusserianism. In his *Manifesto for Philosophy*, Badiou would later describe this situation as the outcome of a misguided yet heroic attempt to relay a first 'suture' of philosophy – that is, the reduction and delegation of its four generic conditions on to politics alone – with a second one, this time on to science. Without becoming the servant of a third condition – poetry or art – as happens so often after Nietzsche and Heidegger, philosophy today must undo this double suture, which is in fact a belated inheritance from the nineteenth century, in order to disentangle the strict compossibility of all four generic procedures of truth.[6] This clarifying extension, though, remains in a way faithful to Althusser's materialist view of philosophy as a theoretical practice conditioned by truths that are produced elsewhere, or on another scene.

The second and third articulations no longer invoke a general principle about science and philosophy, but concern the specific nature of historical and dialectical materialism themselves. The object of historical materialism, as theory of history, includes the various modes of production, their structure and development, and the forms of transition from one mode to another. In principle, the scientific nature of this theory cannot be established by historical materialism itself but only by a philosophical theory designed for the express purpose of defining the scientificity of science and other theoretical practices in their specific difference from ideological practices. This general epistemological theory of the history of the theoretical offers a first definition of dialectical materialism. As Badiou writes: 'The object proper to dialectical materialism is the system of pertinent differences that both and at the same time disjoins and joins science and ideology.'[7] The reconstruction of this general theory would thus seem to take an extremely perilous turn, since few distinctions have provoked more polemical outbursts than the infamous break between science and ideology, the ineffectiveness of which is then often equated with the perceived failure of the entire endeavour of Althusser.

It is indispensable, however, to traverse the very problematic nature of the difference between science and ideology if we want to understand not only Althusser's enterprise but also the systematic foundation of Badiou's philosophy, for the latter hinges on a similar Bachelardian or Platonic distinction between truth and knowledge, or between truth and opinion. In fact, this is exactly the point where we need to address a frequent misunderstanding that affects the reception of both philosophers.

In his review, Badiou himself insists on the primitive impurity of the difference in question: 'The fact that the *pair* comes first, and not each one of its terms, means – and this is crucial – that the opposition science/ideology is not distributive. It does not allow us immediately to classify the different practices and discourses, even less to "valorize" them abstractly as science "against" ideology.'[8] Instead of serving as a simple point of departure or normative guarantee, the opposition must be endlessly processed and divided from within: 'In reality, the opposition science/ideology, as the opening of the domain of a new discipline (dialectical materialism), is itself developed therein not as a simple contradiction but as a process.'[9] Not only is every science dependent upon the ideology that serves merely to designate its possible existence; there is also no discourse known as ideological except through the retroaction of a science. Of this further thesis, the importance of which cannot be overestimated, the following statement from *For Marx* offers a paradigmatic rundown:

> There exists no *pure* theoretical practice, no bare science, which throughout its history as a science would be safeguarded by who knows what grace from the threats and attacks of idealism, that is, of the ideologies that besiege it. We know that there exists a 'pure' science only if it is endlessly purified, a free science in the necessity of its history only if it is endlessly liberated from the ideology that occupies it, haunts it or lies in wait to attack it. This purification and this liberation are obtained only at the cost of a never-ending struggle against ideology itself, that is, against idealism – a struggle which Theory (dialectical materialism) can guide and clarify regarding its reasons and objectives as no other method in the world today.[10]

Always marked by the possibility of false departures and sudden relapses, this contradictory processing of the difference between science and ideology, or between materialism and idealism, is key to a proper reconstruction of Althusser's philosophy, as will likewise be the case for the difference between truth and knowledge, or between fidelity to the event and its obscure or reactive counterparts, in the later philosophy and theory of the subject of Badiou: 'It is not exaggerated to say that dialectical materialism is at its highest point in this problem: How to think the articulation of science on to that which it is not, all the while preserving the impure radicality of the difference?'[11] From this point of view, the materialist dialectic can be redefined as the theory of contradictory breaks, using the same principle of unity in difference to articulate not only science and ideology, or truth and opinion, but also theory and practice, base and superstructure, as well as the very distinction between dialectical and historical materialism.

A third and final articulation of these two disciplines depends, in effect, upon the peculiar unity that ties together the different instances and practices of a determined social formation. While historical materialism approaches this unity from the point of view of its actual existence, mainly under capitalism, its use of a series of concepts and their order of deployment in the course of analysis simultaneously point to a paradigmatic exposition which, though absent as such from the study of history itself, defines in a new way the object of dialectical materialism. The latter is then no longer, or not only, the theory of the complex difference between science and ideology, but the linked system of concepts and their laws of combination that define the specific unity, or type of causality, structuring the whole of any given society.

We know that Althusser elaborates this theory of causality in 'Contradiction and Overdetermination' and 'On the Materialist Dialectic' from *For Marx*, and in 'The Object of *Capital*' from *Reading Capital.* Two concepts in particular, dominance and overdetermination, define the essence of Marx's discovery of a new, structural causality, radically different from its more traditional, linear or expressive, definitions. As for the first of these two concepts, a society always possesses the complex unity of a structure dominated by one of its instances, or articulated practices. Depending on the conjuncture at a given moment in the history of a society, the dominant can be economical, political, scientific, religious, and so on. If a conjuncture is thus defined by the attribution of dominance to one instance or other in the social whole, we can affirm, with Badiou: 'The first great thesis of dialectical materialism – here considered to be the epistemology of historical materialism – posits that the set of instances defines *always* a conjunctural kind of existence.'[12] As for overdetermination, this concept is imported from psychoanalysis to account for the causality of conjunctural change – that is, the displacement of the dominant from one instance or practice to another, as well as the condensation of contradictions into an explosive antagonism. The notoriously controversial argument then holds that such conjunctural variations are the effect of an invariant but absent cause, which is the finally determining instance of the economy. 'Such is, brutally schematized, the second great thesis of dialectical materialism: There exists a determining practice, and this practice is *the "economic" practice.*'[13] In a peculiar decentring, the latter thus fulfils two unequal functions at once, since as determining force it is absent from the structured whole in which it none the less finds a place as one articulated instance among others.

The theory of structural causality is perhaps no less susceptible of misunderstandings than the break between science and ideology. Althusser's structuralism, a common objection then goes, is incompatible with the profoundly historical insights of Western Marxism and, as such, is unable to stave off the dogmatic threats of Stalinism. The great battle of the giants over history and structure, however, remains blind to what is without a doubt the core aspect of the theory of overdetermination – an aspect which, moreover, re-emerges in Badiou's theory of historical situations at the centre of *Being and Event.* This aspect becomes especially clear when Althusser rereads Lenin's analysis, through his famous concept of the weakest link, of the specific conditions that enabled the success of the 1917 revolution in Russia.

The point of Althusser's reading is not simply to reiterate Lenin's well-known analysis but, rather, to ask how a structure actually *seizes* and *becomes* history – or, to put it the other way round, how history '*eventalizes*' and *periodizes* the structure of a given situation at the site of a subjective intervention. Technically foreign to Lenin no less than to Marx, yet supposedly already at work and implied in their analyses, Freud's concept of overdetermination is thus meant to articulate history and structure without separating them in terms of concrete empirical fact and abstract transcendental or ontological principle:

> Overdetermination designates the following essential quality of contradiction: the reflection, within the contradiction itself, of its own conditions of existence, that is, of its situation in the structure in dominance of the complex whole. This 'situation' is not univocal. It is not only its *de jure* situation (the one it occupies in the hierarchy of instances in relation to the determinant instance: the economy in society) nor only its *de facto* situation (whether it is, during the stage under consideration, dominant or subordinate) but *the relation of this de jure situation to this de facto situation*, that is, the very relation that makes of this factual situation *a 'variation' of the structure, in dominance, 'invariant' of the totality.*[14]

This 'situation' is perhaps best understood in the everyday sense in which we say that 'we have a situation' when something happens that no longer fits the natural order of things. If Althusser adds the quotation marks, it is no doubt to distance himself from an overly Sartrean (not to mention Situationist) term, which in contrast will be pivotal to all Badiou's work. Using Badiou's terms from *Being and Event*, we could say that this is indeed the point where the structure of a situation suddenly becomes indiscernible, or newly discernible only through an intervention loyal to the event – in this case a political event – that will have changed the very parameters of what counts or not as discernible in the language of the situation.

To say metaphorically that the gap between history and structure is then bridged would still leave the two in a relation of passive externality. We would still fail to grasp the fact that, through the theory of structural causality, it is not just that dialectical materialism is the systematization of historical materialism, but the latter is also present, as if immanently withdrawn, in the former. Nor is one discipline meant to provide only the empty places, structures or necessary forms which would then have to be applied to, or filled by, the concrete forces, contents and contingent circumstances studied by the other. Rather, what is most striking in the theory of the weakest link as developed and recast in the concept of overdetermination is to see how a structure takes hold of the actual moment, how isolated facts are literally thrown together to form a specific conjuncture and, thus, how necessity, far from realizing or expressing itself in history, actually emerges out of contingency. Any change produced by overdetermination, therefore, exceeds the realm of scientific objectivity and at once becomes the site of a subjective wager, irreducible to the way individuals function ideologically in the normal state of the situation. As Badiou would recall many years later in *Metapolitics*: 'Overdetermination puts the *possible* on the order of the day, whereas the economic space (objectivity) is that of regulated stability, and the space of the state (ideological subjectivity) makes individuals "function". In reality, overdetermination is the place of politics.'[15] Historical materialism could thus still be said to be implicated, or contained, in the hollow spaces of dialectical materialism: not as the objective science of history in a traditional sense, but as the theory and concrete analysis of historical possibility.

Traversing the polemic over history and structure, then, there is the fundamental question of what truly constitutes a historical event. For instance, in politics: 'When, and under which conditions, do we say that an event is political? What is "that which happens" when it happens politically?'[16] For Althusser, at least in his two canonical works, the answer to this question requires the passage through dialectical materialism as the theory of structural causality between the economy, ideology and politics. 'What makes that *such and such* an event is *historical* depends not just on its being an event, but precisely on its insertion into forms that are themselves historical, into the forms of the historical as such (the forms of base and superstructure),' he writes in *For Marx*, obviously struggling with the difficult relation of form and content between dialectical and historical materialism: 'An event which falls within these forms, which has something to fall under these forms, *which is a possible content for these forms*, which affects them, concerns them, reinforces them or disturbs them, which provokes them, or which they provoke, or even choose and select, *that* is a *historical event*.'[17] The theory of structural causality, in this sense, is already an attempt to think through the problem of how the structure of a given situation, in the effective process of becoming historical, will have been transformed as the result of an unforeseeable event. Together with the impure difference between science and ideology, this is the other half of the unfinished task that Badiou draws early on from the canonical works of Althusser: 'In any case, it is on the solution, or at least on the posing, of the problem of structural causality that the ulterior progress of dialectical materialism depends.'[18]

Traversing the Fantasy: Enjoyment Beyond Interpellation

> Lacan institutes himself as the educator of every philosophy to come. I call a contemporary philosopher one who has the unfaltering courage to go through Lacan's antiphilosophy.[19]

One of the most intriguing chapters in the ulterior development of the general theory of structural causality, and of the difference between science and ideology, refers to the unpublished notes for a new collective project, initiated under the guidance of Althusser less than a year after the publication of *Reading Capital*. Thus, in autumn 1966, Althusser sends a series of confidential letters and typewritten drafts to his students Badiou, Étienne Balibar, Yves Duroux and Pierre Macherey, in which he proposes to form a 'group of theoretical reflection' in preparation for what is to become an ambitious work of philosophy, *Elements of Dialectical Materialism* – nothing short of their systematic *Ethics*, in an explicit reference to Spinoza. Although this joint effort never goes beyond the exchange of personal research notes – published only in the case of Althusser, and even then only posthumously, in his *Writings on Psychoanalysis* (not included in the English translation of this title, but now available as part of *The Humanist Controversy and Other Writings*) – in retrospect we might say that this collective project, fostered by the encounter with Lacan's thought, constitutes one of the three major sources for Badiou's *Theory of the Subject*, together with the poetry of Mallarmé and the still-obscure political sequence after May '68 marked by French Maoism. What Althusser could not foresee was that this extraordinary project would lead him, if not the other members of the group, into a theoretical deadlock which, in the opinion of some commentators, sums up the ultimate demise of the entire historical endeavour of Althusserianism.

The fundamental thesis of Althusser's draft, 'Three Notes on the Theory of Discourses', is that the philosophy of dialectical materialism in its contemporary conjuncture must come to terms with the theoretical impact of psychoanalysis, especially through the work of Lacan. To develop this thesis entails a double task: a reflection on the status of the object of psychoanalysis, the unconscious and its formations, in its relation to ideology, and the elaboration of a theory not of language or discourse as such, but of discourses in the plural. Althusser's notes thus start out by distinguishing four discourses, each marked by a certain subject-effect, a particular type of structure, and the use of certain signifiers as its material: the *discourse of ideology*, in which the subject is present 'in person', possesses a specular structure that appears to be centred due to an essential effect of misrecognition, and operates with a variety of materials not limited to concepts but including gestures, habits, prohibitions, and so on; the *aesthetic discourse*, in which the subject is present by the 'interposition' of more than one person, relies on an equivocal structure of mutually exclusive centres, and likewise operates with a diversity of materials, to produce an effect of recognition and perception; the *discourse of science*, from which the subject is absent 'in person', proposes a decentred structure, and operates with concepts and theorems to produce an effect of knowledge or cognition; and, finally, the *discourse of the unconscious*, in which the subject is 'represented' in the chain of signifiers by one signifier that is its 'place-holder', is supported by a structure of lack, or fading, and operates with fantasies to produce a circulation of libido, or drive.

Here I should perhaps add that Badiou's very first publication, 'The Autonomy of the Aesthetic Process', studies the subjectivity that is specific to the discourse of art, in particular the novel, and thus contributes to the theory of four discourses as proposed by Althusser.[20] Although it is essentially mixed and equivocal, as we will see, this theory can be considered an important touchstone not only for Badiou's *Theory of the Subject* but even more so for his recent unpublished seminars on the same topic which are being reworked for *Logics of Worlds* – not to forget Lacan's own theory of the four discourses, which he begins to elaborate in his seminars right after May '68, from *The Obverse of Psychoanalysis* until its last version in *Encore*: the master's discourse, the hysteric's discourse, the university discourse, and the analyst's discourse.[21] In fact, the mixed nature of these theories in the case of Lacan and Althusser can be explained using Badiou's own later terms by seeing how, in the name of various discourses, they conflate two questions of an entirely different nature: the question of the *different figures of the subject* within a given truth-procedure, and the question of the *various types of truth-procedure* in which these figures appear. Althusser's description of scientific discourse, for instance, involves aspects of the subjective figure of fidelity that pertains to every condition of truth, but at the same time, and on another level, pretends to define science differentially in relation to other procedures such as art, or love as seen in psychoanalysis. His ideological discourse does not belong on this same level, since it is not an alternative procedure but designates, rather, a mixture of the act of subjectivation and the obscure and reactive figures which, for any procedure, conceal or deny that a truth actually took place. Lacan's hysterical and masterly discourses, similarly, describe subjective figures that in one sense are universal while in another they are strictly internal to the clinical discourse of psychoanalysis itself, but they cannot be put on a par with the analyst's discourse in an otherwise understandable attempt to differentiate its status from the university discourse – the latter being little more than a codeword for revisionist ideology. Despite the obvious family resemblances, not to mention the recurrent number of four, any attempt to transpose Badiou's theory of the subject directly on to Lacan's or Althusser's theory of discourses is thus doomed to fail.

Althusser himself, however, quickly abandons the idea that there could be such a thing as a subject of the unconscious, let alone a subject of science, and instead reduces the subject-effect to a purely ideological function – a view of which he is later to provide a systematic account, through the theory of interpellation, in what is no doubt his last canonical text, 'Ideology and Ideological State Apparatuses'.[22] In the third and final of his research notes, as well as in the letter of presentation accompanying all three, he thus warns the other members of the group that to him the notion of the subject seems more and more to belong only to the ideological discourse, being a category inseparable from the latter's structure of misrecognition and specular redoubling. Individuals are interpellated into subjects and, at the same time, given the reasons necessary for their identification with those same symbolic or imaginary mandates for which, as a result, they believe they have been predisposed in advance. Without ideology, a social formation would distribute the various instances and practices of its structure, including all the phenomena of dominance and determination studied in the general theory of structural causality, while designating empty places for the function of the bearers of this structure. By interpellating individuals into subjects, ideology then provides those who will fill the blank spaces of this function. Althusser often describes this mechanism by using expressions from everyday life which clearly have a didactic purpose. Ideology is indeed what allows a structure to gain a firm grasp on lived experience: it is the mechanism by which a social formation 'takes hold', as when we say that the mayonnaise 'takes' or 'holds', at least in French. Finally, this mechanism of ideological interpellation does not come about without an unconscious effect of misrecognition and transferential illusion, an effect which is therefore constitutive of the subject. In everyday language, Althusser suggests that the unconscious and ideology are articulated as a machine and its combustible: the unconscious 'runs on' ideology just as an engine 'runs on' fuel. Ideological formations allow the unconscious, through repetition, to seize on to the lived experience of individuals.

Here we arrive at the unsolved problem of Althusser's encounter with Lacan and the combination of the latter's return to Freud with his own plea for Marx. In order to understand the historical effectivity of an event, between its blockage and its irruption, dialectical materialism had to explain how a structural cause takes hold of a specific situation, which is 'eventalized' by the effects of conjunctural change. Similarly, to understand the individual effectivity of the practice of the cure, psychoanalysis must explain how the unconscious functions only when 'repeated' in a variety of situations, between the normal and the pathological, which make up the lived experience of an individual. In both cases, though, Althusser ultimately cannot conceive of these 'situations', which include a peculiar rapport between the structural and the conjunctural, otherwise than as a function of ideology. Hence, even if Freud and Marx, each in his own way, contribute to the new logic, or materialist dialectic, best summed up in the concept of overdetermination by the unconscious and by the mode of production respectively – something Althusser demonstrates as early as 'Freud and Lacan' and as late as 'On Freud and Marx', both published in his *Writings on Psychoanalysis* – he can no longer explain, except by way of ideology, how this dialectic somehow already implies the concepts of history, in the guise of a materialist understanding of historical possibility. Because the efficacy of overdetermination in producing situations for a subject is now perceived to be profoundly ideological, Althusser's philosophy can no longer register any true historical event – not even in principle, let alone in actual fact – as will become painfully evident during and after the events of May '68 in France. Conversely, we can infer what will be needed to think through the possibility of a situation's becoming historicized by virtue of an event: namely, a theory of the subject that would no longer be reduced to a strictly ideological function, but would account for the specificity of various subjective figures and different types of truth-procedure. Ideology could then be said to describe a certain configuration of the subjective space, which besets each and every condition of truth as part of its ongoing process, but it is no longer a symmetrical rival on a par with science, or truth, as such.

With the articulation of ideology and the unconscious, in any case, Althusser hits upon an exception to the rule that humanity poses itself only those problems that it is capable of solving. 'I said that there had to be some links but at the same time I forbade myself to invent them – considering that provisorily this was for me a problem without solution, for me or perhaps not only for me,' he admits in a personal letter: 'Not every question always implies its answer.'[23] Althusser's project thus seems to run aground when he is faced with the question of structure and subject. What is more, in so far as this deadlock is a result of Althusser's dialogue with the discourse of psychoanalysis, there seems to be no easy escape from this impasse by way of a return to Lacan.

As Badiou writes afterwards, in *Metapolitics*:

> The very frequent attempt, anchored in the few Althusserian texts on psychoanalysis, on this point to complete Althusser by Lacan is in my view impracticable. In Lacan's work there is a theoretical concept of the subject, which even has an ontological status, in so far as the subject's being consists of the coupling of the void and the *objet a*. There is no such thing in Althusser, for whom the object exists even less than the subject.[24]

The impossible, though, can sometimes happen, and the impracticable can become real. Back in 1959–60, as he recently recalled, Badiou himself was, after all, the first student to bear witness to the published work of Lacan during Althusser's course at the École Normale Supérieure.[25] And a few years later, after making psychoanalysis the topic of a seminar of his own in 1963–64, Althusser would send another student of his to visit the ongoing seminar of Lacan whereby the latter, upon hearing how he is interrogated about his ontology, promptly sends his colleague a word of praise for the student responsible for this intervention – the same student who is later to become Lacan's son-in-law and official editor, Jacques-Alain Miller.[26]

True, anecdotes do not amount to a theory. Nor do I wish to repeat in a nutshell the well-documented history of the encounter between Althusser and Lacan. What I do want to signal, however, is how, through these and other personal stories, the logic of overdetermination has gradually become the cornerstone for a unified theoretical discourse which today constitutes one of the most powerful doctrines in all theory and philosophy. Miller lays the foundation for this combined doctrine, most clearly in 'Action of the Structure' in *Cahiers pour l'Analyse*:

> We know two discourses of overdetermination: the Marxist one and the Freudian one. Because Louis Althusser today liberates the first from the dangerous burden, which conceives of society as the subject of history, and because Jacques

> Lacan has liberated the second from the interpretation of the individual as the subject of psychology – it now seems to us possible to join the two. We hold that the discourses of Marx and Freud are susceptible of communicating by means of principled transformations, and of reflecting themselves into a unitary theoretical discourse.[27]

Miller adds that the principal injunction behind this ambitious project could be Freud's own *Wo es war, soll ich werden* ('Where it was, I shall come into being') – a succinct condensation, if there ever was one, of the way substance and subject are to be articulated in the new unified theory. Two other articles by Miller, finally, remain essential references for anyone seeking to reconstruct the genealogy of what will become the common doctrine of structural causality: namely, 'Suture' and 'Matrix'.[28] This is precisely the doctrine, however, with which Badiou seeks to come to terms most emphatically and polemically in his *Theory of the Subject.*

While urging on a more coherent account of Miller's overall thought, I will summarize this doctrine by referring to the work of a student of his, Slavoj Žižek, whose doctoral thesis – directed by Miller and published in French in two volumes, *Le plus sublime des hystériques: Hegel passe*; and *Ils ne savent pas ce qu'ils font: Le sinthome idéologique* – provides at once the basic materials for his provocative entry on to the theoretical scene in the English language – above all, in *The Sublime Object of Ideology.*[29] '*Wo es war*', of course, is also the name of the series which Žižek edits for Verso, and in which he published not only his highly critical rejoinder to Badiou's philosophy, as part of *The Ticklish Subject*, but also Peter Hallward's translation of Badiou's very own *Ethics: An Essay on the Understanding of Evil* as well as, more recently, *Metapolitics.*[30] For many readers, Žižek's work thus provides the inevitable perspective from which they will come to read Badiou in English. This makes it even more urgent to understand the fundamental differences between the two in terms of Lacan's legacy – a task that, I believe, cannot be achieved properly unless Badiou's *Being and Event* is read in conjunction with his *Theory of the Subject*, a book which is completely ignored by Žižek. As for the lineage of Marxism, or post-Marxism, the first to elaborate Lacan's and Miller's views on suture and structure, together with Gramsci's thought on the historical bloc, into a programmatic statement of political philosophy are Chantal Mouffe and Ernesto Laclau, in *Hegemony and Socialist Strategy: Towards a Radical Democratic Politics* – a text which, furthermore, links the logic of structural causality to a critique of essentialism that is much indebted to Derrida.[31]

Three points can be made regarding the real, the subject and ideology, which sum up the basic elements of the new doctrine of structural causality:

1. Just as the symbolic order is structured around the traumatic kernel of the real, a social field is articulated around the real of antagonism, which resists symbolization. Like the theory of relativity, the special theory of foreclosure needs to be generalized. To become consistent, not just a psychotic but any symbolic order needs to foreclose a key element which paradoxically incompletes the structure by being included out. The structure is not-all: there is always a gap, a leftover, a remainder – or, if we change the perspective slightly, an excess, a surplus, something that sticks out. A social formation is not only overdetermined but constitutively incomplete, fissured, or barred because of the very impossibility of society which embodies itself in its symptomatic exclusions. 'There is no such thing as a sexual relationship,' declared Lacan in *Encore*, in a formula which Laclau and Mouffe restate, or translate, in *Hegemony and Socialist Strategy*: 'There is no such thing as a social relationship,' or simply: 'Society doesn't exist.'[32] The absence, or lack, of an organic society is, then, the point of the real of politics, but precisely by opening the field of the political, this impossible identity is also the condition of possibility of any hegemonic identification. All this may very well seem to be a supplement to the common textbook idea of structuralism as a flattening out of the social field, but in fact the logic of structural causality, which really constitutes the high point of structuralism, never reduced the effects of overdetermination to a closed economy of grid-like places and their differential relations. The aim was, rather, always to detect and encircle the uncanny element which, in the efficacy of its very absence, determines the whole structure of assigned places as such. 'The fundamental problem of *all* structuralism is that of the term with the double function, inasmuch as it determines the belonging of all other terms to the structure, while itself being excluded from it by the specific operation through which it figures in the structure only under the guise of its *place-holder* (its *lieu-tenant*, to use a concept from Lacan),' writes Badiou in his early review of Althusser, describing what, even today, remains the principal task of the critique of ideology for someone like Žižek: 'Pinpoint the place occupied by the term indicating the specific exclusion, the pertinent lack, i.e., the *determination* or "structurality" of the structure.'[33] As an absent or decentred cause, the determining instance may well have shifted in keeping with the increased attention for Lacan's later works, so that the real is now to the symbolic what the symbolic was to the imaginary before, but after all, we remain firmly within the framework of the common doctrine of structural causality. As Žižek himself concludes in *The Sublime Object of Ideology*: 'The paradox of the Lacanian Real, then, is that it is an entity which, although it does not exist (in the sense of "really existing", taking place in reality), has a series of properties

– it exercises a certain structural causality, it can produce a series of effects in the symbolic reality of subjects.'[34]

2. The subject 'is' nothing but this gap in the structure, the fissure between the real and its impossible symbolization. The new doctrine thus avoids, at the same time, the metaphysical understanding of both substance *and* consciousness. In fact, in so far as metaphysics, in one of its famous Heideggerian delimitations, culminates in the epoch of the image of the world as the representation and manipulation of the object by the subject, the new doctrine can also be said to entail a wholesale deconstruction of metaphysics. This means that the polemic of structuralism and humanism can be avoided, or even turns out to have been predicated on a mistaken premiss, since the doctrine of structural causality already implies a new notion of the subject as well. Subject and substance are then articulated through the lack at the very centre of the structure. In other words, if there is always a leftover in the process of symbolization, a stubborn remainder that signals the failure of the substance to constitute itself fully, then the subject coincides with this very impossibility that causes the inner decentrement of the structure as substance. 'The leftover which resists "subjectivation" embodies the impossibility which "is" the subject; in other words, the subject is strictly correlative to its own impossibility; its limit is its positive condition,' writes Žižek in *The Sublime Object of Ideology*, in a rare typically deconstructive move; while Laclau explains, in his preface to the same book: 'The traditional debate as to the relationship between agent and structure thus appears fundamentally displaced: the issue is no longer a problem of *autonomy*, of determinism versus free will, in which two entities fully constituted as "objectivities" mutually limit each other. On the contrary, the subject emerges as a result of the failure of substance in the process of its self-constitution.'[35] Before adopting any particular position, identity or mandate, in a logical primacy that will guarantee the radical status of the new doctrine, the subject is thus the subject of lack. If to be radical means to go to the root of things, as the young Marx was fond of recalling, what indeed could be more radical than to show the constitutive uprootedness of the very notion of the subject, prior even to any essence of the generic human being as invoked by Marx?

3. Ideology is a fantasy-construct aimed at concealing the essential inconsistency of the sociopolitical field. The fundamental ideological fantasy, therefore, is always some version of the idea that society constitutes an organic, cohesive and undivided whole. By defining society as impossible, strangely enough, the new doctrine thus gives itself an unfailing measuring-

stick to redefine ideology in terms of a structural misrecognition – this time not of some concrete reality hidden behind the veil of false consciousness, but, rather, of the fact that ideology conceals nothing at all, the 'nothing' of the structure which 'is' the subject. As Laclau writes in *New Reflections on the Revolution of Our Time*: 'The ideological would not consist of the misrecognition of a positive essence, but exactly the opposite: it would consist of the non-recognition of the precarious character of any positivity, of the impossibility of any ultimate suture.'[36] Totalitarian ideologies, for instance, fail to acknowledge the empty place of power, which in democracy constitutes the paradoxical object-cause of all political struggles. The critique of ideology, therefore, can no longer consist only in unmasking the particular vested interests hidden behind the false appearances of universality. Instead, two rather different tasks impose themselves, which can be compared to the ends of the psychoanalytic cure as discussed by Žižek. The aim is, first, a traversing of the fantasy, in order to acknowledge how an ideology merely fills out a traumatic void in the midst of the social field and, second, in order that the symbolic order does not disintegrate altogether, the identification with the symptom, with the piece of surplus-enjoyment which continues to resist even after the dismantling of the fundamental fantasy, and which thus somehow gives body to the radical inconsistency of society itself. This obscene enjoyment, which attaches itself to the symptom and is ultimately nothing but pure death drive pulsating around the central emptiness in the midst of the symbolic order, cannot be overcome by means of an old-style symptomal reading of ideology, nor even by a revolutionary social change. As Žižek writes about the drive to enjoyment which, like our human condition, is the ultimate pre-ideological support of all ideology: 'The thing to do is not to "overcome", to "abolish" it, but to come to terms with it, to learn to recognize it in its terrifying dimension and then, on the basis of this fundamental recognition, to try to articulate a *modus vivendi* with it.'[37] What Žižek thus adds to Laclau's cleaner deconstructive version of structural causality is the obscene passionate enjoyment that is the dark underside, or the nightly obverse, of the lack in the symbolic order.

Finally, in a last ironic twist, the doctrine of structural causality is turned against Althusser – himself one of the first to use these terms to bring together Marx, Freud and Lacan! Žižek thus claims that to reduce the subject to an effect of interpellation, as the specular assumption of imaginary and symbolic mandates, misses the traumatic kernel of enjoyment that is the real object-cause of this process of subjectivation itself. Althusser, in other words, fails to understand how the last support of ideology, its ultimate stronghold, is the subject of lack forever trapped in a structure of fantasy, like an unbearable truth that presents itself only in the structure of a fiction:

> This is the dimension overlooked in the Althusserian account of interpellation: before being caught in the identification, in the symbolic recognition/misrecognition, the subject ($) is trapped by the Other through a paradoxical object-cause of desire in the midst of it (a), through this secret supposed to be hidden in the Other: $◇a – the Lacanian formula of fantasy.[38]

Žižek then briefly feigns to retrieve Althusser's original formulation of four subject-effects – in science, art, ideology and the unconscious – only, in his turn, to reduce their variety to a single one of them as their underlying figure:

> there are two candidates for the role of the subject *par excellence* – either the ideological subject, present *en personne*, or the subject of the unconscious, a gap in the structure ($) that is merely represented by a signifier. Althusser opted for the first choice (ideological status of the subject), whereas from the Lacanian standpoint the second choice seems far more productive: it allows us to conceive of the remaining three 'effects-of-subject' as the derivations-occultations of $, as the three modes of coming to terms with the gap in the structure that 'is' the subject.[39]

This is a typical anti-philosophical move of radicalization in which the lack in the structure, a gap that coincides with the subject as such, is turned against the derived question of this subject's empirical ideological positions. Unless this absolutely prior gap is acknowledged, philosophy and the theory of the subject will thus always stumble upon the obstacle of the real that remains unthought. Žižek, who will repeat this move in his critical rejoinder to Badiou, interprets the deadlock of the entire Althusserian enterprise as a failure to come to terms with the subject of lack, caused by an impossible enjoyment before and beyond interpellation. At issue are thus the obscure prior scenarios of guilt, complicity or desire which predispose an individual to become the subject of interpellation to begin with, and will continue to resist its hold ever after. 'In short, the "unthought" of Althusser is that there is already an uncanny subject that *precedes* the gesture of subjectivization,' writes Žižek. ' "Beyond interpellation" is the square of desire, fantasy, lack in the Other and drive pulsating around some unbearable surplus-enjoyment.'[40] We would thus have to conclude that Althusser's thought indeed cannot be completed by a return to Lacan, whose psychoanalysis, rather, *shows* that of which one cannot *speak* in Althusserian Marxism. Except that this revelation, from beginning to end, keeps relying on the unified theory of structural causality – from the real of enjoyment, which is the absent cause of the symbolic law, to the subject as lack, which is strictly correlative to the object of desire itself – with ideological fantasy merely being an occultation of its perverse and uncanny efficacy.

Have we not, perhaps, left the domain of dialectical materialism altogether? If the social field is by definition barred, then the very ambition to produce a universal ontology and epistemology of which the study of history and society would be a regional application might well seem to be the quintessential idiocy. For Žižek, however, this is precisely why we should remain committed to the cause. ' "Dialectical materialism" stands for its own impossibility; it is no longer the universal ontology: its "object" is the very gap that forever, constitutively, renders impossible the placement of the symbolic universe within the wider horizon of reality, as its special region,' he writes in *The Metastases of Enjoyment*. 'In short, "dialectical materialism" is a negative reminder that the horizon of historical-symbolic practice is "not-all", that it is inherently "decentred", founded upon the abyss of a radical fissure – in short, that the Real as its Cause is forever absent.'[41] Althusser, for his part, concludes his research notes for the unfinished *Elements of Dialectical Materialism* by stating that psychoanalysis, in order to be more than a practice or a technique, requires not one but two general theories: the first, already known, historical materialism, which would define the specificity of psychoanalysis in comparison with other discourses, and account for the conditions of its emergence and use in society; and the second, still to be constructed, a general theory of the signifier capable of explaining its function in the case of the unconscious. In letters from the same period sent to his analyst, with copies to the members of his theory group, however, the author shows more interest in understanding how something as radically new as language and the unconscious, for instance, emerges in the life of an infant. For Althusser, this sudden irruption of novelty, which is neither generated nor developed from a previously given origin, but instead introduces another structure into the existing order of things, is the essential object of what he now calls a logic of emergence, which is still none other, he adds, than the materialist dialectic as understood by Marx and Freud.

Badiou's *Theory of the Subject* will consist entirely in confronting these two orientations of dialectical materialism: one for which the act of subjectivation remains irredeemably anchored in the structural causality of lack; and the other, which seeks to map a subjective process on to the rare emergence of a new consistency – on to the appearance of a new structure in which a subject not only occupies but exceeds the empty place in the old structure, which as a result becomes obsolete. Written several years before the key works of Laclau, Mouffe and Žižek, this remarkable yet strangely ignored text thus strikes in advance at the basic shortcoming of what has since become their common doctrine: its inability to register the making of a new consistent truth beyond the acknowledging of the structural lack, or void, that is only its absent vanishing cause.

In fact, taking up a task already announced in 'The (Re)commencement of Dialectical Materialism', all Badiou's subsequent work can be read as a giant polemical effort to untie the eclectic doctrinal knot that even today binds together the works of Marx, Freud, Nietzsche and Heidegger as read by Althusser, Lacan and Derrida:

> Can we think 'at the same time' the reading of Marx by Althusser, that of Freud by Lacan and that of Nietzsche and Heidegger by Derrida? Headline, in our conjuncture, of the most profound question. If we take these three discourses in their integral actuality, I think the answer can only be negative. Better yet: to approach indefinitely that which keeps all three *at the greatest distance* from one another is the very condition of progress for each one of them. Unfortunately, in our instantaneous world in which concepts immediately become commercialized, eclecticism is the rule.[42]

Badiou's philosophy, unlike Deleuze's affirmative style, is indeed polemical throughout. 'I have never tempered my polemics, consensus is not my strength,' he admits, in keeping with the materialist understanding of philosophy: 'It is no doubt more instructive to write with an eye on that which one does not want to be at any cost than under the suspicious image of that which one desires to become.'[43]

The Road to Damascus

The sharp tone of Badiou's polemic against Althusser and Lacan no doubt comes as a response to the incapacity, or unwillingness, of both thinkers to find any significant truth in the events of May '68, while drawing further consequences from these events remains, by contrast, one of the principal aims of Badiou's work in the 1970s and early 1980s. His still widely unknown *Theory of the Subject*, presented in the form of a seminar from 1975 until 1979, with a preface written in 1981 at the time of Mitterrand's accession to power, offers the first massive summary of this ongoing effort.

In the case of Althusser, 'Ideology and Ideological State Apparatuses' contains perhaps his only theoretical attempt to register the effects of the revolt, including examples from the world of education as well as the obligatory scene of a police officer hailing a passer-by in the street. After his much-publicized *Elements of Self-Criticism*, most of Althusser's work can then be read as a double effort – not unlike the two parts in Badiou's later *Can Politics Be Thought?* – of destruction and recomposition of Marxism, respectively, in 'Marx Within His Limits' and 'The Subterranean Current of the Materialism of the Encounter'.[44] These final notes change the terrain once more, this time from dialectical to aleatory materialism, in order to grasp the essence of political events in their purely contingent occurrence, regardless of the so-called laws of historical necessity. One might therefore expect this extremely lyrical inquiry into the materialism of chance encounters, deviating atoms and aleatory conjunctures to have attuned its author in retrospect to explosive events such as those of 1968 in France. At the end of a long list of examples, however, the greatest manifestation of this watershed year still appears as a non-event: 'May 13th, when workers and students, who should have "joined" (what a result that would have given!), pass by one another in their long parallel processions but *without joining*, avoiding at all costs joining, rejoining, uniting in a unity that no doubt would have been without precedent until this day.'[45] Missed encounter of students and workers, or paradoxical failure, on the philosopher's part, to come to grips with the event of their reciprocal transformation?

If Badiou's Maoist pamphlets are unforgiving in their attack against Althusser, the point is above all to counter those among the latter's theses on structure and ideology which, after the events, facilitate the betrayal of students, workers and intellectuals alike. His *Theory of Contradiction* thus opens on a statement of principle: 'I admit without reticence that May '68 has been for me, in the order of philosophy as well as in all the rest, an authentic road to Damascus,' and the impact of this experience is further investigated in *Of Ideology*: 'The issue of ideology is the most striking example of a theoretical question put to the test and decided by the real movement.'[46] The first booklet seeks to redefine the fundamental principles of dialectical materialism in a return to Mao's 'On Contradiction', which already served Althusser, however cursorily, in *For Marx*, while the second takes aim not only at the latter's one-sided views of ideology and the subject in 'Ideology and Ideological State Apparatuses' but also at their alleged rectification in *Elements of Self-Criticism*: 'We have to put an end to the "theory" of ideology "in general" as the imaginary representation and interpellation of individuals into subjects.'[47] Historicity cannot be reduced to the objective inspection of a structure of dominant or subordinate instances, even if it is uncompleted by an empty place of which the subject is invariably the inert and imaginary place-holder. The transformative impact of an event can be grasped only if the combinatory of places and their ideological mirroring play is anchored, supplemented and divided by a dialectic of forces in their active processing.

Such is, philosophically speaking, the experience of Badiou's road to Damascus that would forever distance him from Althusser.

While Althusser's failed encounter remains foreign to the events themselves, Lacan's open indictment of May '68, by contrast, is far more inherently damaging. Before tackling the university discourse as a whole, Lacan clearly hits a central nerve in the student-popular movement in so far as his accusation that it is a hysterical outburst in search of a master anticipates, in a painful irony, the subsequent arguments and apostasies of so many an ex-Maoist turned New Philosopher. At an improvised meeting in 1969 at the newly established campus of Vincennes, in a speech reproduced in *The Obverse of Psychoanalysis*, Lacan thus mockingly provokes his students: 'If you had a little bit of patience, and if you wanted my impromptus to continue, I would tell you that the only chance of the revolutionary aspiration is always to lead to the discourse of the master.'[48] This criticism – which restages much of the battle between anarchists and Party hardliners, if not the ancient struggle between sceptics and dogmatists in their appropriate co-dependence – is clearly the unspoken impetus for Badiou's systematic reply to Lacan in *Theory of the Subject*. To understand this situation is all the more urgent today because Žižek, in *The Ticklish Subject*, will throw the same Lacanian criticism – of deriving a dogmatic masterly philosophy from a politics of short-lived hysterical outbursts – back at the feet of ex-Althusserians such as Badiou.

The Real Not Only As Cause But Also As Consistency

> 'We ask materialism to include that which is needed today and which Marxism has always made into its guiding thread, even without knowing it: a theory of the subject.'[49]

What is then the principal lesson to be drawn, according to Badiou's *Theory of the Subject*, from the political sequence initiated by the events of May '68?

The full effect of these events is first of all registered in philosophy as a humbling lesson in dialectics. Even the double articulation of places and forces, or the sublation of one by the other, is not quite enough. The dialectic is first and foremost a process, not of negation and the negation of negation, but of internal division. Every force must thus be split into itself and that part of it that is placed, or determined, by the structure of assigned places. 'There is A, and there is Ap (read: "A as such" and "A in another place", the place distributed by the space of placement, or P),' as Badiou writes: 'We thus have to posit a constitutive scission: A = (AAp).'[50] Every force stands in a relation of internal exclusion to its determining place. The famous contradiction of the proletariat and the bourgeoisie, or labour and capital, for example, is only an abstract structural scheme, A versus P, that is never given in actual fact. Althusser's argument for overdetermination, of course, already rejected the purity of these contradictions, but his solution was only to move from a simple origin to a complex structure that is always-already given; Badiou's dialectic, by contrast, aims at the actual division of this complex whole. There are notorious contradictions in the midst of the people. 'In concrete, militant philosophy, it is thus indispensable to announce that there is only one law of the dialectic: One divides into two,' Badiou summarizes. 'Dialectics states that there is a Two and proposes itself to infer the One as moving division. Metaphysics poses the One, and forever gets tangled up in drawing from it the Two.'[51]

If determination describes the dialectical placement of a force and its resulting division, then the whole purpose of the theory of the subject is to affirm the rare possibility that such a force comes to determine the determination by reapplying itself on to the very place that marks its split identity. From the slightly static point of departure that is the fact of scission, A = (AAp), in which p is the index of the determination by P within A, so that Ap controls the divided essence of AAp, or Ap(AAp), we thus get the actual process that both limits and exceeds the effects of determination: Ap(AAp) $\rightarrow$ A(AAp), or A(Ap). This is without a doubt the single most important moment in all of Badiou's *Theory of the Subject*: a symptomatic twist, or torsion, of the subject upon the impasses of its own structural placement – a process that we will find again, but in a more succinct and potentially misleading formulation, in *Being and Event*. 'It is a process of torsion, by which a force reapplies itself to that from which it conflictingly emerges,' Badiou explains: 'Everything that belongs to a place returns to that part of itself which is determined by it in order to displace the place, to determine the determination, to cross the limit.'[52] Only by thus turning upon itself in an ongoing scission can a rare new truth emerge out of the old established order of things – a truth-process of which the subject is neither the pre-given origin nor the empty bearer so much as a material fragment, or finite configuration.

Badiou finally suggests that the dialectical process in a typical backlash risks provoking two extreme types of fallout, or *Rückfall* in Hegel's terms: the first, drawn to the 'right' of the political spectrum, remits us to the established order, and thus obscures the torsion in which something new actually took place: Ap(AAp) $\rightarrow$ Ap(Ap) = P; the second, pulling to the 'left' instead, vindicates the untouched purity of the original force, and thus denies the persistence of the old in the new: A(AAp) $\rightarrow$ A(A) = A. These extremes correspond, of course, to the twin 'deviations' of dogmatism ('right-wing opportunism' or 'rightism') and adventurism ('left-wing opportunism' or 'leftism') as diagnosed in the Chinese Cultural Revolution. What is thus blocked or denied is either the power of determination or the process of its torsion in which there occurs a conjunctural change: 'But the true terms of all historicity are rather Ap(A), the determination, and A(Ap), the limit, terms by which the whole affirms itself without closure, and the element is included without abolishing itself.'[53] These distinctions then allow Badiou to propose an extraordinary rereading of Hegel's dialectic – itself in need of a division, and not just the resented victim of a wholesale rejection, as in the case of Althusser.

The complete deployment of this dialectic also provides us with a key that allows us to understand the perceptions of failure and success that left such a heavy stamp on the aftermath of May '68. In fact, both the provocative accusations by outside observers such as Lacan and the contrite turnabouts by ex-Maoists such as Glucksmann remain caught, as if spellbound, in the inert duel between the established order of places and the radical force of untainted adventurism. The world-famous picture of Daniel Cohn-Bendit during one of the demonstrations of May '68, with the student leader smiling defiantly in the face of an anonymous member of the riot police who remains hidden behind his helmet – a picture that will eventually decorate the cover of Lacan's seminar *The Obverse of Psychoanalysis*, from the following year – might serve to illustrate this point. Indeed, the contagious appeal and extreme mobilizing force of this image depends entirely on a limited structural scheme in which there appears to be no scission in the camp of the ironic and free-spirited students, nor any torsion of the existing order of things beyond a necessary yet one-sided protest against the repressive state. Althusser's much-discussed example of the police officer interpellating a passer-by in the street remains bound to this dual structure, as might likewise be the case with the definition of politics in opposition to the police in the later work of Jacques Rancière. For Badiou, however, this view hardly captures any specific political sequence in its actual process. 'There is not only the law of Capital, or only the cops. To miss this point means not to see the unity of the order of assigned places, its consistency. It means falling back into objectivism, the inverted ransom of which consists by the way in making the State into the only subject, hence the antirepressive logorrhea,' the author warns. 'It is the idea that the world knows only the necessary rightist backlash and powerless suicidal leftism. It is Ap(Ap) or A(A) in intermittence, that is to say P and A in their inoperative exteriority.'[54] Lacan's accusation thus merely reproduces a face-off between the two extreme outcomes of the dialectical process, without acknowledging the true torsion of what takes place in between.

In view of this acute diagnosis and the elaboration of an alternative materialist dialectic in the remainder of *Theory of the Subject*, there is something more than just awkward in the criticism according to which Badiou's *Being and Event* would later get trapped in a naive undialectical, or even pre-critical, separation of two spheres – being and event, knowledge and truth, the finite animal and the immortal subject – as clear-cut and as pure as place and force still were in the earlier pamphlets. Not only does this criticism systematically miss an important point even of Badiou's later philosophy, but the whole polemical thrust of his work on the subject consists very much in debunking the presuppositions of such critical postures as they emerge after May '68. The almost cynical irony is that Badiou's theory of the subject arrives at this turning point in a rigorous dialogue and confrontation with Lacanian psychoanalysis, which will then become the authoritative point of reference for the criticisms along these same lines raised against Badiou's later philosophy by someone like Žižek.

With the need to divide the subject in relation to the order in which it receives its place, we may none the less still seem to find ourselves on the familiar grounds of the logic of structural causality, which for Badiou can be summed up in a single statement from Lacan's *Écrits*: 'The subject is, as it were, in external inclusion to its object.'[55] This object can then be read as either the symbolic order itself, following the earlier Lacanian views, or as the uncanny element of the real that has to be foreclosed if such an order is to gain any coherence at all, according to the later teachings of Lacan. In the first instance, the subject's decentred cause would be the unconscious, which is structured like a language; in the second, the subject is the strict correlate of the gap in this structure, the place of which is then held by the piece of the real that is included out and, as such, embodies the impossible object-cause of desire. Regardless of which reading applies to the object, however, Badiou's theory of the subject hinges on how exactly we understand their dialectical relation of external inclusion – whether as a structural given or as a divided process.

For Badiou, most of Lacan's work stays within the bounds of a structural dialectic, which is strikingly similar, as far as its basic operations are concerned, to Mallarmé's poetry. These operations consist, first, in setting up a scene marked by the traces of a disappearance – say a sunken ship or a drowned siren, whose vanishing sustains the whole scene itself. This is the operation of the absent or evanescent cause, which determines the established order of things: 'Nowhere placed, the vanished force supports the consistency of all places.'[56] This vanishing cause then produces a chain effect by leaving behind a series of metonymical terms, such as a white hair or the foam on the surface of the sea, the division of which is the mark of the lack that caused them: 'Thus the absent cause is always reinjected into the whole of its effect. This is a great theorem of the structural dialectic: in order for the causality of lack to exert itself, every term must be split.'[57] Prescribed by the lack of its object, finally, a subject appears only as the unspeakable vacillation eclipsed in the flickering intermittence between two such markings. 'The subject follows throughout the fate of the evanescent term, having the status of an interval between the two signifiers, S_1 and S_2, which represent the subject one to the other,' Badiou concludes. 'Anyone who wants to declare its substance is a swindler.'[58]

Mallarmé's poetry thus offers an illuminating exposition of the doctrine of structural causality as developed in the Lacanian school. For Badiou, however, the problem with this doctrine is precisely that, while it never ceases to be dialectical in pinpointing the absent cause and its divisive effects on the whole, it nevertheless remains tied to the structure of this totality itself, and is thus unable to account for the latter's possible transformation. 'A consistent thought of the vanishing term is the realist peak of the structural dialectic,' which means that there is no temporal advent of novelty: 'The logic of places, even when handled by an absolute virtuoso, would be hard put to deliver anything else than the regular, virtually infinite iteration of that which vanishes and annuls itself.'[59] For Mallarmé, in the end, 'nothing will have taken place but the place itself,' just as Lacan indicates the ineluctable law that forbids the emergence of the new out of a division of the old: 'When one makes two, there is never any return. It does not amount to making a new *one*, not even a *new* one.'[60] Mallarmé's and Lacan's structural dialectic in this sense ends up being profoundly idealist, according to Badiou. It should be noted that this is not the usual objection against the idealism of the signifier or of discourse in the name of some hard referent or concrete human practice. Badiou's argument is, rather, that idealism consists in denying the divisibility of the existing law of things, regardless of whether these things are ideal or material: 'The indivisibility of the law of the place excepts it from the real. To link this exception means in theory to posit the radical anteriority of the rule,' he writes. 'The position of this antecedence is elaborated in philosophy as idealism.'[61]

After the lesson in dialectics, there thus appears to be an even more urgent need to return to the definition of materialism.

If, for Badiou, Mallarmé and Lacan are two of the four great French dialecticians, together with Pascal and Rousseau, then it is also true that their legacy must be divided into its idealist and its materialist tendencies, as happened before with Hegel. In Lacan's case, the dividing line may seem to fall between his earlier and his later work. The determining role of the symbolic order then tends to be idealist, while the persistence of the real guarantees a materialist outlook. 'Just as Hegel for Marx, Lacan is for us essential and divisible,' Badiou observes. 'The primacy of the structure, which makes of the symbolic the general algebra of the subject, its transcendental horizon, is increasingly counteracted in Lacan by a topological obsession, in which all movement and progress depend on the primacy of the real.'[62] Lacan's inquiries into the real would thus have the greatest political resonance for a materialist philosophy.

Several years before Ernesto Laclau and Chantal Mouffe would consolidate this reading in *Hegemony and Socialist Strategy*, the Lacanian real is in fact already understood in a political key in Badiou's *Theory of the Subject*, so that 'if the real of psychoanalysis is the impossibility of the sexual as relationship, the real of Marxism states: "There is no class relationship." What does this mean? It can be said otherwise: antagonism.'[63] Lacan's materialism, from a politico-philosophical perspective, would thus lie in an undaunted insistence on some traumatic kernel of antagonism that always-already fissures every social order.

Upon closer inspection, however, the shift from the symbolic to the real turns out to be a necessary but insufficient condition for a materialist theory of the subject. To recognize in antagonism the real that is the constitutive outside of any society, while also a fundamental strategy of the structural dialectic, at best gives us only half of the process by which a political subject is produced, and at worst can actually keep this process from ever acquiring the coherence of a new truth. From the point of the real as absent cause, indeed, any ordered consistency must necessarily appear to be imaginary in so far as it conceals this fundamental lack itself. For a materialist understanding of the dialectic, however, the decisive question is rather whether the real cannot also, on rare occasions, become the site for a newly consistent truth.

In addition to the real as an evanescent cause, we ought therefore to conceive of the real as a novel consistency. Badiou calls the first conception algebraic, in so far as the real is considered in terms of its relations of belonging and foreclosure, while the second is topological, in terms of adherence and proximity. 'We thus have to advance that there are two concepts of the real in Lacan, as is adequate to the division of the One: the real of evanescence, which is in a position of cause for the algebra of the subject, and the real of the nodal point, which is in a position of consistency for its topology,' with both being required for a materialist theory of the subject: 'From the real as cause to the real as consistency we can read an integral trajectory of materialism.'[64] Lacan's obscure topological investigations, however, are limited by the fact that they remain bound to the constraints of the structural dialectic. For this reason, even his uncompromising insistence on the real threatens to become contemplative and idealist – as though the end of analysis were the mere recognition of a structural impasse, maybe accompanied by an identification with the remaining symptom of enjoyment, but without the actual process of a subject conditioned by truth.

The line of demarcation between idealism and materialism in Lacan's thought must therefore be drawn through the very concept of the real, splitting its core in order to mark off those aspects that remain tied to a structural lack and those that point towards a torsion, or destruction, of the structure itself. 'Our entire dispute with Lacan lies in the division, which he restricts, of the process of lack from that of destruction,' Badiou concludes. 'Destruction means torsion. Internal to the place, it ravages its spaces, in a laborious duration.'[65] This violent language, in fact, only restates the rare possibility, discussed above, of overdetermining the determination, and displacing the existing space of assigned places, while the price to be paid if one seeks to avoid such violence, whether it is called symbolic or metaphysical, is the droning perpetuation of the status quo.

For a truth to take place, therefore, something has to pass through the impasse. 'If, as Lacan says, the real is the impasse of formalization,' then, Badiou suggests, 'we will have to venture that formalization is the im-passe of the real', which breaches the existing state of things and its immanent deadlocks: 'We need a theory of the pass of the real, in a breach through the formalization. Here the real is not only that which can be missing from its place, but that which passes *with force*.'[66] Surely anchored in the real as a lack of being, a truth-procedure is that which gives being to this very lack. Pinpointing the absent cause or constitutive outside of a situation, in other words, remains a dialectical yet idealist tactic, unless and until this evanescent point of the real is forced, distorted and extended, in order to give consistency to the real as a new generic truth.

For Badiou, consequently, there are two parts to the theory of the subject in the long aftermath of May '68. The first, dialectical or algebraic half holds that every force is divided by the law of its structural placement: 'Every *it* that is stands to itself in a relation of distance that is due to the place where it is,' while the second, materialist or topological half accounts for the emergence of a subject out of the forced torsion of its determining law: 'It happens, let us say, that "*it* turns *I*." '[67] This double articulation is, finally, Badiou's way of explicating the old Freudian maxim *Wo es war, soll ich werden*, in such a way that the subject cannot be reduced purely and simply to the impasse of the structure itself, as seems to have become the idealist trend after Lacan.

In Lacanian psychoanalysis, though, there are two subjective figures that do seem to point towards an excess of the real beyond its placement in the existing law of things: anxiety and the superego. The first signals a radical breakdown, due to the irruption of an overwhelming part of the real, in the whole symbolic apparatus. In this sense, anxiety is an infallible guide for a possible new truth, the site of which is indicated precisely by such failure. 'Anxiety is that form of interruption which, under the invasion of the real as too-much, lets the existing order be as dead order,' Badiou summarizes. 'We might say that anxiety designates the moment when the real *kills*, rather than divides, the symbolic.'[68] In this way, anxiety is only the revealing counterpart of a violent superego injunction, which constitutes the obscene and unlawful underside of the public law. 'The superego is related to the law, and at the same time it is a senseless law,' Lacan himself says. 'The superego is simultaneously the law and its destruction. In this regard, it is the word itself, the commandment of the law, inasmuch as only its root is left.'[69] The figure of the superego gives access to that part of non-law that is the destructive foundation of the law itself, but only in order more forcefully to recompose the structural space of assigned places. In conjunction with the barbaric ferocity that serves as its native soil, the superego is a terrorizing call to order that seems almost automatically to fill out the void revealed by anxiety.

Between anxiety and the superego, a subject only oscillates in painful alternation, without the event of true novelty, just as the insufferable experience of formlessness without a law provokes in turn the reinforcement of the law's excessive form. At best, these two subjective figures thus indicate the point where the existing order of things becomes open to a fatal division, but without allowing a new order to come into being.

As early as his first seminar, however, Lacan himself raises the question of whether this analysis should not be extended to include two other figures of the subject: 'Should we not push the analytical intervention all the way to the fundamental dialogues on justice and courage, in the great dialectical tradition?'[70] For Badiou – who, from this point onwards, further elaborates what is only a suggestion in Lacan – courage and justice are indeed outmoded names for the process whereby an existing order not only breaks down, gets blocked or is reinforced in its old ways, but actually expands, changes, and lends coherence to a new truth. Like anxiety, courage stands under the dissolving pressure of the real, but this time it is in order to twist the structure at the point of its impasse. 'Courage positively carries out the disorder of the symbolic, the rupture of communication, whereas anxiety calls for its death,' writes Badiou. 'All courage amounts to passing through where previously it was not evident that anyone could find a passage.'[71] The part of destruction in the figure of courage then no longer provokes the restoration of a senseless law of terror, but instead puts the old order to the test so as to produce an unforeseeable alternative. 'Anxiety is lack of place, and courage, the assumption of the real by which the place is divided,' so that now the old non-law of the law gives way to a new law, one which no longer recomposes the archaic fierceness of the superego injunction but, rather, produces a figure of unheard-of justice. 'Justice is that by which the subject's nodal link to the place, to the law, takes on the divisible figure of its transformation,' concludes Badiou. 'More radically, justice names the possibility – from the point of view of what it brings into being as subject-effect – that what is non-law may serve as law.'[72]

Thus, Badiou's theory of the subject ties four subjective figures into a single knot. The first two figures – anxiety and courage – divide the act of subjectivation that marks a flickering moment of destruction; while the other two – superego and justice – split the moment of recomposition that is the enduring work of a subjective process. Any subject thus combines a destruction with a recomposition, following two possible trajectories, or strands, which an integral materialist theory of the subject needs to combine. The first strand – from anxiety to the superego – is subordinate to the law of the existing order of places and its founding lack; the second – from courage to justice – actively divides the consistency of the existing order to produce a new truth. According to the first strand, which can be called algebraic, a subject fundamentally occupies a position of internal exclusion with regard to the objective structure in which it finds its empty place; according to the second, a subject stands in a topological excess over and above its assigned placement, the law of which is then transformed.

In short, a subject insists on being caused by that which is missing from its place, but it consists in the coherence of a forced lack. As Badiou concludes: 'The theory of the subject is complete when it manages to think of the structural law of the empty place as the anchoring point of the excess over its place.'[73] Lacan's psychoanalysis gives us only half of this theory: that is, the structural and algebraic strand that remains caught in an endless vacillation between the twin figures of anxiety and the superego, or between the vanishing object-cause of desire and the violent restoration of the archaic law, to which a supplementary strand of courage and justice, of a transformative process and a consistent new truth, ought to be added in Badiou's theory of the subject.

A final way to fix the irreducible distance that separates Lacan and Badiou involves a return to ancient tragedy as an ethical source of inspiration behind psychoanalysis. In Freud and Lacan, this source has always been Sophocles, whereas Aeschylus should rather serve as our model of tragedy according to Badiou: 'The whole purpose of critical delimitation with regard to psychoanalysis, as far as its contribution to the theory of the subject is concerned, can be summed up in this question: Why, through Oedipus, has it been so profoundly Sophoclean?'[74] If, in the world of Sophocles, Antigone and Creon name the respective figures of anxiety and the superego – that is, the formlessness of what persists without legal place and the surfeit of form that restores the law as terror – then Badiou's aim in turning to the alternative model of Aeschylus is to find examples of courage and justice in the twin figures of Orestes and Athena, or, the interruption of the vengeful law of things and the recomposition of a new legal order. 'There exist indeed two Greek tragic modes,' Badiou suggests. 'The Aeschylean one, the sense of which is the contradictory advent of justice by the courage of the new; and the Sophoclean one, the anguished sense of which is the search in return of the superego as origin.'[75] Lacan firmly establishes himself in the world of Sophocles while pointing toward its extension by Aeschylus, which is precisely where the theory of the subject must come according to Badiou.

In retrospect, Badiou's *Theory of the Subject* can still be said to suffer the effects of several shortcomings, or possible misgivings:

1. Philosophy, in *Theory of the Subject*, still appears to be sutured on to the sole condition of politics. The procedures of art, science and love – as well as the eternal shadow condition of religion – are already present throughout the book, but they may seem to be mere illustrations rather than conditions in the strict sense, since the subject of truth is defined exclusively in terms of politics: 'Every subject is political. Which is why there are few subjects, and little politics.'[76] Later, in *Conditions*, a collection of essays which builds on the new foundations of *Being and Event*, Badiou would correct this statement: 'Today, I would no longer say "every subject is political", which is still a maxim of suturing. I would rather say: "Every subject is induced by a generic procedure, and thus depends on an event. Which is why the subject is rare," ' while in *Manifesto for Philosophy* the author had already concluded: 'Every subject is either artistic, scientific, political, or amorous. This is something everyone knows from experience, because besides these registers, there is only existence, or individuality, but no subject.'[77] In the new theory of the subject that is part of *Logics of Worlds*, we can expect to see a new account of the

various figures that open up a subjective space for each and every condition of truth.

2. Within the condition of politics, *Theory of the Subject* still considers the Party as the only effective organizational structure. Badiou has since then abandoned this strict identification of the political subject with the Party, which in all its incarnations over the past century has remained bound to the state. In practice, this has led Badiou to leave his former Maoist group, the Marxist–Leninist Union of Communists of France, and to participate in a small alternative militant group, simply called Political Organization, which states in a recent issue of its newsletter, *Political Distance*: 'The balance-sheet of the nineteenth century is the withering away of the category of class as the sole bearer of politics, and the balance-sheet of the twentieth century is the withering away of the party-form, which knows only the form of the party-state.'[78] Philosophically, moreover, this search for a new figure of militantism without a party brings Badiou back to an old acquaintance, in *Saint Paul: The Foundation of Universalism*, as though almost thirty years had to pass before he could finally come to terms with his personal road to Damascus: 'For me, Paul is the poet-thinker of the event, and at the same time the one who practises and voices the invariant features of what we might call the militant figure.'[79]

3. Badiou's *Theory of the Subject* seems to presuppose from the start that there is such a thing as subjectivity, without giving this thought much ontological support. Although at the end the book already introduces the whole question of Cantorian set theory, and in fact locates the subject in the immeasurable excess of inclusion over belonging, only *Being and Event* will systematically elaborate the underpinnings of this thesis from a meta-ontological – that is to say, meta-mathematical – point of view. In the preface to this second major work, the author writes in retrospect: 'The (philosophical) statement according to which mathematics *is* ontology – the science of being-as-being – is the stroke of light that illuminated the speculative scene which, in my *Theory of the Subject*, I had limited by purely and simply presupposing that "there was" subjectivation.'[80] The new task in *Being and Event* will then consist in articulating, by way of the impasse of being, a coherent ontology together with the theory of the subject – a task which dialectical materialism would have accomplished in the old days by means of an homology between the dialectics of nature and the dialectics of spirit, but which today requires a careful reformulation – this time, above all, in a polemic with Heidegger, and not only with Lacan, whose ontology was already questioned by Miller.[81]

4. Finally, much ink has been spilled, including on the part of Badiou himself, to correct the violent language of destruction with which *Theory of the Subject* seeks to displace the structural dialectic of lack in Mallarmé or Lacan. At times the tone of this language reaches chilling heights indeed, while affirming the part of loss that inheres in any new truth. 'Every truth is essentially destruction,' Badiou already writes in one of his early Maoist pamphlets. 'History has worked all the better when its dustbins were better filled.'[82] Towards the end of *Being and Event*, however, the author admits: 'I went a bit astray, I must say, in *Theory of the Subject* with the theme of destruction. I still supported the idea of an essential link between destruction and novelty.'[83] In a strict ontological view, the part of loss in novelty must be rephrased in terms not of destruction but of subtraction and disqualification. A new truth cannot suppress any existence, but by extending a given situation from the point of its supplementation that is an event, an inquiry into the truthfulness of this event can disqualify, or subtract, certain terms or multiples – namely, those inegalitarian ones which are incompatible with the generic nature of all truth. Destruction is then only a reactive name for that part of knowledge that will no longer have qualified as truthful in the extended situation. The distinction between these two paths, destruction and subtraction, is, moreover, a key topic of the author's ongoing inquiries. Much of Badiou's *Ethics*, for instance, deals with the specific restraints that must apply to any process of truth in order to avoid the catastrophe of forcing an entire situation, while the alternative of subtraction is the subject of several lectures in *Le Siècle*. There is thus a limit, or halting point, which cannot be forced from the point of the situation's extension by a new truth. 'Let us say that this term is not susceptible of being made eternal,' writes Badiou. 'In this sense, it is the symbol of the pure real of the situation, of its life without truth.'[84] To force this limit, which is the unnameable or neutral that is specific to each generic procedure, is a major cause of what Badiou defines as Evil. An example of this would be the disastrous suppression of all self-interest, in the guise of total re-education, as proclaimed by certain Red Guards at the height of the Chinese Cultural Revolution. Badiou himself, finally, tends to read his earlier doctrine of lack and destruction as such a disastrous forcing of the unnameable. Everything thus seems to point towards the notion of destruction as the principal misgiving in Badiou's early thought, which was very much sutured onto politics under the influence of Maoism.

In view of this last crucial objection, I simply want to recall how Marx himself defines the scandalous nature of dialectical thinking, in his famous Postface to the second edition of *Capital*: 'In its mystified form, the dialectic became the fashion in Germany, because it seemed to transfigure and glorify what exists. In its rational figure, it is a scandal and an object of horror to the bourgeoisie and its doctrinaire spokesmen, because it includes in its understanding of what exists at the same time that of its negation and its necessary destruction.'[85] What is happening today, however, is a new transfiguration of the given which may well cast itself as radical but which, precisely by trying to ward off the horrifying scandal of thinking in terms of negation – or, rather, of scission and destruction – merely ends up confirming the status quo in the name of a respectful ethical principle devoid of all truth. The mandatory limit of the unnameable, then, far from restraining an ongoing process of truth from within, actually blocks such a process in advance, and thus keeps a truth from ever taking hold to begin with. Even transfigured by an acknowledgement of the real as its inevitable kernel of idiotic non-knowledge, a mortal life without truth is the radically mystified figure of today's structural dialectic. By criticizing the ferocity of destruction, Badiou – perhaps unwittingly – allows his thought to participate in this trend which, guided by the undeniable authority of Lacan or Levinas and their doctrinaire spokesmen, is only too quick to abandon the idea that, in addition to respect for the other or recognition of the real, a truth implies a symptomatic torsion of the existing order of things.

Destruction, in *Theory of the Subject*, means such a torsion whereby a subject is neither chained on to the automatism of repetition nor fascinated by the haphazard breaking in two of history, as in Nietzsche's figure of the overman, or by the sudden death of the whole symbolic order as such, as in the figures of anxiety and the superego in Lacan or Žižek. For Badiou's *Theory of the Subject*, destruction was not to be confused with death or with a total wipeout of the existing law of things. Since *Being and Event*, however, he himself seems to have forgotten that destruction – even as an exaggerated figure of resentment for which the past always remains the heaviest weight – names part of the process of torsion by which a new subject comes into being, and as a result of which something drops out of the old picture.

The Ontological Impasse

> What a marvel of dialectical materialism is Cantor's famous diagonal reasoning, in which what is left over founds what stands in excess![86]

The change between Badiou's two major works thus far may seem proof of a definitive shift from dialectics to mathematics – with the former dominating his *Theory of the Subject*, together with the slender volume *Can Politics Be Thought?*, which in fact already anticipates the intervening doctrine of the event, and the latter appearing systematically in *Being and Event*, for which the accompanying *Manifesto for Philosophy* then provides a readily accessible context. Does this trajectory, however, really imply an irredeemable break, or is there an underlying continuity? Are the earlier misgivings merely abandoned after the so-called mathematical turn, or do we face a more systematic version of previous insights that in essence remain unchanged, or perhaps even become obscured? In what direction, moreover, is this trajectory currently heading?

Badiou's *Being and Event* should be considered the first half of a larger project, the second volume of which is currently announced for publication in 2006 under the title *Logics of Worlds*. The ambitious overall aim of this project is to affirm that philosophy, despite the repeated prophetic declarations of its imminent end, is once more possible. The present times, in other words, are capable of articulating the key philosophical categories of being, truth and subject in a way that requires neither an inaugural return nor a melancholic traversing of an end but, rather, a decisive step beyond: 'One step in the modern configuration which since Descartes links the conditions of philosophy to the three nodal concepts of being, truth, and subject.'[87] For Badiou, what is needed at present to link these basic concepts is a philosophy of the event which, despite an irreducible polemical distance, would be compatible both with the critique of metaphysics, as brought to a close by Heidegger, and with the intervening doctrines of the subject, mostly tied to political and clinical experiences, after Marx and Freud.

In *Being and Event*, mathematics provides the master key to articulate – both to join and, by way of an impasse, to split off – the science of being with the theory of the subject. The book's guiding thesis is deceptively simple: ontology exists, in so far as ever since the Greek origins of philosophy, and as one of its conditions, the science of being has always been mathematics: 'This is not a thesis about the world but about discourse. It states that mathematics, throughout their historical unfolding, pronounce whatever can be said about being-as-being.'[88] For Badiou, the place where the ontological discourse is developed today, at least if philosophy agrees to take on this decision, is in axiomatic set theory, from Cantor to Cohen. The basic result of his meta-ontological investigation into set theory then holds that everything that presents itself, in any situation whatsoever, is a multiple of multiples, or pure multiple, without One.

The One 'is' not, but 'there is' One. The latter is only the result of an operation, the count-for-one, as applied to the pure multiple which retroactively must be supposed to be inconsistent. To exist means to belong to a multiple, to be counted as one of its elements. A given multiple, or set α, acquires consistency only through the basic operation which counts whatever this multiple presents as so many ones that belong to this multiple. Prior to this count, though, we must presume that all being paradoxically inconsists, without any God-like principle or pre-given origin. In this sense Badiou's ontology of pure multiplicity agrees with the critique of the metaphysics of presence, so that his deconstruction of the One is another way of declaring the death of God.

Choosing a strict alternative to Heidegger's hermeneutic path, however, Badiou's inquiry does not submit itself to the language of the poets, who alone would be capable of rescuing the clearing of being. Instead of upending philosophy in the name of poetry, or art, the critique of metaphysics in this case is conditioned by the deductive fidelity of pure mathematics. Badiou seeks thus to avoid the dominant suture of contemporary philosophy in its pious delegation on to poetry; philosophy today must, rather, draw the required consequences from the closure of the age of the poets, which has run its complete gamut from Hölderlin to Celan. The axiom, not the poem, holds the key to a science of being compatible with the theory of the subject, access to which is provided by way of subtraction, not by interpretative approximation.

All the ontological ideas, axiomatically established in set theory, proceed from the void or empty set, named by the letter $\varnothing$, which must be postulated as the only possible proper name of being. The empty set is indeed universally included in every other set, while itself having no elements that belong to it, and as such 'founds' all mathematical sets. In a normal situation, however, the void not only remains invisible or indiscernible, but the operation of the count moreover reduplicates itself in an attempt to establish the metastructure, or the state of the situation, in the guise of an uninterrupted totality. This second operation consists in counting, or representing, as subsets whatever the first count presents as terms of a given set. The count of the count would then hold for parts just as the count-for-one holds for elements, with the latter doing for belonging what the former does for inclusion. What Badiou calls the state of a situation, in other words, operates by way of the power-set $p(\alpha)$, which is the set of all the subsets of a given set α. The true threat – one that almost became real in the 2000 presidential elections in the United States before being averted through the interruption of the count of the count – would be that in some place – say, at the borders of the void – there might be something that escapes this counting operation: singular elements belonging to the situation without being documented as part of its state or – the other way round – nonexistent parts that are included in the state without having any elements that are thought to belong to their mass. As Badiou writes: 'A nonexistent part is the possible support of the following, which would ruin the structure: the One, in some part, is not, inconsistency is the law of being, the essence of the structure is the void.'[89] The emergence of such uncanny phenomena as nonexistent parts or singular elements would fundamentally upset the operation of the redoubled count by which the state seeks to ward off the void that is always the foundation of its precarious consistency. The state of a situation, in effect, is an imposing defence mechanism set up to guard against the perils of the void.

After the initial guiding decision that mathematics provides the science of being, the fundamental thesis of the whole metaontological inquiry in *Being and Event* then affirms that there is an excess of parts over elements, of inclusion over belonging, of representation over presentation. There are always more ways to regroup the elements of a set into parts than there are elements that belong to this set to begin with: $p(\alpha) > \alpha$. The state of a situation, in other words, cannot coincide with this situation. The cardinality of the set of all parts or subsets of a set is superior to the cardinality of this set itself and – in the case of an infinite set, as with most situations in this world – the magnitude of this excess must be assumed to be strictly beyond measure. 'There is an insurmountable excess of the subsets over the terms' which is such that 'no matter how exact the quantitative knowledge of a situation can be, we cannot estimate, except in an arbitrary decision, "by how much" its state exceeds it.'[90] This is, finally, the ontological impasse – the point of the real in the science of being – around which the author builds the entire artifice of *Being and Event*: 'This gap between α (which counts as one the belongings or elements) and $p(\alpha)$ (which counts as one the inclusions or parts) is, as we shall see, the point at which lies the impasse of being.'[91]

In the second half of *Being and Event*, Badiou exploits this point of the real that is proper to the meta-mathematical analysis of being, in order to discern in its deadlock, not some originary lack as a cause for pious ecstasy or postmodern respect before the unpresentable, but the closest site where an event, as a contingent and unforeseeable supplement to the situation, raises the void of being in a kind of insurrection, and opens a possible space of subjective fidelity. In normal circumstances, as we saw above, the structural impasse that is intrinsic to the state of the situation remains invisible, so that the void that is its foundation appears to be foreclosed. This foreclosure is the very operation that allows the smooth functioning of the established order of things – when everyone does what comes naturally, because the state of the situation in effect appears to be second nature. Exceptionally, however, an event can bring the excess out into the open, expose the void as the foundation of all being, and mark the possible onset of a generic procedure of truth. A seemingly natural and well-ordered situation then becomes historical when what is otherwise a structural impasse, proper to the law of representation as such, becomes tangible through the effects of a radically contingent event. As the doctrine of the weakest link already implied, all historicity occurs at the point where a deadlock of structural determination is crossed by the irruption of a rare event – an irruption which, as will become clear, cannot be dissociated from the intervention of a subject.

Perhaps the most important argument in all of *Being and Event* effectively holds that an event, which brings out the void that is proper to being by revealing the undecidable excess of representation, can be decided only retroactively by way of a subjective intervention. In a concise and untranslatable formula, a final thesis thus sums up the trajectory of the entire book: 'The *impasse* of being, which causes the quantitative excess of the state to wander beyond measure, is in truth the *passe* of the Subject.'[92] A subject is needed to put a measure on the exorbitant power by which the state of a situation exceeds this situation itself. Through the chance occurrence of an event, the structural fact of the ontological impasse is thus already mediated by subjectivity; without the intervention of a subject faithful to the event, the gap in the structure would not even be visible. The impasse is never purely structural but also, at the same time, dependent upon a haphazard intervention.

In every subject, as in an equivocal nodal link, a structural law is tied on to the contingent occurrence of an unpredictable wager. 'Everything happens as though between the structure, which liberates the immediacy of belonging, and the meta-structure, which counts for one its parts and regulates the inclusions, a breach were opened that cannot be closed except by a choice without concept,' writes Badiou. 'The fact that at this point it is necessary to tolerate the almost complete arbitrariness of a choice, and that quantity, this paradigm of objectivity, leads to pure subjectivity, that is what I would like to call the symptom of Cantor–Gödel–Cohen–Easton.'[93] A subject, then, is that which decides the undecidable in a choice without concept. Setting out from the void which, prior to the event, remains indiscernible in the language of established knowledge, a subjective intervention names the event which disappears no sooner than it appears; it faithfully connects as many elements of the situation as possible to this name which is the only trace of the vanished event; and subsequently it forces the extended situation from the bias of the new truth *as if* the latter were indeed already generically applicable.

Although it is essentially a repetition of the argument from Badiou's *Theory of the Subject*, the pivotal thesis about the impasse of being as the pass of the subject is nevertheless open to a fundamental misunderstanding, which in my opinion is due to the primarily ontological orientation of *Being and Event*. From a Lacanian point of view, above all, the thesis might as well be inverted in order to reduce the subject's passing to the structural impasse pure and simple. To come to terms with the unbearable kernel of the real, a subject must then not only renounce all imaginary ideals and symbolic mandates, but also assume the essential inconsistency of the symbolic order itself. The end of analysis, in other words, lies not just in accepting the divided and alienated nature of the subject as one's positive condition, but in acknowledging that what divides the subject is nothing but the lack that keeps the symbolic order from ever achieving any meaningful closure. The event, in this case, would be like a symptomatic slippage which exposes the fact that the symbolic order itself is incomplete – unable as much as the subject is to offer any answer to the abysmal question of the other's desire: *Che vuoi?* The subject 'is' nothing but the empty place opened up in the structure by the very failure to answer this founding question. Recognition of this ineradicable void in the midst of the structure would then already coincide with the traumatic truth itself – if, that is, there exists such a thing as a truth of the real in psychoanalysis, which in any case would have to be more than its passing acknowledgement.

Žižek, for instance, describes this passage as a kind of ideological anamorphosis, or change of perspective, whereby that which previously served as an unshakeable guarantee of meaningfulness all of a sudden appears merely to cover a gaping chasm of nonsense. The sole task of the subject, then, lies in the purely formal act of conversion which assumes this immediate speculative identity between absolute power and utter impotence, by recognizing the point where the dazzling plenitude of being flips over to reveal its morbid foundation in a thing-like nothingness. Typically, what at first appears to be a purely epistemological obstacle, owing to the subject's limited capacities for knowing as compared to the ungraspable power of some truly infinite entity, from a slightly different perspective – by looking awry at what is usually overlooked – turns out to be an essential ontological feature, inherent to the blocked structure of being itself.

'Where it was, I shall come into being': for a subject, the formal act of conversion thus consists in somehow 'becoming' what one always-already 'was' beforehand: namely, the very gap or empty place that prevents the symbolic order from attaining full closure. All that happens has already taken place; there is nothing new under the sun, except for the formal gesture by which a subject assumes responsibility for what is happening anyway. 'The "subject" is precisely a name for this "empty gesture" which changes nothing at the level of positive content (at this level, everything has already happened) but must nevertheless be added for the "content" itself to achieve its full effectivity,' as Žižek concludes in *The Sublime Object of Ideology*: 'The only difference lies in a certain change of perspective, in a certain turn through which what was a moment ago experienced as an obstacle, as an impediment, proves itself to be a positive condition.'[94] The subject thus not only posits that what seems to be presupposed as something objectively given is already his or her own doing, but the activity of pure self-positing must in turn be presupposed to be split from within by an insurmountable deadlock that is not external but immanent to its very essence. In a formal turnabout or instantaneous flipover, devoid of any actual change, the subject's pass would immediately coincide with the recognition of the impasse of the structure of being itself – that is to say, the gap between the real and its impossible symbolization.

The essence of truth, from this psychoanalytic perspective, is not a process so much as a brief traumatic encounter, or illuminating shock, in the midst of common everyday reality. This interpretation thus fails to understand the procedure whereby a truth is not something we chance upon in a slight change of perspective, but something that is actively produced, through a step-by-step intervention, after an event. Žižek, for instance, mistakenly sums up Badiou's philosophy by speaking repeatedly of the miracle of a 'Truth-Event'.[95] Even regardless of the awkward capital letters, this syncopated and apocryphal expression collapses into an instantaneous act what is in reality an ongoing and impure procedure, which from a singular event will have led to a generic truth by way of a forced return upon the initial situation. Whereas for Žižek, the appearance of the empty place of the real that is impossible to symbolize is somehow already the act of truth itself, for Badiou a truth comes about only by forcing the real and displacing the empty place, in order to make the impossible possible. 'Every truth is post-evental,' he writes in *Manifesto for Philosophy*, so that the event which, in a sudden flash, reveals the void of a given situation cannot itself already be the truth of this situation – hence the need for a militant figure of fidelity such as the one studied in *Saint Paul*: 'Fidelity to the declaration is crucial, because truth is a process, and not an illumination.'[96]

Badiou's *Being and Event*, however, may still give the false impression that a Lacanian psychoanalytic perspective is sufficient to articulate the impasse of being with the pass of the subject. I would suggest, therefore, that we reread this book's central thesis from the point of view of Badiou's *Theory of the Subject*, which also argues that from the real as the impasse of formalization we should be able to grasp formalization as the forceful passing of the real.

Indeed, the earlier work seems to me much more effective in explaining where exactly this thesis imposes a vital step beyond psychoanalysis – a step which the later work barely indicates in the title of its final part: 'Forcing: Truth and Subject. Beyond Lacan'.[97]

Following the ontological orientation of *Being and Event*, the debate with psychoanalysis indeed depends purely on the *location* of the void: whether on the side of the subject as lack (for Lacan) or on the side of being as empty set (for Badiou). If the polemic were defined only in these terms, though, the answer on behalf of psychoanalysis could still consist in locating an ever more fundamental lack in the midst of the structure of being – before identifying the subject itself with this empty place, as would be the case for Žižek. In fact, the irrefutable radicality of this prior and absolutely originary lack or void, as revealed in the ontological impasse, can then be used as an anti-philosophical rebuttal against any given subject's imaginary confidence and dogmatic mastery over a truth without precedent.

Following the double, algebraic and topological, articulation of *Theory of the Subject*, however, the irreducible difference with regard to psychoanalysis lies, rather, in the *process* of what happens near the borders of the void which will have become the site of a possible event: whether a vanishing apparition of the real as absent cause (for Lacan) or a forceful transformation of the real into a consistent truth (for Badiou). The polemic, then, can no longer be reduced to the simple location of lack but, instead, resides in the inescapable choice between lack and destruction, between a vanishing cause and a symptomatic torsion, or between the determining placement of an empty space and the displacement of the excessive power of determination itself. Seen from this earlier point of view, any purely formal act of conversion or speculative judgement, which makes the subject's pass immediately transitive to an impasse of the structure, would in fact turn out to be as yet devoid of truth. What would be needed for a rare generic truth to emerge, in addition to this initial act of subjectivation, is the forcing of the situation and the gradual sequencing of a subjective process by which the structure is actually transformed from the point of its breakdown.

In this sense, Badiou's *Being and Event* can be said to be both more encompassing and more limited than his *Theory of the Subject*. More encompassing, in so far as the latter work starts from the given that there is subjectivity, whereas the former uses the deductive power of mathematics to give the subject its substructure in ontology. But also more limited, in so far as the ontological definitions of being, event, truth and subject risk remaining caught up in a structural dialectic which in reality is only half the picture. By this I mean that from the strict point of view of what can be said about being, the subject of truth is defined by a lack of being, rather than by the process of giving being to this very lack. The ontological discourse, in other words, gives us the pure algebra of the subject without elaborating the topology of its purification.

From a set-theoretical or ontological perspective, the event can be seen as a vanishing mediator of the void – a revelation of the unpresentable empty set, or non-place, which founds the presentation of each and every placement. Mallarmé, not surprisingly, re-emerges in the later work as the poet-thinker of the event at its purest. From the older logical or topological perspective, however, the doctrine of structural causality is incapable of giving consistency to the actual making of a new truth. What is more, from this last perspective, the subject can no longer be reduced to a unique figure of fidelity in connection with the name of the vanished event, but must be unfolded according to the various figures of a complex subjective space. In short, if *Theory of the Subject* gives us an intricate subjective configuration without much further ontological support, then the systematic meta-mathematical inquiry gives us only a one-dimensional figure of the subject, transitive to the structure, in *Being and Event*. These limitations not only give rise to certain misunderstandings in the reception of this last work, but also constitute the main impetus behind the current continuation of its overall project.

Since the publication of *Being and Event*, and in an implicit return to *Theory of the Subject*, Badiou has thus formulated a triple self-criticism, a more complete answer to which in large part defines the positive table of contents of his *Logics of Worlds*.[98]

1. All the stuff of a given situation cannot be fully accounted for in the sole terms of belonging, which, as we have seen, is the only verb for the ontological discourse. The key to understanding the new work, by contrast, lies in the greater attention given to the question not only of being but also of appearing, or being-there. This logical and topological emphasis will require a remodelling of the concept of the situation, particularly through the theory of categories as opposed to the strict ontological purview of axiomatic set theory. Situations, then, are constructed no longer purely on the grounds of a relation of being as belonging and the impasse of inclusion, but in terms of networks, trajectories and paths, which together give topological coherence to a universe of appearing, or a world. This logic of appearing, which is anticipated in the small unpublished booklet *Being-There*, is the one that will re-emerge as part of *Logics of Worlds*.

2. The ontological perspective risks defining the event exclusively in terms of a sovereign and punctual irruption of self-belonging, $E \in E$. Badiou's

recent work, however, underscores ever more clearly the extent to which the truth of an event not only constitutes a vanishing apparition of the void of being, but also sets off a regime of consequences to which the belabouring of a truth gives way in a forced return to the situation of departure. In addition to the ontological definition of the event, therefore, we must consider its logical aftermath, following the inferences that are the lasting result of the work of the subject. Not only is the event a punctual and self-belonging encounter, it also opens up a process of successive implications; it is true that it emerges in a sudden flash, but its traces must also be elaborated according to a duration that is all its own. Without such a process, by contrast, the event may indeed induce comparisons with the notion of the act in psychoanalysis, as in the most recent works of Žižek or Alenka Zupančič.[99] Badiou has been relentless in his effort to counter this temptation of an anti-philosophical act – not by ignoring its insights but by closely examining its most forceful inner mechanisms, for example, in the unpublished seminar on 'Lacanian Anti-philosophy'.

3. The definition of the subject that corresponds to the ontological perspective of the event is also one-sided. It includes only the effects of fidelity, without considering how any inquiry into the truth of a situation encounters other subjective figures as well, such as those of reaction or denial. It is precisely in this sense that *Being and Event* is more limited than *Theory of the Subject*, where the subject is defined in terms both of the act of subjectivation and of the subjective process in which at least four figures are tied in a knot: anxiety, the superego, courage and justice. Badiou's *Logics of Worlds* will pick up on this older analysis from the point of view of the different conditions of truth, in order to distinguish how, for each one of these conditions, the act of subjectivation likewise opens up a subjective space configured by the complex interplay between the figure of fidelity and its obscure or reactive counterparts. Part of this ongoing investigation can be appreciated in the unpublished seminar 'Axiomatic Theory of the Subject'.

In this recent seminar, Badiou initially defines the act of subjectivation as a hysterical figure, capable of detaching an opening statement from the event itself, which as such disappears no sooner than it appears. From the event, ontologically defined in terms of self-belonging, $E \in E$, the hysterical act of subjectivation thus no longer consists just in naming the void but in extracting or detaching an indispensable first statement as true: $E \rightarrow p$. A declaration of love is no doubt the simplest example of such an operation of detachment. This first figure would be hysterical in so far as the subject of the statement somehow remains personally implicated in the statement itself, as in the

Lacanian formula: 'Me, the truth, I speak.'[100] Every subject of a truth-process, in this sense, would first emerge by being hysterical. To derive a regime of consequences from this initial statement, and thus to give consistency to a universalizable truth about the entire situation in which the event took place, a masterly figure is required through which a series of further statements can be inferred from the first one – statements that are no longer tied to the particular person of the speaking subject. This inferential process follows the simple rules of logical implication: given p, if p → q, then q. While the point of emergence of a new truth is always caught in a hysterical scheme, the operations of the master name the figure of consequent fidelity. Mastery and hysteria would thus appear to be co-dependent in their mirroring relationship – with both being required before a truth can come into existence. In fact, if the implicated person of the hysterical act of enunciation is the unconscious to be repressed beneath the bar of the mastery of consequences, then we can also say that, vice versa, the unconscious of the hysterical figure is a regime of mastered inferences. The act of subjectivation is necessary but also, strictly speaking, inconsequential, yet at the same time the enthralling intensity of the hysterical speech act can always be put forward to denigrate and mock the meagre outcome of the master's inferences. This is how the hysteric, like any good anti-philosopher who is never far removed from this figure, can remind the master of the need always to begin anew.

Badiou himself rather quickly abandons the twin names – though not the processes – of the master and the hysteric in order to avoid any confusion with the theory of the four discourses in Lacanian psychoanalysis. The last two figures of reaction and obscurantism in Badiou's new axiomatic theory of the subject also correspond only vaguely to Lacan's university discourse and the discourse of the analyst. A subjective figure, rather, becomes reactive whenever the logical outcome of a truth-process in retrospect is considered to be indifferent as compared to the event that caused it. This event might as well not have taken place, and the result would still be exactly the same: no matter if p or not-p → q. In a strangely perverse argument, the fact that an event has taken place with unmistakable consequences is thus denied. The subjective support of truth is then no longer split by an emergent speech act, as in the hysterical figure, nor barred by the labour of consequences, as in the figure of mastery, but purely and simply obliterated. In a certain sense, the reactive figure re-enacts the 'rightist' deviation of the dialectical process discussed above, whereas the obscure figure is enraptured by a 'leftist' solution, which turns the event from a singular condition into a radical and unattainable origin that from times immemorial precedes and overwhelms the search for a specific truth in the present. Knowledge of this transcendent origin is then simply imposed and transmitted, instead of being actually detached, which means forever obscuring the possibility that an unprecedented regime of consequences can be initiated in the here and now by a rare temporal act of subjectivation. In this denegation of all present temporality, the obscure figure is fundamentally a figure of death. Is it, then, a coincidence that Badiou's seminar parts ways with the Lacanian theory of the four discourses precisely at this point where the obscure figure is discussed? Should we not consider the passing acknowledgement of sexual difference, of desire and of the death drive, or, in a politicized reading, the recognition of the real kernel of social antagonism, as such a radical and obscene absolutely prior origin, which always-already threatens to render impossible – or merely imaginary and naive – the consequent belabouring of a new and unheard-of truth? At this point, I leave it to the reader to decide how, in this light, we might not only reframe the criticisms raised by someone like Žižek, but also interpret the latter's own thought from within the theory of the subject as it is currently being reworked by Badiou.[101]

By Way of Conclusion

> Fundamentally, really, I have only one philosophical question: Can we think that there is something new in a situation?[102]

For Badiou, in the final instance, everything revolves around one question: how does true change occur in a given situation? Not only: what is being, on the one hand, and what is the event, on the other? But: what truly happens *between* ordinary configurations of the multiple of being and their supplementation by an unforeseeable event? Badiou's principal concern, in my view, is not with a pristine opposition but with the impure difference of being and event, while the subject is precisely that which operates in the equivocal space of this in-between. His critics are mostly one-sided, if not mistaken, in charging his philosophy with dogmatism or absolutism for relying on a sovereign divide separating being from event, or with decisionism for defining the event in terms of a strict self-belonging. Whenever Badiou does seem to establish such a divide as that between truth and knowledge, or between being and event, these should not be taken as two already separate dimensions or spheres, which, moreover, only his critics transcribe with capital letters. Rather, from the point of a subjective intervention, they stand as the extremes of an ongoing process of detachment and scission. Despite a recurrent temptation by Mallarmé's wager, Badiou is rarely taken in by the absolute purity of truth as a voluntaristic and self-constituent decision in the radical void of the undecidable. To the contrary, much of his philosophical work is guided by the hypothesis that the oppositions between being and event, and between structure and subject, far from constituting, in turn, a structural given that would merely have to be recognized, hinge on the rare contingency of a process, an intervention, a labour. Truth as an ongoing process actively destroys the premiss of a simple face-off, no matter how heroic or melancholy, between an established order of being and the untainted novelty of an event. Was this not, after all, the harsh subject lesson in dialectical materialism to be drawn from the events of May '68 according to Badiou himself?

Being and Event, in this respect, admittedly proves itself to be much less decisive and insightful – or rather, as a treatise on ontology, it is of necessity much more purified and decisionistic than *Theory of the Subject* or *Logics of Worlds*. The impure and equivocal nature of all truth-processes, which is not easily grasped in the algebraic science of being as being, is by contrast inseparable from any topological understanding of the subject. When the ontological inquiry is reread from the point of view of the older subject theory, however, as I have tried to do in this study, even Badiou's later philosophy begins to revolve around two key concepts – the *site* of the event and the *forcing* of truth – which his critics and commentators tend to ignore, but which in fact sum up his contribution to a forgotten tradition of the materialist dialectic.

Even from the ontological aspect, the matheme of the event indeed is $E_x = \{x \in X, E_x\}$, that is, not just a pure event of self-belonging, $E \in E$, cut off from the situation S but an event *for* this situation, E_x, as determined by the site $X \in S$. There is little doubt in my mind that the idea of the evental site is a continuation, in ontology, of the search for a dialectic in which every term or multiple, even the otherwise unfounded multiple of the event, is internally marked by the structure of assigned spaces in which this multiple is placed. Otherwise, the ontological discourse risks almost literally leading us back to the false structural or creationist scheme of P versus A, in so far as the event constitutes a pure vanishing insurrection of the void which founds the structure of being and stands revealed in the immeasurable excess of $p(\alpha) > \alpha$. Even Badiou's later thought remains dialectical, despite the mathematical turn, in rejecting such stark opposition between being and event, in favour of the specific site through which an event is anchored in the ontological deadlock of a situation that only a rare subjective intervention can unlock. An event is not pure novelty and insurrection, but is tributary to a situation by virtue of its specific site.

A subject's intervention, moreover, cannot consist merely in showing or recognizing the traumatic impossibility around which the situation as a whole is structured. If such were to be the case, the structural dialectic would remain profoundly idealist – its operation delivering at most a radical, arch-aesthetic or arch-political act that either brings home the unbearable anxiety of the real itself, or ultimately calls upon the annihilation of the entire symbolic order in a mimicry of the revolutionary break, which can then perfectly well be illustrated with examples drawn from Antigone to Hollywood. Badiou's thought, by contrast, seeks to be both dialectical and materialist in understanding the production of a new truth as the torsion, or forcing, of the entire situation from the precise point of a generic truth, as if the latter had already been added successfully to the resources of knowledge available in this situation itself. Without such a process, the real that resists symbolization will only have been the site of a possible truth, but it is not already the given truth of the situation itself; in fact, the real in this case would merely indicate a structural impossibility, not an evental site whereby the regular structure of a situation becomes historicized. The subject, finally, is a laborious material process that requires a putting-to-work of an event. It does not come to coincide, in a purely formal act of conversion, with the impasse of the structure as with the real kernel of its own impossibility – say, through the traumatic symptom, with which a subject can identify only after traversing the ideological fantasy. At best, to acknowledge this radical impasse, as in the case of antagonism for the political philosophy of radical democracy which I have discussed elsewhere, is still only the inaugural act of subjectivation bereft of any subjective process; at worst, it is actually that which forever blocks and obscures the consequential elaboration of a new truth. For Badiou, a subject emerges only by opening a passage, in a truly arduous production of novelty, through the impasse – forcing the structure precisely where a lack is found – in order to make generically possible that which the state of the situation would rather confine to an absurd impossibility. Following a long tradition from Marx to Mao, this means nothing if not bringing the new out of the old – forcing a new consistent truth out of the old order of things from the point where our knowledge of the latter is found wanting.

Badiou's philosophy can be read as an untimely recommencement of dialectical materialism in the sense in which the latter would be a philosophy not of pure and absolute beginnings, but of impure and painstaking recommencements. It is a thought of change situated in whatever can be said of being as pure multiple, yet supplemented by the irruption of an event, the truth of which emerges not in a unique and instantaneous vanishing act that would coincide with the event itself but, rather, after the event in an ongoing process of fits and starts, of destructions and recompositions, of backlashes and resurrections, of fidelity and the extreme fallout of reaction and obscurantism. An event is a sudden commencement, but only a recommencement produces the truth of this event. Badiou's philosophy could thus be said to obey not one but two ethical imperatives: 'Never give up on your desire!', but also 'Always continue!', that is, 'Always rebegin!' As Badiou himself suggests in his latest seminar on the theory of the subject: 'The ethical would be to rebegin rather than to continue.'[103]

Notes

1. Alain Badiou, *Peut-on penser la politique?* (Paris: Seuil, 1985), p. 84.

2. Badiou, 'Democratic Materialism and the Materialist Dialectic,' trans. Alberto Toscano, *Radical Philosophy* 130 (2005): 21. This article is an abridged version of the preface to Badiou's *Logiques des Mondes* (Paris: Seuil, 2006). See also Badiou, 'Le (re)commencement du matérialisme dialectique,' *Critique* 240 (1967): 438–67. In addition to *For Marx* and *Reading Capital*, this review deals with a short article by Althusser, 'Matérialisme historique et matérialisme dialectique', *Cahiers Marxistes Léninistes* 11 (1966).

3. Badiou, *Abrégé de métapolitique* (Paris: Seuil, 1998), p. 72.

4. Althusser, *Pour Marx* (Paris: Maspéro, 1965; La Découverte, 1986), p. 25. For a succinct discussion, see Gregory Elliott, 'A Recommencement of Dialectical Materialism', *Althusser: The Detour of Theory* (London: Verso, 1987), pp. 70–114. In this chapter, despite the use of the same title, Elliott only incidentally refers to Badiou's review article while he completely ignores all of the later work by Althusser's one-time student.

5. Althusser, *Pour Marx*, p. 25.

6. Alain Badiou, 'Sutures', in *Manifeste pour la philosophie* (Paris: Seuil, 1989), pp. 41–8. With regard to Althusser's obligatory lesson about politics as a condition for philosophy, see 'Althusser: le subjectif sans sujet', in Badiou, *Abrégé de métapolitique* (Paris: Seuil, 1998), pp. 67–76. For Althusser's own description of his double suturing of philosophy, see *Éléments d'autocritique* (Paris: Hachette, 1974), pp. 100–101.

7. Badiou, 'Le (re)commencement du matérialisme dialectique', p. 449.

8. Badiou, 'Le (re)commencement', p. 450. In the chapter '"Science et idéologie"' from his *Éléments d'autocritique*, Althusser himself admits that he had reduced the theory of science and ideology, despite the injection of a recurrent dialectical struggle, to a speculative-idealist opposition of truth 'against' errror, of knowledge 'against' ignorance.

9. Badiou, 'Le (re)commencement du matérialisme dialectique', p. 450.

10. Althusser, *Pour Marx*, p. 171. Peter Hallward, in a personal note to the author, insists that for Badiou, mathematics *is* such a pure theoretical practice, in fact the *only* science that is axiomatically set free from the ongoing struggle mentioned by Althusser. To answer

this objection would require us to take up the enormous task of investigating the double status of mathematical science, both as the discourse of ontology and as one subjective condition of truth among others, in Badiou's philosophy.

11. Badiou, 'Le (re)commencement du matérialisme dialectique', p. 452.
12. Badiou, 'Le (re)commencement du matérialisme dialectique', p. 455.
13. Badiou, 'Le (re)commencement du matérialisme dialectique', p. 457.
14. Althusser, *Pour Marx*, p. 215.
15. Badiou, *Abrégé de métapolitique*, p. 75.
16. Badiou, *Abrégé de métapolitique*, p. 155.
17. Althusser, *Pour Marx*, p. 126. Regarding the theory of the event as derived from the idea of overdetermination, see also Étienne Balibar, 'Avant-propos pour la réedition de 1996', in Althusser, *Pour Marx*, new pocket edition (Paris: La Découverte, 1996), p. ix.
18. Badiou, 'Le (re)commencement du matérialisme dialectique', p. 458.
19. Badiou, *Conditions* (Paris: Seuil, 1992), p. 196.
20. Alain Badiou, 'L'autonomie du processus esthétique', *Cahiers Marxistes-Léninistes* 12–13 (1966): 77–89. This article was supposed to become a book-length study on *l'effet romanesque* for Althusser's series Théorie for Maspero. See Louis Althusser, *Lettres à Franca (1961–1973)* (Paris: Stock/IMEC, 1998), p. 691. Actually published in this series the same year, the most systematic investigation of literature along the lines of Althusser's theory of four discourses remains, of course, Pierre Macherey's *Pour une théorie de la production littéraire* (Paris: Maspéro, 1966).
21. See Alain Badiou, *Théorie axiomatique du sujet (Notes du cours 1996–1998)* (author's unpublished typescript). For a succinct exposition of Lacan's theory of four discourses, with clear traces of the influence of Badiou's thought, see Bruce Fink, 'The Status of Psychoanalytic Discourse', in *The Lacanian Subject: Between Language and Jouissance* (Princeton, NJ: Princeton University Press, 1995), pp. 127–46.
22. Louis Althusser, 'Ideology and Ideological State Apparatuses (Notes Towards an Investigation)', in *Lenin and Philosophy and Other Essays*, trans. Ben Brewster (London: NLB, 1971), pp. 127–88.
23. Louis Althusser, *Écrits sur la psychanalyse*, ed. Olivier Corpet and François Matheron (Paris: Stock/IMEC, 1993), p. 12.
24. Badiou, *Abrégé de métapolitique*, pp. 68–69.
25. In a footnote to *Le Siècle* (Paris: Seuil, 2005), Badiou writes: 'Personal testimony: in 1960 I was a student at the École Normale Supérieure, and I had just discovered with extreme enthusiasm the published texts of Lacan, when Althusser, who at the time was in charge of philosophical studies at the École, charged me with providing my colleagues with a synthetic presentation of the concepts of this author who was then utterly ignored. Something I did in two exposés which, even today, continue to guide me from within' p. 76, n. 1.
26. For Lacan's note and Miller's personal recollection of the effect this caused in him, see the correspondence quoted in Althusser, *Écrits sur la psychanalyse*: 'Rather good, your guy. Thanks,' was all Lacan's note said, but this was sufficient for Miller: 'Here, a spark fixated something for me' (p. 304).
27. Jacques-Alain Miller, 'Action de la structure', *Cahiers pour l'Analyse* 9 (1966): 103. The journal *Cahiers pour l'Analyse*, with about a dozen thematic issues, was the remarkable organon of the Cercle d'Epistémologie at the École Normale Supérieure. Badiou started

participating in the journal precisely with this special issue, devoted to the *Généalogie des Sciences*, in which Michel Foucault also formulates his own archaeological theory of discourse and event in response to a questionnaire by members from the Cercle.

28. Jacques-Alain Miller, 'La Suture', *Cahiers pour l'Analyse* 1 (1964); 'Matrice', *Ornicar?* 4 (1975). Badiou will rely on this second article in his *Théorie du sujet* (Paris: Seuit, 1982), and more recently still refers to both texts as canonical, in another footnote to *Le Siècle*, p. 143 n. 1. See also Badiou's critical reading of 'La Suture' in 'Note complémentaire sur un usage contemporain de Frege', in *Le Nombre et les nombres* (Paris: Seuil, 1990), pp. 36–44. Miller recently reissued most of his juvenilia, in *Un début dans la vie* (Paris: Gallimard, 2002).

29. See Slavoj Žižek, *Le plus sublime des hystériques: Hegel passe* (Paris: Point Hors Ligne, 1988) and *Ils ne savent pas ce qu'ils font: Le sinthome idéologique* (Paris: Point Hors Ligne, 1990). Translations of this two-volume work can be found, with numerous changes and additions, in *The Sublime Object of Ideology* (London and New York: Verso, 1989), *For They Know Not What They Do: Enjoyment as a Political Factor* (London and New York: Verso, 1991); and *The Metastases of Enjoyment: Six Essays on Woman and Causality* (London and New York: Verso, 1994). It should be noted that similar titles in English and French by no means cover identical tables of contents. Žižek, furthermore, only seems to stick to the same basic Lacanian concepts, but in fact these terms often receive dramatically different interpretations. His dialogue with contemporary thinkers, finally, offers a superb example of the Machiavellian art of war in philosophy – often presenting an opponent's positions as entirely his own before attacking them for reasons that in fact apply only to his previous position. Many criticisms in Žižek's books can thus be read as self-criticisms of an earlier book of his, so that a coherent overall interpretation of this vast body of work is quickly becoming a fascinating impossibility.

30. Slavoj Žižek, 'The Politics of Truth, or, Alain Badiou as a Reader of St Paul', in *The Ticklish Subject: The Absent Centre of Political Ontology* (London and New York: Verso, 1999), pp. 127–170; Alain Badiou, *Ethics: An Essay on the Understanding of Evil*, trans. and introd. Peter Hallward (London and New York: Verso, 2001). The latter work also contains a useful bibliography and translator's introduction in which Peter Hallward anticipates some of the criticisms from his book *Alain Badiou: A Subject to Truth* (Minneapolis: University of Minnesota Press, 2003). See also, by the same author, 'Generic Sovereignty: The Philosophy of Alain Badiou', *Angelaki: Journal of the Theoretical Humanities* 3:3 (1998): 87–111. Hallward's criticisms, which target above all the sovereign and absolutist tendencies in Badiou's thought, coincide to some extent with the argument against dogmatism made by Žižek. In his introduction to Badiou's *Ethics*, however, Hallward seems to have tempered these criticisms a bit, and pays more attention to the situated specificity of all truth-processes along the lines of the materialist reading I present here.

31. Ernesto Laclau and Chantal Mouffe, *Hegemony and Socialist Strategy: Towards a Radical Democratic Politics* (London: Verso, 1985). For a useful didactic overview of the common doctrine of Laclau, Mouffe and Žižek, see Yannis Stavrakakis, *Lacan & the Political* (London: Routledge, 1999). I have offered a Badiou-inspired critique of the political philosophy of radical democracy, which is tied to the doctrine of structural causality, in 'Por una falta de política: Tesis sobre la filosofía de la democracia radical', *Acontecimiento: Revista para pensar la política* 17 (1999): 63–89; reprinted as 'Democracia radical: Tesis sobre la filosofía del radicalismo democrático', in *Los nuevos adjetívos de la democracia*, a special issue of the Mexican journal *Metapolítica* 18 (2001): 96–115.

32. Laclau and Mouffe, 'Beyond the Positivity of the Social: Antagonisms and Hegemony', in *Hegemony and Socialist Strategy*, pp. 93–148.

33. Badiou, 'Le (re)commencement du matérialisme dialectique', p. 457 n. 23. For further explanations, Badiou refers to Miller's 'La Suture' and to Claude Lévi-Strauss's classic 'Introduction à l'œuvre de Mauss', in Marcel Mauss, *Sociologie et anthropologie* (Paris: PUF, 1950). Compare also with Gilles Deleuze's explanations about the role of the 'empty place' in the structure, in 'À quoi reconnaît-on le structuralisme?', in *La philosophie au XXe siècle*, ed. François Châtelet (Paris: Hachette, 1973; Brussels: Marabout, 1979), pp. 292–329, and Badiou's implicit reading of this text in his *Deleuze: 'La clameur de l'Être'* (Paris: Hachette, 1997), pp. 57–63. For Žižek, however, 'the basic gesture of "structuralism" is to reduce the imaginary richness to a formal network of symbolic relations: what escapes the structuralist perspective is that this formal structure is itself tied by an umbilical cord to some radically contingent material element which, in its pure particularity, "is" the structure, embodies it. Why? Because the big Other, the symbolic order, is always *barré*, failed, crossed-out, mutilated, and the contingent material element embodies this internal blockage, limit, of the symbolic structure' (*The Sublime Object of Ideology*, p. 183).

34. Žižek, *The Sublime Object of Ideology*, p. 163. For Althusser, of course, the finally determining instance of the economy also does not 'exist', nobody ever encounters such a cause 'in person' but only through the effects that are its conditions of existence. This then raises the important question of the ontological priority attributed to the economy – or at least, to the class struggle – in Marxism and refused in post-Marxism. Even when Žižek addresses this question in the book's introduction, he himself, as always, ends up relying on an ontologically prior antagonism – the traumatic kernel of the real whose correlate 'is' the subject.

35. Žižek, *The Sublime Object of Ideology*, p. 209; Laclau, 'Preface', in ibid., pp. xiv–xv.

36. Ernesto Laclau, *New Reflections on the Revolution of Our Time* (London and New York: Verso, 1990), p. 92.

37. Žižek, *The Sublime Object of Ideology*, p. 5. At the end of *Théorie du sujet*, faced with the tiresome question of ideology, Badiou asks: 'What more can we say . . . to the various formulations of the "human condition", dogmatically exalted in its absolute power (art and religion), sceptically cornered to its lack and the inevitability of death? To show that all this sticks to our skin and takes the guise of a transcendent negation of the class struggle does not go further than an establishing of facts by some materialist bailiff' (pp. 317–18).

38. Žižek, *The Sublime Object of Ideology*, p. 44. On the level of theoretical anecdotes, I am tempted to counter this objection by recalling how Althusser explains his absence from Lacan's seminar, which he himself had invited to the École at rue d'Ulm: 'I don't attend: which is the climax of enjoyment. Absence. A funny absence. There are funny absences, good absences,' a thought that no doubt should be tied to this other reflection, in a letter to his analyst: 'I think that you will agree on the very general principle that there is an efficacy to absence, on the condition of course that it not be an absence in general, the nothingness, or any other Heideggerian "clearing", but a determinate absence, playing a role in the very place of its absence. That is no doubt important for the problem of the emergence of the unconscious' (*Écrits sur la psychanalyse*, pp. 11, 90–91). From a more theoretical perspective, moreover, Althusser himself ends these last texts on psychoanalysis by questioning the instability of Freud's two founding notions of fantasy and drive. Finally, the reader will find an exemplary analysis of fantasy as the ultimate support of ideology and identity in Althusser's vitriolic intervention during and after the meeting at which Lacan announced the dissolution of his School.

39. Žižek, *The Sublime Object of Ideology*, p. 62. The fact that there is always a subject *par excellence* (the subject of lack) as well as the real *par excellence* (the real as enjoyment, or surplus-enjoyment) is symptomatic of the mechanism by which Žižek produces the irrefutable radicalism of his anti-philosophical act – an act which should *not* be confused with Badiou's notion of the event.

40. Žižek, *The Metastases of Enjoyment*, p. 61; *The Sublime Object of Ideology*, p. 124. See also Mladen Dolar, 'Beyond Interpellation', *Qui Parle* 6.2 (1993): 73–96; Judith Butler, *The Psychic Life of Power: Theories in Subjection* (Stanford, CA: Stanford University Press, 1997), pp. 106–31; and Alenka Zupančič, *Ethics of the real: Kant, Lacan* (London and New York: Verso, 2000), who concludes the debate most succinctly: 'The (psychoanalytic) subject is nothing but the failure to become an (Althusserian) subject' (pp. 41–2 n. 11).

41. Žižek, *The Metastases of Enjoyment*, pp. 135–6, n. 18.

42. Badiou, 'Le (re)commencement du matérialisme dialectique', p. 445.

43. Badiou, *Deleuze*, p. 8; *Théorie du sujet*, p. 13.

44. These texts are taken up posthumously, under the apt subheadings 'Textes de crise' and 'Louis Althusser après Althusser', in *Écrits philosophiques et politiques*, ed. François Matheron (Paris: Stock/IMEC, 1994), vol. I, pp. 367–537, 553–94, translated in Louis Althusser, *Philosophy of the Encounter: Later Writings, 1978–1987*, translated and introduced by G.M. Goshgarian (London and New York: Verso, 2006). For the importance of these texts, see, among others, Gregory Elliott, 'Ghostlier Demarcations: On the Posthumous Edition of Althusser's Writings', *Radical Philosophy* 90 (1998): 20–32.

45. Althusser, 'Le courant souterrain du matérialisme de la rencontre,' in *Écrits philosophiques et politiques*, p. 584. For a short, slightly bitter criticism of this unfinished text, see Pierre Raymond, 'Le matérialisme d'Althusser', in *Althusser philosophe*, ed. Pierre Ramond (Paris: PUF, 1997), pp. 167–79.

46. Alain Badiou, *Théorie de la contradiction* (Paris: Maspero, 1975), p. 9; Badiou with François Balmès *De l'idéologie* (Paris: Maspero, 1976), p. 7.

47. Badiou and Balmès, *De l'idéologie*, p. 19. For a summary of this early phase of Badiou's writings, see Jason Barker, 'Maoist Beginnings', in *Alain Badiou: A Critical Introduction* (London: Pluto Press, 2002), pp. 12–38.

48. See the appendix in Jacques Lacan, *L'envers de la psychanalyse* (Paris: Seuil, 1991), p. 239.

49. Badiou, *Théorie du sujet*, p. 198.

50. Badiou, *Théorie du sujet*, p. 24.

51. Badiou, *Théorie du sujet*, pp. 32, 40. A whole chapter in Badiou's *Le Siècle* is devoted to the particularly violent episode of this struggle in the ideological history of the Chinese Cultural Revolution, between the defendants of the idea that 'Two fuse into One' and the adherents of 'One divides into Two'. See 'Un se divise en deux', *Le Siècle*, pp. 89–101. See also Badiou's earlier commentary in the footnotes to *Le noyau rationnel de la dialectique hégélienne* (Paris: Maspero, 1978).

52. Badiou, *Théorie du sujet*, pp. 29–30. One of Althusser's most breathtaking texts, 'Le "Piccolo", Bertolazzi et Brecht', in *Pour Marx*, is the closest he comes to Badiou's philosophy and theory of the subject, including the false dialectic of melodrama, which opposes the Hegelian Beautiful Soul to the corrupt outside world, and this extremely condensed version of dialectical time in the process of torsion: 'A time moved from within by an irresistible force, and producing its own content. It is a dialectical time *par excellence.*

A time that abolishes the other one,' that is, the empty time without history, 'together with the structures of its spatial figuration' (p. 137).

53. Badiou, *Théorie du sujet*, p. 30. Badiou illustrates this dialectic with a lengthy excursion into the ancient history of the Christian Church, with its twin heresies: 'rightist' Arianism, for which Christ is wholly mortal, pure P; and 'leftist' Gnosticism, for which God is inhumanely divine, pure A. Given this crucial rereading of Hegel's dialectic and the history of Christianity, it is quite surprising to see that Badiou's *Théorie du sujet* is not even mentioned in Judith Butler's recently reissued *Subjects of Desire: Hegelian Reflections in Twentieth-Century France* (New York: Columbia University Press, 1999).

54. Badiou, *Théorie du sujet*, pp. 60, 30.

55. Jacques Lacan, *Écrits* (Paris: Seuil, 1966), p. 861.

56. Badiou, *Théorie du sujet*, p. 81.

57. Badiou, *Théorie du sujet*, p. 89.

58. Badiou, *Théorie du sujet*, pp. 151–2.

59. Badiou, *Théorie du sujet*, pp. 115, 52.

60. Badiou, *Théorie du sujet*, p. 126; Jacques Lacan, *Le Séminaire XX, Encore* (Paris: Seuil, 1975), p. 79. Following Badiou's own reading, I have added a double emphasis in my version of this sentence, which is nearly untranslatable: 'Quand un fait deux, il n'y a jamais de retour. Ça ne revient pas à faire de nouveau un, même un nouveau.' See Badiou, *Théorie du sujet*, pp. 131–2.

61. Badiou, *Théorie du sujet*, p. 200.

62. Badiou, *Théorie du sujet*, pp. 150–51.

63. Badiou, *Théorie du sujet*, p. 145.

64. Badiou, *Théorie du sujet*, pp. 243–4.

65. Badiou, *Théorie du sujet*, p. 149.

66. Badiou, *Théorie du sujet*, p. 41. In the Lacanian school, the *passe* describes the end of an analysis when the position of the analysand gives way to that of the analyst. Badiou's use of the concept in *Théorie du sujet* and *L'Être et l'événement* is clearly inspired by this definition, but it is not restricted to the therapeutic situation. Among the numerous references on the topic, I want to mention the remarkable testimonies in the collective volume *La passe et le réel: Témoignages imprévus sur la fin de l'analyse* (Paris: Agalma, 1998).

67. Badiou, *Théorie du sujet*, pp. 27, 59. The two sentences are nearly untranslatable: 'Tout ça qui est se rapporte à ça dans une distance de ça qui tient au lieu où ça est', and 'Il arrive, disons, que "*ça* fasse '*je*'".

68. Badiou, *Théorie du sujet*, pp. 172, 307.

69. Jacques Lacan, *Le Séminaire I, Les écrits techniques de Freud* (Paris: Seuil, 1975), pp. 164–65.

70. Jacques Lacan, *Le Séminaire I, Les écrits techniques de Freud* (Paris: Seuil, 1975), p. 309.

71. Badiou, *Théorie du sujet*, pp. 176–7, 310.

72. Badiou, *Théorie du sujet*, pp. 176–7.

73. Badiou, *Théorie du sujet*, p. 277. For a further discussion of this alternative for the sinister future of the Left in the aftermath of 1968, not only in France but also and especially in Mexico, see my 'Travesías del fantasma: Pequeña metapolítica del 68 en México', *Metapolítica* 12 (1999): 733–68. Here I compare Badiou's position, together with José Revueltas and Paco Ignacio Taibo II, to those more akin to the deconstructive

redefinitions of, and retreats from, the political by Jean-Luc Nancy and Philippe Lacoue-Labarthe.

74. Badiou, *Théorie du sujet*, p. 178. In the final theses of his *Rhapsodie pour le théâtre* (Paris: Imprimerie Nationale, 1990), Badiou raises an even more wide-ranging question: Why tragedy? Why not comedy? This brief treatise, I might add in passing, is in many ways the closest relative of *Théorie du sujet* among Badiou's later works.

75. Badiou, *Théorie du sujet*, p. 182.

76. Badiou, *Théorie du sujet*, p. 46.

77. Badiou, *Conditions*, p. 234 n. 41; *Manifeste pour la philosophie* (Paris: Seuil, 1989), p. 91. The political suturing of Badiou's early philosophy has left an unmistakable trace in his later work: the wordplay on the 'state of the situation' and the modern political 'state'. How this play would work for the three other conditions is not always equally clear.

78. 'Sur le XXé siècle et la politique', *La Distance Politique* 35 (2001): 3–4. All articles in this newsletter are anonymous, but for similar arguments about the fate of the party-form, see Badiou's *Le Siècle*. L'Organisation Politique, founded in 1985, gathers members of the Maoist Union des communistes de France marxiste-léniniste (UCFML), which in turn emerged in 1970 amidst the worldwide revolutionary sequence of 1966–76. For more information, see the recently published theses or guidelines of the group, in *Qu'est ce que l'Organisation politique?* (Paris: Le Perroquet, 2001). Badiou discusses some of the recent activities of this group in his interview with Peter Hallward, reprinted as an 'Appendix: Politics and Philosophy', in *Ethics*, pp. 95–144.

79. Alain Badiou, *Saint Paul: La fondation de l'universalisme* (Paris: PUF, 1997), p. 2. Much more careful attention should be paid to this recent rebirth of interest in saintly figures – from Saint Augustine for Jean-François Lyotard or León Rozitchner to Saint Paul for Badiou and Žižek, all the way to Saint Francis for Michael Hardt and Toni Negri.

80. Badiou, *L'Être et l'événement* (Paris: Seuil, 1989), p. 10.

81. For a more detailed discussion of the Heideggerian and Lacanian legacy in Badiou's philosophy, see my 'Vérité et forçage: Badiou avec Heidegger et Lacan', in *Alain Badiou: Penser le Multiple*, ed. Charles Ramond (Paris: L'Harmattan, 2002), pp. 259–93.

82. Badiou, *Théorie de la contradiction*, pp. 27, 86. For a ferocious attack upon these and other comparable statements from Badiou's early Maoist work, see Jean-Marie Brohm, 'La réception d'Althusser: histoire politique d'une imposture', in Denise Avenas, *et al.*, *Contre Althusser. Pour Marx* (Paris: Éditions de la Passion, 1999), pp. 278–87.

83. Badiou, *L'Être et l'événement*, p. 446.

84. Badiou, *L'Éthique* (Paris: Hatier, 1994), p. 76. Much of Badiou's *Le Siècle* is also devoted to this alternative between destruction and subtraction, especially in art, as answers to the question of the end and the beginning that haunts the entire century – or, rather, Badiou's 'brief' twentieth century, from the Revolution of 1917 until the period of what he calls the Restoration in the 1980s.

85. Quoted and commented by Althusser, *Pour Marx*, pp. 87–8.

86. Badiou, *Théorie du sujet*, p. 234.

87. Badiou, *Manifeste pour la philosophie*, p. 12.

88. Badiou, *L'Être et l'événement*, p. 14.

89. Badiou, *L'Être et l'événement*, p.113.

90. Badiou, *L'Être et l'événement*, pp. 113, 309.

91. Badiou, *L'Être et l'événement*, p. 97.

92. Badiou, *L'Être et l'événement*, p. 471.

93. Badiou, *L'Être et l'événement*, p. 311.

94. Žižek, *The Sublime Object of Ideology*, pp. 221, 176.
95. Žižek, 'The Politics of Truth', in *The Ticklish Subject, passim.*
96. Badiou, *Manifeste pour la philosophie* p. 89; *Saint Paul*, p. 16.
97. Badiou, 'Le forçage: vérité et sujet. Au-delà de Lacan', in *L'Être et l'événement*, pp. 427–75. Part of this meditation has been translated into English as 'Descartes/Lacan', in *UMBR(a): A Journal of the Unconscious* 1 (1996): 13–17. In the same issue, see also the excellent introductions to Badiou's work by Sam Gillespie and Bruce Fink.
98. For a good summary of this recent self-criticism, see Badiou's Preface to the Spanish edition of *L'Être et l'événement* in *El ser y el acontecimiento*, trans. Raúl J. Cerdeiras, Alejandro A. Cerletti and Nilda Prados (Buenos Aires: Manantial, 1999), pp. 5–8. See also my review of this translation in *Cuadernos de Filosofía* (forthcoming).
99. See my arguments in 'Badiou without Žižek' (see note 101 below) and 'The Žižekian Act' (forthcoming). Lacan, incidentally, began to develop his own understanding of the act in his seminar *L'acte psychanalytique*, which was interrupted by the events of May '68 in France. A comparison between Žižek and Badiou's theory of the subject, I should add, is seriously hindered by terminological matters – with Žižek calling 'subject' (of lack) and 'subjectivation' (as interpellation) what for Badiou would be more akin, respectively, to (evanescent, hysterical) 'act of subjectivation' and (consistent, masterly) 'subjective process'. Invoking opposite reasons yet using the same terms, each thinker could thus accuse the other for remaining at the level of mere subjectivation!
100. Badiou, *Théorie axiomatique du sujet*, seminars of 4 December 1996 and 9 January 1997.
101. Since the publication of the earlier version of this article, I have taken on this task myself in 'Badiou without Žižek', *The Philosophy of Alain Badiou*, ed. Matthew Wilkins, special issue of *Polygraph: An International Journal of Culture & Politics* 17 (2005): 221–44.
102. Badiou, interview with the author, taped on 10 June 1999. See Bosteels, 'Can Change Be Thought: A Dialogue with Alain Badiou', *Alain Badiou: Philosophy and its Conditions*, ed. Gabriel Riera (Albany, NY: SUNY Press, 2005), p. 252.
103. Badiou, *Théorie axiomatique du sujet*, seminar of 14 January 1998. See also Badiou, *L'Éthique*, pp. 70, 78. In fact, the figure of (re)commencement is a constant throughout Badiou's work. See, for example, the interview with Natacha Michel about *Théorie du sujet*, 'Renaissance de la philosophie', *Le Perroquet* 6 (1982): 1, 8–10; 13–14 (1982): 1, 10–13; or the article about Marxism which anticipates Badiou's arguments in *Peut-on penser la politique?*, 'La figure du (re)commencement', *Le Perroquet* 42 (1984): 1, 8–9.

II Art

8

The 'Concrete Universal', and What Comedy Can Tell Us About It

Alenka Zupančič

In view of the numerous references to Hegel in Lacan's work, it might seem very odd to include Hegel among Lacan's silent partners. And yet, if there is a Hegel who is indeed a very loud partner of Lacan – although his voice is, more often than not, that of Kojève – there is also another Hegel who fully qualifies for the role of Lacan's silent partner – a Hegel who is present most prominently at the very moments when he seems to be furthest away from Lacan's thoughts and words. Both Hegel and Lacan would probably agree that, in order for such silent dialogue and affinity to be properly heard, they have to pass through a third instance in which they can resonate. In what follows, I take comedy to be just such a third instance.

The Absolute on the couch

There is little doubt that among classical philosophers, Hegel was the one to value comedy and the comic spirit most highly. In the *Phenomenology of Spirit* he considers comedy to be the most accomplished spiritual work of art, elaborating on it – briefly but concisely – within the triad epos–tragedy–comedy that concludes the section on 'Religion in the form of art'. The fact that Hegel discusses art within the section on religion demands some preliminary remarks concerning the structure of the *Phenomenology* and the status of the discussion of art in it. Without entering into a detailed account of the construction of this unique philosophical work (which is still subject to considerable debate, partly because Hegel changed his original plans as he went along), let me just point out some general outlines. The *Phenomenology* falls into two big triads. The first is formed by sections on Consciousness, Self-Consciousness and Reason, the second by sections on Spirit, Religion and Absolute Knowledge. I will leave the first triad aside. We thus have Spirit, Religion and Absolute Knowledge in a triad that seems to represent an almost caricaturist peak of idealism, yet with several rather astonishing twists to it.

For Hegel, Spirit is nothing other than the world; as such, it is most material – it is, so to speak, a materialist reversal of the movement Consciousness–Self-Consciousness–Reason, where all shapes of consciousness are still only 'abstract forms of it'.[1] Reason becomes Spirit when it is conscious of itself as its own world, and of the world as itself. The shapes or figures [*Gestalten*] of the Spirit are now 'real Spirits, actualities in the strict meaning of the word, and instead of being shapes merely of consciousness, are shapes of the world' (*PS*, 265). In a word, Spirit is reason as materially existing, above all in the ethical life and practices of a community. The section on Spirit thus covers (from this new standpoint, which is the standpoint of community) history, starting from Greek Antiquity (the immediacy of Spirit – the ethical order); it continues with the process of *Bildung*, Culture, where the world of the Spirit breaks in two and is alienated from itself (this is where the history of Christianity comes in), up to the point where (after the Enlightenment and the French Revolution) Spirit appears in the shape of 'Morality' as 'Spirit that is certain of itself', Spirit that has done away with the Other world. This concludes the section on Spirit. Here, on the threshold of the section on Religion, there is a very significant shift of perspective. If, in the section on Spirit, the emphasis is on how Spirit (as world) appears to consciousness, and how the latter conceives it, in the section on Religion the emphasis is on the question of how Spirit (or the Absolute) conceives itself. We are dealing with two different emphases: the duality or tension between 'in itself' and 'for consciousness', of course, remains, and the way consciousness perceives or grasps the Absolute remains, also in the section on Religion, an important motor of the dialectical movement. For the sake of better conceptual clarity, however, we can sharpen things a little, and say: consciousness and the Absolute, which are indispensable agents in both sections, exchange roles. If, prior to this section, the principal role belonged to consciousness which, in the spirit of the world, had to come to its own Absolute, the main role now goes to the Absolute, which has to achieve its self-consciousness. The section on Religion is thus a peculiar 'Divine Comedy', in which what is at stake is, so to speak, a 'consciousness-raising' of the Absolute itself (that is to say, of the Absolute as materially existing in different forms of religion and art). The question is no longer simply that of how consciousness conceives of or sees the Absolute, but also of how the Absolute sees itself. It is this second, rather unique perspective that prompted one of the great interpreters of Hegel, Jean Hyppolite, to suggest that in the section on Religion we are no longer dealing just with 'phenomenology of spirit' but also, and above all, with its 'noumenology'.[2]

As for the status of the section on Religion (in which the discussion of comedy also appears), we could say that Hegel's paradoxical – and ultimately atheist – wager lies in the following: it is not enough that consciousness comes to know that it is itself the source and the drive of that Absolute Spirit which, from a certain point on, appears to it as its unattainable Beyond, its Other (and that it reappropriates it or declares its illusory character, the fact that it is but a product of consciousness itself). Hegel's point is that Absolute Spirit as the product of consciousness is, precisely as this product, something real, something that has material and historical existence. (One could say that, in this respect, Hegel anticipates the Althusserian thesis about the materiality of ideology – are not what Althusser calls 'Ideological State Apparatuses' precisely one of the forms in which spirit exists as the world?)

And this is the cause of the ultimate impotence of the reason of Enlightenment, the reason which knows that the Other (world) does not exist, yet remains powerless in the face of all the practices (including its own) which, in spite of that knowledge, still keep manifesting some form of religious beliefs. '*Je sais bien, mais quand même . . .*' (I know very well, but still . . .) is a quasi-universal paradigm of the post-Enlightenment belief which, to a large extent, we still share today. Since we will be discussing comedy, it is perhaps not so inappropriate to point out that at stake here is precisely the paradigm of the following joke: a man believes that he is a grain of seed. He is taken to a mental institution, where the doctors do their best finally to convince him that he is not a grain, but a man. As soon as he leaves the hospital, he comes back very scared, claiming that there is a chicken outside the door, and that he is afraid that it will eat him. 'Dear fellow,' says his doctor, 'you know very well that you are not a grain of seed, but a man.' 'Of course *I* know that,' replies the patient, 'but does the chicken?' In a word: it is not enough that we know how things really stand; in a certain sense, things themselves have to realize how they stand. In the context of the confrontation between Enlightenment and religion, this joke could perhaps be reformulated as follows. In the enlightened society of, say, revolutionary terror, a man is put in prison because he believes in God. By various means, but above all by means of an enlightened explanation, he is brought to the knowledge that God does not exist. When he is freed, the man comes running back and explains how scared he is of being punished by God. Of course he knows God does not exist, but does God know too?

In a certain sense, the whole section on Religion in the *Phenomenology of Spirit* represents Hegel's most extraordinary attempt at staging this other movement in which Absolute Spirit itself has to reach the conclusion that it does not exist (outside the concrete consciousness of people and of the world). This section is thus the other (or the obverse) side of the phenomenology of spirit; it is a paradoxical, almost postmodern story about how the narrative of the experience of consciousness is seen and read by what this same experience of consciousness produces in its historic movement. And – if we refer again to the above joke – in this perspective, the 'Absolute Knowledge' that follows the chapter on religion and concludes the *Phenomenology* is nothing but a paradoxical coincidence of the knowledge of the patient with the knowledge of the chicken.

Here we can, of course, note a crucial affinity between this double movement and what is at stake in psychoanalysis. In psychoanalysis (if it is worthy of its name) the main problem also does not lie simply in the subject becoming conscious of her unconsciousness, of all that (often painfully) determines her actions and experiences. This is insufficient: the main problem is precisely how to shift and change the very symbolic and imaginary structures in which this unconsciousness is embodied outside 'herself', in the manner and rituals of her conduct, speech, relations to others – in certain situations that keep 'happening' to her. In short, it is not simply that in analysis the subject has to shift her position (or even 'adapt' herself); the major part of the analytic work consists precisely in shifting the 'external practices', in moving all those 'chickens' in which the subject's unconsciousness (and her relation to herself) are externalized. And one of the major obstacles that can occur in analysis is precisely that the subject can become all too eager to change herself and her perception of the world, convinced that in analysis she will experience a kind of intimate revelation on account of which everything will be different and easier when she re-enters the world. In other words, the subject is ready to do quite a lot, change radically, if only she can remain unchanged in the Other (in the Symbolic as the external world in which, to put it in Hegel's terms, the subject's consciousness of herself is embodied, materialized as something that still does not know itself as consciousness). In this case, belief in the Other (in the modern form of believing that the Other does not know) is precisely what helps to maintain the same state of things, regardless of all subjective mutations and permutations. The subject's universe will really change only at the moment when she attains the knowledge that the Other knows (that it does not exist).

What Lacan and Hegel share in this respect is that they both take this dimension of the Other extremely seriously – not as a subjective illusion or spell that could be broken simply by saying out loud that 'the Other doesn't exist' (just consider how this [nowadays] common theoretical mantra coexists perfectly well with all sorts of secret or not-so-secret beliefs), but as something which, despite its nonexistence, has considerable material effects. Yet they also share their resistance to the opposite move: that of elevating the Other to the dignity of an impenetrable Otherness which, when facing the subject, becomes, for example, the touchstone of the ethical. What can be so traumatic about (encountering) Otherness is its dimension of Sameness. Precisely by being the *same*, the Other is not reducible to the subject. What is at stake here is not the identity of the Otherness but, rather, the Otherness of identity itself. Other(ness) has its place in the very gap that separates or prevents any identity/sameness from coinciding with itself in any immediate way.

This is why, for Lacan, the real point at which something in this relationship can be effectively shifted is not the abolition of Otherness, or its absorption into the subject, but the coincidence of the lack in the subject with the lack in the Other. This is a short circuit of internal external, not an elimination of one or the other. For this short circuit or local covering over of two to occur, work on the subject, as an internal work on consciousness, is not enough; a work on the Other is also needed. In psychoanalysis, the condition of this work on the Other is transference. And transference is ultimately nothing but the subject's trust in her own sameness or identity, working outside her, in the Other. This trust or 'credit' is needed, because the subject has no immediate control over what her sameness does, and how it speaks in this exteriority.

It is this feature that we could call the comic dimension of analytic experience. I am referring here to the autonomy of the (subject's) sameness that is working 'out there'. And the analyst is not – as is sometimes thought – the authority that simply refers the subject back to herself, pointing out how she is in fact responsible for what is so systematically 'happening' to her; the analyst is, rather and above all, the authority that has to give all this 'happening' the *time* (and the space) to come to the subject. This could be one of the main reasons for the long duration of analysis, for the precipitation of knowledge does not really solve anything: we can come to know what there is to know quite soon in this process, yet this insight of knowledge is not enough; the work of analysis is also needed, the work that is not simply the work of analysing (things), but much more the work of repetition, work as 'entropy'. In analysis, the subject very often rushes in different directions, each time expecting to find some salutary knowledge, some secret formula that will deliver her from her pain. And as a rule, she comes again and again, through all these different paths, to the same things and knowledge that keeps repeating itself. The subject often goes along the same paths again and again.

Yet this work, in all its entropy, is precisely not empty, it is not wasted time, it is what is needed for knowledge (that can be present from a very early stage) to come to the place of truth.

But let us return to Hegel. Before we move on to what he has to say on the subject of comedy, just a few final remarks and orientation points. 'Religion in the form of art' appears between 'Natural Religion', with which we start, and 'The Revealed Religion', with which we conclude. Given how Hegel situates it within the historical side of the *Phenomenology*, Religion in the form of art covers exclusively the period of Ancient Greece: sculpture, hymn-lyric, and the movement of Cult ('the abstract work of art'), Dionysian celebrations ('the living work of art'), and the Greek epics, tragedy and comedy ('the spiritual work of art'). In this last complex, which interests us, we are thus actually dealing with a very narrow and precise segment of art, represented by the names of Homer (the epics), Aeschylus and Sophocles (tragedy), and Aristophanes (comedy). So, not only does Hegel discuss art in the section on religion, he is also discussing a very specific moment of art. And we might ask what we should expect from this kind of overdetermined (by the question of religion) and at the same time extremely limited (in its references) discussion of art? Is it not all too obvious that Hegel simply and skilfully uses certain forms of art to fill in the speculative framework that he develops and constructs independently of them, the framework of self-representation of Absolute Spirit? To a certain extent, this is entirely true. Art is not an immediate subject of discussion, but appears and comes to life in the process of discussing something else. This is not exactly what we might call today an immanent approach to art (although one is often led to wonder what this immanent approach is actually supposed to mean); yet it is not a simple gesture of application either. Hegel does not apply his concepts to different forms of art, but introduces the latter as cases of concretely existing moments of the concept, and this indirect approach allows him to propose several very precious insights. This is especially true of his comments on comedy.

Thus, in the few pages dedicated to comedy in the *Phenomenology of Spirit* we must not look for some all-encompassing theory of comedy that would allow us, among other things, to distinguish conceptually between different periods and authors of comedy, as well as different comical procedures that they create and use in their work. What we will be looking for is something else, something that could be a very productive starting point for a philosophical discussion of comedy: what is the singular moment of the Spirit that is at work in comedy? Instead of trying to deduce a common essence from the multiplicity of different comedies, we will rather embark, with Hegel, on a journey of a philosophical construction of the 'comic perspective', which, as I hope to show, not only significantly challenges and undermines many of the received ideas on what comedy is and how it works, but also invites a broader discussion of several central points of religion, philosophy and psychoanalysis, and especially those related to claims about human finitude, which will be addressed (and also questioned) in the last section of this chapter.

Comedy as the Universal-at-work

If we are properly to appreciate Hegel's comments on comedy, it is now necessary briefly to sketch out his remarks on the epic and on tragedy, which immediately precede and lead to the discussion of comedy.

The key issue of the entire section on the spiritual work of art is representation. It is precisely the (gradual) abolition of representation that puts the three genres of epic, tragedy and comedy in a succession that is not simply historical, but also dialectical. The starting point of the 'spiritual work of art' is a split or duality that has several names: human/divine, subject (self)/substance, contingency/necessity, individual/universal, self-consciousness/external existence, essential world/world of action. We are thus dealing with a rather brutal duality of the world where notions such as essence, substance, necessity, universal (and the corresponding entities – gods) stand opposed to those of appearance, the subject, contingency, the individual (and, of course, the entities that correspond to these notions – human beings). The key question concerns the relationship between these couples, and it is precisely with this question that the destiny of representation will be played out. All three forms of spiritual art mediate – each in its own way – the terms of this duality.

In the universe of the epic we thus have, on the one hand, ordinary people and, on the other, the gods, the epic being precisely a 'synthetic linking together' of the two terms, their 'mixture' [*Vermischung*]. What characterizes the formal structure of the epic is, first, that the content (the relation between the human and the divine) is, for the first time, *presented* to consciousness (i.e. represented). The mode of the epic is thus the mode of narrative as representation, and the process of mixture appears at that level. How? As the mixture of universal and individual: the medium of the epic is language, which belongs to the universal, yet – and at the same time – the Minstrel is an individual who, as a subject of this world, produces and bears this language. The extreme of universality, the world of gods, is linked with individuality, with the Minstrel. They are linked through the middle term of particularity, which is simply the nation embodied in its heroes, who are individual men like the Minstrel, yet present and thereby at the same time universal. This is basically the form of syllogism that Hegel recognizes in the epic. At its core, the representation is thus nothing but 'a synthetic combination of the universal and the individual'. Yet this combination or linking remains external: the principle of action, which belongs to the subject or the self, is, so to speak, projected on to universal powers (gods) from the outside ('from the other side'); it is applied to them. The universal powers have the form of individuality and the principle of action: their actions are identical to those of men; universal powers act like humans. But, at the same time, these universal powers remain the universal that withdraws from the connection with the concrete: they are the universal that remains unrestricted in its own specific character (gods are individual gods, set up one against the other, yet their divine existence is independent of individuality). To put it simply: the limitation of this kind of universal is precisely that it is *not really limited* by its own concrete individuality, but remains above it. This, for Hegel, is the weakness (and not, perhaps, the strength) of this universal. It is the kind of universal that 'through the invincible elasticity of its unity effaces the atomistic singleness of the doer and his constructions, preserves itself in its purity and dissolves everything individual in its fluid nature' (*PS*, 442). Concrete subjects, with their determinate nature, cannot find themselves in this purity. As such, this universal and its powers remain a 'void of necessity' that floats above the heroes and everything else.

We now come to the next form of spiritual work of art, tragedy, which – far from being an antithesis of the epic, as one sometimes too automatically expects from Hegel – gathers closer together the dispersed moments of the inner essential world and the world of action. In Greek tragedy, the language is no longer simply a universal medium of representation, it ceases to be narrative and enters into the content: instead of being spoken about, the heroes now speak for themselves, they are the speakers. So the content ceases to be representative, although, as we shall see, the moment of representation remains present in tragedy on another level. The performance displays to the audience – who are also spectators – 'self-conscious human beings who *know* their rights and purposes, the power and the will of their specific nature and now how to *assert* them' (*PS*, 444). These are now *characters* that exist as actual human beings who impersonate the heroes and portray them not in the form of narrative, but in the actual speech and action of the actors themselves. In other words, via the actors, the universal itself starts to speak. We could say that if the epic introduces and practises the form of *narrating* the Essence, tragedy introduces and practises the form of *(en)acting* or staging it.

With tragedy, we are dealing with real human beings, the actors, who put on their *masks* and represent the essence with the help of the mask. The self of an individual (the actor) puts on a mask and, with it, puts on the character he is playing. In this way we come to a new mode of representation, which is not narrative (and in this sense figurative, imaginary), but is linked to the Real of the mask itself as the gap or the interval between the actor and the character. The mask as such has no content, it is more like pure surface – or, most literally, it is the inter-face – that separates the self of the actor from his stage character as (represented) essence. When the actor puts on the mask, he is no longer himself; in the mask, he brings to life the (universal) essence he represents. This means, however, that here also the essence ultimately exists only as the universal moment, separated by the mask from the concrete and actual self, and that as such this essence is still not actual. The self appears merely as *assigned* to the characters.

The union between self-consciousness and substance or faith thus remains external, it is 'a hypocrisy, . . . the hero who appears before the onlookers splits up into his mask and the actor, into the person in the play and the actual self' (*PS*, 450). We could also say that the actor, who is there to represent the essence, has to make us forget his actual self, and see only the sublime character as essence. All that can remind us of the actual existence of the actor behind the mask (for instance, his body functions, slips, and so on) is disturbing to the effect of representation; it is bad representation, bad performance.

Now, how do things stand with comedy? There are many authors who see in comedy precisely the emphasis on this other, human side of representation which is a reminder of the 'physical' residue that the mask can never completely sublimate or absorb, a reminder of an irreducible (real) refusal of the symbolic gesture of representation, a kind of 'objection of conscience' that finds its voice in comedy. Unlike those authors who see comedy as representing or giving voice to the other side of representation, to its failure, Hegel goes considerably further and introduces a rather spectacular shift of perspective that one could formulate as follows: the comic character is not the physical remainder of the symbolic representation of essence; it is *this very essence as physical.* And this is precisely why, according to Hegel, the comic work of art does away with representation. How, and what does this mean?

With (Greek) tragedy and its mode of representation, we had, on the one side, abstract universality and Fate and, on the other, self-consciousness, the individual self that represented this fate as a stage character. With (Greek) comedy, says Hegel, 'the actual self of the actor coincides with what he impersonates (with his stage character), just as the spectator is completely at home in the drama performed before him and sees himself playing in it' (*PS*, 452). This passage is crucial, and demands commentary. We should not understand Hegel to be claiming that, in comedy, actors no longer act, but simply appear as themselves. A performance is still a performance, as Hegel himself is careful to point out. What loses the form of representation (that is, the form of being separated from the actual self) are universal powers, gods, Fate, essence. In comedy, 'the *individual self* is the negative power through which and in which the gods, as also their moment, . . . vanish' (*PS*, 452). However, continues Hegel, the individual self is not the emptiness of this disappearance but, on the contrary, preserves itself in this very nothingness, abides with itself and is the sole actuality. Through the fact that it is individual consciousness in the certainty of itself that exhibits itself as this absolute power, it has lost the form of something *(re)presented to consciousness*, something altogether *separate* from consciousness and alien to it (like the content of the epic or the essential characters in tragedy). This emphasis is absolutely essential. Absolute powers lose the form of things represented by appearing themselves as subjects or as concrete beings.

In order to unravel this highly condensed speculative argument, I propose the following reading. When comedy exposes to laughter, one after the other, all the figures of the universal essence and its powers (gods, morals, state institutions, universal ideas, and so on) it does so, of course, from the standpoint of the concrete and the subjective; and, on the face of it, we can indeed get the impression that in comedy, the individual, the concrete, the contingent and the subjective are opposing and undermining the universal, the necessary, the substantial (as their other). And this is, to be sure, the view that a great many authors propose as the paradigm of comedy. Hegel's point, however, is that in this very 'work of the negative' (through which comic subjectivity appears) comedy produces its own necessity, universality and substantiality (it is itself the only 'absolute power'), and it does so by revealing the figures of the 'universal in itself' as something that is, in the end, utterly empty and contingent.[3]

Comedy is not the undermining of the universal, but its (own) reversal into the concrete; it is not an objection to the universal, but the concrete labour or work of the universal itself. Or, to put it in a single slogan: *comedy is the universal at work.* This is a universal which is no longer (re)presented as being in action, but *is* in action. In other words, 'the negative power through which and in which the gods vanish' is precisely the power which has been previously (in the mode of representation) attributed to gods, and has now become the acting subject. To recapitulate: in the epic, the subject narrates the universal, the essential, the absolute; in tragedy, the subject enacts or stages the universal, the essential, the absolute; in comedy, the subject is (or becomes) the universal, the essential, the absolute. Which is also to say that the universal, the essential, the absolute become the subject.

In comedy, says Hegel, 'the Self is the absolute Being' (*PS*, 453). In comic consciousness, 'all divine being returns, or it is the complete alienation of substance' (*PS*, 455). That is to say: in comic consciousness, the substance is not alienated from the self or the subject (as it is in the 'unhappy consciousness'), it is alienated from itself, and this is the only way it comes to self-consciousness and to life in the strict meaning of the word. Comedy is not the story of the alienation of the subject, it is the story of alienation of the substance, which has become the subject.

It is hardly possible to overemphasize this crucial point. At first sight, it seems that in comedy all that is concrete, and belongs to the content, refutes/rebuts the universal-formal. There is no sacred thing or solidity that comedy could not rock to its foundations. Just think, for instance, of Monty Python's *The Meaning of Life*: a delirious comedy in which we, so to speak, laugh out, one after another, all human certainties and universal values. Yet Hegel's point is that this movement of revealing the universal as a 'play of the caprice of chance individuality' is possible only through a radical shift in the fundamental structure: in comedy, the universal is on the side of undermining the 'universal'; the comic movement, its 'negative power', *is the movement of the universal itself* (and precisely as *movement*, this universal is also the subject).

This also helps us to explain one rather paradoxical feature of comedy; 'paradoxical', since it appears to be in contradiction with the generally recognized materialism of comedy, its emphasis on the concrete and on the Real of human limitations and deficiencies. The comic universe is, as a rule, the universe of the indestructible (this feature is brought to its climax in cartoons, but is also present, in a more subtle way, in most comedies). Regardless of all accidents and catastrophes (physical as well as psychic or emotional) that befall comic characters, they always rise from the chaos perfectly intact, and relentlessly go on pursuing their goals, chasing their dreams, or simply being themselves. It seems that nothing can really get to them, which somehow contradicts the realistic view of the world that comedy is supposed to promote. To take a kind of archetypal example: a toffee-nosed baron slips on a banana skin (thus demonstrating that even he is subject to the laws of gravity), yet the next instant he is up again and walking around arrogantly, no less sure of the highness of His Highness, until the next accident that will again try to 'ground' him, and so on and so on. (Take, for example, Sir John Falstaff in Shakespeare's comedy *The Merry Wives of Winsdor.*)

How are we to understand this consistent feature of comedy, the surprising fact that in this genre of the concrete, the concrete does not seem really to get to people? As a matter of fact, the answer is quite simple. The constellation described looks like a paradox, in so far as we do not notice that in comedy, the abstract and the concrete have switched places at the very outset. What do we mean by this? Let us stay with the archetypal character of a buffoonish baron who implacably believes in his aristocratic superiority, although all through the comedy he stumbles, so to speak, from one muddy puddle to another. We have only to think about it a little in order to see that what we are dealing with here is in no way an abstract-universal idea (belief in the elevated nature of his own aristocratic personality) undermined, for our amusement, by intrusions of material reality. Or, to put it differently, we are not dealing with an abstract perfection, belied by human weaknesses and limitations to which this VIP is none the less subjected. On the contrary, is it not only too obvious that the capital human weakness here – what is most human, concrete and realistic – is precisely the baron's unshakeable belief in himself and his own importance: that is to say, his presumptuousness? *This* is the feature that makes him 'human', not the fact that he falls into a muddy puddle or slips on a banana skin. Banana skins, muddy puddles, and all the other devices through which reality reminds the comic character of its existence are ultimately much more abstract (and, let us not forget, often much more unrealistic) than the baron's very vivid and palpable belief in his own aristocratic Self. And, of course, we should not overlook the fact that what is really funny and makes us laugh most in our archetypal (imaginary) comedy is not simply that the baron falls into the puddle but, much more, that he *rises* from it and goes about his business, as if nothing had happened. The puddle itself is thus not the site of the concrete reality (in which anybody turns out to be only human), but one of the props or devices through which the very concreteness or humanity of the concept itself – in our case, the concept of baronage or aristocracy – is processed and crystallized. In other words, what is indestructible in comedies and comic characters is this very *movement* of concrete universality.

Here we also come to an important distinction between, I would venture to say, true and false comedies (a distinction that broadly corresponds to the distinction between subversive and conservative). It is not a question of *what* (which content) is subjected to comical treatment – Mother Teresa, Lenin, machismo, feminism, the institution of the family or the life of a homosexual couple – it is a question of the mode of comic processing itself. False, conservative comedies are those where the abstract-universal and the concrete do not change places and do not produce a short circuit between them; instead, the concrete (where 'human weaknesses' are situated) remains external to the universal, and at the same time invites us to recognize and accept it as the indispensable companion of the universal, its necessary physical *support.* The paradigm of these comedies is simply the following: the aristocrat (or king, or judge, or priest, or any other character of symbolic status) is *also* a man (who snores, farts, slips, and is subject to the same physical laws as other mortals). The emphasis is, of course, precisely on 'also': the concrete and the universal coexist, the concrete being the indispensable grounding of the universal. This is the great wisdom of those comedies which actually get stuck halfway down the path to the comical: we have to consider and accept the material, physical, concrete and human aspect of things, otherwise we will be carried into a dangerous abstract ideality, extremism, if not even fanaticism (for instance, that of forgetting our own limitations and our mortality) – as if this perspective of combining the universal and the concrete, the aristocrat and the man, were not in itself something utterly abstract. It runs out of steam precisely at the point where true comedy begins, and leaves all the universals, the human side of which it tries to expose, fundamentally untouched in their abstract purity, since the dirt is absorbed by the human side, which is then forgiven as belonging to the 'necessary evil'. (Thus, for example, in this case the comedy of baronage would never be exactly the comedy of baronage as such, but always that of its contingent bearers, particular individuals, who are 'only human'.) This kind of comedy remains caught in an abstract dualism of the concrete and the universal and, much as it may emphasize the side of the concrete, this concrete remains but one element in the constellation of the universal versus the concrete, which is itself purely abstract. The conservatism of this paradigm springs, of course, from the fact that it offers the audience, via the 'human' aspect, an identification with the baron as Ego-Ideal, which as such remains not only untouched, but even reinforced. We identify with heroes' weaknesses, yet their higher calling (or universal symbolic function) remains all the more the object of respect and fascination (instead of being the object of comic laughter).

So what, in this respect, is a true comedy? Comedy which does not try to seduce us into deceptive familiarity with the fact that His Highness is *also*, at the same time, or 'on the other hand', as human as the rest of us. A true comedy about a presumptuous baron has to produce the following formula in all its materiality: an aristocrat who believes that he is really and intrinsically an aristocrat is, *in this very belief*, a common silly human. In other words: a true comedy about aristocracy has to play its cards in such a way that the very universal aspect of this concept produces its own humanity, corporeality, subjectivity. Here, the body is not an indispensable basis of the soul; an inflexible belief in one's own baronage is precisely the point where the soul itself is as *corporeal* as possible. The concrete body of the baron, which repeatedly falls into the puddle of human weaknesses, is not simply the empirical body that lies flat in the mud, but much more the belief in his baronage, his 'baronness'. This 'baronness' is the real comic object, produced by comedy as the quintessence of the universal itself. To put it into psychoanalytic terms: here, the Ego-Ideal itself turns out to be the partial (comical) object, and ceases to be something with which we identify via the identification with one of the partial features of its reverse side. The Ego-Ideal directly *is* a human weakness – which is to say that, in this kind of comedy, the process of identification with the partial feature is, by virtue of its comic character, always also the process of disidentification. The point is not that an aristocrat is also an ordinary man. He is an ordinary man precisely *as an aristocrat*, at the very peak of his aristocracy. Here we should recall Lacan's famous remark that a lunatic is not some poor chap who believes that he is a king; a lunatic is a king who believes that he really is a king. Does this not hold even more for comedy? It is not some poor chap who believes himself to be a king who is comical (this is rather pathetic), but a king who believes that he really is a king.

Thus, the difference between subversive and conservative comedies does not lie in their content, in what is subjected to the comical procedure. This also means that we will not find it where some authors, following a sort of ascetic ethics, place it: in other words – and to put it simply – in the question of whether we are making fun of ourselves and our own beliefs, or of others and their beliefs. This distinction is invalid for several reasons, but principally for the following one. The direct parody of oneself and one's beliefs can very well flourish within the conservative paradigm of 'combining' the concrete and the universal. It can successfully promote the very ideology whose human side and weaknesses are being exposed. There are plenty of examples of this in several veins of Hollywood comedy, in which derision of our own beliefs and of the 'American way of life' produces the very distance necessary to sustain these very same beliefs and this very same way of life. Or – an even more obvious example – President Bush and his media strategy of mocking his own presidential self, which of course aims precisely at portraying the inflexible war President as 'the guy next door', as a fallible individual who is aware of his faults and imperfections. In this case, the wittiness functions precisely as a way of distancing oneself from one's own concreteness (which, of course, is the very opposite of the primacy of the concrete): one gets evacuated, so to speak, into one's wit or spirit, and the message sent out is that one is something *more* than one's miserable concrete self. The real comedy of

George W. Bush can be seen at times when he makes no effort to be funny, but solemnly appears as an American president who believes that he really is an American president. It is at these moments that he comes up with the most comical lines, the collection of which has become an Internet sport. Take a few examples: 'You teach a child to read, and he or her will be able to pass a literacy test' (Townsend, Tennessee, 21 February 2001). The following, probably most famous one, is almost worth the Freud-Heine 'famillionar' joke: 'They misunderestimated me' (Bentonville, Arkansas, 6 November 2000). Or one of the latest: 'Our enemies are innovative and resourceful, and so are we. They never stop thinking about new ways to harm our country and our people, and neither do we' (Washington, DC, 5 August 2004). Contrary to this, the other kind of Bush humour, with which he likes to demonstrate his ability to laugh at these miracles of wit that he keeps producing, is already a refashioning of the self-undermining power of 'Bushisms' themselves into a conservative way of accepting and tolerating pure stupidity ('What can we do? The President's only human').

So, to summarize, the difference between subversive and conservative comedy does not not lie in its content, or in the ideological position of the authors, or in the question of who the target is (our own ideological universe or the universe of others); it lies in the question of whether it touches the very universality of what it is showing – touches it, gets to it, sets it in a motion in which universal contents are particularized one after the other, and the only universal left is this very concrete *movement* of the universal.

But let us return to Hegel. Comedy is the moment in which substance, necessity and essence all lose their immediate – and thus abstract – self-identity or coincidence with themselves. This emphasis is important because it reminds us that the end of the mode of representation does not imply a return to immediacy or to an organic fusion of opposites. The substance becomes subject in the moment when, through a split in itself, it starts relating to itself. In this way we come not so much to the abolition of representation but, rather, to its new notion, which is in fact very close to the Lacanian concept of representation. Could we not say that in comedy, one moment of the substance represents the subject for another moment of the substance? If so, we could perhaps answer an objection that might be raised in relation to the Hegelian distinction between comedy and tragedy, as cited above. We saw that, according to Hegel, the main (formal) problem of tragedy is that it preserves the interval between the subject or the self and the character or stage person that the self is representing. With comedy, this interval is supposed to disappear. One might object to this by pointing out that it is precisely in comedy that we find a whole arsenal of various characters that exist quite independently of the concrete subjects, and they are occasionally assumed by these subjects as masks, for the purposes of comedy ('idiotic master', 'cunning servant', 'miser', 'shrew', 'tramp' . . .). On the other hand, tragedy seems to be much closer to an organic fusion of the actor and his character.

We will answer this objection by clarifying the misunderstanding that generates it. Tragedy can appear as an organic fusion or synthesis of the actor-subject and the character precisely because the subject represents the character (and the better the representation, the more powerful will be the feeling of fusion of these two, of the individual and the universal). Hegel would entirely agree with this, and he says as much himself. The problem is that, convincing as this fusion-in-representation might be, it still remains exactly that: a fusion of the two, an individual representation of the universal, without reaching the point where one of the two terms would generate the other from within itself, and become this other. To put it more precisely: we are still dealing with the classical mode of representation, a constellation of two elements in which one represents the other. What happens in comedy is that the subject changes its place. The subject is no longer the one who represents something (as actor, and with the help of his mask) and to whom (as spectator) something is represented. Recall Hegel's thesis that in comedy, 'the actual self of the actor coincides with what he impersonates (with his stage character), just as the spectator is completely at home in the drama performed before him, and sees himself playing in it'. This coincidence of the self (the actor) and his character means nothing but that the split between these two now moves to and inhabits that character itself (i.e. the essence), and it is precisely this inner split that constitutes the place of the subject in the character. This is why, when speaking of comedy, we cannot say that the subject-actor represents a (comic) character for the spectator, but that the subject-actor appears as that gap through which the character relates to itself, 'representing itself'.

We have a great example of this, which I like to cite, in one of the best (if not the best) film comedies ever made, Ernst Lubitsch's *To Be Or Not To Be.* At the beginning of the film, there is a brilliant scene in which a group of actors are rehearsing a play featuring Hitler. The director is complaining about the appearance of the actor who plays Hitler, insisting that his make-up is bad, and that he does not look like Hitler at all. He also says that what he sees in front of him is just an ordinary man. Reacting to this, one of the actors replies that Hitler *is* just an ordinary man. If this were all, we would be dealing with the logic of revealing 'fundamental truths', which remains stuck halfway in relation to the properly comic way of transmitting truths. So, the scene continues: the director is still not satisfied, and tries desperately to name the mysterious 'something more' that distinguishes the appearance of Hitler from the appearance of the actor in front of him. He searches and searches; finally, he sees a picture (a photograph) of Hitler on the wall, and triumphantly cries out: 'That's it! That's what Hitler looks like!' 'But sir,' replies the actor, 'That's a picture of me.' This, on the contrary, is really comical. The mysterious charisma of Hitler, the thing in Hitler more than a man-named-Hitler, emerges before us as the minimal difference between the actor who plays, represents, Hitler and the photograph of this same actor. In other words, the fact that the universal of the representation is related to *itself* produces the very concrete of the represented. In the form of a gag, this same procedure already appears immediately before the scene just described, in a rehearsal of the same play. We are in Gestapo headquarters, and somebody announces Hitler. The doors open, and everybody raises their hands with the salute 'Heil Hitler'. Hitler walks in, raises his hand, and says, 'Heil myself!'

It is precisely this relating of the 'universal essences' (characters) to themselves and to other 'universal essences' (the relating that always succeeds either too much or not enough – this is the surplus with which most comic situations and dialogues build) that creates the movement in which the universal becomes concrete, and becomes the subject. 'Stereotypical' characters as abstract universalities are set in motion and, through different accidents and events, the concrete, subjective universality is condensed or produced – the universal as subject, so convincing and powerful in good comedies. Just think of Chaplin's character, the Tramp. As such (or 'in itself') this character is perfectly stereotypical, and has been seen hundreds of times (if nowhere else, in Chaplin's own numerous silent comedies). Yet at the same time it would be hard to find something more concrete, subjective and universal in the same gesture as precisely the Tramp. But not only the Tramp. Just think of *The Gold Rush* or *Modern Times* – in both cases Chaplin appears with a generic name: 'Lone Prospector' in the first; 'Worker' in the second. We thus start with an abstract universality, which is not so much 'represented' by Chaplin as forced to rise/descend to the concrete universality of the individual we see on the screen. 'The Tramp', 'Lone Prospector' and 'Worker' are, in comedy, the very movement of becoming-'trampship', 'prospectorship', 'workership' – that is to say, (their) subject. If we think about it for a moment, we can see how in tragedy we are in fact dealing with an opposite motion. Here we always start with a very concrete and strong personality, a significant individual with a proper name that often gives the tragedy its title. It would be hard to imagine to have, as titles of tragedies, universal or generic names – to change, for example, the title *Antigone* into *The (Untamed) Shrew*, *Othello* into *The Jealous Husband, Romeo and Juliet* perhaps straight into *Love's Labour's Lost*. It would indeed be hard to do this and still remain on the territory of tragedy. This, of course, is no coincidence: the two dramatic practices involve opposite motions. In tragedy the acting subject, via the various ordeals that befall her, has to let – often at the price of her own death – some universal idea, principle or destiny shine through her. In comedy, in contrast, some universality ('tramp', 'worker', 'misanthrope' . . .) has to let a subject in all his concreteness shine through it – not as the opposite of this universal (or as its irreducible support), but as its own inherent truth, its flexibility and life.

This is why, for Hegel, comedy is not simply a turn from the universal (from universal values of the beautiful, the just, the good, the moral . . .) towards the individual or the particular (as always and necessarily imperfect, limited and always slightly idiotic), but corresponds instead to the very speculative passage from the abstract universal to the concrete universal. For Hegel, it is the abstract universal itself that is, by definition, imperfect and limited, because it lacks the moment of self-consciousness, of the self, of the concrete; it is universal and pure only at the price of being ultimately empty. The turn or shift at stake here is thus not a shift from the universal to something else, but a shift within the universal itself. The turn towards the individual is the turn of the universal itself, it is the risk and the trial of the universal. It is only as a concrete self that the universal comes to its own truth via the gap of self-consciousness. The concrete is not some unavoidable deformation of the universal, some often idiotic incorporation of an otherwise impeccable universal 'spiritual' Idea or Concept, but the touchstone of Spirit itself. This is to say – and to put it bluntly – that the universal itself is precisely as idiotic as its concrete and individual appearance. The universal that does not go through this process is not a true universal, but a mere general abstraction from the concrete. It is only with the concrete that we come to the real spirit of the universal, and we could say that the materialism of comedy is precisely the materialism of the spirit. (Linguistically, we are very well aware of this: language recognizes that comedy, precisely in its materialism, is a matter of spirit; this is evident in numerous terms that link the comic mode with spirit. Let me mention just a few: *wit* in English; *geistvoll* or *geistreich* in German, as well as *witzig* and *Witz*, which have the common root with the English *wit*; French is especially eloquent in this regard – *avoir de l'esprit, être spirituel, faire de l'esprit, mot d'esprit*, or just simply *esprit*.)

With this attested affinity between spirit and comedy, it comes perhaps as no surprise that comedy ranks high in the 'phenomenology of spirit'. And not just because of the term spirit – could we not say that the entire movement of the *Phenomenology of Spirit* is surprisingly akin to the comic movement as described by Hegel: different figures of consciousness which follow one upon the other in this gigantic philosophical theatre go, one after the other, through a twist in which a concrete universal is being produced and self-consciousness constituted – that is, in which substance becomes a subject. No wonder, then, that a good many of the chapter titles in *Phenomenology of Spirit* read as perfect comedy titles: 'Lord and Bondsman', 'The Unhappy Consciousness', 'Pleasure and Necessity', 'The Law of the Heart and the Frenzy of Self-Conceit', 'Absolute Freedom and Terror', 'Dissemblance or Duplicity', 'The Beautiful Soul' – not to mention the ultimate comedy (and this is not meant ironically!) bearing the title 'Absolute Knowledge'.

So it is not surprising that Lacan described Hegel's *Phenomenology* as *un humour fou*, a crazy humour.[4] This humour of Hegel's might strike us as especially crazy at the point where he works out and establishes a direct passage from comedy to the very core of Christianity (as revealed religion). At a time when, thanks to Mel Gibson, everybody has been talking about the Passion of Christ, his unimaginable suffering, it would perhaps be the right moment to lend an ear to the Hegelian story of the 'comedy of Christ'. But I will leave this until another time, and move on to the last part of my argument.

Physics of the infinite against metaphysics of the finite

Against the background of some of the crucial points about comedy developed above, I am prompted to challenge a somewhat pivotal point that is being all but constantly made, repeated, reaffirmed in the modern (and postmodern, or let us simply say post-Hegelian) discussion of comedy, a point which also situates this genre in a wider philosophical, political and ideological context. This point has various different formulations, which can be summed up as follows. Comedy is a genre that strongly emphasizes our essential humanity, its joys and limitations. It invites – or even forces – us to recognize and accept the fact that we are *finite, contingent* beings. It teaches us that we are *only human*, with all our faults, imperfections and weaknesses; and (for some authors) that beauty is in small, trivial, simple things (not in 'cold' universal ideals). Comedy is a monument to the awkward innocence of essential humanity, and it helps us to deal affirmatively and joyfully with the burden of human finitude.

It is rather amazing how these 'modern' views on comedy are irresistibly driven towards pathos (an affect which is, in fact, as far as possible from the true comic spirit), and how comedy's supposed celebration of human finitude often seems to be the principal argument when it comes to justifying serious theoretical or philosophical attention to this traditionally rather underrated genre. And if modern readers are often taken aback by Hegel's discussing comedy (and art) in the context of religion, they seem to have fewer problems embracing this kind of discussion, which can hardly be said to be any less overdetermined by a very similar set of questions. For quite some time, a lot of critical philosophical work has been dedicated to various ways of undermining the metaphysics of infinitude, and of transcendence. Yet we should not overlook the fact that there is also a considerable (modern) corpus of what I would call a *metaphysics of finitude* in which, often in the tone of pathos, mentioned above, finitude appears as *our* (contemporary) great narrative. The range of this metaphysics of finitude is considerable; it stretches from very complex and highly elaborate philosophical enterprises to an utterly common-sense 'psychotheology of everyday life' (to borrow Eric Santner's expression), in which finitude appears as consolation for, and explanation of, our little (or not so little) disappointments and misfortunes, as a new Master-Signifier summoned to make sense of our ('acknowledged') senseless existence, as a new Gospel or 'good news': You're only human! Give yourself a break! Nobody's perfect!

Those who recall the famous last scene from Billy Wilder's *Some Like It Hot* (the last sentence of the movie is precisely 'Nobody's perfect') know how spectacularly, and at the same time most precisely, comedy can subvert this great wisdom (which is even supposed to be the wisdom of comedy): nobody's perfect, therefore it doesn't matter what you say or do, or what you are; you'd better shut up and let us do exactly what we have in mind with you (for instance: marry you, as the gag goes in the movie). Or, in another comic twist on the theme of perfection: 'Nobody's perfect. I am nobody.'

The prizing of comedy as an exemplary case of finitude (and of everything that is supposed to be related to it: acceptance of our weaknesses, limitations and imperfections; reconciliation with the absence of the transcendental and acknowledgement of the equation 'a human is [only] human', 'life is [only] life') is conceptually highly problematic. Such perspective on comedy is much too simplistic, and soon turns out to be pretty useless. Is it not, rather, that the exact opposite rings truer? If humans were 'only human(s)' (and life 'only life'), if the human equation indeed added up so neatly and with no remainder, *there would be no comedy.* Is not the very existence of comedy and of the comical telling us most clearly that a man is never just a man, and that his finitude is very much corroded by a passion which is precisely not cut to the measure of a man and of his finitude? Most comedies set up a configuration in which one or several characters strongly depart from the moderate, balanced rationality and normality of their surroundings and of other people in it. And, if anything, it is precisely these other, 'normal' people who are 'only human' or 'only men', whereas this is far from the case with comic characters. Flaws, extravagances, excesses and so-called human weaknesses of comic characters are precisely what accounts for their *not* being 'only human'.

Thus, although it is true that comedy incites a certain good-humoured attitude towards human 'weaknesses', the important additional emphasis is that these weaknesses are precisely something on account of which a man is never only a man. We are not merely playing with words here, reversing their meaning. What is at stake is a point that is essential for the understanding of comedy: 'man', a human being, interests comedy at the very point where the human coincides with the inhuman; where the inhuman 'falls' into the human (into a man), where the infinite falls into the finite, where the Essence falls into appearance and the Necessary into the contingent. And if it is true that the comic universe – much more than the tragic universe – builds within the horizon of immanence, that it abandons the reference to the Beyond and always situates the Essence in a concretely existing situation, it does not do so simply by closing off its finite self in relation to the (infinite) Beyond, by excluding it from its field of reference. On the contrary, it does so by including it in the immanence, in the given situation. The Beyond is included in the world and in the human as the heterogeneous element on account of which a man is never simply and only a man. 'Man is only man' is the axiom of abstract idealism; basically, it states nothing but 'man is not God'. Whereas the true materialistic axiom, promoted by comedy, is, rather, 'a man is not (only) a man'. This is what the above-mentioned metaphysics of finitude fails to see when it encloses itself within a heart-stirring humanism of accepting human weaknesses and flaws.

To sum up: there is a significant attempt to think comedy through the notion of finitude (that is to say, of its acknowledgement and acceptance) and to promote comedy as the exemplar of the contemporary metaphysics of finitude. Contrary to this, one should insist that the true comic spirit, far from being reducible to this metaphysic of the finite, is, rather, always a 'physics of the infinite', (or even a 'corporeality of the infinite'). Moreover, it is precisely this physics of the infinite that situates comedy on the ground of true materialism, exempts it from all forms of spiritualism, and also gives it its contra-religious thrust – not in any simple sense of static opposition, or of mocking the infinite Other, but, rather, by deploying this infinite Other as the very material Real of human life as such.

What is the problem with the claim that comedy is fundamentally about accepting and becoming reconciled with our human finitude, and in what sense can this claim be seen as metaphysical? First, we note that it actually combines two fundamental claims: the claim about human finitude and the claim that this finitude is something that human beings cannot really accept and be reconciled to; this is supposed to be the core and the source of most problems and misfortunes of humanity, and of most of the ideologies it has produced in the course of history. Confronted – or so the story goes – with the cruel and irreversible fact of death, and the finitude that death implies, humanity, not being able to accept it, has set in motion an increasingly elaborated metaphysical machinery of another or parallel world (be it that of eternal Ideas or of God's kingdom), which helps it to deal with and surmount the thought of its own mortality, as well as to enslave a large portion of this same humanity with the promise of redemption. This narrative can take more elaborate and sophisticated forms, but it mostly comes down to an opposition or duality of the *Real* of death (the ultimate traumatic point) and a symbolic shield or network that we raise and/or use in dealing with it, in transforming it into something else. This account, far from explaining anything, actually fails to deal with the fundamental question: how do we come to experience our real death as traumatic – or, to put it even more directly, how do we come to experience our eventual death as real (as that Real which demands symbolic sheltering)? If death is simply this pure Real beyond all Symbolic and Imaginary, and also beyond our experience strictly speaking, how is it that we have any relation to it, whether of fear, anxiety, or anything else? Lacan's answer is that death enters our lives *as real* by virtue of the signifier – that is, precisely by virtue of the Symbolic:

> How can man, that is to say a living being, have access . . . to his own relationship to death? The answer is, by virtue of the signifier in its most radical form. It is in the signifier and insofar as the subject articulates a signifying chain that he comes up against that fact that he might be lacking from the chain of what [he] is.[5]

In other words, far from shielding us from death, the Symbolic is precisely our emphatic encounter with death as *real.* It introduces death into life (as part of our 'life experience') – not in the sense that we die only 'symbolically' (or that we can imagine ourselves dying or can talk about it: Lacan is not talking about the signifier 'death', but about any signifying chain), but in a much more fundamental sense in which by way of the signifier, of speech, death literally enters our life, the midst of our life, becomes part of our fundamental experiences, and gives form to whatever anxieties and feelings we might have in relation to the fact that one day, we will in fact die. Our way of entering speech and becoming subjects of the signifier is what constitutes our experience of death, and also provides the frame or paradigm of our relation to it. We are thus dealing with two levels or two dimensions of the Symbolic, which are intrinsically connected, but nevertheless different: that of going through 'death by the signifier', and that of being able to talk about it and relate to it. The first level is strictly speaking transcendental, or constitutive of our subjectivity and our experience as such. The fact that it comes from an altogether immanent dimension of human life – speech – does not make it any less transcendental in the sense defined above. (And one could maintain that there is no conceptually tenable theory of immanence that does not include this transcendental dimension, whatever name it gives it.)

In conclusion, I know death because I speak, and not necessarily of death. If I have anxieties about my death, it is because I speak. But this is also precisely what complicates the story about human finitude and our reluctance to accept it. How, then, does the Lacanian (and Hegelian) perspective differ from the contemporary *doxa* of human finitude? Certainly not by nurturing a belief in immortality, nor by maintaining that there is a part or a dimension of men – call it the soul or subject (as opposed to the individual or ego) – which is as such infinite. The difference is much more interesting. The predominant contemporary concept of human finitude is, of course, also not simply that of reminding us that sooner or later we will drop dead, and no soul will leave our body to join its heavenly Father. It refers – to put it simply – to limits and limitations of *living* human beings. Here finitude is but the emphatic notion or a Master-Signifier of all that human life implies in terms of limitations, of incompleteness, division, out-of-jointness, antagonism, exposure to the others, 'castration'; of impasses of desire, of two or more ends that never exactly coincide to form a perfect circle. It is about a chiasm that fundamentally determines human condition. Is it not also, however, that in this discourse, in the way it uses finitude as its Master-Signifier, the latter appears precisely as the closure of that which is said to resist any closure? This is most clearly detectible precisely in the redoubling of a description by prescription, in the passage from 'We are limited, divided, exposed beings' to 'Be limited, divided, exposed!' (i.e. you *must* accept this) – whereby the latter constitutes the ethical part of contemporary thought about human finitude. One can see here a kind of reversal of Wittgenstein and his 'Whereof one cannot speak, thereof one must remain silent'; it is not a paradoxical prohibition of the impossible but, rather, a paradoxical injunction of the possible, of what there is. Despite numerous references, in this ethics, to the possibility of change and of emancipatory politics, this possibility is largely blocked precisely by the imperative of the possible. In relation to this, the Lacanian stance is not – as it is sometimes described, or criticized – that of an imperative of the impossible, of forcing oneself (or others) beyond the limits of what is humanly possible; it concerns the ontological/conceptual status of these limits – and, more importantly, of death. The crucial difference between the Hegelian/Lacanian perspective and that of the contemporary *doxa* of finitude is that in the former, death is the *condition of possibility* of what is human (but also of what is inhuman); whereas in the latter, death is the *limit of possibility* of what is human (and it is also in this sense that I used the term 'closure' above).

A very significant characteristic (or symptom) of this ethics of human finitude is the way it usually approaches the question of excess. Different forms of excess (and especially that of violence and hatred) are seen not as belonging to the chain defined by human finitude (division, incompleteness, limitations . . .), but as resistance to finitude or to its acceptance. Violence and hatred cannot count as human weaknesses, for in this case we would be under an ethical imperative to 'tolerate' and accept them. Therefore, they must be a reaction and resistance to our weakness, forms of its disavowal, and hence disavowal of our basic humanity. Yet if there is one fundamental lesson of psychoanalysis, it is precisely that of recognizing excess at the very core of humanity – not simply as egoist, aggressive, self-interested attitudes towards others, but also, and more interestingly, as the human inclination to act against one's own self-interest. And by that I am referring to the abandonment of self-interest not in pursuing some higher ethical goals, but in pursuing one's own enjoyment. *Jouissance*, with its always excessive, 'surplus' nature, as well as desire in its radical negativity, necessarily complicate the story of accepting one's finitude, since they introduce (or indicate) a fundamental *contradiction in this finitude itself.* One could of course retort that this human contradiction *is* the very mark of its finitude. Yet this move is precisely that of closure. Instead, one should take a further conceptual step: it is not simply that, as human beings, we are marked by a fundamental contradiction, and are therefore finite – the contradiction applies, or stretches, to the very finitude which is our 'human condition'. For what is at stake is that our finitude is always-already a *failed finitude* – one could say, a finitude with a leak in it. Lacan situates the 'leak' in the point of incidence of the signifier, in its double effect. On the one hand, the signifier uproots us, pulls us out of an immediate immersion in our natural substance, and exposes us to the fluid course of the signifying chain. On the other hand, it induces our passionate, stubborn attachment to a specific link of the signifier and enjoyment (or desire), leaves us 'stuck' with it. Not only does the signifier introduce death in the midst of our life (thus transforming it from an outer limit, or a final stop to life, into its inherent limit and condition of possibility) – by doing so, it also introduces a gap into our finitude. And we could say that it is there that we can ultimately locate the powerlessness or inefficiency of just asserting and reasserting the fact of human finitude in the face of religious discourse – this discourse uses and exploits precisely the contradiction of human finitude, it exploits some fundamental human experience, which the 'metaphysics of finitude' mostly refuses to acknowledge or take into account as real.

It is here that comedy is much more far-reaching. The conceptual point – deployed, in a theatrical way, by comedy – is none other than this: the finitude of human reality is, at the very outset, a paradoxical finitude, a finitude with a flaw. For human beings as beings of speech (and therefore also of enjoyment and desire), there is no such thing as an unproblematic finitude (which, for some mysterious reason, they would refuse to accept). Would it not be more correct to say that humankind would be more than happy to be able to live peacefully in its finitude, but that there is something that gnaws away at this finitude from within, erodes it, puts it into question?

Human finitude has a hole in it, and it is precisely this 'hole' that has been posited, in religious discourse, opposite man as his other, eternal Essence. In this respect, if immanence means anything, it means that the one thing 'modern' man needs to accept or take upon himself is not (simply) finitude, but precisely this 'hole in finitude', which is the topological space of the metaphysical notions of the Soul and God (instead of 'filling in' this hole by more or less pathetic assertions about human finitude, hoping that they will cast out religious representations of the Soul and God). The problem is thus not simply finitude, but the inherent surplus or lack that is parasitic on it, as well propelling it in its most spectacular achievements and creations, in which human consciousness and thought is being incessantly incorporated outside itself.

So perhaps the most accurate way to articulate the question of human finitude/infinitude would be to say: not only are we not infinite, we are not even finite.

If we stop here and think again about comedy, we can perhaps see more clearly that the stuff that comedies are made of is precisely this hole in finitude, in its different and various forms. Comic characters, as well as comic situations, do not only expose this fact, but also use it abundantly as the very generative source of what they themselves create.

Two brief remarks must be added here.

The first is that the 'failed finitude' is but another term for what I previously called the 'physics of the infinite' (as opposed to both metaphysics of the infinite and metaphysics of the finite). 'The infinite' refers to the very contradiction involved in the human condition, a contradiction which can precisely not be qualified as finite (that is to say, as something with a necessary and *inherent* end to it), whereas 'physics' refers to the fact that this infinite contradiction is always materialized in very concrete and finite objects and actions, and that it exists only through and with them.

The second remark concerns the relation between the concrete and the universal at work in the art of comedy. If we stop briefly to consider the difference between irony and comedy proper, we will notice that this difference is very much the one between pointing out limits and limitations of, for example, the universal, and endorsing these limits by transforming them into the very points of the infinite and generic power of the universal. Let us first take the famous double graffiti:

'God is dead.' Nietzsche
'Nietzsche is dead.' God

This is irony at its purest, in its minimal formula. The ironic turn brings out the limitation, the particular, concrete determination of the place of enunciation, which then belies the universality of the statement. The point of the quoted ironic twist is of course not simply to reaffirm God against Nietszche; the supplement it introduces is there to foreground the gap between the statement (its content, which is supposed to be universal) and the place of enunciation (which is supposed to be always particular), and this gap is used to 'prove' the impossibility (the internal contradiction) of universal statements or truths. Any universal statement could be disproved by pointing to the particular (concrete) place of its enunciation. Yet does not the limit of this kind of irony lie in the fact that it does not recognize the possibility of a 'concrete universal' (as well as the possibility of an 'abstract particularity'), and remains within the parameters of the opposition between abstract universality and concrete particularity? The twist introduced by the true comic spirit is precisely to cut across this opposition, and to bet on the possibility of a concrete universal. In the context of our example, the true comic twist would thus take the following form:

'God is dead. And I'm not feeling very well either.'

This is a splendid example of the 'singular universality', which could be defined as follows: what is at stake is not simply the universal value of a statement (of its content), but the universalizability of the place of enunciation itself. In this case, the place of enunciation does not undermine the universality of the statement, but becomes its very internal gap, that which alone generates the only (possible) universality of the statement.

Notes

1. *Hegel's Phenomenology of Spirit*, trans. A. V. Miller (Oxford and New York: Oxford University Press, 1977), 264. Further references in the text to *PS*, followed by page number, refer to this edition.

2. See Jean Hyppolite, *Genèse et structure de la Phénoménologie de l'esprit de Hegel* (Paris: Aubier–Montaigne, 1978), 522–3.

3. 'The pure thoughts of the Beautiful and the Good thus display a comic spectacle: through their liberation from the opinion which contains both their specific determinateness as content and also their absolute determinateness . . . they become empty, and just for that reason the sport of mere opinion and the caprice of any chance individuality.' (*PS*, 452)

4. Jacques Lacan, *Le séminaire XVII: L'envers de la psychanalyse*, ed. Jacques-Alain Miller (Paris: Seuil, 1991), 197.

5. Jacques Lacan, *The Ethics of Psychoanalysis* (London: Routledge, 1992), 295; translation slightly modified.

9

The Familiar Unknown, the Uncanny, the Comic: The Aesthetic Effects of the Thought Experiment

Robert Pfaller

1 THE CONSIDERABLE CHARM OF A DUBIOUS METHOD

I am a poet.
That makes me interesting.[1]

The very expression 'thought experiment' catches the attention. Its usage contains a bold statement: namely, that one can discover unknown facts or principles purely in thought – an assertion that may either provoke contradiction or motivate experiments on oneself. The uncertainty of this statement does not seem to detract from its appeal. On the contrary: the thought experiment becomes an even more fascinating idea, the less its effectiveness is beyond question. Whereas the concept of proven methods of arriving at knowledge may leave us quite indifferent, the idea of a method of such uncertain value seems oddly interesting. The first paradox of the thought experiment consists in this disproportion – in this unbalanced ratio between appeal and performance, so to speak.

The ambiguity of the concept may well contribute significantly to the appealing uncertainty that surrounds the idea of the thought experiment. What exactly does this concept signify? Does the thought experiment proceed along the lines of empirical methods, with the aim of preparing empirical experiments, defining their meaning or even predicting their possible results? Can an experiment carried out in thought replace real experiments when these are not feasible? Is it a journey into fiction with (possibly unforeseen) scientific value? Is it an instrument of ethics that facilitates individual decision-making with the help of unrealistic assumptions?[2] Or is it the artistic representation of an unreal world by which, strangely enough, real people – without having attained any kind of knowledge – are nevertheless influenced and moved at least as strongly as they are by other artistic representations?

The heterogeneity of the kinds of thought experiments that first come to mind in the course of a brief mental review shows that the non-being dealt with in thought experiments can be expressed in at least as many ways as Aristotle determined for being.

1.1

The philosopher Ludwig Wittgenstein also places emphasis on the questionableness of thought experiments – while, simultaneously, this concept emerges in his work in all its ambiguity. Concerning theoretical value, Wittgenstein firmly opines that it is not possible to experiment in thought: 'Looking up a table in the imagination is no more looking up a table than the image of the result of an imagined experiment is the result of an experiment'[3]. On the other hand, Wittgenstein might be one of those philosophers who most strongly and impressively operate with something that could be referred to as thought experiments; that is why he almost always appears in discourses on the topic. The attractiveness of his philosophy derives largely from the fact that he again and again develops the most amusing, absurd and surprising ideas in order to twist his lines of argument (among them, even his rejection of the thought experiment itself): 'Why can't my right hand give my left hand money?' 'Imagine a servant dropping the tea-tray and everything on it with all the outward signs of carefulness.' 'Why can't a dog simulate pain? Is he too honest?'[4]

Wittgenstein nevertheless points out the use of these paradoxical interventions and their locations: for what separates us from truth is not merely lack of knowledge. It is more often preconceived and familiar opinions: 'ein Bild hielt uns gefangen' ('a picture held us captive'[5]). Wherever this is the case, another picture, a counter-picture, must be interposed:

> I wanted to put that picture before him, and his *acceptance* of the picture consists in his now being inclined to regard a given case differently: that is, to compare it with *this* rather than *that* set of pictures. I have changed his *way of looking at things.*[6]

This counter-picture is Wittgenstein's thought experiment. Its use consists not in gaining knowledge about the previously unknown, but in doing away with theoretical presuppositions that were previously taken for granted.

Thus the matter treated with the help of this thought experiment is not the object about which we wish to know something, but the fixed idea that we had about this object. After a successful thought experiment, we usually know less about the object than we did before; we can only formulate better questions. Empirical experiments provide answers to questions, whereas thought experiments enable questions where previously only premature answers existed.

With its imaginative strength, the thought experiment intervenes in the field which the philosopher of science Gaston Bachelard terms the 'imaginary of the scientific spirit'. Thought experiments break through the epistemological obstacles raised by the imaginary.[7] These breakthroughs are of vital value: only through them does a theory attain an object and become able to ask questions about it. According to Bachelard, no science has ever established itself without this preliminary breakthrough.[8] Since that time the constructivist theories of science, in agreement with Bachelard, regard the power of the theoretical construction to estrange our familiar assumptions and views as one of the most crucial performance criteria for theoretical work.[9]

1.2

The reason the thought experiment seems to appear so fascinating, despite the greatest uncertainty about its theoretical use, may be its strength, which is directed at what is imaginary. Contrary to the impression that it may give, the Imaginary deals not with objects, but with the subjects who imagine these objects. And it has far less to do with realizing than with wishing. Bachelard notes:

> It suffices to speak about an object to make us believe that we are objective. But, through our first choice, the object rather designates us, than us designating it, and what we consider our fundamental ideas of the world, often are nothing but confidential revelations about the youthfulness of our spirit.[10]

Whereas real cognitions are of no interest to most people, and can therefore virtually be relegated to an 'encyclopaedia of useless knowledge',[11] the thought experiment always has to do with ourselves, our ideas and wishes, and is therefore immensely interesting even if the cognition gained is marginal or trivial.

Thus the central thesis of the Stoic Epictetus seems to be proven: people are never excited by facts, but always by their imaginary notions of those facts.[12] It is precisely because the thought experiment deals with imagination, not with facts, that it can cause excitement (usually pleasant). In this respect, the effects are aesthetic, not theoretical. The interest in overcoming imagination and cognitive obstacles is consequently also aesthetic: ridding oneself of illusions – being able to switch between images rather than persisting in a fixed idea – is a pleasant feeling. This does not yet complete the cognition, but the aesthetic approach gives it vital encouragement.

This may be one of the reasons why philosophical criticism aimed at overcoming cognitive obstacles – as Jonathan Culler, for example, observes[13] – has detached itself from philosophy as well as from the sciences, and has become mainly a concern of art (and associated theoretical practices) over recent decades.

1.3

Thomas Macho and Annette Wunschel pose a stimulating question in their book on the thought experiment: 'What do we actually want to know, when we raise such questions [in a thought experiment]?'[14] In order to find an answer, we would like to deduce conclusions from these considerations: namely, that people who conduct thought experiments are often not really aiming to attain knowledge. Lacanian psychoanalysis (contrary to Freud's assumption of the 'Wißtrieb', the drive for knowledge) notes that one of the strongest human endeavours concerning cognition aims at not knowing certain things.[15] A large number of thought experiments in literature and film, therefore, deal not with the principles of an unfamiliar world (albeit one that is, for some obscure reason, still interesting to us) that enriches our previous knowledge, but with our present world in a recognizably distorted, parodic way. That is why the preamble 'How would it be if . . .' is simply a charming disguise for the statement: 'That is how it is here and now'.

For example, the basic idea of the film *Minority Report* (USA, 2002) – that criminals can be detected before they commit their crimes – describes a hypothesis that is already being followed up in social sciences; with the help of recent test procedures, attempts are made today to distinguish between, for example, latent psychotic, aggressive offenders and other characters that are more overtly dangerous and easier to discern. The science-fiction film *Planet of the Women*, made in Czechoslovakia in the 1970s, describes a world in which men and real marmalade are respectively abolished and forbidden. It deals in a humorous way with easily identifiable elements of the world of actually existing socialism: with dissident circles who secretly eat real marmalade, as well as with the betrayal of principles by the elite, who in reality are male. *Matrix* (USA, 1999) not only deals with a current feeling among the residents of the so-called 'First World' that they are living in an artificial economy, as well as in a world based on fake information,[16] but also – read against the grain – with a bunch of pleasure-hating metaphysicians who, for no reason, prefer to swallow the red pill of assumed truth rather than the blue pill of a comfortable life. Here it is easy to detect in current everyday culture the ascetic tendencies so conducive to neoliberal politics, according to which everything that gives pleasure (smoking, drinking, 'adult language', sex, and so on) increasingly becomes an abhorrence liable to prosecution (similar to the world of *Planet of the Women*).

Thus these kinds of thought experiment never carry us away to unfamiliar, but always to 'familiar strange worlds'.[17] The effects aimed at by these thought experiments are not theoretical, but aesthetic. They are not intended to bring cognition, but to give us pleasure – for example, the pleasure of gaining distance through recognition.

2 TO LAUGH OR BE FRIGHTENED

All my plays are tragedies – they become funny only because they are uncanny.[18]

If it is possible to estrange one's own familiar world in such a thought experiment by means of the preamble 'What if . . .', then two types of pleasure can emerge: either, when imagining a strange world, we are reminded of our own world in a peculiar, uncanny way, or we burst out laughing because in what has just appeared to be a strange world (at a previous moment, or for someone else) we clearly recognize our own.

The thought experiment, as a way of creating aesthetic effects based on the principles of the familiar unknown, plays a decisive role within two specific aesthetic genres: in the comic of comedy, and in the uncanny. These two genres feature a peculiar structural analogy, which has so far hardly been mentioned. Yet everyday speech shows a certain sensitivity to it – for instance, the phrase 'I had a funny feeling', which refers rather to something *uncanny* than to the familiar characteristics of comedy. Conversely, things are sometimes described as 'uncannily funny'; this again refers less to something really scary – of which the uncanny consists – than to the enhanced funny side of things.[19]

In at least four aspects, the comic of comedy and the uncanny coincide. Let us term these four aspects the *occurrence of symbolic causality, success, repetition*, and *double*. In order to indicate, at least, how far these points form a system, I will try to develop a coherent pattern, starting with a very obvious genre feature of comedy.

One of the most outstanding and remarkable features of comedy seems to be its *polygamous position.* Polygamy in comedy is obvious. Not only are there frequent occurrences of adultery, multiple marriages or love affairs involving more than two people (none of which is necessarily amusing *per se*[20]), but comedy often proclaims such polygamy as a concept of happiness.[21] Many happy endings – in Lubitsch's work, for instance – consist in the fact that a *ménage à trois* has prevailed over monogamy, and triumphantly moves on. The recent trio Cate Blanchett/Billy Bob Thornton/Bruce Willis in Barry Levinson's wonderful gangster comedy *Bandits!* (USA, 2001) is a rare current example (this is true of the comedy genre in general).

This is based on a first structural attribute of comedy: namely, the rule 'fun turns deadly serious', or 'representation turns into what is represented'. Many of the polygamous adventures in comedy arise because the plot demands that love should be acted, and this acted love then becomes reality. In Jack Conway's screwball comedy *Libeled Lady* (USA, 1936), for instance, William Powell has to go through a sham marriage with Jean Harlow, on the instructions of a daily newspaper, in order to ruin, as a married man, the reputation of millionaire's daughter Myrna Loy by feigning love in an affair with her. Of course, in accordance with the laws of comedy, true love develops – on the part of both ladies, as well as on Powell's side – leading to highly amusing fast-paced complications.

This principle whereby a game becomes reality can also be termed the *occurrence of symbolic causality.*[22] This is equivalent to the anti-psychological position maintained by comedy. Unlike tragedy, comedy concedes to the actual, the represented, the appearance, the obvious, not to the actors' intentions. Comedy argues that 'love always exists when it is acted'. In this respect comedy is materialist and (which is the same in this case) structuralist. Tragedy, on the other hand, basically suggests that the actors are in the right with their intentions, feelings and beliefs, as opposed to the represented, the appearance, and the obvious. Tragedy argues that 'it is not the performance that is decisive, but what the actors feel within themselves'.[23] The position of tragedy is therefore idealistic and metaphysical. The fact – familiar from everyday life – that what is represented can result from representation cannot therefore be represented in tragedy. For tragedy, which is so concerned with seriousness, the idea that seriousness can result from play is intolerable.

Things are quite different again within the genre of the uncanny. Just like the comic in comedy, the uncanny often arises because the represented itself results from the representation, or seems to do so. Freud, for instance, mentions an English story, where

> a young married couple . . . move into a furnished house in which there is a curiously shaped table with carvings of crocodiles on it. Towards evening an intolerable and very specific smell begins to pervade the house; they stumble over something in the dark; they seem to see a vague form gliding over the stairs – in short, we are given to understand that the presence of the table causes ghostly crocodiles to haunt the place, or that the wooden monsters come to life in the dark, or something of the sort.[24]

Thus the story is about the occurrence of symbolic causality or, as Freud says, about the case that 'a symbol takes over the full functions of the thing it symbolizes' (ibid.). The anti-psychological moment, which appeared in the symbolic causality of comedy, recurs here. The actor's better intrinsic 'psychological' judgement (for example, that the carved crocodiles are 'mere symbols') loses out against the superficial impression that things might be different. In terms of the uncanny, this can be shown more clearly as follows.

Besides the rule of 'play becomes reality', a second structural feature can be deduced from the comedy of polygamy: the paradigm of *success.* In comedy, everything succeeds – often too much so. Poor William Powell in *Libeled Lady* succeeds in having two real amorous conquests instead of one merely faked one. Josef Tura, the brave actor in *To Be Or Not To Be*, is able to prove at Gestapo headquarters that he himself is Professor Siletsky and not the dead, real and also apparently more authentic Siletsky, who is also present. Not only this – soon after, his fellow actors, disguised as an SS squad, manage to rescue him by 'unmasking' him and marching him off as an impostor.

Comedy works with the principle of success, whereas tragedy is based on the principle of failure. Love, as far as it exists in tragedy, is doomed to failure – which is considered proof of its authenticity. In tragedy (owing to its metaphysical position), nothing authentic belongs to this world. On the other hand, thanks to the paradigm of success there is always plenty of successful love in comedies – even abounding love, 'surplus-love',[25] so to speak, and here its success is absolute proof of its authenticity, because everything that is wonderful in comedy (owing to its materialist position) belongs to this world.

As in comedy, the genre of the uncanny is based on the principle of success. Freud writes about what he considers one of the 'undeniable instances of the uncanny':

> In the story of 'The Ring of Polycrates', the King of Egypt turns away in horror from his host, Polycrates, because he sees that his friend's every wish is at once fulfilled, his every care promptly removed by kindly fate. His host has become 'uncanny' to him.[26]

What is striking here is that the uncanny appears as pure success, yet without any obvious addition of evident dreadfulness. Polycrates' guest explains his feeling by the idea that 'the too fortunate man has to fear the envy of the gods'.[27]

Because this information is questionable, Freud illustrates the uncanniness of such success with a further example, in which the dreadfulness is also evident.

> In the case history of an obsessional neurotic, I have described how the patient once stayed in a hydropathic establishment and benefited greatly by it. He had the good sense, however, to attribute his improvement not to the therapeutic properties of the water, but to the situation of his room, which immediately adjoined that of a very accommodating nurse. So on his second visit to the establishment he asked for the same room, but was told that it was already occupied by an old gentleman, whereupon he gave vent to his annoyance in the words: 'I wish he may be struck dead for it.' A fortnight later the old gentleman really did have a stroke. My patient thought this an 'uncanny' experience.[28]

With the success of this curse, the uncanny element becomes obvious. Were the extent of the disaster less drastic, the situation could shift into being humorous – as, for instance, when a spectator at a football match succeeds in casting a spell on the penalty-scorer of the opposing team. In Polycrates' success, on the other hand, the reason for the uncanny feeling is less evident. Here, however, opportunities open up for comedy, since there is often a comic element in unexpected success in games of skill, or in a lottery win after the chance acquisition of a ticket.

But Freud's examples seem to differ on one point: Polycrates *does nothing* to earn his amazing luck; he simply lives in a world that conforms to his wishes. (This must seem uncanny to anyone who, like the guest, opines that the world is not like that.) The Rat Man, on the other hand, actually *does* something – but not to earn his luck. He does not really want the old man to drop dead. The uncanny thing about this success is, rather, that the curse takes effect, although it was not intended in earnest. In the Rat Man's case, success is at the same time the occurrence of symbolic causality.

The symbolic causality, moreover, occurs not only against his intentions, but also against his intellect. He thought that his remark was only a joke, mere words, but reality answers as though it had understood differently. His reasonable knowledge that he cannot perform miracles, that his words cannot kill, seems here to be suspended. This shows very clearly the anti-psychological element of the uncanny, which we noticed in comedy. The intentions, the knowledge and the understanding of the actors are not what matters. Reality seems to follow the appearance – in this case, the superficial interpretation of what the man said. In addition, there arises an uncanny anti-psychological type of guilt that runs contrary to our common sense: the Rat Man feels guilty, even though he neither meant nor did any harm. The guilt of the uncanny is based, rather, on symbolic causality; for such *magical guilt*,[29] appearance is what counts.

The repetition of scenes is the third genre element that comedy shares with the uncanny. In Lubitsch's *To Be Or Not To Be* there is a legendary example in the duplicated meeting of Professor Siletsky and Concentration Camp Erhardt, in which the actor Tura has to appear first as Erhardt and then as Siletsky.[30] Repetition also takes place in the uncanny – and here it also makes occasional reference to polygamy. Freud himself reports on his embarrassing walk through an Italian city, which repeatedly led him back to that very street 'in a quarter of whose character I could not long remain in doubt. Nothing but painted women were to be seen at the windows of the small houses'.[31] On this occasion Freud also points to the possibility of a shift into the comic.

Finally, the structural identity of comedy and the uncanny is revealed in the device of doubling characters. In Chaplin's comedy *The Great Dictator* (USA, 1940), not only one but two Hitlers exist. And Lubitsch's classic on the same topic provides a downright riot of doubling: two Hitlers, two Erhardts, and two Professor Siletskys, with two false beards. As an element of the uncanny, doubling appears as the figure of the doppelgänger.[32] Here doubling of the self may play a privileged role, unlike the doppelgänger of comedy, but the other forms of human multiplicity can also have an uncanny effect. For the uncanny effect to arise, it is sometimes enough for a figure to appear in duplicate. Near Vienna there were once twin brothers, who were both policemen. They are supposed to have had fun in the following way: one of them stopped all speeding cars, and reprimanded the drivers for their risky driving. A few kilometres down the road, the other brother was waiting. Informed by phone, he stopped the same cars again and said sternly: 'Didn't I just tell you not to drive that fast?' What was fun for the brothers may well have been a rather uncanny situation for the drivers. Pascal's famous comment that 'two faces which resemble each other make us laugh, when together, by their resemblance, though neither of them by itself makes us laugh'[33] could therefore easily be reformulated in accordance with the uncanny effect.

If I am correct in my four-point statement about the structural identity of comedy and the uncanny, then the question arises of whether the thought experiment is appropriate to explain it. It could perhaps provide the key to understanding this recurrent uncanny or comical encounter between the uncanny and the comic.

3 THE THOUGHT EXPERIMENT IN THE UNCANNY AND THE COMIC: WAYS OF DEALING WITH ILLUSIONS

Suppose I say of a friend: 'He isn't an automaton'. – What information is conveyed by this, and to whom would it be information?[34]

Why is the thought experiment so appropriate for generating the aesthetic effects of the uncanny and the comic? Or, conversely: in what way are the uncanny and the comic based on a thought experiment?

What strikes us first is that the subject of a thought experiment often also constitutes the subject matter of the comic and the uncanny: for Descartes, for instance, the idea that human figures could actually be machines is a thought experiment.[35] For Bergson, on the other hand, this idea is the source of the comic.[36] Finally, for Freud, the automatism of man is the reason for the feeling of the uncanny – although, referring to E.T.A. Hoffmann's story 'Der Sandmann', Freud declares (contrary to the opinion of E. Jentsch) that he cannot think 'that the theme of the doll Olympia, who is to all appearances a living being, is by any means the only, or indeed the most important, element that must be held responsible for the quite unparalleled atmosphere of uncanniness evoked by the story'.[37] Yet undeniable instances of the uncanny are, for Freud, those cases where compulsive repetition asserts itself as a relentless mechanism in human behaviour, rendering people helpless.[38]

This identity of motive between the thought experiment on the one hand and the uncanny/comic on the other is enabled through a simple principle: both the uncanny and the comic presuppose a thought experiment. The impression of the uncanny or comic always results *when, at a certain moment and at a particular point, the world itself seems to correspond to a thought experiment* – for instance, when people move for a moment as if they were those machines that Descartes tries to imagine in his thought experiment. Freud states the general formula for this structure concerning the uncanny as follows: 'that an uncanny effect is often produced when the distinction between imagination and reality is effaced, as when something that we have hitherto regarded as imaginary appears before us in reality'.[39] This means that two conditions are required for the uncanny and the comic: first, the world itself must give the impression of being a thought experiment; yet at the same time, the unreal, 'fantastic', 'experimental', fictive character of that impression must remain. Should one merely conclude from such a strange impression that the world is so (for example, people are simply machines), then neither an uncanny nor a comic effect would result.

There must therefore be a contradiction between singular experience and general belief, and the singular, strange experience must be part of a whole ('fantastic') story, which is incompatible with our ('realistic') view of the world. After all, not every strange detail is uncanny or comic – some merely arouse our interest, stimulate us to further exploration, and so on. Only if the inconsistent element points to a whole fantastic, thought-experimental story which is familiar to us and which we know with certainty to be fictitious[40] does the uncanny, comic impression arise. Should we not be aware of such a story, the uncanny, comic impression does not come about. (This is why some experiences are uncanny or comic to certain cultures and not to others.[41])

In order for an uncanny or comic impression to arise, it must remain clear that the story suggesting it – contrary to corresponding experience – is an illusion. Consequently, the fiction of a thought experiment must, in both the uncanny and the comic, be generated a priori *as a fiction*, as a *suspended* assumption. The formula 'How would it be if . . .' means here first of all: 'Of course it is not like that, yet it seems as if. . . .'

When a fiction is treated as fiction, it moves as an illusion to the other side – to the side of others. It is not we who believe in what the fiction envisions, but some people or other whom we still occasionally see as persons, or at least think we can imagine – sometimes we do not even spare them a thought.[42] In this way, the preamble of the thought experiment produces exactly what the psychoanalyst Octave Mannoni observed in his clinic, in everyday life and aesthetics, which he aptly describes with the formula: 'I know quite well, but nevertheless . . .'.[43]

'I know quite well, but nevertheless . . .' describes that structure which operates when, for instance, a person who does not believe in horoscopes happens to read in a newspaper horoscope: 'Today is a favourable day for a major change of location' on the day he is moving house, and bursts out laughing, with peculiar satisfaction. Although he has no faith in this horoscope, his laugh – as Mannoni subtly remarks – would have been different had the horoscope designated this day as unfavourable.[44] The knowledge that the newspaper horoscope is nonsense does not by any means override the peculiar satisfaction. On the contrary, a more reliable source reporting advantageous conditions for moving house – such as a favourable weather forecast – would hardly have occasioned such enthusiastic laughter. It can be concluded from Mannoni's formula that better judgement is not only not detrimental to the enthusiastic strength of the illusion of the horoscope, but even oddly beneficial to it.

Mannoni's formula is most illuminating in respect of aesthetic effects. Although Mannoni himself uses it, regarding art, primarily in connection with the amusing illusions of comedy,[45] some of his examples show that the very same structure can just as well bring about the effects of the uncanny.[46]

This raises the question of 'aesthetic choice of neuroses' – that is, the question of the criterion according to which one structure that can express itself in such a variety of ways becomes operative in one effect or another. When does the suspended illusion of a thought experiment produce a comic effect, and when an uncanny one?

4 UNCANNY OR COMIC? WHY NOT SNEEZE, RROSE SELAVY?

> *Sneezing absorbs all the functions of the soul just as much as the [sexual] act, but we do not draw from it the same conclusions against the greatness of man, because it is involuntary. [. . .]*[47]

At first it might appear that the illusion which seems to be suspended in the comic becomes uncanny at the moment when its suspension is lifted. Mannoni's interpretation of a Casanova episode seems to aim in this direction. What for Casanova starts as an amusing conjuring trick with which he wishes to impress other, naive people turns into an uncanny experience for him as soon as the others have fled, and nobody is left to believe what he himself does not. This absence, this 'défaillance des crédules', now excites anxiety in Casanova himself: 'si sa croyance à la magie retombe pour ainsi dire sur lui-même, il est saisi d'angoisse'.[48]

When the others are gone, the illusion turns against him, as it were; its suspension, assured through the presence of gullible spectators, has been lifted. The initially comic episode would consequently cease to be a thought experiment, and thus become uncanny. This fact, regarding the question of a criterion, prompts the following answer: *the comic is what is uncanny for others.* What is comic for us, because it includes an illusion to which we do not succumb, is uncanny for others who are unprotected and naive. On the other hand, when we ourselves are unprotected and succumb to the illusion, it is uncanny for us, and precisely this might make it comic for others.[49]

This finding, however, seems to contradict our previous discoveries: what initially so concerned us was the structural identity of the comic and the uncanny; the fact that in both, a thought experiment, a suspended illusion, seemed to be operative. Now, on the other hand, the thought-experimental element seems to exist only in the comic, not in the uncanny.

There are major objections to this view. Freud states that especially the perception of the uncanny is linked to a suspended illusion: he observes that in order to be able to experience the uncanny, we must have 'surmounted' certain beliefs.[50] Thus, for example, it is necessary to have surmounted the belief in ghosts or symbolic causality, in order to experience as uncanny a ghost story or a story where carved wooden crocodiles come alive. According to Freud, this is precisely what distinguishes the aesthetic of ghost stories from that of fairytales: the ghost story assumes that ghosts do not exist. When they then appear to exist, the uncanny effect is created. In fairytales the assumptions are different:

> In fairytales . . ., the world of reality is left behind from the very start, and the animistic system of beliefs is frankly adopted. Wish-fulfilments, secret powers, omnipotence of thoughts, animation of inanimate objects, all the elements so common in fairy stories, can exert no uncanny influence here. . . .[51]

Just as in the comic, the uncanny is also based on the suspension of illusion, on 'I know quite well, but nevertheless . . .' Only those who 'surmount' the illusion through better judgement can be gripped by the uncanny. The illusion must not turn back on oneself – it must remain the illusion of others, otherwise the distance from it disappears, just as the sense of the uncanny does.

Better judgement, as designated in Mannoni's formula ('I know quite well . . .'), is thus necessary for the effect of the uncanny to result from illusion. Only when illusion is overcome can it be terrifying. The point of Mannoni's formula for the uncanny consists in this paradoxical consequence: *it is not the lack of enlightenment; on the contrary, it is knowledge itself that makes us anxious.*[52] Only when we know that no spirits exist can they frighten us. Therefore one can really frighten only people who do not believe in ghosts.

Although he clearly emphasizes that overcoming illusion is the condition for the uncanny, Freud, unlike Mannoni, tends towards the more familiar, common-sense view that the emergence of the uncanny is due simply to the *insufficient* thorough and final dispatch of the illusory ideas: 'anyone who has completely and finally rid himself of animistic beliefs will be insensible to this type of the uncanny'.[53]

Yet decisive with regard to this theoretical tension in Freud's text is his comment that the uncanny, as something formerly secret – that is, familiar and pleasurable – assumes the unpleasant character of fearsomeness *only after its 'fall'* – that is, after it has been surmounted. Referring to Heine, Freud observes: 'The "double" has become a thing of terror, just as, after the collapse of their religion, the gods turned into demons.'[54] Had the overthrow of illusion by better judgement not already occurred, then the substance of this illusion could not be frightening. Without enlightenment we would be living in the world of fairytales, which is not an uncanny one. As long as we believe in demons, they remain gods; only after we stop believing in them have we reason to fear them. There are no demons other than those we do not believe in.

If, as this evidence shows, the uncanny is also based on the condition of a suspended illusion, can we then rescue our previous formula that the comic is what is uncanny for others? If the comic and the uncanny are based in equal measure upon suspended illusion, then how can the difference between them, which I wished to express in my formula, be contained in a theory?

Perhaps a further example from Mannoni is appropriate to shed some light on this matter. If an actor playing a dead person on stage is lying motionless, gets some dust up his nose and has to sneeze, the audience will laugh.[55] Mannoni acutely analyses the characteristic peculiar to this laugh: the audience laughs not because it is freed from the sad conviction that the man is dead, but because the actor's sneeze has freed it from the obligation to maintain the theatrical illusion. As Mannoni states, everything seems to be there in order to generate the illusion, but *in somebody else* – just as if we (the audience) were the actors' accomplices.[56] The object of this kind of laugh is not the good news that the actor is still alive, but the imaginable astonishment of a naive third party who believes in the theatrical illusion and is fooled by audience and actor together, and for whom the impression of the dead man's sneeze must therefore seem uncanny.

The parameters in this example can easily be changed in such a way that the effect of the uncanny arises. Should somebody we assume to be dead suddenly sneeze, it would be uncanny for us. Now we play the role of the naive person – the third party in Mannoni's example. But our own uncanny fright is based on a non-naivety, a suspended illusion. We have to overcome the illusion that dead people can sneeze so that the experience of an assumed dead person's sneeze can seem uncanny. Only in a culture with a tradition of stories about the living (sneezing) dead could we have encountered this kind of illusion; and only when we have overcome the illusion can we experience the uncanny. Because we do not believe in fairytales (familiar to us through our culture) in which dead people show signs of life, this kind of sign affects us in an uncanny way.

This enables us to tackle both the common ground and the distinguishing element of the uncanny and the comic. Perception of the uncanny always depends on the suspension of an initial illusion – for instance, that dead people can sneeze. I would like to call this initial illusion *the illusion of the uncanny*. In the uncanny as in the comic, this specific illusion is suspended, as a precondition. For both those who are frightened and those who are amused, the idea that dead people can sneeze has to be a fairytale – that is, the illusion of others.

It is only on a second level that the uncanny and the comic separate. There is a second illusion – Mannoni terms it the '*illusion of the comic*' – which is *believed* in the uncanny and *suspended* in the comical. In my example, this is the illusion that the man on stage is dead. If this illusion is our own perception, then the man's sneeze is uncanny. On the other hand, if it is for us the illusion of others, then the sneeze is comic; then we laugh about these others, whom we implicitly presume as soon as we suspend the illusion for ourselves.

What the uncanny and the comic have in common is that they both presume the illusion of the uncanny as suspended. What then separates the comic from the uncanny is the circumstance that only the comic also treats the second illusion – that of the comic – as suspended. The uncanny, on the other hand, is precisely that which remains trapped in the illusion of the comic. With regard to the illusion of the comic, we can now rehabilitate the formula we arrived at previously: that *the comic is what is uncanny for others*. In the comic, we laugh about those who are unable to elude the illusion of the comic, and who therefore are defenceless, at the mercy of the effect of the uncanny.

Now we can also explain the example of human automatism. In this case the illusion of the uncanny consists in the notion that people are machines. This notion has to be suspended as an illusion so that the impression of human automatism can develop its uncanny effect. Only those who consider the notion that people are machines an illusion can be affected uncannily by the opposite impression. One must be familiar with this notion, and at the same time 'know' that people are not machines, in order to be frightened when things appear different.

The peculiar feature of this case is that the very better judgement that suspends the illusion of the uncanny is precisely what constitutes the illusion of the comic. In the comic of human automatism we laugh at the very fact that people think they are something other than machines, and hide the true motives for their actions behind their conscious intentions. This self-deception, which is also the reason for the feeling of the uncanny, is the object of comic amusement. Thus the comic is based on the suspension of the comic illusion of the dissimilarity between people and machines; it is based on the knowledge of human psychological automatism as well as of the tendency to self-deception about it.[57] The general anti-psychological standpoint of the comic of comedy, which we encountered above, appears once again: 'You are far more confusable (i.e. more automatic, reproducible) than you think.'[58]

By differentiating the two levels of illusion – that of the uncanny and that of the comic – we were able to justify the formula of the comic as what is uncanny for others, without deviating from the principle that the uncanny itself is always conditional upon the suspension of illusion. This enables us to explain both these aesthetic effects as the result of a thought experiment. Last but not least, they prove, in this manner, to be forms of a cultured treatment of illusion: such fictions are not developed in order to dispose of fiction once and for all (as Descartes would have liked). In fact, the ability to see through such fictions as fictions, and to retain them with affection, appears in the cultural forms of the uncanny and the comic. This ability has not been shown to an equal extent in all periods of history. The German words *Heidenangst* (cold creeps – literally 'heathen fear') and *Heidenspass* (huge fun – literally 'heathen fun'), which designate the feelings produced by the uncanny and the comic, seem to reveal that a trace of sophistication from the ancient, pagan classical world lives on in these aesthetic effects.

Translated into English by Astrid Hager.

Notes

1. Wladimir Majakowsi, *Her mit dem schönen Leben. Gedichte, Poeme, Aufsätze, Reden, Briefe und Stücke* (Frankfurt am Main: Suhrkamp, 1982).

2. In this sense Lacan uses the term 'thought experiment' (Jacques Lacan [1959–60] *Das Seminar, Buch VII: Die Ethik der Psychoanalyse* [Weinheim, Berlin: Quadriga, 1996], p. 373); see Simon Critchley, 'Comedy and Finitude: Displacing the Tragic-Heroic Paradigm in Philosophy and Psychoanalysis', in *Ethics – Politics – Subjectivity. Essays on Derrida, Levinas and Contemporary French Thought* (London & New York: Verso, 1999), p. 226. Kant's ethical thought experiment of the 'gallows case' (to whose conclusion Lacan is known to have objected) belongs to the very same type: 'Suppose that someone affirms of his inclination for sensual pleasure that he cannot possibly resist temptation to indulgence. If a gallows were erected at the place where he is tempted on which he should be hanged immediately after satiating his passions, would he not be able to control his inclination? We need not long doubt what would be his answer.' (Kant, Immanuel Kant [1788] *Kritik der praktischen Vernunft*, Werkausgabe Vol. VII, 2nd edn [Frankfurt am Main: Suhrkamp, 1977], p. 140; see also *http://www.btinternet.com/~glynhughes/squashed/kant.htm*; Jacques Lacan [1963] 'Kant mit Sade', in *Schriften*, Vol. II, 3rd edn [Weinheim, Berlin: Quadriga, 1991], pp. 152ff.)

3. Ludwig Wittgenstein, *Philosophische Untersuchungen*, 2nd edn (Frankfurt am Main: Suhrkamp, 1980); *Philosophical Investigations*, 3rd edition (Oxford: Blackwell, 2001), 80e (S 265).

4. Wittgenstein, *Philosophical Investigations*, 80e, 60e, 76e (SS 268, 173, 250).

5. Wittgenstein, *Philosophical Investigations*, 80 (S 115).

6. Wittgenstein, *Philosophical Investigations*, 49e (S 144).

7. Gaston Bachelard, *Die Bildung des wissenschaftlichen Geistes. Beitrag zu einer Psychoanalyse der objektiven Erkenntnis* (Frankfurt am Main: Suhrkamp, 1978), pp. 46ff.

8. Bachelard, *Die Bildung*, pp. 46 ff.

9. Fritz Wallner, *Die Verwandlung der Wissenschaft. Vorlesungen zur Jahrtausendwende*, ed. M. Jandl, Hamburg: Dr Kovac, 2002.

10. Gaston Bachelard, *Epistemologie. Ausgewählte Texte*, ed. D. Lecourt (Frankfurt am Main: Ullstein, 1974), p. 134; my translation.

11. See Wilhelm Haefs [1989], *Handbuch des nutzlosen Wissens*, 14th edn (Munich: dtv, 2003).

12. See Epictetus, *Handbüchlein der Moral* (Leipzig: Reclam, 1920), 13 (§ 5); *see also http://www.geocities.com/khs10uk/enchiridion.htm.*

13. See Jonathan Culler, *Dekonstrukton. Derrida und die poststrukturalistische Literaturtheorie* (Reinbek: Rowohlt, 1999), pp. 9ff.

14. See *Science & Fiction. Über Gedankenexperimente in Wissenschaft, Philosophie und Literatur*, ed. Th. Macho and A. Wunschel (Frankfurt am Main: Fischer, 2004), p. 13.

15. See Slavoj Žižek, 'Happiness as an Ideological Category', in *Madam, I'm Adam. The Organization of Private Life*, ed. Piet Zart Institute Kunstuniversität Linz, Bereich Experimentelle Gestaltung (Rotterdam: Linz, 2003), pp. 116ff.

16. See Žižek's analogue interpretations on *The Truman Show*, Slavoj Žižek, *Welcome to the Desert of the Real! Five Essays on September 11 and Related Dates* (London & New York: Verso, 2002), pp. 12f.

17. See Stefan Vockrodt, *http://morgenwelt.de/kultur/000828-filmplaneten.htm.*

18. Odon von Horvath, *Gesannelte Werker*, Vol. 8 (Frankfurt am Main: Suhrkamp, 1978), p. 664.

19. There are three passages in Sigmund Freud's famous essay on the uncanny, where he remarks on the possible shift of the uncanny to the comic. (Sigmund Freud [1919] 'Das Unheimliche', *Studienausgable* Vol. IV [Frankfurt am Main: Fischer, 1989], pp. 237, 247, 252). In Jacques Lacan's theory, the uncanny and comic are determined through the appearance of the *objet petit a* (on this see Jacques Lacan [1958] 'Die Bedeutung des Phallus', in *Schriften*, Vol. II, 3rd edn [Weinheim, Berlin: Quadriga, 1991], p. 130; Lacan [1962–63] *Seminar X: Die Angst* [unpublished], session of 30 January 1963; in comparison to Mladen Dolar, 'The Aesthetics of the Uncanny', in *Mesotes. Zeitschrift für philosophischen Ost-West-Dialog*, Nor. 3, 1991, 51f, 57f.)

20. On the contrary: in recent works on this topic, the whole thing often ends in a catastrophe. See, for example, *The Ice Storm* (USA 1997, Ang Lee); *Marie-Jo et ses deux amours* (France 2001, Robert Guédiguian).

21. Friedrich Engels, *Der Ursprung der Familie, des Privateigentums und des Staats. Im Anschluss an Lewis H. Morgans Forschungen* (Berlin: Dietz, 1973), p. 80.

22. Claude Lévi-Strauss, 'Die Wirksamkeit der Symbole', in *Strukturale Anthropologie*, Vol. I (Frankfurt am Main: Suhrkamp, 1978), pp. 204–25.

23. This is also true, for example, in the question of mistaken identity. Comedy says: you are far easier to confuse than you like to believe. Tragedy, on the other hand, maintains: in reality you are more than anyone thinks (see Robert Pfaller, *Die Illusionen der anderen. Über das Lustprinzip in der Kultur* [Frankfurt am Main: Suhrkamp, 2002], pp. 194f.).

24. Freud, 'Das Unheimliche', p. 244.

25. This is also expressed in numerous 'screwball' titles touching on the theme of

polygamy, such as *My Favorite Wife* (USA 1940, Garson Kanin) or *I Love You Again* (USA 1940, W. S. van Dyke II).

26. Freud, 'Das Unheimliche', p. 239.

27. Freud, 'Das Unheimliche', p. 239.

28. Freud, 'Das Unheimliche', p. 239.

29. In this respect, Durkheim is right when he writes that there is no such thing as 'magical sin' (Emile Durkheim, *Die elementaren Formen des religiösen Lebens.* [Frankfurt am Main: Suhrkamp, 1994], p. 407). Since magic is not based on intentions and actions, there is no sin in it, but there is guilt. Also punishment – automatic self-punishment: see Freud on the taboo society: 'An innocent wrong-doer, who may, for instance, have eaten a forbidden animal, falls into a deep depression, anticipates death and then dies in real earnest' (Freud, *Totem und Tabu, Studienausgabe*, Vol. IX, [Frankfurt am Main, 1912–13], p. 314). This type of guilt is a theme in another aesthetic genre, namely in fate tragedy. Its term *tragic guilt* ('cannot be subjectively taken into account, but exists objectively'; see *http://www.klassikerforum.de/Bodies/gattungen/tragoedie.php*) corresponds to what I have described as *magical guilt.* The ancient fate tragedy is therefore on the side of the uncanny and the comic; it is diametrically opposed to the modern character tragedy.

30. With regard to repetition in comedy, the link with polygamy is easily detectable: at the end of *To Be Or Not To Be*, when the lover of the *Hamlet* actor's wife seems to be somewhat pacified, someone quite different leaves the hall just as the monologu begins.

31. Freud, 'Das Unheimliche', p. 237.

32. See Freud, 'Das Unheimliche', p. 234; Otto Rank, *Der Doppelgänger. Eine psychoanalytische Studie* (Vienna: Turia & Kant, 1993)

33. See Blaise Pascal, *Pensées*, trans. A. J. Krailsheimer (Harmondsworth: Penguin. 1995), p. 5 (§ 13).

34. Wittgenstein, *Philosophical Investigations*, 152.

35. See Descartes: 'Yet do I see any more than hats and coats which could conceal ghosts or mechanical men?' (see *http://www.fas.nus.edu.sg/philo/writings/meditations/second.html*).

36. See Henri Bergson, *Laughter: An Essay on the Meaning of the Comic* (Los Angeles, Green Integer, 1999), where he describes the comical as the simultaneous occurrence of an illusion of life and the impression of a mechanical arrangement.

37. Freud, 'Das Unheimliche', p. 227.

38. Freud, 'Das Unheimliche', p. 237; see also Dolar, 'The Aesthetics of the Uncanny', p. 52.

39. Freud, 'Das Unheimliche', p. 244.

40. A single inconsistent detail might make us unsure, or cause us to refine our theoretical view of the world. The uncanny, on the other hand, as Dolar ('The Aesthetics of the Uncanny', p. 64) correctly emphasizes, has to do not with *uncertainty*, but with *certainty.* The inconsistent element appears to confirm a familiar narration. Its *narrative closure* affects us as that dreadful certainty which overrides the *openness of our knowledge.*

41. Every culture seems to contain a whole repertoire of the 'unbelievable': stories that circulate as 'kid stuff', 'old wives' tales,' and so on, and are used by those who believe themselves grown-up to mark their distance from childhood. Nevertheless, it is not necessarily to be assumed in all cases that these stories have ever been believed. This impression could also be a product of *retroactivity.* The 'homely', 'das Heimliche' in Freud's sense, would then describe a 'home', in which we never have been. For instance, what neurotic men perceive as uncanny about the female genitals cannot therefore, as Freud (1919h: 244)

argues, be ascribed to their being 'the former *Heim* [home] of al human beings'. There must, rather, be old wives' tales about 'castration', and so on, which endow the sight with a 'fantastic' meaning.

42. See Pfaller, *Die Illusionen der anderen.*

43. Octave Mannoni, *Clefs pour l'Imaginaire ou l'Autre Scène* (Paris: Seuil, 1985), p. 9.

44. Mannoni, *Clefs pour l'Imaginaire*, p. 20.

45. See in particular his essay 'L'illusion comique', Mannoni, *Clefs pour l'Imaginaire*, pp. 161–83.

46. On Mannoni's examples, see below. One point in which Mannoni's formula for the uncanny appears in Freud practically word for word is the remark on the crocodile story: It was a naive enough story, but the uncanny feeling it produced was quite remarkable' (Freud, 'Das Unheimliche', p. 244) – this means, in Mannoni's terms: '*I know quite well* that this is silly, *but nevertheless* it is really frightening.'

47. Pascal, *Pensées*, p. 241 (§ 795).

48. Mannoni, *Clefs pour l'Imaginaire*, p. 30.

49. See Freud's explanation: 'In Nestroy's farce, *Der Zerrissene* [The Torn Man], another means is used to avoid any impression of the uncanny in the scene in which the fleeing man, convinced that he is a murderer, lifts up one trapdoor after another and each time sees what he takes to be the ghost of his victim rising up out of it. He calls out in despair, "But I've only killed one man. Why this ghastly multiplication?" We know what went before this scene and do not share his error, so what must be uncanny to him has an irresistibly comic effect on us' (Freud, 'Das Unheimliche', p. 252).

50. Freud, 'Das Unheimliche', p. 247. This term 'surmounting' occupies in Freud's theory of 1919 precisely the place where he later inserts his concept of *disavowal* (Freud [1927] 'Fetischismus', *Studienausgabe*, Vol. III [Frankfurt am Main: Fischer, 1989], pp. 379–88.

51. Freud, 'Das Unheimliche', p. 250.

52. Dolar comes to the same conclusion when he pinpoints the uncanny in Gothic Romanticism as a product of the modern age ('The Aesthetics of the Uncanny', p. 53).

53. Freud, 'Das Unheimliche', p. 248.

54. Freud, 'Das Unheimliche', p. 236.

55. See Mannoni, *Clefs pour l'Imaginaire*, p. 163

56. See Mannoni, *Clefs pour l'Imaginaire*, pp. 163f.

57. The classic philosopher of this comic knowledge concerning the question of automatism is, of course, Blaise Pascal: 'For we must make no mistake about ourselves: we are as much automaton as mind . . . .' (Pascal, *Pensées*, p. 247 [§ 821].)

58. Clearly, here the word 'anti-psychological' does not refer to a position that ignores or denies any psychological life. On the contrary: self-deception, which human beings develop regularly, is itself a psychological phenomenon, and a subject of psychoanalysis. The latter is anti-psychological in so far as it gives no credence to such deceptions, but takes them all the more seriously as facts (See Slavoj Žižek, *Liebe Dein Symptom wie Dich selbst! Jacques Lacans Psychoanalyse und die Medien* [Berlin: Merve, 1991], p. 49).

10

Burned by the Sun

Slavoj Žižek

On top of Gellert Hill, in the Buda part of Budapest, there is a monument to the Liberation of the city by the Red Army in 1945: the gigantic statue of a woman waving an unfurled flag. This statue, usually perceived as an exemplary case of socialist-realist baroque *kitsch*, was actually made in 1943 on the orders of the Fascist dictator Admiral Horthy, to honour his son who fell on the Russian front fighting the Red Army; when, in 1945, Marshall Kliment Voroshilov, the Soviet commander, was shown the statue, he thought it could serve as the monument of liberation . . . does this anecdote not tell us a lot about the openness of the 'message' of a work of art? Within the horizon of traditional metaphysics, art is about (beautiful) appearances, and science is about the reality beneath the appearances. Today's sciences, however, focus more and more on the weird domain of autonomized appearances, of phenomenal processes deprived of any substantial support; no wonder, then, that, in a symmetrical counter-movement, modern art is more and more focused on the Real Thing. Is not the most succinct definition of modern art that it is art 'beyond the pleasure principle'? One is supposed to enjoy traditional art, it is expected to generate aesthetic pleasure, in contrast to modern art, which causes displeasure – modern art, by definition, *hurts*. In this precise sense, modern art is sublime: it causes pleasure-in-pain, it produces its effect through its own failure, in so far as it refers to impossible Things.[1] In contrast, beauty, harmonious balance, seems to be more and more the domain of the sciences: already Einstein's relativity theory, this paradigm of modern science, is praised for its simple elegance – no wonder the title of Brian Greene's bestselling introduction to string theory is *The Elegant Universe.*

The traditional Platonic frame of reference is thus turned around: sciences deal with phenomena, events, appearances; art deals with the hard Real: this 'Real Thing', the struggle to convey it, is the proper 'object' of art. In his memoirs, Dmitri Shostakovich dismissed Sergei Prokofiev, his great competitor, for refusing to take historical horrors seriously, always playing the 'wise guy'. To name just one supreme example, however, Prokofiev's first violin sonata (Opus 80) clearly demonstrates the obverse of the composer's (in)famous 'irony':

> Throughout its four movements . . . one senses a powerful undertow of struggle. Yet it is not the struggle of a work against something outside itself, but rather the struggle of something within the work, unmanifested, trying desperately to break out, and constantly finding its emergence 'blocked' by the existing, outward form and language of the piece. This blocking of 'something within' . . . has to do with the frustration of a desire for cathartic release into some supremely positive state of being, where meaning – musical and supra-musical – is transparent, unironizable: in short, a domain of spiritual 'purity'.[2]

It is here that Prokofiev pays the price for his ironic stance, and it is such passages that bear witness to his artistic integrity: far from indicating any kind of vain intellectual superiority, this ironic stance is just the falsely bright obverse of the *failure of Prokofiev's constant struggle to bring the 'Thing from Inner Space' (the 'something within') out.* The superficial 'playfulness' of some of Prokofiev's works (like his popular First Symphony) merely reveals, in a negative way, the fact that Prokofiev is the ultimate anti-Mozart, a kind of Beethoven whose 'titanic struggle' ended in disaster: if Mozart was *the* supreme musical genius, perhaps the last composer with whom the musical Thing transposed itself into musical notes in a spontaneous flow, and if in Beethoven a piece achieved its definitive Form only after a long heroic struggle with the musical material, Prokofiev's greatest pieces are monuments to the defeat of this struggle.

Is, then, this 'Thing from inner space' my inner 'genius' (that which is in me but is more than myself, the impersonal force that drives me[3])? The relationship between this 'genius' and my 'ego', the core of my person, belongs to a field which has nothing to do with the Freudian unconscious proper, or, even more, with the strict philosophical notion of subjectivity. Its proper place, rather, is in the *Lebensphilosophie* and Jungian problematic: the ego does not cover the whole of our subjectivity, it is something that can emerge only through a long process of individuation out of and against the background of a vast impersonal field of our 'psychic substance', the id in a more Jungian than properly Freudian sense. That is to say: the Freudian unconscious has nothing to do with the id of *Lebensphilosophie* (and, consequently, the subject of the unconscious has nothing to do with the ego). So what is the subject of the unconscious (or, simply, the subject proper)? Here we should recall Kierkegaard's wonderful short text 'On the Difference between Genius and Apostle', where he defines the genius as the individual who is able to express/articulate 'that which is in him more than himself', his spiritual substance, in contrast to the apostle who, 'in himself', does not matter at all: the apostle is a purely formal function of the one who has dedicated his life to bearing witness to an impersonal Truth that transcends him. He is a messenger who was chosen (by grace): he possesses no inner features that would qualify him for this role. Lacan mentions in this context a diplomat who serves as a representative of his country: his idiosyncrasies are irrelevant, whatever he does is read as a message from his country to the country to which he is posted – if, at a major diplomatic conference, he coughs, this is interpreted as softly indicating his state's doubt about the measures debated at the conference, and so on. And Lacan's paradoxical conclusion is that the Freudian 'subject of the unconscious' (or what Lacan calls 'subject of the signifier') has the structure of the Kierkegaardian apostle: he is witness to an 'impersonal' Truth.

Is not what we encounter in hysteria precisely a 'body of truth': in the bodily symptoms that result from the hysterical 'conversion', the immediate organic body is invaded, kidnapped, by a Truth, transformed into a bearer of truth, into a space/surface on to which the Truths (of the unconscious) are inscribed – hysteria is the ultimate case of Lacan's *c'est moi, la vérité, qui parle.* In short, the structure here is that of a Kierkegaardian apostle: the body is cancelled/suspended as indifferent in its immediate reality; it is taken over as the medium of Truth. And we should not be afraid to draw the line from here to Stalin's notorious words at Lenin's funeral: 'We, Communists, are not like other people. We are made of a special stuff' – this 'special stuff' is precisely the body transubstantiated into the body of Truth. In his famous short poem 'The Solution' (1953; published in 1956), Brecht mocks the arrogance of the Communist *nomenklatura* faced with the workers' revolt:

> After the uprising of the 17th June
> The Secretary of the Writers' Union
> Had leaflets distributed in the *Stalinallee*
> Stating that the people
> Had forfeited the confidence of the government
> And could win it back only
> By redoubled efforts.
> Would it not be easier
> In that case for the government
> To dissolve the people
> And elect another?[4]

However, this poem is not only politically opportunistic, the obverse of his letter of solidarity with the East German Communist regime published in *Neues Deutschland* (to put it brutally, Brecht wanted to cover both his flanks: to profess his support for the regime as well as to hint at his solidarity with the workers, so that whoever won, he would be on the winning side), but also simply *wrong* in the theoretico-political sense: one should bravely admit that it *is* in effect a duty – even *the* duty – of a revolutionary party to 'dissolve the people and elect another', that is, to bring about the transubstantiation of the 'old' opportunistic people (the inert 'crowd') into a revolutionary body aware of its historical task, to transform the body of the empirical people into a body of Truth. Far from being an easy task, to 'dissolve the people and elect another' is the most difficult of them all.

Thus we have two couples of opposites which should be strictly distinguished: the axis *ego–id* and the axis *subject–Truth*. The subject has nothing to do with ego as the expression and organizing agency of a reservoir of psychic forces and drives: it is rather, in an almost bureaucratic sense, a functionary of anonymous Truth. When, at the very end of Shakespeare's *Tempest*, after freeing Ariel, his genius, Prospero stands alone ('Now my charms are all overthrown, /And what strength I have is mine own'), does he not thereby leave behind not only his genius, but also his ego? Does he not enter a different field, that of subjectivity proper? The subject is the one who can say 'what strength I have is mine own'. The subject proper is empty, a kind of formal function, a void which remains after I sacrifice my ego (the wealth that constitutes my 'person'). The shift from ego to the subject, from the axis *ego–id* to the axis *subject–Truth*, is synonymous with the emergence of the ethical dimension proper: I change from an individual, a person, into a subject the moment I turn into the agent of an impersonal Truth, the moment I accept as my task the endless work of bearing witness to this truth.[5] As such, I am nothing in myself: my entire authority is that of Truth – or, as Kierkegaard put it apropos of Christ: with regard to their content, Christ's positive statements are no more profound than the statements of an average student of theology; what accounts for the abyss that separates them is that one was the ultimate apostle of Truth while the other was not. The structure here is extremely 'dogmatic': what matters is *who* said it, not *what* he said. This may appear to contradict my previous point that what matters is Truth, not the subject propagating it; however, therein resides the paradox of the authority of Truth: Truth is characterized not by the inherent features of true propositions, but by the mere formal fact that these propositions were spoken from the *position* of Truth. Consequently, in an exact parallel to the fact that the subject is a pure messenger, an apostle of Truth, with no regard to his inherent properties, Truth itself is not a property of statements, but *that which makes them true.* Truth is like ready-made art: a urinal is a work of art when it occupies the place of a work of art – no material property distinguishes Duchamp's urinal from the urinal in a nearby public toilet.

What, then, *is* this 'thing from inner space', in so far as it stands for Truth as *agency*? The famous 'stolen boat' episode from Wordsworth's *Prelude* provides the precise co-ordinates of its emergence:

> One summer evening (led by her [Nature]) I found
> A little boat tied to a willow tree
> Within a rocky cave, its usual home.
> Straight I unloosed her chain, and stepping in
> Pushed from the shore. It was an act of stealth
> And troubled pleasure, nor without the voice
> Of mountain-echoes did my boat move on;
> Leaving behind her still, on either side,
> Small circles glittering idly in the moon,
> Until they melted all into one track
> Of sparkling light. But now, like one who rows,
> Proud of his skill, to reach a chosen point
> With an unswerving line, I fixed my view
> Upon the summit of a craggy ridge,
> The horizon's utmost boundary; far above
> Was nothing but the stars and the grey sky.
> She was an elfin pinnace; lustily
> I dipped my oars into the silent lake,
> And, as I rose upon the stroke, my boat
> Went heaving through the water like a swan;
> When, from behind that craggy steep till then
> The horizon's bound, a huge peak, black and huge,
> As if with voluntary power instinct,
> Upreared its head. I struck and struck again,
> And growing still in stature the grim shape
> Towered up between me and the stars, and still,
> For so it seemed, with purpose of its own
> And measured motion like a living thing,
> Strode after me. With trembling oars I turned,
> And through the silent water stole my way
> Back to the covert of the willow tree;
> There in her mooring-place I left my bark,
> And through the meadows homeward went, in grave
> And serious mood; but after I had seen
> That spectacle, for many days, my brain

Worked with a dim and undetermined sense
Of unknown modes of being; o'er my thoughts
There hung a darkness, call it solitude
Or blank desertion. No familiar shapes
Remained, no pleasant images of trees,
Of sea or sky, no colours of green fields;
But huge and mighty forms, that do not live
Like living men, moved slowly through the mind
By day, and were a trouble to my dreams.

It is clear what 'actually happened' in this episode: the young boy was a victim of an optical illusion:

> When he rowed away from the cave the boy had fixed his gaze upon the top of a ridge, behind which there initially seemed to be nothing but the sky. As he rowed further out on to the lake, however, a more distant peak, behind the ridge, came into view. The further he is from the shore (and his first instinct is to row faster: 'I struck, and struck again') the more he can see of the mountain; it therefore seemed to be 'growing still in stature'. There is, then, an extremely rational explanation for what the boy sees. His imagination, however, transforms the mountain into a 'living thing' which 'strode after me'.[6]

This is how a 'thing from inner space' emerges. All the ingredients of a fantasy-staging are here – the noumenal 'shines through' in what is 'actually' just an optical illusion. That is to say: far from being a simple descendant of the Kantian Thing-in-itself, the Freudian 'Thing from Inner Space' is its inherent opposite: what appears as the excess of some transcendent force over 'normal' external reality is the very place of the direct inscription of my subjectivity into this reality. In other words, what I get back in the guise of the horrifying-unrepresentable Thing is the objectivization, the objectal correlate, of my own gaze – as Wordsworth put it, the Thing is the 'sober colouring' reality gets from the eye observing it:

The Clouds that gather round the setting sun
Do take a sober colouring from an eye
That hath kept watch o'er man's mortality.[7]

Perhaps, from this perspective of the Thing as Evil, one should turn around the well-known Augustinian notion of Evil as having no positive substance or force of its own, but being just the absence of Good: *Good itself is the absence of Evil*, the distance towards the Evil Thing. To put it in transcendental terms: the Good is the mode of appearance of Evil, 'schematized' Evil. The difference between Good and Evil is thus a parallax. The common definition of parallax is an apparent displacement of an object (the shift of its position against a background) caused by a change in observational position that provides a new line of sight. The philosophical twist to be added, of course, is that the observed difference is not simply 'subjective', due to the fact that the same object which exists 'out there' is seen from two different stations, or points of view. It is rather that, as Hegel would have put it, subject and object are inherently 'mediated', so that an 'epistemological' shift in the subject's point of view always reflects an 'ontological' shift in the object itself. Or, to put it in Lacanese, the subject's gaze is always-already inscribed into the perceived object itself, in the guise of its 'blind spot', that which is 'in the object more than object itself', the point from which the object itself returns the gaze.

The 'action' of Juan José Saer's *Nobody Nothing Never* (*nadie nada nunca*, 1980), this masterpiece of pure parallax, is minimal, practically nonexistent: during a stifling Argentinian summer, Cat Garay, heir to a once-prosperous, now declining family, and his lover Elisa try to protect their horse from a horse-killer on the loose; their intense affair and the hunt for the killer on the banks of the Parana river take place in the atmosphere of political anxiety and disintegration. The story progresses so that every event is told twice, first in the voice of an 'objective' narrator, then in Cat's voice – with the same phrases often repeated verbatim. Is this not like Malevich's *Black Square on White Background* the marking of a purely formal minimal difference, gap, against the background of the 'nothing' of narrated content? We are dealing here not with a substantial difference between two particular contents, but with a 'pure' difference that separates an object from itself and, as such, marks the point at which the subject's gaze is inscribed into the perceived object. The same minimal difference is the point around which the poems of Alejandra Pizarnik, another supreme Argentinian writer, turn. Three short poems from her supreme achievement, *Arbol de Diana* ([*Tree of Diana*], 1962), fully display her almost Zen-like succinct precision:

> like a poem buried in [*enterrado del*: by]
> the silence of things
> you speak to ignore me [*para no verme*: in order not to see me][8]
>
> far beyond any forbidden zone
> is a mirror for our sad reflections [*transparencia*][9]
>
> This song of regret [*arrepentido*], alert, behind my poems:
> This song denies me, chokes my voice.[10]

These lines are interconnected in a way which becomes discernible if one adds a line from 'Signs', a poem from a later collection, *El infierno musical* ([*The musical hell*], 1971):

Everything makes love with silence.[11]

Pizarnik is arguably *the* poet of subtraction, of minimal difference: the difference between nothing and something, between silence and a fragmented voice. The primordial fact is not Silence (waiting to be broken by the divine Word) but Noise, the confused murmur of the Real in which there is not yet any distinction between a figure and its background. The first creative act is therefore to *create silence* – it is not that silence is broken, but that silence itself breaks, interrupts, the continuous murmur of the Real, thus opening up a space in which words can be spoken. There is no speech proper without this background of silence: as Heidegger knew, all speech answers the 'sound of silence'. Hard work is needed to create silence, to encircle its place in the same way as a vase creates its central void. This is how the death drive and sublimation are strictly correlative: the death drive has first to erase the murmur of the Real, and thus open up the space for sublime formations. Where poetry is concerned, this difference is not between poems, but between poem(s) and the song which, of course, has to remain unsung, unspoken, since it is the song of silence.

It is here that the visual dimension enters; recall Nietzsche's complaint: 'Must one smash their ears before they learn to listen with their eyes?' (*Thus Spake Zarathustra*, Prologue, 5). Is this complaint about the difficulty of teaching people how to listen not ambiguous? Does it mean that it is difficult to learn to *listen with one's eyes*, or that it is simply difficult to learn to *truly listen*? In other words, if we follow Wagner's Tristan (who, while dying, shouts: 'I see her [Isolde's] voice!') and accept, as one of the definitions of modern art, that one has to listen to it with one's eyes, does this mean that one can truly hear (hear the silence, the silent Message-Thing covered by the chatter of words) only with one's eyes? As a result, is not modern painting (as indicated already by Munch's *The Scream*) a 'sound of silence', the visual rendering of the point at which words break down? And, incidentally, this is also how the critique of ideology (whose Platonic origins we should unabashedly admit) functions: it endeavours to smash our ears (hypnotized by ideology's siren song) so that we can start to hear with our eyes (in the mode of *theoria*).

Back to Pizarnik: avoiding fake obscurantism, we should not be afraid to read these four fragments 'logically', as parts of a complex *argument*, providing clues for each other. So let us begin with the last line, 'everything makes love with silence': this, of course, does not mean that there is a sexual relationship between Something and Nothing, but, precisely, its failure: this lovemaking has failed. That is to say: the voice of silence, that of 'a poem buried in the silence of things', is not a silent support, protective and caring of the poet's words, but that which speaks 'to ignore' the poet, a brutal malevolently neutral entity which 'alert, behind my poems . . . denies me, chokes my voice'. So when Pizarnik refers to this song of silence as a 'mirror for our sad reflections', located 'far beyond any forbidden zone', this, again, makes it an inaccessible threatening entity, in Kantian terms: a song which dwells in the terrifying noumenal domain of the Real in which a kind of 'objective' truth (or, rather, a totally objectifying knowledge) about me is inscribed.

In order to clarify this key point, let us recall a wonderful scene in *The Matrix*, when Cipher, the traitor, the agent of the Matrix among the rebels, who is located in reality, kills rebels (who are immersed into the VR of the Matrix) one after the other by simply unplugging them from their connection to the machine. While the rebels are experiencing themselves as fully immersed in ordinary reality, they are actually, in the 'desert of the Real', immobilized on the chair on which they are connected to the Matrix: Cipher has the direct physical approach to them as they 'really are', helpless creatures just sitting on the chair, as if under narcosis at the dentist's, who can thus be mishandled in any way the torturer wants. Cipher is communicating with them via the phone which serves as the communicating link between virtual reality and the 'desert of the Real', and the horror of the situation is that while the rebels feel like normal human beings freely walking around in reality, they know that, at the Other Scene of the 'desert of the Real', a simple unplugging of the cable will cause them to drop dead in both universes, virtual and real. This situation, while it is parallel to that of all humans who are plugged into the Matrix, is worse in so far as here, humans are fully aware not only of their true situation but also of the threat posed in reality by the evil agent who intends to kill them soon. It is as if here the subjects obtain the impossible direct link with the Real of their situation, the Real in all its threatening dimension. This Other Scene is 'a mirror for our sad reflections . . . far beyond any forbidden zone'.

This, of course, brings us back to Plato's cave: how can one survive a direct confrontation with the Sun, the ultimate Real, without getting burned by the rays of its heat? Among the poets, it was Hölderlin who focused on the risks of this confrontation, paying for it the highest price: madness. And we are in a domain in which the fall into madness has a clear political connotation. Georg Lukács deserves to be cited here – we should recall 'Hölderlin's *Hyperion*', his weird but crucial short essay from 1935, in which Lukács praises Hegel's endorsement of the Napoleonic Thermidor against Hölderlin's intransigent fidelity to the heroic revolutionary utopia:

> Hegel comes to terms with the post-Thermidorian epoch and the close of the revolutionary period of bourgeois development, and he builds up his philosophy precisely on an understanding of this new turning-point in world history. Hölderlin makes no compromise with the post-Thermidorian reality; he remains faithful to the old revolutionary ideal of renovating 'polis' democracy and is broken by a reality which has no place for his ideals, not even on the level of poetry and thought.[12]

Here Lukács is referring to Marx's notion that the heroic period of the French Revolution was the necessary enthusiastic breakthrough followed by the unheroic phase of market relations: the true social function of the Revolution was to establish the condition for the prosaic reign of bourgeois economy, and true heroism lies not in blindly clinging to the early revolutionary enthusiasm, but in recognizing 'the rose in the Cross of the present', as Hegel liked to paraphrase Luther – that is, in abandoning the position of the Beautiful Soul and fully accepting the present as the only possible domain of actual freedom. It was thus this 'compromise' with social reality which enabled Hegel's crucial philosophical step forward, that of overcoming the proto-Fascist notion of 'organic' community in his *System der Sittlichkeit* manuscript, and engaging in the dialectical analysis of the antagonisms of bourgeois civil society. (That is the properly dialectical paradox of the proto-Fascist endeavour to return to a premodern 'organic' community: far from being simply 'reactionary', Fascist 'feudal Socialism' is a kind of compromise-solution, an ersatz attempt to build socialism within the constraints of capitalism itself.) It is obvious that this analysis by Lukács is deeply allegorical: it was written a couple of months after Trotsky launched his thesis of Stalinism as the Thermidor of the October Revolution. Lukács's text has thus to be read as an answer to Trotsky: he accepts Trotsky's characterization of Stalin's regime as 'Thermidorian', giving it a positive twist – instead of bemoaning the loss of utopian energy, one should, in a heroically resigned way, accept its consequences as the only actual space of social progress. . . . For Marx, of course, the sobering 'day after' which follows the revolutionary intoxication reveals the original limitation of the 'bourgeois' revolutionary project, the falsity of its promise of universal freedom: the 'truth' is that universal human rights are the rights of commerce and private property. If we read Lukács's endorsement of the Stalinist Thermidor, it implies (arguably against his conscious intention) an utterly anti-Marxist pessimistic perspective: the proletarian revolution itself is also characterized by the gap between its illusory universal assertion of freedom and the ensuing awakening in the new relations of domination and exploitation, which means that the Communist project of realizing 'actual freedom' had failed.

Hölderlin's starting point is the same as Hegel's: the gap between (the impossible return to) traditional organic unity and the modern reflective freedom – how are we to overcome it? His answer is what he calls the 'eccentric path': the insight into how the very endless oscillation between the two poles, the very impossibility and repeated failure to reach the final peace, *is* already the thing itself – that is, this eternal way *is* man's fate. What Hölderlin fails to do, however, is to accomplish the next properly *Hegelian* step into the true speculative unity of the two poles: his limitation is best epitomized by the title of his philosophical fragment, 'Being and Judgement (*Ur-Teil*, primordial division)'. For Hölderlin, being is the always-already lost pre-reflexive Ground to which we eternally long to return – what he does not do is to conclude that this very presupposed Ground is already retroactively posited and, as such, already (a name for) *pure difference*. In short, what eludes Hölderlin is the true nature of Hegelian Universality as the site of the structural deadlock, of an impasse which particular formations endeavour to resolve. It is for *this* reason that, towards 1800, he definitely turns to poetry as the most appropriate way to describe the 'eccentric path' of man – so, in his case at least, the turn to poetry is an escape, an index of the failure to accomplish the work of thought.

The solution of *Hyperion* is that of a narrative: what in reality cannot be reconciled is reconciled afterwards, through its narrative reconstruction. (The interesting and crucial feature of *Hyperion*, this novel composed of letters, is that *all* the letters are written *after* the 'actual' events.) Is it adequate, then, to read this solution as *Hegelian* – that is, to claim that, in a clear parallel to Hegel's *Phenomenology of Spirit*, Hölderlin sees the solution in a narrative which retroactively reconstructs the very 'eccentric path' of permanent oscillation between the loss of the Centre and the repeated failed attempts to regain the immediacy of the Centre as the process of maturation, of spiritual education? Read in this way, Hölderlin's later shift can easily be interpreted as a farewell to the metaphysics of subjectivity, as breaking out of the metaphysical closure and the assumption of an irreducible gap covered by metaphysics. The model of such a reading is Eric Santner's book on Hölderlin: for Santner, the late Hölderlinian break occurs when this narrative synthesis and *Aufhebung* of tension is threatened, even abandoned, by the 'sober' acceptance of irreducible multitude which can no longer be reconciled in an overall narrative scheme. And, as Santner points out, this abandonment of the encompassing narrative frame leads not to abandonment of links between fragments but to the discovery of a new level of interconnectedness, a 'paratactic' field of secret links, of echoes and reverberations between monadic elements – something, I am tempted to claim, not unlike the inner links of Plato's *chora* which precede the grid of Ideas.[13]

Here I should introduce a triple, not just bipolar, structure: the narrative procedure is neither the direct exposure to 'fire from heaven' (the ecstatic throwing-oneself into the lethal bliss of the divine Thing) nor the deadly sobriety of icy everyday life, with its meaningless multiplicity, but a mediation of the multiplicity itself. In other words, while Santner locates 'narrative vigilance' on the side of the 'fire from heaven', treating it exclusively as a defence against the dispersed multitude of sober and icy ordinary life, would it not be even more appropriate to treat it as a defence against the ecstatic dissolution of all structure in the 'fire from heaven', as an attempt to retain a minimal structure of life? Is the narrative not ultimately a narrative about what Hölderlin called the 'law of succession', the paternal symbolic order which keeps the chaotic abyss of the Sacred at a proper distance?[14] Furthermore, are not paratactic coexistence and a mystical experience of Oneness on the same side, both opposed to narrative organization? Is not the ecstatic experience of Oneness something which emerges only when we step outside the grid of a narrative and confront absolutely particular monadic entities?

The shift in Hölderlin, deployed by Santner, from 'narrative vigilance', from subordinating everything to the grand narrative of the westward movement of gods, and laying the foundation for the arrival of new gods, to 'sobriety', to the marking of the signs of daily life, can be perfectly well explained in the Heideggerian terms of the shift from onto-theology, from an all-encompassing metaphysical narrative, to the post-metaphysical attitude of *Gelassenheit*, of 'letting things be' outside any frame of metaphysical justification – like Angelus Silesius' rose, which is 'ohne Warum'.[15] The irony here, however, is double. First, Santner himself develops this shift in a book which totally ignores Heidegger (and to write a book on Hölderlin ignoring Heidegger is an achievement in itself). Secondly, Heidegger himself, in his detailed readings of Hölderlin, also ignores this 'Heideggerian' aspect of the texture of Hölderlin's poetry – the paratactic disintegration of the narrative unity – and focuses precisely on the grand narrative of the withdrawal and possible new arrival of gods.

What if we read Hölderlin's shift as a shift from desire to drive? 'Vigilance' is vigilance for partial objects around which drives circulate. Such a reading has a precise sociopolitical background: we should approach Hölderlin's openness to the signs of everyday life through the perspective of one of the key features of capitalism: namely, the permanent production of piles of waste. The obverse of the incessant capitalist drive to produce new objects are thus the growing accretions of useless waste, piled-up mountains of used cars, computers, and so forth, like the famous aeroplane 'resting place' in the Mojave Desert – in these ever-growing heaps of inert, dysfunctional 'stuff', whose useless, lifeless presence cannot fail to affect us, we can, as it were, perceive the capitalist drive at rest. Here we should recall Benjamin's insight into how we encounter historicity proper precisely when we observe cultural artifacts in decay, in the process of being reclaimed by nature. In November 2003, after a visit to Poland, where he participated in the Camerimage festival and opened an exhibition of his own paintings and sculptures in łódź, David Lynch was completely fascinated by this truly 'post-industrial' city: the big industrial centre with most of the steel works and other factories in decay, full of crumbling grey concrete housing developments, with extremely polluted air and water. . . . Lynch wants to invest money there to create his own cinema studio, and help to transform łódź into a thriving centre of cultural creativity (Peter Weir and Roland Joffe are also linked to this project). Lynch has emphasized that he 'feels very much at home in Poland' – not in the Romantic Poland of Chopin and *Solidarność*, but precisely in this ecologically ruined Poland of industrial wastelands. This news once more confirms Lynch's extraordinary sensitivity, on account of which we should be ready to forget his reactionary political statements, as well as his ridiculous support for a New Age megalomaniac project of a mega-centre for meditation. The post-industrial wasteland of the *Second* World is in effect the privileged 'evental site', the symptomal point from which we can undermine the totality of today's global capitalism. We should *love* this world, up to and including its grey decaying buildings and sulphurous smell – all this stands for *history*, threatened with erasure between the post-historical First World and the prehistorical Third World.

Notes

1. Is postmodern art, then, a return to pleasure?

2. Ronald Woodley, accompanying text to the recording by Martha Argerich and Gidon Kremer (Deutsche Grammophon 431 803–2).

3. Do not the three emblematic figures of musical genius, Bach–Mozart–Beethoven (vaguely corresponding to the painter's triad of Leonardo–Raphael–Michelangelo), stand for the three modes, of coping with the traumatic-excessive Thing in me which is my genius? One can either practise one's genius as an artisan, unburdened by any divine mission, just doing one's hard work (Bach); or one can be lucky enough to be able to deploy one's genius into an unencumbered flow of creativity, with an almost childish spontaneity (Mozart); or one's genius is a kind of inner demon which compels the artist to create his work in the process of painful titanic struggle (Beethoven), enforcing its will against and on to the resisting stuff.

4. Bertolt Brecht, *Gedichte in einem Band* (Frankfurt: Suhrkamp, 1982), pp. 1009–10.
5. Reference to Alain Badiou's notion of truth is crucial here, of course.
6. Alan Gardiner, *The Poetry of William Wordsworth* (Harmondsworth: Penguin, 1990), p. 84.
7. See also: '. . . the midnight storm / Grew darker in the presence of my eye'.
8. Alejandra Pizarnik and Susan Bassnett, *Exchanging Lives* (Leeds: Peepal Tree, 2002), p. 20.
9. Pizarnik and Bassnett, *Exchanging Lives*, p. 25.
10. Pizarnik and Bassnett, *Exchanging Lives*, p. 26.
11. Pizarnik and Bassnett, *Exchanging Lives*, p. 32.
12. Georg Lukács, 'Hölderlin's *Hyperion*', in *Goethe and His Age* (London: Allen & Unwin, 1968), p. 137.
13. See Eric Santner, *Friedrich Hölderlin: Narrative Vigilance and the Poetic Imagination* (New Brunswick: Rutgers University Press, 1986).
14. What cannot but appear as the most radical opposite of Heidegger's reading, the Oedipal reading of Hölderlin's breakdown (developed in the 1960s by Jean Laplanche), is thoroughly convincing: as Hölderlin himself clearly noted, he was unable to *locate the lack*, that is, he was living in a permanent state of ontic-ontological short circuit in which every experience of (even a minor) ontic failure or imperfection threatened to explode into an ontological catastrophe, into a disintegration of the entire world. Instead of dismissing this reading as psychologically reductionist, ontic, missing the ontologico-historical level, we should, rather, elevate the unfortunate 'Oedipus complex' to the dignity of ontology.
15. Why does Heidegger focus almost exclusively on Hölderlin's poems? Why does he totally ignore his philosophical fragments and the novel *Hyperion*? There is a good reason: his late poems signal the breakdown of the solution Hölderlin tried to articulate in *Hyperion* and his philosophical fragments from the late 1790s.

11

The Politics of Redemption, or, Why Richard Wagner Is Worth Saving

Slavoj Žižek

The Wagnerian Sublime

With Romanticism, music changes its role: it is no longer a mere accompaniment to the message delivered in speech, it contains/conveys a message of its own, 'deeper' than the one delivered in words. It was Rousseau who first clearly articulated this expressive potential of music as such when he claimed that music, instead of merely imitating the affective features of verbal speech, should be given the right to 'speak for itself' – in contrast to deceptive verbal speech, in music it is – to paraphrase Lacan – the truth itself which speaks. As Schopenhauer put it, music directly enacts/expresses the noumenal Will, while speech remains limited to the level of phenomenal representation. Music is the substance which goes to the true heart of the subject, which is what Hegel called the 'Night of the World', the abyss of radical negativity: music becomes the bearer of the true message beyond words with the shift from the Enlightenment subject of rational *Logos* to the Romantic subject of the 'Night of the World', that is, the shift of the metaphor for the kernel of the subject from Day to Night. Here we encounter the Uncanny: no longer external transcendence, but, following Kant's transcendental turn, the excess of Night at the very heart of the subject (the dimension of the Undead), what Tomlinson has called the 'internal otherworldliness that marks the Kantian subject'.[1] What music conveys is no longer the 'semantics of the soul', but the underlying 'noumenal' flux of *jouissance* beyond linguistic meaningfulness. This noumenal is radically different from the pre-Kantian transcendent divine Truth: it is the inaccessible excess which forms the very core of the subject.

After such a celebration of musicality, we cannot but agree with Vladimir Nabokov when he characterized the ideal state as the one in which there is 'no torture, no executions, and no music'. . . .[2] Indeed, the line of separation between the sublime and the ridiculous, between a noble act and a pathetic empty gesture, is ultimately untraceable. Recall the beginning of the first movement of Beethoven's Ninth Symphony: was there ever a more succinct declaration of the resolute stance, the stubborn stance of the uncompromising will to enact one's decision?[3] However, is it not true that, if one just barely shifts the perspective, the same gesture cannot fail to appear as a ridiculous exaggeration, a hysterical handwaving which betrays the fact that we are actually dealing with an imposture? What, however, if we read the stance of the first movement not as dignity, but as the *obstinacy* of the 'undead' drive? What this oscillation of ours means is that there is no kitsch in itself: what Bartók achieves in his 'Concerto for Orchestra' is to *redeem* the ultimate kitsch melody from Lehár's *The Merry Widow* – the quotation of Lehár is in no way meant ironically, since setting it in a different context de-fetishizes it, providing it with a proper musical environment out of which this beautiful melody emerges 'organically'. Fortunately however, the problem with this expressive potential of music is that, brought to its conclusion, to the end, it cancels itself: when we progress to the very core of the subject, we encounter the fantasmatic kernel of enjoyment which can no longer be subjectivized, affectively assumed by the subject – the subject can only stare, with a cold transfixed gaze, at this kernel, unable fully to recognize himself in it. Recall 'Der Laienmann', the last song of Schubert's *Winterreise*: at the very nadir of despair, emotions are frozen, we are back at the non-expressive mechanism, the subject is reduced to the utter despair of mimicking the automatism of mechanical music.

In the history of opera, this sublime excess of life is discernible in two main versions, Italian and German, Rossini and Wagner – so maybe, although they are the great opposites, Wagner's surprising private sympathy for Rossini, as well as their friendly meeting in Paris, does bear witness to a deeper affinity. Rossini's great male portraits, the three from *Barbiere* (Figaro's 'Largo il factotum', Basilio's 'Calumnia' and Bartolo's 'Un dottor della mia sorte'), together with the father's wishful self-portrait of corruption in *Cenerentola*, enact a mock self-complaint, where one imagines oneself in a desired position, being bombarded by demands for a favour or service. The subject shifts his position twice: first he assumes the roles of those who address him, enacting the overwhelming multitude of demands which bombard him; then he feigns a reaction to it, the state of deep satisfaction in being overwhelmed by demands he cannot fulfil. Let us take the father in *Cenerentola*: he imagines how, when one of his daughters is married to the Prince, people will turn to him, offering him bribes for a service at court, and he will react first with cunning deliberation, then with fake despair at being bombarded with too many requests. . . . The culminating moment of the archetypal Rossini aria is this unique moment of happiness, of the full assertion of the excess of Life which occurs when the subject is overwhelmed by demands, no longer able to deal with them. At the high point of his 'factotum' aria, Figaro exclaims: 'What a crowd /Of the people bombarding me with their demands/ – Have mercy, one after the other [*Uno per volta, per carità*]!', referring to the Kantian experience of the Sublime, in which the subject is bombarded with an excess of data that he is unable to comprehend. The basic economy here is obsessional: the object of the hero's desire is the other's demand.

This excess is the proper counterpoint to the Wagnerian Sublime, to the 'höchste Lust' of the immersion into the Void that concludes *Tristan*. This opposition of the Rossinian and the Wagnerian Sublime perfectly fits the Kantian opposition between the mathematical and the dynamic Sublime: as we have just seen, the Rossinian Sublime is mathematical, it enacts the subject's inability to comprehend the sheer quantity of the demands that overwhelm him, while the Wagnerian Sublime is dynamic, it enacts the concentrated overpowering force of the *one* demand, the unconditional demand of love. One can also say that the Wagnerian Sublime is the absolute Emotion – this is how one should read the famous first sentence of Wagner's 'Religion and Art', where he claims that when religion becomes artificial, art can save its true spirit, its hidden truth – how? Precisely by abandoning the dogma and expressing only the authentic religious emotion, that is, by transforming religion into the ultimate aesthetic experience. (And the paradox of *Parsifal* is that it turns *Tristan* around: the intimate metaphysical experience is again forcefully externalized, turned into, precisely, *ritual* – the high points of *Parsifal* are undoubtedly the two Grail rituals.)

Tristan should thus be read as the resolution of the tension between sublime passion and religion still operative in *Tannhäuser*. The entreaty at the beginning of *Tannhäuser* enacts a strange reversal of the standard entreaty: it is not an entreaty to escape the constraints of mortality and rejoin the beloved, but an entreaty, addressed to the beloved, to let the hero go and return to the mortal life of pain, struggle and freedom. Tannhäuser complains that, as a mortal, he cannot bear the continuous enjoyment ('Wenn stets ein Gott geniessen kann, bin ich dem Wechsel untertan; nicht Lust allein liegt mir am Herzen, aus Freuden sehn ich mich nach Schmerzen/Though a god may incessantly savour enjoyment, I am subject to change; pleasure alone does not lie close to my heart – in the midst of joy I crave after pain'). A little later, he makes it clear that what he is longing for is the peace of death itself: 'Mein Sehnen drängt zum Kampfe, nicht such ich Wonn und Lust! Ach mögest du es fassen, Göttin! [*wild*] Hin zum Tod, den ich suche, zum Tode drängt es mich!/my longing drives me to combat; I do not seek pleasure and rapture!

Oh, if you would understand, Goddess! [*wildly*] Hence I seek after death, I am drawn to death!' If there is a conflict here between eternity and temporal existence, between transcendence and earthly reality, then Venus is on the side of a terrifying *eternity* of unbearable excessive *Geniessen.*

This provides the key to the opera's central conflict: it is *not*, as is usually claimed, the conflict between the spiritual and the physical, the Sublime and the ordinary pleasures of the flesh, but a conflict inherent to the Sublime itself, splitting it up. Venus and Elisabeth are *both* metaphysical figures of the Sublime: neither of the two is a woman destined to become a common wife. While Elisabeth is, obviously, the sacred virgin, the purely spiritual entity, the *untouchable* idealized Lady of courtly love, Venus also stands for a metaphysical excess, that of excessively intensified sexual enjoyment; if anything, it is Elisabeth who is closer to ordinary earthly life. In Kierkegaard's terms, one could say that Venus stands for the Aesthetic and Elisabeth for the Religious – on condition that one conceives here of the Aesthetic as included in the Religious, elevated to the level of the unconditional Absolute. And that is Tannhäuser's unpardonable sin: not that he engaged in a bit of free sexuality (in this case, the severe punishment would have been ridiculously exaggerated) but that he elevated sexuality, sexual lust, to the level of the Absolute, asserting it as the inherent obverse of the Sacred. This is why the roles of Venus and Elisabeth should definitely be played by the same singer: the two *are* one and the same person; the only difference lies in the male hero's attitude towards her. Is this not clear from the final choice Tannhäuser has to make between the two? When he is in his mortal agony, Venus calls him to join her again ('Komm, O komm! Zu mir!/Zu mir!' Come, O Come! To me! To me!); when he gets close to her, Wolfram cries from the background: 'Elisabeth!', to which Tannhäuser replies: 'Elisabeth!'

In the standard staging, the mention of the dead sacred Elisabeth gives Tannhäuser the strength to avoid Venus's embrace, and Venus then leaves in fury; would it not be much more logical, however, to stage it so that Tannhäuser continues to approach *the same* woman, discovering, when he is close to her, that Venus really is Elisabeth? The subversive power of this shift is that it turns around the old courtly love poetry theme of the dazzlingly beautiful lady who, when one gets too close to her, is revealed to be a disgusting entity of rotten flesh crawling with worms – here, the sacred virgin is discovered at the very heart of the dissolute seductress. So the message is not the usual desublimation ('Beware of the beautiful woman! It is a deceptive lure which hides the disgusting rotten flesh!') but the unexpected sublimation, an elevation of the erotic woman to the mode of appearance of the sacred Thing. The tension of *Tannhäuser* is thus the tension between the two aspects of the Absolute: the Ideal-Symbolic and the Real; Law and Superego. The true topic of *Tannhäuser* is that of a *disturbance in the order of sublimation*: sublimation starts to oscillate between these two poles.[4]

Wagner with Kierkegaard

We can see, now, in what precise sense *Tristan* embodies the 'aesthetic' attitude (in the Kierkegaardian sense of the term): refusing to compromise one's desire, one goes to the end and willingly embraces death. *Meistersinger* counters it with the ethical solution: true redemption lies not in following the immortal passion to its self-destructive conclusion; one should, rather, learn to overcome it via creative sublimation and to return, in a mood of wise resignation, to the 'daily' life of symbolic obligations. In *Parsifal*, finally, the passion can no longer be overcome through its reintegration into society, in which it survives in a gentrified form: one has to deny it completely in the ecstatic assertion of religious *jouissance*. Thus the triad *Tristan–Meistersinger–Parsifal* follows a precise logic: *Meistersinger* and *Tristan* represent the two opposite versions of the Oedipal matrix, within which *Meistersinger* inverts *Tristan* (the son steals the woman from the paternal figure; passion breaks out between the paternal figure and the young woman destined to become the partner of the young man); while *Parsifal* gives the co-ordinates themselves an anti-Oedipal twist – the lamenting wounded subject here is the paternal figure (Amfortas), not the young transgressor (Tristan). (The closest one comes to lament in *Meistersinger* is Sachs's 'Wahn, wahn!' song from Act III.) Wagner planned to have Parsifal visit the wounded Tristan in the first half of Act III of *Tristan*, but he wisely decided against it: not only would the scene have ruined the perfect overall structure of Act III, it would also have staged a character's *impossible* encounter with (the different, alternative reality, version of) *itself*, as in time-travel science-fiction narratives where I encounter *myself*. One can descend to the ridiculous here by imagining the *third* hero joining the two – Hans Sachs (in his earlier embodiment, as King Mark, who arrives on a ship before Isolde), so that the three of them (Tristan, Mark, Parsifal), standing for the three attitudes, debate their differences in a Habermasian context of undistorted communicational exchange.

The way to read Wagner is thus with a 'horizontal' interpretation, not a 'vertical' one: we should look for structural variations on a gesture or an object, not directly for its meaning. Kundry kissing Parsifal is to be compared to Siegfried kissing Brünnhilde; the Grail to the Ring, and so on. The first step in a proper understanding of Wagner's work is to establish the multiple series of features which serve as lateral links between different operas by Wagner himself, as well as between Wagner's operas and other composers' operas. The feature that links *Meistersinger* and *Tannhäuser*, for example, is the central place of a singing competition: Wagner came to the idea to do *Meistersinger* in 1845, immediately after he finished *Tannhäuser* – what about a comic counterpart to the tragic singing competition at the centre of *Tannhäuser*? Another passage to *Meistersinger* starts from *Tristan*: in contrast to the *Tristan*, in *Meistersinger* the explosion of excessive desire is tamed, contained. Crucial here is the parallel between King Mark and Hans Sachs: they both offer the beloved woman to the younger man; in *Tristan*, however, the offer comes too late (Mark makes it to the dead Tristan), while in *Meistersinger* the offer is accepted, ensuring the happy outcome. No wonder, then, that in Act III Scene 4 of *Meistersinger*, just before the sublime quintet, there is an outburst of a quasi-incestuous erotic tension between the young Eva and the fatherly figure of Hans Sachs, in which King Mark is directly mentioned:

> *Eva:* 'If I had the choice, I would choose none but you; you were my husband, I would give the prize to none but you. – But now I am chosen . . . if I am married today, then I had no choice: that was obligation, compulsion!'
> *Hans Sachs:* 'My child, from Tristan and Isolde, I know a sad fate. Hans Sachs was clever and did not want anything of Herr Marke's lot. It was high time that I found the right man for you.'

The quintet which follows thus not only stands for the moment of inner peace and reconciliation that precedes the crucial struggle; it also marks the resolved incestuous tension. And, along these lines, I am tempted to claim that the triad *Tristan–Meistersinger–Parsifal* is reproduced in three exemplary post-Wagnerian operas: Richard Strauss's *Salome*, Puccini's *Turandot* and Schoenberg's *Moses und Aron*. Is not *Salome* yet another version of the possible outcome of *Tristan*? What if, at the end of Act II, when King Mark surprises the lovers, he were to explode in fury and order Tristan's head to be cut off; the desperate Isolde would then take her lover's head in her hands and start to kiss his lips in a Salomean *Liebestod*. . . . (And, to add yet another variation on the virtual link between *Salome* and *Tristan*: what if, at the end of *Tristan*, Isolde were not simply to die after finishing her 'Mild und leise' – what if she were to remain entranced by her immersion in ecstatic *jouissance*, and King Mark, disgusted by it, were to give the order: 'This woman is to be killed!'?) It has often been noted that the closing scene of *Salome* is modelled on Isolde's *Liebestod*; what makes it a perverted version of the Wagnerian *Liebestod*, however, is that what Salome demands, in an unconditional act of caprice, is to kiss the lips of John the Baptist ('I want to kiss your lips!') – contact not with a person, but with a partial object. If *Salome* is a counterpart to *Tristan*, then *Turandot* is the counterpart to *Meistersinger* – let us not forget that they are both operas about a public contest, with the woman as the prize won by the hero.

Salome twice insists to the end in her demand: first, she insists that the soldiers bring Jokanaan to her; then, after the Dance of the Seven Veils, she insists that King Herod bring her the head of Jokanaan on a silver platter – when the king, believing that Jokanaan is actually a holy man, and that it is therefore better not to touch him, offers Salome in exchange for her dance anything she wants, up to half of his kingdom and the most sacred objects in his possession, just not the head (and thus the death) of Jokanaan, she ignores this explosive outburst of outbidding, and simply repeats her inexorable demand: 'Bring me the head of Jokanaan.' Is there not something properly Antigonean in this request of hers? Like Antigone, she insists without regard for the consequences. Is Salome not therefore, in a way, no less than Antigone, the embodiment of a certain ethical stance? No wonder she is so attracted to Jokanaan – it is a matter of one saint recognizing another. And how can one overlook the fact that, at the end of Oscar Wilde's play on which Strauss's opera is based, after kissing Jokanaan's head, she utters a properly Christian comment on how this proves that love is stronger than death, that love can overcome death?

What, then, would be the counterpart to *Parsifal*? *Parsifal* was from the very beginning perceived as a thoroughly ambiguous work: the attempt to reassert art at its highest, the proto-religious spectacle bringing the Community together (art as the mediator between religion and politics), against the utilitarian corruption of modern life, with its commercialized kitsch culture – yet at the same time drifting towards a commercialized aesthetic kitsch of an ersatz religion – a fake, if there ever was one. In other words, the problem of *Parsifal* is not the unmediated dualism of its universe (Klingsor's kingdom of fake pleasures versus the sacred domain of the Grail) but, rather, the lack of distance, the ultimate identity, of its opposites: is not the Grail ritual (which provides the most satisfying aesthetic spectacle of the work, its two 'biggest hits') the ultimate 'Klingsorian' fake? (The taint of bad faith in our enjoyment of *Parsifal* is similar to the bad faith in our enjoyment of Puccini.) For this reason, *Parsifal* was the traumatic starting point which allows us to conceive of the multitude of later operas as reactions to it, as attempts to resolve its deadlock. The key among these attempts is, of course, Schoenberg's *Moses und Aron*, the ultimate pretender to the title 'the last opera', the meta-opera about the conditions of (im)possibility of opera: the sudden rupture at the end of Act II, after Moses' desperate 'O Wort, das mir fehlt!', the failure to compose the work to the end. *Moses und Aron* is, in effect, anti-Parsifal: while *Parsifal* retains a full naive trust in the (redemptive) power of music, and finds no problems in rendering the noumenal divine dimension in the aesthetic spectacle of the ritual, *Moses und Aron* attempts the impossible: to be an opera directed against the very principle of opera, that of the stage-musical spectacle – it is an operatic representation of the Jewish prohibition of aesthetic representation.

Is not the buoyant music of the Golden Calf the ultimate version of the bacchanalia music in Wagner, from *Tannhäuser* to the Flower Maidens' music in *Parsifal*? And is there not another key parallel between *Parsifal* and *Moses und Aron*? As Adorno noted, the ultimate tension of *Moses* is not simply between divine transcendence and its representation in music, but – inherent to music itself – between the 'choral' spirit of the religious community and the two individuals (Moses and Aaron) who stick out as subjects; in the same way, in *Parsifal*, Amfortas and Parsifal himself stick out as forceful individuals – are not Amfortas's two 'complaints' the strongest passages of *Parsifal*, implicitly undermining the message of the renunciation of subjectivity? The musical opposition between the clear choral style of the Grail community and the chromaticism of the Klingsor universe in *Parsifal* is radicalized in *Moses und Aron* in the guise of the opposition between Moses' *Sprechstimme* and Aaron's full song – in both cases, the tension is unresolved.

What one should always bear in mind apropos Schoenberg's *Moses und Aron* is that it is a sequel to another operatic project which, while dealing with the same problem, remained only a draft: *Der biblische Weg*, a musical drama about the fate of the Jewish people. In order to regain a new homeland, the Jews colonize an African country; when they are threatened by the rebellion of the indigenous population, they develop a mysterious new weapon of mass destruction (deadly rays which suffocate all living beings) – how are we to locate *this* fantasy, for the most part gracefully ignored in the literature on Schoenberg? Although, in the planned finale of the drama, the Jews renounce the use of this weapon, this renunciation takes place in what is undoubtedly the weirdest case of the Hegelian *Aufhebung* of brutal destruction into spiritual conquest: the Jews promise that, instead of using the deadly rays, they will only radiate the spiritual power of their pure belief – in short, the spread of their belief is the sublated form of deadly chemical warfare. . . .[5]

Schoenberg imagined a leader who would try to incorporate elements of Moses, the bearer of the divine message who had a speech impediment, and of Aaron, a political activist who knew how to prepare the people for the fulfilment of their dreams, not shying away from the 'performance of miracles', and planning an actual fight for possession of the land. *Moses und Aron* thus follows *Der biblische Weg*: we get first the synthesis, then its failure. Max Aruns, the hero of *Weg*, is (as the sound of his name already indicates) the impossible synthesis of Moses and Aaron, and in Schoenberg's development, 'One divides itself into Two': Max Aruns is split into Moses and Aaron.

In Schoenberg's play, the exiles first spend a period maturing in a land of preparation, as the Hebrews did in the desert. Schoenberg calls this land Asmongaea, and Max Aruns is promised protection and help for his people by the ruler of that country. In an exchange between Max Aruns (the astute political thinker) and a former sceptic, the dialogue has a prophetic ring: 'People cannot take a position in a country inhabited by enemies,' says Aruns (who has chosen a kind of New Palestine as a territory for the gathering of the exiles). In a rousing speech at the 'Immigration Centre', Aruns asserts: 'As He did for the Hebrews at Jericho, God has given us a powerful weapon with which to overpower our enemies: we have our own trumpets of Jericho! An invention . . . enables us to aim rays at any point around the globe, and at any distance rays which absorb the oxygen in the air and suffocate all living creatures.' (This was written in 1926.) When relations with the host country get complicated, Jewish crowds revolt, Aruns is overpowered, and young Guido takes over the biblical Joshua's role. He will lead the nation into the Promised Land; and

> as little as we intend to send these newly discovered, death-carrying rays of material power to any point of this earth, as little as we intend to seek revenge or use violence against any nation, so much do we, on the contrary, intend to radiate . . . the world [with] the illuminating rays of our belief . . . so that they may bring forth new spiritual life. . . . We have an immediate goal: we want to feel secure as a nation. We want to be certain that no one can force us to do anything, that no one can hinder us from doing anything.

The profound ambiguity of this solution is indicated by the very persistence of the signifier 'radiation': in a kind of mock-Hegelian *Aufhebung*, the chemical-warfare radiation is internalized/spiritualized into radiating Jewish spirituality on to others. How, however, will the Jews 'feel secure as a nation' if not through some kind of military defence which will guarantee the place from which they will be able to radiate their spirituality? If nothing else, the Jews will have to rely on the death-carrying rays as a permanent threat guaranteeing their security: we do not intend ever to use them, but we have them. . . .

What, then, can follow this breakdown? It is here that I am tempted to return to our starting point: to Rossinian comedy. After the complete collapse of expressive subjectivity, comedy re-emerges – but a weird, uncanny kind. What comes after *Moses und Aron* is the imbecilic 'comic' *Sprechgesang* of *Pierrot Lunaire*, the smile of a madman who is so devastated by pain that he cannot even perceive his tragedy – like the smile of a cat in cartoons, with birds flying around its head after the cat gets hit on the head with a hammer. The comedy enters when the situation is too horrifying to be rendered as tragedy – which is why the only proper way to do a film about concentration camps is a comedy: there is something fake about doing a concentration-camp tragedy.

Wagner as a Theorist of Fascism

Perhaps such a reading enables us also to cast a new light on the link between *Parsifal* and the *Ring*. The *Ring* depicts a pagan world, which, following its inherent logic, *has* to end in a global catastrophe; however, there are survivors of this catastrophe, the nameless crowd of humanity which silently witnesses God's self-destruction. In the unique figure of Hagen, the *Ring* also provides the first portrait of what will later emerge as the Fascist leader; however, since the world of the *Ring* is pagan, caught in the Oedipal family conflict of passions, it cannot even address the true problem of how this humanity, the force of the New, is to organize itself – of how it should learn the truth about its place; *this* is the task of *Parsifal*, which therefore logically follows the *Ring*. The conflict between Oedipal dynamics and the post-Oedipal universe is inscribed within *Parsifal* itself: Klingsor's and Amfortas's adventures are Oedipal, so that what happens with Parsifal's big turn (his rejection of Kundry) is precisely that he leaves Oedipal incestuous eroticism behind, opening himself up to a new community.

The dark figure of Hagen is profoundly ambivalent: although he is initially depicted as a dark plotter, both in the *Nibelungenlied* and in Fritz Lang's film, he emerges as the ultimate hero of the entire work and is redeemed at the end as the supreme case of the *Nibelungentreue*, fidelity until death to one's cause (or, rather, to the Master who stands for this cause), asserted in the final slaughter at Attila's court. The conflict here is between fidelity to the Master and our everyday moral obligations: Hagen stands for a kind of teleological suspension of morality on behalf of fidelity; he is the ultimate '*Gefolgsmann*'.

Significantly, it is *only* Wagner who depicts Hagen as a figure of Evil – is this not an indication of how Wagner none the less belongs to the modern plane of freedom? And is Lang's return to the positive Hagen not an indication of how the twentieth century marked the re-emergence of a new barbarism? It was Wagner's genius to intuit prophetically the rising figure of the Fascist ruthless executive who is at the same time a rabble-rousing demagogue (recall Hagen's terrifying *Männerruf*) – a worthy supplement to his other great intuition, that of a hysterical woman (Kundry) well before this figure overwhelmed European consciousness (in Charcot's clinic; in art from Ibsen to Schoenberg).

What makes Hagen a 'proto-Fascist' is his role of unconditional support for the weak ruler (King Gunther): he does for Gunther the 'dirty jobs' which, although necessary, have to remain concealed from the public gaze – 'Unsere Ehre heisst Treue'. As such, Hagen is not 'Gunther's phallus' – it is, rather, Siegfried himself who obviously assumes this role in overcoming, taming and raping Brünnhilde for him; what makes him phallic is the very fact that he acts as Gunther's spectral double. (When, in the recent German bestseller *Hagen von Tronje*, by Wolfgang Hohlbein, Hagen is finally fully rehabilitated, we should not read this as an assertion of Nazi authoritarianism but, rather, as the rejection of Siegfried's hero cult: Hohlbein's Hagen is a complex person deeply in love with Kriemhild. In other words, what we get here is the 'psychologization' of Hagen as the price of his rehabilitation – something akin to what John Updike did in his *Gertrude and Claudius*.)

We find this stance, a kind of mirror-reversal of the Beautiful Soul which refuses to dirty its hands, at its purest in the Rightist admiration for the heroes who are ready to do the necessary dirty work: it is easy to do a noble thing for one's country, right up to sacrificing one's life for it – it is much more difficult to commit a *crime* for one's country when it is needed. . . . Hitler knew very well how to play this double game apropos of the Holocaust, using Himmler as his Hagen. In the speech to the SS leaders in Posen on 4 October 1943, Himmler spoke quite openly about the mass killing of the Jews as 'a glorious page in our history, and one that has never been written and never can be written', explicitly including the killing of women and children: 'I did not regard myself as justified in exterminating the men – that is to say, to kill them or have them killed – and to allow the avengers in the shape of children to grow up for our sons and grandchildren. The difficult decision had to be taken to have this people disappear from the earth.'

This is Hagen's *Treue* brought to the extreme – was not the paradoxical price for Wagner's negative portrayal of Hagen, however, his *Judifizierung*? A lot of recent historicist work has tried to bring out the contextual 'true meaning' of Wagnerian figures and topics: the pale Hagen is really a masturbating Jew; Amfortas's wound is really syphilis. . . . The idea is that Wagner is mobilizing historical codes known to everyone in his epoch: when a person stumbles, sings in cracking high tones, makes nervous gestures, and so on, 'everyone knows' that this is a Jew, so Mime from *Siegfried* is a caricature of a Jew; the fear of syphilis as an illness in the groin caused by having intercourse with an 'impure' woman was an obsession in the second half of the nineteenth century, so it was 'clear to everyone' that Amfortas had really contracted syphilis from Kundry. . . . Marc Weiner developed the most perspicuous version of this decoding by focusing on the micro-texture of Wagner's musical dramas – manner of singing, gestures, smells: it is at this level of what Deleuze would have called pre-subjective affects that anti-Semitism is operative in Wagner's operas, even if Jews are not explicitly mentioned: in the way Beckmesser sings, in the way Mime complains. . . .

Marxism Against Historicism

The first problem here, however, is that such insights, even if they are accurate, do not contribute much to a pertinent understanding of the work in question. We often hear that, if we are to understand a work of art, we need to know its historical context. Against this historicist commonplace, we should argue that too much of a historical context can blur the proper contact with a work of art – in order properly to grasp, for instance, *Parsifal*, we should *abstract* from such historical trivia, *decontextualize* the work, tear it from the context in which it was originally embedded. Even more, it is, rather, the work of art itself which provides a context enabling us to understand a given historical situation properly. If, today, someone were to visit Serbia, direct contact with raw data there would leave him confused. If, however, he were to read a couple of literary works and see a couple of representative movies, they would definitely provide the context that would enable him to situate the raw data of his experience. There is thus an unexpected truth in the old cynical wisdom from the Stalinist Soviet Union: 'he lies as an eye-witness!'

There is another, more fundamental problem with such historicist decoding: it is not enough to 'decode' Alberich, Mime, Hagen, and so on as Jews, making the point that the *Ring* is one big anti-Semitic tract, a story about how the Jews, by renouncing love and opting for power, brought corruption to the universe; the more basic fact is that *the anti-Semitic figure of the Jew itself is not a direct ultimate referent, but already encoded, a cipher of ideological and social antagonisms.* (And the same goes for syphilis: in the second half of the nineteenth century, it was, together with tuberculosis, the other big case of 'illness as a metaphor' [Susan Sontag], serving as an encoded message about socio-sexual antagonisms, and this is why people were so obsessed by it – not because of its direct real threat, but because of the ideological surplus-investment in it.) An appropriate reading of Wagner should take this fact into account and not merely 'decode' Alberich as a Jew, but also ask: *how does Wagner's encoding refer to the 'original' social antagonism of which the (anti-Semitic figure of the) 'Jew' itself is already a cipher?* What complicates the picture is thus its circular structure: while the figure of 'the Jew' is the referent encoded in Wagner's condemnation of the lust for power and wealth, and so on, the social content of the figure-cipher 'the Jew' is, again, the capitalist lust for wealth (what the reference to the 'Jewish plot' provides is a kind of naturalized false genealogy of capitalism). There is thus no need to search for another, 'deeper' content hidden beneath the figure of 'the Jew' – everything is here, we should only shift the perspective to capitalist dynamics, discern in it a cipher for these dynamics.

A further counter-argument is that Siegfried, Mime's opponent, is in no way simply the beautiful Aryan blond hero – his portrait is much more ambivalent. The short last scene of Act 1 of *Götterdämmerung* (Siegfried's violent abduction of Brünnhilde; under the cover of *Tarnhelm*, Siegfried poses as Gunther) is a shocking interlude of extreme brutality and ghost-like nightmarish quality. What makes it additionally interesting is one of the big inconsistencies of the *Ring*: why does Siegfried, after brutally subduing Brünnhilde, put his sword between the two of them when they lie down, to prove that they will not have sex, since he is simply performing a service to his friend, the weak king Gunther? *To whom* does he have to prove this? Is Brünnhilde not supposed to think that he *is* Gunther? Before she is subdued, Brünnhilde displays to the masked Siegfried her hand with the ring on it, trusting that the ring will serve as protection; when Siegfried brutally tears it off her hand, this gesture has to be read as the repetition of the first extremely violent robbery of the ring in the Scene 4 of *Rheingold*, when Wotan tears the ring off Alberich's hand. The horror of this scene is that it shows Siegfried's brutality naked, in its raw state: it somehow 'de-psychologizes' Siegfried, revealing him as an inhuman monster, that is, the way he 'really is', deprived of his deceptive mask – *this* is the potion's effect on him.[6]

In effect, there is in Wagner's Siegfried an unconstrained 'innocent' aggressivity, an urge to pass directly to the act, and just go ahead and squash anything that gets on your nerves – as in Siegfrid's words to Mime in Act I of *Siegfried*: 'When I watch you standing, / Shuffling and shambling, / Servilely stooping, squinting and blinking, / I long to seize you by your nodding neck / And make an end of your obscene blinking!' (The sound of the original German is even more impressive: 'Seh'ich dich stehn, gangeln und gehn, / Knicken und nicken, / Mit den Augen zwicken, / Beim Genick möcht'ich den Nicker packen, / Den Garaus geben dem garst'gen Zwicker!'). The same outburst is repeated twice in Act II: 'Das eklige Nicken / Und Augenzwicken, / Wann endlich soll ich's / Nicht mehr sehn, / Wann werd ich den Albernen los?' ('That shuffling and slinking, / Those eyelids blinking – / How long must I / Endure the sight? / When shall I be rid of this fool?'), and, just a little later: 'Grade so garstig, / Griesig und grau, / Klein und krumm, / Höckrig und hinkend, / Mit hängenden Ohren, / Triefigen Augen – / Fort mit dem Alb! / Ich mag ihn nicht mehr sehn.' ('Shuffling and slinking, / Grizzled and grey, / Small and crooked, / Limping and hunchbacked, / With ears that are drooping, eyes that are bleary . . . / Off with the imp! I hope he's gone for good!') Is this not the most elementary disgust, repulsion, felt by the ego confronted by the intruding foreign body? We can easily imagine a neo-Nazi skinhead uttering just the same words to a worn-out Turkish *Gastarbeiter*. . . .[7]

Finally, we should not forget that, in the *Ring*, the source of all evil is not Alberich's fatal choice in the first scene of *Rheingold*: long before this event took place, Wotan disturbed the balance of nature, succumbing to the lure of power, giving preference to power over love – he tore out and destroyed the World-Tree, transforming it into a spear on which he inscribed the runes fixing the laws of his rule; he also plucked out one of his eyes in order to gain insight into inner truth. Thus evil does not come from the Outside – the insight of Wotan's tragic 'monologue with Brünnhilde' in the Act II of *Walküre* is that the power of Alberich and the prospect of the 'end of the world' is ultimately Wotan's own guilt, the result of his ethical fiasco – in Hegelese, external opposition is the effect of inner contradiction. No wonder, then, that Wotan is called the 'White Alb', in contrast to the 'Black Alb', Alberich – if anything, Wotan's choice was ethically worse than Alberich's: Alberich longed for love, and turned towards power only after being brutally mocked and turned down by the Rhinemaidens; while Wotan turned to power after fully enjoying the fruits of love, and getting tired of them. We should also bear in mind that, after his moral fiasco in *Walküre*, Wotan turns into 'The Wanderer' – a figure of the Wandering Jew, like the first great Wagnerian hero, the Flying Dutchman, this 'Ahasver des Ozeans'.

The same goes for *Parsifal*, which is not about an elitist circle of the pure-blooded threatened by external contamination (copulation by the Jewess Kundry). There are two complications to this image: first, Klingsor, the evil magician and Kundry's Master, is himself an ex-Grail knight, he comes from within; second, if we read the text really closely, we cannot avoid the conclusion that the true source of evil, the primordial imbalance which derailed the Grail community, resides at its very centre – it is Titurel's excessive fixation on enjoying the Grail which is at the origin of the misfortune. The true figure of Evil is Titurel, this obscene *père-jouisseur* (perhaps comparable to giant wormlike members of the Space Guild from Frank Herbert's *Dune*, whose bodies are disgustingly distorted because of their excessive consumption of the 'Spice').

This, then, undermines the anti-Semitic perspective according to which the disturbance always ultimately comes from outside, in the guise of a foreign body which throws the balance of the social organism out of joint: for Wagner, the external intruder (Alberich) is merely a secondary repetition, externalization, of an absolutely immanent inconsistency/antagonism (Wotan's). With reference to Brecht's famous 'What is the robbery of a bank compared to the founding of a new bank?', I am tempted to ask: 'What is a poor Jew's stealing of the gold compared to the violence of the Aryan's (Wotan's) grounding of the rule of Law?'

One of the signs of this inherent status of the disturbance is the failure of big finales in Wagner's operas: the formal failure here indicates the persistence of the social antagonism. Let us take the biggest of them all, the mother of all finales, that of *Götterdämmerung*. It is a well-known fact that, in the last minutes of this opera, the orchestra perform an excessively intricate cobweb of themes, basically nothing less than the recapitulation of the thematic wealth of the entire *Ring* – is not this fact the ultimate proof that Wagner himself was not sure about what the final apotheosis of the *Ring* 'means'? Not being sure, he took a kind of 'flight forward', and threw *all* the themes together. . . . So the culminating theme of 'Redemption through Love' (a beautiful and passionate melodic line which previously appeared only in Act III of *Walküre*) cannot fail to remind us of Joseph Kerman's acerbic comment about the last notes of Puccini's *Tosca*, in which the orchestra bombastically recapitulates the 'beautiful' pathetic melodic line of Cavaradossi's 'E lucevan le stelle', as if, unsure what to do, Puccini simply desperately repeated the most 'effective' melody from the previous score, ignoring all narrative or emotional logic.[8] And what if Wagner did *exactly the same* at the end of *Götterdämmerung*? Not sure about the final twist that should stabilize and guarantee the meaning of it all, he had recourse to a beautiful melody whose effect is something like 'whatever all this may mean, let us make sure that the concluding impression will be that of something triumphant and upbeat in its redemptive beauty. . . .' In short, what if this final theme enacts an *empty gesture*?

The ending of *Götterdämmerung* has not only two but, rather, three versions, best designated by the names Feuerbach, Bakunin and Schopenhauer: the reign of human love, revolutionary destruction of the old world, resignation and withdrawal from the world. Along the same lines, it is by no means clear how we are to conceive of the crowd of men and women who, 'in deepest emotion', bear witness to the final destruction in fire and water – who are they? Do they really embody a new liberated society?[9] The change from early revolutionary to 'mature' Schopenhauerian Wagner is usually understood as the shift from a humanist belief in the possibility of a revolutionary change in existing social reality – that is; a belief that our reality is miserable for contingent historical reasons – to a more 'profound' insight into how reality *as such* is miserable, and the only true redemption lies in withdrawing from it into the abyss of the 'Night of the World' – and it seems easy to denounce this shift as the most elementary ideological operation, that of elevating a contingent historical obstacle into an a priori transcendental limitation. What, however, if things are not so simple? What if a revolutionary stance towards the existing social order can also be sustained by a 'pessimistic' notion of a corrupted universe, as seems the case even with Brecht? In short, the key question is: is Wagner's early notion of revolution really 'sublated' completely in Wagner's late metaphysical turn? What if the shift to a 'pessimistic' metaphysics compels us to raise the question of social change again, from a new perspective?

What we should render problematic in Wagner is the very naivety of his early 'revolutionary' theory of the original 'betrayal' of love which gave birth to power, the entire historicization of the Feuerbachian anthropology of love.[10] Is not the notion of the primordial harmony, out of which power emerges through an act of usurpation which disturbs the balance, to be rejected? Is not the core of Fascism precisely the re-establishment of this balance by liquidating the excessive element which introduced imbalance and antagonism (the Jew)? To put it briefly: in clinging to the myth of pristine nature thrown out of joint by some original act of evil, of choosing power over love, Wagner forgot to take into account the basic lesson of Darwin, which is precisely that there is *no* such nature:

> Where Lamarck had made much of the reasonableness and truthfulness of nature, Darwin savored its eccentricities and quirks, even occasionally its silliness. He looked for the marginal, the out-of-kilter, to bolster his argument for natural selection. . . . One might say that nature has taken delight in accumulating contradictions in order to remove all foundation from the theory of a preexisting harmony between the external and internal worlds.
>
> Here we have the quintessence of Darwinism. No special creation, no perfect adaptation, no given attunement of mind to world. It was precisely the disharmonies that caught Darwin's fancy.[11]

In terms of this archi-ideological notion of primordial imbalance, the shift is from the early 'revolutionary' Wagner, who wanted the harmony of love restored through the abolition of state power, and the late 'Schopenhauerian' Wagner, who perceived the 'really existing' external reality of social life *as such* as the false domain to be overcome not by installing a new social order, but by abandoning reality itself and immersing oneself in the ecstatic realm of the Night. If anything, the second version is to be preferred, since it is based on the insight that 'reality' *as such* emerges as the result of a certain disturbance, imbalance – here we should focus on the basic narrative frame of the *Ring*: things happen, the story goes on, as long as the ring circulates – that is, they begin when the ring (or, rather, the gold) is stolen, and they end when the ring is returned to the Rhine (so, perhaps, the proper subtitle of the tetralogy should have been, in the style of eighteenth-century novels, 'A sad story about how three lascivious but innocent girls living in the depths of the Rhine lost and then regained their treasure'). Does this not account for the 'rejection of castration', for the anti-Oedipal pro-incest stance of Wagner detected by Claude Lévi-Strauss? Perhaps the primordial catastrophe for Wagner is not so much the betrayal of love through power but, rather, the Oedipal rule of circulation? So what if what Wagner perceives as the Fall is in effect (not so much Salvation as) the explosive opening, the emergence of human freedom proper? And is it along these lines that we should interpret the attempts to rehabilitate Hagen? Is it, then, that what Wagner does not see is the violent nature of love itself – love *is* the primordial act of violence, the ruthless privileging of one object at the expense of all others which puts the lover in a kind of emergency state?

This brings us back to Wagner's anti-Semitism: when Wagner is defended along the lines of 'one should not judge nineteenth-century works retroactively, casting the shadow of the Holocaust back on them', the reply should be that here, precisely, we should apply Benjamin's notion that some texts are like an unfinished texture of traces, or undeveloped films which become fully readable only afterwards, in a later epoch, when their consequences are actualized. Anti-Semitism is none the less not the hidden ultimate 'truth' of Wagner's universe: first, it is not hidden, it is openly displayed, out there for everyone to see; secondly, even when the anti-Semitic message is discernible in his work, Wagner undermines it, acquires a distance towards it, through his very artistic practice. Mime may be the portrait of a repulsive Jew contrasted to the heroic youth and strength of Siegfried, but is Siegfried's brutal display of repulsion at Mime not (implicitly, at least) presented as repulsive in itself? The third and crucial moment: let us not forget that the first full-blooded Wagnerian hero, finding himself in the archetypal Wagnerian position of being undead, condemned to endless wandering, unable to find (and longing for) redemption in death, is the Flying Dutchman, and he is clearly a Jewish figure, modelled on Ahasver, the Wandering Jew (and, incidentally, the main source for this is Heine, a Jewish poet!). All other Wagnerian heroes are variations on the Dutchman, including Lohengrin (is he also not waiting restless in Montsalvat for the call of a lady in need by whom he expects to be redeemed from the boring and sterile life there, from 'Monsalvat's frigid joys'?), Wotan turned into The Wanderer, and Kundry herself as the wandering Jewess (this, perhaps, is how we should read the mysterious 'redemption to the Redeemer' from the finale of *Parsifal*: what if we refer this formula to Kundry, the woman-redemptrix who should be redeemed?[12]). We can imagine Lohengrin in a parallel with the Dutchman: is he also not in a kind of limbo at Monsalvat, in a situation not so different from the Dutchman's wandering around, desperately waiting for a damsel in distress to call for him so that he can escape the monotony of Monsalvat? We can easily imagine him singing his own version of the Dutchman's 'Die Frist is um . . .', bemoaning his fate and longing for a woman who will not ask him the fateful question. And, like the Dutchman, once he is involved with a woman, he secretly longs for her to ask the prohibited question, unable to confront the prospect of dull married life, glad to perform the dignified withdrawal again after telling the assembled crowd who he is. . . .

In *Lohengrin*, we should insist on the opposition between *must* and *ought*, 'müssen' and 'sollen'. When Lohengrin enjoins Elsa: 'Nie sollst du mich befragen!', we are dealing here with the moral injunction prohibition – not 'you must not!', but 'you ought not!' (or 'you should not!'). Elsa's asking the question is on a different level, that of 'must' – she 'cannot but' ask it, she cannot do otherwise, it is her fundamental character, she is compelled by an inexorable drive (which is the very Freudian *Trieb*) to ask it. 'Must' and 'Ought' thus relate as the Real and the Symbolic: the Real of a drive whose injunction cannot be avoided (which is why Lacan says that the status of a drive is ethical); the Ought as a symbolic ideal caught in the dialectic of desire (if you ought not to do something, this very prohibition generates the desire to do it). When you 'must' do something, it means that you have no choice but to do it, even if it is unpleasant, horrible: Wotan is cornered by Fricka, and he 'must' ('cannot but') allow the murder of Siegmund, although his heart bleeds for him; he 'must' ('cannot but') punish Brünnhilde, his dearest child, the embodiment of his own innermost striving.[13] Here Wagner encounters the paradox of the 'killing with *pietà*', from the Talmud (which calls us to dispense Justice with Love) to Brecht's two key *Lehrstücke*, *Der Jasager* and *Die Massnahme*, in which the young comrade is killed by his companions with loving tenderness.

Love and its Vicissitudes

Only *Das Rheingold* is pure musical drama – at two points in *Die Walküre*, opera re-emerges at its most glorious, as a male aria – Siegmund's 'Winterstürme wichen' and Wotan's 'Der Augen leuchtendes Paar'. It is easy to imagine both sung as a popular song. (At least, in the first case, the 'aria' gradually changes into a properly Wagnerian musical drama.) *Das Rheingold* is Wagner 'as such', at his purest: in Hegelese, 'in his notion' – it is unique in that it is the only pure example of Wagner's theory of musical drama, the piece where Wagner fully respected his own rules elaborated previously in *Opera and Drama*; with *Die Walküre*, the 'human, all too human' passion (and operatic aria!) (re-)emerges forcefully, and explodes the constraints of Wagner's theoretical edifice. No wonder *Rheingold* is set among gods, monsters and dwarfs only, with no humans (and, according to Wagner's Feuerbachian notion in this epoch, humanity is the only reality): *Rheingold* is a kind of virtual pre-ontological theatre, giving us a display of pure potentialities (the divine, the monstrous . . .) prior to the emergence of the actual human world.[14] The whole tetralogy then follows a precise inner logic: *Siegfried* returns to the innocent fairytale magic, while *Götterdämmerung* throws us into the vulgar universe of political intrigues and power play. There is a kind of Greimasian square here: an axis opposes *Rheingold* and *Siegfried* to *Walküre* and *Götterdämmerung*. Furthermore, there is a parallel between *Walküre* and *Götterdämmerung*: in both cases, Act I finishes with a sex-act situation (the act itself being consummated in the first case, renounced in the second).

It is a cliché of Wagner studies that the triumphant finale of *Das Rheingold* is a fake, an empty triumph indicating the fragility of the gods' power and their forthcoming downfall – however, does the same not go also for the finale of *Siegfried*? (Furthermore, is the finale of *Das Rheingold* really shallow, built on fragile foundations and thus doomed to fail? What if it is precisely this fragile character that provides the tone of tragic grandeur to it? What if it is so effective not in spite of but *because of* its fragility?) The sublime duet between Brünnhilde and Siegfried which concludes the opera fails a couple of minutes before the ending, with the entry of the theme announcing the couple's triumphant reunion (usually called the theme of 'happy love' or 'love's bond') – this theme is obviously false (not to mention the miserable failure of the concluding noisy-bombastic orchestral *tutti*, which lacks the effectiveness of the gods' entry to Valhalla in *Rheingold*). Does this failure encode Wagner's (unconscious?) critique of Siegfried? Recall the additional curious fact that this theme is almost the same as – closely related to – the Beckmesser theme in *Meistersinger* (I owe this insight to Gerhard Koch; Act III of *Siegfried* was written just *Meistersinger*)! Furthermore, does not this empty bombastic failure of the final notes also signal the catastrophe-to-come of Brünnhilde and Siegfried's love? As such, this 'failure' of the duet is a structural necessity.[15] (We should none the less follow the inner triadic structure of this duet closely: its entire dynamic is on the side of Brünnhilde, who twice shifts her subjective stance, while Siegfried remains the same. First, from her elevated divine position, Brünnhilde joyously asserts her love for Siegfried; then, once she becomes aware of what his passionate advances mean – the loss of her safe, distanced position – she shows fear of losing her identity, descending to the level of a vulnerable mortal woman, man's prey and passive victim. In a wonderful metaphor, she compares herself to a beautiful image in the water which gets blurred once man's hand directly touches and disturbs the water. Finally, she surrenders to Siegfried's passionate love-advances and throws herself into the vortex.) Excepting the last notes, however, Act III of *Siegfried*, at least from the moment when Siegfried breaks Wotan's spear to Brünnhilde's awakening, is not only unbearably beautiful, but also the most concise statement of the Oedipal problematic in its specific Wagnerian twist.[16]

On his way to the magic mountain where Brünnhilde lies, surrounded by a wall of fire which can be penetrated only by a hero who does not know fear, Siegfried first encounters Wotan, the deposed (or, rather, abdicated) supreme god, disguised as a Wanderer; Wotan tries to stop him, but in a half-hearted way – basically, he *wants* Siegfried to break his spear. After Siegfried disrespectfully does this, full of contempt, in his ignorance, for the embittered and wise old man, he progresses through the flames and perceives a wonderful creature lying there in a deep sleep. Thinking that the armoured plate on the creature's chest is making its breathing difficult, he proceeds to cut off its straps with his sword; after he raises the plate and sees Brünnhilde's breasts, he utters a desperate cry of surprise: '*Das ist kein Mann!* /This is no man!'. This reaction, of course, cannot fail to strike us as comic, exaggerated beyond credulity. However, we should bear a couple of things in mind here. First, the whole point of the story of *Siegfried* up to this moment is that while Siegfried spent his entire youth in the forest in the sole company of the evil dwarf Mime, who claimed to be his only parent, mother–father, he has nevertheless observed that, in the case of animals, parents are always a couple, and thus longs to see his mother, the feminine counterpart of Mime. Siegfried's quest for a woman is thus a quest for sexual difference, and the fact that this quest is at the same time the quest for fear, for an experience that will teach him what fear is, clearly points in the direction of castration – with a specific twist. In the paradigmatic Freudian description of the scene of castration (in his late short text on 'Fetishism'), the gaze discovers an absence where a presence (of the penis) is expected, while here, Siegfried's gaze discovers an excessive presence (of breasts – and need I add that the typical Wagnerian soprano is an opulent soprano with large breasts, so that Siegfried's 'Das ist kein Mann!' usually gives rise to hearty laughter in the audience?).[17]

Secondly, we should bear in mind an apparent inconsistency in the libretto which points the way to a proper understanding of this scene: why is Siegfried so surprised at not encountering a man, when, beforehand, he emphasizes that he wants to penetrate the fire precisely in order to find a woman there? To The Wanderer, he says: 'Give ground, then, for that way, I know, leads to the sleeping woman.' And, a couple of minutes later: 'Go back yourself, braggart! I must go there, to the burning heart of the blaze, to Brünnhilde!' From this, we should draw the only possible conclusion: *while Siegfried was in fact looking for a woman, he did not expect her not to be a man.* In short, he was looking for a woman who would be – not the same as man, but – a symmetrical supplement to man, with whom she would form a balanced signifying dyad; what he finds, however, is an unbearable lack/excess. . . . What he discovers is the excess/lack not covered by the binary signifier – that is, the fact that Woman and Man are not complementary but asymmetrical, that there is no Yin–Yang balance – in short, that there is no sexual relationship.

No wonder, then, that Siegfried's discovery that Brünnhilde 'is no man' gives rise to an outburst of true panic accompanied by a loss of reality, in which Siegfried takes refuge with his (unknown) mother: 'This is no man! A searing spell pierces my heart; a fiery anxiety fills my eyes; my senses swim and swoon! Whom can I call on to help me? Mother, Mother! Think of me!' He then summons up all his courage and decides to kiss the sleeping woman on the lips, even if this will mean his own death: 'Then I will suck life from those sweetest lips, *though I die in doing so.*' What follows is the majestic awakening of Brünnhilde, then the love duet which concludes the opera. It is crucial to note that this acceptance of death as the price for contacting the feminine Other is accompanied musically by the echo of the so-called theme of 'renunciation', arguably the most important leitmotiv in the entire tetralogy. It is first heard in Scene 1 of *Rheingold*, when, answering Alberich's query, Woglinde discloses that 'nur wer der Minne Macht versagt /only the one who renounces the power of love' can take possession of the gold; its next most noticeable appearance occurs towards the end of Act 1 of *Walküre*, at the moment of the most triumphant assertion of love between Sieglinde and Siegmund – just before pulling the sword out of the tree trunk, Siegmund sings it to the words: 'Heiligster Minne höchste Not /holiest love's highest need.' How are we to read these two occurrences together? What if we treat them as two fragments of the complete sentence that was distorted by 'dreamwork', that is, rendered unreadable by being split into two – the solution is thus to reconstitute the complete proposition: 'Love's highest need is to renounce its own power.' This is what Lacan calls 'symbolic castration': if one is to remain faithful to one's love, one should not elevate it into the direct focus of one's love, one should renounce its centrality.

Perhaps a detour through the best (or worst) of Hollywood melodrama can help us to clarify this point. The basic lesson of King Vidor's *Rhapsody* is that, in order to gain the beloved woman's love, the man has to prove that he is able to survive without her, that he prefers his mission or profession to her. There are two immediate choices: (1) my professional career is what matters most to me, the woman is just an amusement, a distracting affair; (2) the woman is everything to me, I am ready to humiliate myself, to forsake all my public and professional dignity for her. Both are false; both lead to the man being rejected by the woman. The message of true love is thus: even if you are everything to me, I can survive without you, I am ready to forsake you for my mission or profession. The proper way for the woman to test the man's love is thus to 'betray' him at the crucial moment of his career (the first public concert in the film, the key exam, the business negotiation which will decide his career) – only if he can survive the ordeal and accomplish his task successfully, although he is deeply traumatized by her desertion, will he deserve her, and will she return to him. The underlying paradox is that love, precisely as the Absolute, should not be posited as a direct goal – it should retain the status of a by-product, of something we get as an undeserved grace. Perhaps there is no greater love than that of a revolutionary couple, where each of the two lovers is ready to abandon the other at any moment if revolution demands it.

What happens, then, when Siegfried kisses the sleeping Brünnhilde, so that this act deserves to be accompanied by the Renunciation theme? What Siegfried says is that he will kiss Brünnhilde '*though I die in doing so*' – reaching out to the Other Sex involves accepting one's mortality. Recall here another sublime moment from the *Ring*: Siegmund and Brünnhilde's duet towards the end of Act II of *Walküre*, when Brünnhilde, in her cold majestic beauty, approaches Siegmund, informing him that every mortal who sees her will soon die – she is here to tell him that she will take him to Valhalla, the eternal dwelling of dead heroes, after he loses the battle with Hunding. Siegmund refuses her offer if Sieglinde cannot join him in Valhalla, preferring the love of a miserable mortal woman to 'Valhalla's frigid joys / *Walhalls spröden Wonnen*'. Siegmund thus here literally renounces immortality – is this not the highest ethical act of them all? The shattered Brünnhilde comments on this refusal: 'Do you value everlasting bliss so little? Is she everything to you, this poor woman who, tired and sorrowful, lies limp in your lap? Do you think nothing less glorious?' Ernst Bloch was right to observe that what is lacking in German history are more gestures like Siegmund's.[18]

But which *love* is renounced here? To put it bluntly: incestuous maternal love. The 'fearless hero' is fearless in so far as he experiences himself as protected by his mother, by the maternal envelope – what 'learning to fear' amounts to, in fact, is learning that one is exposed to the world without any maternal shield. It is essential to read this scene in conjunction with the scene, from *Parsifal*, of Kundry kissing Parsifal: in both cases, an innocent hero discovers fear and/or suffering through a kiss located somewhere between the maternal and the properly feminine. Until the late nineteenth century, the Montenegrins practised a weird wedding-night ritual: in the evening, after the marriage ceremony, the son got into bed with his mother and, once he was asleep, the mother silently withdrew and allowed the bride to take her place: after spending the rest of the night with the bride, the son had to escape from the village to a mountain and spend a couple of days there alone, in order to get accustomed to the shame of being married . . . does not something very similar happen to Siegfried?

The difference between *Siegfried* and *Parsifal*, however, is that in the first case the woman is accepted; in the second she is rejected. This does not mean that the feminine dimension disappears in *Parsifal*, and that we remain within the homoerotic male community of the Grail. Syberberg was right when, after Parsifal's rejection of Kundry which follows her kiss, 'the last kiss of the mother and the first kiss of a woman', he replaced Parsifal-the-boy with another actor, a cold young woman – did he not thereby enact the Freudian insight according to which identification is, at its most radical, identification with the lost (or rejected) libidinal object? We *become* (identify with) the *object* of which we were deprived, so that our subjective identity is a repository of the traces of our lost objects. This means that the conflict in *Parsifal* is not between sexuality and spirituality, nor (as it is sometimes claimed) between heterosexuality and the closed homosexual community (as, so the story goes, the libidinal foundation of a totalitarian community). It is, rather, the conflict between intersubjective desire and partial drive caught in its closed circuit of *jouissance*: Monsalvat is a perverse paradise of partial drive making its circuit around the Object.[19]

Intermezzo: Janáček as Anti-Wagner

A way out of these Wagnerian deadlocks is deployed in Janáček's *Katja Kabanova*. This opera is based on *The Storm*, the most popular play by Alexander Nikolayevich Ostrovsky, the nineteenth-century Russian writer who was also a passionate social reformer, deeply concerned about the greed, superstition and narrow-mindedness of the Russian society of his day.[20] The characters at the centre of his plays are exponents of what the Russians call *samodurstvo*: narrow-minded, blinkered, stubborn, unshakeable and immovably self-righteous, with closed minds and inclined to domestic tyranny. The tragic irony and point of *The Storm* is that Katerina (Katja) Kabanova, its heroine who rebels against *samodurstvo*, is already too deeply indoctrinated with the poison against which she rebels: so terribly strong and so deeply ingrained is the sense of sin, the superstition that pervades that narrow society, that Katerina cannot escape their consequences. During a thunderstorm, when the townspeople have to seek shelter in a ruined church covered in ancient frescoes of the Torments of Hell, she hears the wrath of the heavens in the thunder and lightning, and breaks down and confesses her transgression; from the ruin of her life which this self-accusation causes there is only one escape for her: suicide. To nineteenth-century Europeans, Katerina thus could not but seem a weak and passive victim; but to the Russians, in whom passivity and fatalism were ingrained after generations of serfdom, she was a symbol of revolt, since her actions explode the horizon of those bound by tradition. For example, tradition insisted that a wife wail loudly when her husband went away as proof of her devotion: embracing a husband in public and leaving the house to meet another man were unbelievable breaches of proper behaviour.

So what does Janáček do with this story? Fundamentally, the whole aspect of social rebellion, of the Enlightenment struggle against religious prejudices, disappears: Janáček's Katja is a victim of fate in the guise of a blind uncontrollable passion – why? We should take into account the shift in historical situation: Janáček wrote his opera in the early twentieth century, when peasant *samodurstvo* was no longer a direct reality to be fought but a thing of the (nostalgic) past, a closed universe of passions and their repression no longer present in modern industrialized society. Does this make him an ideological mystifier, somebody presenting a historically determined oppression as eternal fate? The comparison with another Katerina in another twentieth-century opera based on a similar Russian narrative – Shostakovich's *Lady Macbeth* – seems to confirm this conclusion: Shostakovich's Katerina

Ismailova rebels, she kills her husband and father-in-law, in contrast to Janáček's Katerina Kabanova, who is only able to turn her violence against herself.

Lady Macbeth is based on a famous horror story by another nineteenth-century Russian writer, Nikolai Leskov, about the real-life case of Katerina Ismailova, a merchant's wife in the middle of the great Russian nowhere, who rebels against her patriarchal surroundings by murdering her husband, her father-in-law and her husband's saintly nephew. She and her lover, Sergei, are discovered in the act of killing the little boy, and sentenced to exile in Siberia. On the way there, Sergei gets entangled with another younger woman-prisoner, whom Katerina murders by jumping with her into a freezing river in which both of them drown. Shostakovich turned this creepy tale into a Soviet morality play: the objective conditions under which Katerina was forced to live justify her acts of violence, which are not crimes but acts of feminist liberation. (Of course, in such a reinterpretation, the third murder had to be left out.) In order to achieve this reinterpretation, Shostakovich combined Leskov's Katerina with Ostrovsky's Katerina, offering as the motivation of her acts libidinal awakening:

> A whole scene from Ostrovsky's play (Katerina's oath of fidelity) is inserted into the libretto to make the point; and Shostakovich referred to his heroine with the same famous epithet – 'a ray of light in the Dark Kingdom' – by which a nineteenth-century radical writer had honored Ostrovsky's gentle heroine sixty years before. . . . Shostakovich . . . described the difference between Ostrovsky's meek heroine and their rampageous one as that between the mild protests of a czarist writer and the triumphant achievements of Socialist Realism. Their Katerina, they proudly announced, was no mere ray of light but the full radiance of the Marxist sun.[21]

Leskov's approach to his story is indicated by its first sentence: 'Certain characters are sometimes found in our regions whom we cannot remember without shuddering, however many years may have passed since the day we met them.' Following the murder of her father-in-law, his Katerina is swept into a whirlpool of almost inevitable crimes which will take her to her death: everything starts with a blunder, a first crime, which is why the motto at the beginning of Leskov's story is a popular saying: 'Think twice before you take the first step!'. Hence it is in fact a moral, exemplary tale. In the opera, this tone of a true-to-life, horrifying, moralizing chronicle is replaced by a view-point of the main character, who is offered as the figure of our identification. Katerina Ismailova is a kind of Madame Bovary going wild, reacting to her stultifying condition of an unsatisfying marriage with a wild explosion of murderous violence, in a long tradition that reaches from the naturalism of Zola's *Thérèse Raquin* to American *film noir* (*The Postman Always Rings Twice*). Within this tradition, misogyny is inextricably linked to feminist potential: it is the desperate patriarchal condition that drives a wife to such an outburst of violence.

We can thus establish a matrix of four positions with regard to how Janáček and Shostakovich relate to their literary models: Shostakovich transforms Leskov's naturalistic-moralistic depiction of a moral monster into a story of aggressive feminine rebellion; Janáček transforms Ostrovsky's sympathetic story of the victim of religious superstition and social oppression into a drama of elementary passions. One way further to elaborate the comparison between Janáček and Shostakovich is with regard to the sexual act, the consummation of the affair, which takes place in the middle of both operas: Shostakovich displays it fully on-stage, while in Janáček's opera it occurs behind the stage, in the 'off' space. Does this feature epitomize Shostakovich's 'progress' over Janáček's prudish restraint, which is also reflected in the opposite resolution of Katerina's predicament? In Janáček's opera, Katerina breaks down, confesses her act and kills herself; while Shostakovich's Katerina rebels violently against her oppressors – again, is this 'progress' or not? And what about the third, modern secular, resolution of the same tension, with Katerina simply leaving her husband and his family, not to mention the comic version (Katerina going on cheating her husband) – would this still be the stuff of opera?

Let us return to Act II of *Kabanova*: the couple of Katerina and her lover Boris is presented as one in a series, in clear contrast to two other couples: the failed relationship of Katja and Boris is situated between two well-functioning couples, the 'normal' couple of Varvara and Kudrjash, two young people whose relationship is a simple joyful love affair and who, at the end, decide to leave for Moscow in order to lead a free life there; the 'pathological' couple of Kabanicha and Dikoy – outwardly respectful moral monsters who practise cruelty through 'good manners', and whose relationship is based on the sadomasochistic game of finding satisfaction in self-humiliation and torturing the other. The paradox of Katja is that her subjective attitude is the very opposite of that of an easy flirtatious woman: she is a perfect wife, religious, humble, loving, serving – *this is why* Kabanicha, her mother-in-law, hates her as it were ontologically, striving to destroy her in her very being. Kabanicha cannot tolerate true affection, the overlapping of inner affects and external form – for her, there must be a gap between the two, the form *must* be 'hypocritical'. So when, at the beginning of Act II, Kabanicha criticizes Katja for not making a display of grief over her husband's absence, she is reproaching her not for her insincerity but, precisely, for her lack of insincerity, for failing to perform a hypocritical ritual of grief.

Recall Pascal's well-known advice to those who cannot bring themselves to believe: 'Kneel down, act *as if* you believe, and belief will come by itself!' We should attempt a kind of inversion of Pascal's formula – what if its true underlying message is: 'Do you believe too much, too directly? Do you find your belief too oppressive in its raw immediacy? Then kneel down, act as if you believe, and *you will get rid of your belief* – you will no longer have to believe yourself; your belief will already exist objectified in your act of praying!'? That is to say: what if one kneels down and prays not so much to regain one's own belief but, quite the opposite, to *get rid* of one's belief, of its overproximity – to acquire the breathing space of a minimal distance towards it? To believe – to believe 'directly', without the externalizing mediation of a ritual – is a heavy, oppressive, traumatic burden which, through exercising a ritual, one has the chance to transfer on to an Other. . . . And what if the same goes for marriage? The standard Catholic lesson 'You don't love your woman? Go through the ritual of marriage, perform the acts of love prescribed for married life, and love will come by itself!' should also be inverted into: 'Are you too passionately in love, does this passion disturb your life, making it impossible for you to lead a calm, normal existence? No problem: ritualize your love in marriage, transform it into a marital duty, and you will get rid of its excess, turning your life back into a boring but satisfying daily ritual, with no great passions to disturb it!'

Both *Katja Kabanova* and *Jenufa*, Janáček's other masterpiece, are set in a matriarchal universe which turns out to be no less oppressive than the patriarchal one; however, while in *Katja* matriarchy is presented as malevolent, as the reign of perverted and hypocritical Evil, in *Jenufa* it is a benevolent force: Kostelnička, Jenufa's mother-in-law, sacrifices herself for Jenufa, killing her newborn son in order to make her marriage possible – in *Jenufa*, the confession is not Jenufa's but Kostelnička's. It was Max Brod, together with none other than Kafka, Janáček's personal friend and admirer, who noticed this key common feature of *Jenufa* and *Katja*: the public confession.[22] This shared feature, however, only makes all the more palpable the contrast between the two cases: in *Jenufa*, the crime is truly a crime, but justified as an act of love that, in effect, saves Jenufa (by getting rid of the unwanted child, Jenufa can marry and lead a normal life), and the confession itself is also done out of love (to save Jenufa, who is suspected of killing her child); while in *Katja*, the crime (love affair) is not truly a crime at all, and its public confession is 'irrational' – far from saving the heroine, it brings about her destruction.

It is within such a premodern matriarchal universe that natural forces (the river Volga and the storm) can play a role which is much more than that of a metaphor for human passions. The river is the peaceful all-embracing Substance, the Great Mother which pursues its path indifferent to our human strivings and adventures; while the storm stands for its opposite, the moment of vengeful rage and violent outbursts against our human efforts. This natural force is what Jacques Lacan called the 'big Other', the substantial Real, the compass of our entire existence, that which 'always returns to its place', and thus provides the basic co-ordinates of our lives – as befits a matriarchal agricultural society, the rhythm of life is structured by reference to natural cycles (the seasons; day and night). With modern patriarchal industrial society, this reliable big Other disappears, as is exemplified by the use of electricity, which abolishes night, its impenetrable depth – the paradox is that the core of the modern subject becomes the 'Night of the World' at the very moment when the real night disappears. For the hysterical heroine of Schoenberg's *Erwartung*, there is no night, no natural compass that would provide a firm point of orientation to her life.

However, the question still remains: *why* does the storm shock Katja so strongly that it makes her publicly confess her affair and then kill herself by rejoining the river, the all-encompassing maternal Substance? The place where the storm strikes and brings Katja to confess her act is changed in Janáček's opera: in Ostrovsky's story it is a ruined church, and Katja is terrified when lightning illuminates the images of sinners suffering in hell; while in Janáček's opera it is simply 'the vaultings of an old decrepit building', with no religious connotation which would make Katja's breakdown dependent on 'religious oppression'. So why does Katja confess and then kill herself? It is not just 'internalized religious morality' which prevents her from liberating herself; it is rather that, after consummating her affair, she 'realizes that she cannot remain locked in a loveless marriage having once experienced true happiness. . . . Katya's suicide, then, is both an acceptance of defeat and a liberation. . . . While there is sadness in death, for Katya the real tragedy would have been to continue living.'[23]

Is this not a situation similar to the one at the end of Cameron's *Titanic* (another affair which ends in death by drowning)? The true tragedy would have been for the couple to stay together. . . .

The crucial element in the long aria of Katja's suicide is the repeated insistence on her blocked intention-to-signify, on her failure to put into words what she wants to say. First, she explains to Boris why she publicly confessed their affair: 'I did not mean to harm you! I must have lost all my senses when I disclosed everything. It's not that! It's not that! I wanted to tell you something different!' And a little later: 'But no, no! Here I am talking about something else! And I wanted to tell you something else!' And again: 'What it is I wished to say? There's such chaos in my head! I can't remember anything.' What does Katja find so difficult to put into words? Which deadlock bothers her? It concerns precisely the status of her confession: far from being caused by a religious feeling of guilt, of committing a mortal sin, her confession enacts a *utopian dream of publicly admitting/symbolizing her love*, her refusal to treat it as a secret affair. So it is not that Katja is a half-educated country girl unable to articulate her feelings, or that these feelings are in themselves too profound for the medium of speech; what she finds so difficult to express is the key role of the symbolic medium itself. The difficulty lies not in some ineffable transcendence, but in the self-referential immanence of the symbolic medium to love: love becomes what it is only through being publicly recognized as what it is. In this precise sense, Katja Kabanova is a true antipode to Wagner's *Tristan*. The myth of Tristan and Isolde was the first to give full expression to the axiom of courtly love: love is an act of radical transgression which suspends all socio-symbolic links and, as such, has to culminate in the ecstatic self-obliteration of death. (The corollary to this axiom is that love and marriage are incompatible: within the universe of socio-symbolic obligations, true love can occur only in the guise of adultery.) Why is this notion of the adulterous ecstatic self-obliteration which transgresses the bounds of marriage inadequate? There is something in marriage which gets lost when we locate it in the opposition between, on the one hand, its legal-economic role (guaranteeing inheritance, and so on) and its emotional psychic role: the symbolic act of publicly declaring the mutual unconditional attachment of the two people involved. This act should *not* be reduced to the expression of emotions: in a way, it declares: 'We are committed to each other, whatever the fluctuations of our sentiments!' So when Judith Butler, for example, insists, against the demand for the recognition of gay marriages, on the need to dissociate the form of marriage from the actual entitlements that are legally bestowed on the married couple (healthcare, childcare, inheritance . . .), the problem is still what remains of this form itself, of the formal symbolic act of marriage which publicly proclaims the most intimate commitment. What if, in our postmodern world of ordained transgression, in which the marital commitment is perceived as ridiculously out of time, those who cling to it are the true subversives? We should again recall G.K. Chesterton's perspicuous remark, in his 'A Defense of Detective Stories', about how the detective story

> keeps in some sense before the mind the fact that civilization itself is the most sensational of departures and the most romantic of rebellions. When the

> detective in a police romance stands alone, and somewhat fatuously fearless amid the knives and fists of a thief's kitchen, it does certainly serve to make us remember that it is the agent of social justice who is the original and poetic figure, while the burglars and footpads are merely placid old cosmic conservatives, happy in the immemorial respectability of apes and wolves. [The police romance] is based on the fact that morality is the most dark and daring of conspiracies.[24]

What, then, if the same goes for marriage? What if, today, marriage is 'the most dark and daring of all transgressions'? The implicit presupposition (or, rather, injunction) of the standard ideology of marriage is that, precisely, there should be no love in it: one gets married in order to cure oneself of the excessive passionate attachment, to replace it with boring daily routine (and if one cannot resist passion's temptations, there are extramarital affairs . . .) Consequently, the ultimate subversion is to *nominate* the love-union, to proclaim it publicly instead of concealing it.

Flaubert took a crucial step in undermining the co-ordinates of the transgressive notion of love. That is to say: why was *Madame Bovary* dragged to court? Not, as is usually claimed, because it portrays the irresistible charm of adultery, and thus undermines the basis of bourgeois sexual morality. *Madame Bovary*, rather, inverts the standard formula of the popular novel, in which the adulterous lovers are punished at the end for their transgressive enjoyment: in this kind of novel, of course, the final punishment (mortal illness, exclusion from society) only enhances the fatal attraction of the adulterous affair, at the same time allowing the reader to indulge in this attraction without penalty. What is so profoundly disturbing and depressing about *Madame Bovary* is that it takes even this last refuge away from us – it depicts adultery in all its misery, as a false escape, an inherent moment of the dull and grey bourgeois universe. This is why *Madame Bovary* had to be brought to trial: it deprives the bourgeois individual of the last hope that an escape from the constraints of meaningless everyday life is possible. A passionate extramarital liaison not only poses no threat to conjugal love; rather, it functions as a kind of inherent transgression which provides the direct fantasmatic support to the conjugal link, and thus participates in what it purports to subvert. It is this very belief that, outside the constraints of marriage, in the adulterous transgression, we can really obtain 'that', full satisfaction, which is questioned by the hysterical attitude: hysteria involves the apprehension that the 'real thing' behind the mask of the social etiquette is itself void, a mere mirage. If there is a feature which serves as the clear index of modernism – from Strindberg to Kafka, from Munch to Schoenberg's *Erwartung* – it is the emergence of the figure of the hysterical woman which stands for the radical disharmony in the relationship between the two sexes. Wagner does not yet venture this step into hysteria: the problem with him is not his hysteria (as Nietzsche thought) but, rather, that he is not hysterical enough. Although his dramas provide all possible variations on how 'love can go wrong', all this takes place against the fantasmatic background of the redemptive power of a full sexual relationship – the very catastrophic outcome of the stage action seems to assert *per negationem* the belief in the redemptive power of sexual love. It is clearly more than a coincidence that Schoenberg's *Erwartung*, the first true masterpiece of atonal music, set to tones the poem commissioned by Schoenberg from Marie Pappenheim, a minor poetess who belonged to Freud's inner circle (with a connection to Bertha Pappenheim, Freud's Anna O., the patient who coined the expression 'talking cure'?) and wrote the poem following Schoenberg's detailed instructions.

So where does Janáček's *Katja* belong? In the era limited, on the one side, by Romanticism, its notion of radical Evil ('pleasure in pain') and, on the other, by Freud, by the direct impact of psychoanalysis on arts – why? Lacan located the starting point of the movement of ideas which finally gave birth to psychoanalysis in Kantian ethics (his critique of practical reason), and the Romantic notion of 'pleasure in pain'. It is this epoch which provides the only proper ground for what is deceitfully called 'applied psychoanalysis'. Prior to it, we were in a universe where the Unconscious was not yet operative, where the subject was the Light of Reason opposed to the impersonal Night of drives, and not, in the very kernel of its being, this Night itself; afterwards, the very impact of psychoanalysis transformed artistic literary practice (Eugene O'Neill's plays, for example, already presuppose psychoanalysis, whereas Henry James and Katherine Mansfield do not). And this is also the horizon within which *Katja Kabanova* moves – this space of the heroic innocence of the Unconscious in which irresistible passions roam freely. It is only in this space that one can use the storm as a metaphor for the explosion of frustrated feminine sexuality. This is why *Katja Kabanova* is still an opera: the moment of the birth of psychoanalysis (the beginning of the twentieth century) is also the moment of opera's death – as if, after psychoanalysis, opera, at least in its traditional form, is no longer possible. No wonder, then, that Freudian resonances abound in most of the pretenders to the title of the 'last opera' (say, Berg's *Lulu*).

This insight allows us to account for the basic enigma of works like *Katja Kabanova* and *Jenufa*: are they really simply the condemnation of oppressive mores which thwart feminine sexuality? Why this resort to external oppression at the very moment when, in social reality, we fully enter the industrial era? Is it not that, beneath the condemnation, there is a nostalgic resort to a situation in which *real passions were still possible*, and were thwarted only by the oppression? Schoenberg's *Erwartung* tells the bitter truth about the longing of Jenufa and Katerina: that it is thwarted *in itself*.

Parsifal as a Learning Play

Is, however, the reading of *Parsifal*'s finale as that of a hysterical identification with the object the only consistent one? The problematic nature of Nietzsche's critique of *Parsifal* indicates that Wagner's last work is full of surprises: is the scene (the 'dispositif') of Nietzsche's critique of Wagner not already staged in *Parsifal*? No wonder *Parsifal* provoked such a strange mixture of rage *and* admiration in Nietzsche. Klingsor's kingdom fits Nietzsche's notion of Wagner: an impotent hypnotic Master manipulating hysterical women, and thus seducing the public; and, against this kingdom and its musical aspect (chromaticism, immersion in an endless flow lacking proper or inner form), the hero without guilt who leads the Grail community, reasserting firm marching rhythm and heroic hierarchical relations. . . . Nietzsche's critique of Wagner is thus in fact a case of 'the frame itself being part of the enframed content': the very frame of Nietzsche's critique is already staged in the criticized content.[25]

What then, if, *Parsifal* also points in another direction, that of the emergence of a new collective? If *Tristan* enacts redemption as the ecstatic suicidal escape *from* the social order, and *Meistersinger* resigned integration *into* the existing social order, then *Parsifal* concludes with the invention of a new form of the Social. With Parsifal's 'Disclose the Grail!' ['Enthüllt den Graal!'], we pass from the Grail community as a closed order where the Grail is revealed, in the prescribed time and ritual, only to the circle of the initiated, to a new order in which the Grail has to remain revealed all the time: 'No more shall the shrine be sealed!' ['Nicht soll der mehr verschlossen sein!']. (This, perhaps, is the only truly Christian moment of *Parsifal*: the permanent shining of the Grail turns it into a *lux aeterna*, breaking with the pagan circular movement of disclosure and withdrawal.[26]) As for the revolutionary consequences of this change, recall the fate of the Master figure in the triad *Tristan–Meistersinger–Parsifal* (King Mark, Hans Sachs, Amfortas): in the first two works, the Master survives as a saddened melancholic figure; in the third he is *deposed*, and dies.

Why, then, should we not read *Parsifal* from today's perspective: the kingdom of Klingsor in Act II is a domain of digital phantasmagoria, of virtual amusement – Harry Kupfer was right to stage Klingsor's magic garden as a video parlour, with the Flower Girls reduced to fragments of female bodies (faces, leg . . .) appearing on dispersed TV screens. Is Klingsor not a kind of Master of the Matrix, manipulating virtual reality, a combination of Rupert Murdoch and Bill Gates? And when we pass from Act II to Act III, do we not pass, in effect, from fake virtual reality to the 'desert of the Real', the 'waste land' in the aftermath of ecological catastrophe which has derailed the 'normal' functioning of nature? Is Parsifal not a model for Keanu Reeves in *The Matrix*, with Samuel Jackson in the role of Gurnemanz?[27]

I am thus tempted to offer a direct 'vulgar' answer to the question: what the hell was Parsifal doing on his journey in the long time which passes between Acts II and III? The true 'Grail' are the people, their suffering. What if he simply got acquainted with human misery, suffering and exploitation? So what if the *new* collective is something like a revolutionary party, what if one takes the risk of reading *Parsifal* as the precursor of Brecht's *Lehrstücke*, what if its topic of sacrifice points towards that of Brecht's *Die Massnahme*, which was put to music by Hans Eisler, the third great pupil of Schoenberg after Bert and Webern? Is not the theme of both *Parsifal* and *Die Massnahme* that of learning: the hero has to learn how to help people in their suffering? The outcome, however, is the opposite: in Wagner compassion, in Brecht/Eisler the strength not to give way to one's compassion and directly act on it. This opposition itself, however, is relative: the shared theme is that of *cold/distanced compassion*. Brecht's lesson is the art of *cold* compassion, compassion with suffering which learns to resist the immediate urge to help others; the lesson of Wagner is cold *compassion*, the distanced saintly attitude (recall the cold girl into which Parsifal turns in Syberberg's version) which none the less retains compassion. Wagner's lesson (and Wotan's insight) about how the greatest act of freedom is to accept and freely enact what necessarily has to occur is strangely echoed in the basic lesson of Brecht's 'learning plays': what the young boy about to be killed by his colleagues has to learn is the art of *Einverständnis*, of accepting his own killing, which will occur anyway.

And what about the misogyny which obviously sustains this option? Is it not that *Parsifal* negated the shared presupposition of the first two works, their assertion of love (ecstatic courtly love, marital love), opting for the exclusive male community? What if here also, however, Syberberg was right: after Kundry's kiss, in the very rejection of (hysterical-seductive) femininity, Parsifal turns into a woman, adopts a feminine subjective position? What if what we actually get is a dedicated 'radical' community led by a cold ruthless woman, a new Joan of Arc?

And what about the notion that the Grail community is a closed elitist initiatic circle? Parsifal's final injunction to disclose the Grail undermines this false alternative of elitism/populism: every true elitism is universal, addressed to one and all, and there is something inherently vulgar about initiatic secret Gnostic wisdoms. There is a standard complaint by the numerous lovers of *Parsifal*: a great opera with many passages of breathtaking beauty – none the less, Gurnemanz's two long narratives (taking up most of the first half of Acts I and III) are Wagner at his worst: a boring recapitulation of past deeds already known to us, lacking any dramatic tension. My proposed 'Communist' reading of *Parsifal* entails a full rehabilitation of these two narratives as crucial moments of the opera – the fact that they may appear 'boring' is to be understood along the lines of a short poem by Brecht from the early 1950s, addressed to a nameless worker in the GDR who, after long hours of work, is obliged to listen to a boring political speech by a local Party functionary: 'You are exhausted from long work / The speaker is repeating himself / His speech is long-winded, he speaks with strain / Do not forget, tired one: / He speaks the truth.'[28] This is the role of Gurnemanz – no more and no less than the agent – the mouthpiece, why not? – of truth. In this precise case, the very predicate 'boring' is an indicator (a vector, even) of truth as opposed to the dazzling perplexity of jokes and superficial amusements. (There is, of course, another sense in which, as Brecht knew very well, dialectics itself is inherently comical.) With regard to the general economy of Wagner's work, however, the long narratives which interrupt the flow of events, especially in Wagner's late operas, where the singer recapitulates what went on before the opera or, often, simply in the previous opera or act, are a *symptom* of Wagner, the symptom of the inherent failure of the *Gesamtkunstwerk* project: instead of the organic *Darstellung*, the direct rendering of events, we get the artificial *Vorstellung*, representation.[29]

And what about the final call of the Chorus, 'Redeem the Redeemer!', which some read as the anti-Semitic statement 'redeem/save Christ from the clutches of the Jewish tradition, de-Semitize him'? What, however, if we read this line more literally, as echoing the other 'tautological' statement from the finale: 'The wound can be healed only by the spear which smote it [Die Wunde schliesst der Speer nur, der sie schlug]'? Is this not the key paradox of every revolutionary process, in the course of which not only is violence needed to overcome the existing violence, but the revolution, in order to stabilize itself into a New Order, has to eat its own children?

Wagner a proto-Fascist? Why not leave behind this search for the 'proto-Fascist' elements in Wagner and, rather, in a violent gesture of appropriation, reinscribe *Parsifal* in the tradition of radical revolutionary parties?

When one approaches the *Festspielhaus* during intermissions, the first impression, of course, is that of a scene from a Fellini film: aseptic old men in dark suits silently roaming around, accompanied by ladies with too much make-up, a true dance of the vampires, a reunion of living dead playing high society. . . . Is this, however, the whole truth? Or was Boulez right when, back in the 1960s, in one of his memorable anarchic-avant-garde outbursts, he said that all opera houses should be bombed – except Bayreuth?

The fact remains that the Bayreuth stagings (or, rather, the stagings of Wagner in general) provide the most accurate registration of our global spiritual and political preoccupations. Recall the *Parsifals* of the last decades: everything was there, from ecological concerns to New Age spirituality, from space-technology to political revolutions and youth rebellions. . . . More generally, do the great shifts in Wagner stagings not condense the triad of Traditionalism–Modernism–Postmodernism? Before the Second World War, traditional settings of the *Ring* predominated: naturalistic background of wild rocks and trees, Viking-like heroes. . . . Then, in 1950, there occurred the New Bayreuth explosion of radical modernism: ascetic, pseudo-Ancient Greek tunics, empty stages with strong lights and just some minimal simple objects with runes here and there. In the 1960s, Wagner stagings were at the forefront of postmodernism in all its versions: the inconsistent mixture of heterogeneous styles and settings (Rhinemaidens as prostitutes, the conflict between Siegfried and Hagen as a conflict between SA and SS, Valhalla's executive offices . . .), the changes in the narrative (Isolde stays at home and Tristan dies alone, the Dutchman is Senta's hysterical hallucination . . .).

In this way, Bayreuth – and Wagner's work itself – is more and more emerging as an insurpassable *canon*, comparable only to Greek tragedy and Shakespeare: not a foundation with a fixed meaning, but the permanent frame of reference which calls for ever new stagings, which has to be fed by them in order to remain alive. It is through a new staging of Wagner that we make it clear to ourselves where we stand, in the most radical existential sense, and the power of Wagner's opus is precisely that it survives ever new interpretations.

Imagine – my private dream – a *Parsifal* taking place in a modern megalopolis, with Klingsor as an impotent pimp running a whorehouse; he uses Kundry to seduce members of the 'Grail' circle, a rival drug gang. 'Grail' is run by the wounded Amfortas whose father, Titurel, is in a constant delirium induced by too many drugs; Amfortas is under terrible pressure from the members of his gang to 'perform the ritual', that is, deliver the daily portion of drugs to them. He was 'wounded' (infected by AIDS) through Kundry, his penis bitten while Kundry was giving him fellatio. Parsifal is the young inexperienced son of a single homeless mother who does not get the point of drugs; he 'feels the pain', and rejects Kundry's advances while she is performing fellatio on him. When Parsifal takes over the 'Grail' gang, he establishes a new rule for his community: the free distribution of drugs. . . .[30] Such experiments, of course, are risky; they often ridiculously misfire – *not always*, however, and there is no way of telling in advance, so one has to take the risk.

Bayreuth, which was proclaimed dead, dismissed as outdated, at its very conception, is today more alive than the majority of those who organized its funerals. Again and again, it re-emerges as the Mecca of European cultural fundamentalists – the site of their *hadj*, sacred pilgrimage – you have to go there at least once in your lifetime if you want your soul to be saved. And the core of these fundamentalists is no longer composed by hardcore conservatives: as an American critic recently remarked, Wagner's *Ring* was almost kidnapped in recent years by Leftist Jewish directors – in a weird case of poetic justice, you have to go to the American West (to Seattle) in order to enjoy the 'authentic' Teutonic *Ring*. . . .

In 2003, after public letters from Jürgen Habermas, Jacques Derrida, Richard Rorty and other philosophers, there was a lot of talk about the revival of core European values as an antidote to the Americanized New World Order. If there is a cultural event in which, today, this European tradition condenses and embodies itself, it is Bayreuth – so, to paraphrase Max Horkheimer, those who do not want to talk about Bayreuth should also keep silent about Europe.

Notes

1. Gary Tomlinson, *Metaphysical Song* (Princeton, NJ: Princeton University Press; 1999), p. 94.
2. Vladimir Nabokov, *Strong Opinions* (New York: McGraw-Hill, 1973), p. 35.
3. Unfortunately, the same cannot be said for the infamous fourth movement. In one of his essays, Adorno mentions a wonderful example of the vulgarity of *Halbbildung*: an American manual which should help people to recognize the best-known classical music pieces, and thus avoid embarrassment in intellectual society – how? The author proposes for each best-known classical melody words (allegedly illustrating its 'content') which should help us remember it – the four-note theme at the beginning of Beethoven's fifth is thus rendered/translated as 'Hear how fate knocks! Hear how fate knocks!', the main melodic line of the first movement of Tchaikovsky's sixth as 'The storm is over, Tchaikovsky's calm but sad again. . . .' Adorno, of course, explodes with rage (obviously mixed with extreme obscene enjoyment) at this barbarism. The problem with the fourth movement of Beethoven ninth, which sets to music Schiller's ode about the brotherhood of all men, and so on, is that, in it, he does this to himself: Schiller's words, in effect, function as precisely such a vulgar reminder of the 'deep' content. . . .

4. In the 2002 Bayreuth staging of *Tannhäuser*, Wolfram is excluded from the crowd at the end, a mere profile in darkness, an embittered loser. This detail rests on an ingenious insight: that Wolfram, this proverbial 'best friend' trying to help Tannhäuser and enable him to redeem himself, is in effect a thoroughly *bad* character: the – no less proverbial – man in love with his best friend's girl, who tries to win the girl by working for the destruction of the friend while feigning sympathy and help. Wolfram is a thorough hypocrite secretly pushing his best friend towards misfortune, so that he can then publicly present himself as a devastated mourner and supporter of the unfortunate girl.

5. See 'Der biblische Weg', *Journal of the Arnold Schoenberg Institute*, vol. XVII, nos 1–2, ed. Paul Zukofsky (Los Angeles: University of California Press, 1996).

6. Does not Wotan's idea of Siegfried in the *Ring* – only a free human being conceived against the will of the gods, not bound by their law, can redeem them of their guilt – also point to the Christological dimension? Is Siegfried not the man who sacrifices himself for the guilt of the gods?

7. When, in *Der Fall Wagner*, Nietzsche mockingly rejects Wagner's universe, does his style not refer to these lines? Wagner himself was such a repulsive figure to him – and there is a kind of poetic justice in it, since Mime is, in effect, Wagner's ironic self-portrait.

8. Joseph Kerman, *Opera as Drama* (Berkeley: University of California Press, 1988).

9. There is a further interesting feature of Wagner's *Ring*: Wagner used only the first part of the *Nibelungenlied*, that is, the *Ring* ends with Siegfried's death – so what about the second part, Kriemhild's revenge, in which Kriemhild marries Attila and uses him to kill Hagen, Gunther and all their kin? Is this topic of betrayal and passionate revenge not Verdi at his purest (no wonder that when, in the finale of Act II, *Götterdämmerung* approaches the topic of passionate revenge, we get a triumphant Verdian trio, strictly prohibited by Wagner's self-imposed rules!) – and the surprise is that Verdi *did*, in effect, write *Attila*: it is one of his early works (premiered on 17 March 1846 in Venice) with a plot full of passion and revenge which is by no means inferior to *Nibelungs*. The opera opens to Attila's army celebrating victory over the city of Aquileia. Praise is raised to Wodan and their general, who arrives and takes his seat on the throne. Odabella leads a group of women-prisoners in proclaiming their invincible spirit. They fought next to their men, unlike Atilla's women. Attila becomes enthralled with her, and offers her any gift she desires. She asks for a sword, and he gives her his own. She declares that with the sword she shall exact vengeance for all she has lost. Ezio arrives and offers the world to Attila as long as Italy remains his. Attila declares it shall all be his, and wages war. During a truce, Attila comes to marry Odabella and finds her in the arms of Foresto and in the company of Ezio. Attila reproaches all three, and is stabbed to death by Odabella.

10. There is, however, one thing to be said for the young revolutionary Wagner. In 1848, Wagner basically demanded social revolution in order to create the conditions for the proper staging of his operas – yet this is not an argument *against* him. Why should this not be a fully valid argument? First, bearing in mind the antagonism of art and society, to create the conditions of their reconciliation *is* the ultimate goal of revolutionary politics. Secondly, one does not make revolution for ideal abstract goals, but out of singular needs, each individual for particular reasons which can go up to extreme idiosyncrasy (personal jealousy) – this multitude in no way affects the 'objective' revolutionary goal.

11. Jeremy Campbell, *The Liar's Tale* (New York: Norton, 2001), p. 27.

12. Furthermore, what if we read the three figures of Kundry (in Act I the naive helper, in Act II the seductress, in Act III the repentant servant) along the lines of the classic theme of three women – three caskets?

13. The truth of Nietzsche's biting remark that all Wagnerian heroines are versions of Madame Bovary is fully confirmed if we take a glance at the second act of *Die Walküre*: is there not something inherently comic in how, after the larger-than-life battles of heroes, Wotan is afraid to face his wife's wrath? And does the same not go for *Götterdämmerung*, where Siegfried is brought down by family plotting? (The same pattern is already discernible in *Lohengrin*.)

14. The passage, at the beginning of *Rheingold*, from the orchestral interlude to the singing of the Rhinemaidens should be done properly: a cut and at the same time continuity, that is, a totally inherent explosion/inversion, a release of inner tension. (The same goes for Moussorgsky's *Pictures at an Exhibition*, the passage, at the end, from 'Baba Yaga' to 'The Great Kiev Doors'.)

15. This love-duet is also one of the Verdi-relapses in Wagner (the best-known being the revenge trio that concludes Act III of *Götterdämmerung*, apropos which Bernard Shaw remarked that it sounds like the trio of conspirators from *Un ballo in maschera*) – Gutman designated it as a farewell to music drama towards the 'rediscovered goal of the ultimate grand opera' (Robert Gutman, *Richard Wagner* [New York, 1968], p. 299).

16. Does not the couple Gutrune (Kriemhilde) and Brünnhilde belong to the series, which starts with Antigone and Brünnhilde, of a cold 'inhuman' woman accompanied by her 'human' passionate/pathological shadow (Juliette and Justine, Gudrun Ensslin and her sister)?

17. As if referring to this scene, Jacques-Alain Miller once engaged in a mental experiment, enumerating other possible operators of sexual difference which could replace the absence/presence of the penis, and mentions the absence/presence of breasts.

18. With regard to his Germanness, Wagner occupies a special place among great composers. Apropos of Tchaikovsky, Richard Taruskin aptly characterized the double-bind predicament of composers from the 'peripheral' countries (Eastern Europe, Scandinavia): the very vehicle which sustains their international appeal (their national roots) is at the same time the guarantee of their secondary status with regard to the unmarked 'universal' composers (from Germany, Italy or France) (Richard Taruskin, *Defining Russia Musically* [Princeton, NJ: Princeton University Press, 1997], p. 48). In other words, the very feature which sustains their inclusion *into* the canon commits them to secondary status *within* the canon. If a great 'universal' composer was a ferocious nationalist, this is as a rule dismissed as secondary, ultimately irrelevant, while, even if a 'peripheral' composer is not a nationalist, this absence is perceived not as the sign of his universality but as a sign of his troubled relationship towards his ethnic group. The big exception is Wagner: although he is the 'big' composer, his national roots *do* matter in his case – and this is what makes him ideologically suspect.

19. So what about Syberberg's cinema version, which stages Amfortas's wound itself as a vaginal partial object? Is its irony not that the vagina itself, the feminine 'threat' to masculine identity, is reduced to a fetishist partial object?

20. Incidentally, Janáček was not the first to set *The Storm* to music: none other than Tchaikovsky wrote the overture 'Storm' (Opus 76).

21. Ricard Taruskin, 'A Martyred Opera Reflects Its Abominable Time', *The New York Times*, 6 November 1994.

22. Max Brod, 'Katia Kabanova', in *Katia Kabanova. L'Avant-Scène Opéra* (Paris: Éditions Premières Loges, 1988), p. 5.

23. David Hurwitz, in accompanying notes to the Supraphon recording of *Katja Kabanova* (Czech Philharmonic Orchestra/Charles Mackerras).

24. G.K. Chesterton, 'A Defense of Detective Stories', in H. Haycraft, ed., *The Art of the Mystery Story* (New York: The Universal Library, 1946), p. 6.

25. It is easy to demonstrate the inner split of Nietzsche's relationship to Wagner – that is, how his vicious attacks on Wagner bear witness to the fact that Nietzsche was unable to rid himself of Wagner's shadow; however, in spite of (or, rather, on account of) this split, Nietzsche's subjective position was much more authentic than the assured self-reliance of the late Wagner.

26. It is the myth of *Hamlet* whose structure is basically pagan (the 'circle of life', as they put it in *The Lion King*, the circular movement of the order disturbed by the uncle and the balance re-established by the son), while Oedipus (as Jean-Joseph Goux made clear) is a strange exception among myths, the atypical myth in which the normal course of things is interrupted.

27. What if – along the same lines – the entire action of *Siegfried* and *Götterdämmerung* is Brünnhilde's dream, while she is sleeping surrounded by fire? When, twice afterwards (at the end of both operas), fire appears in her dream, she incorporates into the dream the external stimuli of fire raging around her all the time. And the traumatic last scene of Act I of *Götterdämmerung* is the moment of the disintegration of the fantasy, a brutal inconsistent ambiguity – she then quickly concocts the complex narrative of Act II in order to account for this traumatic intrusion.

28. Bertolt Brecht, *Die Gedichte in einem Band* (Frankfurt: Suhrkamp, 1999), p. 1005.

29. For this idea, see David J. Levin, *Richard Wagner, Fritz Lang, and the Nibelungen* (Princeton, NJ: Princeton University Press, 1998).

30. The same could be done for *Tristan*: imagine the action transposed into a conflict between two patriarchal-gangster-fishermen Sicilian families, a kind of *Tristan* transposed into *Cavalleria rusticana*. The *capo* of one of the families ('Mark') sends his nephew ('Tristan') across the bay to the other family to bring him 'Isolde': the marriage is arranged to end a family feud. On the boat, the two recall their past encounter and, after the servant accompanying Isolde gives here a placebo drink instead of poison, declare their mutual love. In the second act, 'Mark' goes on a drinking spree with his friends, while 'Tristan' secretly visits 'Isolde'. . . .

12

Forfeits and Comparisons: Turgenev's 'First Love'

Sigi Jöttkandt

Love has so honeycombed today's ethical discourse that it is as though we have been taken hostage by an Other whose escalating demands on our affection now carry the full force and weight of the original superegotistic injunction from which Freud so famously recoiled.[1] Yet the proper answer to this loving impasse is not, as Slavoj Žižek has recently suggested, to respond with a fully 'ethical' violence that shatters the loving circle but, rather, *more* love.[2] Or, to put it more accurately, as the recent spate of divorces attributed to the website Friends Reunited attests, the proper response to love's spiralling demands is to return to one's first love. Why our first love? Because by returning us to the originary, primary imbalance, the primordial experience of being seized by an other, the One is fractured in Two and from there, as Badiou has suggested, the (truly ethical) vistas of infinity open out: 'One, Two, infinity: such is the numericity of the amorous procedure.'[3] I will return to Badiou's loving count presently, but let us first note with Kierkegaard how, because of this imbalance, one's first love must remain qualitatively different from the merely quantitative succession of all subsequent loves. This is witnessed by its remarkably labile ability to shift places within this numerical series, as Kierkegaard's narrator shortly discovers: 'I had not seen [my first love] for a long time, and I found her now, engaged, happy, and glad, and it was a pleasure for me to see her. She assured me that she had never loved me, but that her betrothed was her first love, and . . . that only the first love is the true love.'[4]

For this reason, too, one's first love can never become a partnership, with the reciprocity that this implies. Instead, our first love haunts us as the failure of what Lacan, in his seminar on transference, calls love's 'signification'. In first love, there is no mysterious flower-turned-hand stretching back as one grasps towards it in the dark, as Lacan famously described the loving relationship in this seminar. There is no transmogrifying loving 'miracle' that converts the loved object, *eromenos*, into the desiring subject, *erastes* willing, like Achilles with Patroclos, to take the place of the lover and assume his

Symbolic 'debt'.[5] What the entire literary tradition has dedicated itself to showing in not inconsiderable detail is the way first love offers nothing but the sublimity of a deep and lasting torment from which we never fully recover – even if, for some unknown reason, our 'first love' miraculously loves us back.[6] First love thus remains a deeply asymmetrical relation. It permanently defeats the closure of the ethical 'metaphor of love' that subjectifies the object and, in the work of love that is analysis, transforms the particularity of individual misery into the universality of common unhappiness. Even so, this initiation into heartache that is first love plays a fundamentally important role, as we will shortly see. For first love is ultimately what prevents love's 'metaphor' from fully crossing over into becoming a perverse circle with its accompanying escalating superegotistic demands.

A case in point right now is psychoanalysis itself. Psychoanalysis is increasingly beset on all sides by demands that it justify itself in relation to a host of competing discourses. 'The psychoanalytic subject is the subject of science,' goes one oft-repeated refrain. Opposing demands are heard from the recent religious recrudescence that has long tried to appropriate the psychoanalytic concept of the big Other for its own. Philosophy, too, has apparently claimed its own special place in the pantheon of psychoanalytic knowledge under the guise of the ethical turn. In a situation like this, psychoanalysis can perhaps be forgiven for returning to its own 'first love', literature.

Set in early-nineteenth-century Russia, Turgenev's short story 'First Love'[7] describes the narrator's first 'summer of love' when he meets the mercurial young Princess Zinaida, whose impecunious mother has taken rooms in the summer residence next door to his family. As merely one of a band of six ardent suitors, the narrator despairs of being selected for Zinaida's special attentions, and he devotes himself to trying to discover which of the group is the favoured one. One night, having received a hint that the successful suitor is to meet Zinaida for a midnight tryst by the fountain, he slips into the garden to confront his rival. Hearing footsteps, the narrator poises himself for the attack – only to discover at the last minute, in a moment of utter confusion and astonishment, that the stranger is none other than his own father. Shortly afterwards, upon receiving an anonymous letter detailing an affair between the princess and the narrator's father, the family leaves in haste for Moscow. Several weeks later, still nursing his emotional wound, the narrator and his father take a ride to the outskirts of town. The father leaves his horse with his son and disappears down a narrow alleyway. Eventually getting bored, and tormented by an old Finn wearing an absurd military helmet, the narrator follows the path his father had taken, and finds him talking to

Zinaida through a window. They appear to be arguing, with Zinaida 'saying words of only one syllable, without raising her eyes and simply smiling – smiling submissively and stubbornly' (198). All of a sudden, the unbelievable happens: 'my father suddenly raised his riding-crop, which he had been using to flick the dust off the folds of his coat, and I heard the sharp blow as it struck the arm bared to the elbow'. Instead of crying out, however, Zinaida merely shudders, gazes at her lover, and kisses the 'scarlet weal' that has appeared on her arm. The father then flings the riding-crop aside and dashes into the house, while the narrator himself flees from the scene back to the river. 'I stared senselessly at the river and didn't notice that there were tears pouring down my cheeks. "They're whipping her," I thought, "whipping her . . . whipping her . . ." ' (199). Later that evening, the narrator muses on the scene he has witnessed. ' "That's what love is," I told myself again, sitting at night in front of my desk on which books and notebooks had begun to appear. "That's real passion! Not to object, to bear a blow of any kind, even from someone you love very much – is that possible? It's possible, it seems, if you're in love . . ." ' (199–200).

Eight months later the father dies unexpectedly from a stroke following the receipt of another upsetting letter, and a large sum of money is mysteriously dispatched to Moscow. The son reads his father's final words in an unfinished letter addressed to him: ' "My son, . . . beware a woman's love, beware that happiness, that poison . . ." ' (200). The narrator never sees Zinaida again, but four years later he hears that she had apparently become a Mrs Dolsky, who has died recently in childbirth. 'So that's how it's all worked out!' the narrator reflects. 'It's to this that that young, ardent, brilliant life has come after all its haste and excitement!' (201). The story then ends with the narrator attending the death of an old woman and marvelling at the strength of the body's resistance to its approaching end. 'And I remember', he says, 'that as I stood there, beside the death-bed of that poor old woman, I began to feel terrified for Zinaida and I felt I wanted to pray for her, for my father – and for myself' (202).

Let us begin with a simple question: who is the 'first love' of the tale? The first, and most obvious, answer is of course Zinaida, the object of the narrator's first youthful passion. The premises of the story itself – a group of friends sitting around after dinner agreeing to tell each other the story of their first love – urges this interpretation on us as we escort the narrator through the soaring ecstasies and piercing torments that issue from Zinaida's impulsive and capricious dealings with him. The second answer, no less patent, can be found in Zinaida's love for the narrator's father. In this older, elegant, sophisticated man – the narrator is unstinting in his admiration for his father, who is invariably described as 'intelligent, handsome' (164), the 'ideal example of a man' (163) – Zinaida finally discovers someone she can't 'look down on' (167), a man who can 'break [her] in two' (167). In contrast to the band of rivals, the father is evidently of an order apart, and it is for his sake that she sacrifices her all, suffering torments which even the narrator, despite the abyssal soundings of his own wretchedness, can scarcely gauge:

> I knelt down at the edge of the path. She was so pale and such bitter sorrow, such profound exhaustion showed in every feature of her face that my heart sank and I muttered: 'What's wrong?' . . . At that instant, I think, I would gladly have given up my life simply to make sure she stopped feeling so sad. I gazed at her, and though I didn't understand why she was so miserable I vividly imagined to myself how she had suddenly, in a fit of overwhelming grief, gone into the garden and fallen to the ground as though scythed down. (169)

The third, and perhaps less immediate, answer can be found in the father's own love for Zinaida, a love which similarly seems to be distinguished from the rest of his erotic adventures. This, perhaps his first, real passion is what ultimately seems to have killed him. The fourth answer is then easy to find in the competing band of rivals, each of whom strives to become 'first' in Zinaida's affections. Each rival thus appeals to a different part of Zinaida's nature and although each, as the narrator observes, 'was needed by her', none succeeds in her eyes (166).

> Belovzorov, whom she sometimes called 'my beast' . . . would gladly have flung himself into the flames for her. Placing no hopes on his intellectual resources and other attributes, he was always making her proposals of marriage, hinting that the others were so many talkers. Maidanov appealed to the poetic strings of her spirit: a man of fairly cold temperament, like almost all writers, he strove to assure her – and perhaps himself as well – that he adored her, wrote endless verses in her honour and declaimed them to her with a kind of unnatural and yet sincere enthusiasm. . . . Lushin, the mocking, cynical doctor, knew her better than them all and loved her more than the others, though he scolded her to her eyes and behind her back. She respected him but didn't let him off scot-free and occasionally took a particularly malicious pleasure in making him feel that he was in her hands. . . . I least understood the relationship which existed between Zinaida and Count Malevsky. He was good-looking, capable and clever, but something dubious, something false was apparent in him even to me, a sixteen-year-old boy, and I was amazed that Zinaida didn't notice it. . . . 'Why do you want to have Mr Malevsky about the place?' I asked her once.
>
> 'He's got such beautiful little moustaches,' she answered. 'Anyhow, it's none of your business.'[8] (166)

There is a fifth answer, however, that I would like to venture here: namely, that the 'first love' of the tale lies in the psychoanalytic love of literature – literature, in so far as she proudly carries the scars of the signifier. Let me try to elucidate this somewhat enigmatic statement.

During the course of their wild evenings in the summer residence, Zinaida invents two games. One is a game of forfeits where each suitor picks a ticket from a hat, and the one who wins has the right to demand a forfeit from her. Zinaida determines the forfeits herself – a kiss, perhaps, or standing immobile as a statue using the 'ugly Nirmatsky' as a pedestal. On one occasion, on winning the forfeit, the narrator relates how

> I had to sit next to her, the two of us covered by a silk scarf, and I was ordered to tell her *my secret*. I remember how close our heads were in the stuffy, semi-transparent, perfumed shade, how closely and softly her eyes shone in this shade and how hot the breath was from her open lips and how I could see her teeth and felt the burning, tickling touch of the ends of her hair. (160–61)

The other game is called comparisons: some object is named, everyone has to try to compare it with something else, and the best comparison wins a prize (174). The merry band play comparisons one day not long after the narrator has gleaned that Zinaida must be in love:

> 'What do those clouds look like?' Zinaida asked and, without waiting for one of us to answer, said: 'I think they look like those purple sails on Cleopatra's golden ship when she sailed out to meet Antony. Do you remember, Maidanov, you recently told me about that?'
>
> We all agreed, like Polonius in *Hamlet*, that the clouds reminded us of those very sails and that not one of us would be able to find a better comparison.
>
> 'How old was Antony then?' asked Zinaida.
>
> 'He was probably a young man,' Malevsky remarked.
>
> 'Yes, he was young,' Maidanov confidently confirmed.
>
> 'Excuse me,' exclaimed Lushin, 'but he was over forty.'
>
> 'Over forty,' repeated Zinaida, shooting a quick glance at him.
>
> I soon went home. 'She's in love,' my lips whispered despite themselves, but with whom? (174)

It is not difficult to make out two of the three psychoanalytic psychic economies operative in these two games. The first game, forfeits, proceeds according to the logic of perversion: within the band of rivals, one person must assume the position of the exception, someone who is singled out from the pack and wins a special favour from the princess. What distinguishes this from the structure of neurosis, equally founded upon an exception, is the way this game takes place within an entirely closed environment. In a forfeiture economy, there are only positives and negatives; one has either won or lost, and the entire game revolves around the princess as a regionally central Other who is forced to dispense favours and perform certain absurd acts on cue. The exception – or, to put it into Hegelian terms, the negative – thus appears as a local event: one member of the band of rivals assumes a position that momentarily sets him apart from the rest before being jettisoned and reabsorbed once more into the general facelessness of the pack. There is no meaning to the structure apart from the chance event of winning the ticket: one cannot buy or sell one's location in the arrangement (' "Sell me your ticket", Belovzorov suddenly bellowed in my ear. . . . I gave the hussar such a look of disapproval that Zinaida clapped her hands and Lushin exclaimed: "Splendid!" ' (160)). And, despite Belovzorov's subsequent complaint, the game is in fact entirely 'fair' to the extent that it is played among true equals. Everyone has an equal chance of assuming the position of the exception.

Comparisons, on the other hand, entail something quite different, and its structure mirrors that of neurosis. In comparisons – a game which, we note, was invented *after* the princess has fallen in love with the narrator's father – the exception is located outside the circle of the rivals. One effect of this is to enable objects to stand in for one another without losing their original place in the game. Clouds can become Cleopatra's sails, Cleopatra can stand in for Zinaida, and the entire comparison can become an oblique reference to the princess's desire to comparably 'sail out' to her lover, another Antony who, like the original, is 'over forty'. All these substitutions can take place simply because the exception (the lover, the narrator's father) is in a position of perpetual exclusion outside the game. Such an expulsion frees up the earlier, binary logic of positives and negatives to allow objects or words to refer to two different things at the same time. The signifier has become detached from its signified, and can now circulate in multiple – that is, non-binary – relations and compositions. Furthermore, if the game of forfeits depended on the blind machinery of chance, comparisons relies on a relation of resemblance, introducing an element of necessity into the ludic equation.

Stated in this way, the economic structures of the two games fail to tell us anything particularly new or psychoanalytically striking. What is interesting, however, is the way the figure of literature makes its appearance in the game of comparisons. The comparative economy is one that depends upon a body of literary knowledge in order for the comparison to work. The clouds cannot be just any sails, but must be *Cleopatra's* sails – and the rivals themselves must be ridiculously sycophantic not just in any ordinary way, but in a *Polonius in Hamlet* kind of way. What might this literary underpinning of the comparative – or, as we might as well call it, Symbolic – economy tell us about the psychoanalytic psychic structures? Freud, of course, made no secret of the fact that many of his discoveries concerning the unconscious are sourced from the literary tradition – from Sophocles, Shakespeare, Jensen, Hoffmann, Dostoevsky, Goethe, to name just the immediate ones, not to mention the well-documented presence of Greek myth, the biblical tradition, and so forth in his thinking. Still, my intention here is not to try to argue for some kind of literary 'primacy' for psychoanalysis – as if all the psychoanalytic insights discover their Ur-texts in literature, and it is simply a matter of digging out their references. This would, to all intents and purposes, be a strictly perverse argument, one that inserts the psychoanalytic first love of literature into the circular, forfeiture economy of priority and belatedness. Although, as we have seen, this is certainly one of the structures operative in Turgenev's text, it is not the only one, and in order to explore the others, let us go back in a little more detail to 'First Love'.

As far as the neurotic structure is concerned, for example, it is well known that Turgenev was profoundly fascinated by the complex relations between *Fathers and Sons*, to name only one of his better-known novels. 'First Love' is thus by no means unique within his *œuvre* in its exploration of the theme of the 'superfluous man' (the title of another Turgenev short story). The superfluous man is the man who never fully emerges from the long shadow cast by his father – the would-be lover collapsing back into a ridiculous impotence at the first appearance of the father's desire. Of the momentous scene by the fountain in 'First Love', for instance, the narrator recounts how

> The jealous Othello who had been ready to commit murder was suddenly turned into a schoolboy . . . I was so frightened by the unexpected appearance of my father that at first I didn't even notice where he had come from or where he had gone. . . . From fear I dropped my penknife in the grass, but I didn't even start looking for it: I was very ashamed. I had come to my senses in a flash. (190)

The Turgenev man is without question only a semi-Oedipalized man, unable fully to recover from the cut of paternal castration and inhabit the 'comparative' economy of Symbolic desire. He remains caught somewhere between the perverse band of duelling rivals and the neurotic realm of the exception. He is both inside and outside the circle at the same time, as the narrator's unusual position in relation to Zinaida makes clear. By turns encouraged and repelled by her capricious flirtations and inexplicable rebuffs, at first the narrator merely supplies one more member to the band of rivals. But after the princess falls in love with his father, the narrator becomes a unique favourite on the basis of father and son's mutual resemblance: ' "Yes. The very same eyes," she added, becoming thoughtful and covering her face with her hands' (169), while later, in their final, unexpectedly passionate farewell, the narrator reflects: 'God knows who it was this prolonged farewell kiss sought to find, but I greedily savoured all its sweetness. I knew it would never be repeated' (196). The name Zinaida bestows on this unique position is that of 'pageboy' (182).

Despite its own potential for becoming ridiculous (the threat to which our Volodya, like other heroes of the Russian literary tradition, is acutely sensitive), this title conveys something very important about the narrator's position. As Zinaida explains while presenting him with a rose for his buttonhole as the 'sign' of his 'new position': 'pageboys must never be separated from their mistresses' (182). In the game of forfeits, the favour was always contingent, momentary and elusive, but this time the narrator is decorated with a Symbolic signifier that marks out his special relation (even if, like all tumescent flowers, it is soon destined to wither). While not quite King to her Queen, like his father, he is nevertheless set apart from the eternal merry-go-round of unpredictable and nonsensical favours suffered by the rivals.

The question I would now like to introduce is what kind of economy psychoanalysis represents, what is its own deep psychic structure? We know from Lacan that in the analytic discourse, the object (a) occupies the position of agent, the split subject is in the position of the other, the product is the master-signifier while its truth is unconscious knowledge. We know, too, that the analytic discourse, as Lacan puts it, is the 'sign of love' that emerges whenever a quarter-turn shift occurs in the three other discourses (the hysterical, university and master discourses).

My question is why, their structural uniformity notwithstanding, the psychoanalytic discourse is not functionally perverse even though it similarly positions the object (a) in the place of the agent. What prevents the desire of the analyst from becoming perverse despite its being articulated on the same structural plane as perversion? In his twelfth seminar, 'Crucial Problems for Psychoanalysis', in a session that has remarkable resonance for the present discussion, Lacan refers to the game the subject plays with its unconscious knowledge. Like the children's game of paper, stone, scissors with which Lacan analogizes it, this is a game of 'rotating dominance' that pivots around the central stumbling block of sexual difference. Every time the subject believes it has beaten this stumbling point and finally become 'determined' – that is, acquired being, through knowledge – this new certainty finds itself overturned, so that Lacan can say that the subject discovers his refuge in the 'pure default of sex'. The game's ruling principle is to try to anticipate the unexpected but, as Lacan observes, the unexpected is thus not truly unexpected, since it is precisely what one readies oneself for: 'one prepares oneself for the unexpected . . . what is the unexpected if not what reveals itself as being already expected, but only when it arrives'.[9]

It is this circular game of the discordance between knowledge and being that engages the subject when it enters analysis. In fact, Lacan says that it 'grounds' the analytic operation which is, interestingly, similarly described as a game in this seminar. The two games, however, operate in different ways. Lacan explains how the subject's game with its unconscious knowledge is reliant on a hidden sleight of hand that allows the subject, to the extent that he supposes the analyst to be the knowing subject, to secretly keep his 'hand in knowledge'. As he puts it, 'the person holding the marbles knows whether their number is odd or even'. This then enables the subject to anticipate the unexpected and, consequently, to keep his distance from it. The analytic game, however, is characterized by an altogether different principle which Lacan describes in terms of waiting. The analytic 'game' is nothing but a waiting game in which the analyst waits for the patient to show him how to act: 'this is what the desire of the analyst is in its operation. To lead the patient to his original fantasy is not to teach him anything, it is to learn from him how to act.' While the subject anticipates, and in anticipating defends himself against the unexpected, the analyst merely waits and, consequently, opens herself to surprise.

From here it is not difficult to see how the analyst's 'supreme complicity' with surprise, as Lacan calls it, is another way of formulating the famous emptiness of the analytic position as the object (a), which is thereby distinguished from that of the pervert. The pervert, as object (a), is characterized by a supreme conviction that enables her to act on behalf of the Other's *jouissance* and become the instrument of its will. Perverse love is a love that circles around knowledge, as the perverse formula of disavowal expresses very clearly: 'I *know* very well [that woman does not have the phallus], but all the same . . .'. Analytic love, on the other hand, is not interested in knowledge and its games of deception but, rather, in truth.[10] Hence while the relationship of the pervert to the object (a) is one of identification – convinced that it knows what the Other wants, the pervert identifies with the object (a) and becomes the instrument of the Other's will – the analyst, in the waiting game that is analysis, 'ends up with something other than an identification' to the extent that the analyst is able to recognize the object (a) as a 'semblance'. 'Love', Lacan explains in his twentieth seminar 'is addressed to the semblance. And if it is true that the Other is only reached if it attaches itself . . . to *a*, the cause of desire, then love is also addressed to the semblance of being.'[11]

To unpack the implications of this, let us now imagine the analytic situation. Analyst and patient are engaged in the analytic work of love. The patient tries desperately to establish his or her own priority in the analyst's affections, wondering about the analyst's likes and dislikes, trying to comprehend the seemingly random acts of kindness and cruelty that the analyst capriciously doles out. What makes the analytic circle of rivals different from the game of forfeiture played by Zinaida with her suitors? The difference is that, like Zinaida, the analyst is in love with another, with a figure who is beyond the immediate circle. Literature, as the first love of psychoanalysis, provides the conditions under which the game of (Symbolic) comparisons can begin (and whose other name is interpretation).

Let me try to explain. The crucial scene in the tale is when the narrator secretly follows his father down the alley and watches the older lover strike his beloved. Recall how the narrator then rushes from the scene back to the river and, with tears pouring down his cheeks, repeats to himself 'They're whipping her . . . whipping her, whipping her' (199). Yet despite displaying the hallmarks of a perverse scenario (including its ironic echo of an earlier scene in the garden when the princess lightly taps each suitor's forehead with a pale-mauve flower), this scene differs from perversion in one crucial respect: rather than positioning the narrator as the Other for whom the perverse scenario is being staged (and whose ultimate function, as we know, is to deny or disavow feminine castration by momentarily singling out a winner (or fetish) who temporarily assumes and fills out the lack), this scene serves instead finally to extricate the narrator from the overpowering shadow of his father: by revealing that his father is castrated.

Two elements of this scene are important here. One is Zinaida's role in causing the violent eruption. Recall how Zinaida, 'saying words of only one syllable . . . and simply smiling – smiling submissively and stubbornly', finally forces the father to act. It is Zinaida's interminable, senseless repetition of a word, along with her simultaneously stubborn and submissive smile, that goads the father into striking her, and in that instant of acting he reveals his true impotence: 'My father flung the riding-crop aside and, hurriedly running up the porch steps, dashed into the house' (198). But it is this very impotence that Zinaida ultimately provokes and loves – it is indeed what every woman loves – and this is what distinguishes the narrator's father from the rest of the band of rivals, namely, his castration. Zinaida loves the father's castration precisely because it is evidence of the fact that there is someone or something beyond him who is not castrated. His castration is the guarantee of the presence of an other 'father', an exceptional, castrating but uncastrated father whom Zinaida loves in and through her love for her impotent and castrated lover. I must point out here how radically different this is from the perverse play of the game of forfeits. In forfeits, the exceptional – that is, castrated –

position always remains a temporary favour. Forfeits requires a black-and-white game of simple positives and negatives that always returns the (missing) phallus back into the unbroken circle. Any member of the band can momentarily assume the castrated position, but he will always fall back afterwards into the undifferentiated whole. The lack, in other words, is Imaginary, and circulates internally within a fetishistic economy. With the narrator's father, however, the lack is Symbolic and therefore – and most vitally, if we remember the lesson of Little Hans – *detachable*, enabling it to be 'flung aside'.[12] As a Symbolic lack, it bears witness to the father's Real impotence.

Secondly, although Zinaida desires a lover who will 'break [her] in two', it is the narrator who ultimately comes out of the story in two halves. The evidence of this lies in the other striking aspect of this scene: namely, the very curious use of the plural form in the narrator's riverside wail: '*They're* whipping her . . . whipping her, whipping her.' Why this sudden intrusion of the multiple into what is plainly an exchange between only two people? The first answer, which is clearly the narrator's own unconscious one, is that by this act the father has himself now entered the perverse circle of rivals, and become merely one of the 'many'. The dream the narrator has that night reveals just how incapable he really is of psychically assuming the new knowledge he has acquired:

> That very night I dreamed a strange and awful dream. I dreamed that I went into a dark low-ceilinged room. My father was standing there with a whip in his hand and stamping his feet. Zinaida was crouching in a corner and there was a bright red weal not on her arm but her forehead. And behind both there rose the figure of Belovzorov all covered in blood, and he opened his pale lips and angrily threatened my father. (200)

Unable psychically to consent to what he has just seen, the narrator immediately resorts to the first game Zinaida has taught him, and inserts the father into the band of rivals with its forfeiture economy.

But I would like to suggest another interpretation of the narrator's interesting slip.[13] When he cries out that 'they' are whipping Zinaida, it is hard not to think of the classic Freudian study 'A Child is Being Beaten'. In his fifth seminar, Lacan reads this fantasy as a kind of allegory of subject formation which takes place in three logical rather than temporal stages: my father is beating a child whom I hate; I am being beaten by my father; and finally – the fantasy's title – a child is being beaten. The second moment, however, is permanently excluded and must be reconstructed through a complicated, atemporal movement that goes from the third moment to the first, and only then to the second.

In his reading, Lacan sees the first moment as articulating the primary intersubjective relation between a child and a rival whereupon I, seeing my father beating the other child (a sister or brother), take this to mean that the father does not love my rival, who is thereby negated, a statement which simultaneously contains its elated obverse: namely, that I, in contrast, am loved – I exist.[14] The third moment – which, as I said, occurs prior to the first and the second moments – presents an objectification of this primary relationship in the form of an external scene or an image – *a* child (that is, an unnamed other rather than my brother or sister or myself) is being beaten, and I am watching as a spectator. The second moment is the moment of crossover between the first and third stages and is, for this reason, both necessary and fugitive, as Lacan says,[15] and must be reconstructed – in other words, it can never be represented in either memory or words. Here the yet-to-be subject is itself being beaten and, judging by the pleasure with which the subject invests the other two moments, is also *enjoying* it. In Lacan's interpretation of 'A Child is Being Beaten', this second, occluded moment thus speaks of a fundamental masochistic enjoyment that accompanies the subject's entry into language. For the fantasy, as Dominiek Hoens puts it, 'is an imaginary representation of what happened to the child symbolically. The child brings into play and, one could say, fantasizes about what it means to be a subject of the Symbolic order: one is beaten away, rubbed out, by something from outside.'[16] Furthermore – and particularly relevantly for our purposes here – this primordial perverse enjoyment of the pounding by the paternal signifier has the result, as Lacan points out, of permanently investing language with an element of eroticism.[17]

Hence when the narrator uses the plural form in his agonized wail that 'they' are 'whipping her', I suggest that here we might find traces of evidence of an occlusion or repression comparable to the second moment of the 'A Child is Being Beaten' fantasy. That is, the narrator's peculiar use of 'they' provides unconscious testimony to the fact that a moment of subjectification has occurred. Although, as in the fantasy, this second moment can never be represented or put into conscious form, we can glean from the presence of the third moment – whose element of spectatorship Turgenev quite deliberately highlights when he has Zinaida framed in the windowsill and half screened by a curtain – that this must indeed have occurred. Two consequences immediately follow from this. One is that we see now that it is not Zinaida, nor the father, nor any member of the band of rivals but language itself, in its primary form of the signifier, that is the 'first (perverse) love' of the text – language, that is, to the extent that in it resides the fundamental masochistic erotic fantasy in which all subsequent fantasmatic desiring 'scenes' or loving representations participate. The other consequence is that it is this (per-)first love that succeeds in fracturing the One into Two, as Badiou put it earlier. Now that the subject has literally been broken in two – that is, irretrievably split between the first and third components of the fantasy – the 'numericity' of the amorous procedure may begin in the form of the quantitative count to infinity of all possible successive loves.

If my construction is correct, is analytic love a (per-)first love after all? Here we must recall Lacan's assertion that (analytic) love is addressed to a *semblance*. A semblance is a counterfeit, a double, a wraithlike form that may possess either an actual or an apparent resemblance to something real. A semblance thus has no being in itself apart from that which it resembles – one could say that it is *nothing but* a relation (of similitude), which brings us back to the question of the emptiness of the analytic object (a). To the extent that it is a semblance, the analyst as object (a) can be inhabited effectively by anyone. That is to say: any analyst can, in principle, be 'my' analyst. Analytic love does not depend upon any particular likeness (or difference) to the Real object in my life that is the support of my desire. As a semblance, the analyst as object (a) is, quite literally, 'nothing' apart from a relation; that is, it is a purely formal similitude, possessing no particular content. Despite the potential for confusion between the two terms, then, the analyst as the 'semblance of object (a)' embodies (the desire for) an 'absolute difference', as Lacan puts it in Seminar XI, by which I understand him to mean this: to the extent that the semblance has nothing grounding itself beyond its purely formal relation of similarity, it can never be the object of an identification. In the transference, there is nothing to identify with beyond the formal relation of likeness itself.[18]

But let us return to the third moment of subjectivity. When Freud discovered the deep structures of psychoanalysis in literature, he invented an Other scene for psychoanalysis in whose dim reddish light the singular shapes of his patients could emerge. The images that surfaced from this developing process are the classic psychoanalytic case histories whose doubles can be found hovering in the larger backdrop of literature. Every subject of analysis thus enters analysis against this literary scene, but it is important to emphasize that analysis has nothing to do with mapping individual subjects on to a literary template – analysis does not take place inside the black-and-white economy of forfeits but, rather, in the semblances of comparisons; interpretations are not identity-seeking metaphors but likenesses, similes. Nevertheless, without the presence of this literary Other, analysis would be caught in either an imaginary or a perverse game. The literary knowledge upon which comparisons is founded prises open what would otherwise be the closed analytic circle: either an imaginary round of hatred and rivalry, or a sadomasochistic scene of enjoyment. To change the metaphor a little, we might say that literature supplies a partially transparent, imaginary screen on to which the third moment of subjectivity can be projected, a screen that enables the generation of a plural 'they' whose principal feature is that it can refer simultaneously to the singular suffering individual of analysis *and* to its exemplary double in the literary typology.

What is it that prevents literature, then, from becoming either just another fetish – that is, a temporary exception or forfeit whose sole function is to reclose the analytic circle – or a religion, in other words, a founding exclusion that guarantees the comparison economy by ensuring that all signs, all signifieds, ultimately converge upon a single point, whether we call that point God, the father, the Master-Signifier, or the phallus? The answer lies in literature itself which, in addition to being a discourse of love, is also the discourse of subjectivity *par excellence.* The two things are in fact the same: the discourse of love is nothing other than the discourse of the subject *as such.*[19] But for this reason, literature, as psychoanalysis's Other, remains perpetually split and, as split, can never serve entirely on one or the other side of the circle. Like a pageboy, literature is always neither fully inside nor outside the analytic loop; it constitutes an Other, but this is an Other that will be eternally incomplete and self-divided. It is this internal self-division of literature, whose scars of the signifier it proudly bears, that defends the analyst as object (a) against the acquisition of (perverse) content.

Could we not say, then, that literature is the 'pageboy' of psychoanalysis? Literature must never be separated from psychoanalysis, but it may never become King to her Queen either. It is marked out from all other rival discourses by a singular relation, precisely because they both possess the same first love for the signifier, for the primordial scarifying letter of language. Hence when Zinaida sees Cleopatra's sails in the purple clouds, or when an analyst discovers a 'veritable Hamlet' in one of her patients, or when a literary critic perhaps comes across an 'Antigone' in a Jamesian heroine, such comparisons are no straitjackets of the imagination. Instead they are testimonies to the presence of analytic love, the love of letters in both its senses, whose ethical function at the end of the day is to prevent the closure of the analyst and analysand's potentially perverse loving circle. We are narrative subjects, after all, and it is only our uniquely singular narratives, awkwardly traced out in relief against our uncanny doppelgängers in the backdrop of the literary Other, that slow down – if not actually stop – the inexorable closing of the blind, senseless machinery of contingency that makes up life's perverse cycle of birth and death.

> Covered in rags, laid on hard boards, with a sack placed under her head [the old woman] was dying painfully and with difficulty. . . . She had seen no joy in her life, had never tasted the honey of happiness – why, then, I thought, shouldn't she be glad of death, of its freedom and its peace? And yet so long as her frail body still struggled, so long as her chest rose and fell agonisingly beneath the ice-cold hand resting on it, so long as her final strength remained the old woman went on crossing herself and whispering: 'Dear God, forgive me my sins,' and it was only with the last spark of consciousness that there vanished from her eyes the look of fear and horror at her approaching end. And I remember that as I stood there, beside the death-bed of that poor old woman, I began to feel terrified for Zinaida and I felt I wanted to pray for her, for my father – and for myself. (202)

Given that the despair of prayer has long since ceased to be an option for most of us, how, then, ought one to respond ethically to the escalation of the Other's demands for more and more love? My earlier metaphor of the hostage might suggest an answer. One is a hostage, after all, only in so far as one desires to leave one's hostage-taker. Yet what would happen if one suddenly, unexpectedly, assumed the hostage-taker's 'cause'?[20] What if one were to turn to one's hostage-taker and pronounce, in a preposterous and ridiculous evocation of the lover's solemn promise: 'I swear I will never, ever leave you. Even if you kill me, my love for you will only have been made stronger, because I will have become a martyr to your cause'? Yet is it not something like such a radical shift in the parameters of discourse that love, to the extent that it is a *metaphor*, as Lacan tells us, succeeds in effecting? Like a metaphor, love's substitution of *erastes* for *eromenos* produces a decisive change in the ordinary logical distance between things.[21] From having been an object, one is transformed by the loving substitution into a subject that reaches back in desire. Not only does this give a new twist to the psychoanalytic imperative to become one's own cause – that is, one must become or adopt the particular cause that, as a hostage, one clearly already 'is' (and, in the process, 'give' what one doesn't 'have', another Lacanian definition of love). It also provides a succinct illustration of how loving someone is, strictly speaking, an intensely *political* (rather than purely ethical) act in so far as it radically transforms existing power relationships. As your lover-hostage, I meet your suspension of the law with an equally exceptional suspension; I subjectify – that is, '*politicize*' – your objectifying appropriation of me through an equivalently political return embrace.

To close this discussion, let us turn back to another of the narrator's peculiar formulations. Recall how, after watching the strange scene between Zinaida and his father, the narrator reflects on the nature of love: ' "That's what love is," I told myself again, sitting at night in front of my desk on which books and notebooks *had begun to appear*. "That's real passion!" ' (199; emphasis added). It is surely no coincidence that, following the (reconstructed) moment of subjectification, books and notebooks begin, as if spontaneously, to propagate themselves on the narrator's desk. For while our narrator has yet to realize it, the truly loving partnership, it seems, lies in the mutual sharing of the 'real passion' for the signifier that first individually marked us as speaking subjects, and whose scarlet welts we now lovingly caress in our beloved's tragic scars. Yet as it traces out the now faint ravages of the signifier, love's hand simultaneously discovers surprising new shapes, patterns and comparisons on the body's page. For that is what love is: the infinitely generative source for the stories we tell about ourselves, which ultimately compose us as narrative subjects.

Notes

1. I am thinking of the recent turn towards 'feeling in theory', to give it the name of Rei Terada's splendid exemplar of it in her *Feeling in Theory: Emotion after the 'Death of the Subject'* (Cambridge, MA: Harvard University Press, 2001). This 'turn' is seen in such divergent philosophical approaches as Luce Irigaray's *The Way of Love* (London: Continuum, 2003); Martha Nussbaum, *Love's Knowledge* (Oxford: Oxford University Press, 1990); and Julia Kristeva's classic, *Tales of Love*, trans. Leon S. Roudiez (New York: Columbia University Press, 1989). A brief glance over recent titles confirms our current ethical steeping in the loving affect; see, for example, Stella Sandford, *The Metaphysics of Love: Gender and Transcendence in Levinas* (London: Continuum, 2001); Roger Burggraeve, *The Wisdom of Love in the Service of Love. Emmanuel Levinas on Justice, Peace and Human Rights* (Wisconsin: Marquette University Press, 2002). Derrida's recent work on mourning, John Protevi argues, can be regarded as one long meditation on love as the experience of originary difference. See his essay 'Love', in *Between Deleuze and Derrida*, ed. Paul Patton and John Protevi (London: Continuum, 2003), 195–202. Note also the recent reprint of Niklas Luhmann's *Love as Passion: The Codification of Intimacy*, trans. Jeremy Gaines and Doris L. Jones (Stanford, CA: Stanford University Press, 1998); Paul Verhaeghe, *Love in a Time of Loneliness: Three Essays on Drive and Desire*, trans. Plym Peters and Tony Langham (London: Rebus, 1999); Michael Stocker and Elizabeth Hegeman, *Valuing Emotions* (Cambridge: Cambridge University Press, 1996). 'The Passions' was the subject of a recent UCLA Humanities Seminar (1998–99), while it seems similarly telling that the first event of Research Group on Formations of the Clinic in the Lacanian Field's 'Lacan in English' seminar in 2003 was devoted to the transference, Seminar VIII and the second, in 2005, was devoted to the Ethics Seminar.
2. Slavoj Žižek, 'A Plea for Ethical Violence', *Umbr(a): War* (2004): 75–89.
3. Alain Badiou, 'What is Love?', trans. Justin Clemens, *Umbr(a)* 1 (1996): 37–53. 45.
4. Søren Kierkegaard, *Either/Or*, vol. 1, trans. David F. Swenson and Lillian Marvin Swenson, rev. and foreword Howard A. Johnson (New York: Anchor, 1959), 242.

5. See Jacques Lacan, *Le Séminaire, Livre VIII: Le transfert*, text established by Jacques-Alain Miller (Paris: Seuil, 1991, 2001), 70.

6. In such a case, one must make a distinction between the 'first love' proper, and the moment of choice where one 'chooses' one's first choice again. It is only through such a structure of repetition that one can properly marry one's first love. For a discussion of this paradox in Henry James, see my essay 'Portrait of an Act: Aesthetics and Ethics in *The Portrait of a Lady*', *The Henry James Review* 25.1 (2004): 67–86. Stanley Cavell has also devoted some attention to this seeming paradox. See his *Pursuits of Happiness: The Hollywood Comedy of Remarriage* (Cambridge, MA: Harvard University Press, 1981).

7. Ivan Turgenev, *First Love and Other Stories*, trans. and intro. Richard Freeborn (Oxford: Oxford University Press, 1990). All page numbers given subsequently in parentheses in the text refer to this volume.

8. Interestingly, the fifth rival, the 'retired captain' Nirmatsky, is left out of this litany of Zinaida's 'needs', but we know from elsewhere in the text that he is 'ugly', was made to dress as a bear and drink salt and water (161). The other four, the Hussar, the Poet, the Doctor, and the Count, each appeals respectively to the competing claims made on Zinaida by warring masculinity (and economic security), art, science and class status. Furthermore, these are all instances of what Freud called 'the narcissism of minor differences': while each rival is distinguished from the others by the possession of certain unique characteristics, they are all materially the same when it comes to the signifying difference of the signifier, as Zinaida's mocking reply to the narrator nicely conveys: that is, to imagine that one is loved for one's particular phenomenal qualities is quite as absurd (and at the same ontic level) as imagining one is loved for one's moustache.

9. *The Seminar of Jacques Lacan, Book XII: Crucial Problems for Psychoanalysis, 1964–65*, unpublished seminar, session of 19 May 1965.

10. 'Indeed, the analyst . . . is the one who, by putting object (a) in the place of semblance, is in the best position to do what should rightfully [*juste*] be done, namely, to investigate the status of truth as knowledge': *The Seminar of Jacques Lacan, Book XX: On Feminine Sexuality: The Limits of Love and Knowledge 1972–1973*, ed. Jacques-Alain Miller, trans. with notes Bruce Fink (New York: Norton, 1998), 95.

11. *The Seminar of Jacques Lacan, Book XX*, 92.

12. Recall Little Hans's fantasy of a detachable penis that would screw into his belly. For Lacan, this detachability is the primary characteristic of the Symbolic phallus, enabling it to light upon any empirical object or signifier without losing its power of negation. See Lacan's discussion of this fantasy in Jacques Lacan, *Le Séminaire, Livre IV: La relation d'objet*, text established by Jacques-Alain Miller (Paris: Seuil, 1994), 266–7.

13. Technically, in the original Russian, this is not really a slip. The Russian reads: 'Ee b'jut, – dumal ja, – b'jut . . . b'jut', which my colleague Thomas Langerak explains can be translated in two ways. The most literal is the one Richard Freeborn provides: 'They are whipping her . . .', where an impersonal action is expressed in Russian in the third person plural. The other translation possibility is 'she is being whipped'. Even with this second translation, however, we continue to retain the sense of impersonality and objectivity that is typical of the third moment of the 'A Child is Being Beaten' fantasy, and whose significance I discuss below.

14. Jacques Lacan, *Le Séminaire, Livre V: Les formations de l'inconscient*, text established by Jacques-Alain Miller (Paris: Seuil, 1998), 242.

15. Lacan, *Le Séminaire, Livre IV*, 116.

16. Dominiek Hoens, '*Hamlet* and the Letter a', *(a): the journal of culture and the unconscious* 2.2 (2002): 91–101. 94.

17. Lacan, *Le Séminaire, Livre IV*, 117.

18. 'The analyst's desire is not a pure desire. It is a desire to obtain absolute difference': Lacan, *The Four Fundamental Concepts of Psycho-Analysis*, ed. Jacques-Alain Miller, trans. Alan Sheridan (New York: Norton, 1979), 276.

19. This is how I interpret Lacan's statement in *Encore* that love is a 'subject-to-subject relationship', whose formula Bruce Fink writes as S <> S. See Bruce Fink, 'Knowledge and Jouissance', in *Reading Seminar XX: Lacan's Major Work on Love, Knowledge, and Feminine Sexuality*, ed. Suzanne Barnard and Bruce Fink (Albany, NY: SUNY Press, 2002), 21–45, 45. See also Lacan's statement 'In love what is aimed at is the subject, the subject as such', which he qualifies as being 'nothing other than what slides in a chain of signifiers' as an 'effect' of the signifier (*Seminar XX*, 50).

20. Like, perhaps, the two French journalists Christian Chesnot and Georges Malbrunot, who were taken hostage in Iraq in protest at the French ban on Muslim headscarves in French schools in 2004. Although they were released in the meantime, there had been rumours on the Internet that they had been freed but had chosen to remain with their captors, the better to cover the Iraq war from the Iraqi perspective. It should be clear that the (impossible) gesture I am describing is radically different from what is known as the Stockholm syndrome. In the Stockholm syndrome, the hostage *identifies* with the hostage-taker, in an ultimate form of self-defence. In 'love', the hostage gives up precisely all forms of identification. In the loving substitution, identity is radically suspended.

21. '[The] decisive problem that an interaction theory of metaphor has helped to delineate but not solve is the transition from literal incongruence to metaphorical congruence between two semantic fields. Here the metaphor of space is useful. It is as though a change of distance between meanings occurred within a logical space. The *new* pertinence or congruence proper to a meaningful metaphorical utterance proceeds from the kind of semantic proximity which suddenly obtains between terms in spite of their distance. Things or ideas which were remote now appear as close': Paul Ricoeur, 'The Metaphorical Process as Cognition, Imagination, and Feeling', in *On Metaphor*, ed. Sheldon Sacks (Chicago: University of Chicago Press, 1979), 141–57, 145. What Ricoeur ultimately calls 'feeling' in this essay is thus not so far from what Lacan would call 'love'. Ricoeur writes: 'To *feel*, in the emotional sense of the word, is to make *ours* what has been put at a distance by thought in its objectifying phase. . . . Its function is to abolish the distance between knower and known without canceling the cognitive structure of thought and the intentional distance which it implies' (154).

13

Kate's Choice, or, The Materialism of Henry James

Slavoj Žižek

It may sound surprising to designate Henry James as the ultimate writer of history, of the impact of history on the most intimate spheres of experience; this properly historical dimension, however, can be discerned even at the level of style: the main feature of James's late style is what Seymour Chatman has called 'psychological nominalization',[1] the transformation of 'John observed X' into 'John's observation was X'; of 'You are not proud enough' into 'Your pride falls short'. Verbs that designate psychic activity or experience are nominalized, and such a procedure puts on stage an abstract entity where previously there had been only a human actor – characters themselves (diegetic persons) tend to evolve into 'anchors for abstractions': 'Thoughts and perceptions in James' world are entities more than actions, things more than movements'(22). Psychological abstractions thus acquire a life of their own; they are not only the true topic of his texts, but even their true agents which interact – in *The Wings of the Dove*, consciousness can 'breathe in a sigh', an impression can become a 'witness'.... Consequently, in several forms of ellipsis that James practised, the human agent of an action tends to disappear completely – witness his heavy use of the expletive *it*. Linked to this is James's distaste for adjectives, since they seem to add a qualification to some pre-existing entity; his favoured way of avoiding them was to replace the standard adjective–noun form with the nominalized adjective followed by 'of' and the noun: in *The Wings of the Dove*, we find not a charming demonstration of Kate's and Merton's need for each other, but the 'charm of the demonstration' of this need; Kate does not display graceful gaiety, but the 'grace of gaiety'; she does not have a free fancy, but the 'freedom of fancy' – in all these cases, again, the quality itself becomes a thing.

James's widespread use of deixis points in the same direction, especially in its extreme form of what Chatman called 'appositive deixis' (63), in which a pronoun is given first, anticipating the real subject which follows in apposition, as in the very first sentence of *The Wings of the Dove*: 'She waited,

Kate Croy, for her father to come in . . .' – a minimal gap is thus introduced between the nameless 'she' and her determinate qualification, indicating the uncertain and vacillating character of every qualification. Deixis is not merely an ersatz for a previously introduced determinate person or thing; rather, it stands for an unnameable X (a kind of Kantian noumenal Thing – and let us not forget that 'thing' is another favourite James term) which eludes all its qualifications. In a strict parallel to nominalization of verbs, here, again, the subject is reduced to an anonymous 'anchor of abstractions'. The subject is not a thing to which attributes are attached, or which undergoes changes – it is a kind of empty container, a space in which things can be located.

To anyone versed in the Marxist critique of the speculative-Hegelian ideological inversions in which an abstract predicate turns into the Subject of the process, while 'real individuals' are reduced to its subordinated predicates, it is difficult here to resist the temptation to (dis)qualify these stylistic procedures as indications of James's fall into 'bourgeois ideological reification', especially since his shift of accent from nouns to their properties does not rely on the standard 'dialectical' notion of the priority of the process over things caught into this process, of 'becoming' over 'being'. If anything, James is a true antipode here to Proust's 'Bergsonism': instead of presenting the flux of Becoming as the truth of fixed Beings, as the process which generates them, he turns verbs and predicates themselves – signs of the process of becoming, of what happens to things or what specifies/qualifies them – into 'things'. At a deeper, properly Hegelian, dialectical level, however, things are much more complex: it is James's very nominalizing of predicates and verbs, their change into substantive agents, which effectively *de-substantializes the subject*, reducing it to a formal empty space in which the multitude of agents interact – somewhat like today's neo-Darwinist theories of subjectivity as the space in which memes fight their battles for survival and reproduction.

In so far as the paradigmatic case of the above-mentioned Marxist critique of the reification of an ideological abstraction is money, we should none the less not be surprised that the ultimate topic of Henry James's work is the effect of capitalist modernization on ethical life: indeterminacy and contingency undermine the old reliance on stable forms prescribing how we are to act and to evaluate our own and others' acts; there is no longer a fixed frame which enables us to find our (ethical) way. The greatness of James, however, is that while he fully accepts this rupture of modernity, and emphasizes the falsity of any retreat to old mores, he also avoids ethical relativism and historicism – that is, the relativization of norms and ethical values to an expression of some more fundamental underlying (economic, psychological, political) historical process. Far from throwing us back into ourselves, into our individualistic experience, this decline of stable social-normative framework makes our radical *dependence* on others even more palpable:

> this altered situation of indeterminacy and contingency might itself reveal an altered social state, one wherein [others'] claims are experienced differently, mean something new, are more directly necessary for me to lead my own life, to give it sense, to assess, and judge. The key issue in morality might not be the rational justifiability with which I treat others, but the proper acknowledgment of, and enactment of, a dependence on others without which the process of any justification (any invocation of common normative criteria at all) could not begin . . . this uncertainty and doubt and profound ambiguity, unresolvability about meaning . . . makes possible and even requires a form of dependency, a dependency even at the level of possible consciousness itself, and some 'lived out' acknowledgment of such dependency, that now makes up the new moral experience, the claims and entitlements of each on others, that [James] is interested in.[2]

This shift is, of course, properly Hegelian: the uncertainty itself, the lack of a fixed socio-ethical frame of reference, far from simply condemning us to moral relativism, opens up a new 'higher' field of ethical experience: that of intersubjectivity, the mutual dependence of subjects, the need not only to rely on others, but also to recognize the ethical weight of others' claims on me. Ethics as a system of norms is thus not simply given; it is in itself the result of the ethical *work* of 'mediation', of me recognizing the legitimacy of others' claims on me. That is to say: in the Hegelian passage from Substance to Subject, the substance (at the social level, for example, the ethical substance, the mores that sustain a way of life) does not disappear, it is just that its status changes: the substance loses its substantial character, it is no longer experienced as a firm foundation given in advance but as a fragile symbolic fiction, something which exists only in so far as individuals treat it as existing, or only in so far as they relate to it as their ethical substance. There is no directly existing 'ethical substance'; the only 'actually existing' thing is the incessant activity and interaction of individuals, and it is only this activity that keeps it alive.

There is a saying that some things can be found only if, before finding them, one gets lost – does not this properly Hegelian paradox provide the formula of the Jamesian search for the ethical position? It can be 'found', formulated, only after one gets lost – only after one accepts that there is no given ethical substance which provides the fixed co-ordinates for our ethical judgement in advance, that such a judgement can emerge only from our own work of ethical reflection with no external guarantee. It is not that we are dealing here with the simple 'Hegelian' movement into alienation (getting lost) and recuperation of oneself (finding a firm position); the point is a more precise one: *it is the very movement of 'getting lost' (of losing ethical substance) that opens up the space for the ethical work of mediation which alone can generate the solution.* Thus the loss is not recuperated but fully asserted as liberating, as a positive opening.[3]

This means that the space of James's novels is thoroughly secular, post-religious. The great act of renunciation at the end of *The Portrait of a Lady* (Isabel Archer decides to stay with her repulsive husband, although she is free to leave him) is the ultimate proof of James's materialism: it has nothing whatsoever to do with any kind of religious transcendence; what makes this renunciation so enigmatic is that it is, on the contrary, conditioned by the very lack of any transcendence – *it can occur only as a kind of empty gesture in a Godless universe.* And it is this passage to the (feminine) act that fails in *The Princess Casamassima*, Henry James's neglected masterpiece.[4] *Casamassima*'s limitations are obvious: approaching the topic of revolutionary anarchists in the London slums of the 1880s, James engaged in a kind of intellectual test, in 'an exercise in the sheer power, the grasping power, of intelligence to divine that which it did not really know'.[5] Therein lies the difference from his masterpieces, like *The Portrait of a Lady* or *The Wings of the Dove*, where he is really at home in the material; in *Casamassima*, James is simply unable directly to confront the contours of revolutionary politics – he does not know the inner texture of this explosive topic. This is why, to mask his ignorance, he engages in elaborate sets of impressions of the London slums, written with great sympathy for the speechless suffering poor. This failure emerges at its purest apropos of the novel's characters: James can provide brilliant descriptions of individual revolutionary types (Poupin, Schinkel, Muniment), but what is totally missing is a picture of the collective revolutionary movement as such: 'He made the mistake of supposing that the whole was equal to a sum of its parts; that if you exhausted the radicals you had gotten at radicalism.'[6]

However, there is still a fundamental, often overlooked and misunderstood, lesson to be learned from *The Princess Casamassima*: to express the deadlock in its radicality is much more pertinent than simple progressive solutions. The *doxa* on this book is that it stands for the conservative James at its purest: its message is aesthetic conservatism – great monuments of culture, and the 'civilized' way of life of the upper classes, justify the suffering of millions. Today, this problem confronts us, if anything, in a much more aggravated way: liberal-democratic affluent societies with their culture versus billions living in poverty in the Third World; the recourse to terrorist violence. . . . In the way it approaches its topic, however, the book is much more radical and ambiguous than it may appear; the first clue is provided by the rather superficial fact that all lower-class revolutionary characters are portrayed as basically sympathetic, while the upper-class ones are clearly presented as vain and vulgar. James is thus far from endorsing a resigned conservative attitude of 'let us preserve what we can of the great cultural heritage, even if it was paid for by the suffering of the anonymous millions': all individuals who stand for this heritage are fake, following an empty ritual; their finesse is a mask of vulgarity. Thus the deadlock is real; there is no easy way out. Hyacinth Robinson's suicide, with which the book concludes, is the sign of an unsolvable antinomy: the impossibility of choosing between the rights of the dispossessed and high culture. More pertinently, what Hyacinth cannot bring together are the two sides of a parallax view – a feature that characterized James himself, with his 'power to see both sides of a question. Hyacinth also, to his destruction, can see each side of the question so well that the only action available to him is self-destruction, which is itself a symbolic statement, the only work of art available to him.'[7] The key difference between Hyacinth and James was that James was able to 'work through' his inability to act, his withdrawal from participation in life, to transpose it into the art of writing. This is why, paradoxically, Hyacinth's failure to pass to the act (and murder an upper-class figure) is also a sign of his lack of creativity: 'Hyacinth's refusal to destroy is also an inability to create, and reflects deeper internal conflicts in the story.'[8] We should thus turn around the well-known platitude according to which destructive rage is a sign of creative impotence: every authentic creative breakthrough starts with the negative gesture of destruction, of clearing the slate.[9]

Far from concerning only the intricacies of intimate libidinal investments, the parallax gap is therefore of the utmost political importance – suffice it to recall the narrative structure of the novels of Henning Mankell, arguably today's foremost detective writer, an author with no affinity whatsoever for James's universe. Most of Mankell's detective novels – set in the southern Swedish town of Ystad, with Inspector Kurt Wallander as their hero – follow the same formula: they start with a brief prologue set in a Third World poor country, then the novel proper moves to Ystad. The Other of today's World History, the poor Third World countries, is thus inscribed into the universe of Mankell's Wallander novels; this big Other of World History has to remain in the background, as the distant Absent Cause. There is one novel (*The Dogs of Riga*, the second book in the Wallander series) in which Mankell violates his rule and allows Wallander to intervene directly into the Other of History: in the course of investigating the murder of a couple of Russians whose corpses were found on the coast close to Ystad, Wallander visits Latvia, where he gets involved in the *imbroglio* of big Story of the Day, the explosion of national independence and the collapse of the Soviet Union – no wonder the novel is a clear failure, contrived and ridiculously pretentious. To add insult to injury, Wallander finds there his (temporary) love-partner, the widow of an honest Latvian police investigator whose name is Liepa Baiba ('liepa' is Slavic for 'beautiful', so we get a 'beautiful babe' . . .).

This absent Third World Other is, however, present in Mankell's artistic universe and life in another surprising way: the 'real' Mankell divides his time between Ystad and Maputo (the capital of Mozambique), where he runs a small theatre for which he writes and directs plays performed by local actors; he has also written a couple of non-detective novels which take place in the desperate conditions of today's Mozambique. And it is only this that brings us to Mankell's true achievement: among today's writers, he is a unique *artist of the parallax view*. That is to say: the two perspectives – that of the affluent Ystad and that of Maputo – are irretrievably 'out of sync', so that there is no neutral language enabling us to translate one into the other, even less to posit one as the 'truth' of the other. All we can ultimately do in today's conditions is to remain faithful to this split as such, to record it. Every exclusive focus on the First World topics of late capitalist alienation and commodification, of ecological crisis, of the new racisms and intolerances, and so forth, cannot but appear cynical in the face of raw Third World poverty, hunger and violence; on the other hand, attempts to dismiss First World problems as trivial in comparison with 'real' permanent Third World catastrophes are no less impostures – focusing on Third World 'real problems' is the ultimate form of escapism, of avoiding confrontation with the antagonisms within one's own society. Recall, back in the 1980s, Fredric Jameson's subtle description of the deadlock of the dialogue between the Western New Left and the Eastern European dissidents, the absence of any common language between them: 'To put it briefly, the East wishes to talk in terms of power and oppression; the West in terms of culture and commodification. There are really no common denominators in this initial struggle for discursive rules, and what we end up with is the inevitable comedy of each side muttering irrelevant replies in its own favorite language.' Does the same not go for Mankell himself, for his work as well as his life? Aware that there is no common denominator between Ystad and Maputo, and simultaneously aware that the two stand for the two aspects of the same total constellation, he shifts between the two perspectives, trying to discern in each the echoes of its opposite. It is because of this insistence on the irreparable character of the *split*, on the failure of any common denominator, that Mankell's work provides an insight into the *totality* of today's world constellation.

Back to the final deadlock of James's *Casamassima*: perhaps we should introduce sexual difference here: far from indicating some kind of 'feminine' indecision and passivity, Hyacinth's deadlock reveals precisely his inability to perform a properly feminine act. The negative feminine gesture would be the only way to break out of this deadlock, to cut its Gordian knot, repeating *mutatis mutandis* what Isabel Archer does at the end of *The Portrait*. It is in *The Wings of the Dove* that we find what is arguably the final and supreme version of this gesture – but where? This novel is one case in which the only way to interpret a scene or story properly is to read it in multiple ways, repeatedly, each time focusing on the perspective of one of the heroes. *The Wings of the Dove* is a novel about a moral trial – but *whose* trial? Recall Delmer Daves's *3.10 to Yuma*, one of the great late Westerns in which the key Act is performed not by the central character who appears to be the focus of the ethical ordeal, but by the secondary character who may even be the very source of temptation. The film tells the story of a poor farmer (Van Heflin) who, for 200 dollars that he needs badly in order to save his cattle from drought, accepts the job of escorting a bandit with a high price on his head (Glenn Ford) from the hotel where he is being held to the train that will take him to prison in Yuma. What we have here, of course, is a classic story of an ethical ordeal: throughout the film, it seems that the person submitted to the ordeal is the farmer himself, exposed as he is to temptations in the style of the (undeservedly) more famous *High Noon* – all those who promised him help abandon him when they discover that the hotel is surrounded by the bandit's gang, sworn to save their boss; the imprisoned bandit himself alternately threatens the farmer and tries to bribe him, and so on. The last scene, however, in retrospect totally changes our perception of the film: near the train, which is already leaving the station, the bandit and the farmer find themselves face to face with the entire gang waiting for the right moment to shoot the farmer, and thus free their boss. At this tense moment, when the situation seems hopeless for the farmer, the bandit suddenly turns to him and tells him: 'Trust me! Let's jump on the wagon together!' In short, the person actually suffering the ordeal was the bandit himself, the apparent agent of temptation: at the end, he is overcome by the farmer's integrity, and sacrifices his own freedom for him . . . and we should approach *The Wings of the Dove* in the same way. This question has to be unambiguously resolved; any recourse to platitudes about the allegedly 'undecided', 'open' character of the narrative is an excuse of weak thought. Again, Pippin is right to emphasize how James's achievement is fully to assert, as the basic defining feature of modernity, a lack of any transcendent ethical Substance, while simultaneously avoiding the easy position of ethical relativism.

The most obvious candidate is Milly, the mortally ill American heiress: *The Wings of the Dove* can be read as a novel about how Milly, after learning of the plot she is the target of, finds the space of an autonomous act not by sabotaging it, taking revenge, but by playing along with it to the end. The novel's moments of decision occur when an unwanted knowledge (even knowledge about knowledge) is imposed on people – how will this knowledge affect their acts? What will Milly do when she learns about the link between Densher and Kate, and of the plot part of which Densher's display of love for her reveals itself to be? How will Densher react when he learns that Milly knows about his and Kate's plan? The one on trial here is Milly: upon learning of the plot, she reacts with a gesture of sacrifice, leaving her fortune to Densher. This utterly altruistic gesture is, of course, manipulative in a much more profound way than Kate's plot: Milly's aim is to ruin the link between Kate and Densher through her bequest to Densher. She freely assumes and stages her death itself as a self-obliterating sacrifice which, together with the bequest, should enable Kate and Densher to live happily ever after . . . the best way to ruin any prospect of happiness for them. She leaves her wealth to them, at the same time making it ethically impossible for them to accept her gift.

We all know the elementary form of politeness, that of the empty symbolic gesture, a gesture – an offer – which is meant to be rejected. In John Irving's *A Prayer for Owen Meany*, after the little boy Owen accidentally kills John's – his best friend's, the narrator's – mother, he is, of course, terribly upset, so, to show how sorry he is, he discreetly delivers to John a gift of his complete collection of colour photos of baseball stars, his most precious possession; however, Dan, John's delicate stepfather, tells him that the proper thing to do is to return the gift. What we have here is symbolic exchange at its purest: a gesture made to be rejected; the point, the 'magic' of symbolic exchange, is that although at the end we are where we were at the beginning, the overall result of the operation is not zero but a distinct gain for both parties, the pact of solidarity. And is not something similar part of our everyday mores? When, after being engaged in a fierce competition for a job promotion with my closest friend, I win, the proper thing to do is to offer him to my retraction, so that he will get the promotion; and the proper thing for him to do is to reject my offer – in this way, perhaps, our friendship can be saved. . . . Milly's offer is the very opposite of such an elementary gesture of politeness: although it is also an offer meant to be rejected, what makes her different from the symbolic empty offer is the cruel alternative it imposes on its addressee. I offer you wealth as the supreme proof of my saintly kindness, but if you accept my offer, you will be marked by an indelible stain of guilt and moral corruption;

if you do the right thing and reject it, however, you will also not be simply righteous – *your very rejection will function as a retroactive admission of your guilt*, so whatever Kate and Densher do, the very choice Milly's bequest confronts them with makes them guilty. As such, Milly's 'ethical' sacrifice is a fake:

> By willing death in this way, Milly in effect dies in order to 'keep dreaming', to maintain the fantasy that has sustained her as a desiring subject. Milly's death thus recalls, albeit inversely, the dream Freud recounts of the father whose child cries out that he is burning. In the Freudian dream, the father wakes up, *in order to continue dreaming*, that is, in order to avoid the traumatic confrontation expressed by the child's cries. Milly, in reverse, dies to avoid waking up; she dies in order to sustain the desiring fantasy. . . . Her 'hysterical' solution, then, is nothing but a cleaving to the sustaining barrier that prevents us from ever achieving the full realization of desire. Milly's death is thus, in Lacan's very precise sense, an ethical death, a death died in accordance with desire.[10]

While I agree with Jöttkandt's description of Milly's sacrificial gesture as a hysterical solution, I am tempted to propose the opposite ethical judgement. Jöttkandt relies on a simplified notion of the Lacanian ethics of desire as hysterical: as if, since desire is primarily the desire for its own non-fulfilment, for its own continuing desire, the ethical act proper is the one of continuing to dream, to postpone satisfaction, to sustain the desiring fantasy . . . what about *traversing* the fantasy?

The second perspective from which the novel can be read is that of Densher. As Milly's perfect counterpoint, he falls into the trap set by her sacrificial goodness: he cannot accept happiness (money plus beloved woman). The trial is here that of Densher: by rejecting Milly's money, he displays 'moral growth' . . . or does he? At the end of the novel, the envelope containing the money functions as one of the Hitchcockian objects in James: not the proverbial MacGuffin, but the 'dirty' Hitchcockian object which circulates among the subjects, casting a bad spell on its possessor.[11] Densher's burning of the letter, his refusal to accept Milly's gift, far from standing for an ethical gesture, is – no less than Milly's sacrifice – a fake, and Kate is right in claiming that, while Densher did not really love Milly when she was alive, he loves her dead – a false love if there ever was one.[12]

This brings us to the novel's true ethical hero, Kate, who should in no way be dismissed as either a cold manipulator or a mere victim of social circumstances – *hers* is the 'No' at the end of the novel (leaving Densher), a properly Kierkegaardian moment in which *the ethical itself is the temptation.* Kate is right to dismiss Densher's 'ethical' rejection of money as false, she is right in guessing that the only *truly* ethical thing for Densher to do, even with regard to Milly, would be to *accept* her gift. Her ethical act – the only true one in the entire novel – is her refusal to marry Densher under the conditions dictated by his acceptance of the terms of Milly's fantasy. She understands the paradox: it is precisely by refusing Milly's money that Densher attests to his fidelity to Milly's fantasy.

Alejandro Inarritu's *21 Grams* (scenario by Guillermo Arriaga) displays a surprising formal parallel with James's *Wings*. Its three main characters find themselves 'between the two deaths': Paul is living on borrowed time; he is dying because his transplanted heart is failing; Cristina is one of the living dead, totally devastated by the accidental death of her husband and two sons; Jack, who accidentally caused their death, is an ex-con who has found his way back into family life by becoming a born-again Christian. As in *The Wings*, each person involves his or her perspective from which the whole story can be read; and, as in *The Wings*, the story focuses on the sacrificial gesture of selling an inevitable death as a free act. At the end of the film, Jack enters the motel room in which Paul and Cristina are staying and asks them, in an outburst of desperate violence, to kill him; Cristina complies and starts beating him with a poker, almost killing him; at this moment, Paul, who is helplessly watching the scene, grabs the gun and shoots *himself*:

> He's going to die because of his failed heart transplant, so if he shoots himself it will be so powerful that it will stop any further violence. If he shoots the gun into the air maybe they'll stop for a moment, I don't know. But if he shoots himself he knows that his action is so sacrificial that there will be no further violence between Cristina and Jack . . . the only method he has of taking the attention of Cristina away from killing Jack is for him to shoot himself. I think of it as an act of love.[13]

Thus *21 Grams* confronts us with an interpretative dilemma that is strictly homologous to that of *The Wings*: is the suicidal sacrificial gesture a true ethical act, or not? In contrast to *The Wings*, the answer here is yes: there is no narcissistic staging of one's death at work in Paul shooting himself, no manipulative strategy of using one's death as a gift destined to secretly sabotage what it appears to make possible. Paul finds himself in a paradoxical predicament in which the only way to change the situation, to interrupt the catastrophic flow of violence, is not to intervene in it but to turn back on himself, to target himself.

Back to James's Kate: the true contours of her act can be discerned only through a close reading of the novel's final pages. Before this scene, Densher has received a thick envelope full of money from Milly's lawyers in New York

– Milly's bequest of the bulk of her wealth to him; he has sent the envelope unopened to Kate. The last scene starts with Kate coming into Densher's room and and ostentatiously laying on the table the envelope, which she has obviously opened. Densher shows his disappointment in Kate who, by opening the envelope, has failed his test; he refuses to have anything to do with the money, and challenges her to marry him without it, or to lose him and have her freedom and the money – he wants to escape any knowledge of the tainted money. She believes that he is afraid, and suggests that although he did not love Milly before her death, he does so now, after it: he is in love with Milly's memory. He offers to marry her immediately 'as we were' but she, leaving, says: 'We shall never be again as we were.'

This abrupt ending is to be read as something akin to the analyst's intervention which concludes the session, a sudden unexpected closure which elevates a marginal detail into the significant Cut. Among recent films, the otherwise rather mediocre and pretentious *Before Sunset* is one of the few which displays such an art of the unexpected ending. A couple (Ethan Hawke and Julie Delpy) who once spent the night together in Vienna accidentally meet again nine years later in Paris; they have only a short time to talk, since Hawke, a successful writer, has a plane to catch in a couple of hours. Their easy conversation gradually turns serious when it becomes clear that neither has recovered from the trauma of their previous encounter; when he is already on the way to the airport, Delpy invites him to drop in at her apartment while his limousine waits outside. As they drink tea, their conversation turns light again – they discuss Nina Simone's songs, and, in a mocking imitation of Simone's dancing style, Delpy comments ironically: 'This boy is gonna miss his plane.' Cut to Hawke, who nods with a smile: 'I know'. Cut into darkness, the end of the film. . . . In the same way, Kate's remark which concludes *The Wings* is a passing remark which none the less, through its strategic placing at the end, functions as a *point de caption* which 'quilts' the novel's meaning. Here are the brilliant final pages of the novel, arguably James's supreme achievement,[14] starting with a direct jump *in medias res*, to the Hitchcockian object:

> She had laid on the table from the moment of her coming in the long envelope, substantially filled, which he had sent her enclosed in another of still ampler make. He had however not looked at it – his belief being that he wished never again to do so; besides which it had happened to rest with its addressed side up. So he 'saw' nothing, and it was only into her eyes that her remark made him look, declining any approach to the object indicated. 'It's not "my" seal, my dear; and my intention – which my note tried to express – was all to treat it to you as not mine.'

The object is clearly established here in its 'Hitchcockian' quality, as the materialization of an intersubjective libidinal investment – note the key sentence: 'So he "saw" nothing, and it was only into her eyes that her remark made him look, declining any approach to the object indicated,' which directly presents the object as the relay of an intersubjective tension. Such an object is never possessed: we do not manipulate it, it is the object itself which determines what *we* are, its possession affects us in an uncontrollable way. Note the paradigmatically Jamesian 'unnatural' syntactic order (not the standard 'She had laid on the table the long envelope from the moment of her coming in . . .' or, even more, 'From the moment of her coming in, she had laid on the table the long envelope . . .'): in order to create a proto-Hitchcockian suspense, the object – the libidinal focal point – is named only at the end; its appearance is delayed. Furthermore, a rapid first reading creates a grammatical confusion: one tends to read the sentence as 'She had laid on the table [from the moment of her coming] in the long envelope', giving rise to a nonsensical quasi-surrealist scene of Kate herself wrapped up in the long envelope on the table; it is only when we get to the end of this passage – that is, when we realize the nonsense of the outcome of our first reading, and then reread it – that we draw the proper meaning. The elegance of this complication is that it shifts the emphasis from the person (Kate) to the object (the envelope). Not only is this object Hitchcockian; we can also easily visualize this paragraph as a scene in a Hitchcock film: first the exchange of gazes, only then, slowly, does the camera approach the object, the focal point of the scene. . . .

> 'Do you mean that it's to that extent mine then?'
> 'Well, let us call it, if we like, theirs – that of the good people in New York, the authors of our communication. If the seal is broken well and good; but we *might*, you know,' he presently added, 'have sent it back to them intact and inviolate. Only accompanied,' he smiled with his heart in his mouth, 'by an absolutely kind letter.'

Since the object-letter is cursed, as in Poe's 'The Purloined Letter', the first reaction is to escape its hold by refusing to act as its receiver and, in this way, to avoid being caught in its circular path – to *stay out* of it.

> Kate took it with the mere brave blink with which a patient of courage signifies to the exploring medical hand that the tender place is touched. He saw on the spot that she was prepared, and with this signal sign that she was too intelligent not to be, came a flicker of possibilities. She was – merely to put it at that – intelligent enough for anything. 'Is it what you're proposing we *should* do?'
> 'Ah it's too late to do it – well, ideally. Now, with that sign that we *know* – !'

'But you don't know,' she said very gently.

'I refer,' he went on without noticing it, 'to what would have been the handsome way. Its being dispatched again, with no cognizance taken but one's assurance of the highest consideration, and the proof of this in the state of the envelope – *that* would have been really satisfying.'

She thought an instant. 'The state of the envelope proving refusal, you mean, not to be based on the insufficiency of the sum?'

Densher smiled again as for the play, however whimsical, of her humor. 'Well yes – something of that sort.'

'So that if cognizance *has* been taken – so far as I'm concerned – it spoils the beauty?'

The *intersubjective* status of knowledge, of 'cognizance being taken', is crucial here: not simply knowledge, but *knowledge about the Other's knowledge.* Remember the final reversal of Edith Wharton's *Age of Innocence*, in which the husband who for long years has harboured an illicit passionate love for Countess Olenska is, after his wife's early death, free to join his love; when, however, on the way to her, he learns from his son that his young wife *knew* about his secret passion all the time, union with the Countess becomes impossible for him. . . . That is the enigma of knowledge: how is it possible that the whole psychic economy of a situation changes radically not when the hero directly learns something (some long-repressed secret), but when he *gets to know that the other* (whom he mistook for ignorant) *also knew it all the time*, and just pretended not to know in order to keep up appearances – is there anything more humiliating than the situation of a husband who, after a long secret love affair, learns all of a sudden that his wife knew about it all the time, but kept silent about it out of politeness or, even worse, out of love for him? In exactly the same way, for Densher, marrying Kate while accepting money from the dead Milly becomes impossible the moment he learns that Milly knew about his and Kate's plot. . . .

'It makes the difference that I'm disappointed in the hope – which I confess I entertained – that you'd bring the thing back to me as you had received it.'

'You didn't express that hope in your letter.'

'I didn't want to. I wanted to leave it to yourself. I wanted – oh yes, if that's what you wish to ask me – to see what you'd do.'

'You wanted to measure the possibilities of my departure from delicacy?'

He continued steady now; a kind of ease – from the presence, as in the air, of something he couldn't yet have named – had come to him. 'Well, I wanted – in so good a case – to test you.'

She was struck – it showed in her face – by his expression. 'It *is* a good case. I doubt whether a better,' she said with her eyes on him, 'has ever been known.'

'The better the case then the better the test!'

> 'How do you know,' she asked in reply to this, 'what I'm capable of?'
> 'I don't, my dear! Only with the seal unbroken I should have known sooner.'
> 'I see' – she took it in. 'But I myself shouldn't have known at all. And you wouldn't have known, either, what I do know.'

Here are the terms of Densher's hypocritical test: he forwarded her the unopened letter, expecting her *not* to open it – his hope was that, in this way, they would conclude a kind of pact of ignorance, cementing their relationship (marriage) in the refusal not only to accept the gift, but even to know what the gift was. Here we encounter a properly melodramatic moment which is a key (and often ignored) part of James's imaginary, and which we find, among others, also in the fourth episode of Krzysztof Kieslowski's *Decalogue*, in which the daughter 'honours her father' in the guise of a burning incestuous desire for him. Again, the question is: is it better not to know certain things? At the end, father and daughter together burn the letter that answers the question whether he is really her father, thereby endorsing ignorance as the basis of their relationship – not a lie, but a consensual withdrawal from truth, the attitude of 'it's better not to know' the truth about the fatherhood contained in the 'letter from an unknown mother' (she was unknown to the daughter, since she died days after giving birth to her). Here, in order to maintain the fragile and delicate libidinal balance of daily life, the letter should *not* reach its destination. In contrast to this solution, Kate, by opening the letter, signals her refusal to 'live a lie'.

> 'Let me tell you at once,' he returned, 'that if you've been moved to correct my ignorance I very particularly request you not to.'
> She just hesitated. 'Are you afraid of the effect of the corrections? Can you only do it by doing it blindly?'
> He waited a moment. 'What is it that you speak of my doing?'
> 'Why the only thing in the world that I take you as thinking of. Not accepting – what she has done. Isn't there some regular name in such cases? Not taking up the bequest.'
> 'There's something you forget in it,' he said after a moment. 'My asking you to join with me in doing so.'
> Her wonder but made her softer, yet at the same time didn't make her less firm. 'How can I "join" in a matter with which I've nothing to do?'
> 'How? By a single word.'
> 'And what word?'
> 'Your consent to my giving up.'
> 'My consent has no meaning when I can't prevent you.'
> 'You can perfectly prevent me. Understand that well,' he said.

She seemed to face a threat in it. 'You mean you won't give up if I *don't* consent?'

'Yes. I do nothing.'

'That, as I understand, is accepting.'

Densher paused. 'I do nothing formal.'

'You won't, I suppose you mean, touch the money.'

'I won't touch the money.'

It had a sound – though he had been coming to it – that made for gravity. 'Who then in such an event *will*?'

'Any one who wants or who can.'

Again a little she said nothing: she might say too much. But by the time she spoke he had covered ground. 'How can I touch it but *through* you?'

'You can't. Any more,' he added, 'than I can renounce it except through you.'

'Oh ever so much less! There's nothing,' she explained, 'in my power.'

'I'm in your power,' Merton Densher said.

'In what way?'

'In the way I show – and the way I've always shown. When have I shown,' he asked as with a sudden cold impatience, 'anything else? You surely must feel – so that you needn't wish to appear to spare me in it – how you "have" me.'

'It's very good of you, my dear,' she nervously laughed, 'to put me so thoroughly up to it!'

'I put you up to nothing. I didn't even put you up to the chance that, as I said a few moments ago, I saw for you in forwarding that thing. Your liberty is therefore in every way complete.'

The stakes of this cat-and-mouse game between Kate and Densher in this passage are very precise: they concern the delicate interplay between a formal (explicit) symbolic act and an implicit act of consenting (of accepting by 'doing nothing formal'). Densher wants Kate neither to accept Milly's bequest nor to reject it in a grand symbolic gesture, but passively to consent to his not touching the money – to join him in his hypocritical attempt to sell avoidance, escape, as an ethical gesture, to sell the refusal to choose as a choice. In short, Densher wants to *deceive the big Other*, to accomplish a gesture that would not be noted as such by the big Other. The ultimate irony, of course, is that Densher's concluding point – 'Your liberty is therefore in every way complete' – names the exact opposite of freedom: the utter cornering of Kate, her total enslavement to the co-ordinates of his 'test'. He puts himself into her power in such a way that *he* totally dominates her: what, to the big Other, will appear Kate's free choice should conceal the brutality of a forced choice imposed by him on her.

It had come to the point really that they showed each other pale faces, and that all the unspoken between them looked out of their eyes in a dim terror of their further conflict. Something even rose between them in one of their short silences – something that was like an appeal from each to the other not to be too true. Their necessity was somehow before them, but which of them must meet it first? 'Thank you!' Kate said for his word about her freedom, but taking for the minute no further action on it. It was blest at least that all ironies failed them, and during another slow moment their very sense of it cleared the air.

There was an effect of this in the way he soon went on. 'You must intensely feel that it's the thing for which we worked together.'

She took up the remark, however, no more than if it were commonplace; she was already again occupied with a point of her own. 'Is it absolutely true – for if it is, you know, it's tremendously interesting – that you haven't so much as a curiosity about what she has done for you?'

'Would you like,' he asked, 'my formal oath on it?'

'No – but I don't understand. It seems to me in your place –!'

'Ah,' he couldn't help breaking in, 'what do you know of my place? Pardon me,' he at once added; 'my preference is the one I express.'

She had in an instant nevertheless a curious thought. 'But won't the facts be published?'

' "Published"?' – he winced.

'I mean won't you see them in the papers?'

'Ah never! I shall know how to escape that.'

It seemed to settle the subject, but she had the next minute another insistence. 'Your desire is to escape everything?'

'Everything.'

Here Densher blurts out the lie of his subjective position: his manoeuvre of putting Kate to the test was done in order for *him* to escape – what, precisely? Confronting the predicament into which Milly's bequest put him. It was Densher himself who failed the ethical test – how?

'And do you need no more definite sense of what it is you ask me to help you to renounce?'

'My sense is sufficient without being definite. I'm willing to believe that the amount of money's not small.'

'Ah there you are!' she exclaimed.

'If she was to leave me a remembrance,' he quietly pursued, 'it would inevitably not be meager.'

Kate waited as for how to say it. 'It's worthy of her. It's what she was herself – if you remember what we once said *that* was.'

He hesitated – as if there had been many things. But he remembered one of them. 'Stupendous?'

'Stupendous.' A faint smile for it – ever so small – had flickered in her face, but had vanished before the omen of tears, a little less uncertain, had shown themselves in his own. His eyes filled – but that made her continue. She

> continued gently. 'I think that what it really is must be that you're afraid. I mean,' she explained, 'that you're afraid of *all* the truth. If you're in love with her without it, what indeed can you be more? And you're afraid – it's wonderful! – to be in love with her.'
>
> 'I never was in love with her,' said Densher.
>
> She took it, but after a little she met it. 'I believe that now – for the time she lived. I believe it at least for the time you were there. But your change came – as it might well – the day you last saw her; she died for you then that you might understand her. From that hour you *did*.' With which Kate slowly rose. 'And I do now. She did it *for* us.' Densher rose to face her, and she went on with her thought. 'I used to call her, in my stupidity – for want of anything better – a dove. Well she stretched out her wings, and it was to *that* they reached. They cover us.'
>
> 'They cover us,' Densher said.

Here Kate spells out the truth of Densher's betrayal: he does not feel guilty, and refuses to profit from Milly's death, not because he does not love her and is for this reason unworthy of her gift, but because he *does* love her – not while she was alive, but from the moment she died. He fell in love with her gesture of dying *for* him and Kate, with how she turned her inevitable death from illness into a sacrificial gesture. Why, precisely, is this a betrayal? Because such love is fake, a case of what Freud called 'moral masochism'.

> 'That's what I give you,' Kate gravely wound up. 'That's what I've done for you.'
>
> His look at her had a slow strangeness that had dried, on the moment, his tears. 'Do I understand then –?'
>
> 'That I do consent?' She gravely shook her head. 'No – for I see. You'll marry me without the money; you won't marry me with it. If I don't consent *you* don't.'
>
> 'You lose me?' He showed, though naming it frankly, a sort of awe of her high grasp. 'Well, you lose nothing else. I make over to you every penny.'
>
> Prompt was his own clearness, but she had no smile this time to spare. 'Precisely – so that I must choose.'
>
> 'You must choose.'

Now we finally reach the (ethical) crux of the matter, the terms of the choice with which Densher confronts Kate: not 'Here I am, without money, choose me or not!', but 'Me *or* the money!' – you can have Milly's money (without me) or me (without money) – that is, if you do *not* choose me, you get the money. Kate, however, rejects these terms and imposes her own choice, more radical than that of Sophie: 'I want either Densher with money or no Densher no money,' which does *not* mean that she 'really wants money' – she wants neither 'Densher without money' *nor money without Densher*. For this precise reason, *she* is the only ethical figure in the novel: she chooses losing both Densher *and* money. This choice is possible only within an *atheist* perspective; it is the sign of a properly *atheist* ethics.

> Strange it was for him then that she stood in his own rooms doing it, while, with an intensity now beyond any that had ever made his breath come slow, he waited for her act. 'There's but one thing that can save you from my choice.'
>
> 'From your choice of my surrender to you?'
>
> 'Yes' – and she gave a nod at the long envelope on the table – 'your surrender of that.'
>
> 'What is it then?'
>
> 'Your word of honor that you're not in love with her memory.'
>
> 'Oh – her memory!'
>
> 'Ah' – she made a high gesture – 'don't speak of it as if you couldn't be. I could in your place; and you're one for whom it will do. Her memory's your love. You *want* no other.'
>
> He heard her out in stillness, watching her face but not moving. Then he only said: 'I'll marry you, mind you, in an hour.'
>
> 'As we were?'
>
> 'As we were.'
>
> But she turned to the door, and her headshake was now the end. 'We shall never be again as we were!'

Why not? Again, because of their shared *knowledge*: they can pretend that nothing has happened, but they 'shall never be again as [they] were', because the big Other knows it has. . . .

James's last novel, *The Golden Bowl*, a true counterpoint to *Wings*, focuses on this strange status of knowledge. If there ever was a work for which the commonplace that, in order to understand it in all its complexity, one has to read it repeatedly, at least twice, does *not* hold, it is *The Golden Bowl*: it should be read *once only*. Even if one repeatedly returns to the novel, one should trust one's first 'confusing' impressions of it – repeated reading tends to cover over its cracks. Here is the summary of the story: Adam Verver, an extremely rich widowed businessman from a nondescript American city, and his daughter Maggie are enjoying an extended stay in Europe, where he is building up a massive art collection which will become the basis of a fine arts museum in his city. Through the matchmaking efforts of Fanny, their American friend living in Europe, Maggie meets and marries Prince Amerigo, an impoverished Italian nobleman. Maggie invites to her wedding Charlotte Stant, an old school friend, also without means; she is unaware that Charlotte and Amerigo were once lovers. Charlotte and Amerigo keep silent about their past affair (in order not to hurt Maggie, or to protect their secret bond?). The day before the wedding, Charlotte secretly meets Amerigo in order to buy a present for Maggie; she selects a beautiful golden bowl, but Amerigo immediately notices that it is cracked.

After the marriage, Charlotte enters Maggie's household and comes to the attention of Adam; Maggie encourages her father to propose Charlotte, and they also marry. Even after the arrival of Maggie's child, however, father and daughter remain inseparable. Thrown back upon themselves, Amerigo and Charlotte succumb to their old feelings and, at Charlotte's instigation, renew their affair. Here, the golden bowl re-enters the story: by accident, Maggie visits the same store and buys it as a gift for her father. When the shopkeeper, stricken with a bad conscience, pays a call to inform her that the bowl is flawed, has a crack, he notices photographs of Charlotte and Amerigo in her apartment, and tells Maggie about their previous visit to his store. Becoming aware of the secret link between Charlotte and her husband, Maggie does not expose the couple; instead, she manoeuvres to keep things under control and steer them her way. She first tells the story of the bowl to Fanny, who, in a gesture of rage, throws the bowl to the floor, wanting to destroy the object which bears witness to the infidelity; Maggie admonishes her not to say anything to her father, so that he will not worry. Amerigo, who heard Maggie telling the story of the bowl to Fanny, and sees the broken bowl, is confronted by Maggie: he assures her that he loves only her, and wants to live with her. Later, he lies to Charlotte, denying that Maggie knows about their affair. Charlotte suspects a change in Maggie's attitude and asks her if she holds anything against her; in response, Maggie flatly lies to her, telling her that she holds no grudge against her and embraces her warmly – at this point, she experiences a strange solidarity with her lying husband.

In order to cut through this growing web of protective lies, Maggie and her father, in a paradigmatically Jamesian conversation in which unspoken implications have more weight than direct statements, make a silent pact that he will take Charlotte away to America to save his daughter's marriage: although Adam makes the move of proposing his and Charlotte's departure to Maggie, he merely answers her subtle manoeuvring. After learning about this decision, Charlotte lies to Maggie, presenting it as her own: she tells Maggie that it was she who convinced Adam to leave because Maggie opposed their marriage, since father and daughter are in love. To make things easier for her friend, Maggie self-sacrificially lies, falsely admitting the truth of Charlotte's version: she did oppose her father's marriage, but failed to prevent it. The story thus ends with two broken couples: Adam returns home to what he considers a life in hell, never to see his daughter again; Charlotte is totally devastated, losing her lover for ever. Maggie has won: appearances are saved, although there is an emotional desert all around. . . . Maggie, of course, is the strong-willed version of the innocent wife from Wharton's *Age of Innocence*: beneath her fragile, naive and innocent appearance in need of protection is a steely determination to look after herself and pursue her own agenda. This is James's vision of American innocence as opposed to European decadence: it is European corruption which is weak and all too naive, while American innocence is sustained by a ruthless determination.

In *The Golden Bowl*, we have four main characters who twice form two couples (plus Fanny, who stands for common wisdom, for the 'big Other' protective of appearances): there are the two 'official' public couples (Amerigo and Maggie; Adam and Charlotte) and the two 'unofficial' couples linked by true passion (Amerigo and Charlotte; Adam and Maggie). This constellation opens up the utopian prospect of the four of them – an incestuous couple and a licentious couple – living happily together, accepting their illicit passions. Why is this solution not feasible? Because of the bowl. The bowl from the novel's title is not a symbol *à la* Grail, a sublime elusive object of lost perfection: it is, rather, again a Hitchcockian object, a little piece of reality which circulates in the background, the focus of intense libidinal investments. Gore Vidal wrote how the cracked bowl is emblematic of 'the relations between the lovers and their legal mates': to all appearances, the world of the two couples is a rare flawless crystal, all of a piece, beautifully gilded with American money, but beneath this appearance there are deep cracks. The cracked bowl is thus what Lacan called the signifier of the barred Other, the embodiment of the falsity of the intersubjective relations condensed in it; consequently, we should not treat it primarily as a metaphor but as an agent in and of intersubjective relations: its possession, destruction, the knowledge about its possession, and so forth, structure the libidinal landscape.

The first thing to note about this landscape is, of course, that the proverbial Jamesian elliptical procedure, reliance on silences, and so on, is brought to an extreme. What, however, if this *finesse*, this sticking to politeness at all costs, this game of innuendos in which the key decisions are often indicated merely by a ponderous silence, mask – keep at bay – an underlying extreme brutality and violence? The person who stands for extreme consideration, desperately trying not to hurt anyone, ready to do anything to protect his daughter whom he perceives as fragile, is Adam – this proverbial American 'robber baron', a character like a Morgan or a Carnegie, who arguably created his wealth in an extremely brutal way, through cheating, bribery, exploitation and murder? The reason he feels a need to 'give something back' is to cover up for his dark past (not to mention the fact that his attitude towards the works of art he collects is that of possession, not of true sensitivity to their beauty).[15]

We should venture a step further here and introduce another quintessential early-twentieth century American theme: that of incest between a daughter and her rich father. Traces of it are discernible up to Scott Fitzgerald's *Tender Is the Night* and Roman Polanski's film *Chinatown*: the brutal Robber Baron father exercises his unimpeded rights also in the sexual domain, enjoying his precious daughter and ruining her life. It is as if this excess of sexual exploitation is a coded inscription of the wider ruthless economic exploitation – these are '[men] of power who can do anything they want'. And it is significant that the work of Edith Wharton, a feminine counterpart to Henry James if there ever was one, is deeply marked by this topic: among her unpublished texts is 'Beatrice Palmato', a short story which describes father–daughter incest in a most explicit hardcore way, with all the details of fellatio, cunnilingus, and so on.[16] Is this not the hidden reference of *The Golden Bowl*? What, then, if the father's protective attitude masks (and thereby signals) the reality of brutal capitalist exploitation and family rape? What if the ultimate protector is a rapist? In *The Golden Bowl*, the incest is not 'real'; however, it is as if its intensity is felt in the incestuous proximity of language itself: Maggie and Adam communicate almost telepathically, with no need to formulate their thoughts fully, immediately sensing what the other is aiming at.

So the ultimate agent of protection is Adam, ready to do anything to protect his daughter's innocence – the paradox, however, is that he, the agent of their incestuous passion, is simultaneously the greatest threat to her innocence. Incest is both the ultimate protection (the child remains safe from the traps of social circulation) and the ultimate threat – so it is quite consistent that the highest sacrifice falls to Adam: the most radical act of protection is for Adam to withdraw his protective shield, to erase himself from the picture, to let her go into the real world, with all its dangers.

When the truth about the bowl comes out, a network of protective lies explodes: all the four characters get involved in a web of lies, or of pretending not to know what they know in order not to hurt the other. The two lovers keep pretending not to know in order to protect Charlotte and her father; Amerigo lies to Charlotte that Maggie does not suspect them in order to save her from guilt; Adam pretends he does not suspect anything to make it easier for his daughter; Maggie pretends to oppose Charlotte's marriage to allow her an honourable exit, and so on and so forth. Who, then, is protecting whom from what? And who is manipulating whom? It may appear that Charlotte and Amerigo are manipulating the Ververs in order to continue their illicit affair; what, however, if both Adam and Maggie get married as a cover for the continuation of *their* incestuous relationship? Here, the shopkeeper is wrong when he says to Charlotte – who cannot see the crack in the bowl, but suspects it because of its low price – 'But if it's something you can't find out, isn't it as good as if it were nothing?' Applied to the libidinal tensions of the novel, this obviously means: if you don't know about the illicit affair, it is as good as if there was no affair. But about *which* affair are we talking here? Adultery or incest? What is ordinary adultery compared with incest? And *who* is the one for whom it holds that, if he or she does not know what they should not know, it is 'as good as if it were nothing'? It is here that things go wrong with all the protective lies: it does not matter whether he or she knows, what matters is that *others do not know that he or she knows* – if his or her knowledge is not known, it allows him or her to *pretend* not to know, and thus to *keep up appearances.* Ultimately, it is thus the 'big Other', the order of social appearances, that should be kept in ignorance: if the big Other does not know, it is 'as good as if it were nothing'. . . .

The parallel with *The Wings of the Dove* is obvious here, and has often been noted: in both stories, the two lovers decide to keep their link secret in order not to hurt the rich, innocent American heiress; in contrast to Kate, however, Charlotte is decidedly *not* ethical. Neither is she egotistically calculating – she is simply not controlling the situation, being thrown around by her passions. Is it Maggie, then, whose manoeuvring is ethical? Is she a new version of Isabel Archer from *The Portrait of a Lady*? Does her act repeat Isabel's decision to remain in a loveless marriage? Here, also, the ethical difference is insurmountable: Maggie in effect does what Isabel is sometimes falsely accused of – she becomes involved in manoeuvring to keep up social appearances. Robert Pippin is therefore right again: *The Golden Bowl* ends 'in a great moral crash'.[17] The final dénouement offers no solution proper, no act that would tear the web of lies apart – or, in Lacanian terms, disclose the big Other's nonexistence.

Maggie's act endorses a false ethics of the unspoken whose perfect deployment we find in one of James's truly great short stories, 'The Great Condition' (1899): Bertram, who is in love with Mrs Damerel, is bothered by rumours of her obscure scandalous past. He proposes to her, declaring his readiness to marry her on condition that she tells him all about her past; she accepts, but with a condition of her own – she will tell him the truth about her past six months after their marriage. When the shocked Bertram withdraws, Henry, his friend who is also in love with Mrs Damerel, proposes to her unconditionally, and they marry. Later, Bertram returns to visit Mrs Damerel, telling her that he explored her past and discovered that there are no dark secrets in it. Mrs Damerel admits that her past is devoid of scandal, but asks him *not* to tell Henry this: Henry will never ask her about her past; he considers himself noble for this, so telling him about it would deprive him of his *noblesse* . . . This logic of refusing to disclose the whole truth, of keeping a secret as a means of maintaining integrity, is profoundly ambiguous: it can be read as revealing Mrs Damerel's insistence on trust; but it can also be read as the manipulation of feminine secrets, as her awareness that the shadow of an illicit mystery enhances the attraction a woman exerts on men. This logic of 'feminine mystery' is totally foreign to Kate from *Wings* – no wonder some misdirected feminists dismiss her as caught in the masculine logic of exploitative domination, opposing her to Milly's authentically 'feminine' attitude of unconstrained giving, of self-sacrificial goodness, of course! Against such deviations, one should insist that Milly is a figure of *male* fantasy, in accordance with Lacan's key thesis according to which, 'female masochism', far from pertaining to 'feminine nature' or to 'femininity', is a *male fantasy*.

This is also why Kate cannot accept Densher's 'being in love with a memory': it would imply her acceptance of the logic of 'to each his or her own small private secret'. Recall the cliché (which, like all clichés, contains a grain of truth) of the different answers one obtains from men or women to the question: 'What would you prefer your partner to do? To have sex with another person and, while doing it, fantasize about you, or to have sex only with you and, while doing it, fantasize about other partners?' The majority of men prefer the second option, the majority of women the first. In the same way, Kate is ready to swallow the first option (Densher can sleep with Milly; he should simply not think about her . . .), she even pushes Densher into it, and rejects the second option (the two of them married, with Densher thinking about Milly) which, for her, marriage to Densher would have been.

The novel's title, which refers to the 55th Psalm ('Oh that I had wings like a dove! For then would I flee away, and be at rest'), can thus again be read in three ways. The first obvious dove, explicitly referred to as such in the text, is, of course, Milly herself, who flew away and found rest in death. The second dove is Densher, whose desire is 'to escape everything'; the real dove, however, is disclosed in the novel's very last line: Kate, who, throughout, has stretched out her wings, covering Milly and Densher with her plot, and then, when Densher or money is at her disposal, turns towards the door and leaves – refusing the choice, she leaves both options behind, and flies away for ever.

Notes

1. I draw here on Seymour Chatman, *The Later Style of Henry James* (Oxford: Basil Blackwell, 1972). Subsequent page numbers in parenthesis in the text refer to this volume.

2. Robert Pippin, *Henry James and Modern Moral Life* (Cambridge: Cambridge University Press, 2000), pp. 10–11.

3. And perhaps this is where James was not radical enough: despite his sympathetic portrayal of the powerless poor in the slums, he was unable to fully confront the *ethical claim* on society that sustains revolutionary radicalism. (Hegel, on the contrary, was fully aware of this problem: his scornful statements on 'rabble [*Pöbel*]' should not blind us to the fact that he admits that their aggressive stance and unconditional demands towards society are fully justified – since they are not recognized by society as ethical subjects, they owe to it nothing.)

4. The edition used is Henry James, *The Princess Casamassima* (Harmondsworth: Penguin, 1987).

5. Irving Howe, 'The Political Vocation', in *Henry James*, ed. Leon Edel (Englewood Cliffs, NJ: Prentice-Hall, 1963), p. 157.

6. Irving Howe, 'The Political Vocation', p. 166.

7. James, *The Princess Casamassima*, Derek Brewer's 'Introduction', p. 17.

8. James, *The Princess Casamassima*, Derek Brewer's 'Introduction', p. 21.

9. And, perhaps, starting from this point, one could deploy an entire theory of the Aesthetic (like Lévi-Strauss who, in the famous passage from *Tristes Tropiques*, conceived of face-drawings as attempts to resolve social deadlocks).

10. Sigi Jöttkandt, 'Metaphor, Hysteria and the Ethics of Desire in *The Wings of the Dove*', paper presented at the International Henry James Conference, Paris 2002.

11. The Jamesian 'MacGuffin' is, rather, the lost manuscript (or pack of letters) around which the narrative circulates, like the 'Aspern papers' from the story of the same title, or the notorious secret from 'The Figure in the Carpet'. The supreme example of the circulating Hitchcockian object-stain in James is arguably the row of pearls in 'Paste' (a minor story from 1899): they pass from the narrator's dead stepmother to his cousin, then back to him, then to a third lady, and their very suspect authenticity poses a threat to the family honour (if they are authentic, then the stepmother must have had a secret lover who bought them). And, as expected, we find in James also the third Hitchcockian object, the traumatic-impossible Thing which threatens to swallow the subject, like the 'beast in the jungle' from the story of the same title; the Lacanian triad of objects (*a*, S of the barred A, big Phi) is thus completed. On this triad, see the Introduction to *Everything You Ever Wanted to Know About Hitchcock, But Were Afraid to Ask Lacan*, ed. Slavoj Žižek (London and New York: Verso, 1993).

12. In more political terms, Densher is a model of the 'honest' bourgeois intellectual who masks his compromising attitude by 'ethical' doubts and restraints – types like him 'sympathize' with the revolutionary cause, but refuse to 'dirty their hands'. They are usually (and deservedly) shot in the middle stages of a revolution (it is the Millies of this world – those who like to stage their death as a sacrificial spectacle – whose wishes are met in the early stages of a revolution).

13. Guillermo Arriaga, *21 Grams* (London: Faber & Faber, 2003), pp. xiii–xiv.

14. Which is why, of course, the interpretation that follows is merely an improvised first approach, with no pretence of completeness.

15. That is one of the great failures of the Merchant–Ivory cinema version of *The Golden Bowl*: the film goes out of its way to make the 'robber baron' as sympathetic as possible. As befits our politically correct times obsessed with 'hurting the Other', considerate behaviour counts more than brutal capitalist exploitation.

16. The story is available in Gloria C. Erlich, *The Sexual Education of Edith Wharton* (Berkeley: University of California Press, 1992).

17. Pippin, *Henry James and Modern Moral Life*, p. 77.

14
Kafka's Voices

Mladen Dolar

Let us take as a provisional starting point the question of immanence and transcendence in Kafka, which can easily cause confusion. To put it briefly, there is a whole line of interpretation which maintains that the predicament of Kafka's universe can best be described in terms of the transcendence of the law. Indeed, it seems that the law is inaccessible to Kafka's 'heroes': they can never find out what it says; the law is an ever-receding secret; even its very existence is a matter of presumption. Where is the law, what does it command, what does it prohibit?[1] One is always 'before the law', outside its gate, and one of the great paradoxes of this law is that it does not prohibit anything, but is itself prohibited, it is based on a prohibition of the prohibition, the prohibition itself is prohibited.[2] One can never get to the locus of prohibition – if one could do so then one would be saved, or so it seems. The transcendence of the law, on this account, epitomizes the unhappy fate of Kafka's subjects, and the only transcendence there is in Kafka's world is the transcendence of this law which seems like an unfathomable, ungraspable deity, a dark god emitting obscure oracular signs, but one can never figure out its location, purpose, logic or meaning.

On closer inspection, however, this elusiveness of the transcendent law reveals itself to be a mirage: it is a necessary delusion, a perspectival illusion, for if the law always escapes us, this is not because of its transcendence, but because it has no interior. It is always deferred from one instance to another, from one office to the next, because it is nothing but this movement of deferral; it coincides with this perpetual motion of evasion. The unfathomable secret behind some closed door, behind some inscrutable façade, is no secret at all – there is no secret outside this metonymical movement, which can be seen as the movement of desire. If the law has no interior, it has no exterior either: one is always-already inside the law, there is no outside of law, the law is pure immanence – 'the unlimited field of immanence instead of infinite transcendence', to quote Deleuze and Guattari,[3] for this second account has been made justly famous by their book on Kafka, one of the most influential recent interpretations.

So what on the first account appeared as pure transcendence is on the second account seen as pure immanence. On the first account one is always-already and irretrievably excluded; on the second one is always included and there is no transcendence, one is trapped in the immanence of the law, which is at the same time the immanence of desire. Does one have to decide between the two, join one camp or the other? Are the two accounts irreconcilable? Although the second reading is no doubt far more useful, and effectively dissipates the misunderstandings advanced by the first, it still perhaps does not quite cover what is at stake in Kafka. By promoting the dimension of pure immanence, it perhaps eludes, reduces and avoids a paradox: the paradox of an emergence of a transcendence at the very heart of immanence – or, rather, of the way immanence always doubles and intersects with itself. Or, to put it another way: there might be no inside, there might be no outside, but the problem of intersection remains.

Lacan, to my knowledge, never mentions Kafka in his published work, so he indeed seems to be his silent and invisible partner. But we do find a couple of passing references in his hitherto unpublished seminars, and one of them bears directly on our point. In his seminar on 'Identification' (Seminar IX, 1962/63) Lacan develops for the first time, at some length, his use of topology. He takes the 'image' of a torus, and sees the problem of the subject's desire in topological terms, translating his dictum that 'the subject's desire is the desire of the Other' into the problem of establishing a communication, a passage between two tori, that of the subject and that of the Other. This calls for an invention of a certain topological model where the curvature of the space would establish a link between inside and outside. He speaks of an irreducible analogy which is 'impossible to exclude from what [for the subject] is called interior and exterior, so that the one and the other pass into each other and command each other' (session of 21 March 1962). For a striking example of such a topological model he has recourse to Kafka, giving a very precise reference to Kafka's brilliant story 'The Burrow', one of his last.[4] The complicated architecture of the burrow, with its labyrinthine passages and its (true and false) entries, the problem of hiding and escape, of passing from one passage to the next, from interior into exterior – all this affords the perfect paradigm for what Lacan is looking for. The burrow is the place where one is supposed to be safe, neatly tucked inside, but the whole story shows that the most intimate place of shelter is the place of thorough exposure; the inside is inherently fused to the outside. But this structure does not relate only to architecture and space organization, it concerns 'something which exists at the most intimate of organisms', their internal organization and their relation to the outside. Indeed, the man appears to be 'the animal of the burrow, the animal of the torus' [*l'animal du terrier, l'animal du tore*], and Kafka's recourse to animality – one of his favourite devices, to which we will come back – thus hinges on a minimal pattern which links the human being as an 'animal' organism to the social and the symbolic; there is 'an anastomosis'[5] between the two. The one passes into the other in a curved space where they can be neither opposed nor collapsed. There is on the one hand the equivalence of the organism and the burrow, amply demonstrated in Kafka's story, and on the other the exposure of the burrow to the outside, the topological cross-connection between them.[6]

From here one can make a leap to Agamben, for the immediate connection between 'animality' and the law, so central to Kafka, is also the cornerstone of Agamben's endeavours, and in particular of his reading of Kafka, where 'bare life' and the law appear as the front and the flip side of the same thing. But Agamben arrived at this by a very different route – by a reflection on the problem of sovereignty, on what he called 'the exclusive inclusion or the inclusive exclusion', the point of exception inscribed in the law itself, the point which can suspend the validity of laws, and has an immediate 'cross-connection' to bare life. On the first pages of his book he defines sovereignty, following Carl Schmitt, as a paradox:

> The sovereign is at the same time outside and inside the juridical order. . . . The sovereign, having the legal power to suspend the validity of the law, is legally situated outside the law. This means that the paradox can equally be formulated in this way: 'The law is exterior to itself', or rather: 'I, the sovereign, who am outside the law, declare that there is no outside of the law.'[7]

So sovereignty is structurally based on an exception which is included in the law as its own point of exteriority. The sovereign is the one who can suspend the legal order and proclaim the state of emergency where laws are no longer valid and the exception becomes the rule. At the opposite end of the sovereign we have its inverse figure, the converse point of exception, which is *Homo sacer*: bare life excluded from the law in such a way that it can be killed with impunity, yet without entering into the realm of the sacrifice. Being outside the law, his bare life exposed to be killed with impunity, *Homo sacer* is exposed to the law as such in its pure validity. The state of emergency is the rule of law in its pure form – precisely the excess of validity over meaning (*Geltung ohne Bedeutung*, to use the expression from Gershom Scholem's correspondence with Walter Benjamin in the 1930s), the suspension of all laws, and therefore the institution of the law as such. We could say: Kafka is the literature of the permanent state of emergency. The subject is at the mercy of the law beyond all laws, without any defence; he can be arbitrarily stripped of all his possessions, including his bare life. The law functions as its own transgression. Kafka's heroes are always *Homines sacri*, exposed to the pure validity of the law which manifests itself as its opposite. Kafka has turned *Homo sacer* into the central literary figure, thus displaying a certain shift in the functioning of the law which took place at the turn of the twentieth century, and inaugurated a new era, with many drastic consequences which will define that century.

Agamben proposes an optimistic reading, as it were, of the parable 'Before the law', precisely at the point where most interpreters merely saw the defeat of the man from the country. The gate of the Law is always open, the doorkeeper does not prevent the man from entering, yet the man finds it impossible to enter through the open door. The openness itself immobilizes; the subject stands awestruck and paralysed in front of the open door, in a position of exclusion from the law, but this is precisely the form of his inclusion, since this is how the law holds him in its sway. Before the law one is always inside the law, there is no place before the law, the very exclusion is inclusion. It is true that the man never manages to get into the Law; he dies outside the gate and, when he is dying, learns that this gate was reserved only for him. Yet the last sentence reads: 'This gate was made only for you. I am now going to shut it. */Ich gehe jetzt und schließe ihn*' (p. 4). But if the very openness of the law is the pure form of its closure and of its unqualified validity and power, then the man succeeded in a most remarkable feat: he managed to achieve the closure. He managed to close the door, to interrupt the reign of pure validity. The closed door, in this reading, is a chance of liberation, it sets a limit to the pure immanence. Admittedly, he was successful only at the price of his own life, so that the law is interrupted only when he is dead – one reading would be: the law has no power over the dead alone, one does not stand a chance while one is alive. Still, there is a perspective of closure, of invalidating the law if only one persists far enough. Was the man from the country so naive or so shrewd? On the one hand he was very timid, he let himself be subdued very quickly, he was easily diverted from his initial intention, instantly intimidated. But on the other hand he displayed an incredible stubbornness, persistence and determination. It was the struggle of exhaustion; it is true that they managed to exhaust him completely with the open door, yet in the end he is the one who exhausts the law. If one is prepared to persist to the end, one can put an end to the validity of the law.

This seems a desperate strategy, but what other strategies are there in this impossible predicament? If there is always some way out of the closure, there seems to be none out of the openness. This is why Kafka is generally misperceived as the depressing author of total closure with no exit, but this is also where the solution of pure immanence does not quite offer a good answer. In what follows I will examine three strategies which offer an exit, as it were, and they are all connected with the instance of the voice – precisely as a point of paradox.

Why the voice? What is it that places the voice in a structural and privileged position? The law always manifests itself through some partial object, through a glimpse, a tiny fragment that one witnesses unexpectedly and which, in its fragmentation, remains a mystery: by morsels; by servants, doorkeepers, maids; by trivia, by trash, the refuse of the law. The overarching validity without meaning is epitomized by partial objects, and those objects are enough for the construction of fantasies, enough to capture desire. And among them is the voice, the senseless voice of the law: the law constantly makes funny noises, it emits mysterious sounds. The validity of the law can be pinned to a senseless voice.

When the land surveyor K. arrives at the village under the castle, he takes lodgings at an inn, and he is eager to clarify the nature of his assignment. He was sent for, he was summoned and he wants to know why, so he calls the castle – he uses this recent invention, the telephone. But what does he hear at the other end of the line? Just a voice which is some kind of singing, or buzz, or murmur, the voice in general, the voice without qualifications.

> The receiver gave out a buzz of a kind that K. had never before heard on a telephone. It was like the hum of countless children's voices – but yet not a hum, the echo rather of voices singing at an infinite distance – blended by sheer impossibility into one high but resonant sound that vibrated on the ear as if it were trying to penetrate beyond mere hearing.[8]

There is no message, but the voice is enough to stupefy him, he is suddenly paralysed: 'In front of the telephone he was powerless.' He is spellbound, mesmerized. – This is just one example chosen at random among many.

The intervention of a voice at this juncture is crucial and necessary. The voice epitomizes at best validity beyond meaning, it is structurally placed at the point of the exception to the law. For the law is the law only in so far as it is written, that is, given the form which is universally at the disposal of everyone, always accessible and unchangeable – but with Kafka we can never get to the place where it is written to check what it says; access is always denied, the place of the letter is infinitely elusive. The voice is precisely what cannot be checked, it is ever-changing and fleeting, it is the non-universal *par excellence*, it is what cannot be universalized. This is also why the superego, the reverse side of the law, is always represented by a voice.[9] And this is the point of Lacan's use of the shofar: this ancient primitive instrument used in Jewish rituals is the representation of the supposed voice of the dying primal father which keeps resonating, thus endowing the letter with authority. The letter of the law, in order to acquire authority, has to rely, at a certain point, on the tacitly presupposed voice which makes certain that the letter is not 'the dead letter', but exerts power and can be enacted. So the voice is structurally in the same position as sovereignty, which means that it can question the validity of the law: the voice stands at the point of exception, the internal exception which threatens to become the rule, and from this point on it displays a profound complicity with bare life. The emergency is the emergence of the voice in the commanding position; its concealed existence suddenly becomes overwhelming and devastating. The voice is precisely at the unplaceable spot in the interior and the exterior of the law at the same time, and hence a permanent threat of the state of emergency. And with Kafka, the exception has become the only rule. The letter of the law is hidden in some inaccessible place and may not exist at all, it is a matter of presumption, and we have only voices in its place.

If we briefly recall Lacan's use of Kafka, we could go even further and make the claim that the voice is 'the anastomosis', the interconnection between the 'animal' organism and the symbolic. The voice ties the language, the signifier, to the body; it is the passage between the two, the place where the one 'communicates' with the other, passes over into the other, structurally the crossing between inside and outside. It presents a topological problem, since it is not a part of the body, nor is it a part of the signifier, yet the two can hold together only by this passage, which is the point of utter ambiguity.

Ulysses

K. is spellbound by the voice emanating from the castle through the telephone, as the wanderer is spellbound by the song of the Sirens. What is the secret of that irresistible voice? Kafka has an answer in his short story 'The Silence of the Sirens' ('Das Schweigen der Sirenen'), written in October 1917 and published in 1931 by Max Brod, who also provided the title. In this story the Sirens are irresistible because they are silent, yet Ulysses nevertheless manages to outwit them. Here we have the first strategy, the first model of escape from the unstoppable force of the law.

'To protect himself from the Sirens Ulysses stopped his ears with wax and had himself bound to the mast of his ship' (p. 430). The first sentence is already one of Kafka's wonderful opening *coups de force* – like, for example, the opening paragraph of his novel *America*, where we have his hero, Karl Roßmann, arriving by boat in New York harbour, admiring the Statue of Liberty with her sword rising high up in the sun. We almost do not notice, but where is the Statue of Liberty's sword? Here we have Ulysses stopping his ears and tied to the mast, while in the legend it was the oarsmen who had their ears stopped with wax, while Ulysses was tied to the mast. There was a division of labour – indeed, the very model of the division of labour, if we follow the argument developed by Adorno and Horkheimer in *Dialectic of Enlightenment*. There is a sharp division between those who are doomed to be deaf and to work, and those who listen and enjoy, take pleasure in art, but are helplessly tied to the mast. This is the very image of the division between labour and art, and this is the place to start scrutinizing the function of art, in its separation from the economy of work and survival – that is, in its powerlessness. Aesthetic pleasure is always pleasure in chains, it is thwarted by the limits assigned to it, and this is why Ulysses confronting the Sirens is so exemplary for Adorno and Horkheimer.

Kafka's Ulysses combines both strategies, the aristocratic and the proletarian; he takes double precautions, although everyone knows that this is useless: the song of the Sirens could pierce any wax, and true passion could break any chains. But the Sirens have a weapon far more effective than their voice: their silence, that is, the voice at its purest. The silence which is unbearable and irresistible, the ultimate weapon of the law. 'And though admittedly such a thing has never happened, still it is conceivable that someone might possibly have escaped from their singing; but from their silence certainly never' (p. 431). We cannot resist silence, for the very good reason that there is nothing to resist. This is the mechanism of the law at its minimal: it expects nothing of you, it does not command, you can always oppose commands and injunctions, but not silence. Silence is the very form of the validity of the law beyond its meaning, the zero-point of voice, its pure embodiment.

Ulysses is naive; he childishly trusts his devices, and sails past the Sirens. The Sirens are not simply silent; they pretend to sing: 'He saw their throats rising and falling, their breasts lifting, their eyes filled with tears, their lips half-parted', and he believed they were singing, and that he had escaped them and outfoxed them, although their singing was unstoppable. 'But Ulysses, if one may so express it, did not hear their silence; he thought they were singing and that he alone did not hear them' (p. 431). If he knew they were silent, he would be lost. He imagined that he had escaped their power by his naive cunning, and in the first account we are led to suppose that it was his naivety that saved him.

Yet the truth of the story is perhaps not in his naivety at all: 'Perhaps he had really noticed, although here the human understanding is beyond its depths, that the Sirens were silent, and held up to them and to the gods the aforementioned pretense merely as a sort of shield.' The shrewd and canny Ulysses, the sly and cunning Ulysses – Homer almost never fails to accompany his name with one of those epithets. Is his ultimate slyness displayed by putting up an act of naivety? So in the second account he outwitted them by pretending not to hear that there was really nothing to hear. They were going through the motions of singing; he was going through the motions of not hearing their silence.

One could say that his ruse has the structure of the most famous Jewish joke, the paragon among Jewish jokes, in which one Jew say to another at the railway station: 'If you say you're going to Krakow, you want me to believe you're going to Lemberg. But I know that in fact you're going to Krakow. So why are you lying to me?'[10] So by extension one could imagine the Sirens' reaction: 'Why are you pretending that you don't hear anything when you really don't hear anything? Why are you pretending not to hear when you know very well there is nothing to hear? You pretend so that I would think you don't hear anything, while I know very well that you really don't hear anything.' The Jewish joke is Ulysses' triumph; he manages to counter one pretence with another. In the joke the first Jew, the one who simply told the truth about his destination, is the winner, for he managed to transfer the burden of truth and lie on to the other one, who could reply only with a hysterical outburst. One is left with the same oscillation as in our story: was the truth-teller naive or shrewd? This is exactly the question which remained hanging in the air with the man from the countryside dying on the threshold of the law. Ulysses' strategy is perhaps not unrelated to the strategy of the man from the countryside: Ulysses counters pretence with pretence, the man counters deferral by deferral, exhaustion by exhaustion – he manages to exhaust the exhaustion, to bring an end to the deferral, to close the door.

This does not work with the Sirens. Indeed, they are defeated: 'They no longer had any desire to allure; all they wanted was to hold as long as they could the radiance that fell from Ulysses' great eyes' (p. 431). Were they suddenly seized with yearning for the one who managed to get away? 'If the Sirens had possessed consciousness they would have been annihilated at that moment. But they remained as they had been; all that had happened was that Ulysses had escaped them' (p. 432). They have no consciousness, all their behaviour is going through the motions, they are automata, they are inanimate, they are machines imitating humanity, cyborgs, and this is why their defeat cannot have any effect. This one has escaped, but that cannot dismantle the mechanism.

So can one fight the law by turning a deaf ear to it? Can one just pretend not to hear its silence? This is no simple strategy, it defies human understanding, says Kafka, it boggles the mind. It takes supreme cunning, yet it does not introduce a closure of the law. Ulysses was an exception, and everybody else is the rule.

Josephine

Let us now turn to another strategy which again has the voice at its kernel, this time a voice which is placed in a position from which it could counter the voice, or the silence, of the law. 'Josephine the Singer, or the Mouse Folk' ('Josefine die Sängerin oder das Volk der Mäuse') is actually the last story Kafka ever wrote, in March 1924, a couple of months before his death. By virtue of being the last, it necessarily invites us to read it as his testament, his last will, the *point de capiton*, the quilting point, the vantage point which will shed some ultimate light on his work, provide a clue which will illuminate, with finality, all that went before. And it is no doubt ironical that this clue, this suture, is provided not only by the voice, but by the tiniest of voices, the minute microscopic squeak,[11] and one is structurally inclined to take this minuscule peep as the red thread that could retroactively enlighten Kafka's obscurity.

There is the vast question of Kafka's multiple uses of the animal kingdom, which are so prominent in his work – Deleuze and Guattari dwell upon this at some length. There is, most notoriously, the becoming-animal of Gregor Samsa, which features, among other things, his voice, the incomprehensible chirping sounds which come out of his mouth when he tries to justify himself in front of the chief clerk. ' "That was no human voice," said the chief clerk . . .' (p. 98); it is the signifier reduced to pure senseless voice, reduced to what Deleuze and Guattari call pure intensity. The general question can be put in the following way: is animality outside the law? The first answer is: by no means. Kafka's animals are never linked to mythology, they are never allegorical or metaphorical. Here is the well-known line by Deleuze and Guattari: 'Metamorphosis is the contrary of metaphor,'[12] and Kafka is perhaps the first utterly non-metaphorical author. The animal societies, the mice and the dogs,[13] to which we will come in a moment, are organized 'just like' human societies,[14] which means that animals are always denaturalized, deterritorialized animals; there is nothing pre-cultural, innocent or authentic about them. On the other hand, however, they nevertheless represent what Deleuze and Guattari call *la ligne de fuite*, a certain line of flight. The becoming-animal of Gregor Samsa means his escape from the mechanism of his family and his job, the way out from all the symbolic roles that he had assumed; his insecthood is at the same time his liberation. Metamorphosis is an attempt at escape, albeit a failed one. But there is a double edge to this: one can read the becoming-animal on the first level as becoming that which law has made out of subjects, that is, reduced to bare animal life, the lowest kind of animality represented by insects, the crawling disgusting swarm to be decontaminated, the non-sacrificial animality (the insect is the anti-lamb) which evokes the bare life of *Homo sacer*. The law treats subjects as insects, as the metaphor has it, but Gregor Samsa destroys the metaphor by taking it literally, by literalizing it; thus the metaphor collapses, the distance of analogy evaporates, and the word becomes the thing. But by fully assuming the position of bare life, the reduction to animality, a *ligne de fuite* emerges – not as an outside of law, but at the bottom of the full assumption of the law. Animality is the internal outside which is endowed with ambivalence precisely at the point of fully realizing the implicit presupposition of the law, it constantly presents the case of what Lacan called anastomosis.

Josephine's voice presents a different problem. It is a question not of metamorphosis but of the emergence of another kind of voice in the midst of a society governed by the law; a voice which would not be the voice of the law, though it might seem impossible to tell them apart. Josephine's voice is endowed with a special power in the midst of this entirely unmusical race of mice. (A parenthesis: what Freud and Kafka curiously have in common, apart from the obvious analogies of their Jewish origins and sharing the same historical moment and the space of Central Europe, is their claim that they are both completely unmusical, that music is the one thing they do not understand at all. Could one not say that this absence of musical gift is the best entry into susceptibility to the voice?)

So what is so special about Josephine's voice?

> Among intimates we admit freely to one another that Josephine's singing, as singing, is nothing out of the ordinary. Is it in fact singing at all? . . . Is it not perhaps just piping [whistling, *pfeifen*]? And piping is something we all know about, it is the real artistic accomplishment of our people, or rather no mere accomplishment but a characteristic expression of our life. We all pipe, but of course no one dreams of making out that our piping is an art, we pipe without thinking of it, indeed without noticing it, and there are even many among us who are quite unaware that piping is one of our characteristics. . . . Josephine . . . hardly rises above the level of our usual piping. . . . (p. 361)

Josephine merely pipes, whistles, as all mice do, all the time, albeit in a less accomplished manner than the others. 'Piping is our people's daily speech . . .' (p. 370) – that is, speech minus meaning. Yet her singing is irresistible; this is no ordinary voice, though it is indistinguishable from others by its positive features. Whenever she starts singing – and she does so in unpredictable places and at unpredictable times: in the middle of the street, anywhere – a crowd immediately gathers and listens, completely enthralled. So this very ordinary piping is suddenly placed on a special spot; all its power stems from the place it occupies, as in Lacan's definition of sublimation: 'to elevate an object to the dignity of the Thing'. Josephine herself may well be convinced that her voice is very special, but it 'can't be told apart' from any other. This is 1924, ten years after Duchamp displayed his *La roue de bicyclette* (1913), the ordinary bicycle wheel, this art object which mysteriously looks exactly like any other bicycle wheel. As Gérard Wajcman puts it, Duchamp invented the wheel for the twentieth century.[15] There is an act of a pure *creatio ex nihilo* – or rather, *creatio ex nihilo* in reverse: the wheel, the object of mass production, is not created out of nothing; rather, it creates the nothing, the gap that separates it from all other wheels, and presents the wheel in its pure being-object, deprived of any of its functions, suddenly in its strange sublimity.

Josephine's voice is the extension of the ready-made into music. All it does is to introduce a gap, the imperceptible break that separates it from all other voices while remaining absolutely the same – 'a mere nothing in voice' (p. 367). This can start anywhere, everywhere, at any time, with any kind of object: this is the art of the ready-made, and everything is ready-made for art. It is like the sudden intrusion of transcendence into immanence, but a transcendence which stays in the very midst of immanence and looks exactly the same, the imperceptible difference in the very sameness. Her art is the art of the minimal gap,[16] and this is the hardest nut to crack.

> To crack a nut is truly no feat, so no one would ever dare to collect an audience in order to entertain it with nut-cracking. But if all the same one does do that and succeeds in entertaining the public, then it cannot be a matter of simple nut-cracking. Or it is a matter of nut-cracking, but it turns out that we have overlooked the art of cracking nuts because we were too skilled in it and that this newcomer to it first shows us its real nature, even finding it useful in making his effects to be rather less expert in nut-cracking than most of us. (pp. 361–2)

So any voice will do to crack the nuts, provided it can create nothing out of something. Josephine's genius is in having no talent, which makes her all the more of a genius. An accomplished trained singer would never have pulled off this feat.

Josephine is the popular artist, the people's artist, so the people take care of her as the father takes care of the child, while she is persuaded that she is the one that takes care of the people; when they are 'in a bad way politically or economically, her singing is supposed to save' them, and 'if it doesn't drive away the evil, at least gives us strength to bear it' (p. 366). Her voice is a collective voice, she sings for all, she is the voice of the people, who otherwise form an anonymous mass. 'This piping, which rises up where everyone else is pledged to silence, comes almost like a message from the whole people to each individual' (p. 367). In a reversal, she embodies the collectivity and relegates her listeners to their individuality. Her oneness is opposed to the collectivity of people – they are always treated *en masse*, they display the uniformity of their reactions, despite some minor divergences of opinion, and their commonsensical opinion is rendered by the narrator (*Erzählermaus*, as one commentator put it), the bearer of the *doxa*.[17] They are non-individuals, while she, at the other end of the scale, is the exceptional one, the elevated individuality who stands for, and can awaken, the lost individuality of others.

But in her role of the artist she is also the capricious prima donna; there is the whole comedy of her claims for her rights. She wants to be exempt from work, she requires special privileges, work allegedly harms her voice, she wants due honour to be paid to her services, she wants to be granted a place apart. She 'does not want mere admiration, she wants to be admired exactly in the way she prescribes' (p. 362). But the people, despite their general esteem for her, do not want to hear about any of this – they are cold in their judgement, they respect her, but want her to remain one of them. So there is the whole charade of the artist who is not appreciated as she would deserve, she does not get the laurels that she thinks should belong to her, she puts up a preposterous act as the genius not understood by her contemporaries. As a protest, she announces that she will cut down her coloraturas – this will teach them a lesson – and maybe she does, only nobody notices it. She keeps coming up with all sorts of whims, she lets herself be begged, and only reluctantly gives in. There is the comedy of hurt narcissism, megalomania, inflated ego, the high mission of the artist's overblown vocation. So one day she indeed stops singing, firmly believing that there will be some huge scandal, but nobody gives a damn, everybody goes about their business as usual, without noticing that anything is missing – that is, without noticing the lack of the lack, the absence of the gap.

Curious, how mistaken she is in her calculations, the clever creature, so mistaken that one might fancy she has made no calculations at all but is only being driven on by her destiny, which in our world cannot be anything but a sad

> one. Of her own accord she abandons her singing, of her own accord she destroys the power she has gained over people's hearts. How could she ever have gained that power, since she knows so little about these hearts of ours? . . . Josephine's road must go downhill. The time will soon come when her last notes sound and die into silence. She is a small episode in the eternal history of our people, and the people will get over the loss of her. . . . Perhaps we shall not miss so very much after all, while Josephine . . . will happily lose herself in the numberless throng of the heroes of our people, and soon, since we are no historians, will rise to the heights of redemption and be forgotten like all her brothers. (p. 376)

Despite her vanity and megalomania, people will easily do without her, she will be forgotten, no traces will be left of her art; this is not a people composed of historians and archivists, and besides, there is no way one could stack, collect, archivize her art, which consists purely in the gap.

So this is the second strategy, the strategy of art, of art as the non-exceptional exception, which can arise anywhere, at any moment, which is made of anything, of ready-made objects, so long as it can provide them with a gap, make them make a break. It is the art of the minimal difference. Yet the moment it makes its appearance, this difference is bungled by the very gesture which brought it about, the moment this gesture and this difference becomes instituted, the moment art turns into an institution to which a certain place is allotted and where certain limits are drawn. Its power is at the same time its powerlessness; the very status of art veils what is at stake. Hence the whole farce of egocentric megalomania and misunderstood genius, special privileges, and so on which occupies the largest part of the story. Josephine wants the impossible: she wants a place beyond the law, beyond equality – and equality is the essential feature of the mouse-folk, equality in tininess, in their miniature size (hence her claims to greatness are all the more comical). But at the same time she wants her status of the exception to be legally sanctioned, symbolically recognized, properly glorified. She wants to be, like the sovereign, both inside and outside the law. She wants her uniqueness to be recognized as a special social role, and the moment art does this, it is finished. The very break it has introduced is reduced to just another social function, the break becomes the institution of the break, its place is circumscribed and, as an exception, it can fit very well into the rule – that is, into the rule of law. As an artist who wants veneration and recognition, she will be forgotten, relegated to the gallery of memory, that is, of oblivion. Her voice, which opens the crack in the seamless continuity of the law, is betrayed and destroyed by the very status of art, which reinserts it and closes the gap. At best it can be a tiny recess: 'Piping is our people's daily speech, only many a one pipes his whole life long and does not know it, where here piping is set free from the fetters of daily life and it sets us free too for a little while' (p. 370).

Just for a little while – but by setting us free, it only helps us bear the rest all the better. The miniature size of the mouse is enough to open the gap, but once it is instituted and recognized, its importance shrinks to the size of the mouse, despite its delusions of grandeur. It is the voice tied to the mast, and the oarsmen, although they may hear it in the flash of a brief recess, will continue to be deaf. Thus we do not end up with Kafka's version of Ulysses, but are stuck with Ulysses *tout court* – or, rather, with the Adorno-and-Horkheimer version. Josephine's sublime voice will finally be *den Mäusen gepfiffen*, as the German expression has it (and this German phrase may well be at the origin of the whole story) – that is, piped to the mice, piped in vain to someone who cannot understand or appreciate it – not because of some obtuseness of the mass, but because of the nature of art itself. One could say: art is her mousetrap. So the second strategy fails, it is ruined by its own success, and the transcendence that art promised turned out to be of such a nature that it could easily fit as one part into the division of labour; the disruptive power of the gap turned out to accommodate the continuity only too well.

The dog

Let us now consider a third option. 'Investigations of a Dog' ('Forschungen eines Hundes'), written in 1922 (two years before Kafka's death) and published in 1931, the title again being given by Max Brod, is one of the most obscure and most bizarre among Kafka's stories – and that is saying something – apart from being one of the longest. Here we have a dog who lives a normal dog's life, just like everybody else, and is suddenly awakened from this life by an encounter with seven rather special music-producing dogs.

> out of some place of darkness, to the accompaniment of terrible sounds such as I had never heard before, seven dogs stepped into the light . . . they brought the sound with them, though I could not recognize how they produced it. . . . At that time I still knew hardly anything of the creative gift for music with which the canine race alone is endowed, it had naturally enough escaped my but slowly developing powers of observation; for though music had surrounded me as a perfectly natural and indispensable element of existence ever since I was a suckling, an element which nothing impelled me to distinguish from the rest of existence . . .; all the more astonishing, then, indeed devastating, were these seven great musical artists to me. (p. 281)

To start with, the situation is similar to that of Josephine's singing: music is everywhere in dogs' lives, the most run-of-the-mill thing, utterly inconspicuous, and it takes 'great musical artists' to single it out, that is, to produce the break. But there is a twist:

> They did not speak, they did not sing, they remained generally silent, almost determinedly silent; but from the empty air they conjured music. Everything was music, the lifting and setting down of their feet, certain turns of the head, their running and their standing still, the positions they took up in relation to one another . . ., [their] lying flat on the ground and going through complicated concerted evolutions; . . . (ibid.)

Where does the music come from? There is no speaking, no singing, no musical instruments. It just came from nowhere, from the empty air, *ex nihilo*. Music was everywhere in dogs' lives, ready-made, but this one was just created out of nothing. We have seen that Josephine's problem was to create a nothing out of something, in *creatio ex nihilo* in reverse, *creatio nullius rei*, but here it is even better: the problem is how to create nothing out of nothing, the gap of nothing which encircles the ready-made object made out of nothing. There we have the great wonder: the ready-made nothing. The ready-made nothing is epitomized by the voice without a discernible source – what Michel Chion has called the acousmatic voice.[18] It is the voice as pure resonance.

In one of his (rather rare) reflections about the voice in the seminar on anxiety (5 June 1963), Lacan argues for his tenet that the object voice has to be divorced from sonority. He curiously makes an excursion into the physiology of the ear: he talks about the cavity of the ear, its snail-like shape, *le tuyau*, the tube, and goes on to say that its importance is merely topological; it consists in the formation of a void, a cavity, an empty space, of 'the most elementary form of a constituted and a constituting emptiness [*le vide*]', like the empty space in the middle of a tube, or of any wind instrument, the space of mere resonance, the volume. But this is but a metaphor, he says, and continues with the following rather mysterious passage:

> If the voice, in our sense, has an importance, then it doesn't reside in it resonating in some spatial void; rather it resides in the fact that the simplest emission . . . resonates in the void which is the void of the Other as such, *ex nihilo*, so to speak. The voice responds to what is said, but it cannot be responsible for it [*La voix répond à ce qui se dit, mais elle ne peut pas en répondre.*] In other words: in order to respond we have to incorporate the voice as the alterity of what is said [*l'altérité de ce qui se dit*].[19]

I will take up just one thread in this difficult passage. If there is an empty space in which the voice resonates, then it is only the void of the Other, the Other as a void. The voice comes back to us through the loop of the Other, and what comes back to us from the Other is the pure alterity of what is said, that is, the voice. This is perhaps the original form of the famous formula that the subject always gets his own message back in an inverted form: the message one gets back in response is the voice. Our speech resonates in the Other and is returned as the voice, something we did not cater for: the inverted form of our message is its voice, which was created from a pure void, *ex nihilo*, as an inaudible echo of pure resonance, and the non-sonorous resonance endows what is said with alterity. One expects a response from the Other, one addresses it in the hope of a response, but all one gets is the voice. The voice is what is said turned into its alterity, but the responsibility is the subject's own, not the Other's, which means that the subject is not only responsible for what he says, but must at the same time respond for, and respond to, the alterity of his own speech. He said something more than he intended, and this surplus is the voice which is merely produced by being passed through the loop of the Other. This is, I suppose, at the bottom of the rather striking phenomenon in analysis, the dispossession of one's voice in the presence of the silence of the analyst: whatever one says is immediately countered by its own alterity, by the voice resounding in the resonance of the void of the Other, which comes back to the subject as the answer the moment one has spoken. And this resonance dispossesses one's own voice; the resonance of the Other thwarts it, burrows it, makes it sound hollow. The speech is the subject's own, but the voice pertains to the Other, it is created in the loop of its void. This is what one has to learn to respond for, and respond to.[20]

But this is just a digression, made in the wild hope of clarifying one obscurity by another, that of Kafka by that of Lacan; the hope that two combined obscurities might produce some light – *ex nihilo*. If we take up just the slogans of 'the resonance of the Other', 'the void', '*ex nihilo*', then we see that the seven dogs' voices are coming out of a pure void; they spring up from nothing, a pure resonance without a source. As if the pure alterity turned into music, the music that pervades anything and everything, as if the voice of this resonance had got hold of all possible points of emission, not the other way round. The resonance of the voice functions not as an effect but as a cause, a pure *causa sui*, but one which in this self-causality encompasses everything. It is as if the pure void of the Other started to reverberate in itself in the presence of those great musicians, whose art consisted merely in letting the Other resonate for itself.

The hapless young dog is overwhelmed:

> the music gradually got the upper hand, literally knocked the breath out of me and swept me far away from those actual little dogs, and quite against my will . . . my mind could attend to nothing but this blast of music which seemed to come from all sides, from the heights, from the deeps, from everywhere, surrounding the listener, overwhelming him, crushing him, and over his swooning body still blowing fanfares so near that they seemed far away and almost inaudible . . . the music robbed me of my wits . . . (p. 282)

This experience completely shatters the young dog's life; it is the start of his quest, his investigations. His interest in all this is not artistic at all, there is no problem of the status of this voice as art, as with Josephine; his interest is an epistemological one. It is the quest for the source, the attempt to gain knowledge about the source of it all. One of Josephine's endeavours was to preserve the dimension of the child in her art, in the midst of that race of mice which is both very childish and prematurely old at the same time – they are like children infused with 'weariness and hopelessness' (p. 369), and Josephine's voice was like preserving their childhood against their economy of survival, against the always-premature adulthood. But the young dog is at the very opposite end of this; he decides that 'there are more important things than childhood' (p. 286). *Es gibt wichtigere Dinge als die Kindheit*:[21] this is one of Kafka's great sentences, it should be taken as a motto, or indeed as a most serious political slogan. A political slogan in the time of the general infantilization of social life, starting with the infantilization of infants, the age which loves to take the despicable opposite line: namely, that we are all children in our hearts, and that this is our most precious possession, something we should hold on to. There are more important things than childhood: this should also be seen as the slogan of psychoanalysis, which indeed seems to be all about retrieving childhood, but not in order to keep this precious and unique thing, but to give it up. Psychoanalysis is on the side of the young dog who decides to grow up, to leave behind 'the blissful life of a young dog', to start his investigations, to turn to research, to pursue a quest.

But his quest takes a strange and unexpected turn. The question 'Where does the music come from? Where does the voice come from?' is immediately translated into another question: 'Where does food come from?' The mystery of the incorporeal resonance of the voice is without further ado transformed into the mystery of a very different kind, of the most corporeal kind imaginable. The voice is the resonance from nowhere, it does not serve anything (Lacan's definition of enjoyment), but food is at the opposite end, the most elementary means of survival, the most material and bodily of elements. Indeed, it is the question about a mystery where there does not seem to be any mystery. The dog sees a mystery where nobody else sees a mystery; the simplest and the most palpable thing suddenly becomes endowed with the greatest of secrets. A break has happened, from nowhere, and he wants to start his inquiries with the simplest things. In a few sentences, in a few lines, one passes from the enigma of song to the enigma of food – the stroke of Kafka's genius at its best, in a passage which is completely unpredictable and completely logical at the same time. Once one starts asking questions, there is no end to mystery. What is the source of food? The earth? But what enables the earth to provide food? Where does the earth get the food from? Just as the source of the law was an enigma which one could never disclose, so is the source of food an ever-elusive enigma. It seems as though food, pure materiality and immanence, will suddenly point to transcendence, if only it is pursued far enough.

So the dog goes around asking other dogs, who all seem quite unconcerned by such self-evident trivialities – nobody would dream of taking such banal inquiries seriously. When he asks them about the source of food, they immediately assume that he must be hungry, so instead of an answer they give him food; they want to nourish him, they want to stuff his mouth with food, they counter his questioning by feeding him.

(I cannot resist the temptation to quote some Lacan in the parethesis:

> Even when you stuff the mouth – the mouth that opens in the register of the drive – it is not the food that satisfies it. . . . As far as the oral drive is concerned . . . it is obvious that it is not a question of food, nor of the memory of food, nor the echo of food, nor the mother's care . . . (pp. 167–8)
>
> the fact that no food will ever satisfy the oral drive, except by circumventing [circling around] the eternally lacking object. (p. 180)[22])

The dog's mouth cannot be stuffed, he is not put off that easily, and he gets so involved in his investigation that he eventually stops eating. The story has many twists and turns that I cannot go into, all of them illuminating and strangely wonderful; I will just jump to the last section.

The way to discover the source of food is to starve. Like 'A Hunger Artist' ('Der Hungerkünstler'), the story written in the same year – not the starving artist, which is a common enough phenomenon, but someone who has brought starvation to an art. The starvation, as it turns out, was his ready-made, since his secret was that he actually really disliked food. It was an art not adequately appreciated, just like Josephine's, and this is why the hunger artist will die of hunger. But the dog is no artist, this is not the portrait of the artist as a young dog, this dog is a would-be scientist and he is starving on his quest for knowledge, which almost brings him to the same result. But at the point of total exhaustion, when he is already dying (like the man from the country), there is salvation, salvation at the point of the 'exhaustion of exhaustion'. He vomits blood, he feels so faint that he actually faints, and when he opens his eyes there is a dog which appears from nowhere, a strange hound standing in front of him.

There is an ambiguity – is this last part a hallucination of the dying dog? Or, even more radically, is this the answer to Hamlet's question 'But in that sleep of death, what dreams may come'? Is this last section a possible sequel to 'Before the Law', the dreams that may come to the man from the country at the point of his death? Is it all a delusion, the glimpse of salvation only at the point of death? A salvation only at the price that it does not have any consequences? But Kafka's description of this delusion, his pursuit of it to the end, bringing it to the point of science, the birth of science from the spirit of a delusion on the threshold of death: these are all the consequences that are needed, something that affects the here and now, and radically transforms it.

The dying dog tries at first to chase away the apparition of the hound (is it a ghost which intervenes at the end, as opposed to the other one which intervened in the beginning?). The hound is very beautiful, and at first it even appears that he is trying to pay court to the starved dog; he is very concerned about the dying dog, he cannot let him be. But all this dialogue is but a haphazard preparation for the event, the emergence of song, the song again coming from nowhere, emerging without anyone's will.

> then I thought I saw something such as no dog before me had ever seen. . . . I thought I saw that the hound was already singing without knowing it, nay, more that the melody separated from him, was floating on the air in accordance with its own laws, and, as though he had no part in it, was moving toward me, toward me alone. . . . the melody, which the hound soon seemed to acknowledge as his, was quite irresistible. It grew stronger; its waxing power seemed to have no limits, and already almost burst my eardrums. But the worst was that it seemed to exist solely for my sake, this voice before whose sublimity the woods fell silent, to exist solely for my sake; who was I, that I could dare to remain here, lying brazenly before it in my pool of blood and filth. (p. 314)

The song again appears from nowhere, it starts from anywhere, from a void, it is separated from its bearer, it is only *post festum* that the bearer steps in, that the hound can assume it, acknowledge it as his. And this song is directed towards the starving dog alone, it is for his ears only, the impersonal call which addresses only him personally, just as the door of the Law was reserved only for the man from the country. It is like the pure voice of a call, just like the irresistible call of the law, like its irrepressible silence, only this time the very same call as its opposite, the call of salvation.

So this voice from nowhere introduces the second break: the dog suddenly recovers on the threshold of death, the voice gets hold of him and instils new life in him; he who could not move jumps up now, resurrected, the born-again dog. And he pursues his investigations with redoubled force, he extends his scientific interest to the canine music. 'The science of music, if I am correctly informed, is perhaps still more comprehensive than that of nurture' (pp. 314–15) – the new science he is trying to establish encompasses both his concerns, the source of food and the source of the voice; it combines them into a single effort. The voice, the music, like pure transcendence, and the food as the pure immanence of the material world: but they have common ground, a common source, they are kept in the same kernel. The science of music is held in higher esteem than the science of nurture, it reaches the sublime, but this is precisely what prevents it from penetrating 'deeply into the life of the people'; it is 'very esoteric and politely excludes the people' (p. 315). It has been erroneously posited as a separate science, different from that of nurture; its power was powerless by virtue of being relegated to a separate realm. This was Josephine's unhappy fate: her song was separated from food, the art was pitted against survival, the sublime was her mousetrap, just as being immersed in nurture was the unhappy fate of all the rest. Just as the science of nurture had to lead through starvation, so the science of music refers to silence, to '*verschwiegenes Hundewesen*', the silent essence of the dog, or the essence kept in silence, the essence that, after the experience of the song, can be discovered in any dog as its true nature. For penetrating this essence, 'the real dog nature', the path of nurture was the alternative and simpler way, as it seemed, but it all boils down to the same; what matters is the point of intersection. 'A border region between these two sciences, however, had already attracted my attention. I mean the theory of incantation, by which food is called down [*Es ist die Lehre von dem die Nahrung herabrufenden Gesang*]' (p. 315; p. 454 in German): The song can call down, *herabrufen*, the food: the source of food was mistakenly sought in the earth; it should have been searched for in the opposite direction. The voice is the source of food that the dog has been seeking. There is an overlapping, an intersection, between nourishment and voice. One can illustrate it with one of Lacan's favourite devices, the intersection of two circles, the circle of food and the circle of the voice, the music. What do we find at the point where they overlap? What is the mysterious intersection? But this is the best definition of what Lacan called *objet petit a*. It is the common source of both food and music.[23]

Food and voice, both pass through the mouth. Deleuze keeps coming back to that over and over again. There is an alternative: either you eat or you speak, use your voice; you cannot do both at the same time. They share the same location, but in mutual exclusion: either incorporation or emission.

> Any language, rich or poor, always implies the deterritorialization of the mouth, the tongue and the teeth. The original territoriality of the mouth, the tongue and the teeth is food. By being devoted to the articulation of sounds, the mouth, the tongue and the teeth are deterritorialized. So there is a disjunction between eating and speaking. . . . To speak . . . is to starve.[24]

By speech the mouth is denaturalized, diverted from its natural function, seized by the signifier (and, for our purposes, by the voice which is but the alterity of the signifier). The Freudian name for this deterritorialization is the drive (if nothing else, it has the advantage of sparing us that terrible tongue-twister, but it has the same sense). Eating can never be the same once the mouth has been deterritorialized; it is seized by the drive, it turns around this object, it keeps circumventing, circling around this eternally elusive object. The speech, in this denaturalizing function, is then subjected to the secondary territorialization, as it were: it acquires a second nature with its anchorage in meaning. Meaning is a reterritorialization of language, its acquisition of a new territoriality, a naturalized substance. (This is what Deleuze and Guattari call the extensive or representational function of speech, as opposed to the pure intensity of the voice, if I may undertake a small *forçage* here.) But this operation can never be successful, and the bit that eludes it can be pinned down as the element of the voice, this pure alterity of what is said. This is the common ground it shares with food: that in food which precisely escapes eating, the bone that gets stuck in the throat (one of Lacan's formulas is precisely that *objet petit a* is the bone that gets stuck in the throat of the signifier).

So the essence of the dog concerns precisely this intersection of food and voice, the two lines of investigation converge – from our biased perspective, they meet in the *objet petit a.* So there would have to be a single science; the dog, on the last page, inaugurates a new science, he is the founding dog of a new science. Although by his own admission he is a feeble scientist, at least by the standards of the established sciences. He could not pass

> even the most elementary scientific examination set by an authority on the subject . . . the reason for that can be found in my incapacity for scientific investigation, my limited powers of thought, my bad memory, but above all in my inability to keep my scientific aim continuously before my eyes. All this I

> frankly admit, even with a certain degree of pleasure. For the more profound cause of my scientific incapacity seems to me to be an instinct, and indeed by no means a bad one. . . . It was this instinct that made me – and perhaps for the sake of science itself, but a different science from that of today, an ultimate science [*einer allerletzten Wissenschaft*] – prize freedom higher than everything else. Freedom! Certainly such freedom as is possible today is a wretched business. But nevertheless freedom, nevertheless a possession. (pp. 315–16)

This is the last sentence of the story. The last word of it all, *le fin mot* as *le mot de la fin*, is freedom, with an exclamation mark. Are we not victims of a delusion, should we not pinch ourselves – is it possible that Kafka actually utters this word? This is perhaps the only place where Kafka speaks of freedom in explicit terms, but this does not in any way mean that there is unfreedom everywhere else in his universe. Quite the opposite: freedom is there at all times, everywhere, it is Kafka's *fin mot*, like the secret word one does not dare to utter although it is constantly on one's mind. The freedom that might not look like much, might actually look wretched, but is there at all points, and once we spot it there is no way of getting away from it, it is a possession to hold on to, it is the permanent line of flight, or rather, the line of pursuit. And there is the slogan, the programme of a new science which would be able to treat it, to take it as its object, to pursue it, the ultimate science, the science of freedom. Kafka lacks the proper word for it, he cannot name it (this is 1922), but he only had to look around, to examine the ranks of his fellow Jewish Austrian compatriots.

Psychoanalysis, of course.

Notes

1. 'The problem of our laws': 'Our laws are not generally known; they are kept secret by the small group of nobles who rule us. We are convinced that these ancient laws are scrupulously administered; nevertheless it is an extremely painful thing to be ruled by laws that one does not know. . . . The very existence of these laws, however, is at most a matter of presumption. There is a tradition that they exist and that they are a mystery confided to the nobility, but it is not and cannot be more than a mere tradition sanctioned by age, for the essence of a secret code is that it should remain a mystery. . . . There is a small party who . . . try to show that, if any law exists, it can only be this: The Law is whatever the nobles do'. (pp. 437–8). All quotes from Kafka's stories are from *The Complete Stories*, ed. N. N. Glatzer (New York: Schocken Books, 1995).

2. See Jacques Derrida, 'Préjugés, devant la loi', in J.-F. Lyotard, *La faculté de juger* (Paris: Minuit, 1985), p. 122 and *passim*.

3. Gilles Deleuze and Félix Guattari, *Kafka. Pour une littérature mineure* (Paris: Minuit, 1975), p. 79.

4. 'Der Bau', written at the end of 1923 and published after Kafka's death by Max Brod, who also provided the excellent title. The German word is impossible to translate in all its ambiguity. It can mean the process of building, construction; the result of building, the edifice; the structure, the make (of a plant, of a novel . . .); a jail; a burrow, a hole in the ground, a mine. The oscillation is not only between the process and the result (establishing an equivalence between 'process' and 'structure'), but also between erecting an edifice and digging a hole.

5. Lacan uses a highly technical term, used mostly in medicine, which Shorter explains as 'intercommunication between two vessels, channels or branches, by a connecting cross branch. Orig. of the cross connections between the arteries and veins etc.; now of those of any branching system'.

6. There is another passing mention of Kafka in Lacan's seminar 'D'un Autre à l'autre' (1968/69). In the session of 11 June 1969, Lacan proposes the Trojan Horse, with its empty belly, 'the empty set', hiding the dangerous object, as a good model of the big Other, where Troy itself, by extension, appears as 'the Kafkaesque castle'.

7. Giorgio Agamben, *Homo sacer* (Paris: Seuil, 1997), p. 23.

8. Franz Kafka, *The Castle*, trans. Will and Edwin Muir (New York: Schocken Books, 1995), p. 27.

9. Hence one can draw the consequence that the voice stands at the opposite end of the Kantian categorical imperative, and it is crucial to draw the line between the moral law and the superego. See Alenka Zupančič, *Ethics of the Real: Kant, Lacan* (London and New York: Verso, 2000), pp. 140–67.

10. This, of course, is one of the grand examples from Freud's book on jokes. *Jokes and their Relation to the Unconscious* (Pelican Freud Library 6, Harmondsworth, 1976), p. 161. In the 'Index of jokes' at the end of the volume, this joke is laconically referred to as 'Truth a lie (Jewish)', and indeed, as I have tried to argue elsewhere, this joke most economically epitomizes the problem that 'Jewishness' presented for Western culture: the indistinguishable character of truth and lie, the fact that they not only look alike but actually coincide, so that 'Jewishness' seems to undermine the very ground of the truth-telling capacity of language. This is the problem with the 'Jews': they look exactly like us, just as the lie looks exactly like the truth.

11. The German dictionary offers the following expression: *das trägt eine Maus auf den Schwanz fort*, for a quantity so small that a mouse could carry it on its tail (with all the German ambiguity of the word, tail/penis). There is a rather vulgar expression in Slovene, 'the mouse's penis', which means the smallest thing imaginable, one cannot possibly conceive of anything smaller; the mouse's voice is of that order of magnitude. The mouse's penis – a circumlocution for castration? Is Josephine a *castrato* – is this the secret of her voice?

12. Deleuze and Guattari, *Kafka*, p. 40. 'There is no longer a proper sense and a figurative sense, but a distribution of states along the fan of the word. . . . What is at stake is not a resemblance between an animal and a human behaviour, and even less a play upon words. There is no longer a man or an animal, since each deterritorializes the other. . . . The animal doesn't speak "as" a human, but extracts from language the tonalities without meaning . . .' (ibid.).

13. Here one should also recall the badger from 'The Burrow', the story used by Lacan. The badger is the antisocial animal, the solitary digger, the animal of a total exclusion from society, but from that point he has all the more to deal with the oppressive and unfathomable big Other. And we should also recall that the story of the burrow is also the

story of the voice: the big Other ultimately manifests itself as the voice. What utterly disconcerts the badger in his intricately designed burrow is the enigmatic whistling, the constant faint buzzing sound whose origin he cannot discover.

14. On closer scrutiny, both mice and dogs in many respects strangely resemble the Jews and their destiny, as several interpreters have pointed out, but I will not go into this. See 'No creatures to my knowledge live in such wide dispersion as we dogs . . .; we, whose one desire is to stick together . . . we above all others live so widely separated from one another, engaged in strange vocations that are often incomprehensible even to our canine neighbors, holding firmly to laws that are not those of the dog world, but are actually directed against it' (pp. 279–80). In both cases there is also a metaphor – to live like a dog, poor as a mouse – which is destroyed by its literalization. With mice we should also keep in mind the connection of the German word, *Maus*, with *mauscheln*, with all its connotations in German (a verb derived from Yiddish for Moses, *Mausche*, and meaning to speak Yiddish, and by extension to speak in an incomprehensible way, and by extension, secret dealings, hidden affairs, deceit).

15. See Gérard Wajcman, *L'objet du siècle* (Paris: Verdier 2000) for the best comment on Duchamp.

16. I can only add in this note that this resonates with Kierkegaard's problem: how to introduce a gap in the continuity as the transcendence in the immanence.

17. Kafka, in the manuscript, crossed out four instances where the narrator speaks in the first person – his is the voice of anonymity, and must remain without an 'I'.

18. Michel Chion, *The Voice in Cinema* (New York: Columbia University Press, 1999). Chion found its supreme cinematic example in the mother's voice in *Psycho*, another voice *ex nihilo*.

19. Jacques Lacan, *L'Angoisse* (Paris: Seuil, 2004), p. 318.

20. Bernard Baas (*De la chose à l'objet* [Leuven: Peeters/Vrin, 1998]) puts this very well: 'The voice is never my own voice, but the response is my own response' (p. 205).

21. For the German original I use *Die Erzählungen. Originalfassung*, ed. Roger Hermes (Frankfurt am Main: Fischer, 2000), p. 420.

22. The quotes are, of course, from *The Four Fundamental Concepts of Psycho-Analysis*, trans. Alan Sheridan (London: Penguin, 1979). See also: 'The *objet petit a* is not the origin of the oral drive. It is not introduced as the original food, it is introduced from the fact that no food will ever satisfy the oral drive, except by circumventing [circling around] the eternally lacking object' (p. 180).

23. 'If music be the food of love . . .' is another great literary testimony which most economically marks that place, although it immediately obfuscates it with the rhetoric of love.

24. Deleuze and Guattari, *Kafka*, pp. 35–6.

15

Lacan with Artaud: *j'ouïs-sens, jouis-sens, jouis-sans*

Lorenzo Chiesa

The multiple theoretical overlappings between Artaud and Lacan are marked by the silent eloquence of a biographical half-saying. It is possible to locate only a single place in the entire corpus of Lacan's writings, seminars and conferences in which he speaks directly of Artaud: in 'Raison d'un échec', Lacan threatens to 'sedate' those of his followers who would be inclined to behave like him.[1] Indeed, their sole actual encounter had been a clinical one: Doctor Lacan visited the patient Artaud in 1938, shortly after his hospitalization in Saint Anne. On that occasion he declared: 'Artaud is obsessed, he will live for eighty years without writing a single sentence, he is obsessed'.[2] This diagnosis turned out to be completely wrong: Artaud died ten years later; in the meantime, he had written six books and left behind many hundreds of notebooks. At one point in *Van Gogh, the Man Suicided by Society*, Artaud 'has done with' Lacan, half-mentioning him once and for all; he establishes that 'Doctor L.' is an 'erotomaniac', and thus turns the very accusation of madness against the psychiatrist himself.[3]

1 Erotomania

> 'I don't know Freud's or Jung's psychoanalysis very well.'
>
> (Artaud to his psychiatrist in Rodez asylum)

> 'admirers of the theme of the unconscious, of both the Freudian and the American kind, this unconscious of which they imagine they are making a spectroscopy.'
>
> (Artaud, 'Bases universelles de la culture')

The works of Artaud are characterized by a lifelong crusade against sexuality. From a biographical standpoint, the mounting radicalism of such an attack coincides with a sexual abstinence which is deliberately chosen and publicized. Artaud refuses sexuality 'in its present form', he criticizes the fact that it is a historical derivative, a symbolic construct.[4] Another sexuality – either mythically lost or *à venir* – is thereby presupposed. More precisely, historical sexuality should be identified with organic sexuality, and the organic or divided body which is socioculturally produced by the religious soul, medical anatomy and scientific atomism.[5] Organic generation and the phallic *jouissance* it entails are, for Artaud, a priori, a synonym of degeneration in so far as they follow the loss of a primordial unity. He thus speaks of the human body as a '*maison de chair close*':[6] the paradigmatic image of the brothel ('*maison close*', literally 'closed house') is provided by the organically sexuated body–house; by the closure, the framing of our flesh ('*chair*') which entails an act of division, a separation of the inside from the outside.

How, more specifically, is organic sexuality necessarily degenerate? Artaud believes that man is fully perverted by a mental obsession with coitus. Certainly, organic sexuality is concretely omnipresent in our daily life and is, indeed, by no means repressed; for Artaud, however, coitus is primarily a perversion, since it is the ubiquitous form of *thought*. Given that, for him, metaphysics is that which 'one carries for oneself as a result of the emptiness one carries within',[7] he identifies coitus as the supreme metaphysical device: coitus stands for an ideologically conformist apparatus imposed upon us in order to conceal the lack introduced by (symbolic) division. This structural perversion is what Artaud calls, in his late work, 'erotomania' in a clear and ironic contrast with the technical meaning of the term as defined by psychiatry – for which it is 'an obsession with chaste love'.[8] In what appears to be a mocking re-elaboration of the homunculus theory, Artaud states that 'every human-man has a sex beneath his brain, a sort of small sex which he soaks in his consciousness'.[9]

Erotomania *qua* perversion is undoubtedly at the same time a *père-version*, or 'version of the Father', in two overlapping ways: (1) it sustains what Artaud calls the '*idiotic* periplus', the tirelessly repetitive, 'dull' circle of the degenerate lineage of father–son–father of which Artaud claims to be the 'leveller';[10] (2) for the same reason, erotomania supports the stupidity of the Father/Other, its utter inconsistency, and thus paradoxically allows the otherwise impossible emergence of meaning. It is in this precise sense that, according to Lacan, the 'non-duped', those who are not deceived by the symbolic Other – in other words, psychotics – 'err': meaning can emerge only from idiocy (that is, non-psychosis), from an utterly arbitrary Name-of-the-Father, an obliviousness with respect to the lack in the Other supported by a perverse phallic *jouissance*. It is for this reason that Lacan writes the latter '*j'ouïs sens*'.[11] Phallic *jouissance* allows us 'to make sense': by enjoying *père*-versely – that is, *for* the Father/Other – by thinking that the latter is One, by being able to 'think' *tout court*, 'I hear' [*j'ouïs*] a sense.

This strict Lacanian interdependence between phallic *jouissance*, Other and symbolic thinking/meaning is clearly grasped by Artaud himself. On the one hand, he often identifies God/Father/Other with degenerate phallic sexuality; for instance, he writes: 'They have found a new way to bring out god . . . in the guise of morbid sexuality.'[12] On the other, expressions such as 'not thinking except of coitus', 'thinking with the sex',[13] are recurrent locutions in his works: as I have already suggested, they attempt to describe a structural, mental *père-version* that greatly exceeds a 'will to have sex'. In fact they designate a modality of thought itself, the only modality through which presently, historically, thought can 'think'. More specifically, one could say with Artaud that in the erotomaniacal *père-version*, thought has found its own '*impouvoir*', its (im)possibility of thinking.[14] Thought can 'pre-tend' to think only by establishing a metaphysics of sex; thinking is merely a pre-tending to think, since, at best, thinking amounts to thinking the impossibility of thought. That is to say: the inability to think which characterizes thought, the fact that human thinking is given only by way of a gap, a 'witnessing oneself',[15] through being one's own spectator – something which persecutes Artaud – this thought that can never fully be thought is structurally marked by a metaphysical demand which finds in coitus both a temporary satisfaction and an always-renewed dissatisfaction.

From a Lacanian standpoint, one might well argue that Artaud is suggesting that coitus functions as the epitome of a *semblant*: it both veils and preserves a lack. Thus satisfaction lies less in the physical satisfaction of coitus itself than in the (dis)satisfaction of a mental demand, that is, in erotomania. What is primarily at stake here is not the satisfaction of a specifically pathological perversion but the endless repetition of a structural – albeit 'holed' – *père-version* through partial (dis)satisfaction. Artaud coins a neologism which wonderfully summarizes the mad astuteness of false thinking: he substitutes 'being *satisfaits*' ('satisfied') for 'being *satis-fous*';[16] this 'being *satis-wild*' tries to convey a concept in which libido and symbolic meaning are inextricably mingled. The mental satisfaction of an impotent thought in the guise of erotomania is a dominant (hegemonically ideological) form of madness which must be juxtaposed with that form of madness, madness *tout-court* for society, which is ascribed to those – like Artaud himself – who rebel against erotomania. Erotomania has to be condemned as false thinking and, in parallel, as a partial form of – phallic – *jouissance* which derives from a degenerate sexuality. The Lacanian name for this 'satis-wildness' would inevitably be 'happiness'.[17]

Historical sexuality can only be organic: it must derive from division and, as such, be condemned. Artaud's theoretical enterprise prior to his internment in 1937 could consequently be summarized by one major question: how can we overcome division? We could well propose that, at this stage, Artaud hysterically denounces the (epistemological, sexual) hole in the Other while refusing to accept it as such: his ban on sexuality coincides with a ban on phallic *jouissance qua* 'cork'[18] of the (lacking) Other, *qua* derivative of and substitute for the fact that there is no relation between the sexes. Nevertheless, Artaud still believes, unlike Lacan, that there is another, extra-historical, extra-symbolic *jouissance*.

'What a beautiful *image* is a eunuch!', writes Artaud in *L'art et la mort*.[19] (Real) castration is an attractive imaginary lure, the mirage of a reconquered unity, which accompanies him from the self-identification with Abelard in *L'art et la mort* (1925–27) to the invention of Saint Antonine, who emasculates himself in *Artaud le Mômo* (1946). However, (real) castration ultimately offers a false remedy against the differentiality of phallocentrism: it violently refuses organic sexuality, but does not really undermine it. For this reason, the very term 'castration' usually indicates a form of lack in Artaud's texts: 'That which man today calls human is nothing but the castration of the supreme part of man.'[20] Such a lack is not compatible with Artaud's nostalgic struggle for the One.

We can actually distinguish two distinct meanings of castration in Artaud. The first is associated with the name of Abelard, possibly the most famous eunuch in all history. In a paradoxical move, Artaud seems to suggest that Abelard was castrated by the sexualization of his love-relationship with Héloïse, not by Fulbert's henchmen. His point is sufficiently transparent: those who have (organic) sex are castrated; (symbolic) castration and organic sexuality are co-dependent (as Lacan states, '*sexus* is clearly connected with *secare*').[21] Rather, true virility lies in asceticism, and love between man and woman has to remain Platonic.[22] The mythical scene of pure love is depicted in the following way: 'Héloïse has . . . a beautiful heart'; in this way, 'the question of love becomes simple', and Abelard is able to 'recover the game of love'.[23] On the other hand, organic sexuality entails Héloïse's transformation into a monstrous castrated aggregate of organs: 'Her skull is white and milky, her breasts disreputable, her legs spindly, her teeth make the noise of paper.'[24] Here the reader should be reminded that Artaud himself believed that he 'had been deflowered by [his only lover] Génica':[25] the violent castration-deflowering of Abelard/Artaud is presented as his uncertain entrance into the conformist-erotomaniacal dimension of the Symbolic.

In *Heliogabalus*, Artaud describes another meaning of castration: 'When the Gaul cuts off his member. . . . I see in this ritual the desire to have done with a certain contradiction, to reunite in a single blow the man and the woman, . . . to fuse them in one.' In this case, castration would seek a reconciliation between the two sexes: however, the androgynous union of man and woman necessarily fails, since the same act which (re)finds the woman is also the one which loses the man. Artaud therefore concludes: 'It is a gesture which finishes them', the Gauls bleed to death.[26]

At this stage, it should be evident how these two kinds of castration overlap: the will to have done with a certain contradiction, to get rid of the hindrance of organic sex and go back to the androgynous One, could be read as a will to castrate symbolic castration. In passing, it has to be noted how this longed-for One confronts us with a highly problematic notion of unity; it is ambiguous inasmuch as the cutting (real castration) which reoriginates it literally refragments the body. . . . This One might eventually be identified with the reverse of the Lacanian *corps morcelé*, a fragmented body which Artaud paradoxically considers to be a primordial unity and which, later in his work, will develop into what is obscurely called a 'body without organs' – that is to say, nothing but an a priori 'positive' reading of what could otherwise be defined only as scattered 'organs without body'.[27] In other words, castration *qua* physical amputation, that of the Gauls, coincides with a failed attempt to castrate organic sexuation, which, in turn, has to be understood as the castration of a – mythical – ascetic virility. The unattainable result of this *double* castration which should allow us to return to a prelapsarian state, this absolute *jouissance* that Artaud is seeking despite repeatedly sensing its impossibility, is named with two different and only apparently contradictory terms: 'love' and 'cruelty'.

The double castration invoked by Artaud as the only possible way of attaining absolute *jouissance* should be read as a double alienation, as the act of alienating oneself *from* symbolic alienation. This act both lets the subject authentically emerge in his rebellion against the differentiality of the Other – against being sexuated as much as against 'being spoken' by the Other – and desubjectivizes him, given that the subject is as such a *parlêtre*, a symbolic, desiring being-of-language. It should not surprise us that one of Artaud's incessant mottos is 'becoming an *aliéné authentique*'. For him, it is necessary to render alienation authentic. With this project in mind, he will travel at first to the remote land of the Tarahumara Indians in Mexico, then to the west coast of Ireland, where he will be arrested under unclear circumstances, shipped back to France, and interned in various asylums.

We should recall that '*aliéné*' in French means both 'alienated' and 'mad': what is at stake here for Artaud is producing a madness that would be 'authentic'. As he himself points out after nine years of internment: 'An authentic madman . . . is a man who preferred to become mad, in the socially accepted sense of the word, rather than forfeit a certain superior idea of human honour.'[28] Two notions of madness are juxtaposed here. There is a forced choice of which Artaud seems to be aware: either one accepts erotomania – false thinking, inauthentic madness, symbolic alienation – or one renders erotomaniacal madness authentically mad – that is to say, alienates alienation – thus refusing to compromise one's individual antisocial acts.[29] This choice is forced in the precise Lacanian sense: 'Either I do not think or I am not'; the subject can only choose between two different ways of getting lost: there where I (pre-tend to) think – in the socially alienated unconscious – 'I cannot recognize myself'; on the other hand, 'there where I *am* [in the Real], it is clear enough that I lose myself'.[30]

At this stage we should recuperate the properly Lacanian term for such a double alienation: this moment of pure negativity should be named (further) 'separation'. Artaud often uses the same term in order to explain his refusal of sexuality. Thus, he invokes an 'integral chastity' which corresponds to an 'absolute separation of sexes':[31] any sexuality *à venir* has to presuppose the end of the alienation between man and woman that was introduced by organic sexuality. It is possible to fight against this (symbolic) alienation only through another alienation: 'Sexuality will be put back in its place. . . . This means that the sexes will be separated for a certain time.'[32]

'Authentic alienation' therefore stands here for a synonym of virginal purity; separation must be achieved by erecting a wall of ascetic continence. As we shall soon see, it is a matter of literally opposing the generation gap.[33] Thus, Artaud writes that 'authentic madmen of asylums have guarded themselves against erotic crime, or if not, it was because they were not authentically mad';[34] we could rephrase all this by means of a simple proportion: authentic madness = purity : inauthentic madness = impure erotomania. Against the 'conformism' of erotomaniacal reasoning, Artaud proposes an alternative itinerary: being more chaste than maidens, he says, actively becoming virgin. Non-conquered virginity will therefore remain a merely organic category; this is why old Artaud's sex/penis has 'receded'.[35]

Furthermore, it should be emphasized that erotomania is an illness from which the *whole* of society suffers; only the totalizing effects of structural obscenity can succeed in segregating the specific madness of 'madmen' or, to put it the other way round, it is only the inevitability of the obscene support that can establish society as One, necessarily segregating society. . . . More specifically, Artaud believes that erotomania does not merely define our age as an age pervaded by imposed ideological lust which obliges us to forget love; it is not sufficient to regard it as the most explicit symptom of a generic 'spell cast upon society' (by psychiatrists and priests at first); it does not reduce itself to representing the most tangible sign of a successful operation of 'collective' and 'civic' black magic.[36] Its peculiarity, its being 'beyond' the 'repressive hypothesis', is, rather, demonstrated by the fact that erotomania ends up achieving its most excessive expression in psychiatrists themselves – that is to say, in those who might have been mistakenly identified as 'immunized repressors' (these paradoxical repressors who instigate sex . . .). There is no clear and ultimately pacifying dualism between 'repressors' and 'repressed'; to put it differently, Artaud seems to be aware of the fact that the injunction to enjoy phallically is inextricable from (the w/hole of) society as such, from its *establish-meant*, or its being counted as One: it constitutes society's obscene, superegoic support. In this way, authentic madmen not only 'attack a certain conformism of manners', but also 'attack the conformism of institutions themselves',[37] and should be diametrically opposed to psychiatrists, who are all radical erotomaniacs in so far as they clearly stand as the 'guardians' of false thinking.

All this would also explain why, according to Artaud, sin and social/erotomaniacal satis-wildness are co-implied.[38] The same social imperative (the superego) commands us to enjoy *and* makes us feel guilty for not enjoying enough an enjoyment which corresponds, in the end, to a lack of enjoyment [*jouis-sans*] but *cannot* be revealed as such. Thus the erotomaniac passes from the utterly reassuring *absurdity of the fault* which characterized the 'repressive' discourse of the traditional master – 'Isn't it absurd to feel guilty if I enjoy?' – to a much more unbearable *fault for absurdity* which capitalistic discourse attributes to the subject who never enjoys enough – 'Am I not guilty if I do not *really* enjoy while enjoying? Isn't this absurd?'. In 'Dossier d'Artaud le Mômo', Artaud writes: 'I condemn you,/ you know why I condemn you/ and I, I do not.'[39] The Other is completely stupid. You are guilty, you know why you are guilty (why I think you are), precisely because I (society) who am accusing you do not know why. You are guilty of knowing that I do not know why you are guilty (you are guilty because you found out about my fraud!), you are guilty of not being guilty, ultimately you are guilty of absurdity (*qua* hole in the Other, *qua* nonexistence of the sexual relationship), you are thus responsible for the absurdity which my fraud was avoiding. . . .

Alienation is both sexual and linguistic. It concerns both desire and meaning. In order to be 'authentically alienated' – that is, fully separated – one must therefore also alienate linguistic alienation. According to Artaud, linguistic separation will coincide with the formation of a truly non-alienated 'speech before the words' in which one is not spoken by the Other. Artaud would agree with Lacan that the unconscious that is structured like a language lies outside; thus he writes: 'In my unconscious it is the others that I hear speaking.'[40] As Lacan himself points out while speaking of James Joyce's daughter Lucia (a 'so-called schizophrenic', he says),[41] the 'madman' [*aliéné*] is somehow superior to 'normal' people inasmuch as he is the only one who correctly senses that words and language are *always* imposed by the Other. For Lacan, however, this superiority is not an 'advantage': on the contrary, it corresponds to the psychotic 'worse' of those who 'do not err', who are not fooled by the Other: those whose Symbolic malfunctions.

2 'Une force Antigone'

> 'The others who have died are not separated. They still turn around their dead bodies. I am not dead, but I am separated.'
>
> (Artaud, *The New Revelations of Being*)

It is well known that, according to Lacan, the fictional, mythically impossible character who fully embodies separation is the virgin Antigone. While interned at the asylum of Rodez, Artaud writes a short text entitled 'Antigone chez le Français', in which he describes her act of separation. What does Artaud say about Antigone?

1. Antigone is *the* woman; she is the woman who *is*, 'the *formal* embodiment of a woman'.[42] Artaud implicitly inscribes her name in the list of his seraphic harem of *filles-à-venir*, also named, not accidentally, 'daughters of the *heart*'. Who are they? *Filles-à-venir* are post-sexuated women whom Artaud could love. According to an organic vision of life, they are friends, potential lovers, grannies, an Afghan translator of *Art and Death* who has never existed in any birth register, all bound together by an imaginary 'inmixing of subjects', as Lacan would call it.

An anti-family must be built and chosen: 'You must decide between your parents and me.'[43] Here one recovers an unexpected development of Artaudian asceticism: *filles-à-venir* are daughters of continence. They are perhaps daughters of a *corps-à-venir*, a body without organs, which the androgyne could only erroneously anticipate. A different notion of unity is at stake here, a unity of pure difference. Artaud's daughters are not organically de-generated from him, but neither are they descendent emanations of a capital One which by now appears insufficient. His are all '*first*-born' daughters. 'We won't get out, in the world as it is now made, from this idea of primogeniture, not the first son of his father, but the father of his first son';[44] 'first' is a characteristic of the son/daughter as such. The father can only be father of a son/daughter who was not generated by him: like Artaud in relation to his '*immortal* little girls'.[45] *Filles-à-venir* were never (organically) born and can never (organically) die: they are real and, as such, 'undead'.[46] Therefore one has to emphasize how the decline of the androgyne coincides for Artaud with a re-evaluation of woman who had previously been accused of interrupting the androgyne's binary perfection, once and for all, by detaching herself from man (thus establishing a void, a difference).

2. Artaud and Antigone 'deserve one another' for having both suffered, undergoing a 'supreme inner combat' and being 'tortured' by an 'abominable notion of infinity'.[47] Antigone managed to defeat it: this is proved by her name, 'the name of a terrible victory'.[48] In so far as 'names are not [always] given at random',[49] Artaud can say that Antigone has become her own name, 'Antigone' now embodies an antagonistic force *par excellence*, 'the force-Antigone of being'.[50] He tells us that in order for her to achieve this status – that is, symbolic separation, alienation *from* the Symbolic – Antigone had to defeat 'all of that within us which is not being or ego [*moi*], but persists in wanting to be considered as the being of our ego'.[51] Antigone has therefore succeeded in defeating alienation, both sexual/linguistic alienation in the Symbolic, for which 'I is an Other' – the social unconscious which desires, speaks us and gives us a name – and imaginary alienation, for which the 'ego is an other', a false unity, an object that emerges through an alienated identification with the image of the other. It is also clear that for Artaud there are two kinds of being, a negative and a positive kind: the 'dull [*obtuses*] forces' – once again a reference to stupidity – of the alienating being, the being which 'is' in my place and through which I 'witness myself', are in fact opposed to the antagonism of a 'contrary force'.[52]

3. Artaud himself is attempting finally to defeat 'all other egos which are other than myself'.[53] He needs Antigone to help him in a 'last combat' through which he should be able to become his real name; but he also knows that this same victory would entail the 'burial of his brother the ego [*moi*]',[54] the death of his actual but never actualized 'self'; the 'true' self is itself a brother, a sibling or double, and it can emerge only as an (objectified) unachievable mirage of unity from an alienated standpoint. In other words, Artaud is well aware of the fact that Antigone's victory is cruelly 'terrible', as he says. On this point, Lacan teaches us that the separation of the object from

symbolic identity leads us to a 'loss of reality', in other words, 'subjective destitution'.

4. Artaud also tells us *how* Antigone achieved her terrible victory over the 'other egos': '*Separating* from her soul the force which pushed her to exist',[55] dissociating herself from the alienating force which nevertheless made her exist.[56] Social existence *qua* false being is alienated by definition; it is what Artaud defines elsewhere as '*êtreté*',[57] 'beingbeen', an objectified being, a state [*état*] which is *not*: 'I know that this world is not'.[58] Artaud specifies that Antigone separates herself from alienated existence by 'finding a contrary force', a force contrary to existence which allows her 'to recognize herself as being different from the being she was living and which lived her'.[59] Antigone's terrible victory implies that she dies symbolically *and* in reality: what survives is the name of an antagonistic force of pure negativity which we might well name 'death drive'.

We should also note how elsewhere in his works Artaud describes separation from the Symbolic in completely opposite terms: 'It is me [*moi*], told me my ego [*moi*] which listens to me. And I [*je*] have replied: all egos are at this point since for what concerns me I [*je*] don't listen to you';[60] 'victory' here is equivalent to the uprising of a wild plurality of egos against the domination of a single ego. However, I do not believe that we are facing a mere contradiction here; beyond the apparent irreconcilability of these two alternatives, we should in fact detect what Lacan himself describes as the two opposite but inextricable deadlocks of separation: tragedy and Buddhism.[61] The subject can be separated from the object in two different ways. More specifically, separation *qua* first stage of the traversal of the fundamental fantasy ($\$\diamond a$) should literally be considered as the detachment of the symbolic (barred) subject from the imaginary object of desire. The consequence of this is the emergence of the object (cause of desire) – *objet petit a* – in its real void, which can then lead to two complementarily opposite impasses; either the subject tragically identifies himself with his fundamental lack-of-being, his irreducible scission, precisely by overcoming all contingent alienations, thus losing the object, or the subject identifies himself with *objet petit a*, thus 'turn[ing himself] into a mummy';[62] this nirvanization is by no means ascetic, since it *perversely* takes the void of the object for the Real of the Thing: the radical alternative to tragedy is therefore psychotic perversion. . . . In Artaud's terms, all this means that one can either obtain a cruel I – that is, one's real name – without the other (all other egos are in fact defeated, and what was thought to be the 'true' ego is 'buried'), or a multiplicity of others, a proliferation of (other) egos without the I. Lacan suggests that psychoanalysis is able to overcome this impasse by resubjectivizing the object after its emergence as void, which in Lacanese means individualizing (the lack of) *jouissance* through the imposition of a new Master-Signifier.

In Seminar VII, Lacan's famous reading of Antigone fails to distinguish between tragedy and Buddhism as two distinct negative outcomes of separation. If, on the one hand, Antigone acts tragically by saying 'No!' to Creon, on the other, she also lives an extra-symbolic mummified life 'in between the two deaths'; Lacan reminds us that when she is 'placed alive in a tomb', she is in fact a 'still living corpse'.[63] Here we should note that according to Artaud, who continually invokes the image of the mummy, the latter is 'eternally between death and life, it is corpse and foetus':[64] Antigone – and those who behave like her – is therefore someone who prefers to 'die alive instead of living dead'[65] (that is, existing in a symbolically alienated state).

More importantly, I would argue that Seminar VII does *not* tell us that separation might lead to an impasse; it does not explain how psychoanalysis should overcome the double deadlock of tragedy and mummification, the pure negativity of a destructive – albeit necessary – moment. Antigone 'does not compromise her desire' to bury Polynices and, in so doing, achieves separation: for Lacan in 1959–60, this is the fundamental ethical law of psychoanalysis; what he does not emphasize sufficiently is the fact that Antigone does *not* return, that her act is self-destructive. . . . On the contrary, this fact should be stressed, given that, at least at this stage, Lacan seems to suggest tragedy as a (contradictory) model for the aim of psychoanalytic treatment.[66]

It is for this same reason that Antigone must not entirely be taken as a model: she cannot epitomize the analysand; the analysand must provisionally be hystericized, as Lacan will say in Seminar XVII, but he does not have to become a tragic figure. Ten years after his reading of *Antigone*, Lacan will refute the identification of psychoanalysis with tragedy; as Miller correctly notes: 'In *The Ethics of Psychoanalysis* Lacan had exalted transgression, whereas in *Seminar XVII* he makes fun of the transgressive hero'[67] since, as he himself claims, 'one transgresses nothing', transgression is a 'lubricious babble'. . . .[68] For Lacan it is certainly necessary to assume the Real (of the) lack and the inconsistency of the Other's 'dull forces'. However, separation must be only fleeting. We cannot dwell in the lack. In other words, Lacan is also asking us to *compromise* our desire precisely in order to keep on desiring – that is to say, to dwell in a properly functioning, albeit resymbolized, Symbolic; Lacan is asking us to compromise after not having compromised, to limit our non-compromised desire for the Void in order to impose a *new* way of desiring. . . .

More precisely, I am proposing to read the injunction 'do not compromise your desire!' in two mutually implied ways. Its first moment corresponds to Antigone's assumption of the lack, her distancing from the Symbolic; its second corresponds to carrying on desiring without falling into the void. If desire is the desire of the Other, desire of desire – and for Lacan, desire is the essence of man *qua parlêtre* – 'do not compromise your desire' can and must also mean 'keep on desiring!' . . . 'Do not compromise your desire' also means 'do not give up the Other!', do not give up the dimension of the sociolinguistic, symbolic Other which is made possible only by desiring. . . . 'Change it, but do not give it up!' . . . The desire of the Other, which we are *qua parlêtre*, also corresponds to the desire to remain within the Other. Active subjectivization is possible only in the intersubjective Symbolic after we have temporarily suspended it and 'reshaped' it through the imposition of a new Master-Signifier and the emergence of a new (partly subjectivized) *jouissance* connected to it. In other words, the political truly starts at the very point where the evil purity of an anarchic and destructive ethics – which nevertheless constitutes the precondition of the former – is compromised.

According to Seminar XI, this subjectivization can be achieved through psychoanalytic treatment, in what Lacan defines as the 'traversal of the fundamental fantasy'. Briefly, this means: (1) detaching *objet petit a* from the barred subject $; (2) achieving the void of separation (subjective destitution); (3) resubjectivizing that same void through sublimation. It will then take another six years for Lacan to elaborate this notion into a sketch of a psychoanalytic politics of anti-ideological *jouissance*. Ideology turns out to be nothing but the *jouissance* which fails to recognize the lack – *its* lack, the *jouis-sans* . . . – and, as a consequence, individually to subjectivize it; the control of *jouissance* is left to the Other. Such a politics is outlined in Seminar XVII with the elaboration of the four discourses, a significant political contribution which still awaits in-depth analysis. In this renewed theoretical context, the tragic figure of Antigone would stand for the embodiment of a radicalized, self-destructive hysteric (an impossibly mythical figure) who, having discovered that the Master/Other is barred, would decide to sacrifice herself in a gesture that reacts against its inconsistencies: as a consequence, she would not undermine the existing Other, but would ultimately sacrifice herself *for* its maintenance or, at best, for the *père-verse* mirage of another consistent Other; precisely by deciding to collapse into the void of the lack, Antigone refuses to accept it.

The results Lacan achieved in Seminar XVII are then further complicated by his reworking of the symptom in 1975–76: this seems to suggest that any possible subjectivization of *jouissance* has to undergo the radical destabilization of 'non-triggered' psychosis and the successive creation of a (partly) 'personalized' Symbolic – one's 'non-tragic' name – by means of one's writing, the marking of one's *jouissance* through the written letter. In other words, what I am also suggesting here is that Lacan's reading of Joyce, far from being a literary-clinical case study, represents his most mature formulation of a psychoanalytic ethics and politics.

3 'Suffer in order to affirm yourself!'

Unlike Antigone, Artaud *returns* after nine years of internment, and he returns with *his name*, which Antigone – according to both Lacan and Artaud himself – had acquired only at the price of disappearing for ever in perpetual subjective destitution. Artaud returns as 'Artaud-le-Mômo', that is to say, literally as a madman ['*mômo*'] who writes about his return, and is able to return only by writing about it – one of the chapters of the book *Artaud-le-Mômo* is indeed entitled 'Le retour d'Artaud-le-Mômo'; Artaud keeps on repeating that the old Artaud is dead. . . . His main theoretical achievement in the years of his return – his last – should be identified with the elaboration of a cosmological ontology of suffering: 'real' being amounts to an authentic '*douleur*' which has been stolen by God. In parallel, this same *douleur* corresponds to an Other, absolute *jouissance* which must be opposed to phallic *jouissance* – which Artaud simply calls '*jouissance*'.

In 1946, shortly after his release, Artaud affirms: 'I *am* there [*là*],/ there means pain.'[69] I am there where I suffer. Being is suffering: in order to be, one has 'to suffer being, all of being'. Suffering, the immediacy of pain, which leaves the false dichotomy between the corporeal and the mental aside, becomes the sole and most immediate proof of my being-real. It is in this sense that pain overlaps with the 'purest reality', as Artaud had called it in *The Nerve Meter*: 'This *douleur* driven into me like a wedge at the centre of my purest reality, at that region of sensibility where the two worlds of body and mind come together.'[70] The immanence of suffering entirely characterizes real being, without any risk of transcendent doubling. Suffering is one.

Pain not only overcomes the division between body and mind, cancelling the specific subjectivity which prospers in the hiatus that separates them, but also suspends any possible transcendence as well as any transcendental. Thus an ahistoric history of pain exists, a continuity without place which is to be opposed to God's/the Other's organically sexuated history: 'Yes, there is a certain history of suffering of which my life is part, whereas it was never able to be part of ordinary life, which has never done anything but run away (putting oneself in a state of detachment [*recul*], calculated, curled up, methodical and premeditated) from suffering.'[71] Life based on eudaimonistic criteria *is not*. Pain should be lived, and in living it, in being, no possibility of calculation would be left for us. Suffering *qua* anti-representation cannot be thought, it can only be lived. Thus Artaud writes: 'The question is to locate oneself in the beyond of [negative] being and of its *reflective* notion of consciousness./ . . . It is the only way of being there ['*être là*', again],/ hitting, suffering, tearing oneself to pieces, not thinking,/ *dis-imagining images*!.'[72] In order to put an end to what he repeatedly calls the 'scandal' of a life which witnesses itself, we should immerse ourselves in *douleur*. In parallel, suffering also functions as a detector of what is not but seems to be (false being). 'Being burnt,/ torn to pieces,/ quartered/ are facts which correspond not to a state [*état*] but to being [*être*].'[73]

Outside of *douleur*, there seems to be nothing:

> One does not do anything, one does not say anything, but one suffers, one despairs at oneself and one fights. . . . – Shall we appreciate, judge, justify the fighting?/ No./ Shall we name it?/ Neither,/ naming the battle means killing nothingness, perhaps./ But above all it implies stopping life. . . ./ We shall never stop life./ But shall we come out to . . . the embankment of the after battle, in order to breathe the memories of the battle?/ Never./ The battle restarted deeper, then what? The perpetual stripping of the flesh? The indefinite scraping off of the wound? The infinite work of the fissure from whence the wound emerged?/ Maybe.[74]

Supposing one chooses *douleur*, what strategy should be adopted during and after the battle? Artaud replies abruptly: no judgement, no justification should be given, no critical operation should be carried out: these would all put us in what was defined as 'detachment' from *douleur*. One must always remain in the immanence of the battle; this is why even one denomination alone would be enough to stop life. This would already be a dangerous retreat – not by chance; it is precisely on the name and judgement of God that, in the same years, Artaud concentrates his attack, his faecal (materially anti-transcendent) discharge: 'I shit on the Christian name'.[75] The act of naming which initiates the intersubjective dimension and the subsequent operation of writing is not just unable to reveal *douleur*–life but also blocks it, annihilates it. Here Artaud is implicitly recalling the fundamental contradiction of his own bio-graphy: in fact this determines him both with the *douleur* that he continually claims to suffer (the 'bio' component) and with his role as a writer who is constantly tempted to symbolize this *douleur* (the 'graphic' component). This oscillation generates a complex operation of writing:

'Authenticity/ of pain/ which is me',[76] Artaud paradoxically *writes*. Endless paradox of a writing which 'kills the [symbolic] nothingness' of suffering by naming it, nailing it to the black and white of the written page and, at the same time, through the same process, 'stops [real] life' *qua* suffering.

It is now important to emphasize how, according to Artaud, avoiding the encounter with pain can only imply a provisional postponement. Pain soon comes back by another route, that of the Other. If one does not choose pain, one then suffers it through God and His '*suppôts*' (henchmen). Artaud's choice of *douleur* is therefore not part of a deliberately masochist programme. 'I chose the dominion [*domaine*] of *douleur*':[77] this affirmation, which has both ethical and ontological implications, does not merely mean that 'I chose the *territory* of *douleur*'. Dominion also implies a certain control. Only by choosing *douleur* can one control it, without suffering it passively. Thus there are two kinds of *douleur*: the first is the one which is 'up to us' – in other words, it corresponds to our share of existential suffering, which, given its immediate immanence, is equivalent to our personal share of being. If we choose *douleur*, we are as much as we suffer. On the contrary, if we try to avoid it, *douleur* returns in a different, *père-verse* form (in a strictly Lacanian sense): the self-redoubling which is one with what Artaud calls 'the detached state' with respect to *douleur* creates a transcendence, an empty space in which God easily manages to insinuate Himself – for Artaud, the organic body is indeed a body divided by God *qua* 'sinker of wells'.[78] In this case, we are passively subjected to a *douleur* which is not up to us; we suffer *for* God / the Other. A nothingness that 'did not want to suffer being'[79] now wants to be and will 'be' as long as someone continues to suffer for it. In this case, we are *not* as much as we suffer, since the share of being proportionate to our suffering is expropriated by God. In *Suppôts et Supplications*, Artaud specifically notes that when God – defined as a 'sorcerer' – deprives us of the share of being which is consubstantial with our suffering, we lose the '*benefit* of *douleur*'.[80] In other words, once suffering perversely becomes suffering *for* God, the '*bene*fit' – which is literally 'what-makes-good' – turns into a spell, a curse, a '*malé*fice' – which, on the contrary, is 'what-makes-evil'. . . . This distinction should give us a plausible avenue into the contorted Artaudian obsession with 'spells' and 'collective black magic'.

Something else is certain for Artaud: the transcendent/organic man who refuses actively to choose pain has learnt how to take God as a model; he does not want to suffer being any longer – while continuing to suffer it for Him – and he is therefore tempted to make the other (man) suffer (for) it. Thus Artaud writes: 'There are millions [of people] . . . who take away . . . the spirit of other people's pain in order to achieve a consciousness, an I, a soul, a duration.'[81] By operating in milieus where pain is canalized and forced to circulate – hospitals, asylums, where 'death is cherished' – the doctor-psychiatrist represents, among organic-transcendent men, all of whom aggressively discharge their own suffering on to others, the apotheosis of sadism: 'Asylums' doctors are conscious and premeditated sadists.'[82] Everywhere in everyday social life one makes the other suffer in one's place, but it is only in an asylum that one can succeed in dis-charging the other completely, reaching the point at which the conformism of 'collective' or 'civic' black magic – that is, the intersubjective spell [*maléfice*] of expropriating pain – literally turns into *possession* of the other. Again, a libidinous element clearly emerges in this process: 'Modern medicine . . . makes its dead men undergo electroshock or insulinotherapy . . . every day it empties its heaps of men from their I,/ thus presenting them as empty . . . to obscene atomic and anatomic solicitings.'[83] As we have seen, psychiatrists are also, for Artaud, erotomaniacs *par excellence*. Erotomania *qua* phallic *j'ouïs-sens*, perverse suffering for the Other, and sadism all ultimately coincide. Because of this, the active acceptance of one's own suffering – that is, real *jouissance* – presupposes, in contrast to the passivity required by God, the interruption of the sadistic chain through one's disengagement from the phallic *j'ouïs-sens* of the Other: 'Suffer in order to affirm yourself,/ establish your own body all alone, without thinking of taking anything away from/ that of anyone else/ above all not through *jouissance*.'[84]

4 j'ouïs-sens, jouis-sans, jouis-sens

At this stage, a concise definition of Lacan's notion of *jouissance* is necessary. *Jouissance* is definitely not pleasure: on the contrary, it is precisely that which 'goes beyond' Freud's pleasure principle. The main characteristic of *jouissance* is suffering: however, we are dealing here with a kind of suffering which is not simply unpleasant, and consequently cannot merely be related to pleasure in an oppositional way. As a first approximation, we could define *jouissance* as 'pleasure in pain'. Against the usual objection: 'At the end of the day, we're not all depraved masochists, speak for yourself . . .', one should refer here to the undecidable nature of what Spinoza beautifully named, in Latin, *titillatio*, tickling. Who does not like being tickled? Does being ticklish correspond to a supreme form of pleasure, or does it coincide instead with radical suffering? We all know that when we are adequately tickled, we literally risk 'dying of laughter'. . . .

Contrary to Miller's claim according to which Seminar VII is problematic in so far as it introduces a 'profound disjunction between the signifier and *jouissance*',[85] I believe that, in this seminar, Lacan analyses both the allegedly 'massive' *jouissance* of mythical transgression *and* the 'brief satisfaction'[86] of the *jouissance* which is structurally inherent in the superegoic component of any symbolic/signifying order. Furthermore, these two 'degrees' of *jouissance* are intimately related, since the *jouissance* of transgression should itself be conceived, first and foremost, as the *jouissance of* the (Sado-Kantian) universalized Law. Here we approach what is possibly the main ambiguity of Seminar VII: Lacan definitely thinks that the Pauline dialectics between the Law and desire – supplemented by inherent phantasmatic transgression/ *jouissance* – can be overcome by a radical transgression *of* the (Sado-Kantian) superegoic Law itself; at the same time, however, he also seems to imply that we can reach beyond such a dialectics by means of a transgression which *opposes itself* to the superegoic Law. In particular, the ethics of psychoanalysis does not 'leave us clinging to that dialectic [of Law and desire]'; it is concerned with a (pure) desire which, beyond morality, 'transgresses interdiction' and 'rediscovers the relationship to *das Ding* somewhere beyond the law':[87] the 'true duty' of psychoanalytic transgression is in fact 'to go against the command' of the 'obscene and ferocious figure' of the superego.[88]

Now, the big question is: how does the Antigonian 'transgressive' ethics of pure desire advocated by Lacanian psychoanalysis in Seminar VII differ concretely from the superegoic transgression of Sado-Kantian *jouissance*? Is such a distinction adequately defended, or do Lacan's arguments, rather, risk confusing these two kinds of transgression? In my opinion, Seminar VII ultimately fails to elucidate the way in which the Lacanian ethics of 'pure' desire is separated from the Sado-Kantian anti-ethics of (mythical) 'massive' *jouissance*. More specifically, I believe that the unclear status of *jouissance* in Seminar VII – bluntly, 'Does Antigone "enjoy herself" through pure desire?', 'Can *jouissance* be good?' – is the consequence of Lacan's mistaken assumption of the existence of a 'primordial Real' *qua* 'totality'[89] which, despite being relegated to a mythical pre- or post-symbolic domain, necessarily entails the postulation of a correlative 'massive' *jouissance*. In other words, at this stage Lacan has not yet completely overcome the (Sadeian; Artaudian) idea that Nature is One (differential, 'fermenting') being that enjoys *per se*: this notion structurally contradicts all theoretical (and clinical) elaborations which presuppose the a priori of the barring of the Other and the logically concomitant reduction of Nature to the Not-One of the undead.

Not without oscillations, in his late work Lacan progressively acknowledges that 'inherent' *jouissance* is, in a radical sense, the only possible *jouissance*; we may well theorize the mythical horizon of an extra-symbolic condition, yet, at the same time, this very theorization is itself logically inconsistent with that of any increase in *jouissance*. In this final section it is therefore my intention to explain the different ways in which inherent *jouissance* functions, as well as to propose some preliminary remarks on the intricate issue of the individual subjectivation of *jouissance*: how should the subject resist the imposition of the superegoic – and always potentially criminal – imperative of the law? With this aim in mind, I shall now enunciate a series of fundamental theses regarding *jouissance*, adopting the privileged standpoint of Seminar XXIII (1975–76): in my opinion, it is in this work that Lacan finally assumes the full consequences of the fact that there is no Other of the Other.

1. We need to remember that the dictum 'there is no Other of the symbolic Other' means primarily that – in so far as the symbolic Other is not legitimized by any Other external guarantor (that is, the universalized Law of the Name-of-the-Father), in so far as the Symbolic is non-All – real otherness with respect to the Symbolic is no longer possible. In other words, in opposition to Seminar VII, finally for Lacan there is no 'primordial One' which was originally 'killed' by the Symbolic; there is no 'pure' primordial Real (no 'real Real') beyond the dimension of the Real-in-the-Symbolic, that is, of the leftover of the Real which 'holes' the Symbolic (in conjunction with the Imaginary). To go further, I must emphasize how, for Lacan, the 'primordial One' – or 'real Real' – is not-One precisely in so far as, in Badiou's terms, it cannot be 'counted as One': it actually corresponds to a *zero*. In a key passage from Seminar XXIII, Lacan points out that 'the Real must be sought on the side of the absolute zero', since 'the fire that burns [the mirage of 'massive' *jouissance*] is just a mask of the Real.'[90] We can think this 0 only retroactively from the standpoint of the 'fake' symbolic/imaginary One (what Lacan calls a '*semblant*'): even better, we can retrospectively think this 0 *as if* it were a One – *the* One *par excellence* – only from the standpoint of the 'fake' One. To put it differently: 0 is *nothing per se*, but it *is* something from the determinate perspective of the 'fake' One; the Thing-in-itself is *in-itself* nothing (as Lacan says, it is *l'achose*).[91] In other words, the 0 equates with the always-already lost mythical *jouissance* of the real Real: the 'fake' One needs the 'fake' *jouissance* of *objet petit a* in order to 'make One' – to cork the hole in the symbolic structure – and thus retrospectively create the *illusion* of an absolute *jouissance* which was originally lost.

2. *Jouissance* is 'pleasure *in* pain'. More specifically, this is *always* equivalent to the *jouissance* of *objet petit a*, which is a remainder of the Real which tears holes in the symbolic structure. *Objet petit a qua* real hole in the Other is both the hole *qua* presence of a surplus-leftover Real (*jouissance* of '*a*') *and*

that hole *qua* absence of the Whole Real (the primordial Real which was never there in the first place), that is, *qua* absence of *jouissance*. Of what does this presence of a real leftover actually consist? At its purest, the *jouissance* of '*a*' *qua* surplus-*jouissance* (the partial drive) can only mean enjoying the *lack* of enjoyment, since there is nothing else to enjoy. This explains why, in Seminar XVII (1969–70), Lacan can state: 'One can pretend [*faire semblant*] that there is surplus-*jouissance* [i.e. *jouissance* of *objet petit a*]; a lot of people are still seized by this idea.'[92] *Jouissance* is suffering, since it is *jouis-sans* – to use a neologism which, to the best of my knowledge, was not coined by Lacan. Enjoying the lack of enjoyment will therefore mean suffering/enjoying the lack of the Thing, the fact that the Thing is no-thing [*l'achose*].

3. One of the major tasks of psychoanalysis is to make the subject accept the real '*a*' *qua lack*. If *jouissance* is *jouis-sans*, enjoying 'more' or 'less' makes sense only from a perverse standpoint which takes the *presence* of *jouissance* for granted. There is only one fundamental difference at work here: one can either accept or fail to accept the lack that *jouis-sans* is. Even when the subject's fundamental fantasy (*qua* barrier) is undone once and for all, as happens in the case of psychosis, what is at stake is not an 'increase' of *jouissance* but an incapacity of the Symbolic to manage the potentially destructive lack of *jouissance* that *jouis-sans* is.[93] In other words, *jouissance* cannot be accumulated because it relies on lack; we cannot objectively accumulate lack, we can only say that $(-1) + (-1) = -2$ if we tacitly assume that -1 is something 'more' than sheer lack, if, from the very beginning, we deceitfully turn -1 into $+1$. . . . According to Lacan, the capitalist discourse epitomizes perversion precisely in so far as it pre-tends to enjoy real '*a*' (the lack) as accumulated *jouissance*.[94]

4. *Jouissance* is a *conditio sine qua non* of the inextricable relationship between the drive and desire. More precisely, the drive supplies a partial 'masochistic' satisfaction of unconscious desire precisely through the dissatisfaction of *jouis-sans*. As a consequence, *jouissance* is generally a necessary precondition of human beings *qua* desiring beings of language. Most importantly, *jouissance* (of *objet petit a*) is not only that which, so to speak, inevitably 'accompanies' the signifier yet remains detached from it: *jouissance* also emerges *in* the signifier itself. That is to say: the drive is not unspeakable, it 'utters itself' in language in the guise of *jouis-sens*. Enjoyment (or, better, its lack) is also enjoy-meant. *Jouis-sans* also indicates a linguistic lack of *sense*, an intrinsic limitation of symbolic knowledge as such – inasmuch as, by definition, symbolic knowledge is Not-All in the unconscious, it should also be regarded as a 'means of *jouissance*'. The reason for this dual nature of

jouis-sans is straightforward: the Symbolic (in its interplay with the Imaginary) that the Real of *objet petit a* tears holes in the structures of both the 'libidinal' realm of desire/sexuality and the 'epistemological' realm of knowledge. The basic Lacanian a priori for this parallelism can be found in the famous motto according to which 'the unconscious is structured like a language': desire and knowledge are the same unconscious linguistic structure, and both partake of *jouis-sans*. Putting together the 'libidinal' acceptation of *objet petit a* with its 'epistemological' counterpart, we may argue that the fact that there is no Other of the Other entails the 'nonsense' (or, the 'epistemological' side of *objet petit a*) of the lack of *jouissance*, the lack of relation between the sexes (that is, the 'libidinal' side of *objet petit a*).

5. In his last seminars – most noticeably in Seminar XXIII – Lacan avails himself of at least four different variants of the notion of *jouissance* which, in my opinion, should nevertheless all be linked, directly or indirectly, to *objet petit a*. The first variant concerns the phallic *jouissance* of *objet petit a* in the fundamental fantasy: Lacan uses the algebraic sign J to express it. In brief, this is the *jouissance* that allows the subject to 'make One' *qua* individuated *parlêtre*, the non-eliminable real supplement of phantasmatic symbolic identification. It is only on the basis of a *j'ouïs-sens* that the barred subject is able to 'hear' [*ouïr*] the sense of the symbolic order: we could render *j'ouïs-sens* as 'I enjoy, therefore I can make sense'.

The second variant relates to the *jouissance* of the Other under the hegemony of which we 'make One' and 'make sense'; this is therefore nothing but the ideological *j'ouïs-sens* which 'corks' the holed symbolic structure itself. As Lacan observes as early as Seminar X, '*j'ouïs*' is nothing but the answer the subject gives to the superegoic commandment '*Jouis!*' ('Enjoy!').[95] It is easy to see that the *jouissance* of the Other is actually equivalent to phallic *jouissance*: the *jouissance* of the Other corresponds to ideological phallic *jouissance* considered, as it were, from the standpoint of structure, not from that of the (alienated) subject who is interpellated by a given ideology.

The third variant refers to what Lacan names Other-*jouissance*, which he denotes with the algebraic sign JA; in the early 1970s, Other-*jouissance* is famously associated with feminine *jouissance*. Other-*jouissance* should definitely *not* be confused with the *jouissance* of the Other. Should we, then, regard it as extra-symbolic? If, on the one hand, it is true that, in Seminar XX, Other-*jouissance* seems to indicate the pure *jouissance* of the Real beyond any symbolic contamination (indeed, it is located 'beyond the phallus'),[96] on the other, it should be evident by now that such a definition of Other-*jouissance* is highly problematic for any serious attempt to develop a consistent theory out of Lacan's anti-structuralist move. The first versions of the so-called Borromean knot – a topological figure which Lacan uses to represent the interdependency of the orders of the Real, the Symbolic and the Imaginary – show us precisely where the difficulty, if not the contradiction, lies: JA (Other – feminine – *jouissance*) lies outside the ring of the Symbolic, but it is *not* outside all the rings! In other words, without the ring of the Symbolic it would not be possible to have the Borromean knot (*qua* topographical representation of the subject-*parlêtre*) and, consequently, not even JA. . . . The important point to grasp here is that feminine *jouissance* remains *indirectly related* to the Symbolic: the feminine Not-All is ultimately *both* different from *and* dependent on the phallic Symbolic, precisely in so far as it stands as the Not-All *of* the Symbolic, its constitutive point of exception. . . . Consequently, JA cannot stand for the *jouissance* of the 'real Real', in other words, there is *no* Other-*jouissance* given that there is no Other of the Other.

Lacan seems to become aware of this deadlock in Seminar XXIII, in which in fact JA barred – a fourth variant of *jouissance* – takes the place of JA in the Borromean knot.[97] In one of the most important lessons of that year, Lacan says: 'JA barred concerns *jouissance*, but not Other-*jouissance* . . . there is no Other-*jouissance* inasmuch as there is no Other of the Other.'[98] The passage from the notion of Other-*jouissance* (JA) to that of the *jouissance* of the barred Other (JA barred) epitomizes the fundamental distance that separates the image of Saint Theresa's holy ecstasy – as referred to by Lacan in Seminar XX – from the 'naming' of lack carried out by Joyce-*le-saint-homme* – as analysed in detail in Seminar XXIII. In this seminar, JA (of Woman; of God) becomes impossible: however, feminine *jouissance* could be redefined in terms of JA barred.[99] JA barred is therefore a (form of) *jouissance* of the *impossibility of JA*. Most importantly, I must emphasize that the *jouissance* of the barred Other *differs from phallic jouissance without being 'beyond' the phallus.*

The elaboration of the notion of JA barred also has a significant repercussion for Lacan's late key motto according to which '*Y a d' l'Un*' ('There's such a thing as One').[100] In Seminar XX, Lacan seems to identify this One with JA, with the idea of a pure Real conceived of in the guise of 'pure difference', a 'fermenting' Nature; although in Seminar XXIII he declares that JA is meant to designate the fact that there is a Universe, he nevertheless specifies that it is quite improbable that the Universe is, as such, a Uni-verse, that the Universe is a One (of pure, Other-*jouissance*).[101] That is to say: a pure, mythical Real – the undead – must be presupposed retroactively, but it cannot be counted as (a self-enjoying, divine) One, not even as the supposedly 'weaker' One of 'pure difference'.

At this stage, we should ask the following crucial question: how does the *jouissance* of the impossibility of Other-*jouissance*, the *jouissance* of the barred Other, distinguish itself from 'standard' phallic *jouissance*? After all, the latter is also, in its own way, a form of barred *jouissance*, of *jouis-sans*. . . . Lacan's straightforward answer is: phallic *jouissance* '*makes One*', whereas JA barred '*makes the individual*'. If phallic *jouissance* (of *objet petit a*) makes the symbolic One, increasingly pre-tending to obliterate the lack, on the other hand, JA barred (which also enjoys *objet petit a*) makes the individual who, as it were, develops 'his own' Symbolic *from* that lack. Joyce is 'the individual' for Lacan in so far as he succeeds in subjectivizing himself by (partially) individualizing *objet petit a*, the lack in the Symbolic;[102] the individual is not the ideological One but stands for another modality of the One, another (non-psychotic) way of inhabiting the Symbolic, 'starting' from its real lack.

Here I should emphasize particularly the way in which Lacan closely associates the emergence of JA barred – which he also, more famously, calls the *sinthome* – with the issue of the *naming* of the Real and the 'marking' of *jouissance*, with the long-deferred question concerning the way in which the subject should bring about a reinscription in and resymbolization of the Symbolic after he has temporarily assumed the real lack in the Other.[103] For Lacan, Joyce is indeed '*Joyce*-le-sinthome'.[104] If, on the one hand, it is true that Joyce 'abolishes the symbol',[105] on the other, it is equally the case that the 'identification with the *sinthome*' (*qua* naming of one's Real) advocated in Lacan's last works as the aim of psychoanalysis could never amount to a permanent subjective destitution, a psychotic non-functioning of the Symbolic. In opposition to such a mistaken conclusion, I should stress that:

(a) Joyce is – to adopt a formula proposed by Darian Leader – a 'non-triggered' psychotic. He is initially 'in between' neurosis and psychosis, and subsequently manages to produce a (partially) individualized Symbolic;
(b) neurotics can eventually turn their ideological symptom – the *jouissance* imposed by hegemonic fundamental fantasies – into a non-psychotic *sinthome* when they undergo the traversal of the fantasy, the moment of separation from the Symbolic and the subsequent process of symbolic reinscription through a new, individualized Master-Signifier. This also means that, despite not being a psychotic, Joyce does not initially need to traverse any fundamental fantasy. Unlike neurotics, he is *already* separated from the Symbolic; instead, he needs to 'create' his founding Master-Signifier. As Miller puts it: '[Joyce's] authentic Name-of-the-Father is his

> name as a writer . . . his literary production allows him to relocate himself within the meaning he lacked.'[106]

To conclude, I would like to comment on a thought-provoking question concerning the *sinthome* formulated recently by Hoens and Pluth: 'From what point of view can the Name of the Father be seen as identical to the *sinthome*?'.[107] The authors deliberately leave their question open, in order to indicate that we are confronted with what remains unconcluded in Lacan's work, and to urge new reinventions of his own reinvention of Freudian psychoanalysis.

Here we should remark that by the early 1960s, *le Nom-du-Père* ceases to be exclusively a prohibitive *Non!-du-Père*; in fact, in the standard situation of neurosis, it also allows the regulation through the symptom of an otherwise destructive *jouissance* – that is to say, its 'No!' lets us (ideologically pre-tend to) enjoy (the lack which holes the Symbolic). What Lacan seems further to suggest with his later work on Joyce is that, in the case of 'non-triggered' psychosis, this same regulation, which allows the subject to inhabit the social space, can eventually be carried out by the *sinthome* itself. In other words, the relativization of the Name-of-the-Father which follows the barring of the Other – that is, the emergence of a structural lack – ultimately entails two complementary consequences where the symptom is concerned: on the one hand, the Name-of-the-Father, in so far as it occupies a place which actually lies outside its competence – since the lack 'belongs' to the domain of the Real – can itself be considered as a symptom (hence in Seminar XXIII, Lacan states: 'The Oedipus complex, as such, is a symptom');[108] on the other hand, 'everything else that manages to orient and localize *jouissance*, i.e. symptoms themselves'[109] can carry out the containment action which is usually accomplished by the 'standard' Name-of-the-Father if the latter does not function properly. Joyce's paternal metaphor was defective: it had to be supplemented by the writer. Thus, the name 'Joyce' literally embodies a subjective placeholder for the lack in the Other, and it does so by means of a particular way of writing. The name 'Joyce' is a 'singular universal': Joyce reaches a substitutive version of the Name-of-the-Father – thus individualized/individuated and anti-ideological by definition – precisely by writing his *jouis-sens*.[110]

A similar process operates in Artaud's late work. He is the one who endlessly deplores any kind of writing as 'garbage'[111] and who, precisely in order successfully to carry out this condemnation, feels constrained to struggle continuously between his awareness of the uselessness of writing and the will to write about it. Artaud writes *against writing*; he keeps on repeating: 'Don't write! Writing goes against being, which is the immanent suffering of one's own *douleur* . . .'. He realizes, however, that this paradoxical writing is in the end the only means through which one can individuate one's own suffering against a perverse suffering for God, and also against the utter separation of psychosis (which, ultimately, does not allow any individuation).[112] How, more precisely, does this transvaluation of writing – from representing the epitome of God's apparatuses of expropriation to standing for a unique means of individuation of suffering – occur?

- Writing is at first diametrically opposed to being *qua* authentic, immanent *douleur.*
- Writing *against writing* coincides with *writing douleur*, given that *douleur* is by definition opposed to writing.
- Writing *douleur* (being) is *impossible*; it is impossible to write about what, by definition, cannot be written.
- Writing *douleur* may therefore be equated with writing the *impossibility* of writing *douleur* (being).
- *This same impossibility* autonomously *generates douleur*. . . . This is where writing is transvaluated; at first, it was by definition opposed to *douleur*/being/life, then it generates *douleur*/being/life.

Artaud thus writes the *douleur* of writing *douleur*, which means that he both *writes* the suffering of writing and lives the individuated *suffering* of writing suffering. Artaud writes because he suffers an expropriation of suffering/*jouissance*, and in this writing he perpetually reiterates this expropriation brought to the paroxystic point at which it becomes the individuated, truly subjectivized, writing of the painful incapacity of writing the suffering of expropriation. 'One can invent one's own language and make pure language speak with an extra-grammatical meaning, but this meaning must be valid *per se*, it must come out of horror . . . the uterine being of suffering.'[113]

On this key issue, there is a clear shift from the early to the late work of Artaud; his internment should be considered as a dividing line. Artaud's late work underlines the *writing* in the writing against writing, since it generates authentic *douleur*/being, it generates '*contra* writing' (by way of its impossibility of expression): in this way, he does not confine himself to an utterly sterile condemnation of writing. What sort of writing is this truly individuated writing of authentic *douleur*/*jouissance*? 'One has to defeat the French language without departing from it':[114] the shift between early and late Artaud is perfectly summarized here; one must not search for a real language 'before' the words, which can lead only to the being-spoken of psychosis; instead, one should write in a language 'in between' the words, a *jouis-sens.*

Finally, it should be noted that Artaud performs this playing with language, which takes place in opposition to but nevertheless *within* its ex-propriating functions, primarily on his own name. As Dumoulié has correctly pointed out, Artaud's 'first gesture of *désaliénation* was a reinvestment of the proper name.'[115] While at the time of his Irish breakdown and the first years of his internment Artaud refused his name and preferred a collapse into anonymity,[116] regressively adopting his childhood nickname (Neneka) or his mother's name, he then 'returns' as 'Artaud-le-Mômo' by continuously reshaping his 'real name'; as he himself claims, he is 'a.r.t.o.',[117] he embodies his real letters, as Joyce is for Lacan the individual, '*l.o.m.* . . . a structure which is that of the *homo*'.[118]

Notes

1. Jacques Lacan, 'La psychanalyse. Raison d'un échec', in *Autres écrits* (Paris: Seuil, 2001), p. 349.
2. Alain and Odette Virmaux, *Antonin Artaud – Qui êtes-vous?* (Lyon: La Manufacture, 1996), p. 60.
3. Antonin Artaud, *Selected Writings* (Berkeley: University of California Press, 1988), p. 484. On the identification of Lacan with 'Dr L.', see G. Scarpetta, 'Artaud écrit ou la canne de saint Patrick', *Tel Quel* 81, 1979, p. 67.
4. Antonin Artaud, *Œuvres complètes* (XII), p. 211. Unless otherwise specified, quotations are taken from *Œuvres complètes* (Paris: Gallimard, 1956–1994), vols I–XXVI.
5. I have further elaborated these topics in the first two chapters of Lorenzo Chiesa, *Antonin Artaud. Verso un corpo senza organi* (Verona: Ombre Corte, 2001).
6. *Œuvres complètes* (XII), p. 214.
7. *Selected Writings*, p. 91.
8. A condition with which Artaud himself might even have been diagnosed, and which we know Lacan diagnosed Aimée with in his doctoral thesis (see Jacques Lacan, *De la psychose paranoïaque dans ses rapports avec la personnalité* [Paris: Seuil, 1975], pp. 262–3).
9. *Œuvres complètes* (XII), p. 229.
10. *Selected Writings*, p. 540. '*Artaud wanted to erase repetition in general*' (Jacques Derrida, 'The Theatre of Cruelty and the Closure of Representation', in *Writing and Difference* [London: Routledge, 1978], p. 245).
11. Jacques Lacan, *Le séminaire livre X. L'angoisse, 1962–1963* (Paris: Seuil, 2004), p. 96.
12. *Selected Writings*, pp. 569–70 (my trans.).
13. *Œuvres complètes* (I), pp. 57, 98, 103.
14. 'The impossibility of thinking which is thought' (Maurice Blanchot, 'Artaud', in *The Blanchot Reader*, ed. M. Holland [Oxford: Blackwell, 1995], p. 131).
15. See *Selected Writings*, p. 84 (my trans.).
16. *Œuvres complètes* (XII), p. 144.
17. Indeed, happiness amounts to the stupidity of 'not wanting to know' the truth about symbolic castration, the inconsistency of the Other, and the actual lack of *jouissance*. As Lacan states in Seminar XVII: 'There is no happiness besides that of the phallus', that is, of the Other. As a consequence, he notes that: (1) happiness becomes a 'political factor';

(2) 'sadly', happiness can mean only that 'everybody is identical to everyone else'; (3) 'it is only the phallus which is happy and not its bearer' (Jacques Lacan, *Le séminaire livre XVII* [Paris: Seuil, 1991], pp. 83–4).

18. Indeed, happiness amounts to the stupidity of 'not wanting to know' the truth about symbolic castration, the inconsistency of the Other, and the actual lack of *jouissance.* As Lacan states in Seminar XVII: 'There is no happiness besides that of the phallus', that is, of the Other. As a consequence, he notes that: (1) happiness becomes a 'political factor'; (2) 'sadly', happiness can mean only that 'everybody is identical to everyone else'; (3) 'it is only the phallus which is happy and not its bearer' (Jacques Lacan, *Le séminaire livre XVII* [Paris: Seuil, 1991], p. 150, 56).

19. *Selected Writings*, p. 135.

20. *Œuvres complètes* (VII), p. 276.

21. Lacan, *Le séminaire livre XVII*, p. 86.

22. Here, Artaud's ironic reversal of the term 'erotomania' finds all its subversive value! . . .

23. *Selected Writings*, pp. 130–31 (my trans.).

24. *Selected Writings*, p. 132.

25. *Œuvres complètes* (XV), p. 164.

26. *Œuvres complètes* (VII), p. 105.

27. However, the notion of an androgynous One differs profoundly from the Unity of pure difference given by the body without organs. For Artaud, the 'first androgyne./ is HIM, the man./ AND *HIM, the woman./* At the same time./ Reunited in ONE' (*Œuvres complètes* [VII], p. 103). It seems to me difficult, therefore, to endorse Deleuze and Guattari's fleeting remark to the effect that here, beyond Hegel, 'multiplicity surpasses all opposition and does away with dialectical movement' (*A Thousand Plateaus: Capitalism and Schizophrenia* [London: The Athlone Press, 1988], p. 532). The only plausible way to rectify an otherwise unsurpassable divergence between two opposite notions of the One is to associate them with two distinct periods of Artaud's production. The (dialectical) androgynous One finds its apex in *Heliogabalus* (1934) and in *The New Revelations of Being* (1937), that is, before Artaud's internment. The One of the pure difference of the body without organs emerges only after Artaud's release from Rodez asylum in 1946.

28. *Selected Writings*, p. 485. See also *Œuvres complètes* (XII), p. 60.

29. In an early letter, Artaud had already pointed out how 'all individual acts are antisocial. Madmen are individual victims *par excellence* of social dictatorship' (*Œuvres complètes* [I], p. 267).

30. Lacan, *Le séminaire livre XVII*, p. 118.

31. Antonin Artaud, *Nouveaux écrits de Rodez*, (Paris: Gallimard, 1977), p. 28

32. *Œuvres complètes* (VII), p. 158.

33. Artaud speaks of the 'microbes of the void' implied in organic sexuality (*Œuvres complètes* [XII], p. 211).

34. *Selected Writings*, p. 485.

35. *Œuvres complètes* (XII), p. 153.

36. *Œuvres complètes* (XII), p. 486.

37. *Œuvres complètes* (XII), p. 484.

38. See *Œuvres complètes* (XII), p. 485.

39. *Œuvres complètes* (XII), p. 199.

40. *Œuvres complètes* (XXI), p. 85.

41. Jacques Lacan, 'Le séminaire livre XXIII', session of 16 March 1976 (unpublished).

42. *Nouveaux écrits de Rodez*, p. 153.
43. *Œuvres complètes* (XIV), p. 139.
44. *Œuvres complètes* (XIV), p. 149.
45. *Œuvres complètes* (XIV), p. 84.
46. There is a 'real Antigone', as Artaud specifies (*Nouveaux écrits de Rodez*, p. 153).
47. *Nouveaux écrits de Rodez*, p. 154. This notion of infinity should be related to the repetitive 'bad' infinity of the phallus in a Lacanian sense . . . Artaud often describes *filles-à-venir* as women raped by 'assassin phalluses' and 'testicles of hatred' (see *Œuvres complètes* [XIV], pp. 19–20).
48. *Nouveaux écrits de Rodez*, p. 154.
49. *Nouveaux écrits de Rodez*, p. 153.
50. *Nouveaux écrits de Rodez*, p. 154.
51. *Nouveaux écrits de Rodez*, p. 154.
52. *Nouveaux écrits de Rodez*, p. 154.
53. *Nouveaux écrits de Rodez*, p. 153.
54. *Nouveaux écrits de Rodez*, pp. 153–4.
55. *Nouveaux écrits de Rodez*, p. 154.
56. For Lacan, the ego *qua* imaginary misidentification is indeed a '*vital* dehiscence' (see *Écrits: A Selection* [London: Tavistock, 1977], p. 21).
57. *Œuvres complètes* (XI), p. 199.
58. *Selected Writings*, p. 413 (my trans.).
59. *Nouveaux écrits de Rodez*, p. 154.
60. *Œuvres complètes* (XIV), p. 20.
61. See Lacan, *Écrits: A Selection*, p. 324.
62. See Lacan, *Écrits: A Selection* p. 324.
63. Jacques Lacan, *The Seminar. Book VII* (New York and London: Routledge, 1992), p. 268.
64. Camille Dumoulié, *Antonin Artaud* (Paris: Seuil, 1996), p. 25.
65. *Selected Writings*, p. 559.
66. See Lacan, *The Seminar. Book VII*, pp. 303, 243, 313.
67. Jacques-Alain Miller, 'La psicoanalisi messa a nudo dal suo celibe', afterword to Jacques Lacan, *Il seminario: Libro XVII* (Turin: Einaudi, 2001), p. 277.
68. Lacan, *Le séminaire livre XVII*, pp. 14, 21.
69. *Œuvres complètes* (XXII), p. 153.
70. *Selected Writings*, p. 91.
71. *Œuvres complètes* (XII), p. 203.
72. *Œuvres complètes* (XXII), p. 19.
73. *Œuvres complètes* (XXII), p. 60.
74. *Œuvres complètes* (XII), p. 236.
75. *Œuvres complètes* (I), p. 13.
76. *Œuvres complètes* (XXII), p. 136.
77. *Selected Writings*, p. 96 (my trans.).
78. *Œuvres complètes* (XII), p. 41.
79. *Selected Writings*, p. 442.
80. *Œuvres complètes* (XIV), p. 99.
81. *Œuvres complètes* (XIV), p. 108.
82. *Œuvres complètes* (XII), p. 216.
83. *Œuvres complètes* (XII), p. 217.

84. *Œuvres complètes* (XXII), p. 138.
85. Jacques-Alain Miller, *I paradigmi del godimento* (Rome: Astrolabio, 2001), p. 18.
86. Lacan, *The Seminar. Book VII*, p. 87.
87. *The Seminar. Book VII*, p. 84.
88. *The Seminar. Book VII*, p. 7.
89. *The Seminar. Book VII*, p. 118.
90. Lacan, 'Le séminaire livre XXIII', session of 16 March 1976.
91. Lacan, *Le séminaire livre XVII*, p. 187. Here Lacan identifies '*l'achose*' with what he calls '*l'insubstance*', and says that these two notions 'completely change the meaning of our materialism'.
92. Lacan, *Le séminaire livre XVII*, p. 93.
93. The psychotic does *not* enjoy 'more' than non-psychotic subjects, rather, he overtly knows that he is *enjoyed* in/by the Other's fantasy. . . .
94. See Lacan, *Le séminaire livre XVII*, pp. 92–5.
95. Lacan, *Le séminaire livre X*, p. 96.
96. Jacques Lacan, *The Seminar. Book XX* (New York and London: Norton, 1999), p. 74.
97. See Lacan, 'Le séminaire livre XXIII', session of 16 December 1975.
98. 'Le séminaire livre XXIII', session of 16 December 1975.
99. In this way, it would be easy to think of *Joy*-cean *jouissance* as a thorough re-elaboration of the *jouissance* of the mystic which Seminar XX had already paired up with feminine *jouissance*. It then also becomes clear why Lacan's recurrent parallelism between Joyce and a saint is far from gratuitous: 'Joyce-the-sinthome is homophonous with sanctity' (Jacques Lacan, 'Joyce le symptôme', in J. Aubert [ed.], *Joyce avec Lacan* [Paris: Navarin, 1987], p. 12).
100. See Lacan, *The Seminar. Book XX*, p. 5.
101. Lacan, 'Le séminaire livre XXIII', session of 13 January 1976. 'I would say that nature presents itself as not being one' (session of 18 November 1975).
102. 'Joyce identifies himself with the *individual*' (Lacan, 'Joyce le symptôme', p. 18).
103. As for the strict relation between the *sinthome* and a particular form of *jouissance*, Lacan writes: 'Joyce is in relation to *joy*, that is, *jouissance*, written in the *llanguage* that is English; this en-joycing, this *jouissance* is the only thing one can get from the text. This is the symptom' ('Joyce le symptôme', p. 17).
104. Lacan, 'Joyce le symptôme'.
105. Lacan, ('Joyce le symptôme', p. 15).
106. Jacques-Alain Miller, 'Lacan con Joyce: Seminario di Barcellona II', *La Psicoanalisi* 23, 1998, p. 40.
107. Dominick Hoens and Ed Pluth, 'The *sinthome*: A New Way of Writing an Old Problem', in L. Thurston (ed.), *Essays on the Final Lacan* (New York: Other Press, 2002), pp. 1–18.
108. Lacan, 'Le seminaire livre XXIII', session of 18 November 1975.
109. Antonio Di Ciaccia and Massimo Recalcati, *Jacques Lacan*, (Milan: Bruno Mondadori, 2000), p. 108.
110. The *sinthome* could thus also be defined as 'positive' *jouis-sens* and opposed to 'negative', ideological *jouis-sens*. The latter should be recuperation on two different levels: (a) a general level for which all (phallic) knowledge is tacitly a 'means of *jouissance*'; (b) particular instances in which the ideological conjunction between hegemonic signifiers and *jouissance* explicitly emerges in *jouis-sens*. In these cases, we are confronted with an idiotic, conformist language which sides with a necessarily idiotic Other. In other words,

although it openly discloses the lack in the hegemonic Other, negative *jouis-sens* does not work subversively in order to denounce it; on the contrary, it fully participates in the Other's ideological homogenization by providing it with a linguistic discharge for its structural and inadmissible *jouissance*. This is why we get so-called 'dirty words': blasphemy and insults might also belong to this category, or, to provide some more prosaic examples, expressions such as 'cool', 'you know', 'check it out', 'I was, like . . .'. It goes without saying that their common feature is compulsive repetition. . . .

111. See *Selected Writings*, p. 85.

112. Contradictorily enough, Artaud will nevertheless continue to call for an absolute communion with JA. . . .

113. *Selected Writings*, p. 449.

114. *Œuvres complètes* (XXII), p. 216.

115. *Antonin Artaud*, p. 108. Dumoulié reminds us that Artaud is also 'Saint Tarto': once again, the individuation of one's real name is associated with sanctity.

116. See *Œuvres complètes* (VII), p. 223, 226, 230.

117. *Œuvres complètes* (XII), p. 53.

118. Lacan, 'Joyce le symptôme', p. 18.

16

Lacan and the Dialectic: A Fragment

Fredric Jameson

I would have liked, in what follows, to accomplish three or maybe even four things, in no special order. I want to try to read Lacan generically, that is, to look at the text of the Seminar as a special kind of genre, one which may or may not have its kinship with immense fragmentary unfinished books like Benjamin's *Arcades Project*, Gramsci's *Prison Notebooks*, Pascal's *Pensées*, and even Pound's *Cantos*. The generic focus means in particular that I will not be trying to reconstruct a system of thought, to be summarized in some more usable conceptual form. It is certainly with Lacan's thinking that we will be concerned here; but only in so far as that thinking is spoken or expressed. That is to say: the traditional relationship between language and thought is to be reversed here: not language as an instrument or a vehicle for conceptuality, but, rather, the way in which the conditions and form of representation (speaking and writing) determine the concepts themselves, and constitute at one and the same time their conditions of possibility and also their limits, inflecting their shape and development. I do not want to prejudge the results or forecast the success of the generic invention itself, except to say that it seems to me desirable to abandon (or, at least, to bracket) loaded terms like unfinished, fragmentary, interminable, and the like.

As if that is not enough, I would also like to use Lacan's work in a different way, as a test case in the construction of theory as such. This word, which came into its distinctive – shall we say post-contemporary – acceptation in the 1960s and the era of structuralism, designates something not only quite different from traditional philosophy, but also from that modern philosophy (Heidegger, say, or pragmatism, or Wittgenstein) that sought to break with traditional philosophizing. This is, no doubt, to degrade Lacan to the status of a mere example, but in a rather different way from that proposed by generic analysis. Here, the example is reconstructed for historical purposes, in order to illustrate the logic of a historical period, or at the very least a historical tendency. Nor is the procedure necessarily redeemed by the conviction that of all the writing called theoretical, Lacan's is the richest, and in many ways (ways that have not all been explored or documented) the source of much that went on around him intellectually and that was published then or has been since. Nor is the question of the structure and dynamics of that kind of writing called theory quite the same as the question of whether Lacan was or was not a structuralist (a question we will also have to deal with); finally, his relationship to the Freudian text (on which the Seminar purports to be one immense commentary) seems at first glance to offer peculiarities not met with in many other 'theoretical' texts (although Althusser's analogous relationship to Marx demands mention here).

A third area of interest seems even more eccentric to these first concerns, and even less relevant to the directions in which they might lead us. This is an interest in what, for want of a better word, I will call Lacan's literary criticism, an interest that can be thought tangential to the very degree to which we believe these moments of literary exegesis to be themselves tangential to Lacan's own work. For all of them are marked in one way or another as examples of the theory; and in all cases the turn to such texts can be documented as matters of sheer accident or the seemingly random association of ideas. The allegorical reading of 'The Purloined Letter' has long since been appreciated, owing in large part to the inaugural position Lacan insisted on for it in *Écrits*; but the even more stunning reading of Freud's own dream of Irma has not attracted much attention. Indeed, the central place of dream analysis in Freud ought to have positioned the issue of narrative interpretation in some space calculated to redeem so-called literary criticism from its marginality here. At the same time, the equally central readings of Hamlet and of Joyce raise another kind of question: the old one about Freudian 'literary criticism' and its traditional relationship to the Oedipus complex generally. The case of Antigone has raised much comment, both old and new, but not particularly of a literary kind. Finally, the most extraordinary of Lacan's commentaries, on Plato's *Symposium*, has scarcely been addressed at all. This body of exemplary interpretation, (in both senses) then, ought to be helpful in determining, on the one hand, whether this is just old-fashioned Freudian criticism, of a type that implies Lacan's own relegation to some old-fashioned doctrinal status, and on the other, whether the concept of allegory does not offer some more productive, and in general undervalued, instrument of analysis and notion of structure than the considerably overused concept of metaphoricity, whose popularity can in part be traced to Lacan himself.

Finally, as if this were not enough, the question should be raised of the dialectical nature of Lacan's thought, a question which presupposes the perennial one of the nature of dialectical thinking itself. It is a question which certainly includes but greatly transcends that of the role and influence of Hegel in Lacan's development, about which it is so often said that in the early years he was palpably stimulated by Kojève's reading of the master–slave dialectic, most notably in the hypothesis of the mirror stage, and of Sartre's (equally Hegelian) notion of the Look and the relations with the Other; but that the mature, as well as the late, Lacan left both Hegel and Hegelian existentialism behind – first for structuralism, and then for his own inimitable formulations on the impossible, on *jouissance* and the *objet petit a*, and on gender.

But perhaps this is to neglect an important principle of precisely that late thinking: namely, the lessons of the four discourses and, in particular, the doctrine of the discourse of the University. The latter posits, indeed, that the driving force of this particular discourse (or structural permutation) lies in the reification of the Other into a proper name. Thus, the discourse of the University always wishes to identify a given thought or truth with that proper name; and is ceaselessly concerned with the affiliation of a thought (which may or may not include the problems of influence, origin, orientation, ideology, and the like) as Hegelian, Lacanian, Sartrean, structuralist (which we may take as shorthand for Lévi-Straussian), Freudian, or whatever. Those of us targeted as 'eclectic' pose a worrisome problem for this kind of discourse inasmuch as the latter observes the various named concepts floating downstream one after the other, pell-mell, like so many unburied corpses, and searches in vain for the reassuring unity of family resemblance. Yet if history is a reconstructed narrative, maybe the problem is not an interesting one, and a given body of thought might well be followed in its development without such a compulsive flurry of attributions. Or perhaps, on the other hand, the introduction of the name in question is to be reconnected to the generic problem we began with, and to be seen as a specific generic set piece or sub-form, a regulated digression designed to adorn or to advance the argument in ways that need to be determined. There are certainly a number of these names that recur fatefully throughout the Seminar: Plato is one (the *Meno*); Aristotle's ethics another; Descartes regularly re-emerges at these moments in which the false problem of consciousness (Lacan *dixit*!) reappears; and there are specific minor roles or cameo appearances assigned to Merleau-Ponty, to Wittgenstein, to Lévi-Strauss himself, not to speak of Saint Anselm, Kant, Bentham, the mystics or Saint Augustine. Many of the references can be explained by the kind of materialist analysis that focuses on the shifting publics of the *Seminar*, their gradual displacement or augmentation of a public initially constituted by younger analysts in training by the arrival of a philosophical (Althusserian-Maoist) group of students centred in the École normale. Many of the references can thus be explained by the dynamics of the appeals that must be made in order to generate a broader type of 'group-in-fusion'. Thus the references to Marx play their role in the construction of a new psychoanalytic theory of value; but also serve as signals and connotations, as well as illustrating a new kind of theoretical imperialism and omnivorousness. There are also, to be sure, the enemies, named or unnamed: ego psychology, the object-relations school, the neo-Freudians and the Americans, Marie Bonaparte, Hartmann and Kris; but presumably their generic role as object lessons is a somewhat different one.

So, for this final kind of inquiry, it would not be a question of Lacan's Hegelianism but, rather, of the hospitality of his thought in general to a new development of dialectical thought itself. In what follows I will organize my observations around the following topics: the function of absence and the paradoxes of castration; incommensurables; the dialectics of semantic slippage; and, finally, relationality and totality.

1.

One of the central issues in Lacan's dialectics turns on absence itself, and on one absence in particular – indeed, the most scandalous one of all. This is, of course, the issue of castration, and one may say that it is doubly scandalous, in two distinct ways. Clearly enough, the hypothesis of castration and a castration complex in Freud himself was always a stumbling block: you could probably tell the story or myth of the Oedipus complex without recourse to the threat of castration, so closely associated with it. At that point, a very specific threat relating to sexuality is generalized out metaphysically, so to speak, and becomes a more diffuse death threat, an evocation of maiming or punishment, or, even more figuratively, a menace to the child's psychic autonomy and the source of a fear which will cripple the subject in later years. But the association of the threat with a desire for the mother tends to relocalize it back in the general area of the sexual, or at least of infantile sexuality.

At that point – and always remaining within the context of Freud's own writing – several objections or complaints are likely to be confronted. The first expresses the fatigue that so many of us have felt at one time or another in the presence of what we may call orthodox Freudian literary criticism (the clearest example of interpretation according to an 'ultimately determining instance' or master code): this is the predictability of the Oedipal theme in a whole range of classical texts from *Hamlet* to *The Brothers Karamazov*, a predictability which certainly resurfaces in Lacan's 'literary criticism', however structurally disguised or modernized (the 'Name-of-the-Father'). The objection has been most forcefully argued by Deleuze and Guattari, whose *Anti-Oedipus* tirelessly (and some may even say, tiresomely) protests against the reduction of everything to the childhood 'Mamma–Papa' situation. It is an objection which is probably not redeemed by the admission (by almost everyone) that Oedipus himself, at least, did not have an Oedipus complex. If truth must always be accompanied by the shock of defamiliarization and demystification, and of the revelation of repressed or forgotten realities, then no doubt the omnipresence of Freud and the Oedipus complex everywhere in 'cultural literacy' today has long since deprived this theme of its original truth value, which we would have to go back to *Studies in Hysteria* to retrieve. Lacan certainly does his bit here, most notably in his insistence that the overt threat of castration is in fact more likely to come from the mother rather than the father, and to constitute a response to the most infantile kinds of masturbation.

But that does not particularly dignify castration as a properly philosophical issue; indeed, to put it that way is to approach the second and more formidable objection: namely, that of sheer contingency. To endow a sheer biological fact of the human organs of generation (which science fiction, at least, might find it perfectly plausible to imagine otherwise) with a determining power of this kind is to challenge the abstractions of philosophy with a kind of irreducible content, which can never be abstracted and philosophically conceptualized without losing its power and drifting into the worst type of metaphysics. But perhaps that is also to challenge philosophy as such, about which it could be argued that it is incompatible with the kind of unity-of-theory-and-practice constituted by Freudianism (and Marxism alike). Still, even in this unusual (second) context, the role conferred on a mere bodily organ may raise the issue of contingency in a different but no less problematical way.

It will be said that Lacan eludes this objection by rethinking the matter of the bodily organ in a dramatic new way: asserting, as is by now well known, that the object of the threat of castration is not the bodily organ called the penis but, rather, that quite different thing called the phallus, which, as the penis in erection, is no longer to be considered an organ but, rather, something closer to an event (or perhaps a power), and which Lacan will now characterize as a signifier (or even as the Signifier, as the privileged signifier, on the basis of the fact that it is the only signifier without a signification or a signified, a qualification which may well turn it back into something closer to a contingent organ again). So far the operation may be counted (or discounted) as yet one more in that series of 'structuralizations' of Freud for which Lacan is well known, the translation into vaguely linguistic terms, on the order of the revision of the Oedipal father into the 'Name-of-the-Father' mentioned above: the structural rose in place of the botanical one.

But even this is to miss everything that is most scandalous about Lacan's 'rewriting' of Freud. It is a scandal effaced by overfamiliarity, that effacement itself reinforced by the overfamiliarity of the Bataille paradox which it borrows and reverses: namely, the relationship between transgression and the Law – each one requiring the other for its reciprocal effect, a kind of strange chiasmus of negativity whereby the negation depends for its force on a reaffirmation of what it negates. But this, in my opinion, is not a dialectic at all but, rather, a vicious circle or, better still, a kind of stamping in place (which is not even a repetition in Freud's own non-dialectical sense); and in any case I think that the frequent interpretation of Lacan's seventh Seminar (the *Ethics*) in terms of Bataille and of transgression is mistaken and misguided.

All of which may perhaps be clarified by returning to the first move in this strange process: namely, Lacan's insistence on the necessity of castration (leaving out of it for the moment the obvious qualifier that the 'castration' in question is merely a figurative one). We have to try to recover the original outrageousness of a position which asserts something nowhere to be found in Freud himself (whose stubborn common sense has little enough in common with these paradoxes): namely, that the 'normal' development of sexuality requires the preliminary experience, at the right moment, of castration; or, if you prefer to avoid words like normal, that the worst kinds of psychic problems – from the neuroses all the way to psychosis – result from a failure to pass through the stage of castration (or try to elude it). It is easy enough to think up psychological or anthropological equivalents for this doctrine: the way in which the death anxiety is necessary for individuality, for example, or the various practices of *rites de passage*, hazing, and the like. But this is surely not the level of truth or conceptuality for which Lacan himself claims to strive, even though he himself also frequently identifies castration and death in ways that facilitate such anthropological or psychological slippage.

The function of castration in Lacan's sense, and what arrests the term in its slippage towards some absolute metaphoricity, even while endowing it with that specifically figurative function it obviously has to retain, is best understood by returning to the peculiarity of Lacan's substitute notion of the phallus. We can in this new framework now say that it is the threat of castration directed to the penis, to the contingent bodily organ, which transforms the latter into the phallus; or, better still, which generates that signifier which is the phallus and enables the bodily organ to fulfil that signifying function from time to time. The lesson is not the empirical one, that there is such a thing as the phallus (and that the man has it, while the woman does not); rather, it is a lesson about absence: namely, that no one has the phallus, neither man nor woman, but that they somehow, from time to time, participate in this signifier, if I may try to put it chastely. Lacan often remarks that there is always something ridiculous about masculine assurance, and that the stances of machismo, necessarily performative, are always threatened by the comic (this male performativity corresponding to that female mascarade identified by Hélène Deutsch, which equally underscores the basis of the Lacanian doctrine that in that sense the 'sexes' or 'genders' are not only not natural, but meaningless and impossible). The point, for masculine development, is that it is the 'experience' of castration (or, in other words, learning that no one 'has' the phallus in the sense of property) that allows the male being to function in the masculine way; or, better still – for I hope it will gradually become clear to what degree the negative formulations are always more faithful to Lacan's doctrine than any positive propositions or assertions – that in the absence of that experience, all kinds of disorders happen to the male being. (One could then, from some clinical or developmental perspective, go on to talk about that privileged relationship to the mother which I have already mentioned in connection with this 'experience': for the first discovery of the possibility of castration comes with her, with her bodily anatomy as well as with her threat, and also the child's experience of himself or herself as the mother's libidinal substitute, not to speak of the innumerable and quite different situations in which the mother can seem to castrate, or make absent or more distant, the father.[2])

But here I am mainly interested in underscoring the constitutive relationship to absence – not even necessarily to lack, although that is certainly a very crucial category (derived from Sartre) – which is central to Lacan's thought, and which indeed documents its claim to dialectical status. The phallus is an absence, and this is what gives it potency as a signifier. Indeed, signifiers themselves are structured dialectically, around absence: following what is probably more a Jakobsonian than a Saussurean linguistics, and certainly in a Hegelian spirit, if not a Mallarméan one, Lacan's examples show over and over again that a signifier can come into being only by virtue of not being present, or at least not being present all the time; this is the deepest meaning of the well-known *fort–da* illustration.[3]

And it is precisely this dialectical requirement which will trace out the path and the strategy of Lacan's most fundamental polemic: the attack on the object-relations school (the official theme of the fourth Seminar). The spirit of this polemic may be quickly formulated: it turns on the notion of the object of desire, to admit the existence of which is also to imply that the desire for it can be fully satisfied (and thereby to dictate a recipe for normality quite different from what is implicit in Lacan's structural accounts). But how do we retain the fundamental emphasis on desire and, at the same time, avoid the unwanted implications that the notion of an object brings with it? One can, for example, insist on the metonymic notion of desire, as it follows a perpetual substitute of one object for another, beginning not with any original or primordial object, but with something that was already a kind of substitution (the so-called *Vorstellungsrepräsentanz*[4]). Or one can posit the enigmatic *objet petit a*, a kind of residue which undergoes all kinds of transformations throughout the Seminar (even if one does not acknowledge its origins in the small *a* of the mirror stage). The fundamental insistence on desire brings with it an equally fundamental insistence that desire is never satisfied (the proof is that its moments of disappearance – *aphanisis*[5] – are catastrophic). But this will gradually determine a shift away from the language of the object in two directions: first, the object (*objet petit a*) will henceforth be given its value by its position within that larger narrative microcosm which is the fantasm: this means that it is henceforth irrelevant to try to evoke the 'object of desire' in purely objectal terms.

On the other hand, this refinement can lead to new differentiations within the very notion of desire itself: and it is at this point that the notion of *jouissance* (omnipresent in the later Seminars) separates itself off from that of pleasure (leaving the 'pleasure principle' itself out of the matter), and indeed becomes specifically defined as being 'distinct from pleasure in so far as it constitutes the latter's beyond'.[6] This dissatisfaction of *jouissance* with mere pleasure, its constant movement beyond the simple satisfactions and achievements of pleasure as such, certainly seems to have something to do with the most famous version of the syntactical formula (beyond or *jenseits*) in Freud, namely the death instinct or Thanatos.

It also determines a whole new rhetorical development in Lacan himself, where the fateful notion of a dimension 'beyond' will colonize a whole species of visual *jenseits*, in the form of veils or tempting coverings of all kinds, which seduce not so much because they have an object behind them as, rather, because they dramatize the absence of an object and are signs and substitutes for just such an absent object, about whose centrality Lacan will invoke the text and premonitory doctrine of early unpublished Freud's *Project*.[7] (The other visual analogue, in Seminar XI, the famous anamorphosis, is, rather, to be grasped as representing the peculiar nature of the phallus.) Here a whole aesthetic opens up – architecture as the setting in place of the void, as shaped absence; and a whole wealth of cultural and literary examples becomes available.[8] Courtly love can thus now be grasped as a very peculiar experiment in keeping the absence at the heart of desire alive; while the mystics then allow us to grasp the way in which absence and negativity extend all the way to the fundamental big Other or God, who, like Freud's primal father, must necessarily be dead in order to function. But it is essential – or so I would argue and insist – that all of these materials be grasped not as some slippage by Lacan towards religion or mysticism so much as instances within his essentially dialectical use of absence. The examples become symptoms of idealism only if we grasp them in positivistic or empirical fashion; they can also, however, be appropriated dialectically.

2.

It does not always seem to be understood that the most telling evidence for the dialectical character of Lacan's thought lies in his awareness of incommensurability. This is a term I borrow from mathematics,[9] even though Lacan himself certainly deploys irrational numbers and their problems in some of his basic analogies (something we will return to). I use it in the larger sense of a radical incompatibility between various explanatory systems or codes: something like an untranslatability between systems. To which we must add: systems between which one cannot choose either; so that the scandal is not so much their incompatibility but, rather, the conviction that one needs both (or all three, or all four) at one and the same time, yet cannot put them together in any systematic way – cannot, in other words, construct some coherent machine out of their very differences. Put this way, the notion of incommensurability might be thought simply to reflect the frustrations of an academic eclecticism, which cannot borrow from various distinct philosophies or theories without longing for their synthesis. Indeed, the very pseudo-concept of incommensurability (which has no positive content, but merely registers and domesticates the necessity of failure) may itself be thought to express such a longing, which may well be the bad yet indispensable motor force of the philosophical project as such.[10] The one, universality, system, totality, synthesis – these, then, are so many names for that currently stigmatized desire; but who is to say that so many ingenious post-contemporary theoretical mechanisms for keeping it in check, or even repressing it, are any less reprehensible, marking as they do the irrepressibility of the unifying impulse (like the Law and its transgression in another familiar paradigm)?

All this may be so; but the stakes become considerably augmented when one decides to read the incommensurability of the codes and theories as so many signs and symptoms of some deeper ontological incommensurability, if I may improperly put it that way. Then it is reality itself which is a coexistence of incompatibles, about which no doubt all kinds of unjustified hopes persist that eventually some 'unified field theory' can unite them. But the hope seems immediately to position us back inside the human mind, and to accuse its theories, rather than reality, of just such incommensurabilities.

This would be the moment to say something about Lacan's conception of science, a status he wants to attribute to psychoanalysis at the same time as he participates in that rather tired and conventional critique of modernity and of modern science, along the lines of Husserl's *Crisis of the European Sciences* or even Heidegger's essay on world-pictures. But it should be said (in Lacan's defence?) that his critique of scientific secularity is not nostalgic for some revival of the big Other, and merely seeks (in an uninteresting way, I believe) to mark the difference between the traditional – the status of the psyche and the Other in religious periods – and the psychic dilemmas faced by a secular and scientific period. The defence of science, on the other hand, on the basis of which the scientificity of psychoanalysis is claimed, does not seem to imply the same kinds of historicism and larger periodizing cultural critiques but, rather, to serve as a weapon against psychology and philosophy: not so much to mark the specificity of Freud, in other words, as to refute those conceptions of coherent system implicit in psychology in particular and philosophy in general. Lacan's formalizations – not merely the graphs, but the later mathemes and topologies, including the knots and the rings – have been thought to be motivated by a desire for a rigour, an effort to avoid the humanism and metaphysics of so much 'orthodox Freudianism', as well as an attempt to pass on a legacy of Lacan's own immune to the revisionisms to which Freud was subjected.[11] That may well be true; but I think we cannot neglect the spatial passion involved in the pursuit of these concentrated hieroglyphs or 'characters', nor can we avoid seeing in them a specific kind of desire, the desire called formalization, which would seem to me to be something quite distinct from scientificity and the claims made for that. That all this takes place within the age of *écriture* lends it an additional or supplementary historical connotation; but the formalizations cannot be reduced to that particular poststructuralist thematic either.

As for incommensurability, whether grasped scientifically or not, I also think it is important to claim that the dialectic comes into being as an acknowledgement of precisely this dilemma, both in its subjective and in its objective forms. If synthesis there be in Hegel, then it seems crucial to insist that there is only one, that of the end, or so-called Absolute Spirit[12] – a stopping point so enigmatic that all kinds of different interpretations have been proposed that satisfy no one: Hegel's own hubris, Hegel himself as the philosophical equivalent of Napoleon, the Prussian state, the end of history, or simply a new historical view of the world and the moment in which the whole human past becomes available to thought (not to speak of the later rewritings as praxis, or the unity-of-theory-and-practice, as socialism or communism, or whatever). For the most part, leaving aside the formal problem of this 'final' moment (and of the problem of the ending which it proposes as implicitly as the great Preface poses the problem of beginning explicitly), Hegel's contradictions are very precisely incommensurabilities which, left behind by history in one way, continue to recur and repeat in others. 'There is no metalanguage', runs one of Lacan's better-known anti-philosophical slogans; vulgar Hegelianism is certainly a kind of metalanguage. But the dialectic is not – or so I argue here – and whatever one chooses to call it, it is a tormented kind of language which seeks to register incommensurabilities without implying any solution to them by some facile naming of them, or the flattening-out of this or that unified philosophical code. It is this provisionality which is sometimes called reflexive (a term which, if it suggests the language of consciousness, is also not satisfactory); and it would, meanwhile, be timely to try to distinguish it from that other more contemporary linguistic strategy so often called theory (something I will not try to do here).

For the moment, what can be suggested as a strategy for dealing with incommensurabilities is to try to wrest them out of the conceptual realm (in which they seem to coexist as so many distinct codes) and to grasp them as projections and intimations, symptoms, of deeper ontological gaps and rifts. This is something which is perhaps easier to do when we move out of the area of the natural sciences and a little closer to the so-called human ones. Here it seems minimally possible to grasp an incommensurability such as that between Marx and Freud, say, both subjectively and objectively: as incompatible theories which at the same time betoken some deeper incommensurability in the historical social world itself. To hold these two perspectives, the subjective one and the objective one, together is not to claim to resolve them back into a single system; but perhaps it does not freeze and eternalize them into some timeless metaphysical opposition either.

At any rate, it is with some such incompatibility that Lacan's Seminar begins, and I want to argue that, whatever the later modifications (and the new concepts, such as that of *jouissance* or drive, which seem to shoot off at some angle which fails to acknowledge the earlier 'system' any longer[13]), this ontological incompatibility obtains throughout; and the various formulations are designed to designate the dilemma rather than to conflate it: 'to explain, rather than to understand', as Lacan repeatedly puts it. The taboo on metalanguage may well be taken as his warning to himself, as well as to his auditors.

For it seems clear that the initial distinction between the Imaginary and the Symbolic (the Real always lurking dimly in the background) is meant very specifically to dramatize an incommensurability of the kind we are discussing – indeed, virtually the primary one in Lacan's view of 'human reality'. Or – to put it the other way round (as one always must) – it is the conflation of these two dimensions into one that generates the pseudo-systems of psychology and philosophy (when the latter offers a theory of 'human nature') as well as the various post-Freudian 'orthodox' revisionisms. The critique of the latter's strategies of intervention in the analytic situation is then, as we shall see, motivated by the new differentiations awakened by this initial disjunction between Imaginary and Symbol.

The Imaginary is a dual system which correlates pure positivities: most notably all those which accumulate around the self and the other (or the subject and the object). Imaginary relationships can thus be grasped as so many positivities (or empirical realities) in their own right, and can be resolved into coherent systems, whether epistemological ones or interpersonal ones. There are numerous conflicts and antagonisms that can be registered in this dimension (most notably the emergence of aggressivity as a function of the mirror stage); but none of them posits dialectical absence or incommensurability. Indeed, it is no doubt the association of Hegel's master–slave dialectic with the mirror stage (the first moment of the emergence of the Imaginary, in which the infant discovers its other self visually in the mirror, at around eighteen months) that is responsible for the characterization of early Lacan as a Hegelian, while the later one leaves the dialectic altogether – first for structuralism, and then for some idiosyncratic form of poststructuralist transgression theory.

But this is to ignore the teachings of numerology: for in fact 'Hegel' stands for the apparition of the Third (as in his American follower, C.S. Peirce); and it is with this Third term that we encounter a dimension that cannot be reduced to Imaginary dualisms and is radically incommensurable with them. That dimension is of course the Symbolic, which we can grasp either in terms of the big Other (A), utterly distinct from the little others (a) of all the Imaginary relationships, or (in terms of language), of the realm of signifiers.

A strange new dialectic sets in at this point, in which the two dimensions can neither be separated nor reduced to one another, nor translated into a unified metalanguage. Thus from a genetic or developmental point of view, it is difficult not to think of stages which would make it possible to distinguish between the onset of the Symbolic and language, and the experience of the mirror stage that presumably inaugurates the Imaginary. Lacan certainly uses stages, particularly in the analysis of the various neuroses and psychoses; but his is an implacable critique of such developmental 'historicism', and he is very reluctant to deploy notions like 'regression' which seem indissociable from some kind of historicist perspective. His solution is the classical – albeit perhaps not altogether satisfactory – one developed by structuralism, in which the ostensible historical or developmental narrative is in fact simply a temporal projection of the possibilities of variation within the 'timeless' structure itself. There is thus no normal psyche, there are elements and relationships whose inflection, distortion, suppression, produce so many types of 'maladjustment' (to use as neutral a term as possible). The (sometimes maddening) typologies of neuroses, perversions, psychoses, then, are not only essential to the strategies of the cure and of the moment of intervention; they are intimately related to the structural hypotheses themselves. (It is worth noting, however, that the structuralist disjunction between the synchronic and the diachronic not only generates such diachronic illusions or projections of development, but returns with a vengeance when the 'structuralist' does finally decide to take temporality into account. Here we encounter Lacan's logical temporalities, along with illustrations like that of the problem of the three prisoners,[14] which are so distinct from the 'structural' analyses that they sometimes strike one as a kind of 'return of the repressed' of the excluded or 'foreclosed' temporality itself.)

Impossible, then, to differentiate the Imaginary from the Symbolic in any way that makes it possible to inspect one dimension in isolation from the other (or from the third dimension of the Real, which cannot even be defined or circumscribed in the way in which we have been able to characterize the other two). The famous Borromean rings of the last years emblematize the interrelationship in which all rings must somehow be interlocked for the human animal to function even in the way it 'normally' does.[15] Thus, we can only speak of a predominance of one dimension over another, and of situations in which a single dimension usurps the function of the others or is, on the contrary, seriously underdeveloped. This would seem at least to secure one fundamental philosophical (or, if you prefer, anti-philosophical) premiss: namely, that we will never be able to have a theory of any of these dimensions in isolation. Yet the Symbolic would seem to present an exception to this rule (and to entitle Lacan to an official position among 'structuralist' theoreticians), for it is identified with language as such, and there are surely any number of systematic theories of language or claimants to a scientific linguistics. But perhaps the project of a linguistics is philosophically more problematic and internally contradictory than the layman imagines (see, for example, the work of Jean-Claude Milner). Inasmuch as we are never out of language, never not in language, it would seem to present the case of a phenomenon that can never (since definition is negation) be defined, since we can never experience its absence. (Ethology offers at best a merely hypothetical approach via so-called animal languages.) In any case, later Lacan slips even these loose traces with his anti-structuralist notion of '*lalangue*' (brilliantly translated as llanguage), a perpetual murmur of our own national language and our own '*idiotismes*' that spills well beyond the boundaries which any self-respecting linguistics would need to assign it. What else the Symbolic is we will see shortly.

As for the Imaginary, its presence can be identified, though even less than language does it offer a realm or an element that might possibly be described in its own right. We have already seen that duality or dualism is one of its markers: and the concept thereby confers on the notion of dualism as ideology (and that of ideology as dualism) a considerable philosophical enlargement: namely, a specification of all dualisms as Imaginary relationships, and thereby somehow 'wrong' or 'bad' concepts, using the familiar Hegelian (or Deleuzian) rhetoric. Indeed, it would seem plausible to identify the Imaginary as occupying that place of Error or, better still, of necessary, unavoidable, well-nigh ontological Error, that *Verstand* occupies in the Hegelian system: the point is that such a peculiar status of Error secures the vocation of the dialectic not only to undo, demystify, and even deconstruct a pre-existing field of error or illusion, but also to posit the latter's reality, its ontological necessity in at least the structural organization of human thought and experience; and thus to ensure the temporal nature of truth, which cannot be arrived at by fiat or correct thinking, but must traverse the moment of error as its necessary precondition. In that sense, the temporality of the psychoanalytic training session would seem to take the place of the various dialectics of history in Hegel.

Another marker of the presence of the Imaginary is to be found in perception as such, and in particular in visuality, as the mirror stage would seem already to foretell. This is the sense in which the ideals of phenomenology come before us as a kind of mirage of the concrete, some illusion of the full body to be achieved perceptually as a Utopia of our being-in-the-world (Merleau-Ponty). The illusions of visuality, so frequently misunderstood as a privileged form of immediacy (not least by the empiricists), thus offer a rich field for demystifying the Imaginary; and no doubt also account for the paradoxical complication of this sense in Lacan's account of the gaze as a part object in Seminar XI (where, in effect, what we loosely take to be the visual is reanalysed and decomposed from the standpoint of the Symbolic).

But clearly enough my presentation has been somewhat perverse here, for I have kept what is for Lacan the strongest form of Imaginary méconnaissance until last in this exposition: it is none other than the ego itself, as the most enduring and ineradicable product of the mirror stage. The polemic against the ego begins at once, in the first Seminar, and may be seen as the source of the most fundamental of all the now familiar structuralist doxa: namely, what is often termed the 'decentering' of the subject (or, more improperly, the death of the subject, along with the 'death' of the author, anti-humanism, and the like). This polemic in turn – and for some no doubt most suspiciously – revives a much older theological tradition in which the sin of pride is tactically denounced, and the self strategically and therapeutically reduced ('*le moi est haïssable*'): a doctrine and a lore to be found in one form or another in the history of most of the great religions. In sociological terms, what we confront here is undoubtedly the waning of that entrepreneurial individualism celebrated by the triumphant bourgeoisie, ambiguously enshrined in its juridical system and its political and social ideologies. In that sense, the vogue of the decentred subject reflects the realities of an increasingly corporate system of economic institutions, and finds its first (more positive) realization in the corporate-collectivist spirit of the 1930s, in fascism, Soviet communism, and the New Deal alike. And no doubt Freud's own 'Copernican revolution' (unlike Kant's, which expresses the pride and bureaucratic achievements of a post-feudal Prussia, foretelling the French Revolution) has something to do not only with the emergence of hysteria as a socially accredited disorder, but also with the decline of Austria as a great power, whose energetic and 'modern' citizenry no longer find fulfilment in the appropriate industrial and imperial tasks.[16]

The degeneration of the Freudian doctrine of the unconscious into the 'ego therapy' of his followers (*dixit* Lacan) certainly positions such concepts of the ego and the self squarely for the Lacanian onslaught. Our initial question, however, must be that of translatability, or in other words, the possibility of substituting a dimension like the Imaginary for a kind of pseudo-object like the ego. Freud certainly drew a picture of this protuberance (a little like the vision of Europe as a tiny promontory of the vast Asian continent), a picture Lacan allows himself to mock, for it is evident that a formula like the famous *Wo es war, soll ich werden* – whatever it does mean – is on most readings a serious threat to his own enterprises and to his claim for Freud's patronage. Reclaiming the swamp of the unconscious and turning it into consciousness and even self-consciousness: this is as ego-centred an Enlightenment recommendation as the old Socratic 'know thyself': at least on a first reading, and without benefit of the contortions with which Lacan's translations and alternative formulations try desperately to reappropriate it (most famously, *là où c'était, dois-je advenir*).

Still, it seems clear that such picture-thinking as the second *topique* – which crudely assigns their places in geographical space to the Ego and the Id, and whose very deployment of spatiality can be instructively contrasted with Lacan's own later 'topologies' – tends to reify this function called the ego, and to suggest that its therapeutic treatment is something on the order of the shrinkage of a tumour. On the other hand, models like that of the mirror stage tend fatally to suggest that the ego is something like an illusion, which one is then tempted to suppose can be done away with altogether. But if it is an illusion or a mirage, a mere projection or image, the ego is none the less something real: a formulation which suggests that one could do without it is as misleading a representation as the old 'death of the subject'. It is perhaps this representational apprehension which determines one of Lacan's most complicated early demonstrations: the optical experiment, involving the illusion of the inverted bouquet,[17] which is redolent of the whole tradition of perspectival assays, very much including the camera obscura and its inversions (along with their various philosophical and metaphorical appropriations for the theory of ideology). However one wishes to restage it in all its complexity, I think the experiment is designed to suggest a fundamental consequence, namely that the projection, the image, the bouquet falsely visualized right-side up and in the empty vase, is nonetheless a real image; it is not an airy nothingness, even though it is sheer illusion. If you want to say that it is false, then it is a necessary falseness, much as for Hegel sheer appearance – the opposite of essence – is also necessary and objective. This is a difficult tightrope to walk; representation can tilt either way: towards a figment one can imagine dissolving altogether, or towards a reified mental function that has all the ontological solidity of the body.

Now I think that the value of the more consequent translational shift, from a language of the ego to one of the Imaginary, lies indeed in redirecting our attention to the text, as it were, rather than to some reified picture of the mental functions, as *Verstand* might imagine it. It also reinstates dialectical relationship at the centre of the analysis, inasmuch as we cannot think the Imaginary without at once calculating it against the dimensions of the Symbolic and the Real from which it is inseparable. And this is a mental operation very different from the kind of freestanding autonomy projected by the noun that claims to name the ego or the self.

But this is perhaps also the moment to say something about an issue that has been touched on only lightly in passing here, but that one would ordinarily – that is to say, from the standpoint of philosophy or common sense – take to be central; and that is consciousness as such. If the ego so often seems to be accompanied by the 'property' of consciousness and, indeed, indissociable from it, the same cannot be said for the dialectical combination of the Imaginary – let us say, for shorthand, perception – and the Symbolic – which can, also for shorthand, be identified as language. Where is consciousness here? It is clear that the introduction of language must subvert any traditional view of consciousness, in so far as thinking in words means vehiculating an externally derived system of some kind – a system which, in addition, threatens the purity and immediacy of perception itself (as in Lévi-Strauss' famous colour systems, in which the nomenclature of a given language inflects our exploration of what we see). Putting it the other way round, we may ask whether this scheme adequately offers us any kind of new theory of consciousness (or, indeed, whether psychoanalysis, and the work of Freud himself, does so successfully).

To put this question is then to understand that Lacan decisively refuses its premisses (and claims that Freud does as well). We might summarize this position as follows: psychoanalysis as a science is predicated on the preliminary bracketing or suspension of the alleged 'problem of consciousness'. The latter is excluded from the problematic of psychoanalysis; and on Lacan's view this is a position Freud himself already reaches in the unpublished *Entwurf* of 1895,[18] which abandons the attempt and turns in a new direction. It is this important move, in turn, which explains the centrality of the debate with Descartes that runs through the seminars (and that includes, implicitly or explicitly, a less significant debate with his followers in Husserlian phenomenology). Perhaps we can formulate the sense of this move as follows: in the philosophical tradition, the data of consciousness, its existential experience, and the like were appealed to in an effort somehow to define the self or the subject: consciousness was felt to be the most immediate and readily available reality to be consulted, whereas it was the self, the thinking subject, the ego or the I, which remained obscure and enigmatic, or unformulable. The Cartesian cogito then assembles and concentrates the materials of consciousness in order to stage the moment of appearance of the subject in its essence. In Lacan (for we cannot really attribute such speculation to Freud himself) it is the reverse: the subject is perfectly tangible and readily available; it is simply the grammatical subject. The ego is meanwhile also quite distinct and far more accessible than in conjectural discussions about identity, the self, and the like: it is the product of the mirror stage, and is something like an object for the consciousness rather than its support (Lacan's reliance here on Sartre's 1936 *Transcendence of the Ego* always needs to be pointed out). At this point, one would seem to have a more reliable path towards the exploration of consciousness than the latter offered in its hypotheses about the self or the ego. Except that at this point as well, speculations about consciousness as such no longer seem necessary or even relevant: consciousness waxes and wanes, knowing its feeblest degree in the consciousness we have in dreams (not to speak of the problems of animal consciousness), and at other times, in the existential decision (or the cogito), concentrated to a point of intensity.

But it is no longer necessary to have a theory of consciousness, since henceforth the unconscious will no longer be defined as the opposite of consciousness, but in completely different ways. (It is confusing to have to talk about the way in which the unconscious is conscious of this or that trauma; yet on the old dispensation it is hard to see how some such formulation can be avoided.)

Perhaps, then, the ambiguity of the exclusion of consciousness needs to be stressed, and left undecided in that form.[19] On the one hand, we may simply take this exclusion as the inaugural or foundational act of psychoanalysis itself as a science, in that sense an act analogous to the radical disjunctions with which the other disciplines have delimited their fields (I am thinking, for example, of the stunning gesture whereby Carl Schmitt 'defines' politics as the positing of the friend–foe distinction). In this form, then, the exclusion of the problem of consciousness would stand as a non-dialectical act, and as the autonomization of a specific field, namely psychoanalysis.

But we may also wonder whether the exclusion of the consciousness does not take place somehow within psychoanalysis, now grasped not so much as a science in the process of constitution as, rather, the Freudian or Lacanian 'system'. Then we may speak of the substitution, for the phenomenological idea of consciousness, of other quite different Master-Signifiers, such as desire. It then becomes evident that to move from a problematic governed by the problem of consciousness to one governed by the notion of desire is dialectically to restructure the former, elements of what was previously identified as consciousness passing into the field and coming before us as new kinds of problems faced by any theory of desire, most notably in the question of sublimation; still others captured by the realm of the Symbolic and returning in the form of syntactical or, more generally, grammatical and linguistic problems (such as the very problem of the subject itself).

Yet it seems best to conclude this discussion of incommensurability with the kind of representational question that has dogged us throughout (and will continue to do so): whether to name an unthinkable phenomenon such as incommensurability is not somehow either to elude the problem altogether (ignoring the fact that it cannot even be named, virtually in advance and by definition) or else to have represented it, after all, by the very concept which was supposed to have named the impossibility of its representation.

Perhaps what I have called Lacan's literary criticism can be briefly invoked here, at least to lay some firmer basis for the problem. Indeed, we remember that the idea of the *sinthome* developed for Joyce (in the 1975–1976 Seminar) was conceived precisely as a kind of supplementary ring that held the three incommensurable Borromean rings together in a situation in which they might otherwise have flown apart, leaving the subject in a state of madness. The idea of art as a kind of heightened therapy is not unfamiliar, to be sure, but this one at least suggests that art has to have something to do with all three dimensions and yet, as it were, also to stand outside them, holding them together – just as, in abstract language, the very term incommensurable sought to do.

From this, the notion of allegory is not far; and everyone has grasped, with varying degrees of admiration or irritation, the allegorical nature of the reading of 'The Purloined Letter'. But most readings of this reading are incomplete, since they see it merely as an allegory of the Symbolic, the tripartite system of positions, and remark on its doubles only to accuse Lacan of leaving that level of structure out.[20] In fact, however, the rectification of this omission restores the larger meaning of Lacan's own allegorical interpretation, which can be described as the surmounting of the Imaginary (the doubles) by the Symbolic as such (the triangular structure).

But as this example is overly familiar, we would do well to consult another; namely, the reading of Irma's dream in the first *Seminar*. Biographical interpretations of this first of all dreams to be analysed have usefully enlarged a personal context Freud was none too eager to disclose in public: thus we know that the guilt Freud felt about his faulty treatment of Irma (and, behind her, his own father) goes a long way towards explaining the kind of wish of which this was a fulfilment. More recently, it has been suggested that the guilt was in reality that of Fliess, so that Freud's own wish-fulfilment finds itself enlarged to include a virtual alter ego (analysts have never quite been sure whether to classify this as an ego-ideal or an ideal ego). Lacan takes a completely different tack here by enumerating the proliferation of triads in the dream, from the ancillary male figures to the female ones, and finally the emergence of the enigmatic formula, trimethalyne (whose odour of sexuality he is also the first to point out). For Lacan, such tripartite stirrings – culminating in the triumphant matheme itself, which obliterates all traces of the first-person or Imaginary narrative – constitutes the very allegory of the installation of the Symbolic order and its hegemony over the Imaginary. At this point, then, the allegory has come to turn on an event rather than a structure, a sense which is confirmed by the extraordinary readings of the Ten Commandments,[21] which in some ways occupy a structural position in Lacan distantly analogous to those of *Totem and Taboo* for Freud. The incest taboo is laid in place by them, but it would be wrong to think, according to Lacan, that they are merely negative instantiations of the Law: in fact (very much like the canonical structuralist interpretation of the incest taboo itself) they are all (but he glosses only a few) markers for the triumph of the Symbolic as such. Thus, the taboo on graven images 'eliminates the function of the Imaginary':[22] the injunction on the Sabbath creates that empty space of absence which, as we have seen, is essential to the construction of a Signifier; that on lying installs the contradictory linguistic levels of the unconscious as such, and so forth. These allegorical readings of a primal event or revelation are very different in spirit from the conventional transgressive function with which Lacan concludes his enumeration (the commandment against covetousness, which is supposed to bring it into being). In any case, this very modern restructuration of allegory from some mere system of parallelisms into a complex new way of registering an event whose levels are otherwise incommensurable, and to that degree unrepresentable, would seem to mark a step beyond that Nietzschean metaphoricity we will shortly find certain of his commentators attributing to him.

3.

But this is the moment to move on to our final cluster of dialectical features, which I have already previewed as the emergence (or re-emergence) of allegory or, if you prefer, the problem of the multiplication of signifieds. This is, on my view, one of the fundamental determinants of the invention of the dialectic as such in the late eighteenth century (the other – detectable as the gradual identification of the problem of modes of production, from Adam Ferguson on – can be described as the new historical content offered by the supersession of feudalism to linguistic and representational expression). I have suggested elsewhere that the following fateful remark by Rousseau can be usefully taken as a revealing designation of the linguistic problems from which the dialectic emerges:

> I have noticed again and again that it is impossible in writing a lengthy work to use the same words always in the same sense. There is no language rich enough to supply terms and expressions sufficient for the modifications of our ideas. The method of defining every term and constantly substituting the definition of the term defined looks well, but it is impracticable. For how can we escape from our vicious circle? Definitions would be all very well if we did not use words in the making of them. In spite of this I am convinced that even in our poor language we can make our meaning clear, not by always using words in the same sense, but by taking care that every time we use a word the sense in which we use it is sufficiently indicated by the sense of the context, so that each sentence in which the word occurs acts as a sort of definition. Sometimes I say children are incapable of reasoning. Sometimes I say they reason cleverly. I must admit that my words are often contradictory, but I do not think there is any contradiction in my ideas.[23]

How can one set of words mean several different things at once, in a kind of semantic punning which, far from disintegrating into an idiosyncratic babble (lalangue), systematically opens up several distinct fields all at once, and serves as the operator for their relationship? Lacan's discussion of metaphor and metonymy – symptom and desire, condensation and displacement – has seemed to offer some critics a handle capable of turning the theory around and reading it as the simple example or subset of an entirely different problem, that of textuality. Thus in a now classical work,[24] Lacoue-Labarthe and Nancy generalize the Lacanian 'system' as kind of unacknowledged Nietzschean metaphoricity which serves to assert the urgency and priority of its own ostensible content above the (for them) more fundamental question of the distinction between philosophy and literature. But the slippage of signifieds which is the principal exhibit here is for Lacan a characteristic of metonymy rather than of metaphor, meant to designate the infinite substitution of new objects of desire, and indeed the movement of *jouissance* itself beyond this or that thematized pleasure and on into the always-absent realm of that 'beyond' which is Thanatos. Nor is metaphor – the symptomatic collapse of signifieds into the body itself – the proper Lacanian designation for what is affirmed here as the space of the literary, a problem which is on my view not the central one, but one which would certainly presuppose some preliminary attention to that related enigma of sublimation.

To pick a more recent example: one of the major critical polemics in Judith Butler's *Antigone's Claim*[25] is based on her premiss that in Lacan the Symbolic is radically separated from the social: this means that (leaving Freud aside) Lacan's structural psychoanalysis will always be implicitly or explicitly ahistorical and thus anti-political – something that has frequently been affirmed in the context of a 'tragic vision' in Lacan, and also on the basis of certain polemics against Marxism. Butler's concern also has to do with the structural complicities between a Lévi-Straussian notion of the signifier and the kinship relations of the 'normal' or heterosexual family. This secondary (or indeed primary) polemic must necessarily also address the gender scheme of the famous twentieth Seminar (*Encore*), sometimes taken to be a relatively more poststructural position than the frequent early appeals to Lévi-Strauss's authority, and to the 'elementary structures of kinship' as one of the fundamental spaces of the Symbolic.

I think that it is best to assess both these (quite unequal) critiques – the formalist one of *Le Titre de la Lettre*, as well as Butler's political one – in terms of the various meanings of big A (the big Other) throughout the Seminar. For it is, allegedly, both language and society, both the Symbolic and the social, and thereby becomes the very nodal point of Butler's case. Perhaps, indeed, her attack needs to be reversed for it to carry its full power: for it is not the separation between language and the social that is Lacan's flaw here but, rather, their too-great fusion and identification with one another, along precisely those lines of kinship which, for Lévi-Strauss, also demonstrated the kinship between marriage classification and language itself. It is this identification which reinforces our sense that for Lacan the social is organized around the heterosexual family, and that it is this normativity which the Lacanian Symbolic carries at its heart. So one wants to undo Butler's moves and to reunite them into a different strategy: to affirm the big A as the locus in Lacan between the Symbolic and the social, and then to introduce historical movement and change back into the social itself, so as to dissociate it from older historical forms of the family, let alone Lévi-Strauss's clan structure. Butler's feeling that any affirmation of this particular Lacanian position on the Law stands as capitulation to the post-AIDS return to order and to the neo-Confucianism of political publics all over the world is certainly justified, and needs to be repeated and insisted on, along with demonstrations of the way in which theory is transformed into ideology over and over again. But such a demonstration is rather different from a philosophical or theoretical critique; and it seems to me more productive to see whether we cannot appropriate this Lacanian thematics (Symbolic and social) for other purposes, rather than simply to denounce it.

What Lacan affirms, in his translation of big A (Other) into the Symbolic and then into the social, is the way in which the infant is surrounded by an element of language, talking, addressing, murmuring, which is at one with his sense of an indeterminable social network in constant movement all around him from the very outset. The two things are the same, and it is only later on that they appear distinguishable, in the form of physical individuals on the one hand and articulated language on the other. Language appears outside, and so does individuality (which, for the self, arrives only at the moment of the mirror stage, and the formation of the ego). But this is so far merely an empirical or developmental account, which takes no notice of what is distinct, unique and incommensurable about A (or the Symbolic order). Nor does it provide us with any description of how conflation or differentiation, identification and separation, between these various realms are to be theorized.

For A is not only the murmur we have evoked: it is, among other things, an Otherness quite beyond the Imaginary dualism of the mother's body, or the other adults of whatever sex who hold the infant. This Otherness then crystallizes into the Father; but also into God, or the Master, or the 'subject supposed to know'. So it is the place of knowledge fully as much as that of language, and power and authority as well (but in Lacan, does that turn on the phallus or on the loss and the threat of loss, the castration, of the phallus?). Meanwhile, is there anything there? Or is big A dead long since, and the space of the Symbolic somehow permanently vacant: an empty yet indispensable function, like Hegel's monarchy? These levels, their content, and their translatability into one another are, of course, the substance of the doctrine itself.

What I am more interested in for the moment is the mechanics of the movement from one level to another; not only the rules of their translatability but the process itself (and only after that, perhaps, its philosophical legitimacy). That we have to do here with something rather different from Jakobsonian metaphor and metonymy can be quickly shown. The shifting of gears whereby big A ceases to be some kind of distant yet anthropomorphic Other and gets identified as Language is not the metonymic movement from one object of desire to another which gets substituted for the first. There is certainly a process of substitution here, in which one discussion and, indeed, one whole code takes the place of another, with the assurance that we are somehow still talking about the same thing; but this is not a movement of desire, nor do we leave behind the previous object with some renewed sense of well-nigh Romantic longing, and of the infinite beyond and non-satisfaction of all desire. Rather, this particular substitution is also an identification which is an enlargement of the previous theme that changes its focus altogether: more like the *Abschattungen* of the phenomenologists, by which one 'aspect' and then a radically different one – the elephant's hide, and then its tail and tusks – are consecutively revealed to us.

Can we, then, somehow speak of the process in terms of so many 'levels' of the psychic event and the structural situation it enacts? Not exactly; for this is a conflation which operates by disjunction and a separation of levels, codes and topics, rather than by the poetic act that brings some wholly new object into the world.

In fact, I think that this process whereby the same modulates into identical yet distinct spaces is a kind of combination of metaphor and metonymy in Lacan's senses: a kind of utopian term to this dualism and opposition, which combines condensation and displacement in the way in which it displaces by way of condensation, and condenses by way of displacement. The process also bears a rhetorical name, I believe, and I will call it allegory: but I think it is more important to show how it enables the very construction of theory itself, at the same time that it is also central to the dialectic.

We can, for example, observe the way in which the Greimasian semiotic square operates, by taking on the opposites of its own synonyms, like the enemies of my friends. This is why it is not exactly correct to describe this as a translation process, for we are simply moving from one term, relatively inert and without the dynamism necessary to set a whole relational system in movement, to its closest semantic cognate, which does possess that dynamism, along with opposites, contraries and contradictories that can speed us on our way. This allows us to speak of two things at one and the same time: it is a scandalous reversal of that philosophical injunction to define rigorously and to eschew multiple meanings. Rather, it is a kind of semantic punning, which allows us to carry the momentum of each discussion on to the next, different one. But it must not be thought that this is some kind of analogy either: for we do not simply attest the formal similarity of two processes in two distinct fields, we complete the mapping of one, incomplete in its context, over into the field of the other, in a kind of conceptual tag which is also a new kind of repetition. Nor is it altogether proper to call this chiasmus, inasmuch as the latter offers the spectacle of an inert transfer, however energetic, without producing the new. Chiasmus may in that sense be thought of as the metaphorization of metonymy (if it is not indeed the reverse), whereas the allegorical process with which we have to do here unites the driving principles of the two tropes in a temporal way which is properly dialectical.

Thus the slippage of meanings within the space of A might better be thought of as a shifting of gears from one power or logic to another, were it not for Jakobson's coinage of the term shifter for a completely unrelated syntactical phenomenon. The movement into a new space then carries properties of the old along with it, so that, for example, the defining position of the Symbolic in a tripartite 'system' is passed on to big A as an opposition with little a (or the Imaginary) at the same time as it opens up an unrelated and rather more metaphysical dimension in the opposition between the Symbolic and the Real.

For it seems to me that the latter (which can seemingly never be looked at directly – let alone theorized – but only glimpsed laterally, out of the corner of the eye) is best understood in terms of the old Sartrean *en-soi*, being-in-itself beyond all consciousness (the *pour-soi*), about which only three meagre propositions can be affirmed: it is; it is what it is; it is in itself.[26] This massive undifferentiated Real is then somehow impacted by language in such a way that we can call any differentiation within it a linguistic or 'symbolic' one. Anything that sets up a rift within the being of the Real is thereby in advance and virtually by definition the Symbolic; and it follows that the first form of the Symbolic will probably be arithmetical. The very word 'one' then triggers an immediate fission throughout Being itself, at the same time as it brings the primal dilemmas of philosophy and metaphysics into existence. But perhaps, even in that example, the word has to precede and include the number: for finally it is nomenclature itself which marks the colonization of the Real by the Symbolic. Names offer the first and the ultimate differentiations; and this is also why it seems unduly restrictive for Judith Butler to identify the Lacanian Symbolic with the Lévi-Strauss kinship systems alone (although they certainly offered a decisive lesson in its theorization). For surely any kind of relational nomenclature, however it functions and whatever social order or disorder it gives rise to, exemplifies the Symbolic; only the absence of nomenclature (or the return to purely Imaginary or dual relationships) would permit escape from it, but by way of what one can only think as a traumatic *Verwerfung* or foreclusion. At any rate, it is clear from this local discussion that even within the chain of slipped signifieds, there will be additional shifts within each term depending on how its relationship defines it.

Meanwhile the process itself can yield a clue to the overall Seminar form, otherwise thought of as a relatively aimless oral delivery, in which (as in the classic serials) the point is never reached but always deferred, and whose fundamental category – alongside the summary of past lessons – seems to be the digression. But if such digressions are now understood to be a shifting of gears predicated on this very 'chain or ladder of signifieds' we have been discussing here, then it becomes clearer that they are enlargements rather than deviations or extraneous incidents, movements up or down into other versions of the same space. The whole seminar, then, with its obligatory new idea or new matheme each year, its local returns and its proleptic topics, designs a unique and massive trajectory across time and across the years, one whose kinship with the temporality of the analytic session Lacan himself has stressed.

4.

Lacan's challenges to the dialectic seem to me to come (predictably) from two different directions. If we posit the dialectic as a way of relating incommensurables, then clearly approaches to the same dilemma can err by either underestimating the incompatibilities in question or overestimating them. Nor are these evasions of the dialectic themselves so incompatible as they might at first seem. Thus, if we identify the former, whereby a differentiation none the less somehow unproblematically identifies itself with what is supposed to be distinguished from it, as irony, then it is noteworthy that so much of what is anti-dialectical today should have been inspired by precisely those German Romantics who made a fetish of Irony in the first place. A lower-level 'ironic' tradition (via Thomas Mann) seems to have been the way in which Germany siphoned off everything most dangerous in its dialectical inspiration, and turned incommensurability back into simple ambiguity or ambivalence.

Insistence on the impossibility of any reconciliation between incommensurables has, on the other hand, seemed to be a French position, traditionally a dualism (from Descartes to Bergson) and today a passionate repudiation of 'totalizations', as pre-eminently in Deleuze (*Différence et répétition* is virtually the manifesto and the summa all together of this stance; but see also Lyotard's *Différend*). Perhaps one could distinguish two main versions of this second anti-dialectical position: the one holding that one cannot totalize, that any vision of system or of the One is necessarily a subjective one. This strikes me as a relatively Kantian note (as are so many anti-Hegelian polemics) that posits the One or the system, the totality, as a noumenon: unless, moving on to Fichte, the noumenon does not exist at all, and there is no totality in the first place (itself a rather metaphysical affirmation, one would think).

But the second mode of dismantling the dialectic acknowledges the impossibility of not totalizing – the necessity of universals, the constant summing up, the irresponsible reflexivity whereby the empirical moves to a higher level in spite of itself – but adds a proviso: that the operation can never be complete, and always leaves a 'remainder' in the form of what is unassimilable. This is seemingly a rather Lacanian move, with the remainder now taking the form of the *objet petit a*, and the dialectic itself being nudged in another direction to recognize that inassimilable *x* as a new philosophical task quite distinct in form and structure from the old claim of transcending everything and then moving on. There are, of course, all kinds of figures available to characterize the mysterious remnant, which evolves from a forever lost object to some kind of obscene or unnameable part object. Why it is incompatible with the mysterious status of what persists in Hegel after a term is *aufgehoben* is not so clear either, except that this particular figure has attracted less attention poetically.

The real Hegelian objection to this objection lies elsewhere, however, and is to be found in his classic doctrine of the limit, directed, appropriately enough, at Kant's noumenon. It is a simple but dialectical observation: namely, that the moment we recognize a boundary or a limit, we are already beyond it – calling something a limit is a way of transcending that very limit towards a plane on which the 'limit' itself is little more than a category and no longer a genuine boundary. So it is that anything identified as the unassimilable gets assimilated by virtue of this very act of identification.

It is a threat and a paradox that does not hold in the same way for an existential perspective: there the brute fact of lived experience transcends anything that can be thought about it; the experience of desire overwhelms the concept of desire, the pain of contradiction resists all conceivable solutions, and something like a density of existence is irredeemably opposed to the most powerful (and power-motivated) hypotheses. But I cannot think that this offers any kind of way out for Lacanian psychoanalysis.

The latter does, to be sure, posit a kind of existential zero degree in that 'pain of existence'[27] with which we are confronted whenever desire ceases (whose function Lacan is sometimes even willing to describe as the masking of that existential zero-degree): it is a very Sartrean conception indeed, and, as in Sartre, the pain of existing and the pain of death are sometimes hard to distinguish from each other as forms of finitude. But more generally for Lacan, affect, although real in whatever existential sense, is also an effect of structure, its existential density as much a by-product as a cause: indeed, affect often seems to share the ambiguity of the ego, both real and a mirage at one and the same time.

Thus the notion of the remainder – a structural concept – continues to fall under the strictures of the Hegelian limit, and under the sway of a dialectic that absorbs it the moment it is identified and named. But the absorption by language suggests two further topics here, which need to be drawn into the problem. The first is the Lacanian term of symbolization, with its obvious connection to the Symbolic order, but about which one still wants to know what it has to do with the production of signifiers on the one hand and with language as such on the other. (The second – not exactly the opposite of this topic – is the question of the matheme, or at least of mathematical language, graphs, knots and the like: I will return to this in a moment.)

Symbolization knows two dramatic moments in Lacan: the first is the very 'definition' of the Real itself, as 'what resists symbolization absolutely'.[28] It is a definition that accords nicely with our previous (metaphysical) discussion of the Real as what has not yet been organized or colonized by language (and in particular, by number). (The accord is scarcely surprising, since it was the resistance to symbolization which inspired this second formulation in the first place.) Here, however, the issues raised by the model of the remainder come back upon us with a vengeance: for does not the Real in this case function exactly like the alleged remainder? It is somehow outside of language or before it, graspable only in so far as we can have some conception of the limits of language and of what could possibly lie beyond it (as 'resisting symbolization'); but it is also something that must be thought occasionally to break in upon us as what we cannot appropriate by way of language: Wittgenstein's silences, the unformulable traumas, affects unrelated to any system or nomenclature of feelings and indeed, inexplicable in any structural fashion. Still, the Hegelian question also continues to arise: is not the very fact of naming all this the Real a first move towards domesticating it and finding it a place within symbolization? Is not the very characterization of the ineffable and the unnameable a way of naming it? And are not the mystics, adepts at this highly specialized dialectic of the language of the unnameable, themselves masters of language itself and of its own peculiarly elastic, not to say infinite, outer limits?

I want to make another point about signifiers as such, a point which needs to be reckoned into any political discussion of Lacan, even though it is a historical issue. For it is important to confront Lacan's repeated insistence on the historical emergence of new signifiers. At one level, this is perfectly obvious and empirical: thus, the Master, fascinated by electric lighting, is led to comment at some length on Socrates's contemplative immobility (in the *Symposium*) in the dark of an ancient world bereft of it. Both the history of everyday life and the nature of modernity are theoretically implicit in such an interest. But on some more metaphysical plane – reminiscent of Plato's Ideas, say, or of the categories of Hegel's *Logic* – Lacan will then posit the alternation of day and night as the emergence of one of the most fundamental of human signifiers, the latter easily identified by the structure of presence/absence (our old friend *fort–da*)[29] that enables them: you would not, in other words, have a conception of night (or day either) if there were not moments in which it was not present.

Still, these are signifiers that have come into being throughout human history and along with the 'development' of language (if we can talk in this way about something that is either there all at once and completely, as a system, or not at all). But it is in the context of the obviously central Signifier in psychoanalysis – namely, the phallus – that all this takes on its suggestiveness and its resonance. Because Lacan's insistence on history, and on the possibility of the emergence of signifiers that are historically original and new, does seem to distance him somewhat from Freud's utterly trans-historical views on the eternity of the Oedipus complex (with the mythic exception of its onset, in the convulsions of the primal horde); and the rather unconvincing recent arguments about the gradual displacement, in Lacan's thought, of the phallus by the *objet petit a* can also be recalibrated, by sexual utopians, as some possibility, within Lacanianism itself, that a new signifier might emerge to displace the phallus in the social organization of human relationships, thereby rendering Freudianism as outmoded as Marxism was argued to have been outmoded by socialism (Lukács, Gramsci).

But perhaps the possibility of genuine historical transformation is to be sought elsewhere, in the reflexivity likely to be generated by Freudian and Lacanian systems and discoveries themselves. Such a utopian perspective is rarely to be glimpsed in Lacan's remarks about psychoanalysts, and even about his own students, many of them analysts in training with him; nor is it confirmed by his always interesting observations about Freud himself, which never challenge Lacan's own transference, nor do they ever come to terms with the dissolution of the 'subject supposed to know'. But utopian curiosity, if not conviction, is to be found in a most interesting and enlightening moment indeed, namely in Roman Jakobson's visit to the Seminar in 1967, when Lacan finds himself impelled to question Jakobson about the kind of new reflexivity or self-consciousness a linguist might be expected to enjoy as someone with a unique relationship to the Symbolic: indeed, a relationship comparable only to that of psychoanalysis itself. Jakobson modestly demurs; but the very fact of the question opens up a vision of at least the structural possibility of the emergence of new human beings – indeed, of some possible mutation of the species with enhanced power over this alien and inhuman force – language itself – which tortures and scars our existence as human animals.

None of which seems very helpful in the more specifically sex-political matter of the phallus and the 'sexual relationship' (or that of gender and gender trouble; French not distinguishing between sex and gender in the Anglo-American fashion). As a Signifier, it is clear not only that the phallus obeys the presence–absence or *fort–da* dynamic mentioned above (for Saint Augustine, it is the very mark of original sin that erections are not subject to free will); but also, that in a way perhaps determined by the construction of psychoanalysis as a discipline, it is the supreme and privileged manifestation of what a signifier is, something all the more unusual in that in this case presumably there is no language involved. Perhaps this is why Lacan posits the phallus as the only Signifier without a signified, without a signification: it knows no semantic slippage, it cannot be subject to a metonymic chain of substitution. Perhaps: but adepts of the system could certainly argue powerfully against either of these propositions, by drawing on fetishism or by adducing sexual projections and allegories. I think it is best, therefore, to talk about this Signifier negatively, in terms of the absence of a feminine equivalent: for it is this absence, literal and figurative alike, which gives the Signifier of the phallus its signifying privilege. The female organ does not know symbolization: this is not to say that, like the Real itself, it 'resists' it; yet in many ways the juxtaposition and the inference are worth making and illuminating, for it leaves the 'feminine' ('Was will das Weib?' asked Freud) in the same kind of mysterious, and yet powerful and even baleful, indistinction as the Real itself.

And this is also finally why – famously, according to Lacanian theory – 'there is no sexual relationship'. The graph in Seminar XX makes it clear that this is, like so much of the descriptions of intersubjectivity in Lacan, a powerful rearticulation of the Sartrean dictum on the ontological impossibility of love (which nonetheless exists existentially): namely, that both parties want the same thing, 'to be loved', a demand that can scarcely be satisfied by its own mirror-image.

But here, in Lacan, each gender wants something else – and this makes out the ambiguity of the Lacanian position, which can be seen as feminist in so far as it posits, for the first time in the psychoanalytic tradition, a genuine desire which is woman's and which is different from man's; or alternatively, sexist, because it seems to endow women's sexuality with an essence (and, of course, does the same for the man's). The existence of flourishing forms of Lacanian feminism (mostly French) and also of violently anti-Lacanian feminisms (mostly American) testify perhaps to the productivity of this ambiguity, but certainly to its undecideability.

At any rate, what the graph is supposed to demonstrate is that, 'woman is the symptom of man', which is to say that in the alleged sexual relationship, what the man wants is *objet petit a*, or, in other words, his fantasm; while what 'woman' wants is divided, according to the graph, between the phallus and the Absolute Other, or God. To which we need to add the reminder that Woman does not exist, only people or individuals of the female sex. At least no one can say, after this, that Lacan failed to take up his own challenge, having pointed out so many times that no one in the psychoanalytic tradition, and in particular none of the great women analysts, ever dared to offer an answer to Freud's question about feminine *jouissance.*

This is perhaps the moment, then, to return to our original topic and ask ourselves some questions about the dialectic, and whether such a view of sexuality might merit such a characterization. We are faced here with two distinct forms of the binary opposition: one in which there is only one term and its absence (the phallus as signifier), and one in which two distinct terms confront each other, if not exactly in opposition, then at least in incommensurable coexistence (the sexual relationship).

What would it mean to answer a question like that? My own inclination is to suggest that both modes are dialectical, yet in different ways (which I do not propose to tabulate and codify here): and this for the fundamental reason that both involve relationality and posit relationality (rather than substance) as their focus or way in. At its most general, then, we can call dialectical any thought mode which grasps its objects, terms or elements as subject to definition, determination or modification by the relationships in which they are by definition seized. This is no doubt a relatively structuralist redefinition of the dialectic; but I would argue that historically – and except for a few decisive surviving remnants, such as Kojève's foregrounding of the master–slave discussion in the 1930s – it was in fact structuralism that made a return to dialectical thought possible in the first place, and this notwithstanding its own occasionally stunted or blocked deployment of the forms of dialectical opposition. I have felt, indeed, that the resurgence of the awareness of antinomies is not itself dialectical (can indeed often be anti-dialectical), but has at least the merit of gradually returning our attention to the nature of contradiction itself (which can be said to be the central dialectical category).

And this is also the spirit in which I would like to approach Lacan's formalizations, or at least characterize them. I do not place any particular stress on their scientificity, nor even on their claim to rigour (although I do not object to other people doing so, or attributing such a desire to Lacan himself). The objection to the equations, and even to the graphs themselves, surely lies in the difference between such formulas and propositions which are enunciated in language. Despite the claims of logical positivism (and speaking as someone who never acquired a mathematical culture), it does seem to me that a mathematical formula is far more open and ambiguous than any philosophical proposition that might offer to translate it into words.

But this is not meant to be an objection: on the contrary. I would want to argue that the equations and the graphs are dialectical precisely because they can be read in a number of different ways or, better still, because what they dramatize is the relationship between the various terms, rather than any single version of that relationship. Once again, it is relationality which is central, not any specific form it might take in this or that concrete case. Thus the graphs allow us to move back and forth between the terms, and to imagine variants of them: it is no accident, for example, that the famous L-schema has much in common with Greimas's semiotic square; but whereas the latter is an empty, purely formal map of all the possible semantic variants on a set, Lacan's graph is an injunction to think all four corners in a complex but necessary relationship to each other. We do have to invent these relationships ourselves, but I hope it is not an invitation to laziness on my part if I say that it does not particularly matter which specific content we decide to confer on them when we do so. Here too, then, Lacan's writing modes, which are somehow themselves dialectically divided between the epigram on the one hand and mathematical formalization on the other, open up a space in which the dialectic can move and develop.

(*to be continued*)

Notes

1. In particular, see *Différence et répétition* (Paris, 1968).
2. *Le Séminaire*, livre V (1957–1958): *Les formations de l'inconscient* (Paris, 1998), p. 208.
3. The reference is to the game whereby Freud's grandson imitated the absence and the return of his mother ('gone'/'there'): *Beyond the Pleasure Principle*, the Standard Edition vol. XVIII (London, 1955), pp. 14–15.
4. Sometimes translated as 'the representational representative', this enigmatic idea (developed in Freud's metapsychological essays on 'Repression' and on 'The Unconscious') seems to designate a representation which has as its object not another object but rather a drive as such (that is to say, something in principle unrepresentable).
5. A term coined by Ernest Jones to designate the disappearance of desire.
6. '*Le Séminaire: La logique du fantasme*', May 31, 1967.
7. Freud's most ambitious pre-psychoanalytic work, *Project for a Scientific Psychology* (*Entwurf einer Psychologie*), was drafted in 1895 and only published in 1950. Lacan's commentary on it is to be found in *Seminar* II (1954–1955).
8. *Le Séminaire* livre VII (1959–1960): *L'éthique de la psychanalyse* (Paris, 1986), pp. 226, 148–152.
9. Arkady Plotinsky, *The Knowable and the Unknowable* (Ann Arbor, Michigan, 2002), pp. 118–119. I suspect, however, that the intended use here is closer to what Bohr called 'complementarity'.
10. See, for example, Alain Badiou, 'Lacan et Platon', in Michel Deguy, ed., *Lacan avec les philosophes* (Paris, 1991), pp. 135–154.
11. Elisabeth Roudinesco, *Jacques Lacan* (Paris, 1993), p. 476.

12. But I am rather inclined to associate myself with Slavoj Žižek's impatience with the standard ideas of 'synthesis': 'does not Hegel's *Phenememenology of Spirit* tell us again and again the same story of the repeated failure of the subject's endeavour to realize his project in social substance . . .?' *The Ticklish Subject* (London, 1999), p. 76.

13. Following Jacques-Alain Miller, Žižek offers a useful (revisionist) account of the various stages in Lacan's teaching of his doctrine: see *The Sublime Object of Ideology* (London, 1989), pp. 131–4.

14. See 'Le temps logique et l'assertion de certitude anticipee' in *Écrits* (Paris, 1966).

15. Here is Jean-Claude Milner's ontological reformulation of the three orders:

> 'There are three suppositions: the first, or rather, the one (for it is already too much to order them; to do so is arbitrary), is that there is. It is a thetic proposition that has no other content than its own position, a position that is a gesture of cut, without which there is nothing that might be. It will be named real or R. Another supposition, named symbolic or S, is that there is language (*il y a de la langue*), a supposition without which nothing, and especially no supposition, could be enunciated. Another supposition, finally, is that there is similarity, where everything that links is grounded: it is the imaginary or I.' Jean-Claude Milner, *Les noms indistincts*, (Paris, 1983) p. 7.

16. The reader will detect the sociological interpretations of Adorno throughout this discussion.

17. See chapters x and xi of *le Séminaire* livre I (Paris, 1975).

18. See note 7 above.

19. I would be inclined to agree with the absolute skepticism of Colin McGinn in *The Mysterious Flame* (New York, 1999), were it not for the Hegelian doctrine of the limit and the certainty that skepticism can also be transformed into a metaphysic.

20. Derrida's essay 'Le Facteur de la vérité' is to be found in the useful collection edited by John B. Muller and William J. Richardson, *The Purloined Poe* (Baltimore, 1988).

21. *Le Seminaire* livre VII (1959–1960): *L'éthique de la psychanalyse* (Paris, 1986), pp. 97–100.

22. *Le Seminaire* livre VII (1959–1960): *L'éthique de la psychanalyse* (Paris, 1986), p. 81.

23. Jean-Jacques Rousseau, *Emile*, Book II, translated by B. Foxley (London, 1911), p. 72.

24. Philippe Lacoue-Labarthes, Jean-Luc Nancy, *Le Titre de la lettre* (Paris, 1973).

25. Judith Butler, *Antigone's Claim* (New York, 2000). Anne Garréta has also indicted the deplorable use of Lacan's term 'le Symbolique' in French political debates on gay marriage, where, even for some left intellectuals it functioned as a concept of a normative human nature: see 'Re-enchanting the Republic: Pacs, Parité and the Symbolique', in *Yale French Studies* 100 (2000), pp. 145–66.

26. See Milner's formulation in note 15, above.

27. *Le Séminaire: 'Le désir et son interprétation'*, December 10, 1958.

28. 'Le réel, ou ce qui est perçu comme tel, est ce qui résiste absolument à la symbolisation'. *Le Séminaire* livre I (1953–1954): *les écrits techniques de Freud* (Paris, 1975), p. 80.

29. See *Seminar* III, op. cit., p. 226.

Notes on Contributors

Alain Badiou is the author of many books, including *Infinite Thought: Truth and the Return of Philosophy* and *Handbook of Inaesthetics*. He teaches philosophy at the Ecole Normale Supérieure. His *Ethics: An Essay on the Understanding of Evil* and *Metapoltics* are also published by Verso.

Bruno Bosteels is Associate Professor in the Department of Romance Studies at Cornell University. His book, *Badiou and Politics*, will be published by Duke University Press. He also serves as general editor of *Diacritics*.

Miran Božovič is Professor of Philosophy at the University of Ljubljana, Slovenia. He is the author of *Der grosse Andere: Gotteskonzepte in der Philosophie der Neuzeit* (Vienna, 1993), *An Utterly Dark Spot: Gaze and Body in Early Modern Philosophy* (Ann Arbor, 2000), and editor of Jeremy Bentham, *The Panopticon Writings* (London, 1995).

Lorenzo Chiesa is a researcher in the Theory Department at the Jan van Eyck Academy. He is the author of *Antonin Artaud: Towards a Body without Organs* (Verona, 2001), and has published numerous journal articles and book chapters on Lacanian theory, Pier Paolo Pasolini, Alain Badiou and Michel Foucault. His book *Subjectivity and Otherness: A Philosophical Reading of Lacan* is currently being considered for publication by MIT Press. He is also completing a collection of papers on Lacan's *Seminar VII* (with Dany Nobus).

Joan Copjec teaches in the Departments of English, Comparative Literature, and Media Study at the University at Buffalo, where she is also Director of the Center for the Study of Psychoanalysis and Culture. Her most recent book is *Imagine There's No Woman*; she is currently writing a book on shame, hejab and cinema.

Mladen Dolar taught for twenty years at the Department of Philosophy, University of Ljubljana, where he is now Senior Research Fellow. Apart from a number of books in Slovene and numerous papers and contributions to edited volumes in several languages his publications include *Opera's Second Death* (with Slavoj Žižek, Routledge 2002) and *A Voice and Nothing More* (MIT 2006, forthcoming).

Timothy C. Huson is presently an independent scholar and teacher residing in Guangzhou, China. His current research interests include language, translation, literature education and labour.

Fredric Jameson is Distinguished Professor of Comparative Literature at Duke University. His most recent book is *Archaeologies of the Future : The Desire Called Utopia and Other Science Fictions* (Verso, 2005).

Adrian Johnston is an interdisciplinary research fellow in psychoanalysis and Lecturer in Philosophy at Emory University in Atlanta, Georgia. He is also a clinical analytic training candidate at the Emory Psychoanalytic Institute. He is the author of *Time Driven: Metapsychology and the Splitting of the Drive* (Northwestern University Press, 2005), as well as of two other forthcoming book projects.

Sigi Jöttkandt is a Flanders Research Council Fellow in the Department of English, Ghent University, Belgium. She is the author of *Acting Beautifully: Henry James and the Ethical Aesthetic* (SUNY, 2005) and is currently writing a book on First Love.

Sylvia Ons is a Lacanian psychoanalyst, Professor of Philosophy at the University of Buenos Aires, and author of numerous essays on Lacanian clinic and on Lacanian approaches to social reality and to philosophy. Her latest publication is *Woman as a Symptom of Man* (Buenos Aires, 2006).

Robert Pfaller teaches philosophy and cultural theory at the University of Art and Industrial Design in Linz and at the Technical University of Vienna, Austria. He is a member of Neue Wiener Gruppe – Lacan-Schule and Forschungsgruppe Psychoanalyse *stuzzicadenti*, Vienna. His publications include *Die Illusionen der anderen. Über das Lustprinzip in der Kultur* (Frankfurt/ Main, 2002) and *Althusser: Das Schweigen im Text* (Munich, 1997).

Slavoj Žižek, a dialectical-materialist philosopher, is Co-Director of the International Centre for Humanities, Birkbeck College, University of London. His latest publications include *Iraq: The Borrowed Kettle* (Verso, 2004), *Interrogating the Real* (Continuum, 2005), and *Neighbor* (with Ken Rinehard and Eric Santner, Chicago University Press).

Alenka Zupančič is a researcher at the Institute of Philosophy, Scientific Research centre of the Slovene Academy of Sciences and Arts, Ljubljana. She is the author of *Ethics of the Real: Kant, Lacan* (2000), *Das Reale einer Illusion* (2001), *Esthétique du désir, éthique de la jouissance* (2002) and *The Shortest Shadow: Nietzsche's Philosophy of the Two* (2003).

Index